WOMEN AND WAR

WOMEN AND WAR

*A Historical Encyclopedia
from Antiquity to the Present*

VOLUME TWO

BERNARD A. COOK, EDITOR

ABC CLIO

Santa Barbara, California   Denver, Colorado   Oxford, England

Library of Congress Cataloging-in-Publication Data is available from the Library of Congress.
ISBN 1-85109-770-8   1-85109-775-9 (e-book)

10   09   08   07   06   10   9   8   7   6   5   4   3   2   1

This book is also available on the World Wide Web as an eBook.
Visit abc-clio.com for details.

ABC-CLIO, Inc.
130 Cremona Drive, P.O. Box 1911
Santa Barbara, California 93116-1911

The acquisitions editor for this title was Alicia Merritt, the project editor was Carla Roberts, the media editor was Ellen Rasmussen, the media manager was Caroline Price, the editorial assistant was Alicia Martinez, the production manager was Don Schmidt, and the manufacturing coordinator was George Smyser.

This book is printed on acid-free paper ∞.
Manufactured in the United States of America

To my children, Bernie and Jennifer;
their spouses, Jen and Bora;
and my grandchildren, Lucy and Emmett

CONTENTS

VOLUME ONE

A

CONTENTS

B

Contents

C

D

Contents

G

CONTENTS

H

I

CONTENTS

J

K

VOLUME TWO

L

M

Contents

N

CONTENTS

R

S

CONTENTS

T

U

CONTENTS

V

W

CONTENTS

FOREWORD

Much of history is shaped by warfare, and women's history is no exception. Across the centuries, noncombatant women have been victims of war, and their multitude of stories have left a sad and enduring legacy. Women's active participation in battle and direct contributions to defense, however, have traditionally been overlooked. Accomplished unofficially, undercover, in disguise, and, until recently, by legislatively limited numbers of participants, women's often obscure activities have been difficult to trace and research and thus have been ignored and forgotten. Within the past twenty years, as military and feminist historians have begun to look more carefully at women in uniform, it has become apparent that historically women have been propelled into ever-increasing military roles by national need.

Limited in the eighteenth and nineteenth centuries to medical and supply-related functions that reflected their societal roles, women served in secret, nursed the wounded, or became involved in the production, collection, and dissemination of food, medicines, clothing, and equipment. Women moved into communications and clerical work at the turn of the century. By 1917, few men possessed these skills, so when the American Expeditionary Force in Europe discovered it needed telephone operators to route commands from headquarters to the front lines and efficient clerks to manage masses of records, the Army recruited women to work under contract. Meanwhile, Army and Navy nurses cared for soldiers and sailors at home and abroad, the influenza epidemic lending increased urgency and importance to their role.

During World War II, a general manpower shortage meant that the nation had to turn to women to serve in widely diverse jobs in both the civilian and military sectors. Servicewomen were assigned not only as nurses and administrators but also to jobs traditionally held by men and became mechanics, truck drivers, and air tower control operators. The function of need even superseded traditional concerns for military women's safety and placed Army nurses on the front lines in North Africa and Anzio and members of the Women's Army Corps in London during the German bombing.

Since then, paralleling women's wider roles in the economic and social sectors of society, servicewomen have entered into a continuously growing array of military occupations, from technical jobs to intelligence, law enforcement, logistics, command, and combat roles. The number of women serving in the Armed Forces has expanded rapidly; women now represent approximately 15 percent of the force. A consequence of this expansion is that women are now an essential part of the force, vital to the mission integrity of a majority of fighting units.

In the recently published memoir of her service in Iraq in 2003, Navy nurse Commander Cheryl Lynn Ruff explained why she wanted to serve with U.S. forces in Iraq: "These guys need us now." In this she speaks for women who served with and in the U.S. Armed Forces across time. Need was the reason that compelled Mary Ann Bickerdyke and Clara Barton to bring food and medicines to soldiers languishing in Army hospitals. Army nurses and female contract surgeons served at casualty clearing stations near the front lines in France and Belgium during World War I because their skills were needed, and Army nurses arrived in North Africa with the invading troops and served under fire at Anzio so that wounded soldiers would receive the best possible medical care. The Navy assigned Lieutenant Commander Bernice Walters, MD, to the hospital ship *Consolation* off the coast of Korea because she was a highly skilled physician anesthetist. The Marine Corps sent Sergeant Barbara Dulinsky to Vietnam because they needed a trained documents manager in Saigon.

During every American war, women sacrificed their lives because they perceived a need and a duty. The roster of their names includes Revolutionary War heroine Jemima Warner, killed by enemy fire during the siege of Quebec, and Civil War Union soldier Rosetta Wakeman who died in disguise during the Louisiana Red River Campaign of 1864. Two Army nurses were among the first U.S. military personnel to die in World War I, and sixteen servicewomen were killed in action during World War II. Army nurse Lieutenant Sharon Lane was killed by an enemy mortar at Chu Lai, Vietnam. Air Force flight nurse Captain Mary Klinker died in the ill-fated Operation Babylift in 1975. As the proportion of women serving in the armed forces grew, so did the numbers of female casualties. Since the beginning of the war in Iraq in 2003, more servicewomen have died from enemy fire than in any past conflict.

Military women's service on the front lines under fire and amid primitive field conditions as well as their deaths in past wars have frequently been overlooked or discounted by military historians, and even some feminist historians, simply because such service did not interest them. Military historians, immersed in battlefield tactics, paid scant attention to women and their activities, and feminist historians were disinclined to write about war. At the Women in Military Service for America Memorial Foundation, our mission is to collect, preserve, and disseminate women's contributions to the defense of the United States. The importance of our efforts was reinforced recently when some politicians questioned how close to the front lines we want our servicewomen assigned and how gender-integrated we want our armed forces to be. During a time when the full extent of women's military roles are being debated, it is essential that we as a nation possess a full and complete understanding of the roles that women have played during times of war throughout the history of the nation.

Historian Bernard Cook of Loyola University has undertaken and brought to fruition the mammoth task of coalescing women's travails during war and their contributions to defense throughout world history. He has included the well known as well as the obscure and missed very few. Readers will quickly realize that the overarching themes of serving because of need and forgotten service remain true no matter which country's history is being studied. This encyclopedia belongs on the reference shelf of every scholar of military history, women's studies, and modern civilizations. May it serve as a starting point for further research in a new and emerging historical field and an inspiration to scholars everywhere.

Judith Lawrence Bellafaire,
Women in Military Service for America
Memorial Foundation

ACKNOWLEDGMENTS

To my wife, Rosemary, I must express my gratitude for her patience and advice. Her invaluable and tireless assistance proofreading has rendered the book more readable. My secretary, Vicki Horrobin, always demonstrated with this project as with others, cheerful support and extraordinary effort. Victoria McCardel, my student assistant, provided most helpful assistance keeping records, handling correspondence, and doing research. Patricia Doran, the Interlibrary Loan Coordinator at the Loyola University Library, offered her talent and assistance on this project, locating needed books and articles.

I am particularly grateful for the suggestions from many of the contributors to this encyclopedia, who have made it a more comprehensive work. Lee Ann Ghajar and Judith Bellafaire at the Women in Military Service for America Memorial in Arlington, Virginia, were encouraging and most helpful. Britta Granrud, the curator of collections at the Memorial's archives patiently provided me with a wealth of unpublished letters, diaries, memoirs, and photographs.

I am grateful for the talent and effort provided by the professionals at ABC-CLIO. My special thanks to Alicia Merritt, the acquisitions editor, for her encouragement and assistance with all sorts of details; to Carla Roberts, the production editor; to Peter Westwick and Alexander Mikaberidze for their assistance and helpful suggestions; to Ellen Rasmussen for her work in locating illustrations; and to all of the other professionals who helped with this project, including Deborah Lynes and the staff of D&D Editorial Services.

INTRODUCTION

This encyclopedia deals with the experiences of women in traditional wars between territorially based armies, but it also approaches war in a much broader sense. It includes the involvement of women in a wide range of organized violence, guerrilla warfare, low-intensity warfare, struggles for national liberation, insurgencies, revolutions, and terrorism. It considers the impact of all sorts of war on women and their role on the home front as well as on the front line. One historian has asserted "women *are* invisible (in history) unless we are looking straight at them" (Rosenhaft 1992, 140). It is hoped that this encyclopedia will contribute to the visibility of women in this unfortunate aspect of the human experience.

War has been a constant plague afflicting humanity. Throughout history, women have been involved in war. Sometimes they were compelled to fight and resist in desperation as their tribes, villages, or towns were under assault. The widow Kenau Hasselaer led the resistance of the women of Haarlem against the besieging Spaniards in 1572–1573 until the city was starved into submission and its defenders massacred. Sometimes a woman would move to the fore to replace male leaders, husbands, fathers, or brothers who had been killed or had failed to provide adequate leadership. Boudicca, who led the Iceni of Britain against the Romans, and Queen Durgautti (Durgawati) of Gurrah (Gondwana) in Hindustan are among the number who fit this category. Trieu Thi Trinh, who led the Vietnamese against the Chinese in 248 and declared, "I wish to ride the tempest, tame the waves, kill the sharks. I want to drive the enemy away to save our people," "merely" rose to the occasion (Bergman 1974, 54).

More frequently and throughout history, women have been the victims of war. They have been forced to grieve slain husbands and children. They have been brutalized and killed. Women have been viewed as property to be seized in war and enslaved. In April 1822, the Turks massacred or enslaved thousands of Greek women on the island of Chios in retaliation for the atrocities perpetrated by Greek insurgents at Tripolitsa. By the time of the rampage of the Turks, which was depicted by Eugene Delacroix in his painting *Massacre of Chios,* was over, the population of the island had been reduced from 120,000 to 30,000. Atrocities against women constantly reoccur in ethnic conflict. Women have been singled out as bearers of the nation. Women were targets of violence in the Bulgarian horrors of 1877 and during the Balkan Wars (1912–1913). Rape has been recurrent in warfare whether or not the warfare was primarily ethnically based. Victorious soldiers felt a right to misuse the women of their conquered foe. Frequently the phenomenon was an act of power, subjecting the enemy, disrupting familial traditions, and inflicting shame on the vanquished—females but also males, who were powerless to protect their women. In World War I, rape and brutality were committed by soldiers of all invading armies—the Germans in the west, the Russians in East Prussia, and even the French when they moved into Alsace (Audoin-Rouzeau and Becker 2002, 34). Stéphane Audoin-Rouzeau and Annette Becker commenting on atrocities committed by

Austro-Hungarian soldiers in Serbia wrote, "facial mutilations, particularly of the eyes, were most frequent, and done to men and women, though women were also the victims of sexual violence and mutilations of the genital organs. Anthropologists of violence have long recorded that such attacks aim at people's most human features, the face and reproductive organs. Women are victimized twice over, as human beings and as future child-bearers, and they are the first whom the invaders want to humiliate" (Audoin-Rouzeau and Becker 2002, 47). The Nazis were single-minded in their desire to wipe out Jewish women to exterminate the Jewish people. Heinrich Himmler, the head of the SS, declared, "How is it with the women and children? I decided to find a clear solution here as well. I did not consider myself justified to exterminate the men—that is, to kill them or have them killed—and allow the avengers of our sons and grandsons in the form of their children to grow up. The difficult decision had to be taken to make this people disappear from the earth" ("Famous Speeches by Heinrich Himmler"). Visibly pregnant women and women with small children were among those selected for immediate gassing on arrival at the death camps.

The dreadful phenomenon of rape in war continued in the twentieth century and into the twenty-first. Wholesale rape was committed by members of the Red Army as it advanced into Germany in 1945, but other Allied forces also raped Germans. Jill Stephenson writes, "foreign troops sometimes regarded Germany's women as part of spoils of war" (Stephenson 2001, 107). Alison Owings writes that U.S., British, and Canadian soldiers "stole, robbed, raped women. It was indescribable" (Owings 1994, 97). French soldiers did the same (Stephenson 2001, 175–176). The rapes committed by the Red Army as it advanced into Germany eclipsed that of the other Allied powers. According to Rita Botwinick, "women were raped without concern or consideration of age or appearance. Many victims felt that the Soviet troops treated such sexual abuse as a victor's justly earned prerogative" (Botwinick 1992, 106). Rape was utilized

as a weapon of demoralization in the wars that accompanied the disintegration of the former Yugoslavia during the 1990s. This occurred as well during the twenty-year civil war between the Sudanese government and rebels in the south of the country and was repeated in Sudan during the bloody rampage of the Janjaweed, government-backed militias, against the people of the Dafur region. Amnesty International accused the Janjaweed of using "rape and other forms of sexual violence 'as a weapon of war' to humiliate black African women and girls" (Lacey 2004). Nicholas Kristof, in one of his many moving and graphic reports on the plight of the people of Dafur, wrote of a refugee in Chad who was "pregnant with the baby of one of the twenty Janjaweed raiders who murdered her husband and then gang-raped her." The Janjaweed told her and the women with her, "You are black women, and you are our slaves." One of the women cried and was killed. Another, who survived gang rape, "had her ears partly cut off as an added humiliation" (Kristof 2004).

If women survived war, many found themselves psychologically and economically ravaged by it. Spartan women reputedly told their men to come back with their shields or on them, but most women have been less sanguine about the loss of fathers, husbands, or sons. Although bereaved women have been universal in time and place, the sheer level of bereavement that accompanied the wars of the twentieth century was unprecedented. World War I left behind numbers of widows and orphans, which eclipsed previous conflicts. "In 1920 600,000 widows in France were eligible for state pensions" (Phillips 1996, 136). In addition, women like Vera Brittain survived burdened with the loss of brothers, fiancées, and friends. Of World War I's impact on France, Audoin-Rouzeau and Becker wrote, "two-thirds or even three-quarters of the population were affected directly or indirectly by bereavement or, more accurately, *bereavements*, the intensity of which was much greater than that experienced in peace time. Young people had died violent deaths, having suffered unprecedented mutilations of the body. Their families often did not even have the corpses of their loved ones to honor. So the mourning process was complicated, sometimes impossible, always protracted" (Audoin-Rouzeau and Becker 2002, 8–9). In addition to the pain of loss, many women were fated to live their lives in involuntary solitude. The imbalance between men and women in the age group between 20 and 35 in 1919 was such that many women who desired to marry were unable to find suitable husbands. Roderick Phillips writes, "In Britain more than a quarter of women in the 30 to 34 age group in 1921 had not married, and almost one-fifth of them never did" (Phillips 1996, 139). For many women, the return of a husband was a mixed blessing. Thousands of surviving soldiers were so physically or psychologically impaired that they were economic, physical, and emotional burdens to their wives. According to Phillips, "A million French soldiers were permanently disabled: Of them 125,000 had lost at least one limb and more than 40,000 had been completely or partially blinded" (Phillips 1996, 137).

Apart from the women whom chance, opportunity, or inclination thrust forward into positions of military leadership, those who were compelled to fight by necessity, and the ubiquitous women survivors and victims of war, other women followed and serviced armies.

One writer has referred to camp followers in the vans of the armies of World War II (Stephenson 2001, 107). However, the phenomenon was more common and even a necessity in earlier wars. Women were historically part of the world of camp and train of European armies. The women entrepreneurs who served as *vivandières* or *cantinières,* in addition to providing food and passing out drink on credit during the heat of battle, cooked and did sewing and laundry between engagements. Some were married to soldiers, but many also provided intimate female companionship to soldiers for a price. In the heat of combat, *vivandières* often replaced fallen soldiers from their unit in battle. The legend of Molly Pitcher is a composite of a number of *vivandières* during the American Revolution. A particularly heroic *vivandière* and medic in the

Union Army during the American Civil War, Annie Etheridge, was decorated for saving wounded under fire.

Through the Thirty Years' War (1618–1648), the women who followed and serviced armies were largely outside the control of military authorities. Until the time of Louis XIV, private contractors were even used to transport artillery. Like transport, which was integrated into the army, the women, who served as *vivandières* or *cantinières* in armies before supply and medical services were organized in a regular fashion, were increasingly supervised by military authorities in the seventeenth and eighteenth centuries.

In addition to the *vivandières,* women fought, disguised as men, as regular soldiers and sailors. Almost 700 did so in the American Civil War. Women disguised themselves for a number of reasons. Some were desperate to escape oppressive relationships. Some were attracted by pay and rations. Some sought adventure. Some followed lovers, and some were patriots. Fighting disguised as men became more difficult in the late nineteenth century as European armies were regularized and put in standard uniforms and recruits were subjected to more than pro forma physicals. Nonetheless, a number of women disguised as men served in the Russian army in World War I. One, Yasha Bochkareva, distraught over the collapse of discipline in the Russian army, organized the first of several women's battalions. Bochkareva felt that men could be shamed into action by the example of women soldiers. Her hopes were shattered. A British woman, Flora Sandes, openly served as a soldier in the Serbian army during World War I and was promoted to the rank of major.

As armies were put in standard uniform and professionalized, the traditional military roles of women as *vivandières* was largely eliminated. Apart from the few women military leaders, camp followers, *vivandières,* and women disguised as men generally came from lower classes. This changed as armies were professionalized. Women, frequently from the middle class, in accord with Victorian view in Great Britain and the United States of women as succorers, increasingly offered their services as nurses. They served as independent contract labor in the Spanish-American War and as volunteer nurses in the Boer War. In the early twentieth century, women, inspired by the ideology of equality, formed voluntary aid societies. Under the aegis of these, women served as nurses in the Balkan Wars and during World War I. The unprecedented dimensions of World War I led to the mobilization of whole nations in support of the war. Women were recruited for war industries in most belligerent states. Thousands of British women served near the front lines as nurses, ambulance drivers, and mechanics. Thousands of others worked in armament factories and replaced men throughout the workforce. Many of the munitionettes worked with dangerous chemicals. TNT yellowed their skin and won them the sobriquet "canary girls." Although the lives of many were, in all probability, shortened by their exposure to hazardous chemicals, several hundred died during the war due to explosions and other accidents. In one explosion at a factory in the Silvertown area of London, the government admitted that 69 workers were killed and 400 injured, but it was suspected that real total was much greater (Adie 2003, 101).

The war forced Great Britain and the United States not only to organize uniformed nursing components but also to put women in uniform as auxiliaries to the regular male military. Great Britain was the first country to place women in formal military service through the formation of the Women's Auxiliary Army Corps (WAAC), the Women's Royal Air Force (WRAF), and the Women's Royal Naval Service (WRNS, referred to as the Wrens). By the end of the war, 100,000 women had volunteered to serve in these auxiliaries.

Although the British and American auxiliary units were frequently disbanded after the end of the war, they were reactivated or vastly expanded during World War II. Women were again encouraged to replace men in the economy in Great Britain and the United States, where Rosie the Riveter became a symbol for war service on the home front. The front lines of total war during World War II were incredibly far flung. World War II brought the violence of war directly to women, who died in the bombardment of cities from London to Tokyo. In addition to the bombing of Hiroshima and Nagasaki, in July 1945, U.S. planes fire bombed 66 Japanese cities killing as many as 500,000 civilians. On August 6 and 9, Tokyo was fire bombed, and another 100,000 Japanese civilians were incinerated (Boggs 2005, 174). Women were caught up as casualties and combatants in street fighting from Warsaw to Stalingrad. In addition, they were directly involved as voluntary or conscripted combatants to an unprecedented extent. In the Soviet Union, women were utilized to supplement numbers in the Soviet military out of necessity and because of the insistent desire of many. Women saw combat duty in both mixed and all-female units. By the end of 1943, the number of women serving in Soviet armed forces numbered between 800,000 and 1 million, 8 percent of the total strength of the Soviet military. Approximately half of these women served at the front (Cottam 1980, 345). Soviet women served as combat pilots, snipers, tank drivers, and regular soldiers. In addition to women volunteers, 400,000 Soviet women were drafted, of these 100,000 served in air defense units (Cottam 1998, xx). Soviet women also played an important role in the Soviet Resistance movement. By February 1944, 26,707 women were serving with partisan units and constituted 16 percent of partisan strength in Belarus (Cottam 1982, 367; Herspring 1997, 47).

Women served in partisan movements in France, Italy, and Poland as well. It was in Yugoslavia, however, that their role was of particular numerical and symbolic significance: 100,000 women served as soldiers in the National Liberation Army (NLA). Initially 1 out of 10 NLA soldiers were women, but the proportion rose to 1 in 8. In addition, 2 million women were mobilized in the Anti-Fascist Front of Women (AFZ). These women ran local government, provided support to the front fighters, and engaged in sabotage. According to Barbara Jancar, "from 1941 to 1945 8.5 percent of the total female population of Yugoslavia was killed or died" (Jancar 1982, 91). Although 25 percent of the women who joined the NLA died, versus 11 percent for the men, there was an even higher casualty rate among the AFZ (Jancar 1982, 93). The AFZ members were not formally soldiers, but this was a guerrilla war, and the front was elusive. When the Nazis and their allies overran villages, AFZ women fought and were killed or captured. Often capture led to rape, torture, and murder. The casualty rate for female Partisans exceeded that for males. Some have asserted that the higher casualty rate for women fighters resulted from their inexperience. Milovan Djilas, a Communist leader within the Yugoslav resistance asserted, however, that the women, in general, fought more bravely than the men (Djilas 1977, 210). Despite their wartime contribution, after the war women were largely excluded from the Yugoslav military. Nevertheless, according to Barbara Jancar "their political and social emancipation was the product of the military campaign" (Jancar 1982, 92).

The British and the French also officially utilized women in combat during World War II. Of the 400 agents recruited and dispatched to Nazi-occupied Europe by the British Special Operations Executive 39 were women. Women were often used as couriers, who, it was hoped, would be less conspicuous on a bicycle in the French countryside or on a train than a young man. In all, 104 agents, 13 of them women, were killed. Some were killed outright; others were captured, tortured, and then killed (see "Atkins, Vera H.").

Because of the increasing insistence for equal rights and opportunities for women, auxiliaries were not disbanded after the war but were, in fact, integrated into the regular military forces of most developed industrial nations. Women gained the right to serve at sea as ensigns and officers, to fly combat aircraft, and to serve with ground forces short of the front line, not that this makes a great difference in wars of insurgency. The role of women in the Israeli military is perhaps a harbinger of future developments in the military of the industrial democratic states. Women played armed roles in the birth of the Is-

raeli state. During the Arab-Israeli War of 1948, more than 12,000 women served in the Israeli military and 114 died in combat (Gal 1986, 46). After independence, this military tradition continued, although in altered form. Israel is the only state in which women are conscripted. The fear of losing women in combat and opposition from Israel's religious parties led the government to exclude women from combat. There was resentment among women against their second-class status in the military. Lawsuits in the 1990s paved the way toward full participation by women in the Israeli military. By the end of 2001, Israeli women held combat positions in air defense, the air force, and artillery; as combat engineers; and in border patrol units.

If states felt compelled to integrate women into their armed forces to one degree or another, insurgent and guerrilla forces, depending on various cultural restraints, tended to utilize women as logistical support or even as fighters. In Latin America, women were involved in the Cuban Revolution. Celia Sánchez and Melba Hernández participated in Fidel Castro's failed attack on the Moncada Barracks in 1953. They subsequently changed his opinion about allowing women to fight with the guerrillas and, later, to participate in the national military. With a number of other women, they joined him in the mountains after his return from exile. Hernández formed the Mariana Grajales Brigade, a platoon consisting exclusively of women. The fact that women worked and fought alongside their male comrades had a significant impact on their place in the revolutionary movement after its victory. After the revolution, women were not drafted by the Cuban military but could volunteer for any branch and many rose to various levels of command. Elsewhere in Latin America, women since the 1950s have constituted approximately 30 percent of the 50,000 or so participants in armed revolutionary struggle (see "Latin America, Women in Guerrilla Movements").

A Vietnamese saying states, "When the enemy comes, even the women should fight" (Bergman 1974, 32). Vietnamese women have fought successive foreign interlopers—the Chinese, the

French, and the Americans. In 1907, Nguyen Thi Ba, a female innkeeper poisoned 200 French soldiers. In 1931, in Nghe Ahn and Ha Tihn provinces, a guerrilla band of 120 fighters, 40 of whom were women, temporarily drove out local functionaries and established a short-lived soviet. When Nguyen Thi Ngia, a twenty-three-year-old Nghe Tinh guerrilla fighter, was captured, she cut off her tongue to avoid breaking under torture. After the French left Vietnam in 1954, Vietnamese women fought for the South Vietnamese regime but, more significantly, for the North Vietnamese and Viet Cong.

Women played a significant role in the thirty-year-long armed struggle of Eritrea for independence from Ethiopia. By the end of the conflict in 1993, women had constituted 30 percent of Eritrea's approximately 100,000 soldiers (Wax 2004, A4). The Eritrean government attempted to rally its people with images of female soldiers, such as a poster with the legend "Mother Eritrea," which depicted a female fighter with a baby on her back brandishing an AK-47.

If women have so often been victims of violence, they have also proved to be capable of being agents of violence. Women historically have been assassins. Judith killed Assyrian general Holofernes, and Charlotte Corday killed the French revolutionary Jean Paul Marat. With the liberatory ideology unleashed by the French Revolution, however, women have increasingly been involved in revolutionary movements, and when the opposed power seemed impregnable, they have resorted to the weapon of the weak and desperate: terrorism. Women were among the populist terrorists who plotted the assassination of Alexander II in Russia in 1881, and one, Sophia Perovskaya, died on the scaffold for the deed. The execution of Gesia Gelfman was delayed because she was pregnant. She died in prison of peritonitis after giving birth. Women terrorists are an increasing phenomenon even in societies with strictly ascribed sexual differentiation. A woman killed the Indian president Rajiv Gandhi and eighteen others when she blew herself up near him in 1991. Women played a significant role in the Italian Red Brigades and were significant not only as participants in Germany's Red Army Faction but also as its leaders. Christian Lochner, a German antiterrorist, has asserted that women terrorists are more ruthless and dangerous. He said, "For anyone who loves his life, it is a very clever idea to shoot the woman first. From my experience women terrorists have much stronger characters, more power, more energy. There are some examples where a man waited a moment before they [sic] fired, and women shot at once. This is a general phenomenon with terrorists" (MacDonald 1991, xiv). In Muslim Chechnya, Palestine, and Iraq, women have been suicide bombers. They were among the Chechen terrorists at a Moscow theater in October 2002 and at the school at Beslan in 2004.

Reflecting on the pictures of Private First Class Lynndie England of the U.S. National Guard, inside the Abu Ghraib prison in Baghdad, Melissa Sheridan Embser-Herbert wrote, "Just as women have proven themselves capable of leading troops in difficult situations, so they have now shown that they can become vulnerable to the power of a role, the power of wielding power. Images of a woman giving a 'thumbs up' beside a hooded, naked man have highlighted the horrors of war in a way I don't believe would have happened had we seen only more traditional images of men at war. Putting a woman's face on war's brutality has I believe, prompted a depth of discussion that might not otherwise have occurred" (Embser-Herbert 2004, B1 and 4).

—*Bernard A. Cook*

References and Further Reading

Adie, Kate. 2003. *Corsets to Camouflage: Women and War*. Published in association with the Imperial War Museum. London: Hodder and Stoughton.

Audoin-Rouzeau, Stéphane, and Annette Becker. 2002. *14–18 Understanding the Great War*. Translated by Catherine Temerson. New York: Hill and Wang.

Bergman, Arlene. 1974. *Women of Vietnam.* San Francisco: Peoples Press.

Boggs, Carl. 2005. *Imperial Delusions: American Militarism and Endless War.* Lanham, MD: Rowman and Littlefield.

Botwinick, Rita S. 1992. *Winzig, Germany, 1933–1946: The History of a Town under the Third Reich.* Westport, CT: Praeger.

Cottam, Jean. 1980. "Soviet Women in Combat in World War II: The Ground Forces and the Navy." *International Journal of Women's Studies* 3 (July/August 1980) 4: 345–357.

———. 1982. "Soviet Women in Combat in World War II: The Rear Services, Resistance behind Enemy Lines and Military Political Workers." *International Journal of Women's Studies* 5, no. 4 (September/October 1982) 367.

———. 1998. *Women in War and Resistance.* Nepean, Canada: New Military.

Djilas, Milovan. 1977. *Wartime.* New York: Harcourt Brace Jovanovitch.

Embser-Herbert, Melissa Sheridan. 2004 "When Women Abuse Power Too." *Washington Post* (May 16): B1, B4.

"Famous Speeches by Heinrich Himmler." On October 6, 1943, Himmler's speech to Gau and Reich chiefs of the party in Posen (Poznan), http://www.scrapbookpages.com/ DachauScrapbook/HimmlerSpeeches.html (accessed March 8, 2005).

Gal, Reuven. 1986. *A Portrait of the Israeli Soldier.* Westport, CT: Greenwood.

Herspring, Dale R. 1997. "Women in the Russian Military: A Reluctant Marriage." *Minerva: Quarterly Report on Women in the Military* 15 (summer) 2: 47

Jancar, Barbara. 1982. "Yugoslavia: War of Resistance." In *Female Soldiers—Combatants or Noncombatants? Historical and Contemporary Perspectives,* edited by Nancy Loring Goldman. Westport, CT: Greenwood.

Kristof, Nicholas D. 2004. "Magboula's Brush with Genocide." *New York Times,* June 23.

Lacey, Marc. 2004. "Rape Used as Weapon in Sudan, Group Says." *Times-Picayune* (New Orleans) (July 19).

MacDonald, Eleineen. 1991. *Shoot the Woman First.* New York, Random House.

Owings, Alison. 1994. *Frauen, German Women Recall the Third Reich.* New Brunswick, NJ: Rutgers.

Phillips, Roderick. 1996. *Society, State, and Nation in Twentieth-Century Europe.* Upper Saddle River, NJ: Prentice Hall.

Reiss, Rodolphe Archibald. 1916. *Report upon the Atrocities Committed by the Austro-Hungarian Army during the First Invasion of Serbia.* Translated by F. S. Copeland. London: Simpkin, Marshall, Hamilton, Kent.

Rosenhaft, Eve. 1992. "Women in Modern Germany." In *Modern Germany Reconsidered, 1870–1945,* edited by Gordon Martel. Pages 140–158. London and New York: Routledge.

Stephenson, Jill. 2001. *Women in Nazi Germany/* Harlow, England: Longman/Pearson Educational.

"Vera Atkins, CBE, Légion d'honneur," 64 Baker Street. http://www.64-baker-street.org/ also/also_vera_atkins_her_story.html (cited January 10, 2006).

Wax, Emily. 2004. "Respected in Battle, Overlooked at Home: Eritrea's Female Veterans Seek Peacetime Role." *Washington Post* (April 2): A4.

TOPIC FINDER

Administrators

Atkins, Vera H.
Bagot, Lady Theodosia
Barton, Clara
Blackwell, Elizabeth
Cleopatra VII, Queen of Egypt
Cochran, Jacqueline
Dix, Dorothea
Eleanor of Aquitaine
Furse, Lady Katherine Symonds
Haverfield, Evelina
Hobby, Oveta Culp
Inglis, Elsie, and the Scottish Women's
    Hospitals
Livermore, Mary Ashton Rice
Lowther, Barbara
McCarthy, Emma Maud
McGee, Anita Newcomb
Nightingale, Florence
Peake, Felicity
Scholtz-Klink, Gertrud
Streeter, Ruth Cheney
Van Kleeck, Mary

American Revolution

American Revolution, Role of Women in the
Bailey, Anne Trotter
Brant, Mary
Corbin, Margaret Cochrane
Fulton, Sarah Bradlee
Greene, Catharine Littlefield
Ludington, Sybil
Martin, Grace, and Martin, Rachel
Molly Pitcher
Reed, Esther De Berdt
Samson, Deborah

Washington, Martha Dandridge Custis
Zane, Elizabeth

Antiquity

Artemisia of Caria
Cleopatra VII, Queen of Egypt
Fulvia
Greek Women and War in Antiquity
Helen of Troy
Japan, Women Warriors in Ancient and
    Medieval Japan
Jewish Women of Antiquity and War
Roman Women and War
Spartan Women
Zenobia, Queen of Palmyra

Atrocities

Armenian Holocaust
Armenian Women Victims of Genocide
Bulgarian Horrors
East Timor, Abuse of Women during War
Germany, Armed Forces, World War II
    Atrocities of
Herero of Namibia, Repression of the
Lidice Massacre
Oradour-sur-Glane Massacre
Rwanda, Women and the Genocide
Smyrna Tragedy, Continuing Ordeal for
    Women Survivors of the
Sudan, Women and the Civil War in

Auxiliary Corps

Ashwell, Lena Margaret Pocock
Australia, Women in Service during World
    War II
Bulgaria, Women and World War II

L

La Pasionaria

See Ibárruri, Dolores

"Lady Haw Haw"
(Margaret Cairns Joyce)
(1911–1972)

British Nazi and expatriate who, together with her husband, produced much of Nazi Germany's English-language radio propaganda during World War II. Margaret Cairns Joyce had been active in the British Union of Fascists in the 1930s. She married the future leader of the break-away National Socialist League, William Joyce, and became the league's treasurer. Once hostilities had broken out between Britain and Germany in 1939, the couple fled to Germany, took German citizenship, and enlisted in Nazi propaganda work. They became known as Lord and Lady Haw Haw, largely because of William Joyce's nasal, vaguely aristocratic-sounding speaking voice, but neither were in fact of elite background. Margaret Joyce was born into a Manchester working-class family and had trained as a typist and dancer.

From early 1940, Margaret Joyce broadcast on the Reichs Rundfunk radio station and on the specially created English-language stations of the Ministry of Propaganda's Bureau Concordia system. These stations' transmissions had been so arranged that they appeared to emanate from within the British isles, and intelligence reports showed that great numbers of British subjects, especially among the youngest and most politically active, listened to the often lurid and always violently anti-Semitic invective of the Haw Haws' broadcasts. Margaret Joyce's specialty was the discussion of women's topics from a Nazi perspective, always replete with the assertion that German women fared better under Nazism than British women under their system of government. She wrote many of her husband's radio addresses as well, for the Bureau Concordia system and the smaller Radio Caledonia, which incited the Scots to rise in revolt against the English; on Christian Peace Movement Radio, which was directed at pacifists; and on Workers' Challenge Radio, which tried to encourage an internal social revolution in wartime Britain.

While in Germany, Margaret Joyce took a German intelligence officer as a lover; she was divorced and severely beaten by her husband but elected to remarry him in 1943. They stayed together thereafter, working at various radio stations until May 1945, when both were arrested by the British military. William Joyce was executed for treason in 1946, but after she had spent some time in Royal Holloway prison, charges against Margaret Joyce were dropped on grounds of compassion. She died in 1972, having spent her last years quietly at home in Britain and in Ireland. Only one of a number of British expatriate women who had collaborated in Nazi propaganda, her role was so prominent a case that, together with her husband, Lady Haw Haw came to be remembered as the English voice of Nazi Germany.

—*Markku Ruotsila*

See also "Axis Sally"; "Tokyo Rose"

References and Further Reading

Dogherty, Martin. 2000. *Nazi Wireless Propaganda: Lord Haw-Haw and British Public Opinion*. New York: Columbia University.

Gottlieb, Julie V. 2000. *Feminine Fascism: Women in Britain's Fascist Movement, 1923–1945*. London: I. B. Tauris.

Martland, Peter. 2003. *Lord Haw-Haw: The English Voice of Nazi Germany*. Kew, England: National Archives.

Selwyn, Francis. 1987. *Hitler's Englishman: The Crime of "Lord Haw-Haw."* London: Penguin.

LAKSHMI BAI (CA. 1830–1858) AND SEPOY REBELLION

Indian freedom fighter. Lakshmi Bai, the Rani of Jhansi, led her compatriots in resistance to British rule during the Indian (Sepoy) Rebellion of 1857–1858 with such courage and skill that she became a figure of mythological proportions in later Indian history. Although Indian and British accounts of her actions differ widely, all agree that she was, in the words of the British commander who fought against her, "the Indian Joan of Arc . . . the best and the bravest of the rebel leaders" (Lebra-Chapman 1986, 114–115).

Lakshmi Bai was born into a Brahman family in the Hindu holy city of Benares about 1830. Some Indian sources give her birth year as late as 1835, adding youth to the mystique of her military exploits, as well as the religious associations of her birth place. Her birth name was Manikarnika, one of the names of the Ganges. Lakshmi Bai's mother died when she was four years old and, as a result of her father's approval (or neglect), she had an upbringing different from that of most proper Indian girls. She learned to read and write, and importantly for her later military exploits, she was trained to ride horses, fight with swords, and fire guns.

In 1842, at twelve years of age, a common age for a Hindu girl at that time to marry, she married the much older Gangadhar Rao, who ruled as Maharaja of the northern Indian principality of Jhansi. On the occasion of her marriage, she took the name Lakshmi (the Hindu goddess of wealth), with the honorific "Bai" added; additionally, she had the title of Rani (queen) of Jhansi. Following the death of their only child, Gangadhar Rao (just before his own death in 1853) adopted a young male relative to be his heir, with Lakshmi Bai designated to serve as regent. With much of India under British control at that time, the governor-general of India did not recognize the boy's succession, because such an adoption—customary in Hindu tradition—was not legal under English common law. According to the hated "doctrine of lapse," the British government, technically still the East India Company, annexed the state of Jhansi on February 16, 1854, and tried to buy off the Rani with a pension and the right to live in the palace.

Lakshmi Bai, resistant to the annexation, nevertheless remained loyal to British rule even after revolt broke out in 1857 among the Indian soldiers (sepoys) in the British army—a revolt that spread throughout much of north-central India. When Indians in Jhansi joined the revolt and massacred the resident British soldiers and civilians, Lakshmi Bai condemned their actions. After the rebels fled from Jhansi, the British asked her to temporarily administer the state, which she did effectively. The British, however, did not trust her, wrongly viewing her as complicit in the revolt, and in March 1858 they led an army against her and laid siege to the fort of Jhansi. The Rani organized the defense of Jhansi, mobilizing all inhabitants, female and male. When the British troops breached the walls of the fort, she managed to escape and joined other rebel leaders in a nearby stronghold.

In this last stage of the Indian Rebellion, Lakshmi Bai, now in open revolt, emerged as one of India's most skilled military leaders. As a female warrior in a male-dominated society, she could draw popular support and protection from identification with powerful Hindu goddesses. Portrayed as wearing either trousers or a sari pulled up between her legs to allow her to ride effectively, she also (according to legend rather than fact) was reputed to ride into battle with the reins in her teeth so both hands were free to wield her sword. Skilled in military strategy as well as combat techniques, she devised plans that, if followed by her male colleagues, might have led to victory rather than defeat of the rebellion—at least in that area of India. Making a last stand at the imposing Gwalior fort in June 1858, the rebels, with Lakshmi Bai in the forefront, engaged in a bloody battle with the British that resulted in her death and the defeat of the rebels. Although her death seemed to end the spirit of resistance, Lakshmi Bai was almost immediately made into an iconic Indian martyr, whose military skill, courage, and defiance became legendary and the subject of multitudinous poems, dramas, paintings, and sculpture. In later years her influence became an important inspiration to both Indian nationalists and feminists. Appropriately, during World War II when a brigade of Indian women was formed to fight against British rule as part of the Indian National Army formed with the encouragement of the Japanese, it was named the Rani of Jhansi Regiment. It was commanded by a doctor, Lakshmi Sahgal (1914–), and engaged in combat against the British. Sahgal was captured during the war but released in 1946 because she was regarded as a heroine by the proponents of Indian independence and her imprisonment was regarded by the British as counterproductive.

—*Nancy Fix Anderson*

See also India to 1857, Women Warriors in

References and Further Reading

Devi, Mahasweta. 2000. *The Queen of Jhansi.* (Originally published in 1956 as *Jhansir Rani,* in Bengali.) Trans. Mandira Sengupta and Sagaree Sengupta. Calcutta: Seagull Books.

Fraser, Antonia. 1989. *Warrior Queens.* New York: Alfred A. Knopf.

Lebra-Chapman, Joyce. 1986. *The Rani of Jhansi: A Study of Female Heroism in India.* Honolulu: University of Hawaii Press.

LANDAU, EMILIA (1924–1943)

Jewish resistance fighter. Emilia (Margalit) Landau was a Jewish resistance fighter who was killed in the first Warsaw ghetto uprising. She was fatally wounded on January 18, 1943, when she threw grenades at Nazis seeking to enforce the removal of the Jews from the ghetto to death camps at Treblinka, Poland.

The Nazis had scheduled an *Aktion* to begin on January 18. The Aktion was to be the final mass deportation of the Jews from the Warsaw ghetto to the extermination camps. Several hundred thousand had previously been transferred to the death camps in the summer of 1942. After the Great Deportation those left in the ghetto were mostly the young and fit, numbering about 65,000.

After the Great Deportation in 1942, Jewish resistance leaders decided that the leaders of the Jewish police force (Judenrat), who were willing agents of the Nazis, should be killed. Emilia participated in the murder of Jacob Lejkin, deputy to Jozef Szerynski, the head of the Jewish Police, who cooperated with the Germans in organizing the mass deportations from the ghetto. The assassination was carefully planned by Emilia Landau, along with Mordecai Grobas and Eliyahu Rozanski, two other members of the *Ha-Shomer ha-Za'ir* (Jewish Self-Defense/Jewish Armed Group, an underground militant Zionist Youth group).

Landau and Grobas trailed Lejkin for weeks to choose the best place and time for the assassination. They studied his habits, his regular movements, the likely opposition, and any escape routes. At dusk on October 29, 1942, Rozanski, who was designated to be the assassin, shot Lejkin to death while he was walking from the Nazi-controlled police station to his home on Gesia Street. Ghetto residents rejoiced while the Nazis ignored the matter.

Most of the people who participated in the Warsaw ghetto uprising were killed, so records are sparse or secondhand. There are two versions of Emilia's death. The first relates that she died when an armed band of the Ha-Shomer ha-Za'ir, commanded by Mordecai Anielewicz, surprised and killed several Nazis. Armed with pistols and hand grenades, members of the group mingled on Niska Street with a long procession of Jews being led away for processing. When a prearranged signal was given, Emilia and the others attacked the Nazis. In the short battle, several Nazis were killed or wounded while the rest fled. Most of the band, led by Anielewicz, were also killed. Emilia was seen throwing a grenade but was shot as she attempted further action.

A second account places Landau's death in the Ostdeutsche Baustelle workshop. The Ha-Shomer ha-Za'ir was based in that workshop, which was managed for a German businessman by Emilia's father, Alexander Landau. The Germans had forced their way into the workshop to seize the Jews there. Emilia threw a hand grenade among the Germans, killing several and wounding more, but she was also killed.

—*Andrew Jackson Waskey*

See also Holocaust and Jewish Women; Kempner, Vitka; Korczak, Rozka

References and Further Reading

Gutman, Israel. 1989. *The Jews of Warsaw, 1939–1943: Ghetto, Underground, Revolt.* Bloomington: Indiana University.

Zucherman, Yitzhak. 1993. *A Surplus of Memory: Chronicle of the Warsaw Ghetto Uprising.* Berkeley: University of California.

LANGE, DOROTHEA (1895–1965)

Photographer of the Japanese detention during World War II. Dorothea Lange is probably most famous for her photographs documenting the Great Depression, but her photographs of change on the home front, especially among ethnic groups and workers uprooted by the war, are equally important. In her early career, Dorothea Lange worked with Arnold Genthe, had her own photography studio in San Francisco, and functioned as part of the West Coast Bohemian photography movement. In the 1930s she participated in the migrant farm workers program of the California Emergency Relief Administration and eventually carried out photographic assignments for the Farm Security Administration (FSA). One of her most famous Depression-era photographs is the "Migrant Mother," taken in Nipomo, California, and now part of the Farm Security Administration and Office of War Information Collection at the Library of Congress.

Later, Lange took photographs for the Office of War Information and the War Relocation Authority (WRA). Three months after Pearl Harbor, President Franklin Roosevelt signed Executive Order 9066 ordering the relocation of Japanese Americans into guarded camps in the western United States. Soon after, the WRA hired Lange to photograph Japanese

Dorothea Lange's photo of school children of mixed ethnicities, including those of Japanese descent, reciting the Pledge of Allegiance while holding an American Flag in San Francisco, just days before the relocation and internment of all Japanese Americans in San Francisco, 1942. (Corbis)

neighborhoods, processing centers, and camp facilities.

Her earlier photographic work did not prepare Dorothea Lange for the disturbing racial and civil rights issues that the Japanese internment raised. In her efforts to capture the spirit of the camps with her photography, Lange created images that combined examples of human dignity and courage with signs of the indignities of imprisonment. Lange found herself immediately at odds with the WRA and the U.S. government, which censored many of her photographs. Her attitude toward internment is reflected in her

statement about a photograph she took of a billboard in Richmond, California. The billboard read, "It takes 8 tons of freight to K.O. 1 Jap, Southern Pacific." Lange said, "The billboards that were up at the time I photographed. Savage, savage billboards. This is what we did. How did it happen? " How could we?" (Her photograph of the billboard is labeled "Richmond, California, 1942," FSA Collection, Library of Congress.)

Two of her most poignant Japanese internment photographs are that of a Japanese American teenager sitting on duffel bags waiting for the bus to an unknown future ("Interrupted

Lives, April 1942," FSA Collection, Library of Congress), and one depicting a class of school children with their hands over their hearts saying the Pledge of Allegiance to the Flag. In the photograph, the children in the front row are Japanese American and the expression of intense loyalty on their faces provides stark contrast to the perceptions of some fellow Americans at the time. ("Prelude to the Japanese Exodus, April 1942," FSA Collection, Library of Congress).

In 1972 the Whitney Museum featured twenty-seven of Lange's photographs in an exhibit about the Japanese internment called "Executive Order 9066." The Library of Congress also featured her photographs of the forced relocation of Japanese American citizens as part of an online exhibit called "Women Come to the Front."

—*Kathleen Warnes*

See also Japanese Interned in U.S. Camps

References and Further Reading

Cole, Robert. 1996. *Dorothea Lange: Photographs of a Lifetime.* New York: Aperture.

Davis, Keith. 1995. *Photographs of Dorothea Lange.* Kansas City: Hallmark Cards.

Meltzer, Milton. 1978. *Dorothea Lange: A Photographer's Life.* New York: Farrar, Straus and Giroux.

Taylor, Paul. 1939. *American Exodus: A Record of Human Erosion.* New York: Reynal and Hitchcock.

LATIN AMERICA, WOMEN IN GUERRILLA MOVEMENTS IN

The important role played by women in guerrilla movements in Latin America since the late 1950s. Though their participation was conditioned by gender, the specific female experience in armed struggle has been ignored by most studies about the guerrillas.

Guerrillas are members of political organizations operating in both rural and urban areas that use armed warfare to achieve their goals. In Latin America, guerrilla war has been linked to revolutionary activism that aims to confront economic inequalities, overturn dictatorships, and foster the structural transformation of society. In virtually all Latin American countries, there has been some degree of leftist guerrilla activity since the late 1950s. The triumph of the Cuban guerrilla fighters in 1959 gave impetus to many other movements, which flourished across the region during the 1960s and 1970s. During its 40-year history, however, the combined strength of leftist guerrilla forces in the hemisphere never exceeded 50,000 members (Gross 1995, 2). Except for successes in Cuba (1959), Nicaragua (1979), and Grenada (1979), armed revolutionary movements failed to overthrow governments. Most leftist guerrilla movements were either annihilated by government security forces, were voluntarily disbanded, or transformed themselves into mainstream political groups. A few cases persist at the beginning of the twenty-first century, such as the Zapatistas (EZLN) in the Mexican province of Chiapas and some revolutionary organizations in Colombia.

Though guerrilla movements played a prominent role in the contemporary history of Latin America, they remain a challenging topic for scholarly study. Sources of information are scarce and not easy to verify largely due to the clandestine nature of their activity. Studies about the guerrillas rarely mention the experience of women, while scholarly work on political attitudes of women in Latin America usually focuses on the conventional political process. This explains the paucity of specifically gender-oriented literature about women in the armed struggle, even if they have comprised up to 30 percent of guerrilla members. Women who decided to take up arms were, akin to their male colleagues, motivated by revolutionary aspirations to change the structures of their societies or to resist dictatorship. While active in these movements, however, they faced gender-specific conflicts and had to face patriarchal prejudices deeply rooted in most Latin American societies. Intended to shape a "new man," revolutionary struggle often ignored personal aspects of political activity that concerned women and usually dismissed gender oppression. Like Ernesto (Che) Guevara's plea for a political formation of the revolutionary character that combines toughness with tenderness, gender discrimination remained another unaccomplished issue in the agenda of most Latin American guerrilla movements.

In all guerrilla movements, women participated less extensively than men. Structural constraints of women's roles in reproductive activities and the patriarchal nature of Latin American society, which reflects and reinforces this role, are the major reasons suggested for this limited participation. A quantum leap, however, seems to have taken place in women's participation in Latin American revolutionary movements roughly between 1965 and 1975 (Kampwirth 2002). Factors influencing the increased female involvement include social structural conditions in their specific country, cultural and political changes, and evolution in the internal organizational characteristics of the guerrilla movements.

Increasing industrialization moved more women into the paid labor force, thus increasing their contact with public issues and facilitating their mobilization. Female migration to cities broke traditional ties and hence made social networking and organizing possible. In some case, the previous existence of women's associations helped women to gain organizational and tactical experience that later facilitated their involvement in broader political issues. Cultural developments, such as the broader diffusion of feminist ideas and the emergence of the Theology of Liberation, offered women a framework for understanding historic injustice and further motivated their will to organize themselves and become involved in politics. Once immersed in political life, women often developed an increasing awareness of their gender-specific oppression and developed a feminist consciousness.

Kampwirth (2002) identifies at least four personal factors that favored the participation of women in guerrilla activity. These are family traditions of resistance, previous membership in social networks, a high educational level, and youth. Women who were active in guerrilla movements were more likely to have been of urban middle-class origin and to have attended high school or college than were their male counterparts. The early participation of middle-class women may be linked to their higher level of education and perhaps greater awareness of political issues. Middle-class women also faced fewer barriers to participation than peasant and working-class women, who were doubly burdened by class and gender constraints. Where working-class or peasant women as well as middle-class women participated, the latter began earlier and were more likely to be at the forefront of guerrilla activity.

The increased participation by women in guerrilla movements is also related to the shift from a *foco* guerrilla structure, which stressed a small band of fighters, to a mass mobilization strategy, which relied on much larger numbers of supporters. Such changes in the political nature of guerrilla struggle would explain why movements such as the Tupamaros (Uruguay), the Sandinistas (Nicaragua), and the Salvadoran guerrilla faction had substantial female participation in contrast to the previous armed groups in Cuba and Colombia (Lobao 1990). The Colombian and Cuban struggles, occurring prior to the 1970s, tended to follow the *foquista* pattern of struggle where revolutionaries act in isolation from the population. In contrast, the prolonged "people's wars" of Nicaragua, Guatemala, and El Salvador strove for mass mobilization and therefore increased the possibility that women (as well as men) from all segments of society would participate.

Once inside the guerrilla organizations, women often had to face gender discrimination and were relegated to support roles. In the midst of highly patriarchal structures, otherwise radically oriented movements tended to reproduce the *machismo* of the larger society. In contrast to the traditional militaries of Latin American states, guerrilla movements did include small numbers of women as combatants. Female members, however, were more likely to occupy support rather than combat positions in the guerrilla struggle. Women were often utilized to manipulate patriarchal images to the guerrilla movements' advantage, distracting security forces or carrying weapons while attracting less suspicion than men. In order to reach leadership positions or accomplish military tasks, women had to show more endurance and capacity than their male comrades. Women's participation and promotion to higher positions in the guerrilla organizations was further undermined by their having to tend homes and children. Motherhood was in itself a complex issue in most guerrilla organizations. Some guerrillas considered having children part of the militant task, viewing reproduction as a means to sustain the revolution. Others dissuaded their members from becoming parents because family life would distract from revolutionary duty and create selfish interests. In the case of women combatants, pregnancy was equated to a "loss" of military capacity. In his writings, Che Guevara revealed ambivalence toward the participation of women. On one hand, he declared himself against the discriminatory attitude toward women in Latin America's colonial mentality and stressed the role of female fellows in revolutionary development. When he described the tasks assigned to female militants in the "tough life of the combatant," however, Guevara followed the patriarchal ascription of domestic, care-giving activities, such as cooking, nursing, and making uniforms, to women (Lobao 1990, 189). Nevertheless, women belonging to guerrilla groups consider themselves to be combatants even if they are not arms-bearing fighters and enjoy a "lower" status in the organizations (Kampwirth 2002). Female participants do not consider the armed struggle as an end in itself, but as one part of the broader frame of their revolutionary activities, not limited to the phenomenon of armed conflict (Diana 1996).

Comparing women's participation in various Latin American guerrilla movements is difficult because of the scarcity of statistical information. Although in Nicaragua 30 percent of the combatants, and many of the top guerrilla leaders, were women, there was a similar percentage of participants in the Mexican state of Chiapas and El Salvador (Kampwirth 2002, 2), where women occupied up to 40 percent of the high-rank positions and enjoyed egalitarian relations with men (Lobao 1990, 198). In Uruguay women, mostly middle class, constituted 25 percent of membership and played a significant role in the Tupamaros during the 1960s, serving in both support and combat roles (Araújo 1980, 33). There are no equivalent studies about female participation in armed struggle in Argentina, Brazil, and Chile, though similarities in structure of the revolutionary movements in these countries during the early 1970s points to similar numbers.

A feminist approach can contribute to theories of revolution. Together with factors such as class, the gender dimension could inform in more complex and more illuminating ways the reasons why some movements succeed in overthrowing dictatorships or reaching their political goals while others fail. The literature already available suggests that the place, role, and treatment that a revolutionary movement assigns to women in its structure can be seen as an indicator of its social competence and ability to take root in the population. The more active and visible role women have in a movement, the better the movement's chances of achieving broad popular support.

—*Estela Schindel*

See also Colombia, Women and Political Violence in; Cuban Revolution, Women in the; El Salvador, Women and the Civil Strife in; Guatemala, Civil Conflict and Women; Nicaragua, Women and War in; Peru: Shining Path

References and Further Reading

Araújo, Ana María. 1980. *Tupamaras: Des femmes de l'Uruguay* [Tupamaras: Women from Uruguay]. Paris: Editions des Femmes.

Carvalho, Luiz Maklouf. 1998. *Mulheres que foram à luta armada* [Women Who Went to Armed Struggle]. São Paulo: Globo.

Diana, Marta. 1996. *Mujeres guerrilleras. La militancia de los setenta en el testimonio de sus protagonistas femeninas* [Guerrilla Women: The Activism of the 1970s in the Testimony of Its Female Protagonists]. Buenos Aires: Planeta.

Gross, Liza. 1995. *Handbook of Leftist Guerrilla Groups in Latin America and the Caribbean*. Boulder, CO: Westview.

Kampwirth, Karen. 2002. *Women and Guerrilla Movements: Nicaragua, El Salvador, Chiapas, and Cuba*. University Park: Pennsylvania State University Press.

Lobao, Linda. 1990. Women in Revolutionary Movements: Changing Patterns of Latin American Guerrilla Struggle. Pages 180–204 in *Women and Social Protest*. Edited by Guida West and Rhoda Lois Blumberg. New York: Oxford University Press.

LAWRENCE, DOROTHY (B. 1896)

Disguised as a man, served briefly in the British Army during World War I. During World War I, Dorothy Lawrence, an aspiring freelance journalist, hoped to gain accreditation from a British newspaper as a war correspondent. Meeting refusals everywhere she turned, she took a channel steamer to France in June 1915. From Paris, Lawrence rode a bicycle to French villages behind front lines but was unable to reach the combat zone. Determined to get to the front to demonstrate her ability as a war correspondent, Lawrence, with the assistance of a number of sympathetic soldiers, acquired a man's uniform. Pretending to bicycle to the French coast in order to return to England, she headed instead

for the area of fighting. At Albert she found soldiers who were willing to help her. Donning her uniform and using the name "Denis Smith," she successfully attached herself to a mine-laying company with whom she spent ten days at the front. Afraid of compromising her collaborators, Lawrence confided to a supposedly sympathetic sergeant that she was a woman. The sergeant, however, turned her in to his superiors and she was arrested. Though some officers suspected that she was a spy, her story was eventually believed. Lawrence was sequestered in a convent for ten days to lessen the immediate impact of any potential revelations she might make on the situation at the front. She was then escorted back to England and had to promise not "to divulge any information till [she] got permission" (Lawrence 1919, p. 189). Her book, *Sapper Dorothy Lawrence: The Only English Woman Soldier*, was published only after the war was over.

—*Bernard Cook*

See also Great Britain, Women in Service during World War I

References and Further Reading

Lawrence, Dorothy. 1919. *Sapper Dorothy Lawrence: The Only English Woman Soldier, Late Royal Engineers, 51st Division, 179th Tunneling Company, B.E.F.* London: John Lane.

LEBANON, WOMEN AND THE FIGHTING IN

Impact of the civil war in Lebanon on women. The civil wars in Lebanon, which raged from 1975 to 1991, reshaped the lives of all Lebanese and left deep wounds in the body politic that are still festering. For Lebanese women of all social, ethnic, or religious backgrounds, the war altered living patterns that had endured for centuries and placed the women at risk to a degree that they had never known. The wars of 1975 to 1991 trapped women in Lebanon between the roles traditionally set for them in patriarchal Christian and Muslim cultures and the unsettled conditions created by conflict. War also gave them increased opportunities to counter traditional stereotypes and transform their standing in Lebanese society.

Women had not attained even minimal sexual, social, and political equality in Lebanon prior to 1975. Although individual women enjoyed success in some fields, particularly education, they could not make any progress in the public sector. They were excluded from decision making at the national level. No woman had ever served as a head of state or as a cabinet minister and only two women had ever served in the national parliament. Prevailing cultural norms kept women in traditional homemaking and childbearing roles. As a group they were in no position to influence the escalating conflicts among Lebanese Christians, Sunni and Shiite Muslims, Palestinians, Druze, Syrians, and Israelis as the country cascaded toward civil war in the early 1970s.

When fighting erupted in Beirut in early 1975, women found themselves facing the travails common to civilians caught in a war zone. Many of their male providers were in militias, leaving women alone with the tasks of childcare and basic survival while experiencing considerable personal risk. Many became activists and a number of organizations appeared that gave women a chance to channel their drive to gain a voice in a war over which they had no control. Most prominent among these groups was the Lebanese Council of Women that worked to raise peace awareness through educational efforts in all parts of the country. Peace agitation among women reached its height on August 1, 1982, when 100 women from all walks of life staged a sit-in at the American University of Beirut campus to protest the Israeli siege and shortages of water, electricity, food, and medicine. This demonstration ended only with the lifting of the siege.

Unfortunately, these peace activities had virtually no impact on the course of the violence in Lebanon. Women continued to be shut out from all political decisions concerning either the unleashing of war or its ending. They found themselves being drawn into the tragedy whether they wanted to be involved or not. Lebanese women could not ignore the highly charged political environment in which they lived. In most areas the fighting raged in their own neighborhoods. Militia fighters moved through homes and farms, destroying or confiscating property. Men and women could not be defined by traditional roles. Not all women were pacifists. Many with husbands, brothers, or sons in the militias rallied to support them. Most acted in supporting functions, providing nursing and medical care, food, and clothing for the male fighters as well as attending to the storage and distribution of ammunition. Many Lebanese women helped with recruitment and communications. Very few, however, did any actual fighting. Although a limited number received training in the use of small arms, the militias did not allow women to fight for fear of their capture. Having women captured would demoralize the fighters because protecting their women was a point of male pride and honor.

Sixteen years of war politicized women's daily lives and forced them into new situations equipped only with the traditional skills that they used to keep their families together. The civil wars in Lebanon raised women's collective social awareness and made them conscious of their importance in developing a dynamic civic society. Participation by women in the country's politics consequently increased. War gave Lebanese women a chance to show what they could do, thus heightening their ability to push into occupations and activities that had previously been closed to them. Many barriers, however, remain. Lebanese women still have not broken into the highest levels of power where men still make critical decisions.

—*Walter Bell*

See also Islamic Resistance Movements, Women and

References and Further Reading

Abu-Saba, Mary Bentley. 1999. Human Needs and Women Peacebuilding in Lebanon. *Peace and Conflict: Journal of Peace Psychology* 5(1):37–51.

Accad, Evelyne. 1989. Feminist Perspective on the War in Lebanon. *Women's Studies International Forum* 12(1):91–95.

Shehadeh, Lamia Rustrum, ed. 1999. *Women and War in Lebanon.* Gainesville: University Press of Florida.

LEBRÓN, LOLITA (1919–)

Puerto Rican nationalist who led an armed attack on the U.S. Congress. On March 1, 1954, Lolita Lebrón led three male members of the Puerto Rican Nationalist Party into the U.S. House of Representatives. From the gallery above the members of Congress the attackers fired shots at the ceiling, unfurled the Puerto Rican flag, and shouted, *"Viva Puerto Rico Libre!"* (Long Live Free Puerto Rico!). No one was killed in the action. Lebrón was convicted and sentenced to fifty-six years in prison.

Puerto Rican nationalists, including Lolita Lebrón, seized by Capitol police after firing into the House chambers from the gallery and injuring eight congressmen, Washington, D.C., March 1, 1954. (Corbis)

Lolita Lebrón was born in Lares, in the mountainous interior of Puerto Rico. In 1868 Puerto Ricans who sought independence from Spain launched their rebellion in Lares. The revolt failed, but the small town carried on the legacy of anticolonial feeling. In the 1940s Lebrón, similarly to many other young Puerto Ricans, left the island looking for work. The United States had made Puerto Ricans citizens in 1917; thus, as a U.S. citizen, she had no difficulty traveling to New York City. There she found low-paying work as a seamstress. While in New York her patriotic feelings and desire to establish an independent Puerto Rico blossomed. She grew to admire Pedro Albizu Campos, the leader of the pro-Independence Nationalist Party, and dedicated her life to ending U.S. colonial control of her land, which had been established in 1898 following the Spanish-American War.

Several events convinced her that a dramatic action in support of Puerto Rican independence was necessary. In 1950 the Nationalist Party had staged an unsuccessful uprising in Puerto Rico, and, as a result, the United States government imprisoned Albizu Campos. In 1952 Puerto Rican Governor Luis Muñoz Marin, working closely with the U.S. government, converted Puerto Rico into a U.S. commonwealth. Also in 1952, in response to the formation of the Commonwealth and U.S. pressure, the UN Committee on Decolonization removed Puerto Rico from its list of colonies, declaring Puerto Rico's status to be an internal matter for the United States to decide. To call world attention to what she and the Nationalist Party considered Puerto Rico's ongoing colonial status, Lebrón organized the attack on Congress.

Lebrón spent twenty-five years in the federal women's prison at Alderson, West Virginia. During her time in jail she did not renounce her act or give up her demand that Puerto Rico be made independent. She did become very religious and wrote a book of poetry, *Sandalo en la celda* (*Sandalwood in the Cell*). Considered a political prisoner by many in the United States

and around the world, she was released from jail in 1979 when President Jimmy Carter granted Lebrón and her fellow Nationalist prisoners clemency.

She returned to Puerto Rico and continued her activism. In 2000 she joined hundreds of Puerto Ricans and North Americans to protest the U.S. Navy's use of the Puerto Rican island of Vieques as a testing ground for conventional weapons. At age eighty she entered restricted land and was sentenced to two months in jail for her act of civil disobedience. Lebrón refers to herself as a patriot, not a terrorist. She condemns the September 11, 2001, attacks against the United States and distinguishes what she did by saying that when she fired on the U.S. Congress, she had no intention of killing anyone.

—*Margaret Power*

See also Latin America, Women in Guerrilla Movements in

References and Further Reading

Lebrón, Lolita. n.d. *Sandalo en la celda*. Cataño, Puerto Rico: Editorial Betances.

Roig-Franzia, Manuel. "A Terrorist in the House." *The Washington Post Magazine*, February 22, 2004.

LEDERER, EDITH (EDIE)

American war correspondent. As the first female correspondent assigned by the Associated Press (AP) to cover the Vietnam War, Edith Lederer did superb work amidst adverse circumstances. She was determined to learn about war and make its horrors known. Covering wars in Vietnam, Afghanistan, and the Persian Gulf during her assignments with AP, her reports were portrayals of the terrible consequences that war brought to people, particularly to women and children. She emphasized that the vast majority of victims of war are innocent men, women, and children.

Edith Lederer was born in New York to Frieda R. Lederer, a kindergarten teacher, and Dr. Samuel B. Weiner, a pediatrician. She graduated with honors from Cornell University in 1963. The next year she received an MA in communications from Stanford University. She worked for *Science Service,* a Scripps-Howard syndicate reporting on science and medicine from Washington, D.C. Her long association with the AP began in 1966 covering student riots at Columbia University and Robert F. Kennedy's Senate campaign. She was transferred to San Francisco two years later to report on Berkeley's student protest movement at the time of Vietnam War, the Angela Davis trial, and the kidnapping of Patty Hearst. Lederer was in her thirties when she received a call from the president of AP, Wes Gallagher, asking her to become the first AP woman assigned full-time to the Vietnam War. Her mother rebuked her for going to cover a war, which had become a hated event in the United States. Although women reporters such as Jurate Kazickas were in Southeast Asia, reporting on the Vietnam War was dominated by men. Lederer was based in Saigon and sent dispatches about conflict in Vietnam, Laos, and Cambodia. For her, Saigon was a city of contradictions; reporting on the war by day and at night getting ready for cocktail parties in diplomatic circles. She was, however, enthralled by her stay in Vietnam. She liked the people, the places, her fellow reporters, and the excitement of covering the war as a reporter and emerged from Vietnam as a well-known correspondent.

After leaving Vietnam in the summer of 1973, Lederer covered the Yom Kippur War from Israel. In 1975 she became the bureau chief in Peru, the first woman to head a foreign bureau for AP. However, after five months Peru's military government expelled her for reporting about military exercises. Her next posting was to Puerto Rico where she served as chief of Caribbean services. From Hong Kong in 1978 she covered China's move toward a liberalized economy. She was sent to Afghanistan after the Soviet invasion in December 1979. Sometimes disguised as a rug buyer, she covered the events in Afghanistan along with her photographer, who was also a woman. Unlike male journalists who were the objects of suspicion, Lederer moved freely about Kabul but sometimes had to sleep in jails with guards protecting her. She witnessed the mass killing of women and gave that wide coverage.

Starting in 1982 she was based in London, where she lived for sixteen and half years. She reported about the downfall of communism in Eastern Europe and the Soviet Union. She was in Saudi Arabia after Iraq's 1990 invasion of Kuwait and told the world about the start of the Gulf War. She was one of the few reporters permitted to move with the U.S. Army.

In 1998 Lederer became the AP's chief correspondent covering the United Nations in New York. From that perspective she has written on crises in the Congo, East Timor, Iraq, Kosovo, and Sierra Leone.

—*Patit Paban Mishra*

See also Gellhorn, Martha; Schuyler, Philippa; Tomara, Sonia; Trotta, Liz; Watts, Jean

References and Further Reading

Bartimus, Tad, et al. 2002. *War Torn: Stories of War from the Women Reporters Who Covered Vietnam.* New York: Random House.

LEE, MARY ANNA RANDOLPH CUSTIS (1808–1873)

Wife of Confederate General Robert E. Lee. Born on October 1, 1808, Mary Lee was the only child of George Washington Parke Custis and Mary Lee Fitzhugh, and the great-granddaughter of George and Martha Washington. She was raised and educated at Arlington, Virginia, the family estate located across the Potomac River from Washington, D.C. In 1831, Mary married Robert Edward Lee, a West Point graduate and lieutenant in the U.S. Army. The couple spent much of their married life at military stations across the United States but frequently returned to Arlington, where six of their seven children were born. In 1846, Mary was afflicted with rheumatoid arthritis, which progressively crippled her until she was confined to a wheelchair in 1863.

Mary and Robert E. Lee came to prominence during the American Civil War, when Robert resigned from the U.S. Army and took a position as the commander-in-chief of the military forces of Virginia, and later, the Confederate States of America. In the opening months of the conflict, Mary remained at Arlington with some of her children but was ultimately forced to relinquish the estate to Federal troops, who used the home as headquarters for the Union Army. The property was later confiscated by the government because of nonpayment of taxes. Mary spent more than a year as a refugee behind enemy lines before relocating to Richmond, Virginia, where she stayed for the remainder of the war. She and her daughters became the toast of elite Richmond society and established a sock-knitting program to encourage support for Confederate soldiers. After the war the family occupied a small farmhouse outside Richmond, where Mary waged a passionate yet unsuccessful campaign to recover the Arlington estate, the grounds of which had been commissioned a national cemetery in 1864. The Lee family later moved to Washington College in Lexington, Virginia, where Robert served as president until his death in 1870. Mary died three years later on November 5, 1873.

—*Giselle Roberts*

See also Civil War, American, and Women

References and Further Reading

Perry, John. 2001. *Mrs. Robert E. Lee: The Lady of Arlington*. Sisters, OR: Multnomah.

LEFORT, CECILY (1903–1945)

British secret agent in World War II. Cecily Marie Mackenzie was born in Ireland in 1903. She married a French doctor, Alex Lefort, and they lived on the coast of Brittany. They fled German occupied France in 1940. In Britain Cecily Lefort joined the British Women's Auxiliary Air Force. Her fluency in French and adaptation to French life were assets when she volunteered to join the French section of the British Special Operations Executive (SOE). After training she was flown, along with Diana Rowden and Noor Inayat Khan, to a site near Le Mans on June 16, 1943. She operated as a courier, code-named Alice, for the "Jockey" network headed by Francis Cammaerts in southeastern France. On September 15, 1943, three months after arriving in France, she was arrested in Montélimar in the Rhône Alps. At a house she was warned not to visit, she fumbled an answer in response to a question by a suspicious German. M. R. D. Foots sarcastically suggested that her "principal contribution" to SOE was her suggestion that the beach below her house at St. Cast, west of Dinard in Brittany, be used by the SOE (Foot 1984, 70). Lefort was subjected to brutal interrogation and eventually sent from the Fresne prison in Paris to the Ravensbrück concentration camp. On May 1, 1945, Lefort died at Ravensbrück, the victim either of starvation or gassing. She was posthumously awarded the Croix de Guerre. Her name is inscribed on the SOE memorial at Runnymede and the Valençay SOE Memorial in France.

—*Bernard Cook*

See also Atkins, Vera H.; Ravensbrück

References and Further Reading

Foot, M. R. D. (Michael Richard Daniell). 1984 (1966). *SOE in France: An Account of the Work of the British Special Operations Executive 1940–1944*. Frederick, MD: University Publications of America.

Nicholas, Elizabeth. 1958. *Death Be Not Proud.* London: Cresset.

Spartacus Web. "Cecily Marie Lefort." http://www .spartacus.schoolnet.co.uk/SOElefort.htm (accessed September 28, 2004).

LEIGH, VERA (1903–1944)

British secret agent in World War II. Vera Glass was born in Leeds on March 17, 1903. She was abandoned soon after her birth, but was adopted by Eugene Leigh, an American, who owned a stable at Maison Laffitte near Paris. She became a designer of dresses and eventually was the part owner of a dress shop on the Place Vendôme in Paris. After the German occupation of Paris, she went to Lyon where she joined the Resistance and helped Allied soldiers to escape. Attempting to escape to England herself, she was interned by the Spanish until her release was obtained by the intervention of a British embassy officer. In England she joined the First Aid Nursing Yeomanry (FANY) and was recruited by the Special Operations Executive. During training she stood out as "about the best shot in the party" and "dead keen" (Foot 1984, 292). After training, Leigh, code-named Simone, was flown to a field in the Cher Valley near Tours, France. There she helped form a new underground network, code-named "Inventor." From a safe house in Paris, Leigh carried messages to groups as far away as the Ardennes. She put herself at risk by going openly around Paris, where she chanced being recognized by former acquaintances. After accidentally meeting her sister's husband at the Gare Saint-Lazare, she helped him guide Allied airmen downed in France to safe houses in the Paris area. She also associated with other agents in public. By the time she was arrested at a café near the Place des Ternes on October 30, her activities had become well known to the Germans.

On May 13, 1944, she was sent from the Fresnes prison with seven other captured British women agents to the Karlsruhe civil prison. On July 6, 1944, on the direct order of Ernest Kaltenbrunner, the head of the SS Security Office, Vera Leigh, Andrée Borrel, Sonya Olschanezky, and Diana Rowden were moved to the Natzweiler-Struthof concentration camp where they were executed the day of their arrival.

—*Bernard Cook*

See also Atkins, Vera H.; Borrel, Andrée; Olschanezky, Sonya; Rowden, Diana.

References and Further Reading

Foot, M. R. D. (Michael Richard Daniell). 1984 (1966). *SOE in France: An Account of the Work of the British Special Operations Executive 1940–1944.* Frederick, MD: University Publications of America.

Nicholas, Elizabeth. 1958. *Death Be Not Proud.* London: Cresset.

Spartacus Web. "Vera Leigh." http://www.spartacus .schoolnet.co.uk/SOEleigh.htm (accessed September 28, 2004).

LEROY, CATHERINE (1944–)

French journalist, one of the most daring combat photographers of the Vietnam War. Born in Paris, Catherine Leroy left for Vietnam in 1966, at the age of twenty-one, carrying a Leica camera. In 1967, with the 173rd Airborne Brigade, she became the first accredited journalist to participate in a combat parachute jump. She was later wounded in action while with a U.S. Marine unit in the Demilitarized Zone, but her photographs of the assault on Hill 881 were published around the world. Early in 1968, during the Tet Offensive, she was captured in Hue by the North Vietnamese Army but was eventually released. She returned to Saigon with photographic documentation of the experience.

She left Vietnam in 1968 and went on to cover some of the major conflicts in places such as Northern Ireland, Cyprus, Lebanon, Afghanistan, Iran, Iraq, Vietnam again, Angola, China, Pakistan, and Libya that marked the second half of the twentieth century. Her photographs were published in magazines such as *Paris Match, Stern, Época, The Sunday Times, Look, Life,* and *Time,* where she worked as a contract photographer from 1977 to 1986.

In 1983, in collaboration with *Newsweek* correspondent Tony Clifton, Leroy published *God Cried,* a book about the Israeli invasion of Lebanon. The volume described events starting with the siege of Beirut in the summer of 1982 to the departure of the Palestine Liberation Organization (PLO) and the massacres by paramilitaries allied to the Israelis at the Sabra and Shatila refugee camps.

Some of Leroy's Vietnam and Lebanon war photographs, along with her commentaries, were published in a chapter dedicated to her in a book entitled *Shooting Under Fire: The World of the War Photographer* (Howe 2002). In 2005, on the thirtieth anniversary of the fall of Saigon, Random House published a book entitled *Under Fire: Great Photographers and Writers in Vietnam,* edited and compiled by Leroy, with a foreword by Senator John McCain (Leroy 2005).

Leroy has received numerous awards, including the Robert Capa Award for her coverage of the fighting in Saigon (she is the first female recipient of this award); the George Polk Award; Picture of the Year Award; the Sigma Delta Chi Award; the Art Director's Club of New York Award; and the Honor Award for Distinguished Service in Journalism from the University of Missouri. In 1996 a retrospective of her work was organized in Perpignan, France, at *Visa pour l'Image,* the prestigious photojournalism festival.

—*Georgia Tres*

See also Friang, Brigitte

References and Further Reading

Howe, Peter, ed. 2002. *Shooting Under Fire: The World of the War Photographer.* New York: Artisan.

Leroy, Catherine. 2005. *Under Fire: Great Photographers and Writers in Vietnam.* New York: Random House.

Lewinski, Jorge. 1978. *The Camera at War: A History of War Photography from 1848 to the Present Day.* New York: Simon and Schuster.

Moeller, Susan D. 1989. *Shooting War: Photography and the American Experience of Combat.* New York: Basic Books.

LESKA-DAAB, ANNA (1921–)

Flight lieutenant of the British Royal Air Force (RAF); ferry pilot of the British Air Transport Auxiliary (ATA); commander of a women's squadron; and the sole ATA pilot to receive the Royal Medal.

At eighteen years old, Anna Leska-Daab qualified as a Category A and B glider pilot and as a balloon pilot at the Warsaw (Poland) Flying Club, which eventually granted her a sports pilot's license. When the Warsaw Flying Club maintained that she had too few points to be admitted to flight training, she implied that the club discriminated against women. Early in 1939 she began to fly at Poland's Pomeranian Flying Club. In June 1939 she qualified as a pilot of the RWD-8. Following Germany's invasion of Poland in September 1939, she was assigned to the Polish Air Force headquarters squadron to fly liaison missions. She also delivered an RWD-13 to an indicated airfield, even though she then had only a few hours of solo flying to her credit. She subsequently flew sixteen wartime missions aboard this type of aircraft.

After her arrival in Great Britain via Romania and France, she initially worked at the headquarters of the RAF and subsequently at the British Air Ministry. Having passed a flying test intended for those with 250 hours of flying, she was immediately recruited by the ATA, even though she had but one-tenth of the flight-time requirement. Along with Jadwiga Pilsudska and Barbara Wojtulanis, Leska-Daab was one of three Polish women to fly with the ATA, which was subordinated to the Ministry of Aircraft Production. Leska-Daab started ferrying ATA aircraft on February 10, 1941, and served until October 31, 1945, longer than the other Poles, delivering the largest number of aircraft.

Stationed at Hatfield and Hamble, Leska-Daab ferried a total of 1,295 aircraft including 557 Supermarine Spitfires. She flew 93 types of aircraft, including flying boats, and was airborne 1,241 hours (Malinowski 1981, 12). When picking up an aircraft at a plant, she had to check its operation both on the ground and in the air and comment in writing on its performance during the flight for the benefit of the destination wing. After landing a multi-engine combat aircraft, such as the Wellington, it took some effort on her part to persuade the male pilots receiving the aircraft that she was, in fact, the pilot. Among her subordinates, whom she instructed and assisted, were five British women and one each from the United States, Chile, and Argentina.

Leska-Daab received many Polish and British decorations, including the Polish Military Pilot Badge and the Royal Medal.

—*Kazimiera J. Cottam*

See also Great Britain, Women in Service during World War II; Polish Auxiliary Air Force

References and Further Reading

Leska-Daab, Anna. 1980. "Z lat wojny—wspomina Anna Leska-Daab" [War Reminiscences of Anna Leska-Daab]. *Skrzydlata Polska,* 20 (May 18): 14.

Malinowski, Tadeusz. 1981. "Z samolotu na samolot" [From Aircraft to Aircraft]. *Skrzydlata Polska* 10 (March 8): 3, 5.

"Polki na wojnie" [Polish Women in the War]. *Skrzydlata Polska,* 10 (October 3, 1985): 12.

LEW, ELIZABETH LOUISE VAN

See Van Lew, Elizabeth Louise

LEWANDOWSKA (NÉE DOWBOR-MUSNICKI), JANIA (1908–1940)

Polish officer murdered by the Soviets. Flight Second Lieutenant Lewandowska was the only woman officer to be incarcerated in the Soviet POW Camp for Polish Officers in Kozel'sk. About 27,600 Polish officers were captured following the Soviet invasion of eastern Poland on September 17, 1939. Of these, 26,000 were executed. The POWs were placed in three camps: Kozel'sk, to the southeast of Smolensk; Starobel'sk, now within the city limits of the Ukrainian city of Kharkiv (formerly known as Kharkov); and Ostashkov, located to the northwest of Moscow. Prisoners sent to Kozel'sk were executed at Katyn Forest in the massacre of Polish prisoners of war by the Russians.

Lewandowska was born on April 22, 1908, in Kharkiv, Ukraine, the elder daughter of Colonel-General Jozef Dowbor-Musnicki, commander of the 1st Polish Corps in 1917–1918 and the Great Poland Army in the province of Poznan in 1919. Lewandowska mastered gliders while still in high school. She made parachute jumps and trained at Poznan Flying Club.

In 1937 Lewandowska was sent to Lwow (now the Ukrainian city of Lviv) to study military radiotelegraphy. In August 1939 she was drafted for service in the 3rd Military Aviation Regiment stationed at No. 3 Air Base near Poznan. On September 1, 1939, after Germany attacked Poland, the base personnel were dispatched eastward by train. The military transport was commanded by Captain Jozef Sidor. After disembarking near Tarnopol on September 22, the Poles were surrounded by Soviet tanks and taken prisoner.

An eyewitness said Captain Sidor and Lewandowska were ordered to leave the group and were placed in a confiscated Polish ambulance, which brought them to Kozel'sk. Althought some evidence of Lewandowska's incarceration in the camp came from survivors, rumors persisted that she used an assumed name because her father was hated by the Soviets. Her name appeared on the so-called Katyn List compiled in 1949 by Adam Muszynski. Lewandowska's name, however, was missing from the German Katyn List of exhumed bodies that had been identified.

According to the testimony of survivor Waclaw Mucho, Lewandowska did not board a vehicle transporting her friends to an unknown destination. Several days later she was taken away in another vehicle. It is now known that the destination of both vehicles was the railway siding at Gnezdovo near Smolensk and Katyn Forest, where Lewandowska was executed.

—*Kazimiera J. Cottam*

See also Polish Auxiliary Air Force

References and Further Reading

Bauer, Piotr. 1989. "Wojenne losy Janiny Lewandowskiej" [The World War II Fate of Janina Lewandowska]. *Skrzydlata Polska, 31* (July 30): 7.

Muszynski, Adam, ed. 1982. *Lista Katynska* [The Katyn List]. 4th ed. London: Gryf.

LIDICE MASSACRE

A mining village near Kladno to the west of Prague that was the site of a mass reprisal killing by the Nazis on June 9–10, 1942. On May 27, 1942, Reinhard Heydrich, second in command of the elite Nazi SS corps, head of the Nazi Security Service, and Nazi administrator of Bohemia and Moravia, was mortally wounded by two agents sent by the Czech government-in-exile in London. The two perpetrators and other members of the Czech resistance were surrounded and killed in the St. Charles Borromaeo Catholic Church in Prague.

An intercepted letter made the Nazi Security Service suspicious that there was a connection between a Lidice family, whose son was serving with the Czech Legion in Britain, and the attack on Heydrich. The Germans launched a punitive raid on the village; the women and children were taken away and 183 men were shot. The majority of the women were sent to the Ravensbrück female concentration camp, where 143 of 195 survived. Only 16 of the 98 children from the village were reunited with their mothers after the end of the war (Zentner and Bedürftig 1991, 543–544). The rest disappeared. Most had been sent to the Chelmno death camp in German-occupied Poland. Others were placed with SS families to be "Germanized."

A radio transmitter belonging to the Czech agents was later found in Lezaky, a village east of Prague. As a result, all of that village's inhabitants were rounded up and brought to Gestapo headquarters in Pardubice. The adults, sixteen men and seventeen women, were all shot. Two little girls were placed with a German family; twelve other children were sent to a death camp where they were gassed. After the removal of its inhabitants, the village was razed.

—*Bernard Cook*

See also Oradour-sur-Glane Massacre

References and Further Reading

Berenbaum, Michael. 1993. *The World Must Know: The History of the Holocaust as Told in the United States Holocaust Museum.* New York: Little, Brown.

Bock, Katrin. "Die Zerstörung von Lezaky [The Destruction of Lezaky]." Czech Radio. http://design.radio.cz/de/artikel/29343 (accessed November 19, 2003).

Zentner, Christian, and Friedemann Bedürftig. 1991. Lidice. Pages 543–544 in *The Encyclopedia of the Third Reich.* Trans. and edited by Amy Hackett. New York: Macmillan.

Literature of World War II, U.S, Depiction of Women in

Women's presence or absence in most important fiction, and of memoirs written by women, during World War II and shortly afterward. Many American novels of World War II, in particular novels of combat with male protagonists, relegate women to secondary roles as love interests, as nearly invisible entities in a male-valorized sphere, or even as antagonistic specters of the world left behind. There are also important texts written during World War II, or shortly afterward—largely written by women—in which females play prominent, and what might now be called "liberated" roles, even if they were victims of war's cruelty and violence.

In the war novels, especially those about soldiers, Irwin Shaw's *The Young Lions* (1948), James Michener's *Tales of the South Pacific* (1947), John Hersey's *A Bell for Adono* (1944), Robert Lowry's *Casualty* (1946), Frederic Wakeman's *Shore Leave* (1944), James Jones' *From Here to Eternity* (1951), John Horne Burn's *The Gallery* (1947), Leon Uris' *Battle Cry* (1957), Jones' *The Thin Red Line* (1962), Norman Mailer's *The Naked and the Dead* (1948), and Sloan Wilson's novel of a post-war veteran, *Man in the Gray Flannel Suit* (1947), women most often play incidental roles, if they appear at all. For soldiers on leave in war zones (Hersey and Burns), women are often the complicated focus of a love life that is almost always a temporary respite from the demands of war. On the home front (Wakeman and Wilson), women are more present, self-conscious, and complicated. In combat novels, women are far more removed— nagging reminders of the toils and tedium of civilian life. The female characters are incapable of comprehending this masculine experience, and, from time to time, are the vicious perpetrators of "Dear John" letters or are otherwise cruel vixens who have given up on waiting, instead taking up with a slacker on the home front. Mailer's novel presents the sharpest hostility. An interesting anomaly is Joseph Heller's *Catch 22*

(1961), far more critical of the authoritarianism of war including misogyny, presenting a rape and murder as one of the inhuman deeds so often dismissed as just one of those things soldiers do. This is, of course, a much later novel, more attuned to the Vietnam period.

Personal narratives by women recount work in factories, their exploits as soldier's wives, their service in the military, in the Office of Special Services, and as internees both on the home front and overseas. Josephine von Miklos, in *I Took a War Job* (1943), and Elizabeth Hawes, in *Why Women Cry, or Wenches with Wrenches* (1944), write with vitality of their factory jobs, their unexpected acumen with tools, and their relations with fellow workers. Hawes, a fashion designer, argues for the full citizenship of women and blacks. Sociologist Katherine Archibald's powerful *Wartime Shipyard: A Study in Social Disunity* (1947) offers a bleak study of workers' prejudice in terms of race and gender, views previewed by a worker in Augusta Clawson's *Shipyard Diary of a Woman Welder* (1944).

Ruth Haskell's *Helmets and Lipstick* (1944) relates her duty as an Army nurse in North Africa before a back injury sent her home. Juanita Redmond's *I Served in Bataan* (1943), and Theresa Archer's *G.I. Nightingale* (1945) also tell of women's wartime nursing. *Citizen 13660* (1946) by artist Mine Okubo is a superb mix of text and drawings that tells of her grim internment with others of Japanese ancestry. A brilliant story of the camps, Hisaye Yamamoto's "The Legend of Miss Sasagawara" was first published in the *Kenyon Review* (1950). Monica Sone's *Nisei Daughter* appeared in 1953.

Margaret Buell Wilder's *Since You Went Away . . .Letters to a Soldier from His Wife* reveals a stoic wife and mother who ultimately takes a war job, pulling through while the husband is at war. Another account was written by Barbara Klaw, *Camp Follower, The Story of a Soldier's Wife* (1943). *Undercover Girl* is the memoir of Elizabeth MacDonald's work in the "morale" division of the OSS, including a stint in China in 1947. Etta Shiber's *Paris Underground* (1944) tells of working with the French resistance and her imprisonment by the Germans. Also significant is Doris Tatier's *The House near Paris: An American Woman's Story of Traffic in Patriots* (1946). American women imprisoned in the Philippines produced many accounts: Shelley Mydans's *Open City* (1945), Doris Rubens Johnston's *Bread and Rice* (1947), and Alice Frank Bryant's *The Sun Was Darkened* (1947). Agnes Keith Newton's *Three Who Came Home* (1947), her horrific account of life in a Japanese prison camp near Burma, includes a near rape. This noteworthy disclosure is unusual in these accounts; in general, discussions of sex, including instances of abuse, are not disclosed by the narrators. What one does encounter are astute and independent minds retelling the interesting experiences of many woman on totally new ground, ground that was brutal and terrifying for some. Kathryn Hulme in *The Wild Place* (1953) writes of her work in a displaced persons' camp in Germany; Gerda Klein's memoir of the Holocaust, *All But My Life,* was published in English in the United States after her emigration in 1957. Eve Curie's *Journey among Warriors* (1943), and Margaret Bourke-White's *Shooting the Russian War* (1942) report their travels to war zones, and Bourke-White gives a grim account of the U.S. invasion and occupation of Germany in *Dear Fatherland, Rest Quietly* (1946).

A contemporary view of black women is provided by the African American press. The *People's Voice*, printed in Harlem until 1948, and the *Pittsburgh Courier* provide insight into the lives of African American women, their social circles, their interests, their activities in the war effort, and the struggle against discrimination— what the *Courier* dubbed the Double V campaign. Ann Petry's *The Street* (1947), "In Darkness and Confusion" (1945, a novella contained in *Miss Muriel and Other Stories,* 1971), and "Like a Winding Sheet" (1947; reprinted in *Miss Muriel and Other Stories*) tell how African American women were alienated during the war and felt the weight of male domination as well as the burdens of racism. Lillian Smith's explosive *Strange Fruit* (1944) is also a crucial novel about race and gender.

Mary McCarthy's short story collection, *The Company She Keeps* (1942), which includes "The Man in the Brooks Brother Shirt," although not addressing World War II (the Spanish Civil War is in the background) introduces a sexually independent woman, noteworthy in part because of such women's effacement during the war. In much wartime fiction, women involved in war work find love, but it is romantic, chaste stuff, quite different from the sexual hunger and activity male protagonists exhibit (although little in men's novels is graphic, either). A decade after McCarthy's book, Margaret Long's *Louisville Saturday* (1950) presents a Dos Passos–like narrative in which numerous Louisville women face choices about sexuality; a mentally ill Victory girl is taken advantage of by a group of soldiers; a middle-aged volunteer turns to lesbianism; and a young wife starts an adulterous affair with an officer.

For their engaged and independent women protagonists who are in war zones or close to them, Martha Gellhorn's first two novels stand out: *The Stricken Field* (1939), in which a woman reporter encounters fascism in Czechoslovakia, and *Wine of Astonishment (1948),* later published as *The Point of No Return,* in which a reporter has an affair with a U.S. officer as the army advances to Germany. In *Liana* (1944), Gellhorn presents a different voice, depicting an Afro-Caribbean woman dominated by a French man in a French colony with the war a distant but significant presence. Kay Boyle, whose writing career began in the modernist society of France in the 1920s, wrote "Defeat," first published in *The New Yorker* in 1944, a cynical story of French women who quickly accept defeat in the earliest days of the German onslaught. This story reappears in her novel *Primer for Combat* (1942). Her *Avalanche* (1944) and *His Human Majesty* (1949), take place primarily in Europe. Boyle's amazing collection of stories about occupied Germany, *The Smoking Mountain,* appeared in 1951. Gertrude Stein, in addition to her memoir, *Wars I Have Seen* (1945), follows two GIs in Germany who cavort with American nurses and others in her final novel, *Brewsie and Willie* (1946).

In "The Lovely Leave," reprinted in *Wave Me Goodbye, Stories of the Second World War* (1989), Dorothy Parker also offers a compelling take on the wife who is confused about the "half life" she has while her flier husband has a whole new life. Other important novels where the war on the home front plays a role are Carson McCuller's *Member of the Wedding* (Boston 1946) and Harriet Arnow's *The Dollmaker* (1954). In addition to these works, another woman, Kathleen Winsor, wrote *Forever Amber* (1944), a historical potboiler entertaining readers at home and in the service with a woman's love conquests. This book was probably the most popular novel of the wartime period though it was set in Restoration England.

—*Page Dougherty Delano*

See also Gellhorn, Martha; Posters, U.S., Images of Women in

References and Further Reading

Rupp, Leila. 1978. *Mobilizing Women for War: German and American Propaganda 1939–1945.* Princeton, NJ: Princeton University.

Sheldon, Sayre P. 1998. *Her War Story: Twentieth Century Women Write about War.* Carbondale: University of Southern Illinois.

Tylee, Claire. 1990. *The Great War and Women's Consciousness: Images of Militarism and Womanhood in Women's Writing.* Iowa City: University of Iowa.

LITVIAK, LIDIIA (LILIIA) VLADIMIROVNA (1921–)

The first woman fighter pilot to shoot down an enemy aircraft in daytime. Lidiia Litviak became a Soviet flying instructor after graduating from the Kherson Flying School and finished training forty-five pilots by mid-1941 (Cottam 1983, 49). In the fall she joined Marina Raskova's Group No. 122, which evolved into three combat wings: Litviak's 586th Fighter Aviation Regiment; the 587th Bomber Aviation Regiment (initially commanded by Raskova herself); and the 588th Bomber Aviation Regiment. Litviak's regiment, which then flew Yakovlev's Yak-1 fighters, became operational in April 1942, at which time it was charged with air defense of the city of Saratov.

In September 1942 Litviak was sent with her squadron to Stalingrad. With fighter pilots Raisa Beliaeva, Ekaterina (Katia) Budanova, and Mariia Kuznetsova, she initially joined the 437th Fighter Regiment, scoring her first two kills on September 13, 1942. As her new wing did not fly Yaks, she soon transferred with Budanova to the 9th Guards Fighter Aviation Regiment commanded by Lieutenant-Colonel Lev Shestakov.

In January 1943, when this unit began acquiring P-39 Cobras, Litviak and Budanova again transferred to the 296th Fighter Aviation Regiment (renamed the 73rd Stalingrad-Vienna Guards Fighter Aviation Regiment) of the 6th Fighter Division, 8th Air Army, to continue flying Yaks. Senior Lieutenants Litviak and Budanova both became "free hunters" searching for targets of opportunity and participated in group combat.

Litviak's final score of twelve autonomous and three group victories (Pennington 2001, 141–142) is now being questioned. The corrected score stands at five autonomous victories and two group victories, including an observation balloon (Polunina 2004, 143), whereas Budanova is credited with six independent and four group victories (Polunina 2004, 139).

Ekaterina (Katia) Vasilíevna Budanova (b. 1916) perished on July 19, 1943, in an engagement with three Messerschmitts and was posthumously awarded the prestigious Hero of the Russian Federation (equivalent to the Hero of the Soviet Union) on October 1, 1993.

Outnumbered in a dog fight, Litviak was shot down on August 1, 1943. There is strong evidence to suggest that she was captured by the enemy and incarcerated in a POW camp. She did not return to the Soviet Union and may have sought refuge in Switzerland.

Her loyalty to the Soviet regime was suspect because her father, former deputy minister of transportation, was executed in 1937, a victim of Stalin's terror. After her alleged remains, buried in a common grave near Krasnyy Luch, were located in 1979, she was rehabilitated in March 1986. Litviak was posthumously awarded the Hero of the Soviet Union on May 5, 1990.

—*Kazimiera J. Cottam*

See also Makarova, Tat'iana Petrovna and Belik, Vera Luk'ianovna; Pilots of the IL-2; Raskova, Marina Mikhailovna; Soviet Air Defense, 586th Fighter Aviation Regiment; Soviet Union/Russian Federation, Women Heros of the

References and Further Reading

Cottam, Kazimiera J. 1983. *Soviet Airwomen in Combat in World War II.* Manhattan, KS: MA/AH Publishing.

———. 2003. Litviak, Lidiia Vladimirovna. Pages 261–265 in *Amazons to Fighter Pilots.* Edited by Reina Pennington. Vol. 1. Westport, CT: Greenwood.

Pennington, Reina. 2001. *Wings, Women and War.* Lawrence: University Press of Kansas.

Polunina, Ekaterina. 2004. *Devchonki, podruzhki, letchitsy* [Girls, Girlfriends, Pilots]. Moscow: OAO Izdatelískii Dom ìVestnik Vozdushnogo Flota.

LIVERMORE, MARY ASHTON RICE (1820–1905)

Author, woman's rights advocate, and suffragist who worked with U.S. Sanitary Commission, an organization set up to coordinate efforts to provide food, clothing, and medical assistance to Union troops and wounded veterans during the American Civil War. Mary Rice was born in Boston on December 19, 1820. She studied at the Female Seminary in Charleston, Massachusetts, and taught there following her graduation.

She was a tutor on a Virginia plantation, where she developed a deep opposition to slavery.

In 1861 the forty-one-year old Livermore, who had married a Unitarian minister, began working with the Chicago branch of the U.S. Sanitary Commission. She had long been a temperance advocate and had also been active in various ladies' aid societies. Wartime involvement brought her new responsibilities, introduced her to skills hitherto unexplored, and increased her confidence in her own abilities as well as those of other women.

Working with the Northwestern Sanitary Commission, Livermore and her co-manager, Jane Hoge, came to symbolize civilian involvement in the war effort for many women and men. During her everyday wartime activities, she helped raise large amounts of money, oversaw business deals, purchased property, traveled extensively, worked with civilians and military personnel, and managed the ever-changing inventory of supplies destined for army encampments in the western United States.

Among the many ways that war involvement took Livermore beyond traditional women's work, public speaking and writing would remain the most prominent in her later life. In the first stages of the Civil War she began speaking before women's groups throughout the Northwest, describing what she had experienced as an army nurse and Sanitary Commission representative. By 1864 she had begun speaking before large mixed audiences. Initially reluctant to address groups that included men, she was nevertheless bolstered by a popular cause filled with the drama of wartime.

She eventually put her experiences on paper, publishing *My Story of the War* in 1889. More than a century later the volume she wrote remains a valuable description of women's involvement in the American Civil War. It describes their interaction with soldiers, their roles behind the battle lines, in hospitals, and as representatives of the U.S. Sanitary Commission. The book gives valuable biographical information about women who were prominent in wartime relief.

Mary Livermore. (Library of Congress)

See also Civil War, American, and Women; Dix, Dorothea

References and Further Reading:

Brockett, Linus P., and Marcy C. Vaughn. 1867. *Woman's Work in the Civil War: A Record of Heroism, Patriotism, and Patience.* Philadelphia: Zeigler, McCurdy.

Livermore, Mary A. 1889. *My Story of the War: A Woman's Narrative of Four Years Personal Experience as Nurse in the Union Army.* Hartford, CT: A. D. Worthington.

———. 1899. *The Story of My Life.* Repr. New York: Arno, 1974.

Willard, Frances, and Mary Livermore. 1975. *A Woman of the Century.* Repr. of 1893 edition. New York: Gordon.

Wood, Ann Douglas. 1972. "The War Within a War: Women Nurses in the Union Army." *Civil War History,* 18 (September): 197–212.

The new skills that Livermore gained doing wartime activities changed her. In 1869 she stood before attendees at a suffrage convention in Massachusetts and asserted that she and her associates in the war had grown to the "stature of men." She went on to explain, "we cannot go back and be the women we were before." (*National Anti-Slavery Standard,* December 25, 1869). The "new persona" that Livermore took on during the postwar years capitalized on the skills she had gained with the Sanitary Commission. Most notably, she became a well-known lecturer on the Redpath Lyceum lecture circuit, delivering a popular speech entitled "What Shall We Do with Our Daughters?" In the years following the Civil War, Livermore became one of the nation's leading suffragists.

—*Nancy Driscol Engle*

LOCKE, ELSIE
(1912–2001)

Historian, children's novelist, community worker, campaigner for peace, women's rights, and environmental alertness. Within New Zealand society, Elsie Locke was a leading advocate for nonviolence. Born in Hamilton in 1912, Locke grew up near Auckland. After receiving a bachelor of arts degree at Auckland University in 1933, she became increasingly involved in socialist organizations and antifascist rallies. Very close to the Communist Party of New Zealand in the mid-1930s, Locke had organized the New Zealand Woman's Convention in 1934 before encouraging the creation of the Sex Hygiene and Birth Regulation Society in 1936. She participated in several international pacifist conferences before the outbreak of World War II. In Christchurch, where she lived with her husband, J. Gibson Locke, she edited the popular magazine, *Woman To-Day.* In 1949 she published an anthology of the antimilitarist writings of Clement G. Watson, a friend killed in battle in April 1945. Somewhat exasperated by Communist Party propaganda, following Hiroshima and Nagasaki she decided to dedicate her life to the struggle against the "evil atom." In the late 1950s she joined with the Quaker Mary Woodward in the formation of a New Zealand branch of the Campaign for Nuclear Disarmament. Assuredly, her favorite weapons remained ink and pen. Laureate of the K. Mansfield Award in 1959 and author of a classic novel, *The Runaway Settlers,* published in 1965, the academic value of her writings was officially recognized in 1987 by the University of Canterbury, which conferred upon Locke an honorary doctorate in literature. Among her twenty books, *Peace People* (1992) was a major contribution to New Zealand's national cultural heritage: It revealed the history of pacifism from the Maori wars to the protest against French nuclear tests. In 2000, Elsie Locke received the UNESCO Peacebuilder Award for her engagement in favor of social peace and her personal efforts in promoting nonviolence between the Maori and Pakeha communities. The mother of four children, Elsie Locke died in 2001 in Christchurch.

—*Jérôme Dorvidal*

See also Street, Jessie

References and Further Reading

Laracy, Hughes. 2004. "Elsie Locke, Historian—An Appreciation." *History Now.* http://www.nzine.co.nz/views/locke.html (accessed May 4, 2004).

Locke, Elsie. 1992. *Peace People: A History of Peace Activities in New Zealand.* Christchurch: Hazard Press.

LOTTA SVÄRD

See Finland, Lotta Svärd

LOWTHER, BARBARA (TOUPIE) (B. 1890)

Founder and administrator of the Lowther-Hackett ambulance unit, officially attached to the French army in World War I. Lowther ranked as a sub-lieutenant in the French army and received the Croix de Guerre.

Frustrated with receiving the brush-off from the British military, Barbara Lowther and Norah Hackett, who had been managing front-line canteens in the French war zone, sought permission from the French army to form an ambulance unit in 1916. The daughter of the 7th Earl of Lonsdale and close relative of Member of Parliament Claude Lowther, her aristocratic connections aided Lowther in establishing her unit.

In 1917 she secured cars by donation, and drivers—from Britain, Ireland, France, and America—via newspaper advertisements. The unit worked in Cugny and Creil, France, for six months. Determined to take her unit to the frontline to work under the same conditions as male soldiers, Lowther convinced French authorities that she and her coworker were not afraid of being killed. Despite their reluctance to place British women in such a dangerous situation, the unit was posted at Compiègne, France. The only all-women corps on French battlefields holding the official status of soldiers, Lowther's unit worked under camouflage thirty-five yards from German lines. The unit served successfully at medical aid stations through the end of the war.

Lowther was well educated, holding a bachelor of science degree from the Sorbonne. Her masculine appearance led many to believe her to be a lesbian. She was friends and associated with many prominent lesbians of the time, including two members of the Lowther-Hackett unit, Eileen Plunket and Enid Elliot. Other members of the unit include Mary Dexter and Katherine Hodges.

—*Barbara Penny Kanner*

See also Great Britain, Women in Service during World War I; Hodges, Katherine

References and Further Reading

Hamer, Emily. 1996. *Britannia's Glory: A History of Twentieth-Century Lesbians.* London: Cassell.

LUCE, CLARE BOOTHE (1903–1987)

Editor, playwright, war correspondent, congresswoman, ambassador, and presidential adviser. Clare Boothe Luce stands as the epitome of a woman who succeeded in a man's world by using her female charms when talent was not enough. At every juncture of her life, the noted beauty relied on men's patronage and sponsorship to help overcome fierce resistance to a woman's advancement. Her romantic affairs were legendary, as was her ambition.

Born in New York in 1903, Clare Boothe had little formal education or financial security. Convinced of the necessity of marrying for money, at age twenty she wed millionaire George T. Brokaw, an alcoholic twenty-six years her senior. After six unhappy years, she obtained a divorce in Reno, Nevada, and a lucrative settlement. She began her ascent in journalism by working at *Vogue* and *Vanity Fair;* an affair with the managing editor of the latter advanced her career. Her most notable lover, however, was financier and presidential adviser Bernard Baruch, who gave her entrée to a political world beyond the glitter of Park Avenue.

Resigning from *Vanity Fair,* she devoted herself for a time to writing plays. *The Women* (1936) ran for 657 performances, toured the country, and became a popular movie. A caustic comedy ridiculing the shallow world of society matrons, Clare's play featured a toxic wit that shocked and offended Eleanor Roosevelt and many drama critics.

In 1935, Clare met publishing magnate Henry R. Luce. Although married, the thoroughly smitten Luce proposed on their second meeting. Their marriage lasted thirty-two years. Marriage did not, however, give Clare the spot of managing editor of *Life* that she had coveted. Frustrated at being kept at arms' length from both *Time* and *Life,* she persuaded Luce to make her a foreign correspondent for *Life* as World War II began.

Her tour through Europe in early 1940 allowed her to visit the Maginot Line and to meet Churchill, Beaverbrook, and Joseph Kennedy. She was in Brussels when the Germans began their juggernaut west. Escaping via car to France just ahead of the invaders, she returned to the United States to write *Europe in the Spring,* which won praise for its clear-eyed evaluation of the European situation.

Clare's interview with General Douglas MacArthur was *Life's* cover story on December 8, 1941, complete with a photo that she had taken. Of the story, which ran seventy-three pages as submitted, *Life's* managing editor complained that it "stunk" because it "gushed about MacArthur" and told nothing about the Philippines (Martin 1991, 209–210). Nevertheless, Henry Luce pushed to have it printed, albeit in severely edited form. During the early years of U.S. participation in the war, Clare filed stories from the Far East as well as North Africa. Her prose was frequently overblown and self-indulgent, but she did include useful information about the Flying Tigers in Burma and the difficulties of desert warfare.

In 1942, Clare began another chapter of her career when she won a seat in Congress, representing a Connecticut district. Though a Roosevelt supporter in 1932, she had quickly become disenchanted with the president. She earned a reputation as one of FDR's most outspoken and abrasive critics, accusing him of having "lied" the United States into World War II (Martin 1991, 239) and calling U.S. plans for postwar cooperation "globaloney" (*Congressional Record* 1943, 761). She won reelection by a narrow margin in 1944, but the sudden death of her only child, Ann, a student at Stanford University, left her badly shaken. She did not seek reelection in 1946.

The postwar years brought Clare's much-publicized conversion to Catholicism and her appointment as ambassador to Italy. She became a respected elder in Republican circles. Her politics drifted ever rightward, as she spoke stridently about Communism, praised General and Madame Chiang Kai-shek, and defended Richard Nixon throughout Watergate. She spent the last years of her life in Hawaii, where she enjoyed scuba diving and painting. She died in 1987 at the age of eighty-four.

—*Pamela Tyler*

See also Chapelle, Dickey; Emerson, Gloria; Friang, Brigitte; Gellhorn, Martha; Higgins, Marguerite; Hull, Peggy, pseud.; Lederer, Edith; Schuyler, Philippa; Tomara, Sonia; Trotta, Liz; Watts, Jean

References and Further Reading

Boothe, Clare. 1937. *The Women*. New York: Random House.

Congressional Record. 1943. February 9, 1943, vol. 89, p. 761. Washington, DC.

Hatch, Alden. 1956. *Ambassador Extraordinary Clare Boothe Luce*. New York: Henry Holt.

Luce, Clare Boothe. 1940. *Europe in the Spring*. New York: A. A. Knopf.

Martin, Ralph G. 1991. *Henry and Clare: An Intimate Portrait of the Luces*. New York: G. P. Putnam's Sons.

Morris, Sylvia Jukes. 1977. *Rage for Fame: The Ascent of Clare Boothe Luce*. New York: Random House.

Sheed, Wilfrid. 1982. *Clare Boothe Luce*. New York: Dutton.

LUDINGTON, SYBIL
(1761–1839)

American Revolution patriot. Sybil Ludington obtained prominence during the American Revolution when she rode horseback through the countryside of eastern New York to alert the local militia that British forces had attacked nearby Danbury, Connecticut.

Born in 1761, Ludington was only 16 years old when she learned that 2,000 British troops had looted and set fire to Danbury on April 26, 1777. Ludington's home in Fredericksburg, New York, was only about 22 miles away, and the Continental army stored much of the region's supplies in Danbury. This alarmed Henry Ludington, Sybil's father, who was a colonel in the 7th Regiment of the Dutchess County Militia, a regiment comprised of volunteer farmers. Colonel Ludington wanted to help protect Danbury against the British, but the more than 400 members of his regiment were scattered throughout the sparsely settled region.

Sybil volunteered to spread the alarm because she, unlike the exhausted messenger who had warned her father, was familiar with the local terrain and the exact locations where the militia members lived. She also knew where many of the region's Tories lived and could thus avoid them on her ride. She left her home around 9:00 P.M. and under the cover of darkness she rode through Putnam and Dutchess counties in Connecticut. She rode for most of the rainy night through Carmel village, Mahopac, Mahopac Falls, Kent Cliffs, Farmers Mills, and back home through Stormville. Along the approximately 40-mile path, she quickly but discreetly knocked on doors, alerted the militiamen and their families of the proximity of British troops, and otherwise mustered the militia. When she returned home the following morning, more than 400 men set off to protect Danbury.

Colonel Ludington's men did not reach Danbury in time to save it from destruction. The town had already been overrun by British troops who had burned most of the homes and destroyed the stockpiles of food and munitions that were there. When the 7th Regiment finally arrived, British General William Tyron and his troops were already leaving Danbury. During the ensuing battle of Ridgefield, however, Ludington's militiamen joined with other patriot soldiers under the leadership of General David Wooster to force the British troops back to their ships in Long Island Sound.

—*Andrew K. Frank*

See also American Revolution, Role of Women in the

References and Further Reading

Berson, Robin Kadison. 1999. *Young Heroes in World History.* Westport, CT: Greenwood.

Bohrer, Melissa Lukeman. 2003. *Glory, Passion, and Principle: The Story of Eight Remarkable Women at the Core of the American Revolution.* New York: Atria.

LUXEMBURG, ROSA (1871–1919)

German radical socialist executed by right-wing paramilitaries for participating in the Spartacus revolt following the end of World War I. Born in Poland to a Jewish family, Rosa Luxemburg experienced a pogrom in Poland at the age of ten, setting the foundation for much of her future ideology. Her politics from that time reflected her humanitarian views as she worked for the social rights of every person. During the 1880s she embraced the ideology of Marxian internationalism as her own. Despite her Polish birth, Luxemburg did not support the Polish nationalist movement, arguing that nationalism detracted from the main goal of internationalism, and that socialist organizations should strive for the rights of all proletarians. Never a feminist or nationalist, Luxemburg believed that the rights of women and oppressed nationalities would be solved by socialism.

In 1889 Luxemburg and her family moved to Zurich, where she attended the University of Zurich and became one of few women at the time to receive an education at the university level. After completing her thesis, *The Industrial Devel-*

Rosa Luxemburg. (Library of Congress)

opment of Poland, she was granted a doctorate of economics in 1898 and left Zurich. Her intelligence, her speaking and writing skills, and her active political life in Zurich had garnered her much attention, though it was not necessarily positive. Her Polish nationality, her knowledge of several foreign languages, and her gender attracted the attention of the German Social Democratic Party (SPD). The SPD utilized her to spread the socialist message to Polish-speaking workers in Prussian-dominated regions and to gain the support of female workers. In comparison to the stagnant politics in Switzerland, activity with the SPD invigorated Luxemburg and she became bored with Zurich. Through her nominal marriage to Gustav Lubeck, a German citizen and the son of two of Luxemburg's comrades, Luxemburg became a German citizen. Luxemburg also had a lover, Leo Jogiches, who was her companion despite periods of discord for most of her life.

She moved to Berlin in 1898 and quickly established herself within the SPD's ranks as a comrade unafraid to assert her opinions. An ideological difference arose within the party between socialists arguing for reform (the revisionists) and those arguing for revolution. The revisionists wanted to work within the established monarchical system to achieve socialism, whereas the revolutionaries believed that extreme action was the only way to bring about socialism. Luxemburg, writing in *Reform or Revolution* (reprinted 1973), openly attacked revisionism and its leading supporters, criticizing the revisionists' willingness to work within a system that reinforced a class-based society. To Luxemburg's disappointment, the revisionist camp eventually dominated the party. Her outspokenness and inability to compromise her political beliefs won her notoriety but also gained for her disapproval among the moderate socialists.

Luxemburg's stubborn refusal to moderate her opinions led to repeated arrests and continual observation by Prussian officials. In 1903 Prussian authorities imprisoned her for insulting Kaiser Wilhelm's treatment of workers. Luxemburg participated in the failed Russian Revolution in Russian-controlled Poland in 1905, and in 1906 authorities arrested her before she left Russian territory. Following a second arrest and imprisonment in Russia, she returned to Berlin to teach at SPD's Central Party School, where she served until 1914. Over time she gained respect within the party as a result of her reputation as an authoritative teacher. In 1910, unhappy with the slow pace of socialist activity in Germany, she continued to disseminate her ideas and called for the creation of a German republic in her work, *Was Weiter* (*What's Next*) (reprinted 1970).

With the onset of World War I, Luxemburg and other socialist opponents of the war split from the SPD to form the Internationale, which she and Karl Liebknecht transformed into the Spartacus League in 1916. Initially an underground organization, the emergence of Spartacus led to another arrest for Luxemburg. She re-mained in prison for the duration of the war. There she wrote *The Russian Revolution* (translated 1940), expressing her disapproval of Vladimir Lenin's methods in Russia, and *The Junius Pamphlet* (reprinted 1967), arguing that socialism should be achieved by the people rather than by an elite party.

Released from prison following the defeat and the collapse of the German Empire, she joined with Liebknecht and other Spartacists to found the German Communist Party (KPD) in December 1918. Against her wishes, in January 1919 Liebknecht prematurely attempted to overthrow the provisional German government led by the moderate socialist Friedrich Ebert. The German Freikorps, under orders of the SPD-led government, quickly crushed the attempted revolution, known as the Spartacus revolt. Luxemburg, along with Liebknecht, was arrested and killed. Freikorps soldiers disposed of Luxemburg's body in a canal in the middle of the night; her body did not surface until May. Luxemburg was then buried with other comrades who had participated in the failed revolution.

—*Rachael I. Cherry*

See also Germany, Revolution of 1918–1919, Women in the

References and Further Reading

Bronner, Stephen E. 2001. *Socialism Unbound.* 2nd ed. Oxford: Westview.

Frölich, Paul. 1972. *Rosa Luxemburg: Ideas in Action.* London: Pluto Press.

Luxemburg, Rosa. 1940. *The Russian Revolution* [*Russische Revolution*]. Translation and Introduction by Bertram D. Wolfe. New York: Workers Age.

———. 1967. *Junius Pamphlet.* London: Merlin.

———. 1970. "Was Weiter," pages 289–299 in volume 2, *Gesammelte Werke* [Collected Works]. Edited by Günter Radczun. Berlin: Dietz.

———. 1973/1974. *Reform or Revolution?* [*Sozialreform oder revolution?*]. Translated by Integer. New York: Gordon Press.

Shepardson, Donald E. 1996. *Rosa Luxemburg and the Noble Dream.* New York: Peter Lang.

M. M. Raskova Borisov Guards Bomber Regiment

See Soviet Union, 125th M. M. Raskova Borisov Guards Bomber Regiment

MacLeod, Margaretha Gertruida

See Mata Hari, pseud.

Madres de la Plaza de Mayo

See Argentina, Mothers of the Plaza de Mayo

Makarova, Tat'iana Petrovna (1920–1944) and Belik, Vera Luk'ianovna (1921–1944)

Soviet night bombing team. Guards Lieutenants Tat'iana Petrovna Makarova and Vera Luk'ianovna Belik usually flew together as pilot and navigator-bombardier aboard the Polikarpov's Po-2, a highly maneuverable former trainer capable of operating from unprepared airstrips.

They served in the 588th Bomber Aviation Regiment, one of the three Soviet women's wings formed by Marina Raskova and redesignated 46th Taman' Guards Bomber Aviation Regiment in 1943; they were among the first in their unit to be decorated. In September 1942 Makarova received the Order of the Red Banner and Belik was awarded the Order of the Red Star.

Makarova was inspired by the famous 1938 nonstop flight to the Far East carried out by Marina Raskova, Polina Osipenko, and Valentina Grizodubova and by a pamphlet urging Young Communist League members to take up flying. Determined to become a professional pilot, she was admitted to a part-time flying course and was encouraged to train as an instructor. In 1940 she was appointed instructor at the Military School of Basic Training in Moscow (her former flying club) and was awarded the rank of sergeant.

In 1939 Belik enrolled at the Karl Liebknecht Pedagogical Institute in Moscow, where she studied mathematics. Her sound judgment, good memory, and the ability to calculate quickly were noted after she had volunteered for military service.

When, in December 1942, a third squadron was formed in their wing, Makarova became the commander and Belik the navigator of No. 2 squadron. After eight members of their squadron were shot down over the Kuban' area on July 31, 1943, at their own request Makarova and Belik reverted to duties of flight commander and navigator.

During difficult mission sorties over the Ukraine, North Caucasus, the Crimea, Belorussia, and Poland, they often descended to very low altitudes to increase their bombing accuracy. On August 1, 1944, they became the first aircrew of their wing to fight above German soil. Attacked by a German fighter near their home airfield in Poland on August 25, 1944, they perished as their aircraft went down in flames. They carried no parachutes. Makarova had flown a total 628 sorties and Belik, 813.

On February 23, 1945, both were posthumously awarded the Hero of the Soviet Union, the highest Soviet military decoration. As a result of lobbying by Makarova's comrades-in-arms, Bolotnaia, the street where her home was located, was renamed for her. In 1965 Lieutenant-Colonel Evdokiia Bershanskaia, Makarova's and Belik's commanding officer, and their biographer, Chief Navigator Larissa Litvinova, witnessed the unveiling of a memorial stone on the heroines' common grave in the Polish town of Ostroleka.

Kazimiera J. Cottam

See also Soviet Union/Russian Federation, Women Heroes of the

References and Further Reading

Cottam, Kazimiera J. 2003. Makarova, Tat'iana Petrovna, and Belik, Vera Luk'ianovna. Pages 271–272 in *Amazons to Fighter Pilots*. Edited by Reina Pennington. Vol. 1. Westport, CT: Greenwood.

Pennington, Reina. 2001. *Wings, Women and War.* Lawrence: University Press of Kansas.

MALTA, WOMEN AND WARS IN

Role of the women of Malta in war. Malta is a small archipelago 60 miles south of Sicily. In 1565 the Turks invaded Malta with 40,000 troops. The defense was led by the Knights of Malta with 600 knights, 2,600 infantry, and 3,000 Maltese militia (Balbi 1965, 41). Elderly men, as well as women and children, were also recruited. Women worked side by side with men repairing breaches in city walls, manufacturing incendiaries, and carrying supplies. Women and children collected wood to keep pots of pitch boiling, ready to tip onto the invaders.

The siege began in late May and extended throughout the summer. By July the Turks were assaulting the cities of Birgu and Senglea, where the majority of the people had taken shelter. The Turks shifted their attacks from one city to another, coming close to success on numerous occasions. The most serious crisis occurred on August 7 when both towns were assaulted simultaneously with 8,000 attacking Senglea and 4,000 coming against Birgu. The attacks, starting at dawn, lasted 9 hours. In time the Turks gained a foothold in Senglea (Balbi 1965, 145).

According to the knight Louis DeBoisgelin's account of the siege, the women of Malta responded vigorously to this threat and "performed actions which in some degree equaled the resolute valor of the knights . . . the women likewise nobly exposed themselves to the greatest dangers, in order, if possible, to save by their exertions husbands, fathers, brothers, and children" (DeBoisgelin 1988, 105–106). Women flung themselves into the battle, attacking invaders with incendiaries, boiling water, and melted pitch.

> The dread of being deprived, not only of their liberty but of their honor, should they be taken by the infidels, made these valiant women rise superior to the fear of death. The Turks . . . were so incensed at being opposed by such weak though courageous enemies, that they showed them no quarter, but slew a great number with the sword, and destroyed others by throwing, in their turn, fire-works amongst them. (DeBoisgelin 1988, II:105–06)

This fierce resistance, coupled with a timely cavalry raid on the enemy camp, forced the Turks to withdraw after having lost 2,200 men (Balbi 1965, 147).

The smaller town of Mdina was also threatened with attack. The governor dressed all the women as soldiers and marched them back and forth along the walls. The Turkish general, thinking Mdina too heavily defended, called off the attack. The invaders left Malta on September 8, which became celebrated as the Feast of Our Lady of Victory. The civilian casualties were high, with 7,000 Maltese men, women, and children killed (Balbi 1965, 189).

Malta suffered another siege during World War II. Malta was the only Allied base in the central Mediterranean and from there British planes attacked Axis convoys in North Africa. In turn, the Axis blocked convoys to Malta and dropped over 15,000 tons of bombs on the 90-square-mile island.

Despite the harsh conditions, life went on. Censa Bonnici recalled her marriage in November 1941. The wedding took place in the remnants of her bombed parish church. An air raid took place during the service, sending the congregation to a shelter, leaving just the priest, the couple, and two loyal witnesses to complete the ceremony (Mizzi 1998, 96).

Although the Bonnicis survived their wedding day, others were less fortunate. Guza Bondin was caring for her nine-month-old daughter while her husband served in the army. One day she and the baby ventured out to get a milk ration. Guza was careful, waiting for the all-clear to sound before venturing into the streets. But an earlier raid had dropped delayed-action bombs that were designed to cause civilian casualties. One of these exploded as she passed nearby. Guza pressed herself against a door and shielded her daughter's body with her own, but it was too late. The infant was hit in the head by a rock shard and killed (Mizzi 1998, 91–93).

By the summer of 1942 the Maltese were starving. The daily ration for adult males was 14.6 ounces (413.9 grams) of food and even less for women and children (Jellison 1984, 221). Mothers often gave their scanty ration to their children, but it could not satisfy their hunger. Nevertheless, Malta did not surrender, and the courage of the Maltese women, along with the rest of the civilian population, was recognized when King George VI collectively awarded them the George Cross.

—*Dennis A. Castillo*

See also Italy, Women in the Resistance during World War II

References and Further Reading

Balbi, Francisco di Corregio. 1965. *The Siege of Malta*. Trans. by Ernle Bradford. London: Hodder and Stoughton.

Boisgelin, Louis de. 1804. *Ancient and Modern Malta*. Vol. I–III. Repr. Valletta, Malta: Midsea Books Ltd. 1988.

Bradford, Ernle. 1961. *The Great Siege: Malta, 1565*. London: Hodder and Stoughton.

Jellison, Charles A. 1984. *Besieged: The World War II Ordeal of Malta, 1940–1942*. Hanover, NH: University Press of New England.

Mizzi, Laurence. 1998. *The People's War: Malta, 1940–1943*. Trans. by Joseph M. Falzon. Valletta, Malta: Progress Press.

MANDELA, WINNIE (1936–)

A leader of the African National Congress (ANC) in the struggle against apartheid. Winnie Mandela's ultimate significance in South African history may be as diverse as her many names. Known variously as Winnie Madikizela-Mandela, Nozamo Winnie Madikizela Mandela, Comrade Nomzamo, Nkosikazi Nobandle, and Nkosikazi Nobandle Nomzano Madikizela, to name a few, Winnie Mandela will probably best be remembered as one of the leaders in the ANC who fought against the racist apartheid governments in South Africa during the cold war.

Born in 1936 to two English-speaking, missionary-educated inhabitants of the Pondo area of the Transkei in South Africa, young Winnie always seemed to want to help people. In 1953 she moved to Johannesburg to pursue a degree in social work, which she obtained in 1955. Her first employer was the Baragwaneth Hospital and one of her roommates was a woman named Adelaide Tsukudu. Tsukudu introduced her to a young attorney and member of the ANC, Nelson Mandela. After a whirlwind courtship, Nelson and Winnie were married in a Methodist ceremony in 1958. The Mandelas settled into their home in the Soweto area of Johannesburg.

Winnie Mandela spent the first three years of her marriage supporting her husband during his trial on charges of treason. One way she showed her support was by wearing traditional tribal dress to the court proceedings, until the authorities prohibited such attire. In 1964, when her husband was arrested, found guilty, and sentenced to life in prison for his continued work with the ANC, Winnie Mandela was forced to live in the Orlando area of Soweto. She had to resign her social work position with the Johannesburg-based Child Welfare Society because she was not allowed by the government to travel outside of Orlando.

Nevertheless, Winnie Mandela did indeed leave Orlando and was subsequently sentenced to jail. She also spent time in jail in 1969 for failing to give her name and address to the city police and for working for the then-outlawed ANC. In 1970 she was arrested on charges of terrorism and spent time in solitary confinement in the Pretoria Central Prison. Between the time her husband was sentenced to life imprisonment in 1964 and 1977, Winnie Mandela spent approximately 17 months in various prisons throughout South Africa. She described what it was like to spend time in solitary confinement:

> Those first few days are the worst in anyone's life that uncertainty, that insecurity . . . The whole thing is calculated to destroy you. You are not in touch with anybody . . . The days and nights became so long I found I was talking to myself. (Mandela 1985, 99)

By the time she was released from prison, Mandela had spent 491 days in solitary confinement (Lipman 1984, 233). According to Mandela, what brought her the greatest pain and suffering was not the torture or imprisonment she endured, but the pain suffered by her daughter, Zindzi: "[that] was the hardest thing for me to take as a mother . . . Of course I was bitter, more than I've ever been" (Mandela 1984, 25).

Mandela supported the ANC and Black majority of South Africa through the creation of several social organizations such as the Black Women's Federation and the Black Parents' Association. The latter organization provided medical and legal assistance in the wake of the 1976 riots in Soweto. Winnie Mandela never did take on any of the executive roles held by her incarcerated husband and that may have to do more with gender relations than her skills or abilities as a leader (O'Brien 1994, 154).

Probably the two most significant events in Mandela's life were the 1976 Soweto uprising and her involvement with the Mandela United Football Club (MUFC). In the mid-June heat of 1976, South African police fought with the town of Soweto over the government's attempt to compel the Black majority to educate their children in the language of the White minority Afrikaans. Officially, a few dozen died. Unofficially, a few hundred were killed. Nevertheless, the violence signaled the beginning of the end of apartheid in South Africa. Thousands of Black leaders were arrested, among them Winnie Mandela, whom the government tried to implicate as orchestrating the riots. As part of her punishment the government removed Mandela from Orlando and forced her to live in the Brandfort area of the Black township of Phatakahle, in the Orange Free State.

As a result of her Brandfort home being firebombed, the government allowed Mandela to move anywhere in South Africa, provided that she did not live in Johannesburg or Roodeport. She decided to move back to Soweto in the mid-1980s. While Mandela continued her work in support of civil and human rights, other Black groups began to distance themselves from her. One reason for this split was her involvement with the MUFC. The sporting group lived with Mandela and tended to play the role of her bodyguard more so than playing football (soccer) matches. The government arrested and found guilty many members of the football club on charges ranging from robbery to murder, including the kidnapping, torture, and murder of fourteen-year-old Stompie Moeketsi Sepei. In 1991 the South African Truth and Reconciliation Commission found Mandela "politically and morally accountable for the gross violations of human rights committed by the MUFC" (Pohlandt-McCormick 2000, 585).

As a result of MUFC's "reign of terror," the Congress of South African Trade Unions and the United Democratic Front both cut all ties with Winnie Mandela and her organizations. Even the Mandelas could not ride out the waves of political and legal intrigue. After more than thirty years of marriage, Nelson Mandela announced in 1992 that he and Winnie had separated a year earlier. In 1996 they divorced, and Winnie Mandela added her maiden name

to her last name, becoming Winnie Madikizela-Mandela.

Despite her legal, professional, and personal problems, Winnie Mandela was honored with the Robert F. Kennedy Humanitarian Award, the Freedom Prize, the first International Simone de Beauvoir Award, and the Third World Prize for her work in advancing civil, human, and gender-specific rights in South Africa. She also was awarded an honorary doctor of law degree from Haverford Quaker College.

In the early twenty-first century, Winnie Madikizela-Mandela served as the president of the ANC Women's League as well as a member of the South African Parliament. She continued to work for the advancement of women's rights throughout the world.

—Jim Ross-Nazzal

See also First, Heloise Ruth

References and Further Reading

Gilbey, Emma. 1993. *The Lady: The Life and Times of Winnie Mandela.* London: Cape.

Harrison, Nancy. 1985. *Winnie Mandela, Mother of a Nation.* London: Gollancz.

Lipman, Beata. 1984. *We Make Freedom: Women in South Africa.* London: Pandora.

Mandela, Winnie. 1984. *Part of My Soul.* London: Penguin.

———. 1985. *Part of My Soul Went with Him.* Edited by Anne Benjamin. New York: Norton.

Meltzer, Milton. 1986. *Winnie Mandela: The Soul of South Africa.* New York: Viking Penguin.

O'Brien, Colleen. 1994. "In Search for Mother Africa: Poetry Revises Women's Struggles for Freedom." *African Studies Review,* 37 (September) 2: 147–155.

Pohlandt-McCormick, Helena. 2000. "Controlling Woman: Winnie Mandela and the 1976 Soweto Uprising." *The International Journal of African Historical Studies,* 33(3):585–614.

Truth and Reconciliation Commission. 1991. *Report II.* Chp. 6: Special Investigation: Mandela United Football Club. http://www.info.gov.za/otherdocs/ 2003/trc/4_1.pdf (accessed June 25, 2005).

MARIANNE

The female symbol of the French republic and French revolutionary and martial ardor. The figure of Marianne is always depicted as wearing a Phrygian bonnet, such as that worn by freed slaves in Greece, as a symbol of republicanism. The figure is often depicted carrying a revolutionary pike, such as the one that held aloft the head of the commander of the Bastille on July 14, 1789; or a gun. At the end of 1792, France's parliament, the Convention, decreed that the seal of France should include this female liberty figure. Marianne was depicted leading representatives of various classes of the people as they fought on the barricades in Eugene Delacroix's famous painting, *Liberty Leading the People,* which he painted to celebrate the French July Revolution of 1830. In 1889 at the centennial of the Revolution, when the *Marseillaise* became the French national anthem, and July 14, the day on which the Bastille fell, became France's national holiday, representations of Marianne were put in place on Paris' Place de la Republic and Place de la Nation. During World War I, Marianne was depicted in a number of patriotic poses: resolute, warlike, or motherly. As a young woman she greeted her suitor and hero, Uncle Sam, when the United States entered the war in

Liberty Leading the People, *by Eugene Delacroix (1798–1863). (Bettmann/Corbis)*

1917. After the end of the war she soberly commemorated the dead. Her image was banned by the antirepublican and collaborationist Vichy regime (1940–1944) but reappeared alongside General Charles De Gaulle on Free French posters.

—Bernard Cook

See also French Revolution, Impact of War on Women's Protest during the; Paris Commune, Women and the

References and Further Reading

Blume, Mary. "The French Icon Marianne à la mode." International Herald Tribune, July 16, 2004.

"Living in the Languedoc: Central Government: French National Symbols: Marianne." http://www.languedoc-france.info/06141211_marianne.htm (accessed March 2, 2005).

MARIE, QUEEN OF ROMANIA (1875–1938)

Queen of Romania during World War I. Granddaughter of Queen Victoria and cousin to Czar Nicolas, the last emperor of Russia, Queen Marie was a proud, very tenacious, perfect English lady, with an unbeatable will. She inspired courage and confidence in her husband, King Ferdinand, during the darkest and most hopeless moments for the country. According to Count Charles de Saint-Aulaire, a French official in Bucharest during that period, "there is only one man in Romania and that is the Queen" (Pakula 1989, 226).

According to her memoirs, she trusted England and had the vision of a united Romanian state. These were the main reasons that she did not loose faith during the terrible years of World War I, when three-quarters of the country was under Austrian, German, and Bulgarian occupation.

During the difficult period of her withdrawal to Moldavia during the winter of 1916–1917, with the support of the Allies' Red Cross service and with the help of Colonel O. Ballif, the Royal House administrator, the Queen energetically worked to establish a network of military hospitals on the front line. She personally attended wounded soldiers, established public canteens for children and refugees in need, and organized warehouses for food, clothing, and medicine.

She modernized the Iasi Railway Marshalling Station, an aid unit that had consisted of dark, cold, bad-smelling barracks. The wounded lay on the floors, infested with lice, until places for them were found in the overcrowded hospitals. Very often the Queen dressed in the white uniform of a nun–nurse and visited the hospitals. She passed among the rows of hospital beds offering cigarettes, a book of prayers, or a slice of bread.

At that time, she was moving constantly along the front or visiting cities such as Bacau, Onesti, and Roman; spending days in campaign hospitals close to areas where artillery fire could be heard. Her car was always loaded with supplies for immediate help. As large quantities of food, clothing, and medicine began to arrive from the Red Cross, the Queen offered them personally to prisoners-of-war met on the road and to hungry Jews in Iasi, as well as to her soldiers. In the autumn of 1917, she established the Queen Mary's Cross Medal for special merit in military sanitation activities.

Although she could not prevent the armistice between Romania and the central powers, Queen Marie pressed the British government to continue supporting the interests of Romania. In Iasi, at the insistence of the Queen and Prime Minister Bratianu, the Allied ministers signed a document asserting that Romania had heroically fought to the extreme limit, and was forced into a retreat and temporary cease-fire by Russia's treasonous lack of promised support.

As the "Queen Mother" of her soldiers and all those who did not stop believing in the causes of Romania and of the *Entente Cordiale,* Marie was the most vivid symbol of the country's resistance during the war.

—*Miodrag Milin*

See also Teodoroiu, Ecaterina

References and Further Reading

Pakula, Hannah. 1989. *Queen of Romania: The Life of Princess Marie, the Granddaughter of Queen Victoria.* London: Eland.

Countess Constance Markievicz, an Irish Republican leader, makes a farewell address in Boston before returning to Ireland, 1922. (Bettmann/Corbis)

MARKIEVICZ (NÉE GORE-BOOTH), COUNTESS CONSTANCE (1868–1927)

Irish nationalist imprisoned for her role in the Easter Rebellion. Constance Gore-Booth was born in London. Her family belonged to the Protestant ascendancy of prosperous landowners and owned a large estate in County Sligo. She was presented at court in London and studied art in London and Paris before marrying a destitute Polish count, Casimir Dunin Markievicz. A daughter, Maeve, was born in the Ukraine in 1901, but the marriage failed after the family returned to Ireland. In 1907 the Countess joined the nationalist women's organization Inghinidhe na hÉireann (Daughters of Ireland), founded by Maud Gonne, and wrote for its newspaper, *Bean na hÉireann.* In 1908 Markievicz and Bulmer Hobson founded a scouting organization, Fianna (Warriors) to train young people to fight for the nationalist cause. She joined the Irish Citizen Army, which was founded in 1913 to protect workers' against police attacks during the Dublin Lockout.

During the Easter Rebellion of 1916, Countess Makievicz, a lieutenant in the Citizen Army, was second-in-command for the rebel forces at St. Stephen's Green. Of the fourteen women fighters among the rebels at St. Stephen's, Markievicz and Margaret Skinnider were reputedly the best snipers, male or female. At the beginning of the rebellion the Countess shot a policeman who refused to leave his post at the main entrance to the Green. When the rebels at St. Stephen's were forced to surrender, Markievicz kissed her Mauser pistol before handing it to a British officer. After executing fifteen male nationalists, the British sentenced Markievicz to death but recommended mercy because of her sex. The sentence was commuted to life imprisonment. She was freed, however, by the July 1917 general amnesty. While in prison, she was elected the president of Cumann na mBan (The League of Women), the main organization of Irish nationalist women.

In December 1918, in the first election in the United Kingdom in which women were allowed to vote, Markievicz was the first woman elected to the British parliament. She, however, with the other Irish nationalists of the Sinn Féin (We Ourselves—the Irish Republican party dedicated to the independence of all of Ireland), refused to take her seat at Westminster. She joined the Dáil, the Irish parliament in Dublin, as the first labor minister of the new Irish government. She opposed the treaty with England agreed to by Michael Collins and opposed the Irish Free State government in the Irish Civil War. She edited a republican newspaper and traveled to America to gain support for the antitreaty Republicans. She was arrested by the Irish Free State in 1923.

With the end of the civil war, Markievicz was elected to the Dáil, but refused to take her seat because of her unwillingness to take an oath of loyalty to the British king. She joined Eamon de Valera's party, Fianna Fáil (Warriors of Destiny), when it was organized in 1926. In 1927 she was elected as a Fianna Fáil candidate to the Dáil but died on July 15 before taking her seat. Some critics regarded her as superficial and self-absorbed, but the common people of Ireland did not share this negative assessment. Three hundred thousand lined the streets for her funeral procession and de Valera delivered the eulogy at her grave.

—*Bernard Cook*

See also Gonne, Maud; Ireland, The Easter Rising of 1916; Ireland, War of Independence

References and Further Reading

Haverty, Anne. 1993. *Constance Markievicz: Irish Revolutionary.* New York: New York University.

McCool, Sineád. 2000. *Guns and Chiffon: Women Revolutionaries and Kilmainham Goal 1916–1923.* Dublin: The Stationery Office.

O'Faoláin, Sean. 1968. *Constance Markievicz, or The Average Revolutionary.* London: Sphere.

Van Voris, Jacqueline. 1967. *Countess Markievicz: In the Cause of Ireland.* Amherst: University of Massachusetts.

MARKOVIC, MIRJANA
(1941–)

Wife of Slobodan Milosevic, nationalist president of Serbia. Mirjana Markovic was the primary influence on Milosevic, who, as a result of the atrocities committed by Serbian forces during the Kosovo conflict, was indicted by the International War Crimes Tribunal for the Former Yugoslavia. On May 27, 1999, Milosevic was accused of being responsible for ordering the ethnic cleansing of the province and for the rape and murder committed by his troops. Milosevic's biographer, Slavoljub Djukic, said that Markovic, whom he regards as the most powerful woman in Serbian history, "invented" Milosevic (Glenny and Hanzic 1999, 13).

Markovic was the daughter of the unmarried secretary of the Belgrade District Communist Party, who was captured by the Germans and executed in 1942. Markovic was raised by an aunt who was a secretary to Tito, the founder of Communist Yugoslavia. When Mirjana was fifteen, Draza Markovic, a leading Yugoslav Communist, acknowledged that she was his daughter. Mirjana met Milosevic in secondary school and they married while they were students at the University of Belgrade. As a sociologist, she subsequently taught Marxist theory at the university. She is regarded as the force behind Milosevic's rise to power during the period from 1987 to 1990, when he became president of Serbia.

In 2003 the Serbian government issued an arrest warrant for Markovic, who had fled to Russia. The warrant was based on allegations of abuse of power during Milosevic's rule and suspicion of involvement in the murder of the former Serbian President Ivan Stambolic in 2000, shortly before Milosevic was ousted from power.

—*Bernard Cook*

See also Yugoslavia, Women and the Wars That Accompanied the Disintegration of Yugoslavia

References and Further Reading

Glenny, Misha, and Edin Hanzic. "Serbia's Lady Macdeath." *Australian,* March 30, 1999.

"Second Warrant Issued for Milosevic's Wife." *Edmonton* (Alberta) *Journal,* April 19, 2003.

"Serbia-Montenegro Expects Russia to Extradite Milosevic Wife, Son." *Financial Times News Service.* June 20, 2003.

MARTIN, GRACE (N.D.), AND MARTIN, RACHEL (N.D.)

American patriots. The wives of American Revolutionary War soldiers who disguised themselves in their husbands' clothes, took up arms, and successfully intercepted a dispatch from British soldiers and handed it over to the American side.

Grace Waring Martin and Rachel Clay Martin endured the war at the home of their mother-in-law, Elizabeth Marshall Martin. The Martin house was located west of Charleston, South Carolina, along the border with the Cherokee nation. Their husbands were the eldest of the seven Martin sons who had all volunteered for service in the Continental Army.

In the absence of men, the women were subject to the abuses of Loyalists, who on one occasion cut open and scattered the feather beds of the house. The women had also provided a safe haven for an injured Continental soldier, hiding him from Loyalists who were searching for him. The fighting soon came close to home for the Martin women, first with the siege of the port of Augusta and afterward the fort at nearby Cambridge, also known as Fort Ninety-Six. Grace's husband, William, was killed during the siege of Augusta, and a British officer passing to Fort Ninety-Six, still under British possession, rode out to the Martin house to deliver the news in hopes that it would devastate the women.

The Martins received word one evening that a courier, guarded by two British officers, would be passing through the area with an important dispatch. Rachel and Grace determined that they would intercept the message and hand it over to General Nathanael Greene. The women disguised themselves in their husbands' clothing, took weapons, and positioned themselves in the bushes at a point along the road where they knew the British party would pass. The women surprised the British and held them at gunpoint, gained their immediate surrender and the handover of the dispatch, then released them. The dispatch was sent by another messenger directly to General Greene.

Later that night the same three British men sought lodging for the night at the Martin home. The women, their disguises never revealed, offered their hospitality, listened to the men's story of being taken prisoner by two rebel boys, and showed the women their paroles. The men departed the next day, not knowing that these were the very women who had held them at gunpoint the night before.

—*Kristen L. Rouse*

See also American Revolution, Role of Women in the; Corbin, Margaret Cochrane; Fulton, Sarah Bradlee; Greene, Catharine Littlefield; Ludington, Sybil; Molly Pitcher; Samson, Deborah; Washington, Martha Dandridge Custis; Zane, Elizabeth

References and Further Reading

Ellet, Elizabeth F. 1849. *The Women of the American Revolution.* 3rd ed. New York: Baker and Scribner.

MARTIN-NICHOLSON, MARY ELIZA LOUISE GRIPPER

See Conquest, Joan, pseud.

MATA HARI, PSEUD. (MARGARETHA GERTRUIDA MACLEOD, NÉE ZELLE) (1876–1917)

Dutch exotic dancer and courtesan accused of spying for the Germans and executed by the French in 1917. Mata Hari, was born Margaretha Gertrud Zelle on August 7, 1876, at Leeuwarden in the Netherlands. She was the daughter of a Dutch shopkeeper, Adam Zelle, and his wife Antje van der Meulen. Margaretha Zelle was forced to leave a training school for kindergarten teachers after becoming romantically involved with the principal. When she was eighteen, she married a Dutch naval officer of Scottish ancestry stationed in the East Indies, Rudolph MacLeod, who was thirty-eight years old. Following the termination of this unsuccessful marriage, she moved to Paris, adopted the name Mata Hari, and began to perform as an exotic dancer. Her shows gained her widespread notoriety.

When World War I broke out, she was in Germany. Some have asserted that she was recruited there as a German spy by a lover, Traugott von Jagow. After returning to Paris, Mata Hari was placed under surveillance by the French. She fell deeply in love with a young Russian officer, Vladimir Masloff. After he was wounded she wished to visit him in the combat zone. She sought the intervention of Captain Georges Ladoux, who worked in French counterespionage, to obtain permission to travel to the war zone. Mata Hari, who was anxious to provide for herself and her young (and now disabled) Russian lover, was recruited by Ladoux to spy for France. She was to go to Belgium where it was hoped that her contacts would enable her to gain access to General Moritz Ferdinand von Bissing, the German in charge of the occupation of Belgium.

As she traveled to Belgium via Spain to neutral Holland, Mata Hari was detained during a stop at Falmouth, England. The British were looking for Clara Bendix, a German spy whom Mata Hari resembled. The British interrogated her and, on instructions from the French, sent her to Spain. There Mata Hari, in need of money, reputedly had an affair with a German military attaché, Major Arnold Kalle. Some assert that Mata Hari was playing the role of a double agent at this point. In any case, Kalle sent a message, which he knew the British would intercept, stating that he had gained valuable information from Mata Hari, whom he identified as spy H-21.

When she returned to Paris, Mata Hari was arrested. She admitted taking money from Germans, but said that it was in return for her physical attention, not spying. Nevertheless, a closed court martial convicted her of spying, and she was executed by a firing squad on October 15, 1917. To the end, Mata Hari protested that she was innocent of spying for the Germans. She refused a blindfold and blew a kiss to her executioners before they fired.

—*Bernard Cook*

See also Cavell, Edith; Petit, Gabrielle

References and Further Reading

Howe, Russell Warren. 1986. *Mata Hari: The True Story.* New York: Dodd, Mead.

Martini, Teri. 1990. *The Secret Is Out: True Spy Stories.* Boston: Little, Brown.

Ostrovsky, Erika. 1978. *Eye of Dawn: The Rise and Fall of Mata Hari.* New York: Macmillan.

MATILDA OF TUSCANY (1046–1114)

Military leader in support of the papacy. Matilda, countess of Tuscany, is an almost unheard-of figure from the European Middle Ages—a woman whose fame is based primarily on her military role. She was the sole heiress of Count Boniface of Tuscany and his wife Beatrice of Lorraine. When her father was assassinated in 1053, Matilda became one of Europe's greatest landholders. In 1076 she gained extensive territory on the northern side of the Alps when both her mother and her husband, Godfrey (the Hunchback of Lorraine) died. Matilda's northern Italian lands were especially important to the power of the German Salian emperors in Italy. Matilda was not only the most important imperial vassal in Italy, but her lands also guarded the route to Rome—control of the papacy was central to the policy of the Salian dynasty. When open war broke out between Emperor Henry IV and Pope Gregory VII in 1077, Matilda was in a position of great strategic importance. The conflict between papacy and empire, known as the Investiture Contest, raged through Germany and Italy for the rest of Matilda's lifetime and was only partially resolved in 1122. It would not have lasted so long nor ended in the centralization of church power under the papacy had it not been for Matilda.

Matilda was a staunch supporter of Gregory VII and his successors. When relations between pope and emperor first deteriorated early in 1077, she mediated between the two at her castle in Canossa. The resulting peace broke down, after which Matilda provided Gregory with military support. Her most important role was in the defense of Tuscany, preventing Henry IV from reaching Rome and denying him supplies and soldiers from her dominions. Matilda appears to have kept active control of her military instead of delegating the fighting to a male commander; contemporary chroniclers marveled at her "manlike" devotion to the papal cause. She was one of the few medieval women to personally lead an army. Henry IV succeeded in driving Gregory VII from Rome and establishing an "antipope" in his place. In 1087 Matilda marched against the antipope and drove him from Rome. Although she did not personally go on the campaign, in the same year the countess also played a major role in planning the Italian assault on Mahdia, a notable center for piracy in northern Africa.

Matilda remained loyal to the papacy until her death, even after her second husband, Welf of Bavaria, joined the Imperial party in 1096. Finally, the childless Matilda willed her personal lands to the Roman church, a bequest that helped the papacy continue its struggle to centralize religious authority in Christendom.

—*Phyllis G. Jestice*

See also Eleanor of Aquitaine

References and Further Reading:

Eads, Valerie. 2002. The Geography of Power: Matilda of Tuscany and the Strategy of Active Defense. In *Crusaders, Condottieri, and Cannon: Medieval Warfare in the Mediterranean Region.* Edited by J. L. Andrew Villalon and Donald Kagay. Leiden, Netherlands: Brill.

Robinson, Ian S. 1999. *Henry IV of Germany, 1056–1106.* Cambridge, UK : Cambridge University.

MAU MAU REBELLION, WOMEN IN THE

Role of women in the struggle for Kenyan independence. During the 1950s an anticolonial struggle took place in Kenya between Africans who had been colonized by the British. The causes of the revolt dated back to the very early days of colonial occupation. From 1895, when Kenya was declared to be a crown colony of Great Britain, Africans were dispossessed of their land, forced to pay taxes to the new colonial state, and compelled to become low-paid laborers for European settlers and various government enterprises. In addition to economic and political changes, the colonial government, often encouraged by European missionaries, introduced social changes that supplanted customary laws affecting marriage, education, inheritance, land ownership, and religious practices. By the end of World War II a vigorous nationalist movement had emerged in Kenya.

This movement was connected to the continent-wide anticolonial movement because Africans in the colonized areas were eager to eliminate European hegemonic control of their politics, economies, and cultures. Kenya was also one of the African colonies that, like Algeria, South Africa, Mozambique, Angola, Namibia, and Guinea-Bissau, had been established as a white settler colony. The presence of white settlers added a special dynamic to colonialism in Kenya. Because the government was controlled by its European settler population, with the exception of South Africa, there was more race-based discrimination in Kenya than in other British colonies. In fact, the conditions in Kenya were very similar to the apartheid conditions in South Africa, where black Africans were forced to carry passes in order to be outside of their assigned areas, were socially segregated, barred from jobs that were reserved for Europeans and Asian immigrants, and unlike Europeans in Kenya, were unable to participate in politics through voting.

The nationalist movement, led by Harry Thuku, Peter Koinange, and Jomo Kenyatta, began shortly after World War I. Leading both rural and urban dissidents, these nationalists established political associations—the East African Association (1920s), the Kikuyu Central Association (1925–1940), the Kenya African Union (KAU; 1944–1951), and the Land and Freedom Army (1950s)—which eventually became broad-based grassroots coalitions. The Land and Freedom Army was commonly known as the Mau Mau movement. During the first thirty years of the nationalist movement, the political associations utilized several strategies to affect social and political change. These included petitioning the government for lower taxes, improved education, and an end to race-based discrimination in voting, land ownership, and employment. The groups also used mass protests and labor strikes. Two decades of associational politics yielded little change. During World War II, even these moderate African political associations were banned by the British government, which argued that their existence would aid the German war effort. After World War II Africans turned to more militant tactics and the the Land and Freedom Army rebellion began. The goals of the Mau Mau movement were to regain land and achieve freedom from Great Britain. The tactics of the Mau Mau fighters included armed insurgency, which had not been seen in Kenya since the first resistance to colonial occupation had ended.

In the late 1940s African militants began to take oaths that required initiates to swear to be loyal to their fellow black Africans, to maintain the secrets of the organization, and to fight Europeans. Because of widespread inductions, mass meetings, and attacks on African loyalists and Europeans, the government declared a state of emergency in October 1952. Thousands of African men and women fled to the forests and established Mau Mau guerilla bases. Over 10,000 Africans lost their lives during the rebellion. Many more were imprisoned during the war that lasted from 1952 until 1956. Although military operations ended in 1956, men and women rebels remained in detention up until 1959 when the imprisonment system ended.

From the beginning of the nationalist movement until the final release of detainees in 1959, women were very much involved in the nationalist movement and its more militant arm, the Mau Mau movement. Their involvement had begun in the 1930s when they established the Mumbi Central Association, a women's nationalist organization. Mumbi Central was created because male nationalists excluded women from participating in the most prominent nationalist organization, the Kikuyu Central Association. After 1933 the Mumbi Central Association merged with the Kikuyu Central Association; this set a precedent that is still visible in Kenya's political parties of having a women's wing and prominent women members of political organizations. In the 1950s women who fought in the independence movement laid the groundwork for the subsequent involvement of women, such as Wangari Maathai, a noted environmentalist and activist in Kenya and winner of the 2004 Nobel Peace Prize for her work in national and local politics.

From the 1950s women participated in all phases of the anticolonial war. They joined the secret Mau Mau organization that emerged after 1948. The new recruits were required to take an oath of loyalty. Though swearing to abide by a solemn promise was traditionally reserved for males, when the Mau Mau movement began women also took oaths and were often able to administer oaths to male and female recruits. Female Mau Mau adherents, by giving and taking oaths, were therefore breaking an important gender barrier from their introduction to the movement.

Gender barriers were also broken in the area of leadership roles and combat roles. The women's wing of Mau Mau had a prominent female leader, Rebecca Njeri Kari. Another leader, Wambui Waiyaki (later Otieno), developed a network of women spies who gathered data on British installations and operations. At the district and village level women also emerged as leaders. During the rebellion, British political and military forces arrested, imprisoned, and detained Mau Mau leadership and rank-and-file members. Women were among those who were arrested and detained. Prominent women leaders, including Kari, Waiyaki, and Wambui Wangarama, spent years in prison for their political beliefs.

The British likewise imprisoned thousands of women because they were armed combatants, as well as noncombatants who performed support functions for the rebels who lived in guerilla camps in the inaccessible forest zones in Kenya's Central Province. Many other women experienced short-term detention and interrogation because they were Mau Mau rebels or accused of being Mau Mau rebels. A special prison wing was built to hold them. Hardcore prisoners were deported to prisons in coastal areas. During their imprisonment, detainees experienced abuses that included physical assault, sexual assault, food deprivation, and other acts of torture. These became so infamous that the British Parliament investigated and reformed the system toward the end of 1959.

Outside of the prisons, the Mau Mau rebellion was ultimately crushed in 1954 through massive roundups, interrogations, and a program of "villagization." Villagization involved the destruction of tradition villages and the forced relocation of the Kikuyu population to new villages that were surrounded by barbed wire fences and armed guards. Although the villagization policy had the ostensible goal of land consolidation, its real aim was to cut off the support Mau Mau rebels obtained from village populations. A crucial part of that support comprised the network of women who smuggled food and arms to the rebel camps in the forested areas of the three Kikuyu districts.

After the war, like other African colonies Kenya was able to gain its independence. The British government spent millions of pounds repressing the rebellion and was rocked by a scandal involving the murder of political detainees. In addition, other British colonies experienced vigorous populist-based nationalist movements. For Kenya, the failed Mau Mau rebellion was a key factor. Although the rebels lost and thousands were killed, the surviving rebels and others credited the movement with being the impetus for negotiations for independence that began in 1960. Jomo Kenyatta, who was the leader of the KAU organization and alleged to be the leader of Mau Mau by the British, was released from detention in August 1961; when independence was achieved in 1963, Kenyatta became the head of the new African government of Kenya. The new government acknowledged women's roles in the nationalist struggle. Although the new regime did not reform laws that disadvantaged women, some were able to assume political roles such as running for office on the district and national level. They also gained the right to own property and to serve in the military. Thus, the legacy of women's participation in the struggle resulted in a shift in traditional gender roles and laid the basis for social and political change in contemporary Kenya.

—*Cora Ann Presley*

See also Algeria, Women in the War of National Liberation; Eritrea, Women and the Struggle for Independence; Mandela, Winnie

References and Further Reading

Kabira, Wanjiku M., and Nzioki, Elizabeth A. 1993. *Celebrating Women's Resistance: A Case Study of Women's Groups Movement in Kenya.* Nairobi, Kenya: African Women's Perspective.

Kanogo, Tabitha M. 1987. Kikuyu Women and the Politics of Protest: Mau. Pages 78–99 in *Images of Women in Peace and War, Cross-Cultural Historical Perspectives.* Edited by Sharon Macdonald, Pat Holder, and Shirley Ardener. Madison: University of Wisconsin Press.

Nzomo, Maria. 1997. Kenya: The Women's Movements and Democratic Change. Pages 167–184 in *The African State at a Critical Juncture: Between Disintegration and Reconfiguration.* Edited by Leonardo Villalon and Phillip Huxtable. Boulder, CO: Lynne Rienner Publishers.

Otieno, Wambui W. 1998. *Mau Mau's Daughter: The Life History of Wambui Waiyaki Otieno.* Edited by Cora A. Presley. Boulder, CO: Lynne Rienner Publishers.

Presley, Cora A. 1992. *Kikuyu Women the Mau Mau Rebellion and Social Change in Kenya.* Boulder, CO: Westview.

———. 2002. Gender and Political Struggle in Kenya, 1948–1998. Pages 173–188 in *Stepping Forward: Black Women in Africa and the Americas.* Edited by Catherine Higgs, Barbara A. Moss, and Erline R. Ferguson. Athens: Ohio University Press.

White, Luise. 1990. "Separating the Men from the Boys: Constructions of Gender Sexuality and Terrorism in Central Kenya, 1939–1959." *International Journal of African Historical Studies.* 23(1):1–25.

Wipper, Audrey. 1989. "Kikuyu Women and the Harry Thuku Disturbances: Some Uniformities of Female Militancy." *Africa*, 59(3):330–337.

McCarthy, Emma Maud (1858–1949)

Matron-in-Chief of the British Armies, 1915–1918. Emma Maud McCarthy, the daughter of a solicitor, was born in Sydney, New South Wales, in 1859. She was educated at Springfield College and the University of Sydney. In 1891 she went to England and trained as a nurse at Whitechapel London Hospital. During the Boer War, Princess Alexandria chose McCarthy and five other nurses from the London Hospital to go to South Africa as her military nurses. At the end of the war, McCarthy returned to London, having served with distinction. In London she was involved in the establishment of Queen Alexandria's Imperial Military Nursing Service and served as matron at the Netley, Aldershot, and Millbank military hospitals.

In 1910 McCarthy was appointed principal matron at the British War Office. In that capacity she sailed to France in August 1914 with the first ship transporting the British Expeditionary Force. In 1915 she was appointed Matron-in-Chief in charge of all British military nurses. She retained that position throughout the war and returned to England only once while recuperating from an appendectomy. Her organizational skill and energy were remarkable. By 1918 she was in charge of administering a nursing force of some 6,500.

After the war, Maud McCarthy served for five years as Matron-in-Chief of the Territorial Army Nursing Service before retiring.

—*Bernard Cook*

See also Great Britain, Women in Service during World War I

References and Further Reading

"Maud McCarthy." www.barbazon.org.uk/barb47 .htm (accessed November 30, 2004).

McDOUGALL, GRACE ASHLEY-SMITH (1889–1963)

Commandant of the British First Aid Nursing Yeomanry (FANY). Grace McDougall was instrumental in reorganizing the FANY corps for overseas service in World War I. She was decorated by the British with the 1914 Star, by the French with the Croix de Guerre, and by the Belgians as a member of the Order of the Crown, the Order of Queen Elizabeth, and as a Knight of Leopold II.

McDougall, the first member of FANY at the front lines, began as a nurse in Antwerp, Belgium. She worked under constant bombardment and frequently went into the trenches to rescue wounded soldiers. In the Allied retreat from Antwerp, McDougall fell behind German lines while helping a sick English officer. She succeeded in escaping German capture and slipped across the Dutch border to safety.

Back in England, McDougall unsuccessfully petitioned the War Office to get a FANY unit accepted for service. She finally offered the unit to the Belgians. In October 1914 she established the first FANY hospital at Calais in addition to dressing station at Oostkirke, one mile behind the trenches. She later established a typhoid hospital, a convalescent camp for British soldiers, and a convoy of ambulance drivers for the British Red Cross.

—*Barbara Penny Kanner*

See also Great Britain, Women in Service during World War I; Stobart, Mabel

References and Further Reading

McDougall, Grace. 1917. *Nursing Adventures: A F.A.N.Y. in France.* London: W. Heinemann.

Popham, Hugh. 2003. *The F.A.N.Y. in Peace and War: The Story of the First Aid Women's Yeomanry, 1907–2003.* Barnsley, UK: Leo Cooper, Pen and Sword.

McDOWELL, MARY STONE (1876–1955)

New York City public school teacher dismissed during World War I due to her pacifist beliefs. Born on March 22, 1876, in Jersey City, New Jersey, Mary McDowell was the daughter of birthright members of the Society of Friends (Quakers). At sixteen she entered the Quaker Swarthmore College. She excelled academically, was Phi Beta Kappa, and won a Lucretia Mott Fellowship for postgraduate studies at Oxford University. After spending a year as a home student in the Association for the Education of Women at Oxford, McDowell returned to the United States where she taught at the Friends' Academy on Long Island. During this period she also received a master's degree in classical languages and education from Columbia University Teachers College.

In February 1905 McDowell received a permanent appointment as a teacher of Latin and Greek in the New York public school system. In April 1917, when the United States entered World War I, the New York board of education demanded that all teachers promote patriotism and demonstrate loyalty to the war effort. McDowell immediately joined the newly established Women's Peace Party, led by prominent women Jane Addams, Emily Greene Balch, and Alice Hamilton. Though opposed to the war on religious grounds, McDowell was careful not to interrupt classroom learning. She did not call on her students to write letters, nor did she publicly criticize government leaders or school officials. When given directives to sign a loyalty pledge, raise money in class to support the war effort, and teach patriotic citizenship, McDowell quietly refused to participate. She felt strongly that her Quaker beliefs would be protected under the principle of academic freedom.

On January 10, 1918, McDowell was summoned before the New York City board of superintendents. Despite years of favorable classroom evaluations, McDowell's supervising principal reported to district officials that she refused to support all school programs favoring the war effort. In late January the board recommended that McDowell be suspended from her teaching duties. The board decided that McDowell's ability to carry out her duties had been seriously affected by her conscientious objection to war. On April 18, 1918, McDowell was formally notified that charges of conduct unbecoming a teacher had been filed against her. On June 19, 1918, by a vote of 4 to 0, the New York City board of education formally dismissed her.

McDowell believed that her firing had raised important civil liberties issues, especially with respect to her religious beliefs. She appealed her case to the New York state court of appeals. New York's highest court sided with school officials, ruling that an essential part of a teacher's job is to promote patriotic citizenship, especially in time of war. McDowell did not return to the classroom until June 1923, when, long after the war's hyperpatriotism had dissipated, the city's board of education reinstated her. The board maintained that the initial punishment was too severe and the product of public hysteria. She continued to teach until her retirement in 1943.

McDowell never abandoned the Quaker "inner spirit" of peace. When World War II broke out, McDowell helped establish the Pacifist Teachers' League in 1940. Until her death on December 6, 1955, McDowell's nonviolent resistance was expressed in a unique way. She mailed to the Internal Revenue Service only that amount of her required taxes not spent for war preparation. Her action antedated the War Tax Resistance Movement of the Vietnam antiwar protests.

Her contribution to women and war lies primarily in her willingness to risk her job and career in the name of freedom of conscience. Her legal battle represented the first in American history involving public pressures of patriotic loyalty versus female pacifism inside the schoolhouse gates. She was the first female pacifist teacher to legally challenge a state's educational authority during wartime.

—*Charles F. Howlett*

See also Addams, Jane; Balch, Emily Green; Catt, Carrie Chapman; Curtis, Cathrine; Dilling, Elizabeth; Mead, Lucia Ames

References and Further Reading

Beale, Howard K. 1936. *Are American Teachers Free?* New York: Scribner's and Sons.
Curtis, Anna L. 1960. *Mary Stone McDowell: A Biographical Sketch.* New York: Society of Friends.
Howlett, Charles F. 1994. "Quaker Conscience in the Classroom: The Mary S. McDowell Case." *Quaker History,* 83 (Fall): 99–115.
Kennedy. Kathleen. 1999. *Disloyal Mothers and Scurrilous Citizens: Women and Subversion during World War I.* Bloomington: Indiana University.

McGee, Anita Newcomb
(1864–1940)

Acting assistant surgeon general of the United States during the Spanish-American War; helped establish a permanent Army Corps of Nurses; and volunteered as a nurse in the Russo-Japanese War. Anita Newcomb was born on November 4, 1864, in Washington, D.C. In 1888 she married a scientist, William John McGee, with whom she had three children. In 1892 she received her M.D. from Columbian University (now George Washington University) and then undertook postgraduate studies in gynecology at Johns Hopkins University. She stopped practicing medicine in 1896 and took on a series of leadership positions in organizations including the Daughters of the American Revolution (DAR).

When the United States declared war on Spain in 1898, McGee, as chairman of the DAR Hospital Corps, devised a method for her committee to screen all applicants seeking work as nurses for the U.S. Army. Overwhelmed by applications, Surgeon General

George M. Sternberg accepted McGee's plan. He established a Nurse Corps Division and appointed McGee acting assistant surgeon general that August. Instead of endorsing a volunteer ethic, McGee emphasized the importance of formal training. At the same time she pragmatically recruited "immunes" (individuals who had survived yellow fever and thus had developed an immunity), even those without medical training, along with graduate nurses. Her stance brought her into conflict both with the American Red Cross and with the recently organized Nurses' Associated Alumnae, a national group of professional nurses.

McGee subsequently worked to recognize and formalize contract nurses' contributions to the war effort. She helped to form the Society of Spanish-American War Nurses and for six years she served as its president. She also lobbied extensively to establish a permanent U.S. Army Nurse Corps, which was finally accomplished through passage of the Army Reorganization Act of 1901. McGee joined a group of Spanish-American War veterans and nursed Japanese troops during the Russo-Japanese War (1904–1905). Japan gave her an officer's rank and awarded her the Imperial Order of the Sacred Crown in recognition for her service.

Afterward McGee withdrew to private life. She died in Washington, D.C., on October 5, 1940, and was buried in Arlington National Cemetery with full military honors.

—*Laura R. Prieto*

See also Barton, Clara; Nurses, U.S. Army Nurse Corps in World War I; Spanish-American War, Women and the

References and Further Reading

Dearing, Mary R. 1971. McGee, Anita Newcomb. Pages 464–466 in *Notable American Women*. Vol. 2. Edited by Edward T. James. Cambridge, MA: Harvard University.

Sarnecky, Mary. 1999. *A History of the United States Army Nurse Corps*. Philadelphia: University of Pennsylvania.

MCWR

See United States, Marine Corps Women's Reserve

MEAD, LUCIA AMES (1856–1936)

Teacher, advocate, organizer, and historian in the U.S. peace movement's effort to replace war with international arbitration. Lucia Ames was born in Boscawen, New Hampshire, on May 5, 1856, attended high school at Salem, Massachusetts, and received private instruction at the college level. She then studied literature, philosophy, and history on her own. While working in her twenties as a piano teacher, she wrote and published essays on progressive subjects and was a popular lecturer in the Boston area. She wrote a novel, *Memoirs of a Millionaire,* that included advocacy for causes such as housing, educational reform, and interracial justice. She joined the movement for women's suffrage, became a notable activist, and contributed articles to Lucy Stone's *Woman's Journal*. At the age of forty she was introduced to the arbitration effort of the peace movement and soon became a leading figure. That became her principal interest during the next forty years.

Ames and her colleagues believed they had found an alternative to war through third-party settlement of disputes by arbitration. The idea had become a popular objective after the success of the administration of U.S. president Ulysses Grant in settling the post-Civil War's *Alabama* claims with Great Britain by arbitration. A tribunal of arbitration in Geneva after the American Civil War had judged that Great Britain had violated its neutrality by allowing the confederate raider, *Alabama,* to be constructed and sail from Birkenhead. The tribunal had awarded the United States $15.5 million for damages inflicted by the *Alabama* and other confederate raiders, and Great Britain paid. Twenty annual meetings devoted to international arbitration began in 1895 at Mohonk Mountain House in New York state. Notable guests participated, including U.S. Supreme Court justices. Ames was invited to the 1897 meeting. She was accompanied by an acquaintance interested in the movement, Edwin A. Mead, a writer and editor. Ames prepared and delivered a lecture on methods for making the cause known and attracting adherents.

At Mohonk, the friendship with Mead ripened into affection, nourished by their mutual interest in activism for arbitration. Within a year they were married. Their lives together were committed to peace and arbitration.

The war with Spain began soon after her marriage and was followed by the sending of U.S. troops to suppress the Philippine liberation movement.

Mead was vice-president of the U.S. "Anti-Imperialist League" that sought to end the military action and support independence for the islands. Her writings for the arbitration movement include an article, "International Police," that gave early recognition of the importance of sanctions (and armed intervention, if needed) to compel arbitration or compliance with its outcome. In her 1906 book, *Patriotism and the New Internationalism,* Lucia Mead linked peace and arbitration and offered ideas for teaching and promoting peace through arbitration.

Mead did not surrender when World War I made their cause seem hopeless. She was an organizer of the Woman's Peace Party, later called the Women's International League for Peace and Freedom. Continuing her work in the 1920s Lucia Mead published her last book, *Law or War,* in 1928, updating her 1912 work, *Swords and Ploughshares; or, The Supplanting of the System of War by the System of Law.* Adjudication among nations by the present World Court was recognized in *The World Court in Action* (Meyer 2002) as fruit of the U.S. arbitration movement.

—*Howard N. Meyer*

See also Addams, Jane; Balch, Emily Green; Catt, Carrie Chapman; Curtis, Cathrine; Dilling, Elizabeth; International Congress of Women: Antiwar Protest of Women in World War I; McDowell, Mary Stone

References and Further Reading

Craig, John M. 1990. *Lucia Ames Mead (1856–1936) and the American Peace Movement.* New York: E. Mellen Press.

Kuehl, Warren F. 1960. *Seeking World Order.* Nashville, TN:Vanderbilt University.

Meyer, Howard N. 2002. *The World Court in Action: Judging among the Nations.* Lanham, MD: Rowman and Littlefield.

MEDICAL SPECIALIST CORPS: U.S. WOMEN IN MILITARY SERVICE, WORLD WAR II

Dieticians, and physical and occupational therapists serving during World War II under the U.S. Army Medical Department. Approximately 1,643 dieticians and more than 1,600 physical therapists served worldwide, while more than 900 occupational therapists served in stateside Army hospitals. Physical therapists were assigned to stateside Army hospitals and overseas to general, station, convalescent, and field hospitals, all of which followed troop movements, as well as to the Army hospital ships USS *Acadia* and *Seminole.* Dieticians served in stateside and overseas hospitals in all theaters of the war, and 42 dieticians were assigned to 25 hospital ships.

Until December 1942, all specialists served as civilian employees of the Army Medical Department with no rank or benefits. This status changed, however, when Public Law 77–828 authorized relative rank for the length of the war plus six months for dieticians and physical therapists assigned overseas. All initial appointments were made in the grade of second lieutenant. Beginning in May 1943, specialists could be promoted after eighteen months of satisfactory service and a recommendation. There were a few male physical therapists working in stateside Army hospitals, but because Public Law 77–828 applied only to women, these men were assigned as enlisted. The status of dieticians and physical therapists changed again in June 1944 with Public Law 78–350, which granted them full commissioned status with the same rights, allowances, benefits, and privileges given to other commissioned officers.

Occupational therapists served in seventy-six general and convalescent hospitals in the United States, where they treated patients who were transferred to recover from amputations; loss of hearing or sight; neuropsychiatric conditions; or orthopedic, nerve, or spinal cord injuries. Because occupational therapists did not need to be assigned overseas, the surgeon general stated that they would not need the protection under international law provided by military status, and they continued to serve with civilian status.

Dieticians and physical therapists who served overseas frequently faced a shortage of supplies, food, and water, and were often forced to improvise their equipment. Where they worked depended on the area and could range from former civilian hospitals to cantonment-type buildings, hotels, museums, or tents. Physical therapists assisted patients recovering from a variety of war wounds including nerve, brain, spinal cord, orthopedic, and thoracic injuries. Physical therapist Lieutenant Metta Baxter, who served at the 21st General Hospital in Italy, was the first physical therapist to receive the Legion of Merit for her exceptional service in the North African campaigns of July to September 1943. In addition to feeding the soldiers in their hospitals, dieticians also provided a variety of therapeutic and special needs diets. Three dieticians and one physical therapist were held as prisoners of war by the Japanese in the Santo Tomas Internment Camp in the Philippines for almost three years. Public Law 80–36 established the three specialties, largely because of

their service in World War II, as the Women's Medical Specialist Corps within the regular army on March 24, 1947.

—*Kara D. Vuic*

See also Nurses, U.S. Army Nurse Corps in World War II

References and Further Reading

Anderson, Robert S., Harriet S. Lee, and Myra L. McDaniel, eds. 1968. *Army Medical Specialist Corps.* Washington, DC: Office of the Surgeon General, Department of the Army.
Hartwick, Ann M. Ritchie. 1995. *The Army Medical Specialist Corps: The 45th Anniversary.* Washington, DC: Center of Military History, United States Army.

MEIR, GOLDA (NÉE GOLDA MABOVITZ) (1898–1978)

Israeli diplomat, politician, and prime minister. Born in Kiev, Russia, on May 3, 1898, Golda Mabovitz was one of eight children, five of whom died in childhood. Her father immigrated to the United States in 1903, and the rest of the family joined him in Milwaukee in 1906. Golda did well in school and studied to be a teacher. Inspired by her sister Sheyna, she joined the Zionist movement and became a delegate to the American Jewish Congress. She married Morris Myerson in 1917 and during World War I volunteered to join the Jewish Legion, an armed unit recruited among Jews to fight for Britain in the Middle East. The Legion had no use for women, but in 1921 the Myersons, nevertheless, moved to Palestine.

The Myersons worked on a kibbutz and Golda became active in the *Histadrut,* Israel's labor movement. She joined its executive in 1934 and helped raise funds internationally for Jewish settlement. Before Israel's War of Independence (1948), she twice met secretly with Jordan's

King Abdullah in an unsuccessful effort to prevent war. During the war, she traveled to the United States and raised $50 million for the new state. Because of this experience, Prime Minister David Ben-Gurion sent her to Moscow as Israel's ambassador.

Elected to parliament in 1949 as a member of the labor party (*Mapai*), Ben-Gurion appointed Meir minister of labor. A strong and decisive leader, her greatest task was finding housing and jobs for the thousands of Jewish refugees arriving from Europe and the Arab nations each week. Ben-Gurion, who once called her "The only man in my cabinet," appointed her Israel's foreign minister in 1956. At Ben-Gurion's urging, she adopted the Hebrew last name Meir (to burn brightly). She held the post of foreign minister until 1965, gaining international fame as one of the few women to hold a prominent position in international affairs. She worked both to strengthen Israel's ties to the United States and with the new nations of Africa to which she dispatched a series of aid missions.

The ruling labor party appointed Meir prime minister following the death of Levi Eshkol on February 26, 1969. Meir's efforts to trade land gained in the 1967 war for peace proved futile. Instead, she presided over one of the most war-filled periods in Israeli history. Terrorist attacks and cross-border raids on Israel increased, and skirmishing with Egypt across the Suez Canal escalated into the War of Attrition, which lasted through August 1970. The following month Syria invaded Jordan to support a Palestinian rebellion but withdrew its forces after Meir threatened to attack Syria. Tensions with Egypt and Syria increased steadily and produced several invasion scares. The morning of October 6, 1973, Israel's director of intelligence warned that an attack was imminent. Meir rejected an air force proposal to attack first as Israel had in 1967. That afternoon Egyptian forces crossed the Suez Canal in overwhelming force and drove back the surprised Israeli army. On the Golan Heights, desperate fighting narrowly averted a Syrian invasion of the Israeli heartland. Israeli counterof-

fensives defeated both Arab armies, and a U.S.-imposed cease-fire ended the war on October 24.

Despite winning the war, the early setbacks, heavy casualties, and rumors that she had considered using nuclear weapons tarnished Meir's administration. She resigned on June 3, 1974, and returned to private life. She died December 8, 1978 in Jerusalem after a fifteen-year battle with leukemia.

—*Stephen K. Stein*

See also Arab-Israeli Wars; Israeli Military, Women in the

References and Further Reading

Mann, Peggy. 1971. *Golda: The Life of Israel's Prime Minister*. New York: Coward, McCann and Geoghegan.

Martin, Ralph G. 1988. *Golda Meir, the Romantic Years*. New York: Scribner.

Meir, Golda. 1975. *My Life*. New York: Putnam.

MEISEL, HILDA

See Monte, Hilda

MEISELAS, SUSAN (1948–)

American photojournalist noted for her documentary photographs of conflicts in Nicaragua, El Salvador, Chile, and Kurdistan. Susan Meiselas received international acclaim as a result of photographs she took in Nicaragua during the 1978–1979 Sandinista revolution. During this time Nicaragua was a country embroiled in revolution as the Sandinista National Liberation Front (FSLN) fought to overthrow the government of Anastasio Somoza Dabayle. These images essentially launched her career as a photojournalist and captured the attention of audiences worldwide. As one reviewer put it, during this year, "Nicaragua held the news and Susan Meiselas held the negatives" (Shames 1981, 42).

Meiselas did not go to Central America on assignment that year, but rather went to Nicaragua to "look around" after hearing about the potentially volatile political situation. When the popular uprising began in the city of Matagalpa during the summer of 1978, she was there to photograph it, and the resulting images were published in newspapers and magazines around the globe. Such international publications as *Geo, The New York Times Magazine,* and *Paris Match* ran her photographs alongside reportage of the revolution. Her use of color film to record scenes of violence and conflict at a time when most photojournalists still preferred to work with black-and-white images added a sense of urgency to these images that heightened their graphic quality.

The Sandinista revolution was extremely bloody and violent—at least 40,000 people lost their lives during the year of fighting and many more were left injured and homeless. In a country of just over 4 million people, the revolution affected every citizen in one way or another. On July 19, 1979, the FSLN emerged victorious; as they claimed the capital city of Managua, President Somoza fled the country, taking refuge in the United States. This victory was celebrated by thousands in Managua's central plaza and by tens of thousands around the world as Meiselas's images defined the conflict for an international audience.

In 1981 Meiselas published a book of photographs made during the revolution entitled *Nicaragua: June 1978–July 1979* (New York, Pantheon). In 1991 she produced *Pictures from a Revolution,* a documentary film in which she returned to spots she photographed during the 1978–1979 uprising. Other publications and projects by Meiselas include: *Carnival Strippers* (1976), *El Salvador: The Work of Thirty Photographers* (1983), *Chile from Within* (1991), *Kur-*

distan: In the Shadow of History (1997), and *Pandora's Box* (1999).

Susan Meiselas became a full member of the internationally-renowned photographic cooperative Magnum in 1980. Her photojournalism has won her numerous awards including the Robert Capa Gold Medal for her photographs of the Nicaraguan revolution; the Leica Award for Excellence (1982); American Society of Magazine Photographers Photojournalist of the Year (1982); the McArthur Fellowship (1992); and the Hasselblad Prize (1994).

—*J. Keri Cronin*

See also Bonney, Therese; Bubley, Esther; Chapelle, Dickey; Lange, Dorothea

References and Further Reading

Franck, Martine, Eve Arnold, Susan Meiselas, Inge Morath, Marilyn Silverstone, and Lise Sarfati. 1999. *Magna Brava: Magnum's Women Photographers.* Munich: Prestel.
Shames, Laurence. 1981. "Susan Meiselas." *American Photographer* 6:42–49.

MERCY SHIP

The nickname given the USS *Red Cross,* a ship that carried American medical units to Europe in September 1914 to care for the sick and wounded in the first year of World War I. The United States remained politically neutral from the beginning of the war in 1914 until April 1917 and through this neutrality offered medical assistance to all belligerent nations. Long before the U.S. government declared war and mobilized its medical service along with the U.S. Expeditionary Forces, there were small groups of American volunteers, mainly female nurses, providing medical care across Europe.

The War Relief Board of the American Red Cross (ARC) met in early August 1914 and decided to offer units made up of three doctors and twelve nurses each, along with equipment and supplies, to any country involved in the fighting. A call went out to ARC chapters for volunteers from the pool of nurses who had already registered with the organization.

Nurses were required to be natural-born U.S. citizens, pass a physical examination, have smallpox and typhoid vaccinations, and commit for a six-month period. Immediately after the initial meeting, ARC-enrolled nurses began receiving their notices to start processing, obtain inoculations, and travel to New York City, where they were mobilized, receiving their equipment and uniforms. The entire group sailed on September 13, 1914, with units designated for Austria, England, France, Germany, Hungary, and Russia. Another unit, headed for Serbia, departed a few days earlier but was considered part of the same mission of mercy.

Some units were assigned to existing military hospitals, while others had to completely set up hospitals in schools, theaters, casinos, and country estates. Most treated large numbers of patients, many with serious injuries, with very low mortality rates. Although some of the doctors and nurses returned home after their six-month commitment, the units were in place for almost one full year before being recalled on October 1, 1915. Many of the doctors and nurses stayed in Europe when the year was up and continued to work on a volunteer basis with the ARC or other relief or medical organizations.

Medical units sponsored by the American Red Cross continued to travel to the war zone over the next few years, offering much needed medical care to soldiers and the affected civilian population, but those on the Mercy Ship were the first to be of service in the "war to end all wars."

—*Katherine Burger Johnson*

See also Nurses, U.S. Army Nurse Corps in World War I; Red Cross of the United States: World War I and World War II

References and Further Reading

American National Red Cross. 1915. *Tenth Annual Report of the American National Red Cross for the Year 1914.* Washington, DC: American Red Cross.

Dock, Lavinia L., et al. 1922. *A History of American Red Cross Nursing.* New York: Macmillan.

Kernodle, Portia. n.d. *The Red Cross Nurse in Action, 1882–1948.* New York: Harper and Brothers.

Volk, Katherine. 1936. *Buddies in Budapest,* Los Angeles: Kellaway-Ide.

MEXICAN AMERICAN WOMEN AND WORLD WAR II

Contribution of women of Mexican ancestry to the war effort of the United States during World War II and the impact of war work on their self-perception. The drafting of males resulted in a shortage of male workers and led to the mobilization of women in order to meet the high demand of wartime production. The Mexican American counterpart to the wartime image of Rosie the Riveter can be imagined as Rosita the Riveter. In the Southwest and Midwest regions of the United States, Mexican American women labored as riveters, welders, airplane mechanics, farm workers, vegetable packers, seamstresses, nurses, secretaries, shipbuilders, and crane operators, and built tanks, trucks, bombs, and ammunition.

The overwhelming response to the initial call for women workers signified women's desire to do their part for the war effort, but many women were equally anxious to take advantage of the wages that war work offered them. Women also often needed to supplement family income due to the absence of husbands serving in the military. Mrs. Henrietta Rivas of San Antonio, who had made $1.50 per week cleaning houses,

MEXICAN AMERICAN WOMEN IN WORLD WAR II

"In the Valley there were these packing sheds where they packed tomatoes and lettuce . . . there were not enough men to work so they started hiring women. So that is when it started to change a little more in women's lives. They were calling from the government for women to go and work in the factories . . . then they started calling women into the army. And first it was like, oh my goodness, *dios mio*, how can these women go over there by themselves? Everybody was shocked because we were not used to seeing women leave the house. You didn't leave the house until you were married. With senoritas, everything was so strict and then came this change . . . and I think that was wonderful because it opened a new world for women. It showed that women can be independent. This was a real break for women."

—Interview with Aurora Orozco, Cuero, Texas,
U.S. Latino and Latina World War II Oral History Project, July 31, 2004.
Contributed by Brenda Sendejo.

earned $90 a month as a civil service interpreter (Interview with Henrietta Rivas, San Antonio, Texas, U.S. Latino and Latina World War II Oral History Project, June 12, 1999).

Women's entrance into defense work shattered previously established gender roles. The onset of the war provided expanded choices for Mexican American women who did not typically work outside of the home and lived amidst a structured set of traditional Mexican values and beliefs. At age nineteen Aurora Orozco went to work at a vegetable packing shed in Mercedes, Texas. She was only allowed by her parents to do this because of the wartime need for workers (Interview with Aurora Orozco, Cuero, Texas, U.S. Latino and Latina World War II Oral History Project, July 31, 2004). Once women acquired new skills, they began realizing their potential and gained independence. As Vicky Ruiz explains, "Women were claiming places for themselves and their families in the U.S. while 'confronting America'" (Ruiz 1998, xv).

After the war ended, women were told that their patriotic duty was to return to their homes. Although many Mexican American women found satisfaction from their war jobs and car-

ried them out with great efficiency, many willingly returned to being homemakers. Henrietta Rivas, who loved her job repairing airplane instruments at Kelly Field in San Antonio, Texas, believed "Raising my children was more important than my job" (Interview with Henrietta Rivas, San Antonio, Texas, U.S. Latino and Latina World War II Oral History Project, June 12, 1999).

Often, men returned from war demanding that their service to their country should afford them equality. Women defense workers also began to see things differently with regard to their place in their homes and communities. Many women, who had endured discrimination before the war, now fought for equitable educational opportunities for their children and against discrimination in their communities. Victoria Morales, who had worked in the defense industry, said, "Just as the war had changed boys into men, the same thing happened to us girls" (Santillán 1989, 138).

—*Brenda L. Sendejo*

See also Rosie the Riviter; United States, Home Front during World War II

References and Further Reading

Campbell, Julie A. 1990. "*Madres y Esposas:* Tucson's Spanish-American Mothers and Wives Association." *The Journal of Arizona History,* 31:161–182.

Gluck, Sherna Berger. 1987. *Rosie the Riveter Revisited: Women, the War, and Social Change.* Boston: Twayne.

Honey, Maureen. 1984. *Creating Rosie the Riveter: Class, Gender, and Propaganda during World War II.* Amherst: University of Massachusetts Press.

Ruiz, Vicki. 1998. *From Out of the Shadows, Mexican Women in Twentieth-Century America.* New York: Oxford University Press.

Santillán, Richard. 1989. Rosita the Riveter: Midwest Mexican American Women during World War II, 1941–1945. *Perspectives in Mexican American Studies.* 1989: 115–147.

U.S. Latino and Latina World War II Oral History Project archives, University of Texas at Austin School of Journalism. Maggie Rivas-Rodriguez, Project Director.

MEYER, GEORGIA LOU, OR MEYER, G. L.

See Chapelle, Dickey

MICHEL, LOUISE (1830–1905)

French revolutionary, teacher, and member of National Guard unit during the 1870–1871 Franco-Prussian War and 1871 Paris Commune. Years associated with revolution, 1830 and 1905, appropriately mark the birth and death dates of the "Red Virgin," Louise Michel. Michel became a teacher, moved to Paris, and fought for justice as an orator, writer, and uniformed member of the National Guard during the Franco-Prussian War and the Paris Com-

mune that followed. Imprisoned several times during her life, Michel's armed Commune activities resulted in deportation to New Caledonia.

Between March 18 and May 28, 1871, lower-class Parisians established a representative government, the Commune, in direct opposition to the newly established Republic, which they found conservative, unresponsive, even threatening. The national government at Versailles, besieging Paris, began bombarding the city on April 3. Troops entered Paris on May 21, and within a week, street-to-street fighting—even massacres—killed 30,000 residents. Many women, including Michel, fought from the early hours of March 18 through the Commune's demise on May 28.

Michel's participation in this civil war included arming herself with weapons and attire of the National Guard, orating in Red Clubs, writing to newspapers, searching for men hiding from National Guard duty, tending the wounded, and fighting. Her involvement began with the insurrection—Parisians' vocal and violent response to French troops attempting to take cannon, for which Parisians had paid and with which Paris had defended itself during the eighteen-week Prussian Siege. From her post with a National Guard battalion, Michel saw early events, tended the first casualty, and ran to warn others. More Parisians arrived, fraternizing with the Versailles troops, and forced their retreat. Over time, Adolphe Thiers, the president of the provisional government seated at Versailles, organized troops from the provinces, who were hostile to Paris, began bombing the city, and engineered the Commune's ultimate destruction.

Witnesses saw Michel in numerous locations among the fighting men during the battles of the Commune. She fired various weapons, her favorite being a Remington carbine; she kept watch, lived in the trenches, and killed enemies. Georges Clemenceau, who later became president of the Republic, observed her in the streets of Paris and in the fighting. When her unit rested, she fought alongside another company. She commented on the bias women experienced,

Louise Michel. (Leonard de Selva/Corbis)

References and Further Reading

Gullickson, Gay L. 1996. *The Unruly Women of Paris: Images of the Commune.* Ithaca, NY: Cornell University.

Lowry, Bullitt, and Elizabeth Ellington Gunter, eds. 1981. *The Red Virgin: Memoirs of Louise Michel.* Tuskaloosa: University of Alabama.

MILOSAVLJEVIC, DANICA (1925–)

Yugoslav partisan. Danica Milosavljevic was born in 1925 near Uzice, Yugoslavia. Her father wanted all of his children, even his two daughters, to receive an education. Influenced by the oppression of women in Yugoslav peasant society, Milosavljevic joined the Communist Youth Movement in secondary school. By the time the Germans invaded Yugoslavia in April 1941, she was a member of the Communist party. Milosavljevic, who had taken a basic medical course offered by the party youth group before the war, was sent to a partisan detachment near Uzice and given ten days of additional training as a nurse. She served as a nurse for six months before directly appealing to Tito to be allowed to fight. The party leadership did not want her to become a soldier, but she prevailed. By the end of the war she was promoted to second lieutenant and was commander of the First Battalion of the Second Proletarian Brigade. Following the war she was proclaimed a National Hero by the Yugoslav Communist government.

—*Bernard Cook*

See also Yugoslavia, Women in the Military during World War II

References and Further Reading

Jancar-Webster, Barbara. 1990. *Women and Revolution in Yugoslavia, 1941–1945.* Denver, CO: Arden.

including illegal exclusion from rations. She wrote to the newspaper, *La Sociale,* on May 6, 1871, "if you knew the obstacles they put in our way, the backbiting, the hostility!" Despite these challenges, Michel recruited women for ambulance service and continued her armed support of the Commune.

After her capture Louise Michel refused to offer any defense at her trial, calling on the judges to put her to death, if they had the courage. Instead, they deported her. When all convicted communards received amnesty a decade later, she returned to France, fighting for anarchist causes. She died at age seventy-four on a speaking trip, still evoking revolutionary violence.

—*Pamela J. Stewart*

See also Paris Commune, Women and the

MITFORD, UNITY
(1914–1948)

British admirer of Germany and Hitler. Unity Mitford—the fifth child of David Mitford, Second Baron Redesdale, and his wife, Sydney Bowles—was born in London on August 8, 1914. She was named Unity after popular actress Unity Moore but given the unusual middle name Valkyrie. Conceived at her father's Canadian gold mine in Swastika, Ontario, Mitford later incorporated her names and birthplace into her Aryan beliefs. Like her sisters Nancy, Diana, Pamela, Jessica, and Deborah, Unity was educated at home by governesses and took part in the eccentric life of her family. In 1930 Unity was the first of the sisters allowed to go to school, St. Margaret's in Bushy, from which she was promptly expelled.

Unity was presented as a debutante in 1932, but instead of dancing, preferred shocking party guests with her pet snakes. She was drawn to the politics of Sir Oswald Mosley, with whom she had contact through her sister Diana, who had recently left her first husband to live with Mosley. In 1933 Unity joined Mosley's British Union of Fascists. That year Unity accompanied Diana to Germany, where she attended the Nazi party rally in Nuremberg. Unity returned to Germany the following year after convincing her parents to allow her a year abroad to polish her German language skills. While in Munich, Unity began to follow Adolf Hitler's movements, hoping to arrange a meeting, which finally took place in February 1935.

Hitler, to the amazement of his inner circle, met Unity more than 140 times over the next 4 years. Hitler allowed her to tease him, and they shared a number of pet names and inside jokes that, when mentioned, reduced both of them to hysterical giggles. Unity was often escorted, for the sake of propriety, by SS Officer Erich Widemann when she attended subsequent party rallies, the 1936 Olympics, and Nazi social events. In order to prove her loyalty, Unity wrote virulent anti-Semitic letters to the Nazi magazine *Stürmer* and took great pride in having been attacked by Spanish Republicans in 1936 for wearing her special gold party badge in Grenada and in being arrested as a "known Nazi" in Prague in 1938. She usually traveled in an MG sports car flying a Nazi pennant. The Mitfords in England were deeply embarrassed by the wide press coverage given to Unity's activities, especially as she was a cousin of Winston Churchill. Her sister Nancy parodied Unity's attachment to Hitler in her novel, *Wigs on the Green.*

In June 1938 Unity, who had already witnessed and approved of several instances of Nazi humiliation and oppression of Jews, accepted from Hitler an apartment vacated by a forcibly evicted Jewish family. Convinced that war between Britain and Germany could not happen, she wrote a full-page editorial in the London *Daily Mirror* and threatened to friends and family to kill herself if war were to break out between Britain and Germany. On September 3, 1939, Unity carried out her threat and shot herself in the head in a Munich park. She survived and was visited by Hitler, Goebbels, and Goering before being transferred to Switzerland where her mother was able to join her and arrange her return to England. Doctors were unable to remove the bullet from Unity's head and she suffered brain damage that left her incontinent, prone to rages, and with the intellectual ability of an eleven- to twelve-year-old. The family, however, so discreetly managed her rare public appearances that a parliamentary committee demanded to know why she was not interned like Diana and Mosley as enemies during the war. On discovering the extent of her disability, the matter was dropped.

Unity Mitford remained in her mother's care until May 27, 1948, when she died after developing meningitis at the family's remote Scottish property, Inch Kenneth.

—*Margaret Sankey*

See also Braun, Eva; Petacci, Clara

References and Further Reading

Guinness, Jonathan, and Catherine Guinness. 1984. *The House of Mitford*. London: Hutchinson.

Lovell, Mary S. 2002. *The Sisters*. New York: W. W. Norton.

Pryce-Jones, David. 1976. *Unity Mitford*. London: Weidenfeld and Nicholson.

MOLLY PITCHER

Mythic heroine of the American Revolution. Molly Pitcher, according to the legend, was a *cantinière* who put down her pitcher and took the place of her wounded husband, William Hays, at an artillery position during the battle of Monmouth on June 28, 1778. Molly reputedly took the rammer staff from Hays and rallied the flagging American artillerymen. According to some embellishments, Molly returned to find her husband wounded after carrying an injured soldier to safety. General George Washington rewarded her with a gold coin, or perhaps a sack of them, and promoted her to the rank of sergeant.

According to Linda Grant De Pauw, this is all a fabrication. The first written mention of this heroine of Monmouth appeared in 1851 and she was not identified as Molly Pitcher until 1859. The character was not specifically identified until 1876. That year, Wesley Miles of Carlisle, Pennsylvania, claimed that his grandfather's maid, a Mrs. Mary Hays McCauley, had been the heroine of Monmouth. McCauley had probably served in some military capacity during the Revolutionary War. She received a pension from the state of Pennsylvania in 1822 "for services rendered." She had, however, requested the pension only because she was the widow of a soldier. De Pauw believes that citizens of Carlisle invented McCauley's past to embellish the renown of their town (De Pauw 1998, 126–130).

According to De Pauw, despite the legendary nature of the Molly Pitcher story, two men pres-

Mary Ludwig Hays—one of the women on whom the legend of Molly Pitcher might have been based—at the Battle of Monmouth during the American Revolution. (National Archives)

ent at the Battle of Monmouth recounted that women served in the battle. One woman was seen passing ammunition at an artillery emplacement, and another replaced her wounded husband in the infantry. These two women provide some basis for the story of Molly Pitcher. According to De Pauw, however, Mary Hays McCauley was in all probability not Molly Pitcher.

—*Bernard Cook*

See also American Revolution, Role of Women in the; Corbin, Margaret Cochrane; Samson, Deborah

References and Further Reading

De Pauw, Linda Grant. 1998. *Battle Cries and Lullabies: Women in War from Pre-History to the Present*. Norman: University of Oklahoma.

"The Story of Molly Pitcher." Fort Still History. http://www.army.mil/pao/pamolly.htm (accessed December 1, 2004).

MONTE, HILDA, PSEUD. (AKA HILDA MEISEL) (1914–1945)

German anti-Nazi resistance. Hilda Meisel was born in Berlin on July 31, 1914. As a young girl she joined the youth section of the left-wing opponents of the German Communist party. Though she did not finish school, at the age of fifteen she was writing for *Der Funke* (The Spark), the journal of the International Socialist Combat League. In addition to her radical opposition to the Nazi regime, she was a Jew. She apparently was able to emigrate to England through a nominal marriage to a British passport holder. In Britain she continued her radical-left opposition efforts under the nom de guerre Monte. In Britain she wrote a short piece, *"Where Freedom Perished,"* in which she stressed that Germans were also suffering from Nazi oppression. The theme was continued in a book, *The Unity of Europe*.

She was determined to return to Germany to work against the regime. As she attempted to cross the German–Swiss border on April 18, 1945, she was shot by a German patrol. Her passion for justice lives on in her poems.

—*Bernard Cook*

See also Niederkirchner, Käthe

References and Further Reading

Leber, Annedore. 1994. *Conscience in Revolt: Sixty-Four Stories of Resistance in Germany, 1933–1945*. Boulder, CO: Westview.

Monte, Hilda. 1943. *The Unity of Europe*. London: V. Gollancz.

von Rauschenplat, Helmutt, and Hilda Monte. 1940. *How to Conquer Hitler, a Plan for Economic and Moral Warfare on the Nazi Home Front*. London: Jarrolds.

MOON, LOTTIE (1829–1895), AND MOON, GINNIE (1844–1925)

Confederate spies during the American Civil War. Lottie and Ginnie Moon were the only sisters who worked as spies, couriers, and smugglers during the American Civil War, and they also played key roles in the Great Northwest Conspiracy. Drawing on their charisma and connections, they gathered information on Union movements and activities from their many suitors.

Cynthia Charlotte (Lottie) was born in Danville, Virginia, on August 10, 1829. The third child and first daughter of Dr. Robert S. Moon, and Cynthia Ann Sullivan, Lottie was independent and strong-willed. As a child, she excelled at riding, shooting, and acting, which were later manifested in her skill as a spy. She married Judge James Clark in 1849 after spurning Ambrose Burnside at the altar. Both Clarks were Copperheads (Northerners who sympathized with the Confederacy), and their home at Jones Station, Ohio, was both a supply base and respite for Confederate soldiers and spies.

In 1862 Lottie delivered a message from General Sterling Price to Colonel Edmund Kirby-Smith in Kentucky at the bequest of Walter Taylor of the Zachariah Taylor family. After her success on this first mission, she was sent to Canada where she delivered dispatches and letters to Toronto. Passing herself off as a British woman en route to mineral springs in Virginia, her uncanny ability to fake joint injury saved her from discovery on several occasions. She was finally captured by General Ambrose Burnside, who recognized her.

Lottie was a prisoner of war for three months. After the war, she wrote for the *New York World* and in 1870 the paper sent her to Paris as a war correspondent during the Franco-Prussian War. After returning to the United States and trying her hand at acting, she became a novelist and wrote under the pen name Charles M. Clay. She died in Philadelphia on November 20, 1895.

Virginia (Ginnie) Bethel Moon, born in Oxford, Ohio on June 22, 1844, was known for carrying a pearl-handled pistol. Expelled from Oxford Female College for shooting out the stars on the U.S. flag, she was sent home to her parents, who had moved to Memphis. While in Memphis, Ginnie attended to sick and wounded soldiers and made bandages. When Memphis fell into Union hands in 1862, Ginnie charmed the Union soldiers and passed along important details to Confederate officials.

Like her sister, Ginnie worked as a courier and delivered updates to General Nathan Forrest on his famous ride into West Tennessee. In the winter of 1863, while visiting Jackson, Mississippi, she agreed to carry a message from General Sterling Price to her brother-in-law, who lived in Jones Station, Ohio.

While heading downriver aboard the steamboat *Alicia Dean*, she was detained and searched in Cincinnati. Drawing her Colt revolver on Captain Rose, she threatened to report him to General Burnside. When Rose departed, Ginnie snatched the wet dispatches from her bosom and swallowed them. On her way to the Custom's Office for questioning, a jingle in her hoopskirt gave her away. Lined with vials of morphine, opium, and camphor, all bound for Confederate hospitals, she was charged with smuggling goods into the Confederacy.

General Burnside followed her case and remanded her into her mother's custody. A prisoner at Burnet House for three weeks, she spent several months confined at Fortress Monroe, Virginia, but she was eventually paroled to Jones Station.

After the war Ginnie was a familiar figure in Memphis. Devoting her life to work with the poor and sick, she was a heroine during the yellow fever epidemic in the early 1870s. She later moved to California to pursue interests in aviation and acting. Ginnie had a brief career as a screen actor and appeared in several movies. She settled in Greenwich Village, New York, where she died September 11, 1925.

—*Rebecca Tolley-Stokes*

See also Boyd, Isabelle; Civil War, American, Women Combatants during; Greenhow, Rose O'Neale

References and Further Reading

Kane, Harnett T. 1954. *Spies for the Blue and Gray.* Garden City, NY: Doubleday.
Kinchen, Oscar A. 1972. *Women Who Spied for the Blue and the Gray.* Philadelphia: Dorrance.

MOORE, ELEANOR MAY (1875–1949)

Pioneer of the Australian peace movement. Intellectual and writer, Eleanor M. Moore was an underestimated pioneer of the Australian peace movement. Born on March 10, 1875, in Lancefield, Victoria, the young Eleanor completed her education at the Presbyterian Ladies' College in the center of Melbourne. Inspired by the work of the influential Reverend Charles Strong, Moore dedicated her life to the Church of Australia and to the fight against militarism from the Boer War to World War II. An absolute pacifist, more liberal and humanitarian than her Melbourne companions, Moore became an attentive observer of the political events of the new century. During World War I her involvement in the women's antiwar movement was finally recognized. Moore was elected international secretary of the Sisterhood of International Peace (SIP), which had been founded in 1915. A leading advocate of the anticonscription movement, Moore's fight as a peace worker did not win her popularity. Most Australians were not only voluble patriots and imperialists, they were hostile toward the aims of the pacifists. An internationalist and fervent supporter of women's suffrage, Moore attended the International Congress of Women held by the Women's International League for Peace and Freedom (WILPF) in Zurich (May 12–17,

1919). When SIP reconstituted itself as the Australian section of the WILPF, Moore accentuated her personal campaign for peace and emerged as an untiring orator during the numerous meetings of the late 1930s. With courage she refused to join the United Front Against Fascism. She was personally irritated by the peace propaganda of the Communist party of Australia and disappointed by the failure of the World Disarmament Movement after 1932. A supporter of the concept of collective security, she was skeptical about the efficiency of the League of Nations. During the last ten years of her life, until her death on October 1, 1949, Moore's loyalty to the pacifist cause remained intact. In her autobiographical volume, *The Quest For Peace* (1949), she described the long fight for international friendship seen from an Australian point of view. Unfortunately, this book was published when the clouds of the cold war undermined the public sympathy for the national peace movement.

—*Jérôme Dorvidal*

See also Locke, Elsie; McDowell, Mary Stone; Olmsted, Mildred Scott; Onions, Maud; Street, Jessie

References and Further Reading

Moore, Eleanor May. 1950. *The Quest for Peace: As I Have Known It in Australia.* Melbourne: NP.
Saunders, Malcolm. 1993. *Quiet Dissenter: The Life and Thought of an Australian Pacifist.* Canberra: Peace Research Centre.

MOREAU-EVRARD, EMILIENNE (1898–1971)

French resister during World Wars I and II. Emilienne Moreau, affectionately known as the Lady of Loos, was born on June 4, 1899, in the town of Wingles in the northern region of Pas-de-Calais. She was the daughter of a miner turned grocery store owner. In October 1914, the town of Loos, where Moreau was living, was occupied by the Germans, who pillaged the village including her family's home. Moreau, who had intended to be a schoolteacher, in February 1915 organized a makeshift school in a cellar for children between the ages of three and sixteen.

In September 1915 the British attempted to retake Loos in four days of fierce fighting. Moreau began her war contribution by distributing chocolates and biscuits to the British soldiers. She transformed her parents' home into a temporary shelter and hospital, caring for wounded soldiers. She observed the German lines and informed the British of their movements. In one instance, in order to save the life of a British soldier, she went into the street armed with grenades and a revolver, killing five German soldiers.

Moreau was recognized by both the French and the British for her war contributions. The French awarded her the Croix de Guerre and issued a famous postcard in her honor depicting her in mourning dress with the caption, "The Lady or Heroine of Loos." The British awarded her the Military Medal, and the Royal Red Cross recognized her treatment of wounded soldiers by giving her a First Class Award. A British commander, Sir Douglas Haig, affectionately called her the Jeanne d'Arc of Loos for her effort to win back Loos for France.

In 1932, she married Just Evrard, the vice secretary general of the Socialist Federation of Pas-de-Calais, and they had two children. With the fall of France in June 1940, Moreau once again became involved in the war effort. Although German authorities had put her under surveillance because of her participation in World War I, this did not prevent Moreau from becoming involved in the Resistance. She began her work by distributing pamphlets and becoming a contact for British Information Services. She founded several Resistance groups with Louis Albert, director of the Liberation of the North network.

When her husband, Just Evrard, was arrested in 1941, Moreau changed her name to Jeanne Poirier and served first as an agent within the Brutus network directed by Pierre Fourcaud and then with the propaganda group France Fights. When forced to hide in the Lyon area in 1942, she organized missions between Lyon and Switzerland. Moreau demonstrated great courage and exceptional energy by playing a pivotal role in the Resistance in the Alps region. Forced to leave occupied France for Algeria in 1944, she sat on the French Provisional Assembly in Algiers. Later that year following D-Day, she returned to France with a Canadian armored unit.

After the war Moreau was awarded the Cross of the Companion of Liberation in her maiden name, as well as being made an officer of the Legion of Honor. She was decorated with the War Cross, 1939–1945, and the Cross of Volunteer Fighter and Resistor.

—Leigh Whaley

See also France, Resistance during World War II, Women and

References and Further Reading

Moreau, Emilienne. 1970. *La Guerre buissonnière. Une famille française dans la Résistance* [The Truant War: A French Family in the Resistance] Paris: Solar.
Walters, Walter W. 1916. *Heroines of the World War.* London: C. H. Kelly.

MORGAN, ANNE TRACY
(1873–1952)

Noted social activist and philanthropist. Anne Tracy Morgan provided immense assistance to France during and after World War I and World War II. Morgan was born in 1873 into wealth and privilege, the youngest child of John Pierpont and Frances Louisa Tracy Morgan. Her brother was to become the famous financier J. P. Morgan, and when their father died in 1913, she became one of the richest women in the world. Educated privately, Morgan excelled at athletics but remained shy into adulthood.

Noted for her work among society women (Morgan was a founder of the Colony Club in New York City), she was also active in the National Civic Federation, helped to found the Working Girls' Vacation Association, and supported the unpopular concept of trade unionism. Morgan shared ownership of the Villa Trianon in Versailles, France, and with the outbreak of World War I in 1914, she offered the house to the French government, as well as establishing a convalescent hospital nearby. Morgan then helped establish the American Fund for French Wounded. Following the United State's entry into the war in April 1917, she organized the American Committee for Devastated France to help restore the Aisne region. From 1918 to 1924 the group raised over $5 million for food, medical aid, and reconstruction. The work was directed from a chateau at Blerancourt that was later converted into a museum honoring French-American cooperation.

In the 1930s Morgan started yet another organization, the American Friends of France (AFF), known in France as the Comité Americain de Secours Civil. By 1938 the AFF had three relief centers operating to assist evacuees from near the Maginot Line. When the war began, the organization evacuated entire regions, often under bombardment. Forced out of France in 1940 following the German victory, Morgan returned to unoccupied Vichy France in 1941 and following the war in 1945 and 1946 to assess needs. The AFF eventually joined with several other groups to form the Organizing Council of French Relief Societies, which later merged with the Fighting French Relief to become the American Relief for France.

Besides the many awards she received for her philanthropic work in the United States, Morgan was awarded a silver medal by the French Academy of Agriculture and the Croix de Guerre with Palm. She was named a Commander of the Legion of Honor, the only American woman to be thus honored. She retired to her New York home due to poor health in 1948 and died there in 1952.

—*Katherine Burger Johnson*

See also Mercy Ship

References and Further Reading

Lewis, Alfred Allen. 2001. *Ladies and Not-so-Gentle Women*. New York: Penguin.

MOTHERS OF THE PLAZA DE MAYO

See Argentina, Mothers of the Plaza de Mayo

MOWLAM, MARJORIE (MO) (1949–2005)

British secretary of state for Northern Ireland, May 1997 to October 1999, who played a leading role in the formulation of the 1998 Good Friday Accord to end the Troubles (period of violence) in Northern Ireland by the establishment of a government representative of the two communities (Catholic/Republican and Protestant/Unionists) of Ulster.

Marjorie Mowlam, who was born in Coventry, was educated in Britain and the United States. After earning a Ph.D. in political science at the University of Iowa, she worked as a research analyst for Tony Benn, the left-wing leader of the British Labour Party. She also taught and served as an administrator for adult education at Northern College, Barnsley, England. She was elected to parliament from Labour in 1987. Prime Minister Tony Blair appointed her secretary of state for Northern Ireland in May 1997. She worked to restore the lapsed cease-fire of the Irish Republican Army (IRA), a terrorist group fighting for the unification of Ireland, and the inclusion in the multiparty talks of Sinn Féin, the republican political party, which served as the political wing of the IRA. She believed that "You have to take risks in a peace process to get it to work" (Fray 2004). Despite subsequent setbacks in Northern Ireland, she remained optimistic because, in her opinion, the people had enthusiastically embraced the peace process.

After stepping down from her post in Northern Ireland in October 1999, Mowlam entered Blair's cabinet. Mowlam subsequently suffered from a brain tumor. In 2001 she resigned from the cabinet and ran again for parliament. She opposed the war against Iraq in 2003 and advocated negotiation with Osama bin Laden.

—*Bernard Cook*

See also Devlin, Bernadette; Peace People Movement; Ulster, Women during the Troubles in

References and Further Reading

Fray, Peter. "Ministry of Sound." *The Sydney Morning Herald*. November 27–28, 2004.

Schoen, Ricki. 2001. Mowlam. Page 881 in *Europe since 1945: An Encyclopedia*. Edited by Bernard Cook. New York: Garland.

N

NANKING, RAPE OF

Orgy of violence that accompanied the Japanese seizure of the Nationalist Chinese (Kuomintang) capital of Nanking in 1937. In a deliberate effort to cow the Chinese, the Japanese pursued a policy of terror during their invasion of China. Between 1937 and 1945, more that 21 million Chinese, most of them civilians, were killed by the Japanese (Greaves et al. 1993, 1035).

In 1937 the Japanese, who had seized Manchuria in 1931, launched an invasion against the remainder of China. They easily occupied Peking (Beijing) but met stiff resistance at Shanghai. When the Chinese withdrew to Nanking, the Japanese executed many Chinese prisoners-of-war and males of military age. After surrounding Nanking and trapping thousands of soldiers and over 200,000 civilians, the Japanese entered the city on December 13. Japanese officers ordered the execution of Chinese POWs. It was, however, undisciplined soldiers who engaged in a rampage of horror against civilians. For a month Japanese soldiers engaged in an orgy of rape. Females, from young girls to elderly women, were raped on the streets and in homes in front of family members. There were gang rapes, mutilations, and murder. According to Robert Greaves, "Survivors described horrifying sights of women impaled on stakes and children sliced in two" (Greaves et al. 1993, 1034). Some estimates for the number of people killed by the Japanese in Nanking—prisoners-of-war and civilians, men, women, and children—range as high as 300,000. More conservative estimates place the figure between 50,000 and 100,000. Many more survived rape, torture, or being wounded.

After the war a tribunal at Nanking convicted and executed three Japanese lieutenants for beheading POWs and a general, who had commanded troops in the city. General Matsui Iwane, the Japanese commander during the campaign, was tried in Tokyo by a war crimes tribunal. General Matsui, despite his orders against atrocities, was condemned to death for failing to end the horrors effectively.

—*Bernard Cook*

See also China, Women and the Communist Revolution; China, Women on the Home Front in World War II

Chinese wife with body of slain husband in Nanking, China, December 30, 1937. (Bettmann/Corbis)

References and Further Reading

Chang, Iris. 1997. *The Rape of Nanking: The Forgotten Holocaust of World War II.* New York: Basic.

Fogel, Joshua A., ed. 2000. *The Nanking Massacre in History and Historiography.* Berkeley: University of California.

Greaves, Robert, et al. 1993. *Civilizations of the World: The Human Adventure.* 2nd ed. New York: HarperCollins.

Hewitt, William L. 2004. "The Rape of Nanking." Pages 119–127 in *Defining the Horrific: Readings on Genocide and Holocaust in the Twentieth Century.* Upper Saddle River, NJ: Pearson/Prentice Hall.

NANYE-HI

See Ward, Nancy

NAPOLEON'S MARSHALS, WIVES OF

Wives of the twenty-six marshals created during the reign of Napoleon I. The women who married Napoleon's marshals crossed the spectrum of social classes, nationalities, religious orientations, and educational levels. Despite these differences, an underlying common bond remained. These women were the constant supporters of husbands who spent the vast majority of their married lives campaigning in the Napoleonic Wars. They were compelled in certain circumstances to accompany their husbands to various posts and even on military campaigns. The marshals' wives would become an integral component of Napoleon's court during the First Empire.

Duty was the creed of the marshals' wives. The role of military wife was unending for the wives of Napoleon's marshals. As a result of the constant campaigning, the women were required to supervise the home life; they maintained their households, raised children, attended to duties at court, and represented their husbands at appropriate activities. In many cases, however, the wives were active in campaigning, tending to wounded husbands, and two would experience the pain of losing their husbands on the field of honor.

The marshals' wives joined their husbands whenever circumstances allowed. Aglaé Ney joined her husband, Michel, who was given command of the 6th Corps at the Boulogne camp, settling first in Montreuil, then in the Château de Recque, which the marshal had procured specifically for her. Consequently, a court-like atmosphere was facilitated by the presence of Madame Ney. Frequent visitors from Paris enjoyed the abundant diversions that were constantly offered (Atteridge 1912, 126–127). When the marshals were on campaign or serving the French government in some other capacity, their wives might be present with them. In many cases, the marshals were appointed as ambassadors and governors throughout France and French-conquered territories. Marshal Jean Baptiste Bernadotte received an appointment as governor and commander-in-chief of Hanover shortly before the coronation of Napoleon as emperor of France in 1804 (Palmer 1990, 119). Bernadotte was to command and administer the army occupying land that had once been under English control. Desirée Bernadotte joined her

husband in the summer of 1805 and settled into the sumptuous Schloss Herrenhausen, the official residence of the governor. The tides of war were such that Desirée was not able to enjoy her new abode for very long. The threat of a Third Coalition, formed by Russia, Austria, and Prussia, forced Napoleon to order Bernadotte to Wurzburg (Palmer 1990, 121–124). The lives of the marshals and their wives were spent constantly adjusting to such sudden changes caused by shifting political alliances and military pursuits.

The Peninsular War bore witness to the truly grim nature of guerrilla warfare. Marshal Louis Gabriel Suchet commanded an army in Catalonia and was awarded his marshal's baton during the desolate war fighting against Spanish guerrillas. Although he celebrated his marriage on November 16, 1808, by December 1, he was departing for Madrid and the commencement of his role in that fateful campaign. By all accounts, the Peninsular War and its ramifications made the lives of the marshals' wives dangerous and unpredictable. As a result, the emperor expressly forbade wives to accompany their husbands to Spain. Ignoring this directive, Honorine Suchet joined her husband in Aragon in 1810, after he had been appointed military governor for that province. The courage of the young wife is further underscored by the fact that she lived in such inhospitable conditions while pregnant with the couple's first child. As her due date approached, it became necessary for Honorine to leave Spain and she returned to Paris in April of 1811 (Horward and Ojala 1987, 490–497).

Not all of the marshals returned home safely at the end of a campaign. The loss of Marshals Jean Lannes and Jean Baptiste Bessières, who played important roles in the success of the empire, was particularly difficult for Napoleon. Adele Bessières received consolation directly from Napoleon and Josephine after her husband fell at the Battle of Lutzen in 1813 (Junot 1893, 212). The widow of Lannes, Louise, received Napoleon's earnest condolences (Horward and Ojala 1987, 212). She retired from court life for a time but returned to serve as lady of honor to Napoleon's second wife, Marie-Louise.

—*Jolynda Brock Chenicek*

See also Frontier Soldiers, U.S., Wives of; Lee, Mary Anna Randolph Custis; Riedesel, Friederike von; Washington, Martha Dandridge Custis

References and Further Reading

Atteridge, A. Hilliard. 1912. *The Bravest of the Brave: Michel Ney, Marshal of France, Duke of Elchingen, Prince of the Moscowa, 1769–1815.* London: Methuen.

Horward, Donald D., and Jeanne A. Ojala. 1987. *Napoleon's Marshals.* Edited by David G. Chandler. London: Weidenfeld and Nicolson.

Junot, Madame (Duchesse d'Abrantès). 1893. *The Home and Court Life of the Emperor Napoleon and His Family.* 4 Vols. New York: Charles Scribner's Sons.

Palmer, Alan. 1990. *Bernadotte: Napoleon's Marshal, Sweden's King.* London: John Murray.

NATIONAL LEGION OF MOTHERS OF AMERICA (NLMA)

American women's antiwar movement. In September 1939, less than a month after Hitler's invasion of Poland triggered the onset of World War II, the National Legion of Mothers of America (NLMA) was established to oppose U.S. entry into the war. Founded by three California mothers of draft-age sons, Frances Sherrill, Mary M. Sheldon, and Mary Ireland, the legion marked the beginning of the "mothers' movement," a generally right-wing coalition of female isolationists. The NLMA, publicized and probably financed by media magnet William Randolph Hearst, quickly established chapters in cities where Hearst newspapers were published. In Hearst editorials the NLMA was praised for its patriotism and determination to fight all at-tempts to send young Americans to fight in foreign wars.

Colonel Robert McCormick's *Chicago Tribune,* also sympathetic to the mothers' movement, attributed 10 million members to the NLMA. The actual number was probably smaller. In June 1940 some 2 million members voted by mail on resolutions to be put forward by the national organization. Its newspaper, the *American Mothers National Weekly,* had several million readers. Chapters were organized in at least 39 states.

The NLMA's founders were not necessarily pacifists but opposed the deployment of U.S. forces for any purpose except defending the nation from attack. One of the legion's New York chapters recruited a paramilitary group, the Molly Pitcher Rifle Legion, to repel foreign invaders. The NLMA welcomed all women with U.S. citizenship regardless of race, religion, or political party. African American women were enrolled. Nonetheless the NLMA's membership could broadly be categorized as white, Protestant, and Republican.

The credibility of the NLMA was enhanced in January 1940 when writer Kathleen Norris became the league's president. A prolific best-selling novelist and short story writer, Norris had been active in the progressive movement of the early twentieth century, supporting pacifism, prohibition, and the abolition of capital punishment. She was also an opponent of Franklin Roosevelt's New Deal and accused the president of trying to dupe the United States into war. Professing the traditional belief that the Atlantic and Pacific oceans were moats deep enough to safeguard the American shores, she supported the 1940 election campaign of Republican presidential candidate Wendell Wilkie, and worked unsuccessfully against the passage of the selective service bill authorizing a peacetime draft. In September 1940, NLMA members protested the draft bill outside the U.S. Senate, wearing black dresses and veils and maintaining a "death vigil." The NLMA generated a letter-writing campaign but failed to prevent passage of the Lend-Lease Act.

Norris tried to keep the NLMA from falling into the hands of the far right, repudiating the endorsement of her organization by the notorious Father Charles Coughlin. Despite her efforts, Coughlinites and the pro-Nazi German-American Bund gained control over some chapters and strident anti-Semitism was often voiced at legion meetings. More radical elements of the NLMA began to denounce Roman Catholics as well as Jews, and to demand the impeachment of Roosevelt. Norris expelled some of the legion's most militant chapters but resigned as president in April 1941 and continued her antiwar work in concert with more moderate isolationists.

With her departure the NLMA splintered into three groups, the National Legion, the Mothers of the U.S.A., and the Women's National Committee to Keep the U.S. Out of War. The new organizations coordinated their efforts to abolish the draft, repeal the Lend-Lease Act, and impeach Roosevelt. Without Norris' leadership the mothers movement became increasingly militant and marginal.

The NLMA was significant because it demonstrated the potential of mobilizing conservative women who opposed U.S. entry into World War II. It was the first major organization to use maternal arguments against Roosevelt's war policy. The group also encouraged a sense of gender solidarity based on the belief that women would suffer from a war whose course was directed by men.
—*Glen Jeansonne and David Luhrssen*

See also Dilling, Elizabeth; United States, Opposition to U.S. Entry into World War II by Right-Wing American Women

References and Further Reading

Jeansonne, Glen. 1996. *Women of the Far Right.* Chicago: University of Chicago.

McEnaney, Laura M. 1994. "He-Men and Christian Mothers." *Diplomatic History* 18, 1 (Winter): 47–57.

Ribuffo, Leo P. 1983. *The Old Christian Right: The Protestant Far Right From the Great Depression to the Cold War.* Philadelphia: Temple University.

NEARNE, JACQUELINE (1916–1982)

British agent, member of the Special Operations Executive (SOE) who participated in numerous missions to assist French Resistance groups in World War II and who was awarded the title of MBE (Member of the Order of the British Empire) for her work.

Jacqueline Françoise Mary Josephine Nearne was born on May 27, 1916, in Brighton, England, but was raised and educated in France and consequently became bilingual. When Germany invaded France in 1940, she escaped to Britain with her younger sister Eileen (codename Didi), who was also to become a SOE agent.

In 1942 Nearne was recruited into the First Aid Nursing Yeomanry (FANY) and soon afterward joined the F Section (France) of SOE. SOE's mission was to provide support for espionage and sabotage operations that took place behind enemy lines. Nearne was among the second group of women recruited by SOE. She was trained as a courier in Scotland, at Garramore House, along with other French-speaking agents. She was taught how to make Morse code transmissions with a suitcase radio. On January 25, 1943, she secretly parachuted in France, as "Josette Norville," to join SOE's "Stationer" network operating in central and southern France, all the way to the Pyrenees. Her work there involved long and dangerous trips, often by train, keeping in contact with the agents and the wireless operators of the Headmaster circuit, carrying spare parts for radios, and organizing reception committees for newly arrived agents. She also maintained contact between several other SOE networks operating in a large area around Paris.

After fifteen months in the field, Nearne was flown back to Britain in April 1944 to rest. In 1945 she starred (as agent "Cat"), along with fellow agent Harry Rée (as agent "Felix"), in a public information and propaganda film produced by the Royal Air Force (RAF) Film Unit, first entitled *Now It Can Be Told*, about the work of the F Section. The film was shot for the most part in newly liberated France while the war was still going on. The film was shown in 1946 as *School for Danger*. In 2001 it was released on video.

Nearne died in London on November 15, 1982.

—*Georgia Tres*

See also Atkins, Vera H.

References and Further Reading

Mackenzie, William. 2003. *The Secret History of SOE: Special Operations Executive 1940–1945.* London: St Ermins Press.

Stafford, William. 2002. *Secret Agent: The True Story of the Special Operations Executive.* New York: Overlook Press.

NICARAGUA, WOMEN AND WAR IN

The role of women in revolutionary struggle in Nicaragua. The modern history of Nicaragua cannot be fully told without recounting the important roles that women played in the various wars. Throughout much of the twentieth century, Nicaragua was afflicted by a series of armed conflicts, including civil wars, revolutions, and foreign interventions. Nicaraguan women were drawn into all of these conflicts as collaborators, combatants, and victims.

The United States became concerned about Nicaragua because it was under prime consideration for an interoceanic canal. U.S. Marines intervened and occupied Nicaragua several times, including in 1926 during a Nicaraguan civil war. It was at this point that Nicaraguan history turned, when a handful of Nicaraguan patriots decided to resist U.S. occupation. Their leader was Augusto C. Sandino, who in 1927 organized the Ejército Defensor de la Soberanía Nacional de Nicaragua (EDSNN, Army in Defense of the National Sovereignty of

Nicaragua) and fought a guerrilla war that lasted until 1933.

Many Nicaraguan women actively participated in the Sandinista struggle. While these women played an essential role, their tasks can be defined as collaborators. Women were not combatants within the EDSNN but were active in a variety of other ways. They served as spies, messengers, proselytizers, nurses, and in domestic services. Sandino called their actions heroic and admitted that many had died. He gave an example of one who was arrested and tortured and whose children were murdered. After leaving jail she joined the EDSNN as a "cook, nurse and washerwoman" (Grossman 1996, 730). According to Sandino, the exemplary Sandinista woman was one who sacrificed all for the cause and whose personal contributions were the traditional gendered labor of women as care providers. Still, this gendered labor was crucial to the conduct of the war.

While some women joined the guerrilla bands, most remained at home. The women who stayed at home played an essential support role. To keep their families alive, they had to do their own daily work as well as that of their missing men. When the guerrillas passed through an area, local supporters were supposed to provide them with food, which meant even more work. These women assumed tremendous extra responsibilities in support of Sandino.

The war ended when the last of the U.S. Marines were withdrawn from Nicaragua in 1933 and the Nicaraguan government signed a ceasefire with Sandino. Before leaving, however, the Marines created a new Nicaraguan army, the Guardia Nacional, and command was turned over to Anastasio Somoza García. Somoza García ordered Sandino assassinated, and using the Guardia, seized control of the government and created a regime that would dominate Nicaragua for the next forty-five years.

While many Nicaraguans opposed the dictatorship, the Somoza family ruled Nicaragua with an iron hand. In 1961 a small group of Nicaraguans formed a new organization which they named after Sandino, the *Frente Sandinista de Liberación Nacional* (FSLN, the Sandinista Front of National Liberation), and began a new guerrilla war. Slowly the FSLN won popular support culminating in a widespread urban insurrection that finally overthrew the Somoza regime in 1979.

By the 1970s many women became active members of the FSLN and were integrated into the guerrilla columns. While there is some question about the actual numbers, more than 30 percent of the armed combatants were women, some of whom died fighting the regime. The first women joined in the mid-1960s and by 1979 there were thousands of women guerrillas. A few of these women became officers of FSLN units.

Many more women were collaborators. As in the earlier conflicts, they actively supported the guerrillas by providing food, medicines, and safe houses, hiding weapons, and carrying messages. These activities were also very dangerous and many of these female supporters of the FSLN were tortured and murdered by the regime.

Women were involved in many other opposition activities. In 1977 women organized AMPRONAC, the Association of Nicaraguan Women Confronting the National Problem—the "national problem" being the Somoza regime. By 1979 the organization had grown to over 8,000 members (Isbester 2001, 42). While they organized demonstrations against the government's repression, AMPRONAC also protested discrimination against women as well as rising food prices. Many AMPRONAC members joined the armed insurrection.

In July 1979 the Somoza regime was overthrown and a new government led by the FSLN was created. Most women combatants were demobilized and many took civilian positions within the new government. Nevertheless, as the Sandinista Popular Army was created, many women stayed in the military. In 1980 about 6 percent of the officers and 40 percent of the soldiers were women but generally they were placed in noncombat duties (Isbester 2001, 55). AMPRONAC transformed itself into the Association of Nicaraguan Women "Luisa Amanda Espinoza" (AMNLAE), named after the first female FSLN member to die in combat. The group was affiliated with the FSLN and actively supported the new government.

Over the decades the United States had been generally supportive of the Somoza regime. Although President Jimmy Carter had finally cut U.S. aid to Somoza in 1979, President Ronald Reagan was very critical of the new FSLN government. In 1981 Reagan ordered the CIA to reorganize the remnants of Somoza's old army that had fled Nicaragua into a new counterrevolutionary force. Backed by the United States, the contras, as they were known, began to attack the Sandinista regime and its supporters in an effort to overthrow it.

Nicaraguan women were again drawn into war. While some joined or were forced into the contras, most supported the new revolutionary government. This time, however, the FSLN tried to keep women in noncombat and support roles. While men were sent to the front lines in the mountains, women's battalions were formed within the militia to help protect the cities. AMNLAE also helped create the Mothers of the Revolution—Heroes and Martyrs as a support organization for those who had lost children in combat. Thus the male FSLN leaders returned to Sandino's vision of women as collaborators and as mothers who could give their sons to the struggle. Nevertheless, thousands of women actively contributed to the war effort.

Nicaraguan women had been transformed and empowered by the decades of war. Their contributions to the fight against invaders and dictators cannot be denied. With the Nicaraguan people exhausted by years of war, the FSLN lost the 1990 presidential election. The fighting finally ended when the contras signed a ceasefire with the new U.S.-backed president, Violetta Chamorro, the first woman president in Nicaragua's history.

—*Richard Grossman*

See also Latin America, Women in Guerrilla Movements in

References and Further Reading

Grossman, Richard. 1996. *"Hermanos en la Patria."* Nationalism, Honor and Rebellion: Augusto Sandino and the Army in Defense of the National Sovereignty of Nicaragua, 1927–1934. Unpublished Ph.D. dissertation. University of Chicago.

Isbester, Katherine. 2001. *Still Fighting: The Nicaraguan Women's Movement, 1977–2000.* Pittsburgh, PA: University of Pittsburgh.

Randall, Margaret. 1995. *Sandino's Daughters: Testimonies of Nicaraguan Women in Struggle.* New Brunswick, NJ: Rutgers University.

NIEDERKIRCHNER, KÄTHE (KATJA) (1909–1944)

German Communist resistance fighter. Käthe Niederkirchner, a seamstress, was born into a working class family in Berlin on October 7, 1909. During World War I Niederkirchner's father, a plumber, became a Communist while he was a prisoner of war in Russia. In 1925 Käthe Niederkirchner joined the German Communist Youth League and in 1929 she became a member of the German Communist Party. She was arrested on March 27, 1933, after Hitler outlawed the Communist Party. Following her release Niederkirchner emigrated to the Soviet Union, where her family had sought refuge from the Nazi regime. In 1941, when Germany invaded the Soviet Union, she joined the Red Army. Her appeals to German soldiers were broadcast by Radio Moscow and she was sent to prisoner of war camps to persuade soldiers to join the antifascist cause. In October 1943 she parachuted from a Soviet plane into German-occupied Poland near Warsaw. Her mission was to work in Berlin with the Communist underground. She made her way to the railway station at Kostiza. Her forged papers, however, lacked a stamp that the Nazis had just issued and she was arrested by the Gestapo. At the Gestapo headquarters in Berlin, Niederkirchner was kept in solitary confinement and subjected to interrogation and torture for several months. She was then transferred to the Ravensbrück concentration camp, where she was chained by a leg-iron to a wall. On September 27, 1944, the camp commandant pronounced her death sentence, and she was executed that night.

In May 1951 the East German Communist regime renamed Prinz-Abrecht-Strasse—the former location of the Gestapo headquarters—Niederkirchner Strasse.

—Bernard Cook

See also Buch, Eva Maria; Harnack-Fish, Mildred; Kirchner, Johanna; Kuckhoff, Greta

References and Further Reading

Kreuzberger Chronik. 2003. Von Westhafen, Werner. *"Käte Niederkirschner—Heldin des antifaschistischen Kampfes* [Käte Niederkirschner—Heroine of the Antifascist Struggle]." http://www.kreuzberger-chronik.de/chroniken/2003juni/strasse.html (accessed October 3, 2003).

Rürup, Reinhard, ed. 2002. *Topography of Terror: Gestapo, SS, and Reichssicherheitshauptamt on the "Prinz-Albrecht-Terrain:" A Documentation.* Trans. by Werner T. Angress. Berlin: Verlag Willmuth Arenhövel.

NIGHTINGALE, FLORENCE (1820–1910)

Reformer of the British army medical service. Popularly known as "the Lady with the Lamp," Florence Nightingale was throughout her long life an active campaigner for high standards of military and civilian nursing and improved conditions in the hospitals of the British Army. She is best known for her tireless work during the Crimean War (1854–1856), during which she made the British public aware of the ghastly conditions facing the sick and wounded troops, and exposed numerous weaknesses within the

RUN THE "APPOINTED COURSE"

"I have no peculiar gifts. And I can honestly assure any young lady, if she will but try to walk, she will soon be able to run the 'appointed course.' But then she must first learn to walk, and so when she runs she must run with patience. (Most people don't even try to walk.) But I would also say to all young ladies who are called to any particular vocation, qualify yourself for it as a man does for his work. Don't think you can undertake it otherwise."

—Florence Nightingale,
letter published in the *Englishwoman's Review,* January, 1869.
http://www.spartacus.schoolnet.co.uk/REnightingale.htm
(accessed January 21, 2006).

army medical services. In the face of entrenched attitudes and deep-seated inertia, Nightingale imposed order out of chaos, filth, and needless deprivation through a new regime of cleanliness, strict standards of hygiene, and regular hot meals for patients.

Through personal example and in the face of determined opposition from conservative officialdom, Nightingale displayed a remarkable flair for organization, eventually establishing nursing as a respectable vocation based on sound principles of hygiene, domestic science, and methodical care. Her work became the stuff of legend even before the war had ended. Although she antagonized many doctors, nurses, and government officials, she was venerated by the troops, and the public and press at home.

Nightingale was born into a wealthy Derbyshire family, which she shocked by her desire to enter nursing, work widely viewed as the preserve of disreputable, ignorant, and frequently drunk women from the lowest classes. Intelligent and well-connected both professionally and socially, Nightingale defied prevailing attitudes and educated herself about public administration and statistics. She inspected hospitals in Britain, studied government reports on health, and worked in several hospitals in France and Germany. As a result of her experience, and her personal friendship with Secretary of War Sidney Herbert, Nightingale was, in October 1854, dispatched with a party of thirty-eight nurses to Turkey to take charge of the Barrack Hospital at Scutari, on the opposite side of the Bosphorus from Constantinople.

She arrived just after the Battle of Inkerman and found appalling conditions of filth, starvation, infection, and an acute shortage of even the most basic amenities. There were few orderlies; clothes, utensils, beds and bedding, soap, medical equipment, and drugs were almost entirely absent. Even food and water were in short supply. Undaunted, Nightingale immediately set about using the large sums of money raised by public subscription through the *Times* (London) relief fund for the sick and wounded, gifts from friends, and even her own resources, to buy all manner of supplies.

The urgent need for cleanliness and proper hygiene was equally apparent. Overflowing sewers, blocked privies, and the human excrement that covered the floors were not merely responsible for an unearthly stench but also for the production of noxious fumes that caused widespread illness among men already weakened by other ailments such as cholera and dysentery, or by wounds.

Nightingale discovered hundreds of men infested with vermin, laid out in rows on filthy floors and denied even basic attention, sometimes for days at a time. Those orderlies who were in evidence showed little compassion and practiced a good deal of roughness. Worse still, many of the doctors, overworked and understaffed, looked on Nightingale's arrival with suspicion and sometimes scarcely veiled hostility.

Florence Nightingale. (Library of Congress)

Yet with patient numbers constantly on the rise, doctors became utterly overwhelmed and were obliged to tolerate the services of her staff.

Under her management—at times overbearing and acerbic—Nightingale had the wards repaired, cleaned, and properly equipped. She instituted a regime for the regular washing of patients' clothes and bedding with soap and warm water—a service previously unavailable. She had boilers installed and established a scheme to pay soldiers' wives to launder clothes and dressings, and she had the kitchen service placed on a proper footing, with a system for feeding invalids who had previously gone without food for days at a time.

Within eight weeks of her arrival the immediate crisis had passed, thanks to the Herculean efforts of Nightingale and her staff. Her transformation of a virtual charnel house brought a radical reduction in the hitherto staggering mortality rate. The eventual arrival of four different commissions sent out by the government to investigate the scandalous conditions under which soldiers lived and died further reduced the death toll. Nightingale was not alone in reporting the shocking conditions of the military hospitals. Soldiers' letters and the dispatches of journalist William Howard Russell supported her findings. Many people admired the Christian zeal that underpinned Nightingale's work, though Elizabeth Gaskell referred unflatteringly to her "visible march to heaven" (Uglow 1993, 365), emphasizing Nightingale's championing of great causes over the cultivation of good relations with individuals.

Nightingale was forced to fight not only disease and squalor, but also the complacent, inefficient, and at times, corrupt officials in the medical services, the commissariat, and other departments. She walked miles a day up and down the wards, functioning with a minimum of sleep; yet, in addition to her ordinary administrative duties at Scutari, she was still able to write lengthy letters to the War Office and other government departments in London in her campaign to improve the soldiers' lot. So relentless were her efforts that she nearly died of fever in June 1855.

For the remainder of her long life, Nightingale devoted herself to the reformation and reorganization of the army medical service, thus securing for herself a place in the pantheon of great Victorians. In 1860 she founded a nursing school at St. Thomas's Hospital in London. In 1881 an Army Nursing Service was formed. Three years later the Army Nursing Reserve was created, and by the time of the Boer War (1899–1902) female nurses were a well-established component of the British Army, both on campaign and at home. Nightingale's legacy continues today, and she is justly credited as the founder of modern nursing.

—*Gregory Fremont-Barnes*

See also Barton, Clara; Great Britain, Women in Service during World War I; Nurses, U.S. Army Nurse Corps in World War I

References and Further Reading

Cook, Sir Edward Tyas. 1913. *The Life of Florence Nightingale.* 2 vols. London: Macmillan.

Goldie, Sue M., ed. 1997. *Florence Nightingale: Letters from the Crimea, 1854–1856.* New York: Mandolin.

Small, Hugh. 1998. *Florence Nightingale: Avenging Angel.* London: Constable.

Uglow, Jennifer. 1993. *Elizabeth Gaskell.* New York: Farrar Straus Giroux.

Woodham-Smith, Cecil. 1953. *Lady in Chief: The Story of Florence Nightingale.* London: Methuen.

NIKULINA, ANNA VLADIMIROVNA (B. 1904)

Soviet military heroine. Anna Vladimirovna Nikulina hoisted a red flag on the roof of the Third Reich's Chancellery in Berlin as the Russians fought to seize the city. At the time she was senior instructor and secretary of the party commission in the 9th Brandenburg Infantry Corps, which had covered 5,000 kilometers (3,107 miles) from Mozdok in the Caucasus to Berlin.

She was born in the Cossack village of Batalpashinskaia (renamed Cherkessk). When she was fourteen, her father, the first chairman of his village's Poor Peasants' Committee, was hanged by men of the counterrevolutionary Denikin army, who ransacked the family's living quarters, mistreating Anna's mother and grandfather. Nikulina, in reaction, became the first member of the Komsomol (Young Communist League) in her village. Elected her district's Komsomol committee secretary, she studied at the Communist University of Saratov and a political-technical college in Rostov. A Party member since 1925, she married Nikolai Vinogradov,

a fellow university student who became a Party official and was subsequently killed by opponents of collectivization.

The widowed Nikulina worked in a factory and held various local Party posts. She eventually attended the Academy of Water Transport. Her dream was to circumnavigate the globe, but instead she covered some 5,000 kilometers (3,107 miles), at least partly on foot, from Mozdok to Berlin. To go to war she left her two children, a son and daughter, with her sister. Initially a political commissar of a hospital, after graduating from the Military Political School in Rostov, Nikulina underwent a baptism of fire at Mozdok along with a tankborne assault force. On another occasion, when an infantry company commander was killed, she led his men under fire, capturing the village of Angelinovskaia in the Caucasus. Her role as political officer was not only to lead and encourage men under fire, but also to interact with them daily as a morale officer.

By the end of April 1945 the fighting in Berlin was carried out by small Soviet assault groups. Summoned by her Corps' commanding officer, Nikulina was ordered to lead an assault team tasked with the mission of hoisting a red flag on the roof of the Chancellery. She was assigned four men from the 1050th Infantry Regiment's No. 2 Battalion commanded by F. K. Shapovalov (whose nephew in 1984 wrote an account of the mission based on an interview with Nikulina, who was then eighty years old).

Nikulina wrapped the flag around her waist under a leather jacket. Early on May 2 Nikulina's party of five forced their way into the building under heavy fire. The fighting was especially intense on the third floor. After Soviet soldiers inside the building cleared the stairs, Nikulina and her men ran up to the attic, where two of them were killed and one was seriously wounded. With the fourth soldier, Nikulina managed to climb through a hole in the attic onto the roof and to secure the flag to a spire with a telephone cable. Later, in the Führer's bunker, Shapovalov offered her his congratulations.

She participated in the Victory Parade in Moscow on June 24, 1945, where she was reunited with her son, a naval cadet. After the war Nikulina played an active role in reconstruction, distinguished herself as Party organizer, and wrote a book. A recipient of at least ten decorations, she did not receive the Hero of the Soviet Union. Instead, for her feat in Berlin, she was presented with the Order of the Red Banner.

—*Kazimiera J. Cottam*

See also Soviet Union, Order of the Red Banner, Women Recipients

Reference and Further Reading

Cottam, Kazimiera J. 1982. "Soviet Women in Combat in World War II: The Rear Services, Resistance behind Enemy Lines, and Military Political Workers." *International Journal of Women's Studies*, 5, 4 (September/October): 374.

Stepichev, Mikhail. 1969. *Skvoz' gody i buri.* Pages 3, 7–20 in *Skvoz' gody i buri. O zhenshchinakh kommunistkakh* [The Stormy Years: The Story of Women Party Members]. Edited by G.V. Kulikovskaia. Moscow: Politizdat.

Szapowalow, Anatol. 1984. "*Sztandar zwyciïstwa nad Kancelarja Rzeszy*" [The Victory Flag above the Reich's Chancellery]. Trans. by Rajmund Kulinski. *Zolnierz Polski*, 19 (May 6): 9.

NIROUET, COLLETTE (1926–1944)

French volunteer soldier during World War II who died fighting in Alsace. Collette Nirouet, a young Parisian woman, joined the 6th company of the Auvergne Regiment of the French First Army on October 15, 1944. Nirouet was an eighteen-year-old student who initially served as a nurse, although there is no evidence that she had any formal medical training. Following her insistence, the captain of her regiment permitted her to fight as a soldier. For the next few months, she participated fully in the activities of the company, both offensive and defensive, in the line of fire in the forests of Oberwald. She wore a woman's uniform of the U.S. army, not civilian clothing.

Nirouet's family background and initial life experiences perhaps explain why she desired to fight for her country. Her father, a genealogist, had fought for France during World War I, earning the Croix de Guerre. Her brother, permanently injured from a bicycle accident, was unable to be a soldier. Collette felt it was her duty to replace her brother at the front. She also may have joined the army because of experiences at her grandmother's home in Pont-de-Pany that served as a refuge for Allied soldiers. Nirouet not only witnessed the crash of an RAF plane, but also helped provide medical aid for the injured pilot.

Nirouet earned an affectionate nickname, Joan of Arc, from her brothers in arms during the course of her service. They so-named her because of her courage and patriotism. She was also known as Evelyne, a name that stuck with her even after her death. It is under the name of Evelyne Meunier that she appears on the list of those killed on November 26, 1944, in the *Journal des Marches* of the 152nd Régiment infanterie, Campaign 1944–1945.

Nirouet was fatally wounded on November 12, 1944, in the battle of Oberwald. She was not, however, decorated by France until August 30, 1985. Her posthumously awarded decorations include the French commemorative war medal for World War II (with a barrette "*libération*"). The delayed recognition of Nirouet stemmed from the fact that her body was never found. Apparently the Germans took her corpse along with their wounded as they retreated from the battlefield. Also because of her nom de guerre, she did not appear among the list of dead from that battle. On February 23, 1984, a fellow World War II veteran, Antonin Cabizolles, began a quest to recognize Collette Nirouet. Through a lengthy and difficult process, Cabizolles was able to piece together the story of her life and military service. He contacted his comrades, who knew Nirouet personally and fought alongside her. These men provided Cabizolles with the testimony required to write her biography.

—*Leigh Whaley*

See also France, Resistance during World War II, Women and

References and Further Reading

Cabizolles, Antonin. 1987. *Eveylne ou l'Etrange disparue des combats de l'Oberwald: récit historique* [Eveylne or the Strange Disappearance from the Battle of Oberwald: Historical Account]. Paris: Entente.

NLMA

See National Legion of Mothers of America

NONGQAWUSE (1841–1898)

Xhosa (South Africa) prophetess who precipitated a millenarian movement among her people known as the Great Cattle Killing. The years preceding Nongqawuse's prophecies had been difficult ones for the Xhosa. They had fought and lost two wars against the Cape Colony, the so-called Seventh (1846–1847) and Eighth (1850–1852) Frontier Wars, and colonial troops had destroyed Xhosa crops, seized their cattle, and annexed large tracts of Xhosa land. Then a lung sickness, contagious bovine pleuropneumonia (CBPP), brought in from Europe in 1853, began to decimate Xhosa livestock herds. Blight was also destroying maize fields, damaging the stalks before the corn had ripened. The Xhosa were experiencing a period of psychological trauma, continual loss of their land to the British, and food shortages due to the combination of military defeat and natural disaster. The circumstances turned the Xhosa to indigenous belief systems for relief. Several prophets arose, including an adolescent orphan girl, Nongqawuse. She lived with her uncle, Mhlakaza, a disillusioned Christian convert who preached a new gospel containing both Xhosa animist and Christian religious elements.

In April 1856, while playing with a friend at a pool on a river near her home, the fifteen-year-old Nongqawuse reported that two strangers identifying themselves as long-departed ancestors told her that Xhosa cattle were rotten, cursed, and must be slaughtered. Xhosa crops, which were infected with a blight, were also to be destroyed. Xhosa ancestors would then arise from the dead and help the living in a holy war against the British, driving both colonial invaders and Xhosa unbelievers into the sea. The Xhosa could then reclaim their land, restore tradition, and the lung sickness devastating their herds and the blight afflicting their maze would cease. New cattle herds would magically appear, grain bins would overflow, and sickness and death, poverty and witchcraft would cease. In response, the paramount Xhosa chief, Sarhili, slaughtered his herds and ordered subordinate chiefs to do likewise.

Mhlakaza, supposedly interpreting his niece's visions, then determined a day of resurrection, by which time all cattle must be killed, crops destroyed, new grain bins built, cattle-folds laid out, and witchcraft ended. When nothing occurred on three separate days of resurrection, the entire situation collapsed. The results, however, were catastrophic. Close to 80 percent of the nation's cattle—more than 400,000 animals—were slaughtered, 40,000 Xhosa died of hunger, and 150,000 were displaced. The Xhosa lost two-thirds of their land, their economic and political independence, and many survivors were forced to seek refuge and ill-paid employment in the colony (Beck 2000, 46).

Debate about the "great cattle killing" continues more than 140 years after the event. One widely accepted interpretation argues that this millenarian movement arose from colonial pressure, Christian and Xhosa resurrection and regeneration beliefs, and the epidemic of CBPP. Some scholars place much of the blame on Nongqawuse's uncle and the tribal chiefs, while many Xhosa continue to fault the Cape colonial governor, Sir George Grey, for the event and its catastrophic consequences. These latter "androcentric" interpretations have been challenged by some who argue that issues of gender, women's rights, and Xhosa male sexual misconduct led to Nongqawuse's prophecies.

—Roger B. Beck

See also Colenso, Harriette

References and Further Reading

Beck, Roger. 2000. *The History of South Africa.* Westport, CT: Greenwood.

Bradford, Helen. 1996. "Women, Gender and Colonialism: Rethinking the History of the British Cape Colony and its Frontier Zones, ca. 1806–1870." *Journal of African History,* 3(37):351–370.

Mostert, Noel. 1992. *Frontiers: The Epic of South Africa's Creation and the Tragedy of the Xhosa People.* New York: Knopf.

Peires, Jeff. 1989. *The Dead Will Arise: Nongqawuse and the Great Xhosa Cattle-Killing Movement of 1856–1857.* Bloomington: Indiana University.

Switzer, Les. 1993. *Power and Resistance in an African Society. The Ciskei Xhosa and the Making of South Africa.* Madison: University of Wisconsin.

NONHELEMA (OR GRENADIER SQUAW) (CA. 1720–1786)

An important cultural mediator and Shawnee leader. White people called her the Grenadier or Grenadier Squaw because of her bearing and height (nearly six foot six).

Nonhelema married first a Shawnee, then a white captive named Richard Butler, and finally the Shawnee Moluntha. Probably born in Maryland, Nonhelema, also know as Katherine, lived in Pennsylvania before she and her brother, Cornstalk, moved to Ohio, where they each led neighboring villages on the Scioto Creek.

Nonhelema was a warrior woman, whose participation in the colonial frontier wars (including the Battle of Bushy Run in 1774), convinced her that Shawnee survival depended on peace. During the American Revolution, many Shawnee aided the British, but Nonhelema and her brother Cornstalk led a peace faction. After her brother's murder by militia at Fort Randolph in 1777, Nonhelema separated from her tribe to support the Americans. She warned Fort Randolph of a Shawnee attack in 1778, negotiated with the attackers for the Fort, and disguised messengers, who were sent to warn Fort Donnally that a Shawnee attack was imminent. Her large herd of cattle and horses were destroyed during the Fort Randolph siege. In 1780, she served as guide and translator for Lieutenant-Colonel Augustin Mottin de la Balme, the U.S. inspector general of cavalry, when he traveled to Illinois to treat with Indians.

The frontier war continued after the Anglo-American Treaty of 1783. Nonhelema petitioned Congress in 1785 for a 1,000-acre grant of the land in Ohio as compensation for her service during the war and the loss of livestock. Instead, Congress voted her a pension of daily rations for life and an annual allotment of a set of clothes and a blanket. In 1786, when General Benjamin Logan led Kentucky militia against the Ohio Shawnee, Nonhelema and her husband and family surrendered to the troops. After they were in army custody, a soldier killed Moluntha, and the Americans detained Nonhelema at Pittsburgh. While at Fort Pitt, she helped the commander compile a dictionary of Shawnee words. She died sometime after her release in December 1786.

—Joan R. Gundersen

See also American Revolution, Role of Women in the; Wake, Nancy; Winema; Winnemucca, Sarah

References and Further Reading

Calloway, Colin. 1995. *The American Revolution in Indian Country: Crisis and Diversity in Native American Communities.* Cambridge, England: Cambridge University.

Thom, Dark Rain. 1994. *Kohkumthena's Grandchildren: The Shawnee.* Indianapolis, IN: Guild Press.

NORWAY, RESISTANCE MOVEMENT DURING WORLD WAR II, WOMEN AND

Resistance of Norwegian women during the Nazi occupation of Norway from 1940 to 1945. Occupation by a foreign enemy means a state of emergency for the occupied society that in many ways calls into question what was previously taken for granted. Among the social relations that become insecure in this exceptional situation are gender relations. As Norwegian pre-war society was organized very traditionally with regard to gender roles, the participation of women in the resistance movement mirrored, to a certain extent, their traditional roles in the social realms. There were "male" and "female" responsibilities—even in the resistance movement. But the state of war moved the borders of those gendered responsibilities and women participated in the movement in ways that by no means conformed with traditional gender roles.

At the beginning of the German occupation of Norway, which lasted from April 9, 1940, until May 8, 1945, King Haakon VII and the government escaped into exile in Britain. In September 1940 a collaborationist regime under fascist leader Vidkun Quisling was installed, which was a starting point of the attempt to reorganize all of Norwegian society according to fascist principles. This was the main reason for the formation of a resistance movement, which grew dramatically during the entire period of occupation. Tactics included civil disobedience and creation of a civil and military resistance organization.

Different parts of the resistance went through various developmental phases. The campaigns of protest and boycott in which tens of thousands of Norwegians protested against measures of the Quisling regime began in the autumn of 1940, and they made up one of the most outstanding features of the Norwegian resistance. People repudiated their membership in institutions or organizations, which were to be Nazified, or they protested by writing letters of dissent to the authorities. Even if the initiative for those campaigns often came from mostly male political leaders (such as in the labor unions), many women participated.

Two sisters initiated one very famous campaign, the so-called school battle in 1942. The school battle involved protest actions against the Nazification ("new ordering," to use a term of the collaborationist Quisling regime) of teaching and the teacher's professional organization. In February 1942, when laws were promulgated that teachers and pupils would automatically become members of Nazi organizations and that education would be in accord with fascist ideology, teachers organized a protest campaign and more than 14,000 resigned from their professional organization. Schools were closed for a month by a de facto strike. Afterward, 1,000 male teachers were arrested and sent to northern Norway for forced labor. Meanwhile, there was a protest campaign in which approximately 10,000 parents protested against the Nazification of education. As a result of these acts of resistance, the regime could not Nazify school education to the extent that it had desired.

Along with these acts of defiance there was symbolic resistance. Many Norwegians wore red "jelly bag" caps representing the *holdningskampen* (the fight for the "real" national attitude). Women, traditionally responsible for managing everyday life under the difficult conditions of material shortages in wartime, were also the producers and bearers of those signs of "patriotic attitudes."

The more organized forms of resistance started at the end of 1940, when the leaders and representatives of some organizations, which were taken over by Nazi-rule, continued their work illegally. There were two central organizations, the Koordinasjonskomiteen (coordination committee) and the Kretsen (circle), which varied in their orientation toward the government-in-exile, but nonetheless worked very closely together. Most of their members were representatives of the Norwegian prewar civil society and because at that time women were still represented by men in politics, only a few women were to be found in the so-called Sivorg (civil organization). They held primarily secretarial positions.

There were many forms of resistance where women did very important work. Their tasks often would be smuggling of information, weapons, or food, and often would occur in public and under the eyes of German patrols. As women they could exploit the image of a naïve girl whom no one would suspect of carrying weapons. Women were active distributors (and, to a minor degree, producers) of illegal newspapers; they were top-agents of the resistance movement's espionage organization XU; and they were couriers for the Milord (the military resistance organization). Moreover, women played a very important role in hiding and accommodating persecuted people traveling to the Swedish border or to England.

Although a large number of women assisted Norwegian troops after the German invasion in April 1940, they were not regarded as part of the military forces. When the Milord was systematically built up toward the end of the war, this realm was a nearly exclusive men's sphere. The few women who played an active role in the Milord (and, as a result, crossed traditional gender borders) were forgotten in the Norwegian culture of commemoration after 1945, as were all the women who simply had done the work of a "patriotic housewife."

—*Claudia Lenz*

See also Norway, Women and the Home Front during World War II; Norway, Women's Collaboration during World War II German Occupation of

References and Further Reading

Dahl, Hans Fredrik, Bernt Hagtvet, and Guri Hjeltnes. 1990. *Den norske nasjonalsosjalismen. Nasjonal Samling 1933–1945 i tekst og bilder* [The Norwegian National Socialism. Nasjonal Samling 1933–1945 in text and images]. Oslo: Pax forlag.

Lenz, Claudia. 2003. *Haushaltspflicht und Widerstand. Erzählungen norwegischer Frauen über die deutsche Besatzung 1940–1945 im Lichte nationaler Vergangenheitskonstruktionen* [Housewife's Duties and Resistance. Norwegian Women's Narratives about the German Occupation 1940–1945 in the Light of Nationalized Constructions of the Past]. Tübingen, Germany: Edition Diskord.

Norges krigsleksikon, nettutgave, slagord NSK [The Norwegian War lexicon, netversion, keyword NSK]. http://lotus.uib.no/norgeslexi/krigslex /n/n1.html#ns-kvinner (accessed October 28, 2004).

Sveri, Elisabeth. 1991. *Kvinner i norsk motstandsbevegelse 1940–1945* [Women in the Norwegian Resistance Movement 1940–1945]. Oslo: Norges hjemmefrontmuseum.

Værnø, Grete, and Elisabeth Sveri. 1995. *Kvinnenes innsats under annen verdenskrig* [Women's Commitments in World War II]. Oslo: Kvinners frivillige beredskap.

NORWAY, WOMEN AND THE HOME FRONT DURING WORLD WAR II

Deep effects of World War II on Norwegian women. If a country is occupied by a foreign power such as Norway was between 1940 and 1945, people's lives are changed dramatically, not only because of the military presence of the occupier, but also because of the regime of occupation. The restrictions concerning politics and culture touched everyday life when newspapers, cinema, and even sports activities were taken over by Nazi rule. As a consequence, many Norwegians boycotted all types of official cultural events, and social life more and more took place in privacy. Other restrictions, such as a curfew after darkness, also changed everyday life. As far as the gender-related consequences of the German occupation of Norway, it is necessary to be informed about the living conditions of the average population at the time of the German invasion. Norway had about 3 million inhabitants, which meant about 10 people per square kilometer (or per 3.86 square miles). The economy was mostly agrarian; most of the approximately 330,000 farms existing in 1939 were very small and often the farmers were hardly able to survive on what they produced.

Families were poor and frequently had numerous children, many of whom died before they were grown. In farming households, everyone—men, women, and children—had to do hard work, but gender roles and responsibilities were still very traditional. Only the bigger Norwegian cities like Oslo were beginning to develop an industrial culture and at the same time a modernization of social life was taking place. Women were able to find work outside of the home, but this also meant that women staying at home with children now were regarded as housewives and no longer as part of a household's economy. Statistically the number of housewives rose from 445,466 in 1930 to 651,230 in 1946. The fact that women were having fewer children but were becoming mothers at a younger age was another effect of modernization.

The German occupation, especially the policy of Nazification starting at the end of 1940, had far-reaching effects on the gender-related organization of the public and private spheres. The totalitarian grip of the occupier and the collaborationist regime under Vidkun Quisling was directed toward political organizations, societies, and culture and media—the traditionally masculine spheres of power within the society. Consequently private lives became the realm of clandestine organization or the circulation of subversive and resistant codes. Men and women—in their everyday behavior and in the choice of cultural and sporting events they would visit or boycott—made decisions that were no longer private.

A very important facet of how the German occupation of Norway particularly influenced women was shortages of food and other goods needed in everyday life as well as confiscation of materials the occupation power needed for warfare (e.g., warm cloth or rubber boots). It was part of a woman's traditional duties to organize or produce substitutes for missing items. Women had the difficult task of supplying food, clothes, and other things needed daily and this led to many strategies and tricks that were not quite legal in the eyes of the occupation power. Black markets flourished. Such nonconformist behavior, however, could not quite be called "resistance."

On the other hand, the line between the private and the political was definitely transcended when refugees were hidden in private households; in this case, women had to supply everything the refugees needed. Gender arrangements changed under the condition of the German occupation. Women's traditional responsibilities demanded more initiative, creativity, and courage than in peacetime and sometimes were even part of a resistance struggle. Paradoxically, after the war the culture of tribute remembered only male resistance heroes and housewives supporting the effort were doing nothing but a woman's duty.

—*Claudia Lenz*

See also Norway, Resistance Movement in World War II, Women and; Norway, Women's Collaboration during World War II German Occupation of

References and Further Reading

Esborg, Line. 1995. *Krigshverdag. Oslo-kvinner forteller* [Everyday Life in Wartime: Oslo Women Recount]. Oslo: Norsk folkemuseum.

Hjeltnes, Guri. 1986. *"Hverdag"* [Everyday-life]. In *Norge i krig: fremmedåk og frihetskamp 1940–1945* [Norway at War. Foreign Rule and Struggle for Freedom 1940–1945]. Edited by Magne Skodvin. Oslo: Aschehoug.

NORWAY, WOMEN'S COLLABORATION DURING WORLD WAR II GERMAN OCCUPATION OF

The active support of some Norwegian women for the German occupiers of their country during World War II. When one speaks about *collaboration* in an occupied country, one at first has to specify what this term really means. Is political and ideological conviction a necessary criterion for regarding certain ways of acting as collaboration? Or is this necessarily to be assumed when people do paid work for the occupation authorities and thereby contribute to the functioning of its rule? Even sexual relations between occupying soldiers and indigenous women are often stigmatized as collaboration. This section will not solve these definitional problems. Instead, it only deals with the most obvious case of collaboration, that is, the participation in the political movement or party supporting the regime of occupation. In the case of Norway the fascist party Nasjonal Samling (National Gathering) was allowed to build a government and thereby was given a certain degree of power by the Germans.

Nasjonal Samling was, like all fascist movements in Europe, built on the Führer principle, an authoritarian hierarchy with its founder and leader Vidkun Quisling at the top. Influential positions in the Nasjonal Samling could only be attained by those who were completely obedient to Quisling's political visions and plans. The higher positions of the party and the government it formed in 1942 were held exclusively by men.

Quisling's ideas about the power relations in his party mirrored his vision for the organization of the whole society. His ideal was a strictly hierarchical and elitist society based on professions and social strata. His authoritarian principles were also patriarchal, as the leaders always should be outstanding men, followed and obeyed by the folk, which, of course, included women. But even if women were by definition excluded from the centers of power, the fascist's social vision also had a certain attraction for women, as they were offered a positive identification as bearers of the nation's biological and cultural or symbolic reproduction.

In 1933 when the Nasjonal Samling party was founded, a women's organization, Nasjonal Samlings Kvinneorganisasjon (NSK) was also organized. It was led by Vidkun Quisling's wife, Maria. In the beginning, members of NSK were mainly recruited among Maria Quisling's friends but soon the organization grew and a third of NSK's members were women. Especially toward the end of the war, when more and more members resigned from the party, the proportion of women was still rising. This can be explained by the fact that many men who were members of Nasjonal Samling sooner or later involved their female relatives in the NSK.

The NSK had its own propaganda section, which published the women's magazine *Heim og Ætt* (*Home and Kin*). In particular it published articles dealing with keeping a household and home economics. The propaganda of the NKS was directed toward the average Norwegian housewife. It transmitted the Nasjonal Samling's ideological program and its ideas about women's duties in the ideal Germanized Norway. In addition to these traditional female concerns there also existed a paramilitary organization, the Kvinnekorps (Women's Corps).

The paradox of the fascist women's organizations in Norway is the fact that they involved female activists in professional work and personal contributions to the political struggle, which fascism ideologically denied to women.

—*Claudia Lenz*

See also Norway, Resistance Movement during World War II, Women and; Norway, Women and the Home Front during World War II

References and Further Reading

Dahl, Hans Fredrik, Bernt Hagtvet, and Guri Hjeltnes. 1990. *Den norske nasjonalsosjalismen. Nasjonal Samling 1933–1945 i tekst og bilder* [The Norwegian National Socialism. Nasjonal Samling 1933–1945 in Text and Images]. Oslo: Pax forlag.

Norges krigsleksikon, nettutgave, slagord NSK. [The Norwegian War Lexicon, netversion, keyword NSK]. http://lotus.uib.no/norgeslexi/krigslex/n/n1.html#ns-kvinner (accessed October 28, 2004).

NURSES, U.S. ARMY NURSE CORPS IN WORLD WAR I

The U.S. Army Nurse Corps sent 10,245 female nurses to the European theater in World War I; on Armistice Day in 1918, 21,480 army nurses were in service around the world. The majority of the Army nurses signed up through the American Red Cross, which ensured that they were registered, examined, and prepared for service. They served in France, Belgium, England, Italy, Serbia, Russia, Hawaii, Puerto Rico, and the Philippines with the U.S. Expeditionary Forces, the British Expeditionary Forces, and the French Forces. One hundred and two nurses died overseas, most from influenza. Three nurses received the Distinguished Service Cross; many others were decorated by the U.S., French, and British militaries.

The Army Nurse Corps organized for World War I with the help of the Red Cross, which provided funding to aid civilian hospitals to organize and prepare nurses for deployment. The first nurses went to France in April 1917 as part of six base hospitals that aided the British Expeditionary Forces. The nurses arrived before U.S. troops. By August 1918, there were fifty base hospitals in Europe and around thirty more were organized. In addition, special hospitals were organized and deployed to treat orthopedic, head, fracture, and psychiatric cases. Because of their service in the war, female nurse anesthetists gained respect for women in their profession. Despite their service in the Army, however, nurses did not hold rank during the war and were only given relative rank after the armistice.

When the United States entered the war, only 403 Army nurses were on active duty. A shortage of nurses existed throughout the war and increased with the influenza epidemic of 1918. To alleviate the shortage, the Army expanded the age requirement from 25 to 35 years old to 21 to 45 years old and allowed married women and citizens of allied nations to serve in the Corps. However, the Army prohibited 1,000 trained, qualified, and willing African American nurses from serving overseas because of regulations requiring segregated living quarters.

Nurses served in hospitals located both close to and far from the battle. Many nurses, believing that it was the height of nursing care to work where they were most needed, aspired to work as close to the battle as possible. The nearest hospitals to the battle were dressing stations, which were located as close as 1.7 miles (2.74 kilometers) from the battle. The dressing stations provided immediate first aid to soldiers who were then classified and put on ambulances to be sent to field hospitals. The field hospitals had 216 beds, were 2 to 4 miles (3.22 to 6.44 kilometers) removed from the line of battle, and were where the wounded were stabilized before transportation to an evacuation hospital. Evacuation hospitals were larger than field hospitals, with 432 beds, and nurses at these hospitals performed a variety of functions involved with emergencies and the first surgeries for the most seriously wounded.

The Army wanted to minimize the chance that nurses would be killed or captured. Therefore, the Army's Table of Organization did not permit nurses to serve at dressing stations, field hospitals, or evacuation hospitals because they were so close to the battle line and moved with the tide of battle. The demands of war, however, resulted in nurses serving in these hospitals despite formal regulations. Mobile hospitals also moved with the troops and treated the most seriously wounded as close as possible to the front lines, including those with head, chest, and abdominal wounds, and those needing treatment for shock. Nurses also worked in teams of three

U.S. Army Nurse Corps in World War I

"Our first assignment was to duty at the base hospital at Mar-Surler, few miles from Never . . . This base hospital was built in a farmer's field, I think. At any rate, there were no solid roads or paths. We waded in the mud to our ankles between the buildings, & shoveled out what we brought in on our rubber boots. The buildings were knock-down shacks & the one I worked in had no windows, also the one we slept in. We were just taking in the overflow from the better equipped wards & helping until the arrival of a base hospital unit that was expected to arrive at any time. At the time we arrived there was a big drive going on at the front & patients were being sent in by the train load."

—May Lanham (later Austin),
Army nurse stationed in France during World War I.
Collection #969 (WWI, ANC #169 IV 969.D1d),
May (Lanham) Austin Collection, Gift of Gloria A. Karow,
Women in Military Service for America Memorial Foundation, Inc.,
Archives, Arlington, VA.

"This morning four teams were chosen for casualty clearing stations and are to be ready at any moments notice. In each team there are one surgeon, one anesthetist, one nurse and one orderly. The C.C.S's are a little behind the lines . . . They stay about two months, come back and are relieved by other teams. It is very exciting and however anxious everyone is to go, they are just as anxious to get back again to civilization. One really finds out a little of what actually is up there and although I'm perfectly willing to go wherever sent I am just as well satisfied here. I see enough of the awful realities. The trip up gives a very realistic picture as they pass through the war zone, thoroughly destroyed villages and of course are in constant danger of bombs etc. C'est la guerre. So far we have been quite lucky. Last summer one clearing station was bombed. Dr. Brewer's tent was blown up while he was doing an operation fortunately for him. Miss MacDonald one of our nurses was wounded losing an eye but has another and works as fine as ever. I think that is a good record considering the numbers we have sent up."

—Letter from Ethel Roxana Arthur (Presbyterian U.S.A) Hospital, B.E.F.,
to friends, February 20, 1918,
Collection #147, Ethel Roxana Arthur Collection, Gift of Diana Andersen,
Women in Military Service for America Memorial Foundation, Inc.,
Archives, Arlington, VA.

"Was up to Verdun and St. Michiel since Nov. 11—stood in No Man's Land within a week after the signing of the Armistice. This place is the limits now—mud everywhere, and it is some *mud*, believe me—Nothing appeals to me like a cozy corner in the U.S.A.—tho I am surely glad I could come over."

—Letter from Anna Grace McCrady, Chief Nurse, AEF,
to her sister, Winifred, December 9, 1918,
from Base Hospital #117, WWI, ANC, #1600,
Women in Military Service for America Memorial Foundation, Inc.,
Archives, Arlington, VA.

on hospital trains that transported up to 1,500 patients from evacuation hospitals to base hospitals. With 500 beds, base hospitals were the largest of all the hospitals and were located in the rear areas. These hospitals provided treatment for patients arriving from other hospitals and were where casualties recovered before being sent back into the field or to the United States. In the United States, nurses in the corps served in post, cantonment, and general military hospitals.

Nurses at each of these hospitals treated a variety of war wounds, as well as wounds caused by the "new" weapon, poison gas. Beginning in the spring of 1918, nurses also treated thousands of victims of the influenza epidemic. They worked fourteen- to eighteen-hour shifts week after week, and often worked for days on end when necessary. They endured the cold in inadequate clothing, with meager living and sanitary conditions, and often became sick themselves. In addition, the nurses lived in dangerous conditions, as hospitals in all areas were shelled and bombed; nurses had to protect both themselves and their patients.

—*Kara D. Vuic*

See also Fairchild, Helen; Mercy Ship; Nurses, U.S. Army Nurse Corps in World War II; Red Cross of the United States: World War I and World War II

References and Further Reading

Bongard, Ella. 1997. *Nobody Ever Wins a War: The World War I Diaries of Ella Mae Bongard, R.N.* Ottawa: Janeric.

Gavin, Lettie. 1997. *American Women in World War I: They Also Served.* Niwot: University Press of Colorado.

Sarnecky, Mary T. 1999. *A History of the U.S. Army Nurse Corps.* Philadelphia: University of Pennsylvania.

Stimson, Julia C. 1918. *Finding Themselves: The Letters of an American Army Chief Nurse in a British Hospital in France.* New York: Macmillan.

NURSES, U.S. ARMY NURSE CORPS IN WORLD WAR II

During World War II approximately 59,000 women served in the U.S. Army Nurse Corps; among them, 32,500 served overseas. U.S. army nurses served in all theaters of the war, including the major campaigns of North Africa, Italy, France, and the Pacific, as well as the minor theaters of China, Burma, India, the U.S.S.R., Iran, Alaska, Iceland, Panama, and the South Atlantic. Army nurses served closer to the front lines than ever before, landing with the troops or only days after the first assaults. Initially nurses were deployed without military training, but beginning in July 1943 nurses completed a four-week training program in military life. Nurse anesthetists and psychiatric nurses were in great demand throughout the war and underwent additional specialized training.

When Pearl Harbor was bombed, the Army Nurse Corps included fewer than 1,000 nurses, but within six months 12,000 women joined the corps. Many of the nurses who served in the war signed up through the Cadet Nurse Corps. Established in 1943, the Corps offered free nursing education in exchange for military or civilian nursing service for the duration of the war. By the end of the war almost 170,000 nurses had joined the Corps. In January 1945, however, because the Army was experiencing a shortage of medical personnel, President Franklin Roosevelt proposed drafting nurses. The Nurses Selective Service Act passed the House of Representatives and was within a single vote of passing in the Senate when Germany surrendered. With the need for nurses alleviated, the measure was never employed.

Despite the need for nurses, the Army limited the number of African American nurses. Those who were accepted endured segregated hospitals and living quarters, and were often assigned to less desirable duties. In all, approximately 500 African American nurses served in Liberia, Burma, the Southwest Pacific, England, and the United States. In addition, the Army Nurse

U.S. Army nurses march to a waiting troop ship carrying medical equipment and their few personal belongings, 1942. (Library of Congress)

Corps did not accept professional male nurses. Male nurses drafted into the military were utilized as corpsmen with less responsibility and rank or in nonmedical units.

The chain of medical evacuation proved successful in the campaigns of North Africa, and thereafter was used in all theaters. After receiving initial first aid provided by medics in the field, casualties came by litter bearers and ambulances to field hospitals. Approximately 18 nurses worked in each field hospital, which held between 75 and 150 patients. Nurses triaged patients and those deemed strong enough were sent to evacuation hospitals; those needing immediate care were sent to surgery. Casualties who were unable to be moved were either stabi-

lized for treatment or sent to shock wards. The next step in the chain was the evacuation hospital, where 53 nurses treated up to 750 patients who were operated on and were recovering from surgery. Both field and evacuation hospitals closely followed the combat troops; thus, the nurses set up the hospitals in tents, moved on short notice, and worked under hostile conditions.

Casualties were moved from evacuation hospitals to station and general hospitals via trains, ships, or aircraft. On hospital trains, a single nurse worked on each car with up to 32 patients. Nurses also worked on hospital ships that were supposed to be safe from attack but nonetheless were bombed in three separate incidents. Approximately 500 Army flight nurses served in war for the first time and underwent special training that emphasized crash procedures, field survival, and the effects of high altitude on patients. Transport planes were subject to enemy attack because they also carried cargo; 17 flight nurses died, most in crashes due to poor weather or landing fields.

The next step in the chain of evacuation was the station hospital, where the critically wounded received specialized treatment. The last step was the general hospital, where those needing more specific diagnosis, laboratory tests, or long periods of recuperation or therapy were treated. Once recovered, patients were then reclassified and sent either back to the field or to the United States. Both station and general hospitals were semipermanent locations, usually with running water and electricity.

During the war, 201 Army nurses died , 16 because of direct enemy action; 83 Army nurses were held as prisoners of war in various locations, of those, 66 were held by the Japanese for almost 3 years in the Santo Tomas Internment Camp in the Philippines. More than 1,600 Army nurses received medals, citations, and commendations for their service. Until 1944 the nurses served with relative rank, but in June 1944 the Army granted nurses officers' commissions, full retirement benefits, dependants' allowances, and equal pay.

—*Kara D. Vuic*

See also Nurses, U.S. Army Nurse Corps in World War I

References and Further Reading

Fessler, Diane Burke. 1996. *No Time for Fear: Voices of American Military Nurses in World War II.* East Lansing: Michigan State University.

Norman, Elizabeth M. 1999. *We Band of Angels: The Untold Story of American Nurses Trapped on Bataan by the Japanese.* New York: Random House.

Sarnecky, Mary T. 1999. *A History of the U.S. Army Nurse Corps.* Philadelphia: University of Pennsylvania.

Tomblin, Barbara Brooks. 1996. *G.I. Nightingales: The Army Nurse Corps in World War II.* Lexington: University of Kentucky.

O

Olmsted, Mildred Scott (1890–1990)

American peace activist. Mildred Scott Olmsted was a committed pacifist and Quaker who devoted her life to peace activism. She joined the Women's International League for Peace and Freedom (WILPF) working as the executive secretary of the Pennsylvania branch. She later joined the executive staff of WILPF's national organization, where she served until her retirement in 1966. Olmsted is best known for her service to WILPF, but she devoted her life to peace causes. She served as a board member on a number of peace organizations, and during the Vietnam War she fought for the rights of conscientious objectors and was very active in the antiwar movement.

Olmsted was born and raised in Pennsylvania. She spent her high-school years at the Friends' Central School in Philadelphia, and in 1912 she graduated from Smith College with a degree in history. While working as a settlement-house worker, she attended the Pennsylvania School of Social Work and Health Work, where she earned a certificate in 1913. During World War I Olmsted joined the American Friends Service Committee to provide relief to war-torn France and Germany. The devastation of war on the population, particularly in famine-wracked Bavaria, led her to pursue a life of peace activism.

In 1922 Olmsted assumed the executive secretaryship of the Pennsylvania branch of WILPF, where she led the branch membership drive. She used her position to launch her participation in the national organization and in 1934 she became the national organization secretary of WILPF. Olmsted believed that local branches served a primary function in the national organization and provided the membership needed to promote peace legislation. A great believer in civil liberties, she actively campaigned with founding WILPF member, Mary Church Terrell, to establish an interracial organization and to work with the National Association for the Advancement of Colored People (NAACP) anti-lynching campaign. In 1946 she replaced Dorothy Detzer as the national administrative secretary of the WILPF and held this position until she retired in 1966.

In the post–World War II era, despite the Holocaust and the atomic bomb, Olmsted continued to work for WILPF and maintained optimism about humanity. In 1946 she supported the United Nations believing that, despite the dominance of the five big powers, a world body was the right step toward the rule of world law. The 1950s brought new challenges, with the cold war and rise of McCarthyism. During this time Olmsted lobbied Congress to adopt an armistice agreement to end the war in Korea. As other peace organizations withered under the anticommunist storm, WILPF survived in part from the capable leadership of Olmsted. After her retirement she continued to promote world peace and was active in the civil rights and antiwar movements. Prior to her death in 1990, she was honored with numerous peace awards.

—*Danelle Moon*

See also Detzer, Dorothy

References and Further Reading

Bacon, Margaret Hope. 1993. *One Woman's Passion for Peace and Freedom: The Life of Mildred Scott Olmsted.* New York: Syracuse University Press.

OLSCHANEZKY, SONYA (1923–1944)

Participant in the French Resistance who worked with the British secret service during World War II. Sonya (or Sonia) Olschanezky was born in Chemnitz, Germany, on December 25, 1923. Her father was a Russian Jew who was a sales representative for a company that manufactured women's stockings. He moved his family to Romania in 1926 and then to France. Sonia joined the Resistance after the Germans conquered France in 1940. As a foreign-born Jew, she was arrested in May 1942 and sent to a detention center at Darcy. Her mother was able to purchase false papers through friends in Germany and bribe a German official to release her daughter. Olschanezky promptly resumed her resistance work. She was part of the Jewish wing, led by her fiancé, Jacques Weil, connected to the British Special Operations Executive "Prosper" network. Under the code name Tania she worked both as a courier and a participant in sabotage. The network was exposed and she was apprehended in January 1944. After interrogation she was held at the Fresnes prison in Paris. On May 13, 1944, she was sent from Fresnes with seven other captured British women agents to the Karlsruhe civil prison in Germany.

On July 6, 1944, on the direct order of Ernest Kaltenbrunner, the head of the SS security office, Olschanezky, Andrée Borrel, Vera Leigh, and Diana Rowden were moved to the Natzweiler-Struthof concentration camp. The women were executed on the day of their arrival. A watercolor of Olschanezky and her three companions, painted by Brian Stonehouse, an SOE agent and prisoner who witnessed their arrival at Natzweiler-Struthof, has a place of honor in the Special Forces Club in London.

—*Bernard Cook*

See also Atkins, Vera H.; Borrel, Andrée; Leigh, Vera; Rowden, Diana

References and Further Reading

Foot, M. R. D. (Michael Richard Daniell). 1984 (1966). *SOE in France: An Account of the Work of the British Special Operations Executive 1940–1944.* Frederick, MD: University Publications of America.

Kramer, Rita. 1995. *Flames in the Field: The Stories of Four SOE Agents in Occupied France.* New York: Viking Penguin.

Nicholas, Elizabeth. 1958. *Death Be Not Proud.* London: Cresset.

Spartacus Web. "Sonia Olschanezky." http://www .spartacus.schoolnet.co.uk/SOEolschanesky.htm (accessed September 29, 2004).

125TH M. M. RASKOVA BORISOV GUARDS BOMBER AVIATION REGIMENT

See Soviet Union, 125th M. M. Raskova Borisov Guards Bomber Aviation Regiment

Oradour-sur-Glane Massacre

ONIONS, MAUDE (B. 1885)

Army signaler with the British Women's Army Auxiliary Corps (WAAC) in France during World War I. After the war Onions became a pacifist.

In 1917 Maude Onions and a small group of women arrived in Boulogne, France, to replace men as signalers at the front. Formed in 1917, the purpose of WAAC was to send women abroad so that men could work closer to the battlefield.

In 1918, the Boulogne building she worked in was destroyed by a German raid. For six months during the last German offensive she was stationed in a small French village near Calais. On November 11, 1918, she signaled to the Allied armies in the field to cease hostilities.

While in France she played the piano at the Red Cross canteen and provided music for the military services at the English church in Boulogne.

Following the war, Onions recollected many of her conversations and encounters with soldiers in a recording, which she considered a pacifist effort to prevent another world war. Onions described the experiences of men at the front as they related them to her, as well as her own emotional transformation, which lead to her pacifism. Her contact with soldiers and work in the war enabled her, though her book, *A Women at War: Being Experiences of an Army Signaller in France 1917–1919*, to provide a link between the public and the battlefield.

—*Barbara Penny Kanner*

See also Great Britain, Women in Service during World War I

References and Further Reading

Kanner, Barbara Penny. 1997. *Woman in Context.* New York: G. K. Hall.

Onions, Maude. 1929. *A Woman at War: Being Experiences of an Army Signaller in France 1917–1919.* London: The C. W. Daniel Company.

ORADOUR-SUR-GLANE MASSACRE

French village, approximately 16 miles (25.75 kilometers) northwest of Limoges, destroyed in a retaliatory measure on June 10, 1944. As it moved from Toulouse toward the Allied invasion site in Normandy in June 1944, the 2nd *Das Reich* SS Armored Division had come under attack by partisan units. Resistance fighters had blown up a railway bridge at St. Junien, 6.2 miles (10 kilometers) from Oradour. Two soldiers had been shot at the bridge. Near St. Junien a truck carrying eight SS men had been ambushed. Three of its occupants had been killed and the rest captured. In another attack near St. Junien, an SS officer, Major Helmut Kämpffe, had been taken captive. In retaliation, the division's 3rd Company of the 1st Battalion executed an action against the inhabitants of Oradour on June 10. Not a single person in Oradour belonged to the resistance and German soldiers had not previously set foot in the village (Kruuse 1968, 6–7). SS Major Otto Dickmann, the commander of 1st Battalion, had already ordered counterterrorist reprisals against French civilians in the area. Three women had been hanged in Frayssinet-le-Gelat on June 8 and on June 9. Dickmann's unit, the 1st battalion of the Waffen-SS (Der Führer) regiment, engaged in random acts of terror against the inhabitants of Rochechouart about 6.4 miles (11 kilometers) from St. Junien. The mayor of St. Junien, when questioned by the SS, reputedly claimed that 1,800 of his town's 10,000 inhabitants were armed members of the resistance (Kruuse 1968, 32).

Why Oradour was chosen as an example is unknown, but its size and lack of a contingent of armed Maquis, the French Resistance, made it a more tempting target. Another possibility is the fact that there were three nearby towns with similar names, and that Oradour-sur-Vayre, 16.16 miles (26 kilometers) from St. Junien, might have been the intended target.

447

Oradour-sur-Glane, September 26, 1944.
(National Archives)

Major Dickmann and many of the SS perpetrators were later killed in military action; others disappeared in the fog of war and the demise of the Third Reich. Twenty-one SS men were tried in France in 1953. Six were former German SS troopers and a lieutenant; however, thirteen of the SS men and a sergeant were Alsatians. The trial resulted in two death sentences and eighteen prison terms for members of the company (Kruuse 1968, 93–94 and 138). One week after the trial, however, all of the sentences were annulled by the French parliament who voted for amnesty to spare the Alsatians from prosecution as war criminals.

—*Bernard Cook*

See also Germany, Armed Forces, World War II Atrocities of; Lidice Massacre

References and Further Reading

Kruuse, Jens. 1968. *War for an Afternoon.* Trans. Carl Malmberg. New York: Pantheon.

Zentner, Christian, and Friedemann Bedürftig, eds. 1991. "Oradour-sur-Glane." Page 677 in *The Encyclopedia of the Third Reich.* Trans. and ed. by Amy Hackett. New York: Macmillan.

The SS unit entered Oradour after driving people from surrounding farms and hamlets into the village. The troops ordered all the people in the village to assemble in the village center for an identity check. The men were separated from the 400 to 500 women and children, who were then forced into the village church (Kruuse 1968, 52). The SS then began the slaughter, shooting the men or forcing them into buildings that were set afire. Killings also began at the church and the building was set afire, incinerating those who had not been shot. More than six hundred men, women, and children were murdered (Kruuse 1968, 81). Few escaped the slaughter.

Charles de Gaulle issued a decree for the ruins of the village to be left as they stood as a memorial to the victims of Nazism.

ORCZY, BARONESS EMMA
(1865–1947)

Promoter of enlistment in Great Britain during World War I. Emma Orczy, the daughter of composer Felix Orczy and his wife Emma Wass, was born on the family's Hungarian estate at Tarnaors on September 23, 1865. The childhood death of a sister and a peasant uprising on the family's estate left profound memories Orczy later used in her writing. Felix Orczy was close to the Austro-Hungarian royal family and traveled frequently to perform, often taking Emma, who formed a lifelong attachment to the monarchies and palaces of Europe. Educated at a Roman Catholic convent in Brussels, she began studying painting in London at the Heatherly School of Art and the London School of Art.

In 1894, Emma Orczy married English painter and illustrator Montague Barstow, by whom she had one child, John Orczy-Barstow, born in 1899. Orczy enthusiastically embraced Britain as her home country and turned from painting to writing. Her career began with a series of magazine serials, and she completed her first successful novel, *The Scarlet Pimpernel,* in five weeks in 1905. This work spawned a series of sequels, which Orczy wrote until 1940. Orczy also authored a mystery series with an aristocratic female protagonist, beginning with *Lady Molly of Scotland Yard* (1910) and historical fiction.

When World War I broke out in August 1914, Orczy was determined to prove her loyalty to Britain, despite her family's Hungarian titles and land. Inspired by the 1904 novel, *The Four Feathers,* by A. E. W. Mason, Orczy wrote editorials to the London *Daily Mail* in September 1914, suggesting that British women refuse to be seen with men not in uniform, and advocating giving white feathers of cowardice to encourage men to enlist. This grew into the "Order of the White Feather" movement, formally organized by Admiral Charles Fitzgerald and headed by Orczy and fellow novelist Mary Ward. The distribution of feathers was heavily publicized, sexually charged, and broadly promoted in the media, and was credited with enlisting 600,000 men for the war. In reality, the giving of feathers was an often disruptive and humiliating experience for men in crucial civilian employment, or wounded men in civilian clothing. Orczy re-ceived a letter of thanks from King George V, but the government officially discouraged the practice after 1915. After the war, many women who had participated in the Order of the White Feather downplayed their participation, upset at their part in sending men to the trenches. Orczy herself does not mention the Order in her memoirs, and downplayed her support for the war afterward.

Orczy and her family lived at their country house in Kent and spent time in Monte Carlo between the wars; Orczy and Barstow were trapped in Monte Carlo by the 1940 invasion of France. Although technically neutral, Monte Carlo was occupied by the Germans, and Orczy suffered as a British citizen from Gestapo harassment and the British bombing of her house. Widowed in 1943, she returned to Britain after the war and died in London on November 12, 1946, shortly after publishing her memoir, *Links in the Chain of Life.*

—Margaret Sankey

See also Great Britain, Women in Service during World War I

References and Further Reading

Gullace, Nicoletta. 1997. "White Feathers and Wounded Men: Female Patriotism and the Memory of the Great War." *Journal of British Studies,* 36 (April): 178–206.

———. 2002. *Blood of Our Sons: Men, Women and the Renegotiation of British Citizenship during the Great War.* New York: Palgrave.

Orczy, Emma. 1947. *Links in the Chain of Life.* London: Hutchinson.

P

PADILLA, JUANA AZURDUY DE

See Azurduy, Juana de Padilla

PANKHURST FAMILY:
EMMELINE, CHRISTABEL,
E. SYLVIA, AND ADELA
PANKHURST WALSH

Leaders in the English suffrage movement who were divided in their attitude toward World War I. Although united in their commitment to English women's suffrage when they formed the militant Women's Social and Political Union (WSPU) in 1903, Emmeline Pankhurst (1858–1928) and her three daughters, Dame Christabel Pankhurst (1880–1958), E. Sylvia Pankhurst (1882–1960), and Adela Pankhurst Walsh (1885–1961), were divided in their beliefs when Britain entered World War I. The Pankhursts were experienced with militancy in that the WSPU, with its motto "Deeds, not Words," pioneered dramatic tactics of illegal protest that resulted in their repeated arrest and imprisonment. The violence of the Great War, however, irreconcilably divided them, with Emmeline and Christabel enthusiastically support-

ing and working for the British war effort, while Sylvia and Adela became leading activists for peace.

When Britain declared war on Germany and its allies in August 1914, the British government released all political prisoners, including the suffragettes. In response, Emmeline announced that the WSPU would suspend all suffrage agitation for the duration of the war. She said that there was no point to women's suffrage if there was no country in which to vote. Demonizing Germany, as did many of her compatriots, she argued that Germany was an "over-masculine country" that denied the basic rights of women: "The Kaiser has already assigned woman's place to the three K's, '*Kinder, Kirche, Küche,*' (children, church, kitchen)" (Purvis 2002, 275). In the struggle for women's liberty, she maintained, it was far better to support the fight against Germany than to fight one's own government. Many, although not all, of the members of the WSPU and other suffrage organizations agreed with Emmeline's position, most enthusiastically her daughter Christabel. For at least one suffragette, "It was almost with a sense of relief that we heard of the declaration of war, and we knew that our militancy, which had reached such an acute stage, could cease" (Pugh 2001, 299). The most prominent dissenter was Emmeline's daughter Sylvia, who, through her own working

PANKHURST FAMILY

"It was a custom of my father and mother to make the round of our bedrooms every night before going themselves to bed. When they entered my room that night I was still awake, but for some reason I chose to feign slumber. My father bent over me, shielding the candle flame with his big hand. I cannot know exactly what thought was in his mind as he gazed down at me, but I heard him say, somewhat sadly, 'What a pity she wasn't born a lad.' . . . I thought about my father's remark for many days afterward, but I think I never decided that I regretted my sex. However, it was made quite clear that men considered themselves superior to women, and that women apparently acquiesced in that belief."

—Emmeline Pankhurst, 1914.
My Own Story. New York: Hearst International Library, 5.

women's organization, the East London Federation of Suffragettes (ELF), continued working for women's suffrage even as she also campaigned against the war. Emmeline's youngest daughter Adela, who in January 1914 had emigrated to Australia, was also active in antiwar protest.

Emmeline's war work involved energetic recruitment and support for compulsory conscription of soldiers to fight and women to do war work. In July 1915 she accepted the government's request that she organize, at public expense, a large "Right to Serve" procession of women. Modeled on her earlier suffrage demonstrations, women would march to demand the right to work in munitions factories, to counter the strong opposition of the male trade unions. Disheartened by her mother's pro-war actions, Sylvia felt Emmeline had betrayed the memory of Emmeline's peace-loving husband, and her own earlier commitment to peace, as in her stand against the Boer War. What brought Sylvia the most anguish, however, was her mother's statement that if her son were still living, she would want him to fight in the war. Remembering her deceased brother as gentle and pacifistic, Sylvia was shocked that her mother could "Know so little of him that she had failed to sense how alien, how hideous this bestial hate and gross materialism, this butchery must have been to him" (Pankhurst 1932, 67).

In 1916 Emmeline made a trip to the United States to urge support for Serbia, and in the summer of 1917 she went to Russia as a British government delegate to meet with the new head of the revolutionary provisional government, Alexander Kerensky, to urge him to keep Russia in the war. Her most personal effort was the plan she announced in 1915 for members of the WSPU to adopt war babies, children born to unmarried women and servicemen. Emmeline personally adopted four babies.

Christabel also actively promoted the war effort through speeches and writings. In October 1914 she toured the United States in an effort to persuade that country to enter the war. She transformed *The Suffragette,* the journal of the WSPU, into the *Britannia,* with "For King, For Country, For Freedom" as its motto. In its pages Christabel condemned both English pacifism and what she considered German barbarism, and urged the complete destruction of the German nation. She also attacked the weak war leadership of Prime Minister Herbert Henry Asquith. When the more dynamic and militant Lloyd George replaced Asquith in 1916, *Britannia* became one of the government's strongest supporters.

In contrast, Sylvia focused her energies on organizing antiwar activities, arguing that the war was simply waged for the interests of capitalists. Until blocked by the British government's refusal to grant her a passport, she planned to attend with other feminist pacifists the International Congress of Women, held in The Hague in April 1915.

Her horrified mother's response to the congress was to label the participants as treasonous.

It is unthinkable that English-women should meet German women to discuss terms of peace while the husbands, sons, and brothers of those women are the men who are murdering our men on the seas and who have committed the awful horrors of the war in Belgium and elsewhere. (Purvis 2002, 274)

Even though Sylvia was not able to attend, she did join the newly formed Women's International League for Peace and Freedom (WILPF).

Concerned about helping working women whose lives were damaged by the war, Sylvia campaigned for equal pay and safer working conditions for women in the factories. She established clinics, nurseries, and milk distribution centers in the East End of London. She protested vehemently when the government reintroduced a policy to forcibly inspect women suspected of being prostitutes for venereal disease. She set up a League for Soldiers and Soldiers' Wives to ameliorate such problems as housing shortages and food scarcity. Still working for women's suffrage but within the broader context of universal rights for adults, in 1916 she changed the name of her organization from the East London Federation of Suffragettes to the Workers' Suffrage Federation (and in 1919 to the Workers' Socialist Federation). In 1917 her suffrage journal *The Woman's Dreadnought* was renamed *The Worker's Dreadnought.*

In Australia Adela agitated against the war by giving speeches throughout the country for various peace and women's organizations, denouncing conscription and promoting socialist ideas. Also a prolific writer, she promoted the cause of peace through journalism and with

such notable antiwar works as a novel (*Put up the Sword,* 1915); a play (*Betrayed,* 1917); and a pamphlet (*After the War, What?* 1917).

After the war ended in November 1918, Christabel unsuccessfully sought to capitalize on the new partial enfranchisement of British women by running for election to parliament on an anti-German platform. Several years later Emmeline also ran unsuccessfully for election. After their defeats, both withdrew from politics. Emmeline, in failing health her last years, died in 1928. Christabel experienced a religious conversion, became an ardent Seventh Day Adventist, moved to California, and was preoccupied for the rest of her life with religious matters. In the years after World War I Adela continued her activism, increasingly as part of a nationalistic xenophobic movement in Australia. Renouncing her earlier communism for right-wing policies, she remained a pacifist and anti-imperialist, and opposed Australia's entrance into World War II. In 1941 she helped found the Australia First movement. Interned briefly in 1942, after her release she withdrew from public activism.

Sylvia remained active in the peace movement throughout the interwar period. As with many of her fellow pacifists, however, her commitment to peace in the 1920s and even more so in the 1930s was complicated by her strong opposition to fascism and to the military aggressions of Mussolini and Hitler. A leader in the Women's World Committee against War and Fascism, she supported the republican cause in the Spanish Civil War. Decrying the destruction caused by fascist bombing, she had an antiwar memorial erected in 1936 on land next to her home, with a plaque condemning those who supported the right of aerial bombardment. When Mussolini invaded Ethiopia in 1935, she tried to rally support for Emperor Haile Selassie's plea for help from the League of Nations. After the invasion she furthered the Ethiopian cause by founding a journal, *New Times and Ethiopian News,* which she edited for twenty years. In 1956 she moved to

Emmeline Goulden Pankhurst on Wall Street. (Library of Congress)

Ethiopia, where she remained active in work for peace and social welfare. When she died in 1960, the grateful Selassie ordered a state funeral. In Britain, however, it was the pro-war Emmeline and not the pacifist Sylvia whose statue was raised in 1930 outside of the Houses of Parliament.

—*Nancy Fix Anderson*

See also International Congress of Women: Antiwar Protest of Women in World War I

References and Further Reading

Pankhurst, E. Sylvia. 1932. *Home Front: A Mirror to Life in England during the First World War.* London: Cresset Library.

Pugh, Martin. 2001. *The Pankhursts.* London: Penguin.

Purvis, June. 2002. *Emmeline Pankhurst: A Biography.* New York: Routledge.

Smith, Angela. 2003. "The Pankhursts and the War: Suffrage Magazines and First World War Propaganda." *Women's History Review* 22:103–118.

Winslow, Barbara. 1996. *Sylvia Pankhurst: Sexual Politics and Political Activism.* New York: St. Martin's.

PARIS COMMUNE, WOMEN AND THE (1871)

Participation of women in the armed defense of the revolutionary Paris Commune (1871) against troops of the national French government, and the resulting arrest, imprisonment, deportation, exile, and death of thousands of women.

The Paris Commune, an insurrection waged by the lower classes of Paris, lasted from March 18 to May 28, 1871, following the conclusion of the Franco-Prussian War (1870–1871). The national government, which had declared a Republic in September 1870, had fled to Bordeaux. The four-and-a-half-month Prussian siege of Paris had further radicalized and organized the lower classes of Paris as they stood alone against the enemy. Early in the morning on March 18 after the fighting with Prussia had ended, women discovered that French troops were attempting to remove cannon purchased and used by Parisians to defend the city against the Prussians. Rousing citizens to the scene, the women and Paris National Guard personnel fraternized with government forces, resulting in their retreat. Later the same day, Parisians executed two of the rival military leaders, resulting in heightened tensions between Paris and the national government, now seated at Versailles and led by Adolph Thiers. Civil war formally erupted on April 3 when government troops began bombing the city and its environs; during the last week of May, known as the "Bloody Week," Versailles troops entered the city. Street fighting and outright massacres ensued, resulting in the deaths of 30,000 Parisians. Women supported, fought, and died in this revolution from the early morning hours of March 18 through its end on May 28.

During the Commune, women fought alongside men, served in front line ambulance corps, and endured all the hardships of battle. Some received public commendations in newspapers, often signed by the men from their battalions; the photographs of quite a few survive, often taken after their sentencing at military trials following the defeat of the Commune. One communard, using the male pseudonym André Leo, published her views in the Commune newspaper, *La Sociable*. Writing to the military leader of Commune forces on May 8, she declared,

Do you know, General Dombrowski, how the [Paris Commune] was made? By the women . . . the necessity of taking one's part in the Revolution, is the liberty and re-

sponsibility of every human being, with no limit except common law, without any privilege of race, or of sex.

Women such as Louise Michel, Hortense David, Christine D'argent, Victorine Rouchy, and Alix Payen fought, cared for the wounded, and left evidence of their participation in the historical record.

Observers also drew illustrations of dozens of women dressed in military attire at rifle practice, marching drills, and aboard cannon boats in the Seine. Although the minister of war for the Commune declared he did not want women in the ranks, they came anyway, serving in wide-ranging capacities and generally demanding to be paid. Many served as canteen and ambulance workers in the city and on the battlefield, discovering that distinctions between those jobs and armed combat existed only theoretically. In at least some cases, canteen workers entering combat with their National Guard units officially began receiving guns as of April 7, only days after bombardment began; many others argued that, as members of a National Guard unit, they had the right, even the obligation, to bear arms for personal and Commune defense.

In the closing days of the Commune, when government troops fought in the Paris streets against barricaded communards, women regularly challenged the courage of their male compatriots, threatening them with death, replacement by women, or both—if they did not fight well. In one case, Nathalie Lemel threatened Commune troops at a barricade, calling them cowards, telling them that if they did not defend the barricade well, the women would—and they eventually did. At her arrest, Lemel and other witnesses reported that she, with hands and lips now blackened with gun powder, had fought for forty-eight hours straight with no food, adding with much contempt, "We are beaten, but not vanquished!"

Women became the targets of attacks by Versailles troops, especially given their association with setting fires to significant buildings in Paris during the last week. Eventually represented as *pétroleuses,* or female arsonists, the truth or falsity of women's activities became less important than the troops' impression that hysterical, "unnatural" women and their grimy children lurked around every corner ready to destroy property. This, combined with recurring discoveries that Commune troops behind barricades included women, led Versailles troops vehemently to search out women for arrest, and often, massacre.

Women generally saw their own participation linked to their tenuous economic circumstances, made worse by months of war and siege. They viewed the Commune as an opportunity to receive jobs and equal pay and status with men, which women often demanded as part of this social revolution. The male leadership needed the support and active assistance of women. Therefore they often listened to their demands.

Although women carried weapons and participated in armed combat for many reasons, their actions became linked to a world turned upside down, and violent repression was the response of the enemy. According to Alexandre Dumas, the women communards or *fils*—to him not truly female—became women "only when dead," when their anatomy alone and not their words or actions determined their categorization. Just as women had "made the revolution" early on and sustained it by their labors, they fought and died for it at its demise.

—*Pamela J. Stewart*

See also Michel, Louise

References and Further Reading

Eichner, Carolyn. 2004. *Surmounting the Barricades: Women in the Paris Commune.* Bloomington: Indiana University.

Gullickson, Gay L. 1996. *The Unruly Women of Paris: Images of the Commune.* Ithaca: Cornell University.

Jones, Kathleen, and Françoise Vergès. 1991. "Women of the Paris Commune." *Women's Studies International Forum* 14(6):491–503.

Northwestern University; Charles Deering McCormick Special Collections Library. "Siege and Commune of Paris, 1870–1871." http://www.library.northwestern.edu/spec/siege/ (accessed October 31, 2004).

PARRISH, MARIE O'DEAN BISHOP (DEANIE) (1922–)

Engineering test pilot and tow-target pilot in the U.S. Women Airforce Service program (WASP). Born and raised in Florida, Marie Deanie Bishop grew up with a determination to prove herself. On her twenty-first birthday Deanie, who had learned to fly, reached the age requirement for admission to the WASP program and applied that day.

After acceptance, Deanie reported to Avenger Field in Sweetwater, Texas, on November 1, 1943, where she began training. As a member of class 44-w-4, she was one of the first women pilots to go from primary training directly to advanced training, bypassing the basic training level. After the women successfully made that training change, skipping the intermediate "basic" level, all pilot training in the Army Airforce implemented this system.

Following graduation from flight school, Deanie was sent to Greenville Army Air Base in Greenville, Mississippi, where she was one of three WASPs on base. As an engineering test pilot, she tested and repaired new aircraft to be re-released for instructors and cadets in training. At Greenville she test-flew a twin-engine aircraft for the first time.

Because of her success in flying twin-engine aircraft, Deanie was soon selected for the B-26 Flexible Gunnery School at Tyndall Army Airforce Base in Florida. She was one of eight women pilots to pass all training tests flying the difficult B-26 Martin Marauder. One of her duties was to hold the B-26 in a flight pattern while B-24s would fly by with gunners shooting live ammunition at the sleeve target towed by the B-26. The training was crucial to prepare gunners for combat. Deanie was stationed at Tyndall for the remainder of her time as a WASP.

After the WASP disbanded on December 20, 1944, Deanie continued to work in base operations as an aircraft dispatcher. She later went to Langley Air Force Base where a civil service position as chief aircraft dispatcher in base operations was created for her. In 1946 Deanie married Bill Parrish, a B-24 pilot from Tyndall Air Force Base, and she accompanied him when his orders sent him to Panama. There she became private secretary for the director of operations for the 6th Air Force.

After the war, she returned to school and graduated summa cum laude with a bachelor of science degree from the University of Houston. She served as national secretary of the National WASP Organization and chair of the WASP Steering Committee for the National WASP World War II Museum. As associate director and primary interviewer for Wings Across America, a project to document and educate others on the history of the WASP, she recorded over 103 interviews with WASPs, preserving the history of the first American women to fly military aircraft.

—*Christiana Biggs*

See also United States, Women's Airforce Service Pilots

References and Further Reading

Parrish, Deanie. 1999. Interview by Barby Williams. Wings Across America Project and the WASP Word War II Museum, Sweetwater, Texas. http://www.wasp-wwii.org/wings/information.htm (accessed November 18, 2004).

PAVLIUCHENKO, LIUDMILA MIKHAILOVNA (1916–1974)

Leading Soviet female sniper of World War II with 309 kills, including 36 enemy snipers. Liudmila Pavliuchenko (Pavlichenko is the Russian version of the name) served with the Second Company, Second Battalion, 54th Razin Regiment, 25th "V. I. Chapaev" Division of the Independent Maritime Army.

Born in Belaia Tserkov, now in the Kyiv (formerly Kiev) region, Pavliuchenko trained in small arms fire with a military club of the Arsenal Factory, her employer in Kyiv, earning a civilian sharpshooter's badge. She was also trained in machine-gun firing by *Osoaviakhim* (Society for Assistance to Defense, Aviation, and Chemical Industry). In 1937, as a student at the State University of Kyiv, she successfully defended her master's thesis on *hetman* (chieftain) Bohdan Khmel'nitsky, a Ukrainian nationalist, soldier, politician, and diplomat.

Pavliuchenko volunteered for combat duty in June 1941. When her 54th Razin Regiment went into action on the near approaches to Odessa on August 8, 1941, Pavliuchenko scored her first two kills. On October 9, 1941, after her platoon commander was killed in the crucial Dal'nitsky sector, and his deputy was wounded, Pavliuchenko assumed command. Wounded and her face covered with blood, she struggled to remain conscious. Considered one of the best snipers of the Independent Maritime Army, Pavliuchenko scored 187 kills in about two months, before Soviet troops were evacuated from Odessa.

In mid-October 1941 the Independent Maritime Army was transferred to the Crimea to fight for Sevastopol alongside the Black Sea Fleet. Operating in mountainous terrain in the Sevastopol area, Pavliuchenko usually began her vigil at 3:00 A.M., waiting a day or two for her prey. Lying motionless under a bush or in a foxhole for up to eighteen hours, she was accompanied by an observer with binoculars who gave her the reference points and monitored the state of her victims. Inspired by her sense of mission, Pavliuchenko stoically withstood hardships greater than those experienced by ordinary soldiers.

She was an exceptional sniper. Her exploits were publicized by the army, and were imitated. In Sevastopol, where the Germans not only had all enemy sniper positions marked and under fire, but also knew Soviet snipers by name, she managed to impart her skill even during the most difficult situations. She was wounded four times, twice seriously. Finally, in June 1942, she was evacuated from Sevastopol on board a submarine. Invited by Eleanor Roosevelt, Pavliuchenko toured the United States in August 1942 after her final wound had healed.

In 1943, following graduation from the Vystrel Courses for Officers, she earned the rank of major. A master sniper instructor, she trained 80 snipers who scored over 2,000 kills. From 1942 to 1953 she served as research officer for the Main Naval Staff. Meanwhile, having graduated from the University of Kyiv in 1945, she became a military historian and journalist. She was awarded the highest Soviet military decoration, Hero of the Soviet Union, on October 25, 1943, and two Orders of Lenin. She died at the age of 58 and was buried at the prestigious Novodevich'e Cemetery in Moscow.

Kazimiera J. Cottam

See also Soviet Union/Russian Federation, Women Heroes of the

References and Further Reading

Allen, Mary. 2003. "Pavlichenko, Luidmila Mikhailova." Pages 338–340 in *Amazons to Fighter Pilots: A Biographical Dictionary of Military Women*. Vol. 1. Edited by Reina Pennington. Westport, CT: Greenwood.

Cottam, Kazimiera J. 1998. *Women in War and Resistance*. Nepean, Ontario, Canada: New Military Publishing.

Pavliuchenko, Liudmila M. 1977. "I Was a Sniper." Pages 51–70 in *Road of Battle and Glory*. Edited by I. M. Danishevsky. Trans. by David Skvirsky. Moscow: Politizdat.

PEACE PEOPLE MOVEMENT (NORTHERN IRELAND)

Organization founded by Betty Williams (1943–) and Mairead Corrigan (Maguire) (1944–), winners of the 1976 Nobel Peace Prize, to promote peace in Northern Ireland. In August 1974 a car went out of control after its driver, a member of the Irish Republican Army (IRA), had been shot by British soldiers. The car plowed into a family and killed three children. Williams, who heard the shots and went to see what had happened, saw the dead and dying children. Corrigan was the aunt of the children. In an effort to put an end to the violence plaguing Northern Ireland, the two women and Ciaran McKeown founded a nonsectarian movement to promote peace. Their movement united Northern Irish Catholics and Protestants in marches for peace and understanding.

—Bernard Cook

See also Ulster, Women during the Troubles in

References and Further Reading

Maguire, Mairead. 1999. *The Vision of Peace*. Edited by John Dear. Maryknoll, NY: Orbis.

PEAKE, FELICITY (1913–2002)

First director of the British Women's Royal Air Force (WRAF). Air Commodore Dame Felicity (Watts Hanbury) Peake, the daughter of Colonel Humphrey Watts, was born on May 1, 1913, at Cheadle Hulme, Manchester. She studied in both England and France. She met Jock Hanbury while on a cruise to the West Indies and they married in 1935 at St. Margaret's, Westminster. Her husband's hobby was flying and Felicity also became interested in it. After flying for only six-and-a-half hours, she made her first solo flight and received a pilot's license.

A career in flying led her to join the 9th Air Transport Service (ATS) of the Royal Air Force (RAF) just before World War II. Her husband became a pilot in the Auxiliary Air Force and lost his life in a flying exercise in October 1939. Felicity became an ATS company assistant and afterward became a code and cipher officer. While the Battle of Britain was raging, she was posted at Biggin Hill in May 1940, commanding a 250-strong Women's Auxiliary Air Force (WAAF) unit.

She rose steadily in the ranks of the WAAF. She was posted to the recruiting staff of the Air Ministry in January 1941, and later became a public relations officer. She was conscious of her gender and tried to give more women in the RAF an equal footing with the men. The Chief of the Air Staff, Lord Arthur William Tedder, supported her fully, as did the director of public relations of the RAF, Air Commodore Harald Peake, who eventually became Felicity's second husband. At Bomber Command she became deputy WAAF administration staff officer in 1943 and subsequently was promoted to the rank of wing commander supervising the WAAF officers' school at Windermere. The following year she served as a senior staff officer looking after the service conditions of women radar officers, and in 1945 was posted to Cairo at the office of commander-in-chief Mediterranean and Middle East Command, with the rank of group captain.

In 1946 she became director of the WAAF at the age of thirty two. She received the Member of the British Empire (MBE) for her services during the war and became a Dame Commander of the British Empire (DBE) in 1949. She had done commendable work in the transitional phase of the post-war period, and when the British government decided to set up a permanent body in the RAF exclusively for women, the natural choice for leader was Felicity Hanbury. She became the first director of the WRAF in 1949, at the age of 35. She contributed immensely to the shaping of the WRAF. She retired from the service in 1950, married Harald Peake the following year, and lived in a farmhouse at Oxfordshire. Peake was connected with the Imperial War Museum from 1963, holding the post of chairperson from 1986 to 1988. She died on November 2, 2002.

—*Patit Paban Mishra*

See also Great Britain, Women in Service in World War II

References and Further Reading

Peake, Felicity. 1993. *Pure Chance.* Shrewsbury, UK: Airlife Publishing.

PEASANTS' WAR

From 1524 to 1526, a series of peasants' rebellions took place in the Holy Roman Empire. In the early sixteenth century, population growth caused wages to fall and unemployment to increase in the countryside. At the same time, the consolidation of territorial states led to legal and administrative reforms that marginalized local autonomy. The aristocratic and ecclesiastical lords imposed higher taxes, tried to gain control over village commons, and reinforced serfdom. Popular interpretations of Luther's early writings strengthened militant anticlericalism and demands for a reform of the church that seemed to be preoccupied with its own political and economical power.

Numerous groups of rebellious peasants and townspeople, some of them led by lay preachers, sought to redress their grievances through direct talks with their lords, through law suits, and through violent protests. Their demands were revolutionary: The communities should exercise full control over the parish church as well as over the commons; serfdom was to be abolished; taxation was to be reformed; and the Bible as interpreted by reformation theologians should become the basis of state and society. In Thuringia, Thomas Müntzer, a radical rival of Luther, became the spiritual leader of the rebels. The peasants formed "Christian Assemblies," army-like regional groups, but never a unified front. In spite of initial successes, the insurgents were no match for the better-equipped mercenaries of the aristocracy. Even though the Peasants' War ended with the total military defeat of the rebels in several territories, subsequent legislation was influenced by their demands.

Contemporaries blamed the start of the Peasants' War on a woman. The Countess of Lupfen allegedly ordered peasants who were busy with the harvest to search for snail shells upon which she wished to wrap newly spun yarn. The countess not only took the service required of peasants for their right to use land to irrational extremes, but she also attempted to make peasants do the work of handmaids, integrating "male" work into the "female" sphere of the household. This anecdote conformed to popular misogynist ideas: Female disrespect and foolishness were the final straws that provoked a violent reaction by the peasants.

The peasant rebels were often absent from their respective villages for weeks or even months, leaving their farms in the care of their wives. In addition to this passive support, on some occasions women actively took part in the insurgence. Women spread news about the revolt and asked men to join the rebellion. The peasants employed female messengers. The rebels attacked and destroyed castles and monasteries. They were accompanied by peasant women who took the opportunity to pilfer. After robbing convents, rebels threatened the nuns with rape. At Heggbach, peasant women threatened to turn the men loose on the nuns and, following the typical early modern motif of a "world turned upside down," demanded that the nuns should bear children and do farm work while the peasant women would live in the comparative luxury of the monastery. There were numerous women among the militant adherents of revolutionary preachers. During tumultuous actions in Thuringia and the Black Forest, women took up arms to defend these preachers. Thomas Müntzer ordered women to arm themselves and do battle for his cause. Instigated by townsmen, a group of women from Windsheim met to attack and pilfer a monastery in 1525. The women named one of their number as their officer. In the same year, a group of women at Heilbronn formed a protest march, carrying with them the *Bundschuh* (a heavy peasant boot connoting solidarity of laboring peasants), the symbol of the peasant rebels.

Two women believed to have magical skills became leaders or at least advisers of the peasant rebels. The first was a soothsayer who lived near Bludenz. She prophesized that even though the lords had gained the upper hand, the rebels would win the war within months. The other, the widow Margarethe Renner (Black Hofmän-nin), accompanied a criminal who had managed to become the leader of a peasant group. Hofmännin had refused to pay taxes and was rumored to be an accessory to murder. She tried to persuade the insurgents to attack the city of Heilbronn, which ruled over her village, and threatened to mistreat the women of Heilbronn's upper class. Hofmännin allegedly claimed that she had used magic to make the rebels invulnerable. After the conquest of the town of Weinsberg, Hofmännin took part in atrocities committed there. The insurgents executed several noblemen, defiled their corpses, and humiliated the countess of Helfenstein by driving her out of town on a dung cart. The Weinsberg outrages were widely reported and used to justify the rigorous action the aristocratic forces took against the rebels.

—*Johannes Dillinger*

See also Thirty Years' War

References and Further Reading

Franz, Günther. 1984. *Der deutsche Bauernkrieg* [The German Peasant War]. Darmstadt, Germany: Wissenschaftliche Buchgesellschaft.

Kobelt-Groch, Marion. 1993. *Aufsässige Toechter Gottes* [Rebellious Daughter of God]. Frankfurt/Main: Campus.

Ulbrich, Claudia. 1998. "Die Heggbacher Chronik" [The Heggbach Chronicle]. Pages 391–399 in *Gemeinde, Reformation und Widerstand* [Community, Reformation and Resistance]. Edited by Heinrich R. Schmidt. Tübingen, Germany: Bibliotheca-Academica.

PERU: SHINING PATH

Peruvian Maoist terrorist movement. Unlike any Peruvian political party before the 1980s, the Sendero Luminoso (the Shining Path; SL), gave women a role in political affairs. Women acted as agents of violence in the civil war waged throughout Peru from 1980 until 1992.

The SL was founded in 1974 by Peruvian philosophy professor Abimael Guzmán Reynoso in Ayacucho, an Andean city in Peru. The movement's armed struggle began in 1980. Guzmán and most of his cadres were captured in 1992. The ideology of SL was defined as Marxist–Leninist–Maoist–Gonzalo-Thought ("President Gonzalo" was Guzmán's nom de guerre). The SL's military hierarchy consisted of four levels. At its base, or fourth level, were the "masses," formed by peasants from the Andes and the Amazon rainforest. The masses initially collaborated with the SL but stopped supporting the movement due to army intervention and the SL's own repressiveness. Above them, the third level consisted of the combatants and subordinate groups formed by the party. Members of this level were high school and university students recruited by SL professors and students. At the second level were the militant cadres (the party). The cadres were initially formed by the "Holy families" from Ayacucho (the Morotes and the Durands), whose members intermarried and founded the organization. Above them all was President Guzmán.

SL activities included the selective assassinations of those who opposed the movement's actions, including leftist leaders, governmental representatives, and community and church leaders. The assassinations were carried out by an "annihilation squad." The squad's modus operandi consisted of members creating a distraction while a second group killed the targeted person. Afterward, a last segment of the squad fired a final shot into the victim and left a note explaining the reasons for the execution. The combatant in charge of the last shot was, in most cases, a woman.

The presence of women in the SL goes back to its creation; women accounted for 50 percent of the militant cadres and comprised 40 percent of its total membership (Peruvian Truth and Reconciliation Commission, 2003). In 1973, seven years before the SL became a clandestine organization, Guzmán founded the Popular

Feminine Movement of Ayacucho (PFM), whose members accompanied him until his detention in 1992. The SL targeted smart and active women, who were recruited in two ways: first, through intellectual indoctrination in the escuelas populares (popular schools) run by SL members or through classmates and professors at the young women's universities, and second, through romance. The SL organized youth parties where targeted young women were seduced by members and brought into the movement. These women had access to the upper levels of the organization and were usually from middle- or upper-class families. On the other hand, women from the masses, who belonged to peasant communities, were forced to join the organization through threats to their families or kidnapping. These women were used to bear and raise children, and as domestic workers.

The SL could have been seen as an opportunity for urban, educated women to achieve important political participation. This can be assumed by the fact that 57 percent of the imprisoned female SL members had a higher education and 10 percent of them held graduate degrees (Peruvian Truth and Reconciliation Commission, 2003). Laura Zambrano, an SL leader, stated that the SL was more liberating for women than feminism because it offered women the possibility of being equal to men in armed struggle (Herzog 1993, 70). Within the three higher levels of the SL's structure, gender differences were transformed and gender relationships were either controlled by the organization or eliminated. Women could achieve high positions within the organization. The children of combatants were raised in the escuelas populares. The idea of having a family was replaced by the sense of belonging to the party, with Guzmán at its pinnacle. Women from the masses, however, did not have the opportunity of achieving a place in the higher levels of the movement and were kept within their "feminine" roles of caretakers and domestic workers.

Despite the fact that the SL presented itself as a liberating alternative for women, it was not an organization where women or men could act freely. The SL was hierarchical and repressive. The militant cadres had control over the lives of the members of the organization. Decisions concerning marriages and divorces were decided based on the interests of the revolution, and family and cultural ties were broken.

—*Laura Balbuena González*

See also Latin America, Women in Guerrilla Movements in

References and Further Reading

Del Pino H., Ponciano. 1998. "Family, Culture, and 'Revolution:' Everyday Life with *Sendero Luminoso.*" In *Shining and Other Paths: War and Society in Peru, 1980–1995.* Edited by Steve J. Stern. Durham, NC, and London: Duke University.

Herzog, Kristin. 1993. *Finding their Voice: Peruvian Women's Testimonies of War.* Valley Forge, PA: Trinity Press International.

Kirk, Robin. 1993. *Grabado en piedra. Las Mujeres de Sendero Luminoso* [Etched on Stone. Women from the Shining Path]. Lima: IEP.

Peruvian Truth and Reconciliation Commission. 2003. *CVR Final Report.* Lima, Peru: http://www.cverdad.org.pe/ingles/ifinal/index.php (Spanish) and http://www.usip.org/library/tc/doc/reports/chile/chile_1993_toc.html (English) (accessed 20 January 2006).

PERUVIAN TRUTH AND RECONCILIATION COMMISSION: WOMEN AND POLITICAL VIOLENCE

Investigation of the violence in Peru from 1980, when the Maoist terrorist movement known as *Sendero Luminoso* (the Shining Path; SL) initiated its war against the state, until 2000 when Peruvian President Alberto Fujimori left the country for Japan. In 2000, the transitional government of President Valentín Paniagua created the Truth and Reconciliation Commission (TRC). The goals of the TRC were to analyze the nature of the armed conflict that had afflicted Peru, and to attempt to determine who was responsible for the multiple violations of human rights. One of the most important findings of the TRC was that, unlike other Latin American situations, the main perpetrator of political violence was the SL, which was responsible for more than 50 percent of the 69,280 deaths. Because of public hearings, many female victims of the political violence could speak their truth and tell the horror they and their children experienced during the armed conflict. These testimonies allowed the TRC to show the gender aspect of the civil war in its final report, presented in August of 2003.

The TRC report has a chapter solely devoted to the gender-related side of the conflict. The chapter analyses the relationship between violence and gender, showing how vulnerable women were because of their gender. Although women comprise only 20 percent of the conflict's victims, the consequences of the political violence in the lives of women and their children were devastating. Their families were destroyed, leaving them as widows to raise their children alone, or as single mothers to raise children who were the products of rape. Their fields and towns were destroyed, leaving them with no means to support their families. Their bodies were affected due to forced abortions or constant rapes. They were exploited either as sexual objects or for domestic purposes. Moreover, 73 percent of the female victims did not speak Spanish as their native language; 80 percent lived in rural areas; and 34 percent were illiterate. The compounded characteristics of being female and indigenous played a crucial role in the discrimination and violence the women suffered from the SL and the state.

As reported by the TRC, Peruvian women actively participated throughout the political conflict as either agents of resistance or perpetrators of violence. The TRC recognized female victims' efforts to overcome difficulties by working together to create *comedores populares* (soup kitchens) and *clubes de madres* (mothers' clubs), grassroots organizations created by women to alleviate the economic situation. Women also joined the *comités de autodefensa* (self-defense committees) created in the Andes to defend themselves against the SL, and they created the ANFASEP (Asociación Nacional de Familiares de Secuestrados, National Association of Relatives of the Disappeared) organization. Furthermore, due to the important role women played in the resistance movement, female leaders were recurrent targets of the SL's annihilation squad. The TRC also showed the relevant role Peruvian women played as agents of violence within the SL. Female participation in the SL accounted for 40 percent of its membership, and women comprised 50 percent of its central committee.

—*Laura Balbuena González*

See also Latin America, Women in Guerrilla Movements in; Peru: Shining Light

References and Further Reading

Macher, Sofía. 2002. "La Comisión de la Verdad y las Mujeres en el Perú" [The Truth and Reconciliation Commission and Women in Peru]. Pages 181–185 in *La mitad del cielo, la mitad de la tierra, la mitad del poder: Instancias y mecanismos para el adelanto de la mujer* [Half the Sky, Half the Land, Half the Power: Applications and Mechanisms for the Development of Women]. Edited by Diana Miloslavich Túpac. Lima: Centro de la Mujer Peruana Flora Tristán.

Peruvian Truth and Reconciliation Commission. 2003. *CVR Final Report.* Lima, Peru: http://www.cverdad.org.pe/ingles/ifinal/index.php (Spanish) and http://www.usip.org/library/tc/doc/reports/chile/chile_1993_toc.html (English) (accessed 20 January 2006).

PETACCI, CLARA (1912–1945)

Mussolini's mistress, who was shot by partisans at the end of World War II. Clara Petacci was born into a prominent Italian family in Rome on February 28, 1912. She first met Mussolini in 1932. Despite visits with Mussolini at his residence, the Palazzo Venezia, she married an officer, Ricardo Federici. Mussolini dispatched Federici to Japan in 1936, and Clara became Mussolini's mistress, taking up residence in a small apartment in the Palazzo Venezia. Though his fidelity was inferior to hers, she remained faithfully devoted to him to the end. Despite widespread gossip, Mussolini did ignore accusations that a member of her family had engaged in financial irregularities (Smith 1982, 285). When Mussolini was overthrown in July 1943, Petacci, who had fled to Lago Maggiore, was arrested and jailed. Crowds destroyed her father's house in Rome and the Villa Camilluccia, which Mussolini had given her. After Mussolini and Petacci were rescued from imprisonment by the Germans, she joined him at Salò in northern Italy, where he headed the puppet Italian Social Republic.

She was with Mussolini at the end of April 1945, as he attempted to flee toward Austria in a German convoy. Partisans stopped the convoy and captured Mussolini and Petacci. Petacci insisted on remaining with her lover, which resulted in her death (Smith 1982, 319). They were shot at Dongo on April 28, 1945, by Captain Valerio (Walter Audisio), a communist member of the Committee for National Liberation (Cassels 1985, 117). Their bodies and those of five other leading fascists, who had also been captured and executed, were taken by truck to Milan where they were hung by their feet from a gasoline station in the Piazzale Loreto, the site of an earlier murder of fifteen Italian partisans by the Nazis. The corpses were then subjected to physical and verbal vilification.

—*Bernard Cook*

See also Braun, Eva; Mitford, Unity

References and Further Reading

Cassels, Alan. 1982. *Fascist Italy.* 2nd ed. Arlington Heights, IL: Harley Davidson.

Petacci, Clara. 1946. *Il mio diario* [My Diary]. Milan: Associati.

Smith, Dennis Mack. 1982. *Mussolini.* New York: Alfred A. Knopf.

PETIT, GABRIELLE (1893–1916)

Belgian spy executed by the Germans during World War I. Gabrielle Petit was born in Tournai, Belgium, in 1893. When the war broke out Petit was working as a sales clerk in Brussels. Her fiancé, Maurice Gobert, a soldier, was captured by the Germans after he was wounded. He, however, escaped and was eventually able to join the Belgian forces fighting in the southwestern corner of the country. Petit, for her part, volunteered to serve as a spy. After a short training period in England, she gathered information about German troop movements in Belgium for the Allies. She also distributed the clandestine Belgian newspaper, *La libre Belgique* (Free Belgium), and helped Belgians cross the frontier into the Netherlands so that they could join the Belgian army in the south.

Petit's activity was reported to the German authorities, who arrested her in February 1916. She refused to gain a more lenient sentence by betraying the identity of others in the resistance and was condemned to death. Petit was executed by a firing squad on April 1, 1916. After the war she was hailed as a national hero, and her remains were transferred from the execution grounds to a cemetery in Schaarbeek, Belgium.

—*Bernard Cook*

See also Belgium, Women during World War I; Cavell, Edith Louisa

References and Further Reading

"Gabrielle Petit," Propaganda Postcards of the Great War, http://www.ww1-propaganda-cards.com/gabrielle petit.html (accessed February 22, 2006).

PHILIPPINES, WOMEN DURING THE AMERICAN SUPPRESSION OF THE INSURRECTION IN

The Philippine Insurrection was a transforming event for women in the Philippines. The Katipunan (the Association—in Tagalog the full name was Kataastaasan Kagalang-galang na Katipunan nang manga Anak ng Bayan or the Highest and Most Venerated Association of the Sons and Daughters of the Land) , a secret society in the Philippines, led the island's struggle for independence from Spain beginning in August 1896. The Filipinos succeeded in establishing a republic for a short period (December 1897 to February 1898), but by the time the United States declared its own war on Spain, fighting had resumed between Filipino and Spanish forces. The United States engaged Spain both in the Caribbean and the Pacific, and took the lead from Filipino insurgents to complete Spain's defeat. The United States then declared sovereignty over the Philippines, a claim that the new Philippine republic, established on January 23, 1899, rejected. The Philippine Insurrection against the United States ensued from February 4, 1899, until July 4, 1902, when President Theodore Roosevelt declared official victory for the United States. Armed resistance to U.S. conquest, however, continued on some islands into the 1930s, and the Philippines did not gain independence until 1946. The brutal war cost over 200,000 lives, the vast majority of which were Filipino civilians.

Late nineteenth-century society and culture in the Philippines mirrored Spanish ideology

THE SUPPRESSION OF THE PHILIPPINE INSURRECTION

"The present war is no bloodless, opera bouffe engagement; our men have been relentless, have killed to exterminate men, women, children, prisoners and captives, active insurgents and suspected people from lads of ten up, the idea prevailing that the Filipino as such was little better than a dog . . ."

—*Philadelphia Ledger,* November 1901,
quoted in Howard Zinn, 1990. *A People's History of the United States.*
New York: Harper Perennial, 308.

when it came to a woman's place in life. Even elite women had few opportunities for education and were expected to confine their interests to the home. Before the independence movement, Filipinas had rarely been part of social or political movements. The anticolonial movement marked a sharp departure from this pattern. In July 1893, very soon after its formation, the Katipunan established a women's chapter. By hosting Katipunan meetings, women helped disguise the gatherings as social events, thereby not capturing the attention of Spanish authorities. Many of the women in the Katipunan had earlier been initiated as Masons. As defenders of liberal thought and individualism, the Masons in the Philippines led the intellectual challenge to Catholicism and Spanish rule. Though most of the women known today as contributors to the insurrection were wives, mothers, and sisters of the movement's male leaders, they served in many different capacities and earned respect as patriots and insurgents in their own right.

Some Filipina contributions, such as sewing and nursing, were extensions of their domestic roles. Women produced potent national symbols, including the first Filipino flag, flown when Emiliano Aguinaldo declared independence on June 12, 1898. Women organized more than a dozen chapters of the Red Cross, beginning with the society founded by Hilaria del Rosario, wife of Emiliano Aguinaldo, in early 1899. Women were particularly important in supporting the army, collecting food and supplies, and raising funds for the revolution. When internal disputes threatened the unity of the insurrection, women

acted as peacemakers. For example, on April 24, 1899, a group of women brought flowers and knelt before General Antonio Luna, pleading his forgiveness for another general who had delayed in sending reinforcements during a U.S. bombardment.

The participation of Filipinas ranged far beyond women's traditional roles. Agueda Estaban y de la Cruz was a courier and spy who conducted surveillance, first of Spanish and later of U.S. officials. Several women fought as soldiers, coming to special prominence in the region of Cavite. Most notable were Bernarda Tagalog y Monson, who battled the enemy alongside her son; Agueda Kahabagan y Iniquinto, the only woman listed as a general by the Army of the Filipino Republic; and Teresa Magbanua y Ferraris. Magbanua joined the army in defiance of her husband and her uncle, a military commander. After the defeat of Spain, she continued to fight against the United States, at Iloilo City and at Jaro. Though apparently never given an official rank, she commanded guerrillas and was popularly accorded the honorific of "general." Magbanua surrendered to the U.S. forces in 1900.

American women did not participate directly in the military action in the Philippines. During the insurrection they did, however, serve as Army nurses supporting the troops. The impetus to form a permanent Army Corps of Nurses in 1901 largely came from the continued need for military nurses in the Philippines. The United States also hired women as government-sponsored teachers not only to educate but to Americanize its new Filipino subjects.

A trench, with Moro victims, after the fight at Mount Dajo, Island of Jolo, Philippines. (National Archives)

Fewer Filipinas were active in the insurrection against the United States than had been in the revolt against Spain. By 1898, many women insurgents had already been captured and exiled (like Melchora Aquino and Segunda Puentes Santiago), or were exhausted and had returned to domestic life. The average Filipina, however, could hardly ignore the war even if she did not assume a visible role in it. The nature of guerrilla warfare and the specific military strategy of the United States led to widespread suffering. U.S. troops regarded all adult men as potential enemies to be shot at the soldier's discretion; Filipinas were also slaughtered, raped, and physically abused. Some U.S. anti-imperialists, including women like Jane Addams, spoke out against the atrocities but incidents of brutality continued through and after the war, such as the 1906 Moro massacre of 900 men, women, and children.

The experience of the war left a decidedly mixed legacy for these women. Filipinas entered the public sphere for the first time in the wake of the failed insurrection. They engaged in civic reform, promoted women's education, and pressed for suffrage. They avoided direct challenges to patriarchal institutions, but all the while struggled as colonial subjects of a foreign power. The pervasive violence of the war and its aftermath affected countless individual women as well, in ways that historians have yet to document.

—*Laura R. Prieto*

See also East Timor, Abuse of Women during War; Herero of Namibia, Repression of the; Spanish-American War, Women and the

References and Further Reading

De Dios, Aurora J. 1996. "Participation of Women's Groups in the Anti-Dictatorship Struggle: Genesis of a Movement." Pages 141–168 in *Women's Role in Philippine History: Selected Essays.* 2nd ed. Quezon City: University Center for Women's Studies, University of the Philippines.

Policarpio, Paz. 1996. "The Filipino Women during the Revolution." *Review of Women's Studies,* 5:2 and 6:1.

Roces, Mina. 2002. "Women in Philippine Politics and Society." Pages 159–189 in *Mixed Blessing: The Impact of the American Colonial Experience on Politics and Society in the Philippines.* Edited by Hazel M. McFerson. Westport, CT: Greenwood.

Soriano, Rafaelita Hilario, ed. 1995. *Women in the Philippine Revolution.* Manila: Printon.

PILOTS OF THE IL-2 (1941–1945)

Heroic Russian attack bomber pilots. Tamara Fedorovna Konstantinova and Anna Aleksandrovna Timofeeva (née Egorova) flew the formidable IL-2 and were the only women IL-2 pilots to be awarded the exclusive Hero of the Soviet Union Medal.

Senior Lieutenant Konstantinova was deputy squadron commander of the 999th Ground Attack Aviation Regiment, 277th Ground Attack Division, 1st Air Army, 3rd Baltic Front. Born in the Tver' region in 1919, she became an instructor at the Kalinin (Tver') Flying Club in 1939. She was initially rejected for active service due to an alleged shortage of aircraft and risked her life as a truck driver delivering ammunition to the front. Konstantinova eventually secured a transfer to a communications subunit, where she flew the unarmed Po-2, a former training aircraft. She soon distinguished herself by skilfully evading German Messerschmitts. Her per-

sistence in applying for a transfer to an operational air unit eventually paid off. After joining the 566th Ground Attack Aviation Regiment in March 1944, she acquired a new IL-2, and, together with gunner Aleksandra Mukoseyeva, formed a cohesive and effective team.

In December 1944 Konstantinova became deputy squadron commander after transferring to the 999th Ground Attack Aviation Regiment. In West Prussia alone, she flew at least twice as many missions as other pilots in a comparable period, maintaining that she was fighting for two—her late husband and herself. By March 1945 she had flown 66 operational missions and earned many decorations. After the war she flew light passenger aircraft out of Voronezh. In 1948 Konstantinova was permanently grounded due to a serious injury received during an emergency landing. She was awarded the Hero of the Soviet Union on June 29, 1945.

Senior Lieutenant Timofeeva was chief navigator of the 805th Ground Attack Regiment, 197th Ground Attack Division, 16th Air Army, 1st Belorussian Front. Born in the Tver' region in 1916, she came to Moscow to participate in the construction of the Moscow subway and took lessons offered by a flying club operated by her employer. Subsequently, after graduating from Kherson Flying School, she became instructor at the Kalinin (Tver') Flying Club.

At the beginning of the war she flew with the 130th Independent Communication Squadron of the Southern Front. After a Messerschmitt set her unarmed machine on fire and she was forced to make an emergency landing, she became determined to fly combat aircraft so that she could defend herself. Her persistence paid off and she became an IL-2 pilot early in 1943. While learning the IL-2 she flew only twice with an instructor, mastering the aircraft more quickly than her male comrades.

Timofeeva received her baptism of fire over the Black and Azov seas. She soon became a skilled combat pilot and was appointed deputy squadron commander. With her regiment she took part in fierce air battles over the Taman'

Peninsula, and flew many missions in aid of Soviet marines defending the Malaia Zemlia beachhead near Novorossiysk. She attacked enemy tanks, ships, rail junctions, and airfields while coping with fatigue and heavy losses in her unit.

On May 26, 1943, she voluntarily participated in the laying of a smokescreen to assist Soviet ground troops to break through the enemy-fortified Blue Line on the Taman' Peninsula (which stretched from Novorossiysk to Temriuk). To this end, she flew at a low level, unarmed, and without maneuvering. For her actions she was subsequently decorated by commander of the 4th Air Army, General Konstantin A. Vershinin.

After completing a two-month course for navigators in Stavropol in the North Caucasus, she received a new version of the IL-2. Dusya Nazarkina was her gunner. When their flight wing reached the 1st Belorussian Front, Timofeeva was appointed chief navigator.

On August 20, 1944, during her 277th mission, Timofeeva was shot down in flames east of Warsaw, captured by the enemy, and incarcerated in Küstrin POW camp. She had suffered severe burns, but her life was saved by fellow inmates, who offered her food, medications, and encouragement. Following liberation from the camp she was transferred to the reserves. Due to her internment—those captured by the enemy were punished by Stalin, who regarded surrender or even capture as treasonous—Timofeeva was not awarded the Hero of the Soviet Union until May 6, 1965, long after Stalin's death.

—*Kazimiera J. Cottam*

See also Soviet Union, 46th Taman Guards Bomber Aviation Regiment; Soviet Union/Russian Federation, Women Heroes of the; Soviet Union Air Defense, 586th Fighter Aviation Regiment

References and Further Readings

Cottam, Kazimiera J. 1998. *Women in War and Resistance.* Nepean, ON, Canada: New Military Publishing.

Timofeeva-Yegorova, Anna A. 1983. *Derzhis,' sestrenka!* [Hang in, Little Sister!]. Moscow: Voyenizdat.

Vershinin, Konstantin Andreevich. 1975. *Chetvertaia vozdushnaia* [Fourth Air Army]. Moscow: Voyenizdat.

PIZAN, CHRISTINE DE

See De Pizan, Christine

PITCHER, MOLLY

See Molly Pitcher

PLATER, EMILIA (1806–1831)

Polish freedom fighter. Emilia Plater was born on November 13, 1806, in Wilno (Vilnius). Her father, Count Francis-Xavier Plater, was of Westphalian descent, but the family had become thoroughly Polish, especially in patriotic sentiment. Emilia's parents divorced when she was a child and she grew up on an Inflanty estate that belonged to her relatives, the Zybereks. Emilia was very interested in history and admired Tadeusz Kosciuszko, but she was especially inspired by Joan d'Arc, who led the French in battle against English aggressors, and Bobolina, who devoted herself and sacrificed her life to the Greek struggle for independence. Emilia had a picture of Bobolina in her room. In addition to her fascination with history, Emilia became adept at horsemanship and shooting. Following the death of her mother, she sought consolation in reading both Polish literature and poetry. She was particularly moved by Adam Mickiewicz's

"Grazyna." She also was fascinated with the life of the common people and gathered their songs and tales. In 1829 she took a lengthy trip through Poland, visiting both Warsaw and Krakow.

When the Polish insurrection against Russia erupted in November 1830, Emilia cut her hair and, with the support of her cousins, Lucien and Ferdinand, who attended a local military academy, joined the revolutionaries. The partisans hoped to take the Russian fortress of Dynaburg (Dünaburg, today Daugavpils in Latvia), but gave up the idea because of the strength of the Russian force there. With another cousin, Cezary Plater, she then joined the Wilkomierz Riflemen led by Karol Zaluski and subsequently a group of partisans led by Constantine Parczewski. On March 30 Emilia's unit engaged a mounted Russian patrol in Dangiele, and on April 2 they forced an enemy company to pull back. On April 4 her unit attacked a relief column commanded by General Shirman and went on to occupy Jeziorosy.

After General Dezydery Chlapowski reached Lithuania, he told Emilia that there was no place for a woman in the Polish army. She reputedly responded, "I will remain a soldier and I will fight until Poland regains full independence" (Emilia Plater Polish School 2005). She stayed, and when Chlapowski organized the partisans into regular units, Emilia became commander of the 1st Company of the 1st Lithuanian Regiment. Due to her heroism in the battles at Kowno and Szawle, Emilia was promoted to captain. When Chlapowski later decided that the military situation was hopeless, Emilia rejected the idea of seeking refuge in Prussian territory. She reputedly said, "It would be better to die than to put up with such a humiliation" (Emilia Plater Polish School 2005). With her cousin Cezary, she was determined to join forces still fighting farther to the west in Poland. During her journey west, however, she succumbed to exhaustion. She was taken in first by peasants, and then by landowner Ignatius Ablamowicz, who brought her to his estate at Kopciowa, near Kapciamiestis, where she died on December 23, 1831.

After Emilia's death, her favorite poet, the romantic nationalist Adam Mickiewicz, honored her in his 1832 work, "The Death of a Colonel." During World War II after the German invasion of the Soviet Union, the Emilia Plater Independent Women's Battalion, consisting of young Polish women volunteers, was founded near Moscow on June 3, 1943. Veterans of the battalion were called "Platerowki."

—Bernard Cook

See also Polish Independent Women's Battalion, Emilia Plater

References and Further Reading

Angelfile.com. Prominent Poles. "Emilia Plater, Military Woman, Fighter for Poland's Independence." http://www.angelfire.com /scifi2/rsolecki/emilia_plater.html (accessed June 27, 2005).

de Plater, Mervyn B. 1998. "Emilia Plater." http:// www.platerowie.com/emilia.php (accessed June 27, 2005).

Emilia Plater Polish School. "Emilia Plater." http:// www.emiliaplater.org/emilia/emiliave1.html (accessed June 27, 2005).

Straszewicz, Joseph. 1842. *The Life of the Countess Emily Plater.* Trans. J. K. Salomonski. New York: J. F. Trow.

PLAVSIC, BILJANA (1930–)

The first woman and most senior politician convicted by the International Tribunal for the Former Yugoslavia at The Hague of a crime against humanity and the laws and customs of war. Biljana Plavsic was born on July 7, 1930, in Tuzla, Yugoslavia (now Bosnia and Herzegovina). On October 2, 2002, Plavsic pled guilty to one count of political, racial, and religious persecution. She was the only person indicted by the Tribunal for crimes against humanity who pled guilty.

Plavsic was a leading member of the Serbian Democratic Party, headed by Radovan Karadzic, from its inception in Bosnia and Herzegovina. From 1990 until April 1992, Plavsic was a member of the collective presidency of Bosnia and Herzegovina. She and other Serbian nationalists refused to acknowledge an independent Bosnia and Herzegovina that did not recognize special rights for Bosnian Serbs, who constituted 31.4 percent of the population (Gallagher 2001a, 140). Fighting erupted between the Serbs and the government of Bosnia and Herzegovina on April 6, 1992—the day that the European Union recognized the independence of Bosnia.

From February 28 to May 12, 1992, Plavsic was one of two members of the acting presidency of the self-proclaimed Serbian Republic of Bosnia and Herzegovina, serving collectively with Radovan Karadzic. When he became sole president on December 17, she became one of his vice-presidents.

Following the 1995 Dayton Accords, which ended the war in Bosnia, Plavsic served as the Bosnian Serb president from 1996 to 1998. Though remaining a Serb nationalist, she cooperated with the North Atlantic Treaty Organization (NATO) occupation forces and supported Western-leaning candidates within the Serbian section of Bosnia. In 2001 she turned herself in to The Hague Tribunal, which had indicted her. Plavsic accepted ultimate responsibility for the killing of non-Serbs and the operation of concentration camps where Bosnians and Croats were mistreated and killed. She admitted that she was responsible for "forced transfer or deportation, unlawful killing, cruel and inhumane conditions in detention facilities, destruction of cultural and sacred objects, plunder, wanton destruction, forced labour and use of human shields" (Gedye 2003). On February 27, 2003, she was sentenced to eleven years imprisonment. On June 26 she was transferred to Sweden where she was to complete the remainder of her sentence.

—*Bernard Cook*

See also Markovic, Mirjana; Yugoslavia, Women and the Wars That Accompanied the Disintegration of Yugoslavia

References and Further Reading

Gallagher, Tom. 2001a. "Bosnia-Herzegovina." Pages 139–140 in *Europe since 1945: An Encyclopedia*. Edited by Bernard Cook. New York: Garland.
———. 2001b. "Bosnian War." Pages 140–142 in *Europe since 1945: An Encyclopedia*. New York: Garland.
Gedye, Robin. "Remorseful Plavsic Gets 11 Years' Jail." *The Telegraph* (London), March 1, 2003.
United Nations. "Case No. IT-00–40-I, The Prosecutor of the Tribunal against Biljana Plavsic." The International Criminal Tribunal for the Former Yugoslavia. http://www.un.org /icty/indctment/english/pla-ii000407e.htm (accessed January 13, 2004).

PLEWMAN, ELIANE (1917–1944)

British agent during World War II. Eliane Sophy Browne-Bartoli was born in Marseilles, France, on December 6, 1917. Her family moved to England when she was a child, and she went to school in Britain and Spain. She was employed by an import firm in Leicester when the war erupted. She then went to work for the British embassies in Spain and Portugal. In 1942 she joined the Spanish Section of the Ministry of Information in London and married Tom Plewman, a British officer. Shortly afterward, she joined the British Special Operations Executive. After training, Eliane Plewman, whose codename was "Gaby," parachuted into France on August 13, 1943, where she operated as a courier in the Marseilles area for the "Monk" network of the Resistance headed by Charles Skepper. In January 1944 "Monk" blocked the main rail line between Marseilles and Toulon by derailing a train in a tunnel. The network disabled thirty other locomotives during a two-week period. The "Monk" network was exposed in March 1944 as a result of betrayal by a Frenchman, who was executed after the war. Plewman was arrested on March 24. She was interrogated by the Gestapo for three weeks. Despite beatings she divulged nothing. Plewman was then transferred with seven other captured female agents to the Karlsruhe civil prison. On September 10, 1944, on the direct order of Ernest Kaltenbrunner, the head of the SS Security Office, Plewman was transferred with Yolande Beekman, Madeleine Damerment, and Noor Inayat Khan to Dachau. There, on September 11, 1944, the day after their arrival, all four were shot.

—*Bernard Cook*

See also Atkins, Vera H.; Beekman, Yolande; Damerment, Madeleine; and Khan, Noor Inayat

References and Further Reading

"The FANY Agents—Eliane Plewman." The Women of the Special Operations Executive. http://www.64-baker-street.org/agents/agent_fany_eliane_plewman.html (accessed September 28, 2004).

Foot, M. R. D. (Michael Richard Daniell). 1984 (1966). *SOE in France: An Account of the Work of the British Special Operations Executive 1940–1944*. Frederick, MD: University Publications of America.

Nicholas, Elizabeth. 1958. *Death Be Not Proud*. London: Cresset.

Spartacus Web. "Eliane Plewman." http://www.spartacus.schoolnet.co.uk/SOEplewman.htm (accessed September 28, 2004).

PLSK

See Polish Auxiliary Air Force

POCOCK, LENA MARGARET

See Ashwell, Lena Margaret Pocock

POLAND, RESISTANCE DURING WORLD WAR II, WOMEN AND

The significant role of Polish women in the anti-Nazi resistance. There were three main choices for Polish women who wished to actively resist the Germans after the invasion of Poland in September 1939: join the Communist Resistance, serve with the Home Army, or become a member of the international resistance. In addition to these options, Jewish women took part in the Warsaw Ghetto Uprising in 1943 and fought alongside Jewish partisans in the forests of Poland.

Helena Wolff (Dr. Anka), and many other women were active in the Communist Resistance. When World War II broke out, she worked at the Holy Spirit Hospital in Warsaw. During the siege of Warsaw, she risked her own life to remove patients from the burning hospital building. In April 1940 she qualified as a physician. While working at the Marie Curie Radiological Institute in the spring of 1942, she joined the Polish Workers' Party and the People's Guard, and began forming underground People's Guard cells in Warsaw's hospitals. In addition to transporting weapons and Party papers, she also trained nurses for the partisans. In July 1943 she became chief of the People's Guard medical department. When the Germans discovered a People's Guard cell at the Radiological Institute, the party sent Dr. Wolff to a partisan unit in Kielce Province. Early in 1944 she was appointed medical chief of the third district (Kielce) by the headquarters of the People's Army (which succeeded People's Guard). In addition to discharging physician's duties, she fought alongside partisans. In May 1944 she participated in the rescue of fifty-six Soviet

POLISH RESISTANCE

"I was taking a message to headquarters. I had the papers hidden in my sleeve and I walked down the street pretending to be an elegant young lady out for a stroll. Then I passed by some SS men. I thought, 'You bloody bastards. You think you are so strong and I am so weak but my work will eventually defeat you. That was my satisfaction.' "

—Black Barbara (Irena Kwiatkowska-Komorowska),
Courier, Home Army, Warsaw. Quoted in Shelley Saywell. 1985.
"Uprising: Poland, 1939–1945." Pages 102–103 in *Women in War.*
Markham, ON: Penguin Books Canada.
With permission of the author and publisher.

soldiers from a POW camp. Subsequently commissioned, in July 1944 Lieutenant Wolff was appointed medical officer of the People's Army's 1st Brigade. She was actively involved in sabotage missions. On September 30, 1944, she was granted the rank of captain and the Grunwald Cross. Wounded in October, she was captured by the enemy. It is unclear how she died on October 31, 1944. She was promoted posthumously to the rank of major.

Eileen Garlinska (1912–1990), born Eileen Frances Short, was the daughter of a Liverpool sea captain. She came to Poland on a holiday in 1935 and decided to stay. Soon after the German invasion of Poland on September 1, 1939, she married a Polish student. She then went to work as a translator at a clandestine Warsaw office of the Polish government in exile. When her husband became a senior intelligence officer with the underground Home Army, she was given false papers and a new name (Helena). While working as an English teacher, she became a courier. The only British woman to take part in the Warsaw uprising of 1944, she also worked as a nurse. She survived her various adventures and after the war emigrated with her family to the United Kingdom.

The Home Army was split into groups specializing in intelligence and sabotage, weapons buying and manufacturing, and training. A women's sabotage school was founded in 1942, with women becoming members of the Grey Ranks,

commando units specializing in diversionary actions and sabotage, including the theft of weapons manuals, which were translated and combined with instructions on how to build simplified models.

According to General Tadeusz Bór-Komorowski, leader of the Home Army, on the eve of the Warsaw uprising in August 1944, women constituted about one-seventh of the group's total 40,000 membership. The revolt, which began on August 1 and lasted two months, resulted in the devastation of the city, the deaths of some 250,000 people (Saywell 1985, 103, 129), and temporary exile for the survivors.

Two all-female units were created during the uprising: a unit of demolition experts and a special detachment intended for duty in the city sewer system. Among Home Army women, many were Girl Guides who reconnoitered escape and supply routes through the sewers of Warsaw, smuggled weapons, and were members of assassination squads. Others carried messages, delivered food, or took part in smuggling small groups of people out of Warsaw and into the forests for their protection. In addition, an unknown number of women nonmembers risked their lives in helping the resisters, offering them food, hiding them in cellars, and keeping quiet. One Home Army girl courier who went to the Warsaw Ghetto regularly was eventually killed. By far the largest number of Home Army women were liaison couriers and medics.

Women did participate in armed combat during the uprising. Men, however, tended to not approve of women bearing arms. Because of the shortage of guns, women were the last to receive them. Despite the onerous tasks being assigned to women, many male veterans do not acknowledge females in the Home Army as soldiers because they did not always bear arms. Ida Dobrzanska-Kasprzak, an officer with the Home Army, later complained,

I think it is about time that people took notice. It should be said, once and for all, that women fought, too. Men believe if you don't shoot or carry a gun you are not a soldier. But we did the most tedious and most dangerous jobs. Women were injured and killed in action. Men just don't want to admit that we fought too. (Saywell, 1985, 102)

Krystyna Skarbek, born in 1915, was the multilingual daughter of a Polish count. Active in several sports, she married Jerzy Giuycki, a mountain climber and author, in 1938, and the outbreak of World War II found them in Africa. They moved to Great Britain, where Krystyna met George Taylor of the Special Operations Executive (SOE). As an alleged correspondent for a London newspaper, she left for Budapest, Hungary—then a German ally—on December 21, 1939. Subsequently she traveled to Poland to make contact with a secret group of Polish officers working for British intelligence and to visit her Jewish mother, whom she was unable to save. After returning to Hungary, she transmitted clandestine information obtained in Poland to England. When the situation in Hungary became difficult, the SOE sent Krystyna to France. She also had a lengthy assignment in Algeria. Later, known as "Pauline Armand," she was airdropped into southern France on July 7, 1944. Disguised as an untidy peasant woman fluent in Italian, she was sent repeatedly to Italy, where she made contact with Italian partisans and proved successful in recruiting Italian soldiers.

She saved an associate named Roger, who had been arrested by the Gestapo, by daring to reveal that she worked for the SOE and offering the Germans 2 million franks for his freedom, which the SOE agreed to pay. After the war, while working as a waitress in a Polish café in Great Britain, she was stabbed to death by a jealous Irishman, who had become obsessed with her on June 15, 1952. Her funeral was attended by two generals: Stanislaw Kopanski, former chief of staff of the Polish Armed Forces, and Colin Gubbins, director of the British Special Operations Executive. Nicknamed by friends "The Queen of the European Underground," Krystyna Skarbek-Gizycka was awarded both the Order of the British Empire and the French Croix de Guerre.

—*Kazimiera J. Cottam*

See also Granville, Christine, pseud.

References and Further Reading

Bialokozowicz, Piotr. 1980. "Doktor Anka." *Úoanierz Polski,* 45 (November 9): 16.

Dixon, W. James. 2003. "Armia Krajowa (AK), Women in." Pages 22–25 in *Amazon to Fighter Pilots.* Edited by Reina Pennington. Vol. 1. Westport, CT: Greenwood.

"Eileen Garlinska" (Obituary). 1990. *Sunday Telegraph,* April 1, 1990.

Saywell, Shelley. 1985. "Uprising: Poland, 1939–1945." Pages 102–129 in *Women in War.* Markham, ON: Penguin Books Canada.

Stanczykiewicz, Eugeniusz. 1985. "Kim bylas Krystyno?" [Who Were You, Christine?] *Zolnierz Polski* 14 (April 7): 15.

POLISH AUXILIARY AIR FORCE (PLSK)

Women's auxiliary founded by order of the minister of defense of the Polish government in exile in mid-December, 1942. Based on the model of the British Women's Auxiliary Air Force (WAAF), the goal of the Pomocnicza Lotnicza Sluzba Kobiet (Polish Auxiliary Air Force or PLSK, 1943–1945) was to cooperate with the Polish Air Force and replace Polish pilots in service and support roles on Polish air bases in the United Kingdom.

Initially, in May 1943 thirty-six women candidates were sent for basic training to Falkirk, Scotland. After undergoing successively higher levels of specialized training, the group qualified as flight instructors. Twelve women graduated from an officers' course and the remainder from a noncommissioned officers' (NCO) program. In October 1943 the women were awarded both Polish and British ranks. General recruitment to the PLSK began in November 1943 (Polish Women in the War 1985, 12).

Apart from Great Britain, where the PLSK recruited most of its members, the PLSK also attracted Polish women from Canada, the United States, France, Argentina, Switzerland, China, and Japan. A large number of volunteers came from Polish military units organized in the Soviet Union, the so-called Anders Army commanded by General Wladyslaw Anders. This unit was subsequently evacuated from the USSR to the Middle East. The women served in twenty-six units of the Polish Air Force.

PLSK recruits were trained in forty-five specialties to which they were directed on the basis of their abilities and preferences, including every area where they could promptly replace men. For example, women were employed in communications, laboratory work, and interpreting aerial photographs. They served as clerks, cooks, mechanics, radio and telephone operators, physicians, dentists, sentries, and parachute folders. Women officers served in administrative, logistical, intelligence, and educational capacities.

There are discrepancies in the total numbers of officers and NCOs. A more recent Polish source (Mleczak 1994, 2) cites the total strength of the PLSK as 1,436, constituting 10 percent of

the Polish Air Force on the western front of the war, with 52 officers and 110 NCOs, while an earlier source cites a total of 1,653, including 52 officers and 163 NCOs (Polish Women in the War 1985, 12).

—*Kazimiera J. Cottam*

See also Polish Independent Women's Battalion, Emilia Plater

References and Further Reading

Cottam, Kazimiera J. 2003. "PLSK." Pages 345–46 in *Amazons to Fighter Pilots*. Edited by Reina Pennington. Vol. 1. Westport, CT: Greenwood.

Mleczak, Eugeniusz. 1994. "Dziewczeta z tamtych lat: Odsloniecie tablicy w Katedrze Polowej WP" [Young Airwomen of Long Ago: The Unveiling of Memorial Plaque at the Polish Armed Forces' Cathedral]. *Polska Zbrojna*, 109 (June 9) V: 2.

"Polki na wojnie" [Polish Women in the War]. 1985. *Skrzydlata Polska*, 10 (October 3): 12.

POLISH INDEPENDENT WOMEN'S BATTALION, EMILIA PLATER (1943–1945)

The first all-female Polish infantry unit. Following the German invasion of the Soviet Union in June 1941, and as a result of the Sikorski-Maisky Agreement of August 18, 1941, Polish citizens who had been interned in the Soviet Union following the Soviet occupation of eastern Poland in September 1941 were granted amnesty and a Polish army was formed under the command of General Wladyslaw Anders. Polish women internees were eager to serve in this army, in part due to their difficult living conditions. Soviet authorities initially objected to the recruitment of women but relented when General Anders argued that Soviet army itself consisted of many women.

General Anders favored creating a volunteer Polish women's corps based on the model of the

British women's auxiliary service. Women recruits were to receive basic and specialized training. Due to epidemics of typhus, malaria, and dysentery ravaging the personnel of the new Polish army, the main emphasis was placed on nursing. Women also produced newsletters, entertained troops on stage, taught literacy, and were employed as telephone operators.

Between September 1941 and August 1942, 4,667 Polish women in uniform were evacuated by land and sea to the western front in Europe via Central Asia and Iran (Biegun 1992, 48). The Polish Women's Auxiliary Service in Great Britain employed approximately 6,700 women (Saywell 1985, 103) and functioned akin to the Free French in cooperation with the British Auxiliary Territorial Service.

The Emilia Plater Independent Women's Battalion, consisting of volunteers from among young women left behind in the USSR, was founded on June 3, 1943, in Sel'tse near Moscow. Ironically, the battalion, named after Emilia Plater, an active participant in the 1830–1831 insurrection directed against Russia, was intended to fight alongside Soviet troops. Battalion veterans were called *Platerowki*, a name often applied to all Polish military women who served on the eastern front.

Initially attached to the 1st Tadeusz Kosciuszko Polish Division, the battalion swore its oath alongside the division on July 15, 1943. The battalion was directly subordinated to the 1st Polish Corps on August 19, 1943, and to the 1st Polish Army on July 17, 1944. Unlike auxiliary female units of Great Britain and the United States, the battalion was not governed by special military regulations. Its commanders and deputy commanders were men, while its political officers were women: Halina Zawadzka, Irena Sztachelska, and Ludwika Bobrowska.

As of August 18, 1943, the battalion consisted of a command element, one fusiliers company, two infantry companies, one machine gun company, a company of handheld anti-tank grenade launchers, and six platoons—mortar, reconnaissance, signals, medical, engineer, and logistics.

By late 1943 one transport platoon was added. The battalion's strength at the time was 691, including 48 officers, 163 noncommissioned officers, and 480 enlisted personnel (Cottam 2003, 150). Troop strength fluctuated, however, as the battalion provided basic training to women subsequently assigned elsewhere.

The alleged inability of some personnel, especially teenagers, to keep up with the very intensive training was used as a pretext to gradually transform the battalion from a first-line combat unit to one assigned mainly sentry and military police duties, which the women carried out in an exemplary fashion. Yet the organizational structure was maintained and members successfully took part in all major combat training exercises alongside male soldiers. It would seem that senior commanders were reluctant to expose women soldiers to the very heavy losses suffered by Polish troops alongside the Russians. One third of the 1st Polish Division was wiped out in the Battle of Lenino in the Smolensk region.

Only the Fusiliers Company took part in the Battle of Lenino, serving in auxiliary capacities such as sentry and police duties, administration of first aid, and escorting German POWs. The battalion as a whole remained at Sel'tse until early January 1944, at which time it was transferred to Smolensk. Two months later the battalion was based in Ukraine. After several additional moves, on October 12, 1944, the battalion was ordered to transfer to Praga, a suburb of Warsaw located on the Vistula River's eastern shore. Here the battalion was charged with guarding military and civilian property. On December 16 all detached subunits returned to the battalion. Finally, on January 17, 1945, following the liberation of Warsaw, the first group of the battalion crossed the frozen Vistula and on March 21 the battalion became directly subordinated to the Polish general staff. Its duties in Warsaw were the same as in Praga.

About 70 members of the battalion were killed during the war (Cottam 2003, 150). In

May 1945 it had roughly 500 members, representing a small percentage of the total number of Polish women serving on the eastern front, with estimates ranging widely from roughly 8,500 to 14,000 (Cottam 2003, 151). These numbers include some former members of the battalion who, like Emilia Gierczak, had been appointed platoon (or company) commanders in all-male units because many of the Polish male soldiers were not suitable to be officers.

On May 25, 1945, the battalion was disbanded in Warsaw, and on July 23, 1945, the discharged *Platerówki* were issued a complete uniform and two towels. Some of them secured employment in military institutions and about fifty became pioneer farmers in Platerówka, a village named after them in the newly acquired Western territories. On June 20, 1993, a commemorative plaque dedicated to the *Platerówki* (women soldiers of the 1st and 2nd Polish Armies formed in the USSR) was unveiled. The ceremony took place in the Cathedral of the Polish Armed Forces in Warsaw.

The following are selected prominent members of the battalion:

Halina Bielawska-Pietkiewicz. Lieutenant-colonel and former commander of the officer cadet corps in the infantry officer school in Ryazan.' She was third in her division to be promoted and her decorations included the Cross of Valor.

Helena Jablonska. Second lieutenant. As a private serving with the Fusiliers Company, she had been wounded in the Battle of Lenino. She was awarded the Virtuti Militari, the highest Polish military decoration, and the Cross of Valor.

Aniela Krzywon. She served as a private with the Fusiliers Company and was killed in the Battle of Lenino. She is the only Polish woman soldier awarded Hero of the Soviet Union, the highest Soviet military decoration.

Janina Wolanin. Major (Ret). She served as commander of a mortar company in the 3rd Polish Division. She was wounded three times, and was awarded the Virtuti Militari and the Cross of Valor.

—*Kazimiera J. Cottam*

See also Polish Auxiliary Air Force; Poland, Resistance during World War II, Women and

References and Further Reading

Biegun, Kazimierz. 1992. "Kobiety w armii gen. Andersa (wrzesien 1941–sierpien 1942)" [Women in General Anders' Army (September 1941–August 1942)]. *Wojsko I wychowanie,* 3:44–48.

Cottam, Kazimiera J. 1986. "Veterans of Polish Women's Combat Battalion Hold a Reunion." *Minerva: Quarterly Report on Women in the Military,* 4 (Winter): 1–7.

———. 2003. "'Emilia Plater' Independent Women's Battalion." Pages 149–151 in *Amazons to Fighter Pilots.* Edited by Reina Pennington. Vol. 1. Westport, CT: Greenwood.

Saywell, Shelley. 1985. *Women in War.* Markham, ON: Penguin Books Canada.

POSTERS, U.S., IMAGES OF WOMEN IN WORLD WAR II

Variety of depictions of women in U.S. World War II posters. Such images, like the narratives in general, were by no means unique to U.S. propaganda. Not all women in U.S. posters were American: some were the victims of Nazi or Japanese rape, ravage, torture, and political repression. By and large, images of American women were seductively favorable. Women in nurse or Red Cross uniforms appeared assertive, attractive, patriotic, and capable. Countless images of strong, hardworking factory employees such as the Rosie the Riveter on recruiting and morale-building posters testified to women's contributions to the war effort. Some images suggested the self-sacrificing, patient woman who stoically suffered through war's home front hardships as she waited at the hearth for a husband or son's return. But other images presented women as naively careless, or even as "enemy agents" or "saboteuses;" women whose loose lips or loose sexual ways put American men in danger, either of being torpedoed or brought down by a venereal disease.

A massive poster campaign by the United States during World War II manifested a combination of advertising, political propaganda, and art. The Office of War Information took command, working with other government agencies, the military, writers, artists, and corporate groups to produce such stunning graphics as the Four Freedom posters by realist Norman Rockwell, modernist artist Ben Shahn's exhortations to oppose fascism, or the more abstract poster urging increased production, "Give 'Em Both Barrels" by Jean Carlu. Millions of posters were slapped up on factory walls, at bus stops, in grocery stores, on billboards, in schools, and offices. They spoke to the nation's total mobilization with 10 million men in uniform, and 7 million women moving to another county or state to work. Printed in huge runs, in black and white or color, from the size of a notebook sheet to immense images, posters were part of "the most intense visual experience in the nation's history" up to that time (Roeder 1993, 62).

The posters addressed all areas of home front life, as well as personnel serving overseas. Some posters were directed at encouraging desired behavior, from daily teeth brushing to saving fats, buying war bonds to planting victory gardens. Others aimed to restrict behavior, curtailing loose talk that might aid the enemy, stopping absenteeism or sloppy work habits, or curtailing the spread of venereal diseases. Clearly the posters suggest a mobilized nation that needed to rely on men and women's conscious involvement in the war effort.

Poster and film images glorified and glamorized the roles of working women and suggested that a woman's femininity need not be sacrificed. Whether fulfilling their duty in the home, factory, office, or military, women were portrayed as attractive, confident, and resolved to do their part to win the war. (From the National Archives Records and Administration exhibit, Powers of Persuasion 1994–1995)

At the same time, many posters relied on restrictively gendered views. Some highlighted traditionally maligned images of women, while the men who did bad things were made to look like bumbling idiots or just plain naïve (the loose talking women and the men who chose the wrong woman). Others depicted the enemy, German and Japanese, as rats and other vicious animals.

Perhaps the most famous wartime image was the "We Can Do It" poster, which shows a muscular woman dressed for factory work. A Norman Rockwell poster shows another "Rosie the Riveter" with lunch box and welding tool at her side, fashioned after Michelangelo's *Isaiah* (initially a cover of *The Saturday Evening Post,* this image helped introduce the iconic Rosie to the nation). Countless posters showed lipsticked, well-coiffed, appealing white women, at times alongside a uniformed man, sometimes peeking out from under a Jeep, urging women to join the Red Cross, Army nursing corps, or other war services.

More sinister images in the security campaign showed women as the ultimate lures to obtain precious military information. The poster "Wanted for Murder" suggested the mugshot of a woman who had perhaps inadvertently passed on war-related information. Posters that spoke about sexual relations offered the most consistently negative images of women. "She looked clean, but . . ." one poster moaned, suggesting that the line between clean and dirty or good and bad was nearly imperceptible. "Saboteuse," a yellowish poster declared, showing an infected

U.S. WAR POSTERS

At least one viewer voiced objection to the negative depiction of women in some U.S. war posters: "American women who are knitting, rolling bandages, working long hours at war jobs and then carrying on with 'women's work' at home—in short, taking over the countless drab duties to which no salary and no glory are attached, resent these unwarranted and presumptuous accusations which have no basis in fact, but from the time-worn gags of newspaper funny men."

—A letter from a resident of Hawaii to the Office of War Information, from NARA "Powers of Persuasion" exhibit. http://www.archives.gov/exhibit_hall/powers_of_persuasion/powers_of_persuasion_home.html (accessed March 4, 2005).

woman lurking in a doorway while near-innocent soldiers sauntered by. These posters, along with those urging men to "take a pro" (a prophylactic), supplemented the military and public health organizations' extensive campaign to curtail prostitution, teenage sexual promiscuity, and the spread of venereal disease, which took a serious toll on work-hours in the military. Such posters did not appeal to any sense of sexual morality other than the underlying fears of the sexually active woman.

—*Page Delano*

See also Literature of World War II, U.S., Depiction of Women in

References and Further Reading

Roeder, George. 1993. *The Censored War: American Visual Experience during World War II*. New Haven, CT: Yale.

Winkler, Alan. 1972. *The Politics of Propaganda: The Office of War Information, 1942–1945*. New Haven, CT: Yale.

RAANC

See Australian Army Nursing Service/Royal Australian Army Nursing Corps

RANI OF JHANSI

See Lakshmi Bai and Sepoy Rebellion

RAPE: RED ARMY IN WORLD WAR II

Fate of German and other women at the hands of the victorious Red Army in World War II. Following the Russian success at the Battle of Kursk in the spring of 1943, the Russians began pushing the Germans back as they headed for Berlin. For women in the regions traversed or occupied by the Russian soldiers, this advance resulted in inescapable brutality suffered at the hands of the Soviets. Estimates of the total number of women raped by the advancing Red Army reach past 2 million (Beevor 2002, 410). Females of all ages, from girls as young as 12 to elderly women approaching the end of their natural lifespan, experienced rape without any hope of protection or intervention. Neither age, nationality, religion, nor political association served to spare women from victimization at the hands of their occupiers or, as was often the case, liberators.

Revenge is attributed as the main motive behind the rapists' crimes. German policy toward Russians, military or civilian, allowed no mercy toward a race viewed as subhuman, and the soldiers of the Red Army used rape and other hate crimes to inflict retribution for this policy. Even some Russian women approved of rape under the same reasoning of punishing an enemy undeserving of mercy. Not all of the rape victims were German, however. Rape occurred wherever the Red Army passed, except for Bulgaria. According to Norman Naimark, the Red Army was less of a problem in Bulgaria due to the "superior leadership and discipline" of Marshal F. I. Tolbukhin and his officers and because the Bulgarians welcomed the Soviet troops, who were regarded by the Bulgarians as liberators (Naimark 1995, 70). Elsewhere the cruelty was due to out-of-control soldiers consumed with lust fueled by alcohol. Gangs of Russian soldiers raped Poles (Beevor 2002, 107), Romanians, Hungarians (Naimark 1995, 70), and even Russian and Ukrainian victims

RAPE COMMITTED BY THE RED ARMY IN GERMANY

"Beginning in East Prussia in January 1945, reaching a crescendo in the two-week battle for Berlin and continuing after the end of hostilities, rape ran at epidemic levels. The Red Army's officers had neither the will nor inclination to stop it. During the battle, 130,000 women were raped, 10 percent of whom committed suicide. In the 1945 campaign in Germany, Beevor establishes, with unimpeachable scholarship, that at least 2 million women were ravished, many in gang rapes. Soviet soldiers violated all in their path, not just young German girls but women in their 70s, and even Russian prisoners."
— Frank McLynn, "The Triumph of Terror," *Independent* (London), May 2, 2002.
Quoted on the website for *Berlin: The Downfall 1945* by Anthony Beevor.
http://www.arlindo-correia.com/040702.html (accessed August 3, 2004).

from the Nazi-run labor camps that the Red Army was supposedly liberating (Beevor 2002, 107). Women emerging from labor camps experienced gang rape, often repeatedly, rather than liberation. Perhaps they were viewed as collaborators.

Rape of German women in Berlin was at its worst during the first week of the occupation but continued into 1948 (Naimark 1995, 79). Anthony Beevor emphasizes that the wave of rape during the initial occupation stemmed from revenge but then became a case of "the spoils going to the victor." Stalin and other officials knew of the problem but took no major action to halt it. Official Soviet policy toward rape did not address the problem as a criminal act but rather as one damaging to the Soviets' international image or as a health concern for the soldiers involved.

Until 1948, when orders confined Russian soldiers to their posts within the Russian zone of occupation in Germany, soldiers were rarely punished for rape. Soviet leaders wanted to halt the growing disdain for the Red Army and the communism that it was purported to represent, but the rampant occurrence of rape by their soldiers proved to be quite damaging. Following the war, women were not inclined to vote for communists, given their memory of them as rapists. Military authorities attempted to disseminate propaganda to dissuade rape, with the reasoning

that Russian soldiers should not want to "soil" themselves with the vile German enemy; this approach, however, proved ineffective. For women and their family members who dared to complain to occupying authorities, the only response was inaction. Authorities punished soldiers more often for looting, arson, and other forms of destruction of property than they punished them for rape.

Attempts of civilians to protect women were futile, but townspeople tried varying methods to warn each other of the approaching Red Army. Citizens sounded alarms, often banging pots and pans, creating a chain reaction of alarms across the town. In some instances, the sheer noise from these warnings served to hurry the exiting of the soldiers, irritated by the cacophonous onslaught of noise. Individually, men attempting to protect women suffered retribution for their actions. Women tried to protect themselves either by dressing as if they were important people or by dressing as dirty, unkempt, and unattractive individuals. These techniques proved fruitless. In some cases, a desperate woman hoping to avoid gang rape would approach a soldier and offer herself for his sole use.

The victims experienced common effects and results of rape, such as post-traumatic stress, unintended pregnancies, sexually transmitted diseases, and abandonment. Many women died, committed suicide, or obtained abortions after being raped. Doctors, attempting to alleviate the problems, set up makeshift clinics to dole out penicillin, if it was available, or to perform abortions, despite legal restrictions on abortion. While some women preferred abortion, others kept their babies or gave them to organizations willing or able to care for their unwanted children. Men returning home also suffered when they discovered that their wives or fiancées had been raped. Their responses were often not supportive, adding to the victims' emotional trauma. Raped women soon found engagements broken off or relationships permanently changed. Though no official estimate of the number of children conceived through rape following the Red Army occupation has been calculated, people knew which children came from Russian fathers.

—*Rachael I. Cherry*

See also Rape in War

References and Further Reading

Beevor, Anthony. 2002. *The Fall of Berlin, 1945.* New York: Viking.

Hlihor, Constantin, and Ioan Scurtu. 2001. *The Red Army in Romania.* Oxford: The Center for Romanian Studies.

Naimark, Norman M. 1995. *The Russians in Germany: A History of the Soviet Zone of Occupation, 1945–1949.* Cambridge, MA: The Belknap Press of Harvard University.

Peterson, Edward N. 1999. *Russian Commands and German Occupation, 1945–1949.* New York: Peter Lang.

Rape in War

Mass rape in war. Rape in war is not a modern phenomenon. It has always occurred during warfare. Opinions explaining this vary considerably. Regardless of the reasons for its occurrence, the failure to punish the perpetrators has remained consistent over time. This lack of accountability is directly linked to the gender-specific nature of the crime.

In the Middle Ages, most people believed that soldiers raped for sexual release. Many cultures and individual men believed that women existed to satisfy men's sexual appetites. Considered men's property, women were treated as part of the victor's booty.

To promote aggressive behavior, it has not been uncommon for armies or individual officers to encourage soldiers to rape or at least to tolerate their behavior. It functions as a form of male bonding. Furthermore, in a perverted way of reasoning, if it is heroic to kill enemy men during war, it must be heroic to rape an enemy woman. Since women began openly joining the military in the twentieth century, male soldiers raping female comrades has become a problem.

Rape is a sexual form of torture with the vast majority of victims being female. As a method of torture, rape (or its threat) is employed to obtain information and to display power and the ability to dominate. It may be in retaliation for the woman's own actions or those of her male compatriots. Enemy males, also sometimes sodomized, often are more reluctant to reveal the abuse than are females. The gendered nature of the crime of rape is a factor in the apparent reluctance to punish perpetrators. There is a gendered imbalance of power in the world, especially in the upper echelons of government and military, the very people with the power to prosecute such wartime offenses.

Raping a woman humiliates not only her but also her male guardian, exposing his inability to fulfill his duty to protect the women of his family. Thus, raping a woman in front of her parents or husband is common practice during war. In cultures placing a high value on women's sexual purity, rape may lead to ostracism from family and community or even to the woman's murder or suicide. In other instances, women are offered to the enemy in an attempt to protect others.

Repeated brutalization in gang rapes sometimes results in the victim's death, often from vaginal bleeding. The likelihood of permanent physical damage, including infertility, increases

RAPE IN WAR

"From conflicts in Bosnia and Herzegovina to Peru to Rwanda, girls and women have been singled out for rape, imprisonment, torture and execution. Rape, identified by psychologists as the most intrusive of traumatic events, has been documented in many armed conflicts including those in Bangladesh, Cambodia, Cyprus, Haiti, Liberia, Somalia, and Uganda."

—UNICEF. "Sexual Violence as a Weapon of War."
http://www.unicef.org/sowc96pk/sexviol.htm (accessed March 8, 2004).

Reports of Rape

"1991–1994: Serbian paramilitary troops used rape systematically as a tactic to encourage Bosnian Muslim women to flee from their land.

"1994: In Rwanda, Hutu leaders ordered their troops to rape Tutsi women as an integral part of their genocidal campaign.

"1997: Secular women were targeted by Muslim revolutionaries in Algeria and reduced to sex slaves.

"1998: Indonesian security forces allegedly raped ethnic Chinese women during a spate of major rioting.

"Late 1990s: Serbian military and paramilitary units systematically raped ethnic Albanian Muslim women during the unrest in Kosovo."

—"Rape of Women during Wartime: Before, during, and since World War II."
Religious Tolerance.org. http://www.religioustolerance.org/war_rape.htm (accessed March 8, 2004).

---

with each assault. The chances of contracting a venereal disease also rise since military infection rates are higher than civilian (Machel 2001, 44). Rape is sometimes even employed as a means of spreading such infections.

Pregnancy can also result. Impregnation, as a means of destabilizing the opposing community, may be the desired result. Moreover, some soldiers, surrounded by the ever-present possibility of death, may rape because of a desire (conscious or not) for the perceived immortality gained by producing a child. Hatred of women's reproductive powers may also be a factor. In addition to psychological and possible physical, social, and economic damage, pregnancy creates more problems for the rape victim. If she herself is not ostracized, the child probably will be. If she is alone in a war-torn country, providing for another mouth will be difficult. Under such conditions, many will choose to abort.

Rape is sometimes employed as a rhetorical tool. Implications of having committed rape emasculate the accused and fuel resistance. Reports of rape are employed to garner the assistance of other neutral groups by harnessing feelings of sympathy, horror, and outrage. This rhetoric, however, can undermine reality through willful exaggeration and desensitization.

In 1998 the U.N. International Criminal Tribunal for Rwanda finally set a precedent by recognizing rape, when it occurred on a massive scale or under orders, as a form of torture. While rape had been recognized as a war crime in the past (for example, in the Fourth Geneva Convention of 1949, Article 27), no one had ever been successfully prosecuted for it until the conviction of Jean-Paul Akeyasu in 1998. At the International Tribunal at The Hague dealing with war crimes in the former Yugoslavia, genocidal rape was also declared an indictable offense.

—*Tonya M. Lambert*

See also Chechnya, Impact on Women of Wars in; East Timor, Abuse of Women during War; Guatemala, Civil Conflict and Women; Kashmir, Conflict in, Women and; Rape: Red Army in World War II; Sudan, Women and the Civil War in; Yugoslavia, Women and the Wars That Accompanied the Disintegration of Yugoslavia

References and Further Reading

Machel, Graca. 2001. *The Impact of War on Children*. Vancouver and Toronto: UBC.

Ryan, Louise. 2000. "Drunken Tans": Representations of Sex and Violence in the Anglo-Irish War (1919–1921). *Feminist Review* 46:73–94.

Tanaka, Yuki. 1996. *Hidden Horrors: Japanese War Crimes in World War II*. Boulder, CO: Westview.

Teo, Hsu-Ming. 1996. The Continuum of Sexual Violence in Occupied Germany, 1945–1949. *Women's History Review* 5(2): 191–218.

Thomas, Dorothy Q., and Regan E. Ralph. 1999. Rape in War: The Case of Bosnia. Pages 203–218 in *Gender Politics in the Western Balkans: Women and Society in Yugoslavia and the Yugoslav Successor States*. Edited by Sabrina P. Ramet. University Park: Pennsylvania State University.

RASKOVA (NÉE MALININA), MARINA MIKHAILOVNA (1912–1943)

Woman Soviet pilot who persuaded Stalin to form three women's combat wings at a time when there was no shortage of male aircrews and combat aircraft were scarce and outdated.

Marina Raskova was a talented organizer and bold dreamer, with a personality that endeared her to subordinates. She acquired specialized knowledge of navigation while employed as draftswoman at the N. E. Zhukovsky Air Force Engineering Academy. The first Soviet woman to earn the diploma of professional air navigator, she became navigation instructor at the academy. She also trained to fly at the academy's expense. A pupil of famous navigators A. Beliakov and I. Spirin, as well as a participant from 1935 in various competitive flights, Raskova became an important navigator in Moscow's May Day air shows.

She gained special fame as the navigator of an ANT-37, Rodina (Homeland), piloted by Valentina Grizodubova and copiloted by Polina Osipenko, during a pioneering nonstop flight from Moscow to the Pacific (6,450 kilometers) executed on September 24–25, 1938. Having failed to reach the destination airfield in Komsomol'sk on the Amur River, the pilot, running out of fuel, was forced to land immediately. (The crew suspected that their mechanics failed to refill the tanks after the aircraft had been tested on the ground.) Fearful of nosing over, the pilot ordered Raskova, located in the forward cabin, to bail out. As a result she unexpectedly spent ten days wandering in the taiga. For their feat, the crew of three were each awarded Hero of the Soviet Union, the highest Soviet military decoration, becoming the first three Soviet women to be thus honored.

After the German invasion, Air Group No. 122 was created. The recruitment of women to the air group began in October 1941 in Moscow and continued in Engels near Stalingrad. The women were at first trained as aircraft and technical support crews (1941–1942). The group evolved into three combat wings: 586th Fighter Regiment, 587th Dive Bomber Regiment (initially commanded by Major Raskova), and 588th Night Bomber Regiment. In 1943 the 588th and 587th were to be renamed, respectively, 46th Taman Guards Night Bomber Regiment and 125th M. M. Raskova Borisov Guards Dive Bomber Regiment.

After Raskova died in a crash during the heavy snowstorm of January 4, 1943, her subordinates pledged to earn the right for their unit to bear her name and qualify as a guards regiment. Both objectives were reached in 1943. Moreover, the regiment's Second Squadron's tactics, as applied in the air battle of June 4, 1943, over the Kuban area, became a model for the entire Soviet bomber aviation.

Raskova's ashes were immured in the Kremlin Wall beside those of fighter pilot Polina Osipenko, who had perished in a training accident in 1939.

—*Kazimiera J. Cottam*

See also Soviet Union, 46th Taman Guards Bomber Aviation Regiment; Soviet Union Air Defense, 586th Fighter Aviation Regiment

References and Further Reading

Cottam, Kazimiera J. 1997. *Women in Air War.* Nepean, Ontario, Canada: New Military Publishing. (Original collection edited by Militsa A. Kazarinova et al., 2nd ed. 1971, under the title *V nebe frontovom.*)

———. 1998. *Women in War and Resistance.* Nepean, Ontario, Canada: New Military Publishing.

Pennington, Reina. 2003. Raskova, Marina Mikhailovna Malinina. Pages 351–354 in *Amazons to Fighter Pilots.* Edited by Reina Pennington. Vol. 2. Westport, CT: Greenwood Press.

RAVENSBRÜCK

Nazi concentration camp for women. The camp was located 56 miles north of Berlin on swampy land near the Havel River. On May 15, 1939, the first prisoners arrived, 867 women transferred from Lichtenburg. The camp was staffed by 150 female SS supervisors (*Aufseherinnen*), male guards, and male administrators. In 1942 and 1943 Ravensbrück served as a training base for women supervisors, and 3,500 women were trained there for work in Ravensbrück and other camps. Among them was Irma Grese.

In late 1939 the camp held 2,000 prisoners. By late 1942 there were 10,800. In 1944 the main camp contained 26,700 female prisoners and several thousand female minors grouped in a detention camp for children. Most of the camp was evacuated in March 1945 as the Russians approached, and 24,500 prisoners were marched into Mechlenburg. When the camp was liberated by Soviet troops on April 29–30, they found 3,500 ill and famished females.

During its existence, at least 107,753 (123,000 according to Tillion 1975, 17) women were interned in Ravensbrück and its satellite detention centers, most of which were industrial slave-labor sites. There was a concentration camp for men near Ravensbrück, but it was connected with the Sachsenhausen camp rather than Ravensbrück. Approximately 50,000 inmates died while imprisoned at Ravensbrück. In addition to general overwork, exposure, malnutrition, disease, and abuse, individual women were subjected to excruciating medical experimentation in the camp, including bone transplants, induced gas gangrene, and deliberately infected incisions. Early in 1945 a gas chamber was constructed at the camp, and between 2,200 and 2,400 women were gassed there. Max Koegel, who had been commandant from the opening of the camp until the summer of 1942, committed suicide in 1946. His successor, Fritz Suhren, was tried and executed in 1950.

Germaine Tillion, a member of the French resistance, was arrested on August 13, 1942. She and her mother, who was also involved in the resistance, were sent to Ravensbrück in October 1943. She wrote,

For a stipulated price the businessman or industrialist received the 500 or 1,000 women requested, along with Aufseherinnen who, equipped with trained dogs and clubs, could force twelve hours of work a day from exhausted and starving women, right up to the point of death. They would be replaced with more of the same, without additional cost to the client. But thanks to the Aufseherinnen, the dogs, and the beatings, it was a perfect cycle, with no waste; the prisoners worked until they could work no more. (Tillion 1975, 42–43)

—*Bernard Cook*

See also Grese, Irma; Holocaust and Jewish Women; Tillion, Germaine

References and Further Reading

Dressen, Willy. 1991. Ravensbrück. Pages 757–758 in *The Encyclopedia of the Third Reich*. Edited by Christian Zentner and Friedemann Bedürftig; translated and edited by Amy Hackett. Vol. 2. New York: Macmillan.

Museum of Tolerance Multimedia Learning Center. "Ravensbrück." http://motlc.weisenthal.com /text/x28/xr2821.html (accessed February 5, 2004).

Spector, Shmuel. 1990. Ravensbrück. Pages 1226–1227 in *Encyclopedia of the Holocaust*. New York: Macmillan.

Tillion, Germaine. 1975. *Ravensbrück: An Eyewitness Account of a Woman's Concentration Camp*. Garden City, NY: Anchor.

Red Army Faction, West Germany, Women of the

Leftist terrorist group in West Germany. The Red Army Faction (RAF) grew out of the West German student movement that began around 1965 as a nonviolent protest against poor conditions in universities, widespread political apathy, and, most generally, the vestiges of authoritarianism that young people perceived in their society. The German movement had at its core a unique psychological dilemma as young, idealistic Germans brought up in postwar peace and affluence felt overwhelming guilt for the crimes of their parents' generation. Within a few years the movement was espousing, in theory at least,

violent struggle against the "fascist" state in imitation of that seen in colonized lands in the Third World. The RAF, officially founded in 1970, aimed, through specifically directed violence, to induce the state to overreact, revealing a true fascist nature that it had carefully hidden behind the mask of democracy.

Women were involved in the leadership of the RAF from its inception. In 1968 Gudrun Ensslin was one of four radicals who set several fires in a Frankfurt department store. Two years later, Ensslin and journalist Ulrike Meinhof, with the help of Irene Goergens, Ingrid Schubert, and Astrid Proll, as well as several men, freed Andreas Baader, one of the arsonists, from prison. The act brought the group, called the Baader-Meinhof gang by the press, into existence. It later adopted "Red Army Faction" as its official title. Although Ensslin, Baader, and a few others formed the core of the group, Ulrike Meinhof, as a well-regarded journalist for the leftist paper *konkret* (Concrete), was the best-known member of RAF, and she wrote most of the group's manifestos and other explanatory material. In 1970 nine RAF members, including five women (Meinhof, Ensslin, Monika Berberich, Brigitte Asdonk, and Petra Schelm), traveled to Beirut to train with Palestinian militants. In the early years of the group's existence, a majority of members were women, and from 1970 to the group's dissolution in 1998, women comprised almost 40 percent of its membership.

As was the case in other left-wing terrorist groups in Europe and the United States, core members of the RAF tended to embrace radical political views and movements but forsook normal political action as they embarked on a policy of direct action. Women in the RAF felt the psychological burden of the Nazi past just as men did; their ideological construction of the state as a fascist entity to be opposed with violence demonstrated their determination to "redo" the past by responding to evil as they wished their parents had done. Of course, the government of West Germany, whatever its faults, did not in any way approach the criminality of the Third Reich.

The presence of women in the RAF had an unintended beneficial effect for the group, as members could satisfy their emotional and sexual needs through relationships with other group members. The RAF was therefore less vulnerable to betrayal by outsiders, and members' loyalties were less likely to be diluted by the pull of personal relationships outside the group. On the other hand, rocky relationships within the group consumed time and energy and at times diminished the effectiveness of the organization.

By including women, the RAF, unlike extremist right-wing groups, doubled the number of potential recruits it could reach. Some female members of the RAF became involved through their relationships with male members, such as Astrid Proll, who was drawn into the group by her brother, Thorwald. Astrid went on to play a central role in the group while Thorwald lost his nerve and was excluded. Monika Berberich was RAF founder Horst Mahler's assistant, and Petra Schelm was the girlfriend of member Manfred Grashof. Eyewitnesses noted that female RAF members were more cruel than male members; the observation may be accurate, or it may reflect a tendency to find female violence more shocking than male.

Women in the RAF carried out activities that men could never have done. Perhaps the best instance occurred in 1985, when a female member of the group met a young U.S. soldier in a bar and lured him to a nearby woods, where he was killed and his military identification stolen. The card was used by a male RAF member to gain access to Rhine-Main Air Base, where a bomb was set off, killing two.

—*Anni P. Baker*

See also Baader-Meinhof Gang; Peru: Shining Path; Red Brigades, Italy, Women of the

References and Further Reading

Becker, Jillian. 1977. *Hitler's Children: The Story of the Baader-Meinhof Terrorist Gang.* Philadelphia: Lippincott.

Horchem, Hans Josef. 1986. *Terrorism in West Germany.* London: Institute for the Study of Conflict.

RED BRIGADES, ITALY, WOMEN OF THE

From 1970 to 1988 the largest and most deadly left-wing terrorist organization in Italy. The Red Brigades (RB) were responsible for most of the 415 deaths through terrorism during that period, including 75 assassinations and twice as many unsuccessful attempts. It also conducted 17 political kidnappings, some of which ended in death, most famously the abduction of former Italian Prime Minister Aldo Moro in 1979. The RB tended to avoid the use of indiscriminate bombing as a tactic, preferring instead to target specific individuals, although others such as police, guards, drivers, and bystanders were wounded and killed as a result of its operations. The RB drew on Marxist ideology to define its goal of destroying the state and creating a proletarian dictatorship.

At its height in the late 1970s, the RB included 600 full-time members as well as thousands of supporters who provided logistical assistance and funds. Most members of the RB had begun with radical politics but, frustrated by inaction, broke away from former associates and took the final step into violence. The group survived four "generations," as imprisoned members were replaced by younger recruits.

As was the case in many left-wing terror groups of the period, women made up at least 30 percent of the RB, and the percentage of female leadership was even higher. They seem to have joined the group for the same combination of ideological and personal reasons as their male comrades. Many RB women grew up having artisan, working-class, or peasant backgrounds, with parents who espoused left-wing or communist views. Others came from middle-class families where religious belief gave them their first impetus toward social transformation. A few had fractious relationships with their parents, but most came from close and contented families; family trauma has not been found to correlate with involvement in terrorism. Female RB members saw women as a distinct group experiencing a particular type of oppression, but they rejected the consciousness-raising activities of the women's movement in the 1970s as time-wasting and fruitless. Instead they embraced the concept of revolutionary violence as the only means of societal transformation and put their faith in the Marxist model that would, they expected, erase gender distinctions along with those of class. Although women often were exposed to radical ideology through boyfriends or husbands, those who became involved in RB terrorism joined the group voluntarily, and many female terrorists were more conversant than men in ideological fine points because they felt compelled to prove and reprove their dedication.

The experience of Margherita Cagol, one of the three founders of the RB in 1970, illustrates many of these trends. Cagol grew up in Trent in a stable middle-class family where she was noted for her religious sensibility and concern for the poor. She attended the University of Trent, where she embraced radical politics wholeheartedly, marrying Renato Curcio, a fellow revolutionary. Although Curcio and Carlo Franceschini are frequently named as the founders of the RB, Cagol's role was equally important. On September 8, 1974, Curcio was arrested by the police in connection with a series of bombings, but five months later, Cagol freed him. On June 5, 1975, she was killed in a shootout with the Italian gendarmerie, the Carabinieri, the first RB militant to die. Curcio was recaptured in January 1976.

Like Margherita Cagol, women in the RB participated in assassinations, bank robberies, and gun battles, but they also acted as lookouts, scouts, drivers, and in other roles where a woman, sometimes with a child in tow, would be unlikely to attract attention. Some resented this unexciting role and wanted to be more directly involved in exciting exploits.

The RB's comradeship and sense of belonging were attractive to women and men and led many members into the group; by the 1980s, however, the RB was decimated by arrests. Many women who found themselves in prison for long periods faced the likelihood that they would not see their children for years; others struggled with the reality that they might never have children. For many RB women both in and out of prison, the years of disillusion following their involvement with the group brought depression, drug and alcohol abuse, and other mental and physical illnesses. In 1987, concerned about the generation of young people who had wasted their lives on destructive activity, the Italian government pardoned RB members who renounced violence; almost 600 men and women did so. But no pardon could retrieve the decades or bring back the hundreds of lives lost to terrorism.

—*Anni P. Baker*

See also Peru: Shining Path; Red Army Faction, West Germany, Women of the

References and Further Reading

Catanzaro, Raimondo. 1991. *The Red Brigades and Left-Wing Terrorism in Italy.* New York: St. Martin's.

Meade, Robert C. 1990. *The Red Brigades: The Story of Italian Terrorism.* New York: St. Martin's.

RED CROSS OF THE UNITED STATES: WORLD WAR I AND WORLD WAR II

U.S. component of the International Red Cross, which provided nurses to the U.S. Army and Navy and organized many war-related relief efforts during World Wars I and II. In September 1914, when an American Red Cross mercy ship sailed out of New York harbor bound for Europe to help soldiers and civilians all over the continent, the U.S. Red Cross organization had 562 chapters and about 500,000 members. World War I transformed the American Red Cross into a powerful social force, and when the war ended in 1918, there were 3,724 chapters, 17,000 branches, and over 31 million members. Although those on the mercy ship were called back home after a year because of insufficient funds, they blazed a path of service for other Red Cross volunteers to follow.

In 1916 the surgeon general of the army and navy requested the Red Cross to organize 50 base hospitals in Europe, and the next year, when the United States entered the war, President Woodrow Wilson appointed a war council to run the Red Cross. Over 30 million Americans became actively involved in Red Cross work, including assembling comfort packages for soldiers overseas and making bandages. The Red Cross began a massive effort to raise funds and recruit members. As part of its effort, it recruited famous artists to produce posters. Alonzo E. Foringer produced a painting entitled "The Greatest Mother in the World," depicting the Red Cross as the ultimate compassionate caretaker.

Red Cross nurses were at the center of the organization's World War I efforts. Eighteen thousand Red Cross nurses served with the Army and Navy Nurse Corps, nearly half of them laboring on the home front to improve health and sanitary conditions. The rest worked at U.S. base hospitals in France, on hospital trains, or in evacuation and field hospitals. Two out of every three navy nurses and four out of five army nurses were Red Cross nurses. The Red Cross also contributed the first contingent of African American nurses certified to the military. The approximately 1,800 African American nurses were restricted by the military to "colored" cantonments, but the situation changed with the influenza pandemic that swept through the United States between 1918 and 1919. The pandemic allowed African American nurses to demonstrate their expertise and

indispensability and join the other Red Cross nurses, who worked tirelessly during the pandemic. Of the 24,000 nurses recruited for war service, 296 died in the line of duty. The Red Cross pioneered psychiatric nursing programs at veterans' hospitals, organized the manufacture of artificial limbs, and helped rehabilitate amputees and blind veterans.

In addition, Red Cross workers provided medical and recreational services for military personnel at home and overseas. The Red Cross established canteens for soldiers in the United States and in Europe. At its twenty two canteens near the front lines, Red Cross volunteers served coffee, donuts, and sandwiches. Canteen workers also comforted wounded soldiers and gave them coffee and water.

By Armistice Day, November 11, 1918, the Red Cross had compiled impressive war service statistics. Overseas, American Red Cross workers labored in over 25 countries and helped millions of civilian refugees as well as Allied soldiers. Over 2,000 American Red Cross workers stayed abroad after the war to continue their work, operating hospitals, convalescent homes, health centers, and clinics.

In the months before Pearl Harbor, Red Cross volunteers in Hawaii staged practice air raids and set up 10 emergency medical stations. When the Japanese attacked, Red Cross medical personnel were on the scene tending the wounded until the doctors could reach them. Twenty-four hours after the Pearl Harbor attack, Red Cross headquarters had organized 1,000 medically trained people for service with the military.

By the time the U.S. Marines landed on Guadalcanal in 1942, over 3 million volunteers were participating in Red Cross activities. More than 70,000 registered nurses served through the Red Cross. The organization created the Nurse's Aide Corps, a strictly volunteer program, to accommodate the nursing needs of the civilian population during World War II. The Nurse's Aide Corps, composed of volunteer women between the ages of 18 and 50, did nontechnical work that gave nurses more time for their professional duties. Volunteers had to pledge to work a minimum of 150 hours a year. The Red Cross recruited nearly 212,000 volunteers who accumulated 42 million hours of service by 1945.

The Red Cross arranged the shipment of food packages for U.S. and Allied prisoners of war. By 1944 Red Cross ships had transported almost 26 million aid packages. The American Red Cross also worked with the International Red Cross to inspect camps and exchange ill and wounded prisoners.

On the home front, the Red Cross organized people of all ages to collect scrap, serve in hospitals, make war relief materials, teach health and safety courses, and assist military people. By 1944 the number of Red Cross volunteers had doubled to 7.5 million. Red Cross blood drives were crucially important. Donating blood for wounded soldiers appealed to the patriotism of ordinary people who were not fighting at the front. By the time the wartime blood donor service was disbanded, the Red Cross had collected 13.4 million units of blood for the wounded.

This service organization provided essential support and relief to sick and wounded combatants and to prisoners of war. It also provided needed morale boosting both for combatants and noncombatants.

—*Kathleen Warnes*

See also Mercy Ship; Nurses, U.S. Army Nurse Corps in World War I; Nurses, U.S. Army Nurse Corps in World War II

References and Further Reading

Davison, Henry Pomeroy. 1920. *The American Red Cross in the Great War.* New York: Macmillan.

Dulles, Foster Rhea. 1971. *The American Red Cross, A History.* Westport, CT: Greenwood.

PBS.org. "Blood in War: Red Cross Blood Donor Service." http://www.pbs.org/wnet/redgold/basics /redcross.html (accessed March 17, 2004).

Redcross.org. "History of the American Red Cross." http://www.redcross.org/museum/19001919bhtml and http://www.redcrossaustin.org/historyhtml (accessed March 19, 2004).

REED, ESTHER DE BERDT (1746–1780)

Organized women's relief work in support of the American Revolution. In 1770, Esther De Berdt, the only daughter of a London trader, married Joseph Reed of New Jersey, who was studying law in England. The newlyweds and her mother settled in Philadelphia. Joseph Reed played a prominent role in the Revolution, serving as president of the first provincial convention in Pennsylvania in 1774 and later as one of Washington's aides.

With six young children (including three born during the war), Esther Reed could have retreated into domestic duties. Instead, in 1780 she formed the Ladies Association to systematically raise money for support of the army. Reed opened their campaign by publishing a pamphlet, *The Sentiments of an American Woman*, on June 10, 1780. The pamphlet listed women in history who had defended their country and called on all women to do so in this hour of need. Members of the association went door to door raising funds and wrote to prominent women in other states urging them to join in the fund-raising. Women in New Jersey, Maryland, and Virginia responded by organizing their own fund drives. The Pennsylvania women raised over $300,000 in Continental dollars (or $7,500 in specie).

Originally the women intended to give each soldier cash, but George Washington opposed this, so the women instead bought cloth, hired sewers, and produced shirts for the soldiers. They sewed many garments themselves. Esther Reed, already weakened from smallpox and the birth of a son in May 1780, died from dysentery on September 18. Sarah Franklin Bache oversaw completion of the task and the delivery of 2,200 shirts to soldiers by December 1780.

—*Joan R. Gundersen*

See also American Revolution, Role of Women in the

References and Further Reading

Gundersen, Joan R. 1996. *"To Be Useful to the World": Women in Revolutionary America, 1740–1790.* New York: Twayne Publishing.

Kerber, Linda K. 1980. *Women of the Republic: Intellect and Ideology in Revolutionary America.* Chapel Hill: University of North Carolina Press; Institute of Early American History and Culture.

Norton, Mary Beth. 1980. *Liberty's Daughters: The Revolutionary Experience of American Women, 1750–1800.* Boston: Little, Brown.

REIK, HAVIVA (1914–1944)

Member of an underground mission sent into Nazi-occupied Slovakia in 1944 by the Yishuv, the Jewish community of Palestine. Born in the village of Shayo Hasso near Banska-Bystrica, Slovakia, Haviva Reik was a member of the Ha-Shomer ha-Tsa'ir Zionist youth movement. In 1938, when Slovakia was annexed by Hungary, Reik became involved in the rescue activities of the Jewish National Fund and the Zionist Organization of Slovakia to help Slovak Jews relocate to Palestine. In December 1938, she left Slovakia for Palestine, joining the Kibbutz Ma'anit. Once there, Haviva enlisted in the Palmah, the fighting branch of the Hagana, the Yishuv's underground military organization.

When Haviva's service to the Palmah was over, she volunteered to become a parachutist for the Hagana, dropping into Nazi-occupied Europe to rescue Jews and to lead them to safety in Palestine. After intensive training, she and other members traveled to Italy to await air transport to Slovakia. Their mission was to reach the Slovak capital, Bratislava, and establish contact with the leaders of the Pracovna Skupina (Working Group), a semiunderground Jewish rescue organization. Although British authorities aided the three male members of her group to parachute into Slovakia, they refused to send a woman behind enemy lines. On September 21, 1944, Haviva parachuted into Slovakia with the assistance of U.S. pilots who were flying to Banska-Bystrica, the heart of the Slovak National Uprising. At the end of September, a fifth member of the group parachuted into Slovakia carrying radio transmitters for the unit.

Because of the upheaval in Banska-Bystrica, Haviva and her Hagana comrades found their time consumed with merely staying alive. They were, however, able to gather the support of forty Jewish partisans. In late October when German Nazis suppressed the Slovak National Uprising, members of the resistance fled to the mountains. They set up a small camp near the village of Bukovice, attempting to gather weapons and fortifying their position.

Six days after they reached the village, the camp was entered by Ukrainian Galacia Waffen, a division of SS troops. Haviva was captured, interrogated, tortured, and sentenced to death as a spy. On November 20, 1944, Haviva was executed in Kremnica, her body thrown into a mass grave with 250 other Jews and Gypsies. Haviva's body was later recovered, and on September 10, 1952, her remains were buried in the Mt. Herzl military cemetery in Jerusalem.

Today, Haviva Reik is considered a Zionist hero. Her courage and loyalty are memorialized in the Kibbutz Lahavot Haviva; the ship *Haviva Reik,* which carried Jewish immigrants to Palestine after World War II; and the Givat Haviva, an Israeli educational center.

—*Joann M. Ross*

See also Bruskina, Masha; Holocaust and Jewish Women; Kempner, Vitka; Korczak, Rozka; Landau, Emilia

References and Further Reading

Laska, Vera, ed. 1983. *Women in the Resistance and in the Holocaust: The Voice of Eyewitnesses.* Westport, CT: Greenwood.

Museum of Tolerance Online Multimedia Learning Center: Simon Wiesenthal Center. "Reik, Haviva." http://motlc.wiesenthal.com/text/x25/xm2537.html (accessed May 20, 2004).

Syrkin, Marie. 1947. *Blessed in the Match: The Story of Jewish Resistance.* Philadelphia: The Jewish Publication Society of America.

Yadvashem.org. Shoah Resource Center. The International School for Holocaust Studies. "Reik, Haviva." http://www.yadvashem.org (accessed May 20, 2004).

REITSCH, HANNA
(1912–1976)

German test pilot. Hanna Reitsch was the only woman to receive an Iron Cross from Hitler and was one of the last people to see him alive in 1945. Born the daughter of a prominent ophthalmologist in Hirschberg, Germany, on March 29, 1912, Reitsch was expected to attend medical school, which she began in 1930. She convinced her parents that her ambition to be a medical missionary required her to take glider lessons at nearby Galgenberg, where she quickly gained a reputation as a fearless and gifted pilot and mechanic. After setting a gilder altitude record in 1933, Reitsch began an aviation career as a flying instructor, film stunt pilot, and member of several scientific crews studying air currents in South America.

In 1934, through her personal friendships with Werner von Braun, Ernst Udet (a World War I fighter ace), and General Robert Ritter von Greim, Reitsch was recruited to do government meteorology testing and public demonstrations of aircraft, including a flight over the 1936 Winter Olympics and an indoor arena flight of a helicopter. In 1937 she moved directly to the Luftwaffe testing labs at Reichlen. She was granted the title *Flugkapitan* (captain of the air) after test flying and offering design suggestions for a Storch fighter and the Messerschmidt ME163 "Rocket Plane." Reitsch's cool thinking allowed her to survive a series of catastrophic design failures that led to numerous crashes. For her bravery, she was awarded the Gold Medal for Flying, with a special diamond addition, by Hermann Goering in March 1941, then the Iron Cross First Class in February 1943 from Hitler himself. Reitsch was only the second woman ever awarded the Iron Cross and the only one to be publicly acknowledged by Hitler.

After seeing conditions on the Russian front during a morale tour in 1943, Reitsch collaborated with Otto Skorzeny in planning suicide flights using a modified V-1 rocket outfitted with a cockpit. Although Reitsch test-flew several of the flying missiles successfully, the Reich never adopted their plan. As the war went on, political tension increased because of her mentor von Greim's rivalry with Goering. Reitsch and von Greim went to great pains to be discreet about their friendship, but it was widely rumored that they were lovers, something Reitsch denied in her memoirs.

On April 26, 1945, Reitsch and von Greim were ordered to fly into Berlin and meet senior Nazi leaders in the underground Chancellery. Von Greim was wounded during the landing approach, and Reitsch brought the plane down at the Brandenburg Gate. She suspected they were to fly out members of the staff or the Goebbels children but was disappointed when she and von Greim were ordered to rally the remaining Luftwaffe for a defense of Berlin. Convinced the city was doomed, they left for Kitzbuhel, where both surrendered to U.S. troops. Reitsch's family, refugees in Salzburg, committed suicide, as did von Greim, who took cyanide while in custody. Reitsch chose not to carry through a suicide plan and instead served as an important witness to the last days in the Berlin Chancellery bunker.

Forbidden from flying after the war, Reitsch wrote her memoirs to support herself and to defend against her portrayal in Hugh Trevor-Roper's *Last Days of Hitler,* which derided her technical skill and painted her as a shrill and besotted acolyte of Hitler and von Greim. Returning to fly gliders in 1951, she left the sport in protest after being banned from traveling to Poland for competition in 1958. Reitsch subsequently traveled to

Africa, where she trained pilots for the new government of Ghana; she became an admirer of Kwame Nkrumah but was forced to flee the country when he was overthrown in 1966. Reitsch died of a heart attack on August 24, 1979, and was buried with her family in Salzburg.

—*Margaret Sankey*

See also Cochran, Jacqueline; Dalrymple, Mildred Inks; Fedutenko, Nadezhda Nikiforovna; Hobby, Oveta Culp; Johnson, Amy; Leska-Daab, Anna; Lewandowska, Jania

References and Further Reading

Piszkiewicz, Dennis. 1997. *From Nazi Test Pilot to Hitler's Bunker: The Fantastic Flights of Hanna Reitsch.* Westport, CT: Praeger.

Reitsch, Hanna. 1954. *Flying Is My Life.* New York: G. P. Putnam's Sons.

———. 1968. *Ich Flog für Kwame Nkrumah* [I Flew for Kwame Nkrumah]. Munich: J. F. Lehmann.

RIDDLE, TOBY

See Winema

RIEDESEL, FRIEDERIKE CHARLOTTE LUISE VON MASSOW VON (1746–1808)

An astute observer and diarist who accompanied her husband, Baron Friedrich von Riedesel, during his service as the senior Hessian general serving with the British in the United States from 1776 to 1783. Delayed by the birth of a son and by transport problems, the Baroness Friederike von Riedesel and her three small children arrived in Quebec in June 1777. She then traveled 150 miles (241 kilometers) through rough countryside to reunite briefly with her husband before returning 85 miles (137 kilometers) to her billet in Trois Rivieres.

In August 1777 the baroness and her children moved forward with General John Burgoyne as he pushed into New York. During the several engagements leading to the British surrender at Saratoga, their quarters became a hospital and at times was under fire. With Burgoyne's surrender on October 17, 1777, the baroness and her husband became prisoners of war.

Although the baroness faced numerous hardships, von Riedesel's rank opened doors. U.S. General Philip Schuyler hosted the family immediately after their surrender. Later they would exchange visits with elite families in Virginia and Maryland, including Thomas Jefferson and Charles Carroll. With each move the baroness scrambled to set up a working farm to supply their table.

After the von Riedesels had been held as prisoners in Boston for a year, the Convention Army, the British army that surrendered at Saratoga, was moved to Virginia. The baroness and her family took 2 months to cover the 550 miles (885 kilometers) to Virginia. They arrived in mid-January, cold and hungry, at their unsupplied, unfurnished rented plantation. After her husband had a stroke, he and the baroness traveled to one of Virginia's hot springs to recover. It was there they learned he was to be exchanged in New York for American prisoners held by the British.

The pregnant baroness and her children set out for New York in August 1779. She arrived at the end of November, having been delayed by visits, illness, and problems with the exchange. Cleared for active service in 1780, the baron was posted to Canada in 1781. The von Riedesels returned to Europe in 1783. The journal that Baroness von Riedesel kept during her travels and published on her return is a rich source describing the experiences of the war and the women who traveled with the army.

—*Joan R. Gundersen*

See also American Revolution, Role of Women in the

References and Further Reading

Leung, Michelle. 2000. Baroness Friederike von Riedesel, "Mrs. General." Pages 267–284 in *The Human Tradition in the American Revolution.* Edited by Nancy L. Rhoden and Ian K. Steele. Wilmington, DE: Scholarly Resources.

Riedesel, Friederike von. 1965. *Baroness von Riedesel and the American Revolution: Journal and Correspondence of a Tour of Duty, 1776–1783.* Translated by Marvin L. Brown Jr. Chapel Hill: University of North Carolina.

Thorpe, Louise Hall. 1962. *The Baroness and the General.* Boston: Little, Brown.

ROLFE, LILIAN (1914–1945)

British agent during World War II. Lilian Vera Rolfe was born in Paris on April 26, 1914. The daughter of George Samuel Rolfe, an accountant working in Paris, she moved to Brazil with her family at the age of sixteen. She worked in the British embassy in Rio de Janeiro. After monitoring German ships in the harbor of Rio de Janeiro, she went to London to participate more actively in the war effort. Rolfe joined the Women's Auxiliary Air Force (WAAF). She was fluent in French, and the Special Operations Executive (SOE) recruited her on November 26, 1943, to be trained as a wireless operator. She was given the code name Nadine and was parachuted with a small radio transmitter and receiver to a location near the city of Orléans on April 5, 1944. She worked with the Historian network headed by Captain George Wilkinson.

Rolfe sent radio messages from the French underground to London. She dispatched sixty seven messages despite the efforts of the Gestapo to find her. Her messages enabled supply drops by the British for the French resistance and provided information on German troop movements. She also participated in missions with the French resistance against the Nazis. Rolfe was involved in a gun battle at the small town of Olivet near Orléans and was finally arrested on July 31, 1944, in a house where her transmitter was located. She was taken to Fresnes prison and was shipped to the Ravensbrück concentration camp on August 8, 1944. After undergoing interrogation and torture, she was executed on February 5, 1945.

For her bravery and sacrifice, she was decorated with the Croix de Guerre in 1946 and listed on the Valençay SOE Memorial, and a street in Montargis was dedicated in her honor. In Great Britain her name was inscribed on the Runnymede Memorial in Surrey.

—*Patit Paban Mishra*

See also Atkins, Vera H.; Borrel, Andrée; Leigh, Vera; Olschanezky, Sonya; Rowden, Diana; Rudellat, Yvonne; Szabo, Violette

References and Further Reading

Binney, Marcus. 2002. *The Women Who Lived for Danger: The Women Agents of SOE in the Second World War.* London: Hodder and Stoughton.

Foot, M. R. D. (Michael Richard Daniell). 1984. *SOE: The Special Operations Executive, 1940–1946.* Westport, CT: Greenwood.

Stafford, David. 2000. *Secret Agent—The True Story of the Special Operations Executive.* London: BBC Worldwide Ltd.

ROMAN WOMEN AND WAR

Indispensable supporters of Rome's military ventures. Ancient Rome was not particularly warlike by ancient standards; what set it apart was the military system the early Romans established, which led to a series of victories that over time created one of the largest empires in world history. This history of expansion put enormous demands on Roman women, who were expected to support the senate and the people of Rome with their patriotism and their wealth, as well as by giving up their sons and husbands for ever-longer periods as the borders of Rome were pushed farther away. Roman women in general were given greater credit than Greek women for intelligence and were often better educated than their menfolk; however, except for camp followers, actual campaigns were normally a strictly masculine pursuit. Roman women, except for very rare exceptions, played their role supporting the military might of the state from behind the scenes.

The foundation myth of Rome provides instructive insight into Roman attitudes toward women and war. When the city was first founded (traditionally dated to 753 B.C.), the community had no women, so the Roman leader Romulus came up with a clever scheme, inviting the neighboring Sabines to attend a religious festival. The Sabines trustingly came with their wives and daughters; at a signal, the Roman men each carried off a woman. The Sabine men went home for their weapons and soon attacked. But the abducted women, by this time pregnant and settled, intervened and made a lasting peace. Thus females are simultaneously presented as helpless prey and as vital peacemakers who, with intelligence and courage, intervene to save both their old and new families.

Roman women were also expected to be brave, as can be seen in the legend of the heroine Cloelia. After Rome won its independence from the Etruscans (ca. 500 B.C.), the Etruscan Porsena invaded. He was eventually forced to withdraw but took a large number of hostages, including the young woman Cloelia. Taking advantage of an opportunity, she led a band of hostage girls back to the Roman lines, swimming the Tiber in the process. Porsena was so impressed that he released half his hostages in her honor. The Romans subsequently erected a statue depicting Cloelia on horseback and wearing a toga—that very masculine symbol of full citizenship.

The role of Roman women in warfare was generally not so visible. Roman legions were originally mustered for a single short campaign, but during the Late Republic period, the rank and file could be away from home for years at a time, fighting as far away as Syria. Until the military reforms of approximately 100 B.C., legionaries were responsible for equipping themselves and thus were normally small property owners. Their wives, therefore, had to stay behind, desperately trying to sustain the family economy in the face of growing pressure from large estates, while their husbands returned for short visits every year or two to impregnate them. Although this situation led to increasing civil rights for Roman women, the sheer workload seems to have been overwhelming in many cases.

Women also occasionally contributed to the war chest; in 390 B.C. Roman women are said to have raised 1,000 pounds (454 kilograms) of gold to bribe the Gauls to leave after troops had occupied the city. For noble women, the main pressure of war lay in the fact that their men were so often away from home for long periods. In times of intense political change such as the first century B.C., the wife often played an indispensable role by protecting her husband's political interests in his absence. Occasionally, this stretched as far as an active military role. The most notorious example comes from the period of the first triumvirate, when Fulvia (d. 40 B.C.), wife of Mark Antony, raised troops and even joined a rebellion in Italy on her husband's behalf. It is extremely clear that "decent" Romans considered her behavior outrageous. She was deeply vilified by Roman authors, as was Rome's enemy Cleopatra VII of Egypt (d. 30 B.C.), another woman who transgressed the boundaries of her gender in military matters. The model for a woman's proper role in warfare was provided by Mark Antony's next wife, Octavia, who was sister to Antony's greatest rival. Octavia refused to take a role in public affairs but put all her efforts into bringing about peace between her husband and brother. This continued to be the model for noblewomen in the imperial period. They were often very powerful behind the scenes but very rarely appeared publicly in matters that had to do with the military.

In general, the role of women in the great Roman war machine and the effects that war had on them is a matter for conjecture. Certainly, warfare would have been impossible without women's religious ceremonies, raising of children, maintenance of family businesses, and fortitude in times of state emergency, but that was all part of being a Roman.

—*Phyllis G. Jestice*

See also Cleopatra VII, Queen of Egypt; Fulvia; Galla Placidia

References and Further Reading

Barrett, Anthony. 2002. *Livia: First Lady of Imperial Rome.* New Haven, CT: Yale University.

Bauman, Richard A. 1992. *Women and Politics in Ancient Rome.* London: Routledge.

Evans, John K. 1991. *War, Women, and Children in Ancient Rome.* London: Routledge.

ROMA/SINTI

Victims of the Holocaust. During World War II the Nazis killed more than 80 percent of the Roma/Sinti (Gypsies) living in the German Reich and more that 50 percent of the Roma/Sinti living in territories occupied by Germany (Thompson 2001, 1069–1070). The Roma/Sinti had been subjected to discrimination and harassment in Germany and elsewhere before the Nazis came to power. At the beginning of the war, approximately 30,000 to 35,000 Roma/Sinti lived in the Nazi German Reich. They constituted Europe's second largest nonterritorial minority, with the Jews being the largest. An estimate of the number of Roma/Sinti living in all of the territory seized by the Germans during the war is approximately 942,000 (Holocaust Museum, 5). Others believe that the figure should be larger. The 1935 anti-Semitic Nuremberg Laws were extended to the Roma/Sinti, depriving them, like the Jews before them, of their civil rights. Regarded as "racially worthless," many Roma/Sinti were forced to undergo sterilization (Stephenson 2001, 116). Beginning in June 1938 a number of Roma/Sinti living in Germany and Austria (which had been absorbed into the Reich in March) were sent to concentration camps, including the Lichtenburg camp for women.

Heinrich Himmler, head of the Nazi SS, called for the resolution of the "Gypsy question" by the "physical separation of Gypsydom from the German nation" (Holocaust Museum, 8). Himmler later expressed his desire that "the Gypsies disappear from the face of the earth," and Joseph Goebbels held the opinion that, as with the Jews, the "Gypsies should simply be exterminated" (Hancock 2004, 163). The deportation of Roma/Sinti to the east, first to ghettos and then to death camps, began in May 1940. Roma/Sinti were among those killed by gas in mobile vans at Chelmno, Poland, in December 1941.

A Gypsy camp called Section B-IIe was set up at Auschwitz-Birkenau. Himmler, who was fascinated by the Roma/Sinti, wished them to be studied. When he lost interest in his experiment due to pressure from Martin Bormann, the Gypsy camp was liquidated. In August 1942, 2,897 Roma/Sinti men, women, and children perished in the gas chambers of Birkenau. Along with those who died in death or concentration camps and ghettos, additional Roma/Sinti, who were placed on an equal footing with Jews (Milton 2001, 225), perished at the hands of German Einsatzgruppen (operational groups) moving through Soviet territory. Others were killed by Romanian and Croatian German allies. Estimates of the number of Roma/Sinti killed by the Nazis and their allies range between 220,000 and 1.5 million (Hancock 2004, 164).

—*Bernard Cook*

See also Holocaust and Jewish Women; Ravensbrück

References and Further Reading

Hancock, Ian. 2004. *O Baro Porrajmos*—The Romani Holocaust. Pages 160–165 in *Defining the Horrific: Readings on Genocide and Holocaust in the Twentieth Century.* Edited by William L. Hewitt. Upper Saddle River, NJ: Pearson/Prentice-Hall.

Kenrick, Donald. 1999. *Gypsies during the Second World War.* Hatfield, Hertfordshire, UK: University of Hertfordshire.

Milton, Sybil. 1995. The Holocaust: The Gypsies. Pages 209–269 in *Genocide in the Twentieth Century: An Anthology of Critical Essays and Oral History.* Edited by William S. Parsons, Israel Charny, and Samuel Totten. New York: Garland.

———. 2001. Gypsies as Social Outsiders in Nazi Germany. Pages 212–232 in *Social Outsiders in Nazi Germany.* Edited by Robert Gellatey and Nathan Stoltzfus. Princeton, NJ: Princeton University.

Stephenson, Jill. 2001. *Women in Nazi Germany.* Harlow, UK: Pearson Educational.

Thomspon, Michál. 2001. Roma. Pages 1067–1071 in *Europe since 1945: An Encyclopedia.* Edited by Bernard A. Cook. New York: Garland.

U.S. Holocaust Museum. N.d. *Sinti and Roma (Gypsies) Victims of the Nazi Era.* Washington, DC: U.S. Holocaust Memorial Museum.

ROOSEVELT, ELEANOR (1884–1962)

Wife of President Franklin D. Roosevelt; U.S. first lady from 1933 to 1945. Eleanor Roosevelt, a niece of U.S. President Theodore Roosevelt, was born on October 11, 1884, in New York City. After her mother died when she was ten years old, Eleanor was raised by her maternal grandmother. She was educated at Allenswood, a school in England. She married Franklin D. Roosevelt, her fifth cousin, in 1905. The contrast between the Eleanor Roosevelt's actions in three wars reveals how much she matured politically over the years. In July 1917, the U.S. Food Administration picked Assistant Secretary of the Navy Franklin Roosevelt's family as a large household model of conservation, and the *New York Times* sent a female reporter to Washington, D.C., to interview Mrs. Roosevelt about her food-saving methods. The *New York Times* quoted Mrs. Roosevelt as saying that training ten servants to be frugal can turn out to be a highly profitable business. The political fallout from the newspaper story taught Eleanor Roosevelt to weather political storms and developed her sense of humor.

By World War II Eleanor Roosevelt had grown sophisticated enough politically to give the Office of Civilian Defense a decidedly New Deal ideological bent after she accepted a position as its deputy director. She insisted that civilian defense also depended on the degree that a community provided its citizens with decent housing, nursery schools, homes for the elderly, and recreational facilities. After she resigned as deputy director for political reasons, she continued to advocate her humanitarian ideals. She persuaded the State Department to let more refugees into the United States, agitated for fair treatment of African Americans in the armed forces and in war industries, and visited Japanese American relocation camps in Arizona to show her sympathy for internees.

Eleanor Roosevelt traveled as her husband's emissary and to boost GI morale during World War II. In 1942 she flew to Great Britain to visit U.S. soldiers. In 1943 she flew to the South Pacific, requesting that Admiral William F. Halsey grant her permission to visit Guadalcanal. The admiral postponed his final decision until she had toured some of the other islands in the area, as well as Australia and New Zealand. He monitored her activities as she made the rounds in her Red Cross uniform and marveled at her physical and mental stamina. He finally accompanied her to Guadalcanal and credited her with accomplishing more good than any other civilian visiting the area. In 1944 she toured U.S. bases in the Caribbean and Central America. Throughout her travels, Eleanor Roosevelt interacted with servicemen with genuine interest and care.

In December 1945 President Harry S Truman appointed Eleanor Roosevelt a delegate to the United Nations. As a member of the U.N. Human Rights Commission she played a major role in drafting a Universal Declaration of Human Rights and getting it adopted by the

U.N. General Assembly. In 1957 she and Soviet Premier Nikita Khrushchev had a spirited debate about the merits of capitalism and communism. Premier Khrushchev considered the debate a success because it was friendly and they did not shoot at each other.

—*Kathleen Warnes*

See also Lee, Mary Anna Randolph Custis; United States, Home Front during World War II; Washington, Martha Dandridge Custis

References and Further Reading

Cook, Blanche Wiesen. 1999. *Eleanor Roosevelt*. New York: Viking Penguin.

Goodwin, Doris Kearns. 1994. *No Ordinary Time: Franklin and Eleanor Roosevelt: The Home Front in World War II*. New York: Simon & Schuster.

Lash, Joseph P. 1971. *Eleanor and Franklin*. New York: Norton.

———. 1972. *Eleanor: The Years Alone*. New York: Norton.

ROSENBERG, ETHEL
(1915–1953)

Convicted of treason and executed by the United States during the cold war. During war or national emergencies, women's roles in society are typically broadened in order to meet the crises. Women become soldiers, factory workers, public speakers, and spies, to name a few. The cold war, however, was a rather unique crisis: anxiety, paranoia, and xenophobia were major characteristics of the decades-long conflict in which proxy contests replaced direct combat among the superpowers. Women were occasionally caught up in the national anxiety of the period; such was the story of Ethel Rosenberg.

Born Ethel Greenglass in New York City on September 28, 1915, her childhood was relatively unremarkable. She attended her neighborhood Hebrew school as well as public school. Her Lower East Side neighborhood was predominately Jewish in character, densely populated by dilapidated tenements, and crowed with sweatshops. In 1932 Ethel, working as a clerk with a shipping company, began her union activities including a strike for better pay and shorter working hours. In 1935 she led 150 women who used their bodies to block the entrance to the company's warehouse. Her employer fired her, but the National Labor Relations Board effected her reinstatement with back pay. Her union activism resulted in the establishment of the Ladies Apparel Shipping Clerk's Union. On the eve of World War II, Ethel Greenglass married Julius Rosenberg, a fellow union activist who had recently received his bachelor's degree in electrical engineering from the City College of New York.

During the war Ethel raised money and supplies for the Allied war effort through the East Side Defense Council. Julius had a job with the Signal Corps but lost his position in 1945 when he was accused of belonging to the Communist Party. He then established his own machine shop with his brother-in-law, David Greenglass.

Although the Soviet Union was an ally of the United States during most of World War II, after the war the United States and the Soviet Union quickly became opponents following the defeat of Nazi Germany. Their opposing socioeconomic systems and objectives in Europe resulted in the cold war. A critical event in that conflict was the Soviet development of an atomic bomb in 1949. The United States was no longer the sole atomic power. U.S. decisionmakers were surprised that the Soviets were able to develop nuclear weapons as quickly as they did. There was a concern that spies must have helped the Soviet Union by delivering atomic technology developed in the United States. Klaus Fuchs, a British member of the top-secret Manhattan Project, was accused of being a spy. Hoping to receive a lesser prison sentence for helping to transfer U.S. atomic secrets to the Soviet Union, Fuchs named others involved in the spy ring. The list of names led to David Greenglass, the brother of Ethel Rosenberg. Greenglass then testified that his brother-in-law was the one who introduced Greenglass to the spy ring. On July 17, 1950, the FBI arrested Julius Rosenberg; Ethel was arrested on August 11. With no viable evidence against her, the FBI apprehended Ethel hoping that Julius would then confess to spying for the Soviet Union to save his wife (Philipson 1988, 266).

While on the witness stand, Ethel Rosenberg repeatedly denied knowing anything about her family member's work for the Manhattan Project or her brother's espionage activities; she also denied knowing any of the other people that the U.S. and British governments had arrested on charges of selling atomic secrets to the Soviet Union apart from what she learned from the newspapers (Rosenberg 1952, 6). She proclaimed, "We are innocent and to forsake this truth is to pay too high a price for even the priceless gift of life—for life thus purchased we could not live out in dignity and self-respect" (Schneir 1965, 187).

The federal government was never able to produce any evidence that tied Ethel into the spy ring (her husband, however, was not as innocent). She was found guilty, primarily on the testimony of her brother. Ethel worked to get her two sons, Robert and Michael, into a stable home. Initially, the boys were cared for by Tessie Greenglass (the boys' maternal grandmother), but their spirits quickly soured, leading Michael to contemplate suicide while Robert began grinding his teeth (Philipson 1988, 263). As most other relatives were either unwilling or unable to take in the boys, Ethel Rosenberg had them placed in the Hebrew Children's Home in the Bronx.

The Rosenbergs' death sentences were carried out on June 19, 1953, by electrocution at Sing Sing prison in New York. Ethel was given three jolts of electricity before she finally died. According to Bob Considine, a witness to the executions, Ethel "was given more electricity which started again the kind of ghastly plume of smoke that rose from her head. After two more little jolts, Ethel Rosenberg was dead" (Philipson 1988, 352).

—*Jim Ross-Nazzal*

See also Mata Hari, pseud.

References and Further Reading

Cohen, Jacob. The Rosenberg File: What Do We Really Know about the Rosenbergs and the Case against Them? *National Review,* July 19, 1993.

Detweiler, Robert. 1996. Carnival of Shame: Doctorow and the Rosenbergs. *Religion and American Culture* 6(1):63–85.

Meeropol, Robert, and Michael Meeropol. 1986. *We Are Your Sons: The Legacy of Ethel and Julius Rosenberg,* 2nd ed. New York: Houghton Mifflin.

Philipson, Ilene. 1988. *Ethel Rosenberg: Beyond the Myths.* New York: Franklin Watts.

Rosenberg, Ethel. 1952. "Testimony of Ethel Rosenberg, Witness for the Defense." http://www.law.umkc.edu/faculty/projects/ftrials/rosenb/ROS_TETH.htm (accessed June 26, 2005).

Schneir, Walter, and Mirian Schneir. 1965. *Invitation to an Inquest.* New York: Doubleday.

Rosenstrasse and Intermarriage of Jews and German Gentiles

A street in Berlin where, in March 1943, several hundred German women who were married to Jewish men protested the Gestapo's detainment of their husbands at a collection center. After a tense week, the Gestapo released the men, demonstrating the potential power of protest that women held in Nazi Germany.

Intermarried couples occupied a unique and important position between Jewish and non-Jewish society. In Nazi Germany, intermarriage (which is the union of a woman and man from different racial, religious, class, or nationality groups) most often referred to marriages between Aryans and Jews (as defined by the government). National Socialism placed anti-Semitism and belief in racial separation at the top of its ideological system. Intermarried couples challenged those beliefs, committing "racial defilement" and creating a racial hybrid, whom the Nazis termed *Mischlinge* (mixed ones). After Adolf Hitler became chancellor in 1933, Aryans were pressured to divorce their Jewish spouses. Many intermarried Germans, both Jewish and non-Jewish, used this pressure as an excuse to end unhappy marriages. Most intermarried couples, however, refused to divorce. Following the 1935 anti-Semitic Nuremberg Laws, pressure on non-Jews to divorce their Jewish spouses increased tremendously. Although many divorces did occur, most couples chose to cope with the obstacles of intermarriage and remained together.

Following the turn of the century, Jewish men overwhelmingly made up the majority of intermarried Jews, meaning most of the women in these couples were non-Jewish Germans (Meiring 1998, 94–95). Under the racial laws established at Nuremberg in 1935, intermarried households with Jewish women married to non-Jewish German men were considered privileged; Jewish women in privileged households largely escaped arrest, and those who were arrested were soon released. Households with Jewish men married to non-Jewish women were considered Jewish, and the men were subjected to many of the same restrictions and abuses as other Jews.

Non-Jewish spouses faced many hardships during the Third Reich. They were forced to be the public face of their family, undertaking all official business, doing all the shopping, and operating as the connection to German society. Restrictions on Jews forced Jewish partners to limit their time outside the home to employment. Non-Jewish women married to Jews had the Star of David posted on their front doors, and their homes were subject to Gestapo searches at any moment. Neighbors and even family members reviled them. Many Germans avoided associating with the wives of Jews for fear that others would denounce them. Non-Jewish spouses of Jews lived in a constant state of fear for their families, always worrying about sudden changes in policies that would force their loved ones to flee. For many of the non-Jewish spouses, constant fear was transformed into determination. When news came that intermarried Jewish men had been included in a round-up, their spouses did not hesitate to help them.

From February 27 to March 6, 1943, the Berlin Gestapo arrested nearly 10,000 Jews, all that remained in the city, in an effort to make the city *Judenfrei* (free of Jews). Between 1,700 and 2,000 intermarried Jewish men were included in the round-up. Because of the unique social position of intermarried Jewish men, they were separated from the other Jews and were relocated and detained in the Jewish community's administration center at 2–4 Rosenstrasse (Stoltzfus 1996, 304, n45). Only the collective public protests of their German wives saved the Jewish detainees from deportation to Auschwitz. Fighting fear and despair, these women appeared in shifts throughout a week of protest, gathering in groups outside the guarded facility. Efforts to disperse the crowd with threats of gunfire would temporarily clear the streets, but the women would return in strength. The visibility of the protests, which grew to as large as 600 people at one time, and the impassioned pleas of women for their husbands were too much to ignore. The Nazi regime, always obsessed with public image and conformity, feared that a crackdown on the protests would lead to more trouble and bad publicity. On March 6 Joseph Goebbels ordered the release of the Jewish men. He rationalized that it would be more efficient and less troublesome to delay the round-up of the remaining Jews until the difficult period following the German defeat at the Battle of Stalingrad had passed (Stoltzfus 1996, 243).

Rosenstrasse had profound implications for the power of protest and the force of women as agents of change in Nazi Germany. It is a unique example of open and successful protest against the anti-Semitic and genocidal policies of the regime. The protestors also demonstrated that even under a repressive, misogynistic regime such as the Nazis', women were able to exert power on the government to bring about change. The concentric roles of the women as wives, daughters, sisters, friends, and employees encouraged the regime to make a series of decisions to temporarily exempt intermarried Jews from deportations to camps until it was too late for the regime to do so. The possibility of a backlash from the families and acquaintances of the protestors was enough to make the government acquiesce to their demands.

The power and success of intermarried German women was further demonstrated at the end of the war. Of the 13,217 registered Jews in Germany in September 1944, 12,987 were married to non-Jews (Stoltzfus 1996, xxvii). By the end of the war, 98 percent of the Jews who survived in Germany were intermarried.

—*Christopher Griffin*

See also Holocaust and Jewish Women

References and Further Reading

Klemperer, Viktor. 1998. *I Will Bear Witness: A Diary of the Nazi Years, 1933–1941*. Trans. Martin Chalmers. New York: Random House.

Meiring, Kerstin. 1998. *Die Christlich–Jüdische Mischehe in Deutschland, 1840–1933* [Christian–Jewish Mixed Marriages in Germany, 1840–1933]. Hamburg: Dölling und Galitz Verlag.

Stoltzfus, Nathan. 1996. *Resistance of the Heart: Intermarriage and the Rosenstrasse Protest in Nazi Germany*. New York: W. W. Norton.

ROSIE THE RIVETER

An icon for a propaganda campaign in the United States during World War II, promulgated by the War Manpower Commission and the Office of War Information. The campaign centered on a call for women to give up the homemaker ideal and to take up occupations that supported the war effort or fill jobs that were left vacant when the men went to war. As large numbers of American males were drafted for service in World War II, Rosie became immortalized in songs, movies, posters, and advertisements. The messages were highly patriotic and viewed women as "production soldiers."

Many depictions of Rosie could be found during the war. The most famous rendition of Rosie was found on the cover of the *Saturday Evening Post* in 1943. In this familiar picture by Norman Rockwell, Rosie, shown eating a sandwich, is clad in coveralls, wearing headgear and goggles, and is supporting a large riveting machine on her legs, positioned just below her massive arms. In the background of this picture is an American flag, over Rosie's head is a halo, and beneath her work shoes is a copy of Hitler's *Mein Kampf*. Rockwell modeled his version of Rosie after Michelangelo's *Isaiah*, significantly modifying his real model's small frame. In another familiar poster often considered to represent Rosie, a young woman adorned in bandana and work shirt is seen rolling up her sleeve, flexing her bicep, and exclaiming, "We Can Do It."

The messages of this propaganda campaign were that women, especially married women who were previously relegated to working at home, should enter male-dominated occupations related to the war effort such as aircraft parts manufacturing, shipbuilding, ammunitions production, and mining. Women were also asked to enter nondefense-related manufacturing occupations in industry and agriculture.

Work in the defense industry normally required long hours, often entailed grueling physical exertion, and was frequently hazardous. Airplane factories were very loud and often caused hearing problems for the workers. Riveting vibrations were rumored to cause breast cancer and other physical maladies in workers; during this period, gynecological problems came to be known as "riveter's ovaries." Some jobs were particularly dangerous, such as those in the munitions industry. Female munitions workers, dubbed "gunpowder girls," worked with the threat of explosions. Those who worked around machines—a large majority of defense employees—were at constant risk of death or dismem-

We Can Do It *poster, featuring Rosie the Riveter.*
(National Archives)

berment. In addition, the work was often monotonous and highly repetitive, causing high levels of boredom that was often relieved through singing. This new image of femininity challenged earlier gender conceptions. Men, who were unhappy to see women do well in occupations that were previously only open to males, often subjected women to harassment and other forms of discrimination.

In spite of the occupations' drawbacks, many women enjoyed the responsibilities of the new jobs and the newfound status of wage earner. The fact that they were able to succeed in these roles opened the door to a greater number of females in traditional male occupations. Although government and industry prompted Rosie to return to the home after the war and many were reluctantly replaced by returning males, the number of women who stayed in the workplace was higher than before the war.

—*Leonard A. Steverson*

See also Mexican American Women and World War II; Posters, U.S., Images of Women in World War II; United States, Home Front during World War II

References and Further Reading

Colman, Penny. 1995. *Rosie the Riveter: Women Working on the Home Front in World War II.* New York: Crown.

Rosietheriveter.org. "Rockwell's Rosie the Riveter Painting Auctioned." Rosie the Riveter Trust. http://www.rosietheriveter.org/painting.htm (accessed April 1, 2004).

Weatherford, Dorothy. 1990. *American Women and World War II.* New York: Facts on File.

ROSS, ISHOBEL
(1890–1965)

Served with the Scottish Women's Hospital service in the Balkans during World War I. Ishobel Ross, daughter of James Ross, was born on the Isle of Skye on February 18, 1890. She attended the Edinburgh Ladies College and the Atholl Crescent School of Domestic Science. When World War I erupted, Ross was teaching cooking at a girl's school. After hearing Dr. Elsie Inglis speak on the Scottish Women's Hospital Unit, Ross volunteered as a cook and was sent to the Salonika front (Greece) in August 1916. She later served in the Balkans for nearly a year. Her diary was published by her daughter after Ross's death.

—*Bernard Cook*

See also Inglis, Elsie, and the Scottish Women's Hospitals

References and Further Reading

Ross, Ishobel. 1988. *Little Grey Partridge: First World War Diary of Ishobel Ross Who Served with the Scottish Women's Hospitals Unit in Serbia.* Aberdeen, Scotland: Aberdeen University.

ROWDEN, DIANA
(1915–1944)

British secret agent during World War II. Diana Hope Rowden was born in Britain on January 31, 1915, but her family moved to France when she was a child. As a teenager she attended school in England, but in 1933 Rowden returned to France and studied at the University of Paris before becoming a journalist. When World War II began in 1939, she joined the Red Cross and served with the Anglo-American Ambulance Corps of the British Expeditionary Force. Cut off by the rapid German victory in 1940, Rowden eventually made her way to Spain and Portugal and then back to Britain. In September 1941, she joined the British Women's Auxiliary Air Force. She was assigned to the department of the chief of air staff and in July 1942 became a section officer.

Rowden's fluency in French and her knowledge of French life led to her recruitment by the British Special Operations Executive (SOE) in March 1943. After her training Rowden was flown on June 16, 1943, to a location near Angers, France; she was accompanied by Noor Inayat Khan and Cecily Lefort. Using the code name Paulette, Rowden served as a courier for the Acrobat network headed by John Starr. Starr was apprehended a month after her arrival. Rowden and a wireless operator, John Young, took refuge in the village of Clairvaux-les-Lacs, where they were informed by SOE headquarters that a new agent was being dispatched to assist them. The expected new agent turned out to be a German spy. Rowden and Young were arrested on November 18, 1943, at Lons-le-Saunier. Rowden was interrogated by the Gestapo for two weeks at their Paris headquarters. On May 13, 1944, she was sent from the Fresnes prison with seven other captured British women agents to the Karlsruhe civil prison. On July 6, 1944, on the direct order of Ernest Kaltenbrunner, head of the SS Security Office, Rowden, Andrée Borrel, Vera Leigh, and Sonya Olschanezky were moved to the Natzweiler-Struthof concentration camp. They were executed on the day of their arrival.

Rowden was posthumously awarded the Member of the British Empire and the Croix de Guerre. A watercolor of Rowden and her three companions, painted by Brian Stonehouse, an SOE agent and fellow prisoner who witnessed their arrival at Natzweiler-Struthof, has a place of honor in the Special Forces Club in London.

—*Bernard Cook*

See also Atkins, Vera H.; Borrel, Andrée; Leigh, Vera; Olschanezky, Sonya

References and Further Reading

Foot, M. R. D. (Michael Richard Daniell). 1984 (1966). *SOE in France: An Account of the Work of the British Special Operations Executive, 1940–1944*. Frederick, MD: University Publications of America.

Kramer, Rita. 1995. *Flames in the Field: The Stories of Four SOE Agents in Occupied France*. New York: Viking Penguin.

Nicholas, Elizabeth. 1958. *Death Be Not Proud*. London: Cresset.

Spartacus Web. "Diana Rowden." http://www.spartacus.schoolnet.co.uk/SOErowden.htm (accessed September 28, 2004).

RUBBLE WOMEN

See Trümmerfrauen

RUDELLAT, YVONNE
(1897–1945)

British operative sent to France during World War II. Yvonne Claire Rudellat (née Cerneau) was born in France in 1897. On May 28, 1942, she joined the British Special Operations Executive (SOE). The SOE had been established in July 1940 to put operatives behind the enemy lines. Winston Churchill, the wartime prime minister of Great Britain, wanted the SOE to "set Europe ablaze." The SOE collaborated with the French resistance movement in gathering intelligence and carrying out sabotage. Because she was French by birth and fluent in French, Rudellat had been recruited to the First Aid Nursing Yeomanry (FANY) for training. With Andrée Borrel, Lise de Baissac, and other women agents, she underwent intensive training, learning about parachute drops and sabotage operations. Rudellat was initially a courier in the Prosper Circuit of F (French) Section of SOE.

Rudellat was sent to the south of France by boat on July 30, 1942. She was the second agent to arrive in France. Lise de Baissac had been parachuted to France in April 1942. Rudellat's activity centered round the Loire Valley area, where she led a Resistance group. She lived in a cottage, working and hiding as the occasion demanded. In March 1943, Yvonne's group blew up the Chaigny power station, two trains in the Le Mans station, and some factories. Authorities were searching frantically for the leader of the operations and zeroed in on her in June 1943. On June 21, she came to a roadblock while attempting to escape the Gestapo dragnet. She did not stop, and in the car chase that followed she was fired on and sustained a severe head injury. She was treated in a hospital in Blois and after interrogations by the Gestapo was sent to Fresnes prison. There she was known as Jacqueline Gautier, a name given her by a fellow prisoner as Rudellat was suffering from amnesia as a result of her head injury.

Rudellat was sent from Fresnes to Bergen-Belsen on April 21, 1945, and died of typhus six days later. The Member of the British Empire (MBE) was conferred on her posthumously. An obelisk at Loire Valley, France, and a plaque at St. Paul's Church, Knightsbridge, in the United Kingdom commemorate her.

—*Patit Paban Mishra*

See also Atkins, Vera H.; Borrel, Andrée; Leigh, Vera; Olschanezky, Sonya; Rowden, Diana; Szabo, Violette

References and Further Reading

Binney, Marcus. 2002. *The Women Who Lived for Danger: The Women Agents of SOE in the Second World War.* London: Hodder & Stoughton.

Foot, M. R. D. (Michael Richard Daniell). 1984. *SOE: The Special Operations Executive, 1940–1946.* Westport, CT: Greenwood.

King, Stella. 1990. *"Jacqueline:" Pioneer Heroine of the Resistance.* London: Arms and Armour Press.

Kramer, Rita. 1995. *Flames in the Field: The Story of Four SOE Agents in Occupied France.* London: Michael Joseph.

RUSSIA, WOMEN IN THE ARMED FORCES (1700–1917)

Women in the Russian military prior to the Bolshevik Revolution (1917). Until World War I, women's participation in the Russian military was sporadic and was attributable to their own efforts. Article 34 of the Russian military regulations of 1716 limited women's service to administrative and medical duties. Those who wished to serve in nontraditional roles dressed as men. For example, Nadezhda Durova, the daughter of a cavalry captain born in 1783, took part in the Napoleonic Wars, served with distinction, and was decorated by the czar himself.

One hundred and fifty nurses served during the Crimean War (1853–1856). The nursing school founded afterward graduated 1,500 nurses for service in the Russian-Turkish War of 1876 (Herspring 1997, 43). During World War I the imperial government dismissed some disguised women soldiers following discovery of their gender, while allowing others to stay.

In June 1917 the 1st Petrograd Women's Battalion, the so-called Women's Battalion of Death, was formed under the command of Maria Bochkareva. Bochkareva's intent was to shame men into not deserting. Some of the women, however, were assaulted or killed by male deserters. Other battalions modeled on Bochkareva's

Members of the Women's Battalion of Death, a branch of the Russian military, 1917. (Underwood and Underwood/Corbis)

were formed in many regions of Russia. A women's detachment in Petrograd defended the Provisional Government (which made women equal before the law), when the Bolsheviks stormed the Winter Palace in November 1917. The number of Russian women who served in World War I was estimated at 5,000 (Herspring 1997, 44).

—*Kazimiera J. Cottam*

See also Bochkareva, Maria; Russia, Women Recipients of the Order of St. George; Russian Republic, Women in the Armed Forces; Soviet Union, Women in the Armed Forces

References and Further Reading

Herspring, Dale R. 1997. Women in the Russian Military: A Reluctant Marriage. *Minerva: Quarterly Report on Women in the Military* 15, no. 3 (Summer):42–59.

RUSSIA, WOMEN RECIPIENTS OF THE ORDER OF ST. GEORGE (1808–1917)

Award created in 1769 by Empress Catherine the Great for Russian officers. Until 1856 it was awarded to officers with at least twenty-five years of service or participation in eighteen to twenty naval campaigns. Two additional awards for enlisted personnel and noncommissioned officers were later added: the Cross of St. George (1807) and a four-level variant of the Cross (1856). Among the women who received these awards were:

Maria Leont'evna Bochkareva (b. 1889). The first Russian woman commander of a military unit, designated the 1st Petrograd Women's Battalion—the so-called Battalion of Death. She was awarded the Cross of St. George, IV

Class, for her previous service with the 28th Polotsk Infantry Regiment as a noncommissioned officer.

Nadezhda Andreevna Durova (1783–1866). Durova, whose married name was Chernova, was also called Cavalry Maid/Maiden, and Alexandrov, the name assigned to her by Czar Alexander I. During the Napoleonic Wars, Durova served in three Russian cavalry regiments: the Polish Horse, the Mariupol Hussars, and the Lithuanian. She saw action against the French in East Prussia in 1807; during the invasion of Russia in 1812; and in the European campaign of 1813–1814. In 1808 Durova was decorated for bravery, at which time she was commissioned by Emperor Alexander I. She was the only woman to be awarded the Cross of St. George before the early twentieth century. In 1836–1841 she published remarkable journals and sensational fiction based on her nine years' experience serving with the Russian cavalry. Two autobiographical works drawn from her sporadic diaries, *The Cavalry Maiden* (1836) and *Notes* (1839), are considered classic contributions to military history.

Rimma Mikhailovna Ivanova (1895–1915). Although a nurse, Ivanova led a successful attack on enemy trenches on September 9, 1915, after all officers from her unit, the No. 1 Company of 108th Orenburg Infantry Regiment, were put out of action. By protesting her participation in combat, the German Military Red Cross authorities made her deed famous. She was posthumously granted the Order of St. George, IV Class, on January 7, 1916.

Antonina Tikhonovna Pal'shina (b. 1897). Disguised as a man and called Anton Pal'shin, Pal'shina served as a private in the Russian army cavalry and infantry during World War I. Pal'shina joined the Cossack cavalry at the beginning the war. After being wounded, Pal'shina's gender was discovered and she was compelled to train as a nurse in a hospital in Lvov (L'viv). She promptly ran away to join No. 6 Company of the 75th Sebastopol Infantry Regiment. Pal'shina is the only Russian woman to have been decorated with both the Order and the Cross of St. George, receiving two of each award.

—*Kazimiera J. Cottam*

See also Bochkareva, Maria; Russia, Women in the Armed Forces; Soviet Union/Russian Federation, Women Heroes of the

References and Further Reading

Cottam, Kazimiera J. 2003. Order of St. George, Women Recipients. Pages 325–326 in *Amazons to Fighter Pilots*. Edited by Reina Pennington. Vol. 1. Westport, CT: Greenwood.

Pal'shina, Antonina Tikhonovna. 1988 (1836). *The Cavalry Maiden: Journals of a Russian Officer in the Napoleonic Wars*. Trans. Mary Fleming Zirin. Bloomington and Indianapolis: Indiana University.

Privalov, Boris. 1980. Dobra i schast'ia ei! [All the Best to Her!]. *Ogonëk* 23 (June):30–31.

RUSSIAN REPUBLIC, WOMEN IN THE ARMED FORCES (1991–)

Following the collapse of communism, more women entered the Russian military, which had difficulty maintaining itself solely with males. By the end of 1992 the number of women in the Russian armed forces climbed to 100,000, including 20,000 warrant officers and 1,100 officers (Herspring 1997, 50). The majority of them served in the ground forces. About 1,000 women were admitted into the elite airborne forces (Herspring 1997, 50–51). One hundred and sixty-nine specialties were opened to women. In 1992, mixed staffing was introduced. By the end of 1992, women volunteers outnumbered male conscripts by 367 to 125 in one motorized infantry unit, and the Moscow Military District announced that it intended to raise the percentage of women in its ranks to 10 percent (Herspring 1997, 51).

The increasingly important role women played was most evident in the Air Defense Forces (ADF), where women occupied 50 percent of key positions in 1992 (Herspring 1997, 51). It was assumed that women had better aptitude than men for detailed work and making precise calculations. When, in 1993, women were allowed to join on the basis of a voluntary contract rather than conscription, the intent was not only to alleviate manpower shortages but also to assist underpaid professional soldiers by providing employment for their wives. Thus, by 1994, the total number of women in the military approached 250,000, but only 1,500 of them were officers (Herspring 1997, 52–53).

Despite their increasing reliance on women, Russian senior officers tended to resist placing them in "men's" jobs and dismissed them at the earliest opportunity. By mid-1997, however, the situation of Russian women soldiers had improved. Out of an army of 1,200,000, women officers numbered approximately 2,400, including 4 colonels and 300 senior officers (ranked major to colonel) (Herspring 1997, 53). Astronaut Valentina Tereshkova was the first woman to be granted the rank of major general. Meanwhile, women had been admitted to communications and chemical warfare schools. Although male commanders acknowledged women's proficiency in carrying out technical, medical, and administrative tasks, they were reluctant to use them in combat, even when they constituted 20 percent of divisional personnel and were appropriately trained (Herspring 1997, 54). Additionally, there was no effective women's lobby group to argue that women were full-fledged members of the Russian armed forces. The recurrent severe shortages of men, coupled with persistent praise of women in the press (citing the superior discipline of women, their more efficient work habits, and their greater devotion to duty), may improve the status of Russian military women in the future.

—*Kazimiera J. Cottam*

See also Chechnya, Impact on Women of Wars in

References and Further Reading

Herspring, Dale R. 1997. Women in the Russian Military: A Reluctant Marriage. *Minerva: Quarterly Report on Women in the Military* 15, no. 2 (Summer):42–59.

RUSSIAN REVOLUTION AND WOMEN

The role played by women in the Russian revolutions of 1917. In 1920 the Russian Communist feminist Alexandra Kollontai wrote, "The future historian will undoubtedly note that one of the characteristics of our revolution was that women workers and peasants played . . . an active important role" (Stites 1978, 317).

As economic, social, and political conditions across Russia worsened in early 1917, czarist officials worried that Russian women were on the verge of open revolt. It was reported that "mothers of families . . . are exhausted by the endless standing in line at the stores. . . . [O]ne spark will be enough for a conflagration to blaze up" (Miller 2001, 182). The spark took place in Petrograd on March 8, 1917, when thousands of women workers took to the streets demanding an end to the war and increases in social services. Over two weeks the crowds grew, more members of the military mutinied, and on March 15, Czar Nicholas II abdicated the throne.

Many Russian women believed that the Revolution would sweep away more than just the czar and the ruling family. Inessa Armand, the head of the Bolshevik Party's women's division, or Zhenotdel, proclaimed that "the bourgeois order is being abolished" and called for the removal of all strategies that maintained the ideology of separate spheres in which women had no control over their lives (Goldman 1993, 3–4).

Eventually, the Communist government would redefine gender relations through the adoption of the 1918 Code on Marriage, Family, and Guardianship. The code abolished the czarist-era status of women as subservient to men by allowing women to sue for divorce, abolishing the stigma of illegitimacy, and mandating child support (Goldman 1993, 51).

During the Revolution, women were portrayed in political iconography as enchained by the czarist policies and helpless to free themselves. For example, Communist leaders of the Petrograd Izhora Works used banners depicting women, in traditional costume and chained to rocks, set free by male workers wielding hammers with the sun shining in the background. The banners were splashed with slogans such as "All Hail the Socialist Republic," "All Hail the Democratic Republic," or "Free Russia." Although the slogans changed, the imagery did not: either women in chains about to be set free by the actions of men or women, or women just set free by the actions of men, standing atop piles of chains (Clements et al. 1991, 229).

As in other conflicts, Russian women played myriad roles from the battlefield to the home front. What was different about their actions during the Revolution was the level of organization (Stites 1978, 318). Communist leaders formed gender-specific combat units such as the Communist Women's Combat Detachment and the Communist Women's Special Purpose Detachment. Women were even recruited into the army of the new provisional government formed after the February Revolution (Stites 1978, 318). One of these combat veterans was Larisa Reisner, who specialized in intelligence gathering. For the Lenin government, formed after the October Revolution, she helped draft the law separating church from state and the Constitution of 1918 (Stites 1978, 319). Women headed the *politotdely* (political sections) in each Red Army unit, where they developed and offered training to all soldiers with regard to the social, political, and economic goals of the Communist leadership (Stites 1978, 32).

Of the thousands of women who participated in the Revolution (such as Nadezhda Konstantinova Krupskaya, Yelena Dmitriyevna Stassova, and Klavdia Nikolayeva), many took public, but certainly not leading, roles. Konstantinova was Lenin's wife. During the Revolution she occasionally spoke at rallies, but she primarily supported her husband. After the Bolshevik seizure of power, Konstantinova became a member of the People's Commissariat of Education and helped launch training and education programs for women. Likewise, Dmitriyevna's role during the Revolution was primarily one of providing support at rallies by standing near Lenin, clapping at the appropriate times. Behind the scenes she worked as secretary for the Party Central Committee. Finally, Klavdia Nikolayeva worked for Russia's first Communist women's magazine, *Kommunistka*. Although Nikolayeva did on occasion speak at public events, her work, like that of other leading Communist women, was primarily behind the scenes (Kollontai 1980).

Possibly the most public woman's voice during the Revolution was that of Alexandra Kollontai, a member of the Party Central Committee. Kollontai spoke publicly in support of women in general and about motherhood in particular. Her typical audience consisted of women, however, not the masses who heard Lenin, Trotsky, and other Communist men speak. For example, on November 6, 1917, she delivered a speech to a conference of women on the necessity of protecting motherhood. Ten years later Kollontai wrote, "These theses were then passed on 'as guidelines' to the People's Commissariat for State Welfare and the People's Commissariat for Labour, which then included the Department of Social Security." Before the end of 1917, Communist leaders issued a declaration ordering the creation of a government bureau dedicated to assessing the needs of women and providing them the necessary support. It was called the Department for the Protection of Mother and Child (Kollontai 1980).

Lenin was supposedly an ardent supporter of women's importance at home. According to Kollontai, Lenin said:

If even the most resolute and courageous fighter on the civil war front returns home and has to listen day after day to the grumbles and complaints of his wife and face in her, as a result of her lack of political consciousness, an opponent to the continuing struggle for Soviet power, the will of even a valiant warrior hardened in battle may weaken, and he who did not surrender to counter-revolution may surrender to his wife and come under her harmful influence. (Kollontai 1980)

In November 1918, the first authorized women's congress was held under the new Communist government. Overall, the congress adopted resolutions regarding the centrality of motherhood, family, and home to Russian women and urged the new Communist government to pass legislation to protect women as mothers and wives. This was the beginning of women's emancipation in Russia. Interestingly enough, Kollontai defined *emancipation* as the ability to be mothers. In other words, emancipation for this Soviet women's activist was seen as a social construct, not a political one.

Immediately following the Revolution and in light of the devastation caused by World War I, Communist leaders cut state funding for social services such as schools and day care centers. According to one source, only 1.8 percent of eligible children attended any type of preschool (Goldman 1993, 74). Although the 1918 code provided for gender equality in all aspects of marriage, family, and divorce, the economic realities of Russia immediately after the Revolution were prohibitive for women seeking divorce. According to Wendy Goldman, "High unemployment, low wages, a lack of daycare not only reinforced women's dependence on the family, they created a sharp contradiction between the harsh reality of life and a legal vision of freedom long promulgated by reformers and socialists" (Goldman 1993, 103).

—*Jim Ross-Nazzal*

See also Kollontai, Alexandra

References and Further Reading

Clements, Barbara Evans, Barbara Alpern Engel, and Christine D. Worobec, eds. 1991. *Russia's Women: Accommodation, Resistance, and Transformation.* Berkeley: University of California.

Goldman, Wendy Z. 1993. *Women, the State and Revolution: Soviet Family Policy and Social Life, 1917–1936.* New York: Cambridge University.

Kollontai, Alexandra. 1980. "The First Step toward the Protection of Motherhood," "V. I. Lenin and the First Congress of Women Workers," and "Women Fighters in the Days of the Great October Revolution." In *Alexandra Kollontai: Selected Articles and Speeches.* New York: Norton. Also available at www.marxists.org/archive/kollonta/works (accessed June 24, 2005).

Miller, Martin, ed. 2001. *The Russian Revolution: The Essential Readings.* Malden, MA: Blackwell Publishers.

Stites, Richard. 1978. *The Women's Liberation Movement in Russia—Feminism, Nihilism, and Bolshevism, 1860–1930.* Princeton, NJ: Princeton University.

RWANDA: WOMEN AND THE GENOCIDE

Genocidal assault of the Hutus against the Tutsis in Rwanda. In barely 100 days between April and June 1994, some 800,000 Rwandans, out of a total population of just over 8 million, were killed by Hutu militias. Most of the victims were Tutsis, but a significant number were moderate Hutus.

Tensions between the Tutsis and Hutus predated the European colonization of East Africa. The Hutus, the majority population of the highland forests of Rwanda, Burundi, and the eastern Congo, were of medium stature physically and were for the most part engaged in subsistence farming. In the 1300s the Tutsis, cattle herders who were typically taller than the Hutus, began to migrate into the Hutu lands from the north or northeast. Between the late seventeenth and early nineteenth centuries, Tutsi kings established hegemony over all of the Hutus. Although the differences between the two peoples have been emphasized for both political and socioeconomic reasons, the Hutus and the Tutsis are quite closely related ethnically, culturally, and linguistically.

In the 1890s Rwanda became part of German East Africa, but in the middle of World War I the colony was seized by Belgian colonials from the Congo, and for the next four decades the colony was administered by the Belgians under a League of Nations and then a U.N. mandate. Lacking any sort of extensive administrative system for managing their colonies, the Belgians found it expedient to control Rwanda through the former Tutsi rulers, compounding the majority Hutus' sense of disenfranchisement. By the late 1950s as independence loomed, the Hutus had organized several radical political parties. In 1959 the Tutsi king was forced into exile in Uganda. In 1963, the year after Rwanda achieved independence, about 20,000 Tutsis were killed by Hutu rioters, and many Rwandan Tutsis fled to Burundi and other neighboring states. In 1988 about 50,000 Hutus were forced out of Burundi as tensions between the two peoples flared in that country.

By 1990 the Tutsi-led Rwandan Patriotic Front (RPF) had amassed sufficient strength to invade Rwanda from Uganda. Within three years the RPF made enough gains to force the Hutu government to sign an agreement that guaranteed the Tutsis a substantial voice in Rwandan affairs and an equal place in Rwandan life. This fragile peace was undermined, however, by a carefully orchestrated hate campaign conducted by extremist Hutu groups that controlled Radio Télévision Libre de Mille Collines (RTLM), the country's independent radio station. This hate campaign struck all-too-familiar themes: the need for racial purity among the Hutus and the verminlike nature of the "foreign" Tutsis. Although the Hutu-dominated government did not control the Hutu extremists, it clearly did nothing to restrain or discourage them. Then, in April 1994,

Rwandan President Juvenal Habyarimana, a Hutu, was killed when the airplane in which he was traveling with the president of Burundi crashed as it approached the Rwandan capital of Kingali. Almost immediately, claims were made that the airplane had been shot down by a rocket fired by Tutsi forces.

Literally overnight, Habyarimana's presidential guard initiated an orchestrated slaughter of Tutsis and moderate Hutus in Kingali and adjacent districts. A militia organization called the Interahamwe (meaning those who attack in unison) had been organized amid the unrest of the preceding years, and it quickly emerged in every corner of the country to greatly expand the slaughter. At its height, the Interahamwe included some 30,000 well-armed militiamen—more than enough to inflame or intimidate large numbers of other Hutus, armed only with clubs, machetes, and knives, into participating in the carnage.

The international community made only token attempts to intercede in order to stop the killing. A small U.N. peacekeeping force was withdrawn after a Hutu mob killed ten of the soldiers. The killing ended only when the RPF, under Paul Kagame, seized control of Kingali and then of the country as a whole. Although a moderate Hutu, Pasteur Bizimungu, was named president of Rwanda, some 2 million Hutus fled into the Democratic Republic of the Congo (DRC, formerly Zaire), which was then on the verge of a violent civil war itself. The Rwandan refugees included many of those who had led the genocide in Rwanda and were wanted for committing crimes against humanity. These war criminals soon seized control of the refugee camps, turning them into fresh killing zones, and they began to recruit, often forcibly, troops with which they launched raids back into Rwanda.

The region and the United Nations thus suddenly faced a double crisis of almost unprecedented proportions. Not only had Rwanda been devastated by a horrible genocide but refugees from Rwanda had flooded into a remote region of a country that was itself politically unstable.

Further complicating matters, the Hutus and Tutsis were the major ethnic groups in districts of the eastern Congo; thus, when Rwanda, Uganda, and Burundi interceded in Congolese affairs, there were many layers of complexity in the political, military, and humanitarian situation. The Rwandan military helped to topple the Congolese government of Mobuto Sese Seko and then that of the rebel Laurent Kabila when both failed to control and then disband the Hutu refugee camps in the eastern Congo.

In the decade immediately following the genocide, the Rwandan government and the United Nations made extensive efforts to bring the chief perpetrators to justice. By 2004 some 500 Hutus had been sentenced to death for their parts in the genocide, and about 100,000 were either serving prison sentences or awaiting trial. In that year Paul Kagame won a landslide victory in the first fully democratic presidential election since the genocide, and the RPF won a clear majority in the legislature. The decisiveness of their victory convinced the leaders of the Forces Démocratiques de Liberation du Rwanda (FDLR), the major insurgent group among Hutu refugees, to announce that their organization would disband.

Of course, as in all terrible conflicts, many of the victims of the Rwandan genocide were women. But the long-standing ethnic tensions in Rwanda provided especially terrible complications for many Tutsi women. Because the similarities between the Tutsis and Hutus often outweighed their differences, particularly in times of relative peace between the groups, intermarriage was not uncommon. But marriages between Hutu men and Tutsi women were much more common than marriages between Tutsi men and Hutu women. Legally, the offspring of the marriages between Hutu men and Tutsi women were Hutus, but at a time of crisis, when issues of racial purity were used to inflame emotions, the Tutsi women in these marriages and their children were especially vulnerable. Indeed, when the genocide began, Hutu men married to Tutsis were often required to prove their loyalty to the Hutus by participating in the murders of their own wives and children.

More broadly, the propaganda of the Hutu extremists portrayed Tutsi women as scheming and predatory sexual figures who undermined the confidence of Hutu men, literally or figuratively seducing them into an abject submissiveness. Thus, when the genocide began, Tutsi women were often viciously gang-raped in order to demean them publicly before they were murdered. Moreover, Hutu women, having been culturally conditioned to view Tutsi women as arrogant individuals who flaunted their supposed superiority, made Tutsi women scapegoats for all sorts of perceived injustices and personal grudges. The torture of Tutsi women became a terrible sport for some Hutu women who participated in the genocide. Some Tutsi women were kept in sexual slavery by the Hutu militias even after the exodus to the eastern Congo occurred. Those women who somehow survived their victimization discovered that their own sense of shame was compounded because they were now socially ostracized. They were reminders of their own husbands' and fathers' failure to prevent their humiliation. If they had become pregnant as the result of the rapes, the stigma was intensified. Abortion and infanticide became horrible denouements to the genocide.

One interesting footnote to the Rwandan genocide is that two Rwandan women became the first plaintiffs in history to sue the United Nations for its failure to prevent a genocide. Anonciata Kavaruganda, the wife of a murdered Supreme Court justice, and Louise Mushiki-wabo, the only Tutsi in Habyarimana's cabinet, both claimed that U.N. forces in Rwanda were not just ineffectual but were actually complicit when the killing began.

—*Martin Kich*

See also Herero of Namibia, Repression of the; Holocaust and Jewish Women; Sudan, Women and the Civil War in

References and Further Reading

Barnett, Michael N. 2002. *Eyewitness to a Genocide: The United Nations and Rwanda.* Ithaca, NY: Cornell University.

Dallaire, Romeo. 2005. *Shake Hands with the Devil: The Failure of Humanity in Rwanda.* New York: Carroll and Graf.

Eltringham, Nigel. 2004. *Accounting for Horror: Post-genocide Debates in Rwanda.* Sterling, VA: Pluto.

Jennings, Christian. 2000. *Across the Red River: Rwanda, Burundi and the Heart of Darkness.* London: V. Gollancz.

Prunier, Gerard. 1995. *The Rwanda Crisis, 1959–1994: History of a Genocide.* New York: Columbia University.

Scherrer, Christian P. 2002. *Genocide and Crisis in Central Africa: Conflict Roots, Mass Violence, and Regional War.* Westport, CT: Praeger.

Taylor, Christopher C. 1999. *Sacrifice as Terror: The Rwandan Genocide of 1994.* New York: Berg.

Waugh, Colin M. 2004. *Paul Kagame and Rwanda: Power, Genocide and the Rwandan Patriotic Front.* Jefferson, NC: McFarland.

S

SALOMON, CHARLOTTE (1917–1943)

German Jewish artist whose autobiographical work, *Life? or Theatre?*, combines paintings, text, and musical cues in a unique chronicle of her life. Salomon's autobiography deals with her childhood in Weimar, Germany, her coming of age during the Nazi years, and her exile in France as a refugee from the Nazi regime. It reveals her battle to define her existence and identity in the face of constant personal and political conflict.

Born into a prosperous family in Berlin in 1917, young Charlotte Salomon struggled to find her own place and voice amid the turbulence of interwar Germany and the anti-Semitic policies of the Nazi regime. She quit school in 1933 but later applied and was admitted to the esteemed Berlin Art Academy. (Her openly avowed Jewish heritage would eventually lead to her dismissal from the institution.) There she learned classical, Nazi-sanctioned methods and techniques of realism, which she broke from almost completely in her own artistic work.

Increasing persecution at the hands of Hitler's government ultimately convinced the Salomon family to leave their homeland. In the immediate aftermath of the anti-Jewish pogrom known as *Kristallnacht* (Crystal Night, the Night of the Broken Glass) on November 9, 1938, Salomon's father, Albert, along with thousands of other Jews, was sent to Sachsenhausen concentration camp outside Berlin. His family managed to secure his release, and from that point forward the Salomons prepared to leave Germany. Charlotte Salomon left in January 1939 to join her grandparents, who had fled Nazi rule in 1933, on the French Riviera. A plan to reunite with her father and stepmother in exile never materialized; her parents ended up in Amsterdam, where they survived World War II and the Holocaust.

After the German invasion of Poland in September 1939, Salomon's grandmother, distressed by the expansion of Hitler's empire, tried to commit suicide (she made another, successful attempt the following year). It was only then that Salomon learned a family secret hidden from her since childhood: six people in her family, including Salomon's mother, had taken their own lives. (Salomon had been told that her mother, who died when Salomon was eight years old, had succumbed to influenza.) Her grandmother's death, the dislocations of war, and her increasing clashes with her grandfather—including an exchange in which he angrily suggested that Salomon kill herself—provided her with the determination to paint the story of her life to avoid falling victim to this fate and as a means of grappling with her family's history. Salomon spent more than a year crafting her autobiography in 1941 and 1942, composing over 1,300 notebook-sized gouache paintings on which text was written directly or on attached overlays. From these, she selected more than 700 for inclusion in *Life? or Theatre?*

In June 1943, Salomon married Alexander Nagler, a Jewish Austrian refugee also living in southern France. Just three months after their marriage they were arrested during intensified Nazi roundups of Jews along the Riviera. Before her apprehension, Salomon had given *Life? or Theatre?* to a friend, with whom it safely remained until war's end. After her arrest, Salomon was transported to Auschwitz, and she apparently was gassed soon after her arrival at the camp on October 10, 1943.

—*Adam C. Stanley*

See also Holocaust and Jewish Women

References and Further Reading

Felstiner, Mary Lowenthal. 1994. *To Paint Her Life: Charlotte Salomon in the Nazi Era.* Berkeley: University of California.
Salomon, Charlotte. 1998. *Charlotte Salomon: Life? or Theatre?* Trans. Leila Vennewitz; ed. Judith C. E. Belinfante, Christine Fischer-Defoy, and Ad Petersen. Zwolle, the Netherlands: Waanders.

Salvation Army in World War I

Nondenominational Christian organization that provided assistance to Allied soldiers during World War I. The Salvation Army was founded in England in 1865 by William Booth (1829–1912), a former Methodist minister. Throughout its history, the group's purpose has been to care for the physical and spiritual needs of all people, regardless of their beliefs. The Salvation Army's effort in World War I was no exception.

Evangeline Cory Booth (1865–1950), daughter of the Salvation Army's founder, was one of the group's most influential members during World War I. Eventually becoming the organization's first woman general, Booth was awarded the prestigious Distinguished Service Medal by President Woodrow Wilson in 1919 for her wartime assistance.

When U.S. troops left for France in 1917, Evangeline Booth immediately began to formulate plans for her officers, male and female, to make the trip overseas. Women officers in the Salvation Army during World War I, commonly referred to as "lassies," were among the first women to be given positions of authority in the sector of social services and often faced physical danger in the frontline areas. Officers of the Salvation Army provided Bible classes as well as religious services for the soldiers. Salvation Army officers also mended torn clothes and helped U.S. soldiers correspond with their families back home. The affection of the "doughboys" was won by the Salvation Army, which provided doughnuts, pancakes, cupcakes, and lemonade to tired and thirsty soldiers.

—*Thomas M. Ethridge*

See also United States, Home Front during World War I; Young Men's Christian Association, World War I

References and Further Reading

Lavine, Sigmund A. 1970. *Evangeline Booth: Daughter of Salvation.* New York: Dodd, Mead.
Wilson, Philip Whitwell. 1948. *General Evangeline Booth of the Salvation Army.* New York: Charles Scribner's Sons.

Samson (Sampson), Deborah (1760–1827)

Veteran of the American Revolutionary War. Deborah Samson volunteered for the 4th Massachusetts Regiment disguised as a man named

Robert Shurtleff or Shirtleff. When her true gender was discovered, she was discharged.

Samson was born in 1760 in Plympton, Massachusetts. Her father died when she was five years old. Because of the family's poverty, Deborah was "bound out" to a farming family until she was eighteen. She was apparently enthused by stories of the Revolutionary War. After being emancipated, she earned enough money to buy cloth and make a man's outfit. Dressed as a male, she volunteered and was accepted into the Massachusetts militia as Timothy Thayer. This first attempt to serve in the military failed when it was discovered that she was a woman. Her second effort was more successful. She served in the 4th Massachusetts Regiment from May 20, 1782, until October 23, 1782. Years of hard work on the farm and a robust physique made her quite fit for the rigors of military life. She was wounded in an engagement near Tarrytown, New York, and again four months later. Neither of these wounds led to the discovery of her gender. When she developed a debilitating fever at Yorktown, however, it was discovered that she was a woman, and she was discharged.

In 1785 she married a farmer, Robert Gannett, and they had three children. She told her story to Horace Mann, who published a fictionalized autobiography of her life, *The Female Review: Life of Deborah Sampson the Female Soldier in the War of the Revolution*, in 1797. It was Mann who added the "p" to her name. A few years after the book was published, Mann wrote a script for Samson to recite on stage and organized a tour. In 1802 she appeared in Boston, New York City, and other towns. After reciting her narrative she would perform the manual of arms.

With the support of her former officers, Deborah received backpay from the state of Massachusetts and a pension from the U.S. government for her military service. After her death in 1827, her husband successfully petitioned for survivor benefits for himself and their children.

—*Bernard Cook*

See also American Revolution, Role of Women in the; Corbin, Margaret Cochrane; Molly Pitcher

References and Further Reading

Crompton, Samuel Willard. 1999. Sampson, Deborah. Pages 230–231 in *American National Biography*. New York: Oxford University.

De Pauw, Linda Grant. 1998. *Battle Cries and Lullabies: Women in War from Pre-history to the Present*. Norman: University of Oklahoma.

Laffin, John. 1967. *Women in Battle*. London and New York: Abelard-Schuman.

SÁNCHEZ MANDULEY, CELIA (1922–1980)

Cuban revolutionary. A native of Manzanilla, located in the eastern province of Granma in Cuba, Celia Sánchez was born in 1922 into a middle-class family. Her revolutionary career began when she helped with the clandestine dissemination of the treatise *History Will Absolve Me*, Fidel Castro's lengthy criticism of Fulgencio Batista's dictatorship and the sole speech Castro used to defend himself after his failed 1953 attack of the Moncada barracks, the headquarters of the Cuban military in the southern part of the country in Santiago.

Charmed by the charismatic young lawyer, Sánchez joined his band of followers, and she is rumored to have been romantically involved with Fidel for many years. During Fidel's exile, Sánchez continued to work to advance the revolution and participated in the 1956 uprising in Santiago de Cuba. Sánchez helped found the July 26th Movement, whose manifesto outlined the original doctrine of the Cuban Revolution. The writings were explicitly based on ten principles taken from writings by poet and martyr for Cuban independence José Martí (Brenner et al. 1989, 35–41). In 1957 Sánchez joined the guerrilla fighters in the Sierra

Maestra, where she and Fidel Castro organized the first all-female platoon. The unit was named after national heroine Mariana Grajales. One of Fidel's closest assistants during the three years of warfare that would culminate in the 1959 victory, Sánchez was instrumental in forming *Radio Rebelde,* the voice of the rebel army. Sánchez, who never had children herself, was said to act as a mother to all rebel fighters (Corona 2004). The historian Pedro Alvarez Tabío emphasizes her high moral standards, profound humanity, and respect for others. She is considered a Heroine of the Revolution and a model for Cuban youth.

—*Sara E. Cooper*

See also Cuban Revolution, Women in the; Grajales Cuello, Mariana; Hernández Rodríguez del Rey, Melba; Latin America, Women in Guerrilla Movements in; Santamaría Cuadrado, Haydée

References and Further Reading

Alvarez Tabío, Pedro. 2003. *Celia: Ensayo para una biografía* [Celia: A Biographical Essay]. Prologue by Armando Hart. Havana: Oficina de Publicaciones del Consejo de Estado.

Brenner, Philip, William M. Leogrande, Donna Rich, and Daniel Siegel. 1989. *The Cuba Reader.* New York: Grove.

Corona Jerez, Martín. "Cubans Pay Homage to Cuban Heroine Celia Sánchez on Mother's Day." AIN Cuba Web. http://www.ain.cubaweb .cu/english/0905boletin.htm (accessed October 26, 2004).

Juventud Rebelde Web. Pedro Alvarez Tabío. "Auténtica flor." http://www.jrebelde.cubaweb .cu/2004/ enero-marzo/ene-11/autentica.html (accessed October 28, 2004).

Sánchez Manduley, Celia, and Haydée Santamaría Cuadrado. 1981. Recuerdos. In *Los dispositivos en la flor: Cuba/Literatura desde la Revolución* [Methods in Flower: Cuban Literature since the Revolution]. Edited by Edmundo Desnoes. Hanover, NH: Ediciones del Norte.

Vega Belmonte, Belkis. 1980. *Celia.* Havana: ICAIC.

SANDES, FLORA (1876–1956)

British woman who fought in the Serbian army during World War I and became an officer. Flora Sandes was the daughter of a Scottish clergyman. When World War I began, she volunteered to work in Serbia with the ambulance service operated by the Scottish Women's Hospitals. She worked for eighteen months with the Serbian Red Cross. When the Bulgarians joined the Central Powers and a joint offensive threw the Serbs into a massive retreat, she returned to Britain to solicit material support for the Serbs. She returned to Salonika in November 1915 and, with great difficulty. made it to the front at Prilep beyond Monastir (Bitolj). There she worked in a hospital and as a nurse with a regimental ambulance corps. As the Central Powers overran the remainder of Serbia, Sandes withdrew with the Serbian army into Albania and traded her role in the ambulance service for a combat role in the regular Serbian army. She had reluctantly offered to return to Salonika rather than be a burden during the retreat, but to her delight, the Serbian

Sergeant Major Flora Sandes, reportedly the only British woman in the Serbian army. (TopFoto.co.uk)

FLORA SANDES

"We met Dr. Nikotitch there again, and he and Commandant Wasitch asked me if I really had made up my mind to go on. They said that the journey through Albania would be very terrible, that nothing we had gone through so far was anything approaching it, and that they would send me to Salonica if I liked. I was not quite sure whether having a woman with them might be more of an anxiety and nuisance to them than anything else, though they knew I did not mind roughing it; and I asked them, if so, to tell me quite frankly, and I would go down to Salonica that night. They were awfully nice, though, and said 'for them it would be better if I stopped [stayed?], because it would encourage the soldiers, who already all knew me, and to whose simple minds I represented, so to speak, the whole of England.' The only thought that buoyed them up at that time, and still does, was that England would never forsake them. So that settled the matter, as I should have been awfully sorry if I had had to go back, and I believe the fact that I went through with them did perhaps sometimes help to encourage the soldiers."

—Flora Sandes, *An English Woman-Sergeant in the Serbian Army*
(London: Hodder and Stoughton, 1916), 91–92.

officers said that the presence of a female Briton would be an inspiration to their men (Sandes 1916, 91). During the retreat, though it was known that she was a woman, Sandes "became attached properly to a company, and became an ordinary soldier" (Sandes 1916, 124). As a member of the 4th Company, 1st Battalion, of the Serbian army, Sandes participated in fighting, and in December 1915 she was promoted to the rank of sergeant major. She was evacuated with her unit from Durazzo to Corfu. When her unit was shipped to Salonika, she briefly returned to England. While there she wrote *An English Woman-Sergeant in the Serbian Army* in an effort to gain support in Britain for the Serbian cause.

Sandes, who later wrote, "I seemed to take to soldiering like a duck to water" (Sandes 1927, 17), rejoined her unit on the Salonika front in the fall of 1916. She was wounded by a grenade in an engagement with the Bulgarians. Though the wound put her out of action for six months, Sandes returned to her unit. She fought until shrapnel remaining in her leg caused further hospitalization and a two-month period of recuperation, which she spent in England. During this period she spoke throughout Britain and to troops in France to acquaint her audiences with

the sacrifices of the Serbs and to garner material support for them. After two months Sandes was back in Macedonia with her unit. When the war ended she remained in the Serbian army. In April 1919 she was promoted to the rank of lieutenant. Demobilized at the end of October 1922, Sandes remained in the reserves. She was promoted to captain in September 1926 and rose to the rank of major before her retirement in 1927. She married Yuri Yudenich, who had been the commander of a White anti-Bolshevik army during the Russian Civil War. He died in September 1941, and Sandes returned to England in 1945.

—*Bernard Cook*

See also Inglis, Elsie, and the Scottish Women's Hospitals; Stobart, Mabel

References and Further Reading

Laffin, John. 1967. *Women in Battle*. London: Abelard-Schuman.

Sandes, Flora. 1916. *An English Woman-Sergeant in the Serbian Army*. London: Hodder and Stoughton.

———. 1927. *The Autobiography of a Woman Soldier: A Brief Record of Adventure with the Serbian Army, 1916–1919*. New York: Frederick A. Stokes.

SANSOM, ODETTE
(1912–1995)

British Special Operations Executive (SOE) operative during World War II. Odette Marie Celine Brailly was born on April 28, 1912, in Amiens, France. In 1931 she married Roy Sansom, an Englishman, and moved to London. After the German occupation of France, despite the fact that she was married and had three daughters, Sansom was recruited to train for the SOE. In 1942 she was put ashore near Cannes to serve as the radio operator for the Spindle network led by Peter Churchill. When the Churchill network was betrayed by a double agent, Churchill and Sansom were imprisoned and tortured by the Gestapo at the Fresnes prison. Hoping to gain leniency, Sansom insisted that Churchill was the nephew of Winston Churchill and that she was his wife. The ruse must have had some effect. Though she was condemned to death, neither she nor Churchill was executed. She was sent with seven other British operatives from the Prosper network, who were later killed, to Karlsruhe. Instead of being transferred with the other agents for execution at Dachau or Natzweiler-Struthof, Sansom was sent to the women's concentration camp at Ravensbrück on July 18, 1944. She survived her imprisonment, as did Churchill. Her husband died during the war, and she married Churchill in 1947. They were divorced in 1956, after which she married Geoffrey Hallowes. For her wartime activity, Sansom was made a Member of the British Empire (MBE) and received the George Cross. She died on March 13, 1995.

—*Bernard Cook*

Odette Sansom, British secret agent, with her former commanding officer, Captain Peter Churchill, after their wedding. (Bettmann/Corbis)

See also Atkins, Vera H.; Beekman, Yolande; Damerment, Madeleine; Plewman, Eliane; Ravensbrück

References and Further Reading

Tickell, Jerrard. 1949. *Odette: The Story of a British Agent*. London: Chapman.

Santamaría Cuadrado, Haydée (1922–1980)

Cuban revolutionary. Haydée Santamaría was born in Esmeralda, Las Villas, Cuba, in 1922. She and Melba Hernández were the only women combatants—among 165 men—in the famous attack led by Fidel Castro on the Moncada Barracks, the headquarters of the Cuban military in the southern part of the country in Santiago, on July 26, 1953. When the dissidents' assault was rebuffed, both Haydée Santamaría and her brother Abel were taken prisoner, along with most of the surviving rebels. Abel was among those tortured and killed by the Batista regime as reprisal; Haydée remained incarcerated for approximately six months. Her subsequent involvement in the underground movement included the clandestine printing of Fidel's speech *History Will Absolve Me*, direction and planning of the July 26th Movement, and participation in the 1956 uprising in Santiago de Cuba. When Fidel Castro returned to Cuba with Che Guevara to lead the rebellion against Fulgencio Batista, Santamaría joined the guerrilla troops stationed in the Sierra Maestra and made history as one of the fiercest rebel soldiers.

After the triumph of the socialist revolution in 1959, Santamaría continued to be intimately involved in Cuban political life, serving on the Central Committee of the Communist Party and the Council of State. Her principal legacy, however, was the foundation and direction of the cultural institution Casa de las Americas, which from its inception has supported revolutionary literature and art both nationally and internationally. In a talk that Santamaría gave at the Universidad de La Habana in 1967, she told the students, "For me to be communist isn't to be a militant in a [political] party; for me, to be communist is to have an attitude toward life" (Rebelión.org 2004; translation by the author). Her writings on the Moncada assault and the Vietnam War, published posthumously, provide an interesting perspective on armed combat, ideology, and sociopolitical responsibility. Haydée Santamaría committed suicide in 1980, twenty-seven years to the day after she participated in the Moncada assault.

—*Sara E. Cooper*

See also Cuban Revolution, Women in the; Grajales Cuello, Mariana; Hernández Rodríguez del Rey, Melba; Latin America, Women in Guerrilla Movements in; Sánchez Manduley, Celia

References and Further Reading

Maclean, Betsy, ed. 2004. *Haydée Santamaría: Rebel Lives*. New York and Melbourne: Ocean Press.

Rebelión.org. "Haydée Santamaría, una mujer revolucionaria" [Haydée Santamaría, a Revolutionary Mother]. Cátedra de Formación Política de Ernesto Che Guevara (Introduction and letters from Santamaría to Che Guevara and to her parents). http://www.rebelion.org/noticia.php?id=133 (accessed October 26, 2004).

Sánchez Manduley, Celia, and Haydée Santamaría Cuadrado. 1981. Recuerdos. In *Los dispositivos en la flor: Cuba/Literatura desde la Revolución* [Methods in Flower: Cuban Literature since the Revolution]. Edited by Edmundo Desnoes. Hanover, NH: Ediciones del Norte.

Santamaría Cuadrado, Haydée. 1985a. *Haydée habla del Moncada* [Haydée Speaks of Moncada]. Havana: Casa de las Americas.

———. 1985b. *Haydée habla del Vietnam* [Haydée Speaks of Vietnam]. Havana: Casa de las Americas.

SAUMONEAU, LOUISE (1875–1949)

French socialist, feminist, and advocate of international peace credited with originating International Women's Day in France. Louise Saumoneau was born in France in 1875 and worked as a seamstress before becoming involved in the socialist-feminist movement in the 1890s as an opponent of class collaboration with bourgeois feminism. Saumoneau believed in class warfare and preached the annihilation of the bourgeoisie.

After the Groupe Féministe Socialiste (Socialist Feminist League) was founded in 1899, Saumoneau, then twenty-four years old, was elected as its leader. In her first speech as group leader, Saumoneau declared that the Groupe Féministe Socialiste's goal was for women to break the chains of their past and to put an end to all injustices directed toward women, as well as other individuals.

At a 1910 conference in Copenhagen, Denmark, organized by the German socialist journalist Clara Zedkin, the proposal of an International Women's Day received considerable attention. In 1914, following the ideas proposed by Zedkin, Saumoneau promoted the celebration of International Women's Day, and on March 8 of that year, 6,000 French women gathered and placed bouquets at Place de la Concorde in Paris. These women also began to voice their desire for the right to vote and for political equality, making this occasion the first public demonstration for women's suffrage in France. Based on this success, Saumoneau convinced some of the women present to participate in an international socialist women's conference for peace that was to take place in Bern, Switzerland. Saumoneau attended this conference as a private citizen in order to avoid partisan conflicts.

During World War I, Saumoneau, true to her pacifist ideals, broke with her party's support for the war and was arrested for antiwar activities. She died in 1949.

—*Stephanie Longo*

See also International Congress of Women: Antiwar Protest of Women in World War I; Luxemburg, Rosa

References and Further Reading

Journée Internationale des Femmes. 2004. http://www.v1.paris.fr/fr/actualites/journee_femmes_2004 (accessed March 1, 2005).

McMillan, James F. "Biographies: Women's Suffrage." http://www.st-andrews.ac.uk/~jfec/cal/suffrage/coredocs/biograp3.htm (accessed March 1, 2005).

Saumoneau, Louise. 1923. *Principes et action féministes socialistes* [Feminist Socialist Principles and Action]. Paris: Publications de la Femme Socialiste.

SCHAFT, JEANNETJE JOANNA (HANNIE) (1920–1945)

Dutch resister executed by the Nazis. Jeannetje Joanna (Hannie) Schaft was born on September 16, 1920, in Haarlem, the Netherlands. Her parents were teachers and socialists. Schaft was studying law in Amsterdam when the Germans invaded on May 10, 1940. Her family's political orientation had prepared her to actively oppose the Nazis. By 1942 Hannie was stealing identity papers from mailboxes and lockers in public places to provide false documentation for Jews. In 1943, when students were required to sign an oath of loyalty to the occupation regime, Hannie refused and had to leave the University of Amsterdam.

She became a member of the Haarlemse Raad van Verzet (RVV, Haarlem Resistance Council). With her friends, sisters Truus and Freddie Oversteegen, Hannie distributed underground newspapers, stole identity papers and weapons, wheedled information from German soldiers about coastal defenses, and placed Jewish children with people willing to hide them. Eventually, Hannie engaged in sabotage and the murder of Nazi agents and collaborators. In

November 1943, Hannie and three others attempted to blow up a power station in the Velsen-Noord district of the northern Netherlands, but some of the explosives failed to detonate. There was some damage to the electrical system, but only part of the electric-powered rail system was affected.

To hide her identity, Hannie dyed her red hair black and wore glasses with plain lenses. Nevertheless, during a routine identity check on March 21, 1945, Hannie was caught with resistance newspapers in her bicycle case. Under intense interrogation she admitted killing a Dutch collaborator. On April 17, 1945, shortly before the end of the war, she was executed by the Nazis on the dunes near Haarlem, where hundreds of other Dutch resisters had been shot.

In 1981 a film was produced based on Theun de Vries's book *Het meisje met het rode haar* (The Girl with Red Hair).

—*Bernard Cook*

See also De Jongh, Andrée

References and Further Reading

"Hannie Schaft: Im Kampf gegen Fascismus [In Struggle against Fascism]." Stiftung Nationale Hannie Schaft-Herdenking. http://www.hannieschaft.nl/21.html (accessed October 9, 2003).

Polsermans, Sophie. "Hannie Schaft: Symbool van vrouwenverzet [Symbol of Female Resistance]." Stiftung Nationale Hannie Schaft-Herdenking. http://www.hannieschaft.nl/21.html (accessed October 9, 2003).

Vries, Theun de. 1956. *Het meisje met het rode haar* [The Girl with Red Hair]. Amsterdam: Querido.

SCHINDLER, EMILIE (1907–2002)

Worked with her husband, Oskar, to rescue Jews during World War II. Emilie Pelsl was born on October 22, 1907, to Catholic farmers in the village of Alt Moletein, Sudetenland, presently in the Czech Republic. Emilie was convent-educated but endured an oppressive family life. She studied agriculture at college. She married fellow Roman Catholic Oskar Schindler (1908–1974) on March 6, 1928, in Zwittau in the Sudetenland after a whirlwind six-week courtship. Their marriage proved to be turbulent. Oskar Schindler had numerous mistresses and two illegitimate children soon after the marriage. He disliked working, enjoyed partying, and never made a dependable income.

In 1935 Oskar found work as a spy with German military counterintelligence, the *Abwehrdienst*. After the 1939 German invasion of Poland, Schindler was offered an administrative post in a Jewish-owned enamelware factory in Krakow that employed Jews from the local ghetto and from the Plaschow concentration camp. Emilie arrived in Krakow in 1941. Unlike Oskar, she did not enjoy the spotlight and performed major tasks at the factory behind the scenes.

Oskar promised the Nazis funds for each Jewish worker for a factory in Brünnlitz. Emilie obtained the formally signed papers from the mayor of Brünnlitz (her former swimming coach), permitting them to retain the Jews. Emilie's role at Brünnlitz was that of German hausfrau. She kept busy entertaining Nazis and secretly finding food on the black market to feed the Jewish workers, who were unable to perform any type of labor due to poor health.

In 1945 Emilie was responsible for single-handedly rescuing 120 Jews from a cattle car bound for Auschwitz concentration camp. She nursed the half frozen, emaciated victims until she became exhausted. These people never worked. By the war's end the Schindlers had spent the earnings from the factory saving over 1,200 Jews. They were penniless and moved to Buenos Aires, Argentina, with Oskar's mistress and some Jewish people they had rescued. After numerous unsuccessful business ventures, Oskar left Argentina in 1957 and returned to Germany, leaving Emilie with his debts. They never saw one another again. Oskar died in 1974. The reclusive Emilie lived in a small cottage with a menagerie of pets. She was financially supported by the Jewish organization B'nai Brith and, eventually, by a small pension from the German government.

Emilie received Israel's Righteous among the Nations Award in 1993 for her efforts to save Jews. She traveled to the United States as director Steven Spielberg's guest at the screening of his movie based on Thomas Keneally's book *Schindler's List*. Despite the fact he gave Emilie scarce mention in the movie, Spielberg paid her $50,000. She also met President Bill Clinton and First Lady Hillary Clinton. Thereafter she traveled to Israel, where she was well received. In 1996 Emilie wrote her autobiography, *In Schindler's Shadow: Where Light and Shadow Meet—A Memoir*. Emilie moved to Germany and lived in a nursing home after suffering several strokes. She died on October 5, 2002.

—Annette Richardson

See also Holocaust and Jewish Women; Wertheimer, Martha

References and Further Reading

Crowe, David. 2004. *Oskar Schindler: The Untold Account of His Life, Wartime Activities, and the True Story behind the List*. Boulder, CO: Westview.

Keneally, Thomas. 1993. *Schindler's List*. New York: Touchstone.

Rosenberg, Erika. 2001. *Ich, Emilie Schindler* [I, Emilie Schindler]. Munich: Herbig Verlag.

Schindler, Emilie. 1997. *In Schindler's Shadow: Where Light and Shadow Meet—A Memoir*. New York: Norton.

SCHMIDT, KITTY (1882–1954)

Owner of a prominent brothel taken over by the *Sicherheit Deinst* (SD, Nazi Security Service). Kitty Schmidt's establishment at 11 Giesebrecht Strasse had a reputation for being the most luxurious and exclusive brothel in Berlin. Walter Schellenberg, head of the SD, was ordered by Reinhard Heydrich, second in command in the *Schutzstaffel* (SS, Defense Echelon), to detect security leaks by infiltrating a high-class brothel. Heydrich was concerned about the disclosure of sensitive information by German bureaucrats and officers. Schellenberg did more than infiltrate the brothel. Kitty Schmidt, the owner of Pension Schmidt, was stopped at the Dutch frontier as she attempted to leave Germany in June 1939. She was brought back to Gestapo headquarters on Prinz Albrecht Strasse in Berlin, where she was confronted with her many offenses, among which were illegally transferring money to England through departing Jews and utilizing a forged passport. She was given the alternative of being sent to a concentration camp or cooperating with the Gestapo; she opted for the latter.

Kitty Schmidt's brothel was commandeered by the SD. They placed listening devices in every room and had a recording center in the basement. After careful psychiatric and other "expert" screening of prostitutes rounded up by a vice squad, Schellenberg selected twenty physically ravishing, talented, and reliable agents. The women were given a wide-ranging seven-week course to acquaint them with domestic and foreign political issues, the significance of military decorations, and the art of extracting secrets from their customers.

In March 1940 the operation was ready. Kitty was instructed to proceed as normal with old customers, utilizing her old staff. When a new customer, German or foreign, arrived with a special referral, she was to offer him an album with pictures of the twenty prostitute-agents. When one was chosen, Kitty would call the SD, who would send the selected agent to gather information.

The British became aware of the operation, and a British spy was able to tap the house's cables from December 1940 until 1943, when the SD operation was terminated. Discipline among the prostitute-agents had become increasingly lax, and a bomb hit the establishment in July 1942. Kitty was moved to the ground floor, but during 1943 the SD decided to end its surveillance operation at the brothel. Kitty stayed, as did many of the agents, but she was sworn to remain silent about the operation. She kept her promise, and the 25,000 disk recordings of the conversations of the brothel's clients disappeared or were destroyed as the Russians fought their way into Berlin.

—*Bernard Cook*

See also Germany, Women and the Home Front, World War II

References and Further Reading

Robson, Dean. "Operation Kitty's." Third Reich Factbook. http://www.skalman.nu/third-reich/ss-operationkittys.htm (accessed October 30, 2003).

SCHOLL, SOPHIE (1921–1943)

Student at the University of Munich executed by the Nazis for her activities with the White Rose resistance group. Sophie Scholl was born into a deeply Catholic family in 1921 in Forchtenberg am Kocker, where her father was mayor. She had two sisters and two brothers but was particularly close to her brother Hans. Though their father counseled caution regarding their devotion to the Nazi government, Sophie and Hans felt a deep sense of German patriotism, and they both participated in the Third Reich's youth programs. Hans became a leader in the Hitler Youth, and Sophie served as a group leader in the League of German Girls. She enjoyed the exercise, field trips, service activities, and camaraderie offered by the organization. It was not until later that she understood her father's sentiment.

In 1937 while attempting to eradicate all non-Nazi organizations, the Gestapo arrested Hans and his siblings Inge, Sophie, and Werner because of Hans's association with a group known as the Young Germans. This group only existed informally, and its activities, based on friendship, outdoor pursuits, and creative expression, were harmless to the regime, but the Gestapo suspected it of being subversively independent. For Sophie and her siblings, their arrest engendered bitterness toward the regime. Like Hans, Sophie began to lose her enthusiasm for the Third Reich and its pervasive control. She became aware of the changes in her country, the restrictions placed on its citizens, and the danger in openly criticizing Hitler and his government.

By the beginning of the war in 1939 Sophie no longer approved of the regime. Ideologically, she disapproved of a powerful nation using its strength against a much weaker nation such as Poland, and in 1940, when the military sent Hans to the front, Sophie's disapproval of the war rose to a personal level. As a student in secondary school, she was particularly interested in art, including forms of modern art regarded as offensive by the regime. Her interests provoked the disapproval of the school's principal, who unsuccessfully attempted to prevent her from graduating and entering the University of Munich, where Hans was a medical student.

Her entry into the university, however, was delayed because of the National Labor Service. In order to avoid directly participating in the war effort, Sophie opted to teach in a kindergarten, believing that six months as a teacher would exempt her from six months of wartime labor. Unfortunately for Sophie, the National Labor Service called on her to work for another six months following her period of kindergarten teaching. She worked on a farm with other National Labor Service women, and the time was not without some enjoyment. During the day she took pleasure in the company of the other women, and at night she read classic works of theology and philosophy. Reading the work of

St. Augustine reinforced her moral outrage at the war and the state of German society.

Sophie finally entered the university in 1942, but she soon became disillusioned with her education at an establishment that sought to reinforce Nazi ideology. In the same year, through one of Archbishop August von Galen's sermons, she learned of the Nazis' euthanasia program, which murdered mentally ill, diseased, and handicapped individuals regarded to be unworthy of life. Shortly after she read the copied sermon, Sophie learned of Hans's participation in the White Rose, a resistance group consisting of a professor and students at the university. She demanded that Hans allow her to participate, lest she miss her opportunity to actively resist a regime that strove to remove citizens' personal rights and integrity.

As a member of the White Rose, Sophie contributed to the production and distribution of leaflets urging opposition to the regime. On February 18, 1943, Sophie and Hans dropped leaflets in broad daylight from an interior balcony in one of the university's buildings. They were arrested, and the People's Court quickly sentenced the siblings, along with other White Rose members, to death by guillotine. Although her prosecutors offered her clemency in exchange for repentance, Sophie refused, and she was beheaded on February 22, 1943.

—*Rachael I. Cherry*

See also Ballestrem-Solf, Countess Lagi; Kirchner, Johanna; Kuckhoff, Greta; Seele, Gertrud; Terwiel, Maria; Von Thadden, Elizabeth; Yorck von Wartenburg, Countess Marion

References and Further Reading

Hanser, Richard. 1979. *A Noble Treason: The Revolt of the Munich Students against Hitler.* New York: G. P. Putnam's Sons.

Michalczyk, John J., ed. 2004. *Confront! Resistance in Nazi Germany.* New York: Peter Lang.

Scholl, Inge. 1983. *The White Rose: Munich 1942–1943.* Middletown, CT: Wesleyan University Press.

SCHOLTZ-KLINK (NÉE TREUSCH), GERTRUD (B. 1902)

Arguably the most influential woman in the Third Reich. By 1939 Gertrud Scholtz-Klink oversaw various women's organizations comprising approximately 8 million German women and 3 million girls in the Hitler Youth. In her own words, Scholtz-Klink believed her responsibility was to "infuse the daily life of all German women with Nazi ideals" (Koonz 1986, xxiv).

When Gertrud Treusch was eighteen, she married Friedrich Klink, a teacher, and bore him six children. Friedrich, a member of the Brown Shirts, became the leader of the Nazi Party in Offenburg but in 1930 died from a heart attack during a street battle. Gertrud stayed involved in the party by organizing other wives. In 1932, she married Günther Scholtz, a country doctor, but was divorced from him in 1938.

Scholtz-Klink rose to prominence within the National Socialist Party by virtue of her contacts with powerful men, including Adolf Hitler, SS leader Heinrich Himmler, Reichsmarshall Hermann Goering, and writer Alfred Rosenberg. In 1934 Scholtz-Klink was asked by Hitler to become chief of women's affairs in the new government. In 1939 she married an SS general (SS Obergruppenführer) August Heissmeyer, further entrenching Scholtz-Klink in the National Socialist state. Historian Claudia Koonz notes that Scholtz-Klink was largely responsible for cultivating the "social side of tyranny" (Koonz 1986, xxxiii). Scholtz-Klink advocated "eugenic purification" by instructing women to choose their mates carefully (Koonz 1986, 168). She considered preserving the German "race" a priority in which women played a special role. Scholtz-Klink helped develop a marriage course that underscored the importance of race and emphasized the importance of women's participation in the domestic sphere as means to achieve a National Socialist state in accordance with Hitler's vision. Scholtz-Klink unreservedly supported the Third Reich's anti-Semitic policies.

As the widow of a Nazi martyr and a mother, Scholtz-Klink was a logical choice to assume the role of organizing German women in the Third Reich. She mobilized women for the German war economy without challenging the Nazi leadership and straying away from women's strictly defined roles of mother, nurturer, and keeper of the National Socialist faith. Scholtz-Klink was adept at cautioning women to avoid appearing careerist and becoming overly cultured, values antithetical to National Socialism.

Under Scholtz-Klink's tenure, 5 million women worked in the Nazi Labor Front, 4 million worked in the *Frauenwerk* (Women's Work) organizations, and 2 million belonged to the elite *Frauenschaften* (Women's Organization). She also supervised 100,000 teachers. Gertrud Scholtz-Klink played a vital role in sustaining the National Socialist movement and, later, the Third Reich. She rose to prominence in part because she never challenged the roles assigned to women; she simply acted as an effective bureaucrat in ensuring that women supported the National Socialist state. Although Scholtz-Klink was not a participant in any of the Third Reich's high-level discussions affecting women, she effectively implemented leadership decisions. After World War II, Scholtz-Klink went into hiding and was not arrested until 1948. Later that year she was sentenced by a French military court to 18 months in prison. In 1949 Scholtz-Klink was declared "de-Nazified" and began receiving a pension by the West German government. She remained unapologetic about her role in the Third Reich, including supporting its anti-Semitic policies.

—*Brian E. Crim*

See also Germany, Women and the Home Front, World War II

References and Further Reading

Koonz, Claudia. 1986. *Mothers in the Fatherland: Women, the Family, and Nazi Politics.* New York: St. Martin's.

Leck, Ralph M. 2000. Conservative Empowerment and the Gender of Nazism: Paradigms of Power and Complicity in German Women's History. *Journal of Women's History* 12(2):147–169.

SCHULZE-BOYSEN, LIBERTAS (1913–1942)

Member of the German anti-Nazi resistance. Libertas Haas-Heye was born in 1913. Her father was a professor, and her mother was the daughter of Prince Eulenburg, a friend of Kaiser Wilhelm. Libertas spent much of her childhood on the Eulenburg estate, Liebenberg. After attending school in Switzerland, she worked as a freelance journalist in the press section of Metro-Goldwyn-Mayer in Berlin and then for the Berlin Cultural Film Center. In 1936 she married Harro Schulze-Boysen, who had been the publisher of a journal, *Der Gegner,* that had been suppressed in April 1933. Their home became a gathering place for like-minded opponents of the Nazi regime. They regarded the war as an unmitigated disaster. In 1940 Greta Kuckhoff introduced Libertas to Mildred Harnack. Libertas and Harro then joined the anti-Nazi resistance group Rote Kapelle (Red Chorus), organized by the Harnacks. Libertas gathered evidence of the mass murder of Jews and other civilians in Poland and Russia. At the Cultural Film Center she made copies of damning film that came into the center so that it might be used later to identify and convict war criminals.

Nazi intelligence deciphered Russian code and discovered the existence of the large resistance group in Berlin. Harro was arrested on August 30, 1942; he was tortured and executed on December 22, 1942. Libertas was arrested on September 8, as she attempted to leave Berlin and was interrogated by the Gestapo. She was betrayed by Gertrud Breiter, a Gestapo secretary, who had convinced Libertas of her sympathy. Libertas told Breiter details of the resistance and asked her to warn members who had not been arrested. Libertas's terrible misjudgment was later revealed to her, causing her great dismay. After the war, however, Nazi prosecutor Manfred Roeder asserted that Libertas's indiscretion had not betrayed anyone "since the officials had known everything already" (Brysac 2000, 339). Libertas was guillotined in the Plötzenzee Prison on the same day that her husband was hanged. Prior to her execution she cried out, "Let me keep my young life" (Brysac 2000, 364).

—*Bernard Cook*

See also Harnack-Fish, Mildred; Kuckhoff, Greta

References and Further Reading

Brysac, Shareen Blair. 2000. *Resisting Hitler: Mildred Harnack and the Red Orchestra: The Life and Death of an American Woman in Nazi Germany.* New York: Oxford University.

SCHUYLER, PHILIPPA (1931–1967)

Vietnam war correspondent. While attempting in an unofficial capacity to rescue and transport schoolchildren to shelter in Da Nang, Philippa Schuyler became the second female correspondent to die during the Vietnam War. As the child of a famous interracial marriage, Schuyler, whose lifelong struggle with her identity informed her work, felt an affinity with mixed-race Vietnamese. She wrote about the demeaning treatment of African American soldiers and was disdained by white soldiers who never accepted her biracial heritage.

Born in the affluent Sugar Hill district of Harlem in 1931, Schuyler was the daughter of George Schuyler, a controversial African American journalist and leader of the Harlem Renaissance, and Josephine Codgel, a white artist

and writer. Educated primarily at home, Schuyler, a musical prodigy and genius, was exposed to her parents' intellectual circle and grew up sheltered from racial problems and the devastation of the Great Depression. Winning prizes and acclaim for her musical performances, she was judged by Detroit's Grinnel Foundation as "the brightest young composer in America." With her father's connections and her mother's determination for Philippa to succeed as an example of interracial progeny, her extraordinary activities received extensive publicity and were documented by *The New Yorker, Look Magazine, Time,* and the *New York Herald Tribune.*

As she grew older, white interest in the novelty of her achievements dissolved, and her appeal lay mainly with African American and international audiences. Performing in more than eighty countries, she never garnered attention at the same level in the United States as she did overseas. After converting to Roman Catholicism in 1958, her destinations abroad changed in focus from glamorous capitals to rustic missions in remote areas.

As her father's health declined, she struggled to support her family with earnings from piano recitals. When opportunities for performances dwindled, Schuyler followed her father's lead and became a professional journalist. As one of the few African American journalists of the 1960s whose work was syndicated by United Press International (UPI), she reached a wider audience as a writer than she had as a performer. Besides writing over 100 articles for newspapers and magazines, Schuyler published 4 nonfiction books, and she was working on a book of fiction at the time of her death. In 1962 Schuyler obtained a passport in the name of Felipa Monterro y Schuyler with the hope of obscuring her racial identity and gaining broader appeal as a performer.

By the summer of 1966 Schuyler arrived in Vietnam as a journalist and ceased working under the name Monterro. Schuyler's father, a noted conservative who supported the troops and U.S. presence in Vietnam, had retired from the *Pittsburgh Courier* and was writing for the *Manchester (NH) Union Leader,* for which Philippa also wrote. Besides working as a foreign correspondent, Schuyler performed for the troops and helped evacuate children, nuns, and priests from besieged missions. Her account of the Vietnam War, *Good Men Die* (1969), was published posthumously.

Schuyler had delayed her departure from Vietnam so that she could bring nine homeless Vietnamese orphans from Hue to Da Nang and enroll them in school. At her request, the U.S. Army supplied her with a helicopter, a pilot, and three crewmen. It was believed that Schuyler had been knocked unconscious by the impact of the helicopter's crash, which was due to a malfunction and not enemy fire.

—*Rebecca Tolley-Stokes*

See also Chapelle, Dickey; Emerson, Gloria; Fallaci, Oriana; Higgins, Marguerite; Hull, Peggy, pseud.; Journalists, American Women, during World War I; Luce, Clare Boothe; Tomara, Sonia; Trotta, Liz; Watts, Jean

References and Further Reading

Schuyler, Philippa. 1969. *Good Men Die.* New York: Twin Circle.

Talalay, Kathryn. 1992. Philippa Schuyler. Pages 983–997 in *Notable Black American Women.* Vol. 1. Edited by Jessie Carney Smith. New York: Gale.

SCOTLAND: WAR WIDOWS AND REFUGEES IN, 1640S AND 1688–1690

Scottish women victims of warfare during the British civil wars of the 1640s and the Glorious Revolution of 1688–1690. Institutions such as the Scottish parliament and privy council and the institutional structure of the Church of Scotland formulated policies that dealt with women as war widows and refugees.

Scotland was faced with a significant refugee problem in the aftermath of the 1641 Ulster Rebellion. By 1641 there was a large Scottish population in Ulster, numbering 20,000 to 30,000 (Young 2001b, 53). Many migrants or descendants of migrants returned to Scotland seeking humanitarian aid. The privy council estimated that in June 1642 there were around 4,000 refugees in the presbyteries of Ayr and Irvine in southwest Scotland (Hume Brown 1906, 267). Financial aid was to be raised via church parishes and presbyteries for distribution to refugees. Regional church records indicate that women formed a core refugee group. In Elgin in northeast Scotland, for example, the widows of ministers who had been killed in the rebellion, widows of soldiers killed in military action in the Irish troubles, and widows whose husbands had been killed by the Irish rebels formed the majority of cases considered by the Elgin kirk (church) session. Often the women had dependents, and their supplications told stories of murder, mutilation, robbery, and loss of goods and property. Anna Griffith, widow of a minister in Ireland named William Murray, appeared before the kirk session on March 18, 1643, where she explained that her husband had been crucified by the Irish rebels. She received financial aid accordingly (Cramond 1908, 245). Later, on May 29, 1645, Christian Balfour, widow of Peter Sharpe, another minister in Ireland, appeared before the presbytery of Lanark. She informed the presbytery not only that her husband had died in prison but also that she herself had been "spoiled by the cruell [*sic*] enemies" (Robertson 1839, 43).

Within the wider context of the British troubles in the early 1640s, there was a Scottish covenanting military force in Ulster from 1642. In addition to receiving financial support from the English parliament, it was supported by voluntary contributions in Scotland. Women were prominent among those who contributed financially to the upkeep of the Ulster army. Merchant accounts for Edinburgh in 1643 indicate that 12 percent of individual contributions (11 of 94) came from women. Ten of these were from widows, and one was from a daughter. Helen Gilchrist, a widow, donated £333 6s. 8d. Scots (approximately US$5,000 in 2006 values), whereas Marion Wilkie, another widow, donated £666 13s. 4d. Scots (approximately US$10,000) (Hume Brown 1906, 85–86).

Following the first civil war in England in 1646 and the subsequent withdrawal of a Scottish covenanting army from English soil in 1647, the financial package agreed to between the Scottish and English parliaments dealt with injured soldiers and the widows and orphans of covenanting soldiers who had been killed in action in England. This model of financial compensation for widows, orphans, and wounded soldiers was also followed in 1649, when compensation was to be provided for casualties of the military invasions of England, excluding the Royalist invasion of England in the summer of 1648 to defend Charles I (Young 2001a, 109–110).

War widows and refugees were also an important social issue in the Scottish context of the Glorious Revolution. In common with the early 1640s, there was return migration from Ulster with refugees bringing back tales of persecution. The administrative structure for raising and providing humanitarian aid was identical to that implemented in the early 1640s—raising money through the church. The records of the Scottish privy council provide many examples of war widows and their dependents seeking humanitarian aid. On May 5, 1690, for example, the council considered the case of Barbara McDonald. Her husband, William Hamilton, a Belfast seaman, had been killed in action fighting for King William at Carrickfergus. She was in a "very miserable and sterving [sic] condition" with no means of support for her children. She fled to Scotland to "seek bread to her cheldrein [sic]" (Balfour-Melville 1967, 227). On August 14, 1690, the council considered the case of Henry Carter from Coleraine. Carter had been in Londonderry during the infamous siege. He had survived but had lost a brother, sister, and young child. All his means and property had also been destroyed. He had a wife and two small children, one of whom was five weeks old, and he was sick and unable to work due to the "long suffering he sustained" in the siege of Londonderry (Balfour-Melville 1967, 385). Thus, he was not able to provide for his wife and family. Women could therefore be victims of warfare within the context of the family unit and not just as widows.

War widows in Scotland between 1688 and 1690 were not exclusively Scottish. On September 5, 1689, the council agreed to provide financial aid to four Dutch women, Closkine Jacobs, Hester Geilmans, Kathrin McLauchlane, and Kathrin Michells. These women had married Scottish soldiers who had probably been serving in the Anglo-Dutch brigade in the Netherlands. Their husbands had been killed in action fighting for the Williamite cause at the battle of Killiecrankie on July 27, 1689, where the Jacobite forces had triumphed.

—*John R. Young*

See also Brittain, Vera Mary; Peasants' War

References and Further Reading

Balfour-Melville, Evan Whyte Melville, ed. 1967. *The Register of the Privy Council of Scotland, 1690.* 3rd series. Vol. 15. Edinburgh: Her Majesty's Stationery Office.

Cramond, William, ed. 1908. *The Records of Elgin, 1234–1800.* Vol. 2. Aberdeen: New Spalding Club.

Hume Brown, Peter, ed. 1906. *The Register of the Privy Council of Scotland, 1638–1643.* 2nd series. Vol. 7. Edinburgh: His Majesty's Stationery Office.

Paton, Henry, ed. 1932. *The Register of the Privy Council of Scotland, 1686–1689.* 3rd series. Vol. 13. Edinburgh: His Majesty's Stationery Office.

Robertson, John, ed. 1839. *Ecclesiastical Records: Selections from Registers of the Presbytery of Lanark, 1623–1809.* Edinburgh: Abbotsford Club.

Young, John R. 2001a. The Scottish Parliament and the War for the Three Kingdoms, 1639–1651. *Parliaments, Estates, and Representation* 21:103–123.

———. 2001b. The Scottish Response to the Siege of Londonderry, 1689–1690. Pages 53–74 in *The Sieges of Derry.* Edited by William Kelly. Dublin: Four Courts Press.

———. 2004. Scotland and Ulster in the Seventeenth Century: The Movement of Peoples over the North Channel. Pages 11–22 in *Ulster and Scotland, 1600–2000: History, Language, and Identity.* Edited by William Kelly and John R. Young. Dublin: Four Courts Press.

SECORD (NÉE INGERSOLL), LAURA (1775–1868)

Canadian heroine during the War of 1812. Laura Ingersoll was born to Thomas Ingersoll and his wife, Elizabeth Dewey, in Great Barrington, Massachusetts, on September 13, 1775. In 1795 the family moved to Upper Canada, where Ingersoll received a land grant and operated a tavern in Queenston, near Niagara Falls. Laura had two stepmothers within a five-year period and numerous siblings. She married Loyalist James Secord in 1794, and the couple had four daughters and one son. During the War of 1812 between the United States and Great Britain, U.S. troops attempted to conquer Upper Canada. U.S. forces seized Fort York (present-day Toronto) and burned the parliament buildings and Government House. The troops then occupied major areas of Upper Canada and were billeted in local houses throughout the Niagara Peninsula.

The Secords provided dinner for several U.S. soldiers one evening. Laura Secord plied the soldiers with liquor. One soldier, Captain Cyrenius Chapin, imbibed too much and boasted about a forthcoming attack by Lieutenant Colonel Charles Boerstler, who was stationed at Fort George. The attack was to be at Captain John De Cew's house at Beaver Dams, which had become a British supply depot. This plan would allow the United States complete control over the Niagara Peninsula. Laura Secord overheard the plan. After the soldiers left, the Secords decided to inform British Colonel James FitzGibbon at De Cew's house.

James Secord was bedridden, recovering from shoulder and knee wounds suffered during the Battle of Queenston Heights on October 13, 1812, so Laura Secord made the journey. After obtaining a permit to visit her half brother Charles, who was ill with fever, she walked to his house early in the morning of June 22, 1813. She had hoped he would be well enough to complete the journey and alert FitzGibbon, but he was still too ill. Laura Secord continued her journey, this time accompanied by her niece Elizabeth. In order to avoid the enemy, Secord chose to bypass main roads and walked instead through bush and swamp. The oppressive heat was unbearable. Elizabeth gave up after three hours. Laura Secord had already walked thirty-two miles when she stumbled into a camp of Mohawk warriors who were British allies. They took her to De Cew's house, where she explained the U.S. plan to FitzGibbon.

The British laid a trap for the U.S. forces. FitzGibbon, with 50 British soldiers and 400 Native Americans, won the Battle of Beaver Dams on June 24, 1813. The U.S. troops were caught in an ambush. Twenty-two officers and 462 soldiers with 2 field guns and their wagons were captured. This battle decisively ended the U.S. quest for control of the Niagara Peninsula.

Secord received no recognition for her efforts after her adventures; her mission was kept quiet, reputedly because the information would have endangered her life. In September 1860, however, she told her story to His Royal Highness Prince Albert Edward, Prince of Wales, son of Queen Victoria, who was visiting the Niagara Peninsula. Following his return to England, he sent her £100 (approximately US$10,000 in 2006). This would be the only financial compensation she would ever receive. Laura Secord died on October 17, 1868, and was buried beside her husband at Drummond Hill Cemetery in Niagara Falls. Two monuments have been erected in her memory.

—*Annette Richardson*

See also Greene, Catharine Littlefield; Ludington, Sybil; Reed, Esther De Berdt

References and Further Reading

Bassett, John M. 2004. *Laura Second*. Rev. ed. Markham, Ontario, Canada: Fitzhenry and Whiteside.

Crook, Connie B. 1993. *Laura's Choice: The Story of Laura Secord*. Winnipeg, Canada: Windflower Communications.

Currie, Emma A. 1900. *The Story of Laura Secord, and Canadian Reminiscences*. Toronto, Canada: Briggs.

McKenzie, Ruth. 1971. *Laura Secord: The Legend and the Lady*. Toronto, Canada: McClelland and Stewart.

SEELE, GERTRUD (1917–1945)

German opponent of the Nazi regime. Born in Berlin, Germany, on September 22, 1917, Gertrud Seele was executed on January 12, 1945, for assisting Jewish people during World War II and for making derogatory statements about Adolf Hitler and his Nazi regime. On October 17, 1952, the 4th Criminal Chamber of the Berlin District Court overturned the conviction.

Seele grew up in a working-class family and attended a secondary school for two years. At age eighteen, she entered nursing school and specialized in public health and social welfare service. She gave birth to a daughter, Michaela, on September 11, 1941, and raised her daughter alone.

In response to the growing persecution of the Jews by the Nazi regime, Seele began hiding Jews in her basement. Her brother Paul, a former labor union secretary, and his wife, Erika, also hid Jews and brought them food and drink. Seele and Michaela were evacuated from Berlin to Merke in 1942. While there, Seele, who had a "healthy sense of justice and fair play" (Leber 1994, 83), expressed outrage against the Nazis. According to her mother, Luise, she also helped Jews. Seele returned to Berlin in 1943 but traveled back to Merke in 1944 to retrieve her belongings. While there, she was arrested for protecting Jews, as well as for making "defeatist statements, designed to undermine the fighting morale of the people" (Leber, 1994, 84).

She was tried before the People's Court in Potsdam, a court designed to judge political crimes. By 1944, though, the "trials [had] lost their last semblance of legitimate legal proceedings . . . [and, the] wording of statues was systematically misinterpreted" (Jewish Virtual Library 2004). This authoritarian court meted out the death penalty for political infractions, and executions were justified after reviewing evidence that at times consisted of only one or two pages of text.

Defended by Dr. Ernst Falck, Seele was convicted and sentenced to death. Falck requested amnesty for his client, but that motion was denied. When Seele asked to see her daughter one last time, this request was also refused, and she was hanged in the Plötzenzee prison.

Seven years after her death, Seele's mother petitioned the court on behalf of Michaela to reverse the conviction and possibly provide compensation under a new law attempting to rectify injustices performed under Hitler's dictatorship. Because many records had been lost, investigation was difficult and it is hard to say with certainly what actions Seele did or did not undertake. Nevertheless, the court eventually ruled that it was "quite clear that the decision of the former People's Court was made on purely political grounds" (Leber 1994, 85). People such as Seele were often "guilty only of exasperated words, hostile opinions, or stray gestures" (Leber 1994, xvii).

—*Kelly Boyer Sagert*

See also Ballestrem-Solf, Countess Lagi; Harnack-Fish, Mildred; Kirchner, Johanna; Kuckhoff, Greta; Von Thadden, Elizabeth; Yorck von Wartenburg, Countess Marion

References and Further Reading

Leber, Annedore. 1994. *Conscience in Revolt: Sixty-four Stories of Resistance in Germany, 1933–1945.* Boulder, CO: Westview.

Miniszewski, Ursula, intern for the Division of the Senior Historian, Center for Advanced Holocaust Studies, United States Holocaust Memorial Museum, Washington, DC. 2004. Personal communication.

"The People's Court." Jewish Virtual Library: A Division of the American-Israeli Cooperative Enterprise. http://www.us-israel.org/jsource /Holocaust/peoplesct.html (accessed May 14, 2004).\Alt}

SEMMER, MARCELLE (1895–CA. 1944)

French heroine during World War I. Following the defeat of the French in the Battle of Charleroi in August 1914, the French were forced to retreat below the Somme River. After the French had crossed the canal at Eclusier, Marcelle Semmer, then 19 years old, opened the lock despite enemy fire and threw the lock key into the canal. The crossing of the Germans was thus delayed nearly 24 hours. In January 1917 Semmer was decorated by the French government with the War Cross and the Cross of the Legion of Honor. Until 1912 approximately only 100 women had received the Legion of Honor. This amounted to only 0.25 percent of the recipients ("L'Ordre Nationale de la Légion d'Honneur" 2004).

—*Bernard Cook*

See also France, World War I, Women and the Home Front

References and Further Reading

"L'Ordre Nationale de la Légion d'Honneur, 2004." http://www.defense.gouv.fr/actualites/dossier/d29/ honneur.htm (accessed August 4, 2004).

SENESH, HANNAH (1921–1944)

Hungarian Jewish partisan who spied for the British in Hungary during World War II and sought to rescue Allied airmen and Jewish people from Nazi occupiers.

In 1939 when anti-Semitism was on the rise in Hungary, Hannah Senesh (also spelled Szenes) left her home and her mother in Budapest to travel to Palestine. Soon after arriving, she began to train as a radio officer and parachutist for the British Special Operations Executive (SOE) (Binney 2002, 315).

In 1938 Senesh became a Zionist when she realized the force of anti-Jewish sentiment in her native country, which paralleled Hitler's increasing power in Europe (Atkinson 1985, 35). Despite her Hungarian patriotism, she came to believe that Jews needed to find safety and sanctity in Palestine because the world was less and less safe for them elsewhere. Therefore, after her high school graduation, Senesh left Hungary for Palestine (Atkinson 1985, 3).

The British SOE organized teams of native speakers from central European countries. In Palestine Senesh volunteered to train as a radio operator and a parachutist with the intention of returning to Hungary with a unit of volunteers. In Egypt she was trained in sabotage and espionage (Atkinson 1985, 112). With her unit, Senesh was to enable captured and hiding Allied flyers and Jews to escape to safety (Binney 2002, 315).

In 1944 Senesh rendezvoused with five male colleagues in Italy; from there they parachuted into Hungary to join underground resisters. Senesh and her unit members were arrested after they landed. The residents of the Hungarian village where she was hiding gave in to police intimidation and turned Senesh over to the authorities. After her arrest by the Hungarian police, German soldiers discovered her radio and took her to Budapest for interrogation (Atkinson 1985, 142–143).

In custody Senesh withstood particularly severe torture but did not reveal any information except her name. The police arrested Senesh's mother to question her about her daughter's work, but they soon realized that the mother did not even know that Senesh had been in Hungary. Once this was discovered, her mother's presence was used in an attempt to manipulate Senesh, but she still refused to give her captors information about the radio transmitter or her mission (Atkinson 1985, 143). In October 1944, Senesh was executed at the age of twenty-three (Binney 2002, 316).

—*Heather E. Ostman*

See also Atkins, Vera H.

References and Further Reading

Atkinson, Linda. 1985. *In Kindling Flame: The Story of Hannah Senesh, 1921–1944.* New York: Lothrop, Lee, and Shepard Books.

Binney, Marcus. 2002. *The Women Who Lived for Danger: The Women Agents of SOE in the Second World War.* London: Hodder and Stoughton.

SICILIAN REVOLUTIONS OF 1820 AND 1848, WOMEN AND THE

Role played by women in nineteenth-century revolutions in Sicily. Despite the subordinate role assigned them in Sicilian society, women played a significant role in the upheavals that Sicily experienced in the nineteenth century, and individual women often stood out for their initiative, bravery, and leadership. For the common people of Sicily, the revolutions of 1820 and 1848 were not primarily about the structure of the political regime. Popular involvement in these upheavals was prompted by social concerns. The people of Sicily wanted food, land, and freedom from oppressive taxation. Common Sicilians, male or female, experienced government as tax collector, ally of the landowner, and brutal police. The violence of poor Sicilian women in 1820 and 1848 manifested their desperation, their anger, and their hope.

Between 1820 and 1821 violence erupted in villages across the island. Disturbances were spearheaded by the poorest segments of the peasant population, and the common demand was an end to taxation. At Grammichele, the town erupted when a tax official tried to impose the hated *macinato* (milling tax) on a poor woman who had come to grind a bit of barley. At Monforte, men and women poured into the square in answer to a church bell's call and forced the prince of Ruffo to abolish the milling tax. During the revolution women figured prominently in the casualties. They were among those killed by the military and police, and they were also among the upper-class victims of popular anger. The anarchic threat of social upheaval unleashed by the revolution so frightened property holders that they were relieved when the Neapolitan monarchy restored its authority.

Revolution erupted on the island again in Palermo on January 12, 1848. The participation of women from the popular strata—the artisans and the poor—was crucial. In the poorer sections of the city women fought alongside men. The broader support and encouragement of women, however, was even more important to the initial victory of the revolution.

Among the women who participated actively in the fighting, few are remembered individually. In Messina, Giuseppina and Paolina Vadalà, whose clothing set them apart as members of the bourgeoisie, fought beside their brothers in the streets. The most celebrated female combatant was Rosa Donato (b. 1808). The forty-year-old Donato came from the poorest segment of Messinan society. She played a singularly heroic role in the first two days of street fighting, and she commanded the citizen artillery during the eight-month bombardment of the city by the Bourbon garrison ensconced in Messina's St. Salvatore fortress. When Messina fell in September, Donato and a male comrade named Lanzetti made their way to Palermo. There the revolutionary government conferred honors on Lanzetti and rewarded him with the commission and pay of a captain of the artillery. Because Rosa Donato was a woman, however, her only reward was work assisting the artillery. After the fall of Palermo in May 1849, she returned to Messina, where she was arrested, placed in solitary confinement, tortured, and then thrown on the street. She died in absolute poverty in 1867.

There is disagreement concerning the real name and background of the most notorious of the female Sicilian revolutionaries. She has been called Maria, Teresa, Maria Teresa, and even Anna but is known as *Testa di Lana* (Wool Head). She has been variously described as a goatherd, a seller of prickly pears, and a milk seller. It is probable that she was all these things. Undoubtedly, she was from the poorest strata in the countryside around Palermo, but she had contacts in town as well. At the beginning of the revolution she already headed an armed band of thirty or forty members. Among them were three of her sons, Francesco, Antonio, and Domenico. Two other sons had been killed by the Bourbon police, and that was the source of her consuming hatred for the Bourbon police administration.

From the beginning of the revolution, Testa di Lana and her band fought the Bourbons. Her service to the cause of revolutionary Sicily initially won the praise of the government and its leader, Ruggero Settimo. The attitude of the revolutionary government and the proponents of order, however, quickly changed. Testa di Lana's force captured a large stock of weapons during the fighting. On February 21 Testa di Lana returned to the convent of St. Anna and led 4,000 enraged people against the facility, where captured Bourbon police officers were being held. The police, whom they seized, were subjected to summary trials. Those judged to be more or less humane were acquitted by acclamation, but those condemned by the crowd were summarily shot.

To the provisional government and the forces of social order, Testa di Lana became a symbol of anarchy and criminality. Her band not only threatened order, it also represented the rage of the common people and was a constant reminder that the disturbances might transform into a truly social revolution. Once the Bourbon enemy had been vanquished, Testa di Lana became a threat to order. There was a bloody clash on April 28 between her forces and a detachment of the Civil Guard, which had been set up on January 28 to protect property and order. Testa di Lana was captured and taken to the fortress of Castellamare. Her release came only when the Bourbon government had regained control of the island; thereafter she and her family were kept under scrutiny.

Although women from the popular classes actually fought during the Sicilian revolution of 1848, groups of noble and bourgeois women took advantage of the revolution to enter the public political sphere. La Legione delle Pie Sorelle (the Legion of Pious Sisters) was created from the desire of the Princess di Scordia to offer real and public support for the revolution. With the assistance of bourgeois women, she and the Duchess of Monteleone e Gualtieri organized hospital care for the wounded. In the middle of February 1848 they established a committee to assist needy women. They saw their chosen activities as compatible with the nurturing role of women, but they were also anxious to demonstrate their ability to organize and carry out beneficial public activities.

Had the Sicilian revolutions of 1820 and 1848 succeeded, it is improbable that the general social aims of women from the poorer strata, which cannot be differentiated from those of poorer males, would have succeeded. The landowning minority, who led both revolutions, worked to thwart social revolution, to restore order, and to maintain property ownership. In the words of Francesco Crispi, they "feared more the victory of the people than that of the Bourbon troops" (Romeo 1973, 334).

—*Bernard Cook*

See also France, Revolution of 1848

References and Further Reading

Cook, Bernard. 1994. Sicilian Women and Revolution in the First Half of the Nineteenth Century. Pages 82–91 in *Selected Papers of the Consortium on Revolutionary Europe 1994*. Tallahassee: Florida State University.

Mack Smith, Dennis. 1988. *Modern Sicily after 1713*. New York: Dorset.

Romeo, Rosario. 1973. *Il Risorgimento in Sicilia* [The Risorgimento in Sicily]. Rome and Bari: Laterza.

selfconscious candor. The result is both one woman's story and a reflection on the larger experience of war for men and women.

—*Carol Acton*

See also Vietnam, U.S. Women Soldiers in

References and Further Reading

Smith, Winnie. 1994. *American Daughter Gone to War: On the Front Lines with an Army Nurse in Vietnam*. New York: Pocket Books.

SMITH, WINNIE (1944–)

Vietnam War nurse and author. Winnie Smith spent her youth in North Carolina and New Jersey. She attended nursing school in New York and joined the army in 1963. In 1966, she was sent to Vietnam for a year's duty.

Winnie Smith's account of her 1966–1967 tour of duty as a nurse during the Vietnam War is an important contribution to American women's war memoirs. Like other nurses' writing from this war, Smith's *American Daughter Gone to War* bears witness to the physical and psychological injuries borne by combatants and nurses and by Vietnamese civilians as well. The book also documents the collapse of her own prewar worldview and the attendant problems of reintegration on her return home.

In the tradition of World War I nursing accounts and Lynda Van Devanter's better-known Vietnam memoir, *Home before Morning,* Smith's book claims the legitimacy of the woman's war experience, challenging the authority of a male-centered war story while at the same time showing the extent to which her own war experience is intimately related to the men she nurses. *American Daughter Gone to War* is not overtly political; the interrogation of the war in Vietnam is primarily revealed through her relationships with her patients and with combatants. She details her own responses with a refreshingly un-

SMYRNA TRAGEDY, CONTINUING ORDEAL FOR WOMEN SURVIVORS OF THE

Armenian victims of Turkish oppression in Smyrna. Unlike Armenians in the rest of the Ottoman Empire, few Smyrna (Izmir) Armenians were deported or killed during the Armenian Holocaust from 1914 to 1918. This tragedy enveloped the city and its surroundings following World War I when the Kemalist forces fighting the Greeks entered Smyrna on September 9, 1922. The Greek and Armenian quarters were set on fire, and the population was driven out and subjected to a prolonged agony on the quayside squeezed between the sea and the burning city.

The lifelong memory of this cataclysmic event has affected the survivors and the generations born to them. Women survivors of the Smyrna tragedy, tape-recorded at the University of California, Los Angeles, spoke of their ordeal, the burning city, and the mass of refugees squeezed against the sea thick with corpses and parts of mutilated bodies while Allied warships stood as soulless spectators.

Atrocities by the Kemalist forces provided an opening for local Turks to join in looting and killing. Turks forced their way into Armenian and Greek homes, burning houses and a church with hundreds of refugees inside. As a child, Malviné Khanjian lost her father and was separated from her mother and siblings during the assault on the Christians of Izmir. She speaks of a feeling of betrayal by Turkish acquaintances: "My father's Turkish partner came to our house and drove us out, confiscating all our money and belongings. We were left in abject poverty, my mother with four orphans" (Armenian Oral History Collection, Malviné Khanjian [née Papazian], born in Aksar in 1912 and interviewed on November 23, 1982).

There was also a sense of betrayal by the Allied powers. Survivors remember how sailors turned on a water hose to chase off those who dared to swim the long distance toward their ship. The beautiful Smyrna seashore had turned into a slaughterhouse. Through it all, the Europeans walked indifferently, filming the gory scenes. Arsenouhi Vrtanessian remembers the warships turning their spotlights on while the Turks were raiding, raping, killing, and abducting pretty young girls. "What the Young Turks did to us in two years, Kemal did in 15 days," Malviné declares. "A massacre like that of Izmir has never happened anywhere." That conviction governed her mind and inspired her life as a survivor of "the greatest tragedy on earth."

Some survivors have dealt with their ordeal by speaking out, telling and retelling their stories, trying to capture every detail that could help them explain the inexplicable, understand the incomprehensible. Others' stories, although revealing from a psychological point of view, are incoherent, unclear, and sometimes contradictory. But testimonies are human documents, and the troubled interaction between past and present manifests a gravity that surpasses concern with accuracy. Occasional lapses and improbabilities are only natural. The paralysis of language is itself evidence of the ghastly ordeal. The women survivors and witnesses break into tears. They have not learned to articulate their ordeal. The mere utterance of a broken word or two draws back the curtain on a scene of utter

suffering: a Turk raping a young woman and then cutting her breasts off and leaving her to bleed to death.

Some have tried to suppress the memory by not speaking about it. Arsenouhi Vrtanessian says, "My daughter asks me to tell her my story, but I don't want to remember my sorrows" (Armenian Oral History Collection, Arsenouhi Vrtanessian [née Martikian], born in Izmir in 1902 and interviewed by Tamar Der-Megerdichian on February 23, 1987). Yet the sorrows are there; the memory is there, deep in the layers of the mind. Arsenouhi is afraid of sharing her memories with her offspring lest she injure their innocent souls. She is afraid of those memories' painful surging to the surface, as she "reconstructs an episode that continues to haunt" her.

These survivors' stories can only enrich an understanding of the Armenian genocide, the childhood memories of places that ceased to exist with the blow of the holocaust, and the traditional cultural traits that were buried with 1.5 million people and forgotten in the New World. They provide a human dimension or a humanistic insight for the Smyrna tragedy, but more important, they show the lasting impact of such catastrophes on women survivors and the generations they raise.

—*Rubina Peroomian*

See also Armenian Holocaust

References and Further Reading

Armenian Oral History Collection, University of California, Los Angeles (UCLA). There are more than 800 interviews of survivors of the Armenian genocide in the UCLA collection. Out of these interviews, some 15 were with survivors of the Kemalist conquest and the sacking of Smyrna. This article is based on recorded interviews totaling about 48 hours.

Dadrian, Vahakn N. 1995. *The History of the Armenian Genocide.* Oxford: Berghahn.

Dobkin, Marjorie Housepian. 1988 (1966). *Smyrna, 1922: The Destruction of a City.* Kent, OH: Kent State University.

SNELL, HANNAH
(1723–1792)

British woman who disguised herself as a man to become a marine. From an unremarkable background, Hannah Snell became a romanticized figure in ballads and stories for being disguised as a male marine using her brother-in-law's name, James Grey. Following her adventures and their subsequent popularity, Snell died at age 69 in the Bedlam Hospital for the mentally ill.

Snell's life is documented in her biography, *The Female Soldier: or The Surprising Life and Adventures of Hannah Snell,* published in 1750 with her permission by Robert Walker. The biography has been the source of subsequent accounts, but their veracity was questioned in the twentieth century by historians who suggested that liberties were taken with the original biography, resulting in some embellishment of the events in Snell's life (Stephens 1997, 57).

According to most accounts, Snell's history as a marine began after her husband, a Dutch sailor, deserted her when she was pregnant. Her baby died soon after birth, and Snell decided to search for her wayward husband at sea. After taking her brother-in-law's clothing and his name, Snell enlisted in the British military just as Scotland was coming under siege from Charles Edward Stuart ("the Pretender," also known as Bonnie Prince Charlie) in 1745 (Forty and Forty 1997, 96). At sea she withstood severe physical conditions, conflicts with superiors, and public punishments—all without revealing her gender.

Snell deserted, however, when she became afraid that her secret might be revealed. She then joined Frazer's Regiment of Marines. En route to India the fleet was hit by a hurricane off the coast of Gibraltar, and Snell's boat was damaged; after repairs were made, its crew joined a siege on Pondicherry. There Snell is said to have received multiple wounds (Forty and Forty 1997, 97). Despite being hospitalized for several months, she extracted the musket balls herself and was able to maintain her disguise.

After recovering, Snell discovered that her husband had died, and she decided to end her travels. She announced her true gender and, after returning to England, began to perform an account of her adventures on stage. Although she maintained a successful public house and married again twice, Snell began to show signs of mental decline and was committed to an asylum for the insane (Forty and Forty 1997, 99–100).

—Heather E. Ostman

See also Great Britain, Women in Service in the Seventeenth, Eighteenth, and Early Nineteenth Centuries; Talbot, Mary Anne

References and Further Reading

Forty, George, and Anne Forty. 1997. *Women War Heroines.* London: Arms and Armour Press.

Stephens, Matthew. 1997. *Hannah Snell: The Secret Life of a Female Marine, 1723–1792.* London: Ship Street Press.

SOPHIE, DUCHESS VON
HOHENBERG (1868–1914)

Wife of Archduke Franz Ferdinand, murdered with him at Sarajevo on June 28, 1914. The murder of the archduke and Sophie served as the spark that ignited World War I.

Sophie Maria Josephine Albina Chotek, Countess von Chotkova und Wognin, was the daughter of a Bohemian member of the lesser nobility, Count Bohuslaw Chotek von Chotkova und Wognin, and his wife, Countess Wilhelmine Kinsky von Wchinitz und Tettau. When Emperor Franz Josef of Austria-Hungary discovered that his nephew and heir to the throne, Archduke Franz Ferdinand, was enamored of Sophie, he forbade the marriage. The heir was required to marry a member of the house of Hapsburg or one of the royal families of Europe. Franz Ferdinand remained adamant, and appeals on his behalf were made by Kaiser Wilhelm II, Czar

Nicholas II, and Pope Leo XIII. Franz Josef relented in 1899 with the stipulation that Sophie would not share Franz Ferdinand's title and that the children of Franz Ferdinand and Sophie would be excluded from secession. The royal family boycotted the 1900 wedding, and Sophie was subjected to discrimination at court. In 1905 the emperor bestowed on Sophie the title Duchess, and in 1909 her title was changed to Duchess, Highness ad Personum, so that she could be addressed as "highness."

Sophie traveled with her husband to Sarajevo in June 1914 to emphasize Austrian resolve in the province of Bosnia-Herzegovina, which, to the dismay of Serbian nationalists, had been annexed by Austria in 1908. On the route from the railway station to a review at the city hall, terrorists threw a bomb at the open touring car in which Franz Ferdinand and Sophie were riding. The bomb exploded under the second car of the entourage, seriously wounding two passengers and nearly a dozen bystanders. After reviewing troops at the city hall the archduke insisted on visiting members of his party wounded in the morning attack. It was suggested that Sophie remain at the city hall rather than expose herself to danger. She insisted, however, on remaining with her husband.

General Oskar Potiorek, the Austrian governor of Bosnia-Herzegovina, decided that the car should avoid the city center but apparently neglected to tell the driver. When the driver made a wrong turn, he was told to stop and back up. He slowly passed within feet of one of the Serbian terrorists involved in the morning attack. Gavrilo Princip drew his revolver and shot the couple. They were rushed back to the governor's residence, where they died.

Sticklers for protocol objected to Sophie's casket being placed next to that of Ferdinand in the chapel. Franz Josef, however, intervened and Sophie's casket was placed beside that of her husband, though lower and with less decoration. The two could not be buried together in the Hapsburg crypt, so they were interred in the chapel of Franz Ferdinand's castle, Artstetten.

—*Bernard Cook*

See also Alexandra, Czarina of Russia; Washington, Martha Dandridge Custis

References and Further Reading

Brook-Shepherd, Gordon. 1984. *Archduke of Sarajevo: The Romance and Tragedy of Franz Ferdinand of Austria.* Boston: Little, Brown.
Cassels, Lavender. 1984. *The Archduke and the Assassin: Sarajevo, June 28th, 1914.* London: Frederick Muller.

SOSNOWSKA-KARPIK, IRENA (1922–1990)

Polish airwoman on the eastern front. Irena Sosnowska-Karpik served with the Polish armed forces formed in the USSR by the Union of Polish Patriots, a predecessor of the postwar Polish communist government, and became an outstanding flying instructor in Poland after World War II.

Sosnowska-Karpik completed a flying course before the war and qualified as a glider pilot, but she had an ambition to fly combat aircraft. Responding to an appeal made by the Union of Polish Patriots, she volunteered for service with the Polish armed forces in the USSR, which she joined on November 10, 1944, with the rank of second lieutenant.

At that time, a group of 717 airwomen, including 80 officers, served in the military aviation of the Polish armed forces on the eastern front. Those who served in Polish military aviation on the eastern front were mainly employed in air force communications, administration, education, staff work, and medical services, including flying medical aircraft. Altogether, almost 3,000 women wore Polish air force uniforms and served in Polish combat aviation on many fronts of World War II (Polki na wojnie 1985, 12).

Serving in the Polish air and air defense forces as a pilot-instructor after the war, Colonel Sosnowska-Karpik was deputy wing commander and pilot-instructor of the Officer Flying School in Dìblin, Poland. She trained almost 1,000 new pilots. When she transferred to the reserves, she had approximately 4,300 flying hours to her credit (Cottam 2003, 408–409), accumulated in both fixed-wing aircraft and helicopters. Decorated with the Knight's Cross of the Order of the Rebirth of Poland, Sosnowska-Karpik was also awarded the Gold and Silver Crosses of Merit as well as various air force medals and badges.

—*Kazimiera J. Cottam*

See also Polish Auxiliary Air Force

References and Further Reading

Cottam, Kazimiera J. 1986. Veterans of Polish Women's Combat Battalion Hold a Reunion. *Minerva: Quarterly Report on Women in the Military* 4, no. 6 (Winter):6.

———. 2003. Sosnowska-Karpik, Irena. Pages 408–409 in *Amazons to Fighter Pilots*. Edited by Reina Pennington. Vol. 2. Westport, CT: Greenwood.

Polki na wojnie [Polish Women in the War]. 1985. *Skrzydlata Polska* 10 (October 3):12.

SOULIÈ, GENEVIÈVE (B. 1919)

Member of the French resistance during World War II. Geneviève Souliè ran the Paris section of the Burgundian Resistance network created and directed by Georges Broussine. The purpose of this network was to repatriate Allied airmen downed by the Germans in occupied territory. More than 300 airmen were returned to their bases in England.

Broussine recruited Souliè, a twenty-one-year-old young woman with blond hair in pigtails whose mother was English. The fact that she was fluent in English was a great asset to the network. She acquired lodging for Allied airmen in Burgundy and kept constant watch on the men under her care, making certain that that they were safe. She made sure that the men kept quiet and that neighbors did not know downed servicemen were lodging in houses next door. She also attempted to make their confinement comfortable until they could be repatriated. She visited with them and brought them cigarettes and books. After a rendezvous had been arranged, she would lead the airmen to their rescuers. She helped 136 servicemen escape France and return safely to England. Eighty-four of them were Americans.

—*Leigh Whaley*

See also Atkins, Vera H.; France, Resistance during World War II, Women and

References and Further Reading

Broussine, Georges. 2000. *L'Evade de la France libre: Le Réseau Bourgogne* [The Free French Escapee: The Burgundy Network]. Paris: Tallandier.

SOVIET UNION, 46TH TAMAN GUARDS BOMBER AVIATION REGIMENT (MAY 1942–MAY 1945)

One of three women's air wings formed by Marina Raskova in October 1941 when male Soviet aircrews were unavailable and aircraft were outdated. Founded in Engels, near Stalingrad, the regiment was initially designated 588th Bomber Aviation Regiment. Its crews flew U-2 biplanes (redesignated Po-2 in 1944), former trainers used as short-range night bombers. The unit was the only women's aviation regiment created by Raskova to remain all-female throughout the war. Initially consisting of two squadrons, the regiment would have two additional squadrons by mid-1943, of which the last functioned as a training squadron under the command of Marina Chechneva.

Personnel of this wing were credited with having flown in excess of 24,000 combat missions on the Southern, Trans-Caucasus, North Caucasus, 4th Ukrainian, and 2nd Belorussian fronts (Cottam 1997, 114). The unit went into action in Ukraine and subsequently operated in the foothills of the Caucasus, over the Kuban area of the North Caucasus, the Crimea, Belarus, and Poland, and finally reached Berlin. Initially subordinated to the 218th Bomber Aviation Division of the 4th Air Army in the Crimea (4th Ukrainian front), the regiment was temporarily attached to the 2nd Stalingrad Guards Bomber Aviation Division of the 8th Air Army. Returned to the 4th Air Army on the 2nd Belorussian front, it was included in the 325th Bomber Aviation Division.

In addition to bombing sorties delivered at the rate of five to eighteen per night, the regiment flew liaison, reconnaissance, and supply missions in support of Soviet ground troops. It was awarded the elite status of Guards on February 8, 1943, and the honorific "Taman" on October 9 for facilitating the German defeat on the Taman Peninsula. This unit was also awarded the Order of Suvorov III Class and the Order of the Red Banner. The unit was disbanded October 15, 1945.

The unveiling of a monument dedicated to its personnel, twenty-three of whom had, by that time, acquired the prestigious title of Hero of the Soviet Union, took place on the Taman Peninsula in October 1967. (In addition, the equivalent Hero of the Russian Federation was belatedly presented to former squadron navigator Tat'iana Nikolaevna Sumarokova in 1995.)

The regiment's successes were due in part to the consistency of leadership provided by its sole commanding officer, Evdokiia Bershanskaia, a competent civil aviation pilot, and her good relationship with Evdokiia Rachkevich, the regimental commissar (deputy commander for political affairs) and one of the very few women graduates of the V. I. Lenin Military Political Academy. In addition, Bershanskaia was ably assisted by her deputy, Serafima Amosova, a former airline pilot; Irina Rakobol'skaia, her chief

of staff; and three successive chief navigators: Sofia Burzaeva, Evgeniia Rudneva, and Larissa Rozanova.

—*Kazimiera J. Cottam*

See also Soviet Union, 125th M. M. Raskova Borisov Guards Bomber Aviation Regiment

References and Further Reading

Cottam, Kazimiera J., ed. and trans. 1997. *Women in Air War: The Eastern Front in World War II.* Russian edition edited by Militsa A. Kazarinova et al. Nepean, Ontario, Canada: New Military Publishing. (The Russian edition was published in 1971 under the title *V nebe frontovom.*)
———. 2003. 46th Taman Guards Bomber Aviation Regiment. Pages 513–515 in *Amazons to Fighter Pilots.* Edited by Reina Pennington. Vol. 2. Westport, CT. Greenwood.
Noggle, Anne. 1994. *A Dance with Death.* College Station: Texas A&M.
Pennington, Reina. 2001. *Wings, Women and War.* Lawrence: University Press of Kansas.

Soviet Union, 125th M. M. Raskova Borisov Guards Bomber Aviation Regiment (January 1943–May 1945)

One of three women's air wings formed by Marina Raskova in October 1941 when male Soviet aircrews were unavailable and aircraft were outdated. Commanded by Raskova herself, the regiment was formed in Engels near Stalingrad and was initially designated the 587th Bomber Aviation Regiment. After Raskova's tragic crash during a heavy snowstorm on January 4, 1943, the unit acquired a new commanding officer, Major Valentin Markov, whose male navigator, Captain Nikolai Nikitin, was to be replaced by a woman, Valentina Kravchenko. There were only two Pe-2 dive bomber squadrons, initially commanded by Nadezhda Fedutenko and Evgeniia Timofeeva, former civil aviation pilots. Each aircrew consisted of a pilot, a navigator-bombardier, and a radio operator–gunner. Because the Su-2 aircraft initially assigned to this unit carried a crew of two and there was no time to train female tail gunners before departing for the front, men often served as rear gunners. A replacement squadron acquired in the spring of 1944 consisted entirely of women. Men, however, partially comprised the regiment's technical personnel throughout its existence.

The regiment went into action near Stalingrad and ended its campaign near the Baltic Sea. It operated over the North Caucasus, the Orel-Briansk sector, Smolensk, Belorussia, the Baltic littoral, and East Prussia. It carried out a total of 1,134 mission sorties on the Southern, Don, Western, 3rd Belorussian, and 1st Baltic fronts (Cottam 1997, 16). In the North Caucasus, the regiment was subordinated to 4th Air Army; on the 3rd Belorussian front to 5th Guards Air Corps of 16th Air Army; and on the 1st Baltic front to 4th Guards Bomber Aviation Division, 1st Guards Air Corps of 3rd Air Army. The regiment acquired the honorific "M. M. Raskova" on May 4, 1943, for successful operations in the North Caucasus and was assigned the new designation, 125th, on September 23, 1943. On July 10, 1944, the unit was granted the honorific "Borisovsky" for its role in the liberation of Borisov, Belarus. It was awarded the Orders of Kutuzov and Suvorov III Class at the level appropriate to aviation regiments. On August 18, 1945, three pilots and two navigators of the regiment became Heroes of the Soviet Union.

Representative participants who were not awarded the Hero of the Soviet Union honor were:

Galina Brok-Beltsova (b. 1925), Guards lieutenant and navigator. With pilot Antonina Bondareva-Spitsyna, Brok-Beltsova joined the regiment with the replacement squadron in the spring of 1944 and received her baptism of fire on June 23, 1944, during the beginning of the Belorussian operation. She flew thirty-six combat missions during the war.

Antonina Khokhlova-Dubkova (b. 1919), Guards senior lieutenant and radio operator–gunner. Khokhlova-Dubkova was the regiment's sole female gunner until the arrival of the all-female squadron in the spring of 1944. In an interview, she described her two machine guns (out of a total of five aboard her aircraft), one of which required her to manipulate 60 kilograms to rearm it.

Elena Kulkova-Maliutina (b. 1917), Guards lieutenant and pilot. She joined the regiment with the replacement squadron in the spring of 1944. On July 24, 1944, although seriously wounded in the abdomen over Lithuania and repeatedly revived by navigator Elena Iushina, Kulkova-Maliutina managed to land safely; two months later she was back in action. A participant in the Victory Parade, she subsequently flew a Tu-2 in a men's aviation regiment until her retirement in 1949.

Marta Meriuts (b. 1909), Guards lieutenant colonel and chief of communications. She was assigned to Raskova's Air Group No. 122 after recovering from a serious head wound and the loss of vision in one eye. In an interview, Meriuts stated that at a postwar Kremlin reception the front commander to whom her regiment was subordinated was unaware that its aircrews consisted of women.

Natalia Smirnova (b. 1924), Guards sergeant and radio operator–gunner. She was a member of the replacement squadron that arrived in the spring of 1944. In an interview, Smirnova told how on one mission the gunner had to stand facing the tail of the aircraft, her head emerging from the hatchway. Once, over Libava, an enemy shell blew open the lower hatch cover, and she was thrown upward out of the aircraft but managed to get back inside.

The unit was disbanded February 28, 1947.
—*Kazimiera J. Cottam*

See also Soviet Union, 46th Taman Guards Bomber Aviation Regiment

References and Further Reading

Cottam, Kazimiera J., ed. and trans. 1997. *Women in Air War: The Eastern Front in World War II.* Russian edition edited by Militsa A. Kazarinova et al. Nepean, Ontario, Canada: New Military Publishing. (The Russian edition was published in 1971 under the title *V nebe frontovom.*)

———. 2003. 125th Borisovsky Guards Bomber Aviation Regiment. Pages 517–520 in *Amazons to Fighter Pilots.* Edited by Reina Pennington. Vol. 2. Westport, CT: Greenwood.

Pennington, Reina. 2001. *Wings, Women and War.* Lawrence: University Press of Kansas.

SOVIET UNION, ORDER OF GLORY, I CLASS, SOVIET WOMEN RECIPIENTS (1943–1948)

Soviet award for "the bravest of the brave." The Order of Glory (III, II, and I Class), intended for Soviet privates, noncommissioned officers, and junior lieutenants of aviation, was created on November 8, 1943. The recipients of the Order of Glory, I Class, numbering about 2,500, received the 3 levels of the order on 3 separate occasions; 4 of them were women.

Sergeant Matriona (Motia) Semenovna Necheporchukova-Nozdracheva (b. 1924) was a medical noncommissioned officer in the 100th Guards Infantry Regiment of the 35th Guards Division, which reached Berlin on May 3, 1945. She distinguished herself dispensing first aid under heavy enemy fire, repelling raids, and defending the wounded entrusted to her. She was awarded her third Order of Glory on May 24, 1945, for bravery demonstrated during the breakthrough of enemy defenses on the west bank of the Oder River and the fierce fighting in Berlin.

Nina Pavlovna Petrova (1893–1945), a senior noncommissioned officer, graduated from snipers' school and participated in the Soviet-Finnish war. During World War II, Petrova, the oldest sniper in the army, had the highest kill record on the entire Leningrad front; she had 100 personal kills and trained 513 new snipers (Cottam 1998, 402). Petrova advanced with the 1st Battalion, 284th Infantry Regiment, 86th Tartu Division, from her native Leningrad through the Baltic lands, East Prussia, and Poland to Schwerin, Germany, where she was killed on May 1, 1945. She was posthumously awarded the Order of Glory, I Class, on June 29, 1945.

Sergeant Danute Jurgievna Staniliéne-Markauskene (b. 1922) served as commander of a machine-gun crew in Company No. 3, 167th Infantry Regiment, 16th Lithuanian Division. She imitated the technique of Anka, a machine gunner in the Russian Civil War, which demanded exceptional self-control. Staniliéne-Markauskene would wait for the enemy to approach closely and only then open fire. She was granted the Order of Glory, I Class, on March 24, 1945, the first Soviet woman soldier so honored, for her role in the fighting for the Klaipeda-Tilsit Highway.

Nadezhda (Nadia) Aleksandrovna Zhurkina-Kiek (b. 1920), a senior noncommissioned officer, was a radio operator–gunner in the Soviet air force. She served in the 99th Independent Reconnaissance Aviation Regiment and was the only woman air gunner in the entire 15th Air Army. Zhurkina-Kiek flew eighty-seven missions, during which she displayed an exceptional ability to spot enemy aircraft and to chase them away or shoot them down. She was awarded the Order of Glory, I Class, on February 23, 1948, for outstanding performance in 1944 over Latvia, at which time she flew ten missions behind enemy lines and shot down a decorated German ace (Cottam 1998, 409).

—*Kazimiera J. Cottam*

See also Russia, Women Recipients of the Order of St. George; Soviet Union, Order of the Red Banner, Women Recipients; Soviet Union/Russian Federation, Women Heroes of the

References and Further Reading

Cottam, Kazimiera J. 1998. *Women in War and Resistance.* Nepean, Ontario, Canada: New Military Publishing.

———. 2003. Order of Glory, I Class, Women Recipients. Pages 324–325 in *Amazons to Fighter Pilots.* Edited by Reina Pennington. Vol. 1. Westport, CT: Greenwood.

Mikora, V. 1976. Zhenshchiny–Kavalery Ordena Slavy [Women Recipients of the Order of Glory]. *Voenno-istoricheskii zhurnal* 3:55–56.

Soviet Union, Order of the Red Banner, Women Recipients (1918–1928)

Award initially given for bravery during the Russian Civil War (1918–1921). Instituted on September 16, 1918, this award was originally intended for the citizens of the Russian Soviet Federated Socialist Republic, with several other Soviet republics adopting their own Red Banners. After the creation of the USSR, a single Order of the Red Banner was announced by the executive committee of the new republic on August 1, 1924. There is no agreement among scholars as to how many Soviet women received the Red Banner for their participation in the civil war, with cited numbers ranging from fifty-three to sixty-three. Recent archival research indicates higher totals. Military medical and political personnel (commissars) predominated within the female component. The order was granted to many additional women during World War II (Cottam 2003, 327). Representative recipients include:

Raisa Moiseevna Azarkh (1897–1971), a senior political-medical officer. Her appointments from mid-1918 to mid-1920 included military commissar of the 1st Special Viatka Division, chief of the Main Military Medical Administration of the Ukraine, chief of the Medical Service of the 5th Army, and chief of the Main Medical Administration of the Far Eastern Republic. She was awarded the Red Banner on February 2, 1928. During the Spanish Civil War she worked with Canadian medical doctor Norman Bethune.

Aleksandra Aleksandrovna (Permiakova) Ianysheva (1894–1983), who served in the Red Guard and the Red Army during the Russian Civil War. One of the outstanding women Bolsheviks, she held the following key posts during the war: chief of the Political Section of the Red Guard Headquarters; chief of the Propaganda Section of the Political Administration of the Red Army; and chief of the Political Section of the 15th Inzenskaia Infantry Division, renamed the Sivashskaia following the division's crossing of the Sivash Gulf in the Crimea. On February 2, 1928, Ianysheva became one of the first recipients in her division of the Order of the Red Banner, which she received for her part in the legendary attack on enemy positions launched after the crossing.

Rozaliia Samoilovna (Zalkind) Samoilova-Zemliachka (1876–1947), dubbed Demon and Osipov. She was senior military commissar of the Red Army during the civil war and served as Soviet deputy premier during World War II. A dedicated revolutionary, an Old Bolshevik, and Lenin's close associate, Zemliachka held crucial military appointments during the civil war, including that of chief of the Political Section of the 8th Army and of the 13th Army. She was awarded the Red Banner on January 23, 1921, for improving the combat effectiveness of the Red Army and facilitating its final victory.

—*Kazimiera J. Cottam*

See also Russian, Women Recipients of the Order of St. George; Soviet Union, Order of Glory, I Class, Soviet Women Recipients; Soviet Union/Russian Federation, Women Heroes of the

References and Further Reading

Baturina, K. S., et al., eds. 1964. *Pravda stavshaia legendoi* [Truth Became a Legend]. Moscow: Voenizdat.

Cottam, Kazimiera J. 2003. Order of the Red Banner, Women Recipients, Civil War. Pages 326–328 in *Amazons to Fighter Pilots*. Edited by Reina Pennington. Vol. 1. Westport, CT: Greenwood.

Johnson, Richard. 1980. The Role of Women in the Russian Civil War (1917–1921). *Conflict* 2(2):201–217.

SOVIET UNION, WOMEN AND THE HOME FRONT DURING WORLD WAR II

The impact of World War II on the women of the Soviet Union. During World War II, Soviet women were unique among the women of the great powers in their large-scale participation as fighters in the armed forces. They also played a proportionately greater economic role than the women of the other major belligerents.

Germany's invasion of the Soviet Union on June 22, 1941, led to the greatest land conflict in the history of warfare. Beginning in 1941 over half of Germany's armored units fought only on the eastern front. At the end of the war three-quarters of the forces left in Germany's 37 armored divisions were fighting on the eastern front. Hitler had asserted, "You only have to kick in the door and the whole rotten structure will come crashing down." He was mistaken. Although the Germans were welcomed in the Baltic states, newly occupied by the Soviet Union, and in parts of the Ukraine, the vast majority of Soviet citizens rallied to the defense of their homeland in its struggle for survival. Women were an essential part of the Soviet war effort and victory. Between 800,000 and 1 million women served in the Soviet armed forces (Cottam 1980, 345). Others participated as par-

tisans in the resistance. More, however, did essential war work on farms and in factories and in preparing defenses in threatened cities. By the end of the war four out of five workers on collective farms were women, and the share of women in public employment rose from two-fifths before the war to nearly three-fifths by 1944 (Harrison 2002).

The suffering of all Russians was intense, but Russian civilians were allotted fewer rations than soldiers. When rationing was instituted in July, workers were allocated 800 grams (1.76 pounds) of bread a day and 2,200 grams (4.85 pounds) of meat a month, supplemented by cereals, sugar, and fat. The ration for older women and children amounted to only 400 grams (14.11 ounces) of bread a day; by the end of 1943 this had been decreased to 300 grams (10.58 ounces). People were reduced to eating dogs and cats. Food crimes—the theft of food and the theft and forgery of ration cards—were widespread. Incidents of cannibalism were even reported. All of these crimes were harshly punished, frequently by summary execution.

In Leningrad, which was besieged by the Germans for 900 days from early September 1941 until January 27, 1944, the rations were much smaller, and the bread that was distributed contained sawdust to give it greater weight. On September 2, 1941, the bread ration for the inhabitants of the city was decreased to 600 grams (1.32 pounds). On September 8, 1941, the Germans bombed the 4-acre Badayev warehouse complex where much of the city's food supply was stored. On September 12 the bread ration was decreased to 500 grams (1.10 pounds); on November 20 it was cut to 250 grams (8.82 ounces) for workers and 125 grams (4.41 ounces), or 460 calories, for civilians. The inhabitants were without fuel, running water, and electricity. During the siege of Leningrad, 1 million of the city's 3 million inhabitants died from starvation and cold, and several hundred thousand were killed by bombing and shelling (Museum of Tolerance 2005).

It is estimated that 7 million Russian combatants, male and female, died during the war. The toll on civilians was at least twice that. Among the millions of civilians who died, women constituted at least half, if not more, of the casualties. In parts of the Soviet Union occupied by the Nazis, Jewish and Roma females and males, adults and children alike, were rounded up and systematically exterminated by mobile killing squads, or *Einsatzgruppen.*

Individual women distinguished themselves in combat. Among the women who contributed to the cultural life of the Soviet Union during the war, Anna Andreevna Gorenko Akhmatova (1889–1966), the great Russian poet, stands out. She expressed the patriotic feelings of the Russian people and their moral outrage at the ravaging of their country by its fascist enemy.

—*Bernard Cook*

See also Einsatzgruppen; Holocaust and Jewish Women; Soviet Union, Women in the Armed Forces; Soviet Union/Russian Federation, Women Heroes of the

References and Further Reading

Barber, John, and Mark Harrison. 1991. *The Soviet Home Front, 1941–1945: A Social and Economic History of the U.S.S.R. in World War II.* London: Longman.

Cottam, Kazimiera J. 1980. Soviet Women in Combat in World War II: The Ground Forces and the Navy. *International Journal of Women's Studies* 3, no. 4 (July-August):345–357.

Glantz, David M. 2002. *The Battle from Leningrad, 1941–1944.* Lawrence: University of Kansas Press.

Harrison, Mark. 2002. "The USSR and Total War." University of Warwick Economic Research Papers, no. 603. http://www2.warwick.ac.uk/fac/soc/economics/research/papers/twcrp603.pdf (accessed August 12, 2005).

Museum of Tolerance. "Leningrad." http://motlc.learningcenter.wiesenthalorg/pages/t04419.html (accessed August 12, 2005).

Pavlov, D. 1965. *Leningrad 1941: The Blockade.* Chicago: University of Chicago Press.

Simmons, Cynthia, and Nina Perlina. 2002. *Writing the Siege of Leningrad: Women's Diaries, Memoirs, and Documentary Prose.* Pittsburgh: University of Pittsburgh Press.

Sparen, Pär. 2004. "Long Term Mortality after Severe Starvation during the Siege of Leningrad." *British Medical Journal* 328:11. http://bmj.bmjjournals.com/cgi/content/abriged/328/7430/11#REF3 (accessed August 12, 2004).

Soviet Union, Women in the Armed Forces (1917–1991)

Apart from their participation in World War II, women in the Soviet Union played an auxiliary role in the Soviet military. Despite the historical record of competent military service by Russian women and recurrent manpower shortages notwithstanding, women have not been treated as a permanent component of the Russian military, and senior officers have resisted placing women in jobs traditionally held by men.

During the Russian Civil War (1918–1920) the recruitment of women was largely limited to medical and political appointments, some of a very onerous nature, as women placed in staff positions had to explain the ideological reasons for combating the opposing Whites (the collective appellation of the opponents of the Bolsheviks in the Russian Civil War). A minority of women received weapons and tactical training. The 1918 draft applied exclusively to women physicians. About 80,000 women served during the civil war, of whom approximately 40 percent were physicians, medics, orderlies, and nurses; the remaining 60 percent were employed in administrative positions, including as political workers (Herspring 1997, 45). By 1919, when the Political Administration of the Revolutionary Military Council of the Republics was created, about 27 percent of all political workers were women, and some of them occupied senior positions. Among those who served in the

The all-female crew of Minesweeper No. 611 *of the Soviet Volga Naval Flotilla.* Left to right: *A. F. Tarasova, E. S. Parkhacheva, A. E. Kupriianova, V. S. Chapova, T. I. Dekalina, and A. P. Shabilina. (Viktorov, S. 1986. "V ekipazhe korablia—tol'ko devushki"* [The Ship Crew Is All-Female]. Morskoi sbornik [Naval Anthology] 3:23–25)

Red Army during the civil war, 1,854 were killed, wounded, or taken prisoner (Herspring 1997, 45).

After the civil war ended, women were expected to go back to civilian life. Between 1925 and 1939 only men were conscripted. The interest of the military with regard to women was largely limited to food service and jobs and education for wives, some of whom received basic military training as dependents of regular military officers. About 100 women studied at military academies in the 1920s and 1930s, a number of whom were to play an important role during World War II, yet these career officers were usually employed in staff positions and had no line troops under their command.

In the late 1930s women often took part in the work of the Red Cross and Red Crescent. In addition to keeping fit through participation in military sports sponsored by the Komsomol (Young Communist's League), women were able to engage in paramilitary training offered by the Osoaviakhim (Society for Assistance to Defense, Aviation, and Chemical Industry), founded in 1927. Women mastered a number of military specialties, especially after World War II began, when they were given enhanced access to weapons training by Osoaviakhim. Women workers also received 110 hours of military training provided by the Vsevobuch (Administration for Universal Military Training) of the ministry of defense (Cottam 1998, xix). In 1942 so-called Vsevobuch Komsomol youth subunits trained 222,000 women as mortar personnel, heavy and light machine gun and submachine gun operators, snipers, and communication specialists (Cottam 1998, xx). Such training took place both before and during the war in military schools, reserve regiments, and field units.

Initially women were sent mainly to air defense and reserve communications units, as well as rear units and establishments of the army and navy, or they were assigned to firefighting, police, and civil defense duties. Such duties were mainly auxiliary and defensive but involved exposure to enemy fire and explosives during air-defense and mine–clearing activities. In the course of the war, women, as a result of manpower shortages as well as their own struggle for equality, moved into new military occupations, including combat duty in both mixed-sex and all-female units. The transfer of women to combat roles often took place despite, rather than because of, official policy. Women volunteering for service at the front were not always motivated by purely patriotic considerations but rather by the loss of loved ones as well as enemy-caused devastation and atrocities. At the end of 1943 the number of enlisted women reached its maximum, estimated at 800,000 to 1 million, or 8 percent of the total strength of the Soviet armed forces; at least half of these women served at the front (Cottam 1980b, 345).

In addition to those who volunteered, more than 400,000 women were mobilized. In 1942, following the state council of defense's decisions of March 23 and April 13, 100,000 women were drafted for air-defense duties. Some 30,000 were sent to logistical units and establishments of the army (decision of April 26), and 25,000 were directed to logistical and coastal units of the navy (decision of May 6) (Cottam 1998, xx). By 1943 all childless women not aiding the war effort were declared eligible for military service.

The first women to leave for the front in early July 1941 had peacetime communications experience. Some were to be charged with very important assignments. For example, the military and civilian authorities in Leningrad cooperated in the laying of an underwater cable across Lake Ladoga, which restored telephone communications with Moscow and other cities. The entire operation, including equipment trials and all installation work, was directed by V. A. Iarchevskaia, a highly qualified female engineer.

In each hero-city (cities threatened by the advancing Germans), hundreds of women volunteered to dig antitank ditches and build fortifications. In Leningrad (the City-Front), there was an unprecedented female construction army of engineer corps, with women in command of sections and platoons. Forty-five thousand women built and maintained permanent strong points, bunkers, foxholes, trenches, and highways. In the summer of 1943 they constructed a belt of powerful fortifications, 25 kilometers (15.53 miles) long, in the 42nd Army zone, as well as five ferro-concrete pillboxes located in the avenue of the probable enemy tank approach (Cottam 1980b, 351). The women worked day and night, in all kinds of weather, under artillery fire and air strikes. Meanwhile, a pipeline for uninterrupted fuel delivery to the blockaded city was laid on the bottom of Lake Ladoga. This project was conceived and executed with the assistance of N. V. Sokolova, a female engineer and diver.

In 1944 and 1945 Leningrad's women engineers were retrained for mine-clearing duties in the huge territory comprising the Leningrad, Pskov, and Novgorod regions. Using dogs to sniff out the explosives, many women perished attempting to disarm the mines. A young woman from Minsk, Iadviga Urbanovich, distinguished herself in mine-clearing work in the Leningrad region. She trained hundreds of other women and personally disposed of more than a thousand shells and over a hundred bombs in Leningrad (Sokolov and Borchenko 1983, 162).

Senior Lieutenant Lidiia Shulaikina, who flew the IL-2 attack aircraft known as the Flying Tank, was the sole woman naval pilot during World War II. The most prominent role in the navy was assigned to women in the Volga Flotilla, created to safeguard shipping. (The Volga River had the transportation capacity of ten railroads.) In addition to working as crew members and captains of cargo ships, women operated antiaircraft guns and served aboard passenger steamships converted to minesweepers. Entire families, including wives and adult children, operated ships in the flotilla.

Very few women served with the large-caliber Ground Forces artillery. An undefined number, however, served in armored units. Women were radio operators, turret gunners, drivers, and tank and subunit commanders. They progressed from lighter to heavier vehicles and either volunteered for tank duty or were transferred, at their request, from other duties. Ekaterina Petliuk was too short to become a pilot so she drove a T-70 tank. Vera Bezrukova was a tank driver. Her baptism of fire took place near the Volga River, after which she fought all the way to Berlin. Managing to extricate herself from the most difficult predicaments, she survived the disabling of eight tanks. Aleksandra and Ivan Boiko, a married couple, served together as tank commander and driver, respectively. Valentina Barkhatova, a native of Siberia, was a radio operator-gunner. She died in a T-34 tank, one of the first to burst into Sevastopol in May 1944. The tank now stands on a cement base in Simferopol as a monument to those who fell during the Crimean operation of 1944. The attractive Aleksandra Samusenko was a tank school graduate, tank commander, platoon commander, and a Guards senior lieutenant. When her battalion commander fell, she led the battalion into battle and out of encirclement. She was killed on the outskirts of Berlin.

There were exceptional female machine gunners and snipers who owed their training to the Osoaviakhim and line units. About 102,333 future snipers attended special Vsevobuch courses and schools (Cottam 1998, xx). The most famous of them was the Central Women's School for Snipers, located near Moscow. Its graduates alone were credited with eliminating 12,000 enemy personnel (Herspring 1997, 46).

Women army scouts were parachuted behind enemy lines or crossed into occupied areas on skis to gather intelligence or to liaison with local underground organizations. Between 1943 and 1944, ninety-four women led underground Komsomol organizations at the regional, district, and urban levels.

By February 1944 there were 26,707 female partisans (Herspring 1997, 47). Women constituted 16 percent of the total partisan strength in Belarus (Cottam 1982, 367). They functioned as radio operators, snipers, machine gunners, and saboteurs and proved invaluable as messengers and scouts.

After the targeted call-ups of March, April, and October 1942 and the sporadic recruitment of women in 1943 and 1944, the proportion of women soldiers was greatest in the land-based Air Defense Forces (ADF), amounting to 30.5 percent in the Moscow area and 34.5 percent on the entire eastern front (Herspring 1997, 46), where women replaced 300,000 men. The average women's participation in the ADF, including in Air Defense Aviation, amounted to 24 percent (Cottam 1980a, 118).

In the spring of 1942 ADF women fully replaced men in the handling of barrage balloons, where teams of 12 were reduced to 6 or 7 women who played a major role in protecting the Soviet capital. In instrument sections of air-defense artillery, women replaced 8 out of 10 men; in machine-gun crews, 3 out of 5; in the Air Warning Service, 5 out of 6; and in the rear services, all male enlisted personnel and noncommissioned officers (Cottam 1980a, 117). The mobilizations significantly affected the entire Soviet armed forces, releasing a large number of men for service at the front and strengthening the ADF, where women constituted more than 50 percent of total strength in some regiments and divisions (Cottam 1980a, 117). During the historic Battle for Berlin massed searchlights were used to blind the enemy at night; at least half of the searchlight operators were women. Additionally, there were all-female gun batteries in the Leningrad Army of Air Defense.

The majority of Soviet women officers were political workers, many of whom served in the ADF, where by 1943 the majority of political workers were women. They involved themselves with every aspect of military life. There were many female political workers in partisan units, mainly at the lower party and Komsomol levels. Those in the underground tried to win over Soviet defectors and troops of Germany's allies, with some success. Above all, political workers were expected to set examples of fearlessness. For instance, Aleksandra Postol'skaia, radio operator and Komsomol battalion organizer of the 88th Rifle Division, replaced her fallen commander and was killed while leading her troops in a successful attack in Rybki in the Smolensk region on August 15, 1943. It was a woman political worker, Major Anna Nikulina, who hoisted the red flag on the rooftop of the Chancellery in Berlin, at considerable danger to herself. Two soldiers in her party were killed, and one was severely wounded. Soviet female political workers of World War II were more numerous than during the civil war, and the tendency for many of them to be line rather than staff personnel was new. Hence their impact on morale was undoubtedly as great or greater than during the civil war.

Women appear to have had a qualitative impact on morale out of proportion to their numbers. Some, at least, were willing participants, full of idealism and enthusiasm. Female partisans and regular army personnel increasingly established themselves in nontraditional roles; those in support and political categories also fought and sometimes assumed command. The result was that mixed-sex crews learned to work harmoniously and all-female groups developed the team spirit and solidarity previously associated only with comradeship among men. Also, some women became attached to their equipment and weapons, which they treated as extensions of themselves. This perceived increase in their physical and mental powers was to them a liberating experience. Often women displayed a strong sense of solidarity and loyalty toward their husbands, brothers, and fathers, and they wished to avenge those who perished.

Although women partisans derailed trains, blew up bridges, and stormed enemy garrisons, they were also frequently expected to cook and do the men's laundry. In the army, women were expected to render first aid regardless of whether they were radio operators, snipers, or machine gunners. This was a wartime version of the female "double shift." Women were drafted as communications specialists or for other nonaggressive duties; even mine clearing fell in that category, though it was at least as dangerous as tank duty or service in Ground Forces artillery. Perhaps never before in the history of warfare

was the line between the combatant and noncombatant less clearly drawn than during the "Great Patriotic War," as World War II was referred to by the Soviet regime and the Russian people.

After the war most women were demobilized and banned from attending military schools and academies. A common belief reasserted itself that women should serve only when the country was endangered. By 1959 there were only 659 military women in the USSR army of 4 to 5 million, serving in women's traditional military occupations such as nursing, political work, communications, and administration (Herspring 1997, 48). The 1967 Military Service Law specified that single women, aged 19 to 40, with medical and specialized training would be accepted for military service in peacetime and could be drafted in wartime to perform auxiliary or specialized duties. By the mid-1970s the estimated number of women in the Soviet armed forces was 10,000 (Herspring 1997, 49). They were, however, prohibited from serving on combat ships and aircraft, and their access to firearms was strictly regulated.

In 1990 women were allowed to teach in military medical institutions. By the end of 1992 (after the dissolution of the U.S.S.R.) the number of women in the Russian military climbed to 100,000, including 20,000 warrant officers and 1,100 officers (Herspring 1997, 50). The majority of them served in the Ground Forces. About 1,000 women were admitted into the elite airborne forces (Herspring 1997, 50–51). One hundred and sixty-nine specialties were opened to women. In 1992 mixed staffing was introduced, and by the end of the year women volunteers outnumbered male conscripts by 367 to 125 in one motorized infantry unit. That same year the Moscow Military District announced that it intended to raise the percentage of women in its ranks to 10 percent (Herspring 1997, 51).

The increasingly important role women played was most evident in the ADF, where women occupied 50 percent of key positions in 1992 (Herspring 1997, 51). It was assumed that women had better aptitude than men for detailed work and making precise calculations. When in 1993 women were allowed to join the military on contract, the intent was not only to alleviate manpower shortages but also to assist underpaid professional soldiers by providing employment for their wives. Thus, by 1994 the total number of women in the military approached 250,000, but only 1,500 of them were officers (Herspring 1997, 52–53).

Despite their increasing reliance on women, Russian senior officers tended to resist placing them in "men's" jobs and dismissed them at the earliest opportunity. Yet by mid-1997 the situation of Russian women soldiers had improved. Out of an army of 1.2 million, women officers numbered approximately 2,400, including 4 colonels and 300 senior officers (major to colonel) (Herspring 1997, 53). Also, astronaut Valentina Tereshkova was the first woman to be granted a major general's rank. Meanwhile, women had been admitted to communications and chemical warfare schools. Though male commanders acknowledged women's proficiency in carrying out technical, medical, and administrative tasks, they were reluctant to use them in combat, even when they constituted 20 percent of divisional personnel and were appropriately trained (Herspring 1997, 54). Also, there was no effective women's lobby group to argue that women were full-fledged members of the Russian armed forces. The recurrent severe shortages of men, coupled with persistent praise of women in the press (citing the superior discipline of women, their more efficient work habits, and their greater devotion to duty), may improve the status of Russian military women in the future.

—*Kazimiera J. Cottam*

See also Soviet Union, 46th Taman Guards Bomber Aviation Regiment; Soviet Union, 125th M. M. Raskova Borisov Guards Bomber Aviation Regiment; Soviet Union Air Defense, 586th Fighter Aviation Regiment; Soviet Union/Russian Federation, Women Heroes of the

References and Further Reading

Cottam, Kazimiera J. 1980a. Soviet Women in Combat in World War II: The Ground Air Defense Forces. Pages 115–127 in *Women in Eastern Europe and the Soviet Union.* Edited by Tova Yedlin. New York: Praeger.

———. 1980b. Soviet Women in Combat in World War II: The Ground Forces and the Navy. *International Journal of Women's Studies* 3, no. 4 (July-August):345–357.

———. 1982. Soviet Women in Combat in World War II: The Rear Services, Resistance behind Enemy Lines and Military Political Workers. *International Journal of Women's Studies* 5, no. 4 (September-October):363–378.

———. 1998. *Women in War and Resistance.* Nepean, Ontario, Canada: New Military Publishing.

Herspring, Dale R. 1997. Women in the Russian Military: A Reluctant Marriage. *Minerva: Quarterly Report on Women in the Military* 15, no. 2 (Summer):42–59.

Pennington, Reina, ed. 2003. *Amazons to Fighter Pilots.* Vols. 1 and 2. Westport, CT: Greenwood.

Smirnova-Medevedeva, Zoya Matveyevna. 1997. *Opalennaia iunost'* [Fire-Scorched Youth]. Translated by Kazimiera J. Cottam under the title *On the Road to Stalingrad: Memoirs of a Woman Machine Gunner.* Nepean, Ontario, Canada: New Military Publishing.

Sokolov, V., and Nikolai Borchenko. 1983. "The Sinister Nights of Leningrad" and "The Score." Pages 153–163 in *The Golden-Tressed Soldier.* Translated and edited by Kazimiera J. Cottam. Manhattan, KS: Military Affairs/Aerospace Historian.

SOVIET UNION AIR DEFENSE, 586TH FIGHTER AVIATION REGIMENT

One of three Soviet women's air wings formed by Marina Raskova in October 1941 when male Soviet aircrews were unavailable and combat aircraft were outdated. An integral part of Soviet Air Defense Forces fighter aviation, the 586th

Marina Raskova, commanding officer of the Soviet 586th Dive Bomber Aviation Regiment. (V nebe frontovom [In the Sky Above the Front]. 1971. 2nd edition. Edited by M. A. Kazarinova et al. Moscow: Molodaia Gvardiia)

flew Yak-series fighter aircraft. Tasked with protecting fixed targets from enemy attacks, the unit was subordinated at various times to the 144th and 101st Fighter Aviation Divisions and the 9th Fighter Aviation Corps. In the course of 4,419 combat sorties, the regiment destroyed 38 enemy aircraft and damaged 42 in 125 air engagements (Pennington 2003, 520). It supported the Battle of Stalingrad and defended Voronezh, Kursk, Kiev, Debrecen, Budapest, and Vienna from enemy air attacks. It was most active during the middle period of the war, while based near Voronezh and Kursk.

Despite including top-ranked pilots, the regiment received little recognition both during and

after the war. Three members of a well-known prewar women's aerobatic team flew with the regiment: Raisa Beliaeva, Valeriia Khomiakova, and team leader Evgeniia Prokhorova. Fighter aces Lidiia Litviak and Katia Budanova were former members of the regiment, which had a very troubled history. The deaths of the first three women mentioned are controversial, as was the transfer of its first commander, Tamara Kazarinova. The unit failed to achieve the elite Guards status, and its pilots never received a single Hero of the Soviet Union award.

The 586th began active service at Saratov, near Stalingrad, on April 16, 1942, under the command of Major Kazarinova, who was later transferred to Air Defense Headquarters following the accidental death of Khomiakova during a night sortie in October 1942. Most of the veterans blamed Kazarinova for the accident. Kazarinova was unpopular and became resentful toward her subordinates, especially after several women pilots sought her removal. She later reputedly took advantage of her staff position to make sure that those seeking her removal received particularly hazardous assignments, and she prevented the unit from gaining the prestigious status of Guards.

On September 10, 1942, Kazarinova sent eight pilots to Stalingrad; their squadron was split into two sections and sent to two different regiments. Among the eight were Lidiia Litviak and Ekaterina Budanova, future aces, but the 586th did not receive credit for their kills (enemy aircraft they shot down). Four of the eight returned within a few months; one perished in Stalingrad. Litviak, Budanova, and Antonina Lebedeva were killed during the summer of 1943 while serving with various men's regiments.

In October 1942 the regiment acquired another squadron staffed by male pilots, as well as a new permanent commanding officer, Aleksander Gridnev. From February 13 to August 16, 1943, the unit was based at Voronezh. This was a very busy period during which pilots Raisa Surnachevskaia and Tamara Pamiatnykh engaged forty-two German bombers and shot down four, thus preventing bombs from being dropped on troop trains passing through the important rail junction at Kastornaia en route to the decisive Battle of Kursk. Surnachevskaia and Pamiatnykh were rewarded with inscribed gold watches by King George VI of England, but they received no Soviet recognition. The regiment also flew high-profile missions escorting important people such as Nikita Khrushchev, then political officer for the Stalingrad front, and Air Defense Forces Commander Major-General Gromadin.

Among the more prominent pilots who died while serving with the regiment were:

Raisa Beliaeva (b. December 25, 1912; d. July 19, 1943, at Voronezh), senior lieutenant, pilot, and squadron commander. A member of a prewar aerobatic team, she participated in the Battle of Stalingrad and escorted Khrushchev's aircraft. Gridnev, her commanding officer, considered her to be a top-rate pilot. Beliaeva's death is attributed to aircraft malfunction.

Valeriia Khomiakova (b. August 2, 1914; d. October 6, 1942, at Saratov), pilot and deputy squadron commander. A member of a prewar women's aerobatic team, Khomiakova was the first woman to shoot down an enemy aircraft at night. On her first combat patrol, September 24, 1942, she destroyed a Ju-88 bomber over Saratov in a nighttime engagement. This was the first official kill credited to the 586th. Khomiakova died in a crash during a night flight on October 5–6, 1942, possibly as a result of being posted to night-alert duty when she was extremely tired.

Evgeniia Prokhorova (b. 1913; d. December 3, 1942, at Uralsk), senior lieutenant, pilot, and squadron commander. A leader of a prewar women's aerobatic team and holder of several world records in prewar competitions, Prokhorova was considered a very competent military pilot. While participating in a fighter escort mission, she was compelled to land during a heavy snowstorm. She was found frozen to

death the next day, trapped in her overturned plane.

—*Kazimiera J. Cottam*

See also Litviak, Lidiia Vladimirovna

References and Further Reading

Cottam, Kazimiera J., ed. and trans. 1997. *Women in Air War: The Eastern Front in World War II.* Russian edition edited by Militsa A. Kazarinova et al. Nepean, Ontario, Canada: New Military Publishing. (The Russian edition was published in 1971 under the title *V nebe frontovom.*)

Pennington, Reina. 2001. *Wings, Women and War.* Lawrence: University Press of Kansas.

———. 2003. 586th Fighter Aviation Regiment. Pages 520–523 in *Amazons to Fighter Pilots.* Edited by Reina Pennington. Vol. 2. Westport, CT: Greenwood.

SOVIET UNION/RUSSIAN FEDERATION, WOMEN HEROES OF THE (1938–1995)

The highest Soviet military award, introduced on April 16, 1934. After August 1, 1939, the title was accompanied by the Hero of the Soviet Union Medal. As of October 16, 1939, the full name of the award was changed to the Gold Star Hero of the Soviet Union Medal (HSU). The recognition was to be conferred on those who distinguished themselves by their heroic deeds. The first Soviet women awarded the title were airwomen Valentina Grizodubova, Polina Osipenko, and Marina Raskova. They were awarded the honor for their pioneering nonstop transcontinental flight to the Far East in September 1938.

As of May 5, 1990, ninety-five military women had been granted the HSU, including Aniela Krzywon (1925–1943), the only Polish woman recipient. Krzywon served with the Polish Emilia Plater Independent Women's

Battalion and was killed in the Battle of Lenino. Of this number, the following Soviet women combatants of World War II were granted the HSU on May 5, 1990, by Mikhail Gorbachev, the reformist Soviet leader and Communist party chief: pilots Lidiia Vladimirovna Litviak and Ekaterina Ivanovna Zelenko (posthumously) and marine Ekaterina Illarionovna Mikhailova-Demina. In addition, two Soviet airwomen—Tat'iana Nikolaevna Sumarokova, squadron navigator of the 46th Taman Guards Night Bomber Aviation Regiment, and Ekaterina Vasil'evna Budanova (deceased), ace fighter pilot who had served in the 73rd Stalingrad-Vienna Fighter Aviation Regiment (the former 296th Fighter Aviation Regiment)—were awarded the Hero of the Russian Federation (HRF) in 1995. In the Soviet era, two women were granted the HSU for postwar performance: Valentina Tereshkova, an astronaut who had attained the rank of major general, and Svetlana Savitskaia, pilot-astronaut, the only woman to be awarded the HSU twice.

The two largest groups of Soviet women recipients of the HSU/HRF for their World War II service were 32 airwomen and 29 partisans and resistance activists. Twelve women HSUs in the ground forces and all three in the navy were medical personnel who took part in combat as well. The total number of Soviet women who received the HSU for their World War II service, 94, appears disproportionately small when compared to the total of 11,500 HSUs earned overall by World War II combatants, considering that women comprised 8 percent of Soviet military personnel in 1943. Apparently senior commanders were not overly generous in awarding the HSU to women soldiers (for example, Mikhailova-Demina). Many women also served in so-called defensive operations, such as engineer preparation of terrain, the building of fortifications, mine clearing, or air defense. Consequently, although exposed to great danger (particularly in the last two categories of military operations), the women were unlikely to receive the HSU reserved for those exhibiting aggressive acts of heroism.

Due to their supposed political unreliability, including arrests of themselves or family members during Stalin's reign of terror, a substantial number of Soviet women who earned the HSU during the war were not decorated until the 1960s and then often posthumously. Representative recipients of the HSU/HRF are discussed, by unit, in the following sections (Cottam 1998).

46th Taman Guards Night Bomber Aviation Regiment

Raisa Ermolaevna Aronova (1920–1982), Guards major. One of several navigators in her regiment with inadequate flying experience, she became a pilot after improving her flying skills in the training squadron. Aronova flew 960 operational sorties and spent 1,148 hours in the air by night. She was awarded the HSU on May 15, 1946.

Marina Pavlovna Chechneva (1922–1984), Guards major and squadron commander. She flew up to 18 night missions and performed 810 short-range combat sorties, with about 1,000 flying hours to her credit. She was assigned especially difficult sorties, including daytime reconnoitering. Only 20 years old, Chechneva commanded a training squadron and trained 18 new pilots and navigators. She authored several books and many articles about her unit and was awarded the HSU on August 15, 1946.

Polina Vladimirovna Gel'lman (1919–), Guards major. Gel'lman served as her squadron's navigator and communications chief. In addition to being very competent, she managed to accomplish a great deal without any fuss and got along well with all of her female comrades. She flew 860 night operational missions, accumulating 1,300 flying hours, and was awarded the HSU on May 15, 1946.

Larissa Nikolaevna Litvinova-Rozanova (b. 1918), Guards captain. Litvinova-Rozanova was chief navigator and, initially, squadron navigator.

She became flight commander after gaining additional flying experience in the training squadron. She replaced Evgeniia Rudneva as chief navigator after the latter's death in April 1944. She was credited with having flown 816 missions and was awarded the HSU on February 23, 1945.

Evdokiia (Dusia) Ivanovna Nosal (1918–1943), Guards junior lieutenant and deputy squadron commander. At the beginning of the war Nosal lost her newborn baby as a result of the bombing of her maternity hospital, which made her determined to fly to avenge the baby's death. She volunteered for and was entrusted with the most difficult missions and was the first to be awarded the HSU in her regiment, posthumously.

Evgeniia (Zhenia) Maksimovna Rudneva (1920–1944), Guards senior lieutenant and chief navigator. In addition to training ground support personnel in navigation, Rudneva successively flew with all pilots of her unit, and she initiated new pilots into their flying duties. A former astronomy student, Rudneva kept an interesting diary. As the regiment's most prominent intellectual, she lectured on the theory of navigation. Rudneva was credited with destroying the headquarters of Field Marshal Baron Ewald von Kleist near Mozdok on the Transcaucasus front. Shot down on her 645th mission, Rudneva was posthumously awarded the HSU on October 26, 1944. An asteroid was later named after her.

125th M. M. Raskova Borisov Guards Bomber Aviation Regiment

Mariia Ivanovna Dolina-Mel'nikova (1920–), Guards major, flight commander, and deputy acting squadron commander. During the initial months of the war, Dolina-Mel'nikova flew about 200 special missions aboard the U-2 in the 296th Fighter Aviation Regiment, in which Lidiia Liviak was to serve. Considered one of the best pilots in her unit, Dolina-Mel'nikova

flew 72 bombing missions. She took part in the Victory Parade on Moscow's Red Square on June 24, 1945, and became one of five in her wing to be awarded the HSU on August 18, 1945. After the war Dolina-Mel'nikova served as deputy commander of a men's aviation wing, from which she transferred to the reserves in 1950.

Galina Ivanovna Dzhunkovskaia-Markova (1922–1985), Guards major and squadron navigator. Initially Dzhunkovskaia-Markova was the navigator for deputy squadron commander Mariia Dolina. During her most memorable battle, in the course of which her squadron shot down four enemy fighters, Dzhunkovskaia-Markova survived a belly landing in her burning bomber. From the spring of 1944 she flew with Squadron Commander Klavdiya Fomicheva. A veteran of 69 medium-range operational missions, Dzhunkovskaia-Markova was resourceful, resolute, and confident. She took part in the Victory Parade on June 24, 1945, in Moscow and became one of five members of this unit to be awarded the HSU on August 18, 1945. She subsequently published several books and articles about her regiment.

Antonina (Tonia) Leont'evna Zubkova (1920–1950), Guards captain and squadron navigator. Zubkova flew 56 missions with Nadezhda Fedutenko, an experienced prewar pilot, and was frequently appointed divisional deputy leader for the duration of bombing missions. On September 2, 1943, Zubkova led fifty-four aircraft onto their target after her divisional leader was shot down, and on April 16, 1944, in the Baltic area, Zubkova again led her divisional column. During the subsequent debriefing at corps headquarters, senior officers and generals were most impressed with Zubkova's aerial photographs. She was one of five from her wing to be awarded the HSU on August 18, 1945. A postwar professor of mathematics at the N. E. Zhukovsky Air Force Engineering Academy, in 1950 she accidentally fell under a train and was killed.

Women in the Ground Forces, Navy, and Resistance

Elena Fedorovna Kolesova (1920–1942), private. Kolesova, a former elementary school teacher, became a partisan leader and saboteur who served in the famous Commando Unit No. 9903, which contributed to the German defeat in the Battle of Moscow. Kolesova was one of this unit's two women members to be awarded the HSU, out of a total of five HSU recipients. (The other female recipient of the HSU, awarded posthumously on February 16, 1942, was the famous partisan Zoia Kosmodem'ianskaia.) Air-dropped in Belarus on May 1, 1942, Kolesova led a handful of young women saboteurs, mistakenly believed by the enemy to number as many as 600. She was credited with instructing hundreds of partisans in mine laying. Kolesova was killed in action and was posthumously awarded the HSU on November 21, 1944.

Natalia Venediktovna Kovshova (1920–1942) and Mariia Semenovna Polivanova (1922–1942), privates and expert snipers. Kovshova and Polivanova, despite their divergent family backgrounds, became close friends before enlisting. Kovshova was born into a family with strong revolutionary traditions, whereas Polivanova came from the nobility and was related to the anarchist Prince Peter Kropotkin and Czarist Defense Minister A. A. Polivanov. Both were graduates of the famous Women's School for Snipers. From the very beginning of their service with the 130th Rifle Division defending Moscow, they were considered model soldiers. On August 14, 1942, in a surrounded platoon decimated by the enemy, they were repeatedly wounded and committed suicide with their last grenades. They were the first Soviet women snipers to be awarded the HSU, on February 14, 1943.

Irina Nikolaevna Levchenko (1924–1973), lieutenant colonel and author. Levchenko was the daughter of a former minister of transportation and victim of Stalin's terror. Appointed as a noncommissioned officer (NCO) at the age of seventeen, senior lieutenant at twenty-one, and major at twenty-eight, Levchenko became lieutenant colonel at thirty-one. She was skilled in tank driving, firing the tank gun, handling small arms, and dispensing first aid. Levchenko received her basic tank training with the 39th Tank Brigade in the Crimea, where she served as a medical NCO. After graduating from the Stalingrad Tank School in July 1942, Levchenko became a tank platoon commander. She also served as assistant tank battalion chief of staff and was liaison officer of the 41st Tank Brigade of the 7th Mechanized Corps. Levchenko ended her army career as a tank corps liaison officer, an appointment granted to the bravest, most resourceful, and most proven in combat. A participant in a reunion of Soviet and U.S. soldiers on the Elbe in 1945, Levchenko graduated from the Moscow Academy of Armored and Mechanized Troops in 1952. The first Soviet recipient of the Florence Nightingale Medal, she was decorated twelve times. She was awarded the HSU on May 6, 1965.

Ekaterina Illarionovna Mikhailova-Demina (1925–), chief petty officer. An outstanding marine and medic, Mikhailova-Demina served in the 369th Independent Naval Infantry Battalion, which advanced from the Taman Peninsula on the Azov Sea through the Balkans to Vienna. Mikhailova-Demina took part in the capture of Belgorod-Dniestrovsky. During the storming of the Yugoslav fortress of Ilok located on the Danube near Bukovar, Mikhailova-Demina was wounded and developed double pneumonia. The recommendation from her immediate superiors that she be awarded the HSU was turned down three times. She was finally awarded the HSU by Mikhail Gorbachev on May 5, 1990.

Mariia Vasil'ievna Oktiabrskaya (1905–1944), Guards sergeant. Oktiabrskaya served as tank driver–mechanic with the 26th Tank Brigade of the 2nd Tatsinsky Guards Tank

Polina Osipenko, Valentina Grizodubova, and Marina Raskova. (Butkov, A. 1978. "Podvigu sorok let" [The Heroic Deed of Forty Years Ago]. Grazhdanskaia Aviatsiia [Civil Aviation] 9:38)

Corps on the 3rd Belorussian front. As the wife of the political commissar of an infantry regiment before the war, Oktiabrskaya became an expert driver and Voroshilov sharpshooter. After evacuation to Tomsk, Siberia, and on learning that her husband, parents, and two sons had been killed, Oktiabrskaya sent all her savings to the authorities in Moscow to cover the cost of manufacturing a tank she wished to drive. Eventually, the authorities complied with her wishes. After training in tank driving, she distinguished herself in her first battle by maneuvering her tank onto enemy positions. Mortally wounded in the head while repairing a damaged track on January 17, 1944, Oktiabrskaya was buried in Kutuzov Gardens in Smolensk with other famous war heroes. She became a posthumous HSU recipient on August 2, 1944.

Neonila (Nina) Andreevna Onilova (1921–1942), senior sergeant. Onilova defended Odessa and Sevastopol. She served in the 54th Razin Regiment of the famous 25th V. I. Chapaev Division, Independent Maritime Army, on the Crimean front. A sharpshooting machine gunner, she trained dozens of fellow soldiers, having perfected the technique of Anka, her civil war role model. Onilova allowed the enemy troops to closely approach and then delivered fire until the front rows were destroyed and those behind were forced to turn back. Initially a medical NCO at the front near Odessa in August 1941, Onilova was soon transferred to a machine-gun platoon, having proven her competence. Seriously wounded in September 1941, she was hospitalized for two months. When she recovered, Onilova insisted on rejoining her regiment situated near

Sevastopol. After learning that she had again been seriously wounded on February 28, 1942, General I. E. Petrov, the army commander, immediately ordered his medical staff to do everything in their power to save her. When her condition began to deteriorate, Petrov himself visited her to say good-bye. The severe, smart-looking, gray-haired general, reportedly with tears in his eyes, said in a slightly hoarse voice, "Well, little daughter, you fought gloriously. Thank you, on behalf of our entire Army and Nation. Everyone in Sevastopol knows about you. The entire country will learn about you, too. Thank you, little daughter" (Cottam 1998, 129). Onilova, however, was only granted the HSU posthumously on May 14, 1965.

Nina Ivanovna Sosnina (1923–1943), leader of the underground in Malin, Soviet Ukraine, during World War II. Sosnina planned and organized resistance based on missions assigned to her from the nearby Kutuzov Partisan Detachment and intelligence obtained by her brother Valentin and others. Along with her father, a surgeon, Sosnina died in a house fire set by enemy soldiers. She and her father were in the home, which belonged to a local teacher, performing an operation on a wounded partisan. Initially blamed for associating with enemies of the people, Sosnina was posthumously rehabilitated: her reputation and honor were restored after being defamed by the Stalin regime, and she was granted the HSU on May 8, 1965.

—*Kazimiera J. Cottam*

See also Soviet Union, Order of Glory, I Class, Soviet Women Recipients; Soviet Union, Order of the Red Banner, Women Recipients

References and Further Reading

Cottam, Kazimiera J. 1991. Yelena Fedorovna Kolesova: Woman Hero of the Soviet Union. *Minerva: Quarterly Report on Women and the Military* 9, no. 2 (Summer):69–75.

———. 1998. *Women in War and Resistance.* Nepean, Ontario, Canada: New Military Publishing.

Lebedev, Z. 1979. Znak osobogo otlichiia [An Award of Special Distinction]. *Voenno-istorichesky zhurnal* 10:84–87.

Markova, Galina Ivanovna. 1971. *Iunost' v ogne* [Youth under Fire]. Moscow: Moskovskii Rabochii.

Smirnov, Sergei Sergeevich. 1975. Katiusha. Pages 122–138 in *Docheri Rossii* [Russia's Daughters]. Edited by I. Cherniaeva. Moscow: Sovetskaia Rossiia.

Smirnova-Medevedeva, Zoya Matveyevna. 1997. *Opalennaia iunost'* [Fire-Scorched Youth]. Translated by Kazimiera J. Cottam under the title *On the Road to Stalingrad: Memoirs of a Woman Machine Gunner.* Nepean, Ontario, Canada: New Military Publishing.

Spanish Civil War, Women and the

From 1936 to 1939 Spanish women participated in a civil war that convulsed their nation. Women fought on both sides of the struggle; however, a surprisingly large number of Spanish women supported the Nationalist forces (Smith 1989, 474). The Nationalists, led by General Francisco Franco, represented conservative sectors like the Falange, a mass-based fascist organization, and were backed by much of the military, the Catholic Church, and large landowners. The Republicans, opponents of the Nationalists, were the governing coalition. They ruled Spain from their 1931 election, at which time they established the Second Republic, until their 1939 defeat. They received support from peasants, workers, and sectors of the middle class; the coalition included communists, socialists, anarchists, and liberals.

In the 1920s and 1930s most of Spain was mired in poverty. Unlike much of the rest of Europe, it had failed to industrialize, except in the north, or carry out agricultural reforms. As a result, the population was malnourished and lacked good housing or health care (Smith

1989, 472). Women worked in agriculture, sweatshops, and factories. Rates of infant mortality were high, as were the number of children born out of wedlock (Koonz 1998, 471). The Republican forces came to power pledging to modernize Spain and improve the population's standard of living.

When the Republicans took control of the government, Napoleonic legal codes and conservative Catholic practices governed how most Spaniards lived. Families could "force their daughters into marriage" (Smith 1989, 473). Divorce was illegal, and husbands could imprison their wives for "disobedience and verbal insults." Women's literacy rate (50 percent) was much lower than that of men (70 percent) (Koonz 1998, 471). As part of its modernization project, the Republican government passed a series of laws that granted women equal status as full citizens. Women obtained suffrage rights and maternity benefits, the option of no-fault divorce, and civil marriage (Koonz 1998, 472).

Republican women fought to maintain the social gains they had won and to preserve the overall political and economic program of the government. In order to counter the threat that the growing power of fascism posed, antifascist Spanish women joined the Worldwide Committee of Women against War and Fascism (Smith 1989, 473). Initially, Republican women joined militia units and took up arms against the Franco forces. Lina Odena was the first Republican to die in battle when she committed suicide rather than surrender to the Nationalists as they overran her position (Smith 1989, 454). Dolores Ibárruri, known as *La Pasionaria*, called on women and men to fight against the fascists. When the Nationalist forces attacked Madrid, one of the last Republican strongholds, she urged women and men to take up arms against them.

Neither the social changes instituted by the Republicans nor their attempts to break up the large estates and set up peasant cooperatives, increase wages, or undermine the power of the Catholic Church pleased conservative forces

within Spain. In 1936 the military under General Franco rebelled and initiated the civil war that, three years later, would defeat the Republican forces.

The majority of Spanish women rejected the Republicans and sided with the Franco forces. Unlike the Republican women, they embraced conservative ideas about gender and heeded the call of the Catholic Church to rally to its defense in opposition to the Republic. In the 1930s José Antonio Primo de Rivera started the Falange, using Benito Mussolini's fascism as a model. In 1934 Pilar Primo de Rivera, José Antonio's sister, organized the *Sección Femenina* (Women's Section) of the Falange, under the leadership of her brother. It was started to "give aid to Falangist prisoners and assistance to the families of fallen members" of the movement (Enders 2002, 86). The organization grew rapidly and exponentially: from an initial group of 300 women in 1934 it grew to 400,000 in 1938, according to its own estimates. The vast majority of these women worked in *Auxilio Social* (Social Assistance), the Falange organization that "provided food, clothing, and shelter to widows, orphans and the destitute, and taught them to 'love God and understand the Falange'" (Enders 2002, 87). They supported separate spheres for men and women and believed that the most important quality a woman could possess was *abnegación* (self-sacrifice).

Although these women engaged in very public activities, such as nursing, running soup kitchens, and in some cases taking up arms, they never did so in order to challenge male power or gender relations, as was the case with some of the Republican women. Instead, their goal was to "strengthen the family within a 'New Spain'" (Keene 2002, 184). They fought to restore conservative ideas about gender; to establish the woman's role in life as a wife and mother within the home, not in the streets; and to uphold the spiritual teachings of the church over all aspects of their lives.

In 1939 Nationalist forces defeated the Republic, and General Franco ruled Spain dictatorially until his death in 1975. Some of the Republican women, especially the most visible leaders like Dolores Ibárruri, went into exile. The lives of most women who stayed in Spain came under the strict control of the Franco government and the Catholic Church. The fascist government rescinded women's right to vote, made divorce illegal, and instituted the Charter of Labor that said "women's only proper sphere is in the nursery" (Koonz 1998, 473). Pilar Primo de Rivera continued to head the Sección Femenina of the Falange, which became the official women's organization until Franco's death. If women wanted to work for the state, "obtain a driver's license, a passport, or the like, [they were] obligated to serve six months with the *Sección Femenina*" (Enders 2002, 87).

—*Margaret Power*

See also Ibárruri, Dolores; Kea, Salaria

References and Further Reading

Enders, Victoria. 2002. "And We Ate Up the World": Memories of the *Sección Femenina*. In *Right-Wing Women: From Conservatives to Extremists around the World*. Edited by Paola Bacchetta and Margaret Power. New York: Routledge.

Keene, Judith. 2001. *Fighting for Franco. International Volunteers in Nationalist Spain during the Spanish Civil War, 1936–1939*. London and New York: Leicester University.

———. 2002. Foreign Women in Spain for General Franco. In *Right-Wing Women: From Conservatives to Extremists around the World*. Edited by Paola Bacchetta and Margaret Power. New York: Routledge.

Koonz, Claudia. 1998. The "Woman Question" in Authoritarian Regimes. Pages 463–492 in *Becoming Visible: Women in European History*. Edited by Renate Bridenthal, Susan Mosher Stuard, and Merry E. Wiesner. Boston and New York: Houghton Mifflin.

Smith, Bonnie G. 1989. *Changing Lives: Women in European History since 1700*. Lexington, MA: D. C. Heath.

SPANISH-AMERICAN WAR, WOMEN AND THE

Role of women in the Spanish-American War. Men and masculinity dominate popular conceptions of the Spanish-American War (April to December 1898). Popular culture idolized women almost exclusively as sweethearts and mothers. Nevertheless, women played significant roles both on the home front and in the war zones. Their most crucial direct contributions to the war effort were as nurses and as relief workers. Women also helped to document and commemorate the war and were symbolically important to propaganda and mobilization.

Between 1895 and 1898 increasing calls for the United States to aid Cuba in its revolt against Spanish rule came from both women and men. Public support for intervention was aroused by newspaper reports of the brutal treatment of Cuban women by Spanish authorities. Women and children were featured prominently as victims of starvation caused by Spain's military policies. The fact that Spain had a queen regent—María Cristina, mother of the underage Alfonso XIII—who seemingly allowed such atrocities, made the situation appear all the worse to U.S. readers, who believed in women's superior morality. The U.S. press also publicized and sometimes exaggerated moral outrages such as the *Olivette* incident, during which Spanish officials in February 1897 strip-searched three Cuban women passengers aboard a U.S. ship. The Spanish press responded in kind, with cartoons of a lascivious Uncle Sam pursing the lovely maiden Spain. Meanwhile, some Cuban women, such as Rosa Castellanos, Josefa Agueros, and Luz Noriega, served as *mambisas* (insurgents) against Spanish forces. So did Filipinas, such as Segunda Puentes Santiago and Gregoria de Jesus y Alvarez, in what would become the Pacific front of the Spanish-American War.

Eventually, the momentum of public opinion, pressure from U.S. officials including Assistant Secretary of the Navy Theodore Roosevelt, and

Spanish-American War

"[After being assigned to the army hospital at Montauk Point, Long Island, New York] we had to hustle to . . . get into uniform then we returned to the Colonel's tent and were ordered to line up outside and a group of doctors were told to choose the nurse each wanted. It was positively funny and yet humiliating to stand there and wonder who would choose you. I don't know how they sized us up. . . . We worked from 5 o'clock until about 8 o'clock without food of any kind, and when we went to breakfast we would get black coffee and some kind of mush, Indian meal or oat meal, then back to work [until 8 P.M.]. I remember one dinner I went to where there was nothing but boiled cabbage and black coffee."

—Rose M. Heavren, speech given at Spanish-American War Nurses (SAWN) meeting,
Pratt High School, March 28, 1950.
SAWN Collection no. 317, Rose M. Heavren Collection,
Gift of Mary (Heavren) Budds,
Women in Military Service for America Memorial Foundation, Inc.,
Archives, Arlington, VA.

events such as the explosion of the battleship USS *Maine* in Havana's harbor propelled the United States into war against Spain. Several women's groups immediately stepped forward to offer their services to the federal government when Congress declared war on April 25, 1898. Existing women's organizations, from the Daughters of the American Revolution (DAR) to the Catholic Sisterhoods, mobilized their members while new women's groups formed specifically for war relief.

The most prominent of the new groups, the Women's National War Relief Association (WNWRA), was formed in New York in May 1898 largely under the impetus of Ellen Hardin Walworth, previously a founder of the DAR. The WNWRA's leadership brought together socially prominent, wealthy women such as Helen Gould, daughter of financier Jay Gould and heir to his fortune, with the wives of influential politicians from across the country. The association followed the model of the U.S. Sanitary Commission from the American Civil War. Its mission was to collect monetary donations and to provide material aid to U.S. troops, especially to the sick and wounded. Its nationwide network

of auxiliaries raised over $50,000 to equip hospital ships, among other projects. The WNWRA also collected donations of food staples and "delicacies," established rest homes for convalescent veterans, and produced thousands of articles of clothing and linens for the soldiers. Other local groups engaged in similar work—fund-raising, sewing, collecting supplies—without necessarily affiliating with any national associations. Similar to these organizations, the Spanish Red Cross and the Cuban White Cross balanced relief efforts with a nationalistic agenda.

The American Red Cross, by contrast, aided not only U.S. troops but also Cuban troops and refugees and Spanish prisoners of war. It engaged in relief work in Cuba and, to a lesser extent, in Puerto Rico and the Philippines, as well as in U.S. military camps. Like the WNWRA and other groups of women volunteers, it sometimes had difficulty in its relations with federal government agencies. As the public became aware of the lamentably unsanitary conditions at some military camps, women began to demand a larger part in what they called the housekeeping side of war: providing and managing food, caring for the sick and wounded, and nurturing the

Nurses aboard an Army hospital ship doing medical work in Cuba during Spanish-American War.
(Bettmann/Corbis)

convalescent. Red Cross president Clara Barton, already beloved for her efforts during the American Civil War, became a revered public icon, the single figure who best represented what women could and should do to alleviate suffering during wartime.

The U.S. military's search for nurses to meet its escalating needs was coordinated by Anita Newcomb McGee. As chair of the Hospital Corps Committee of the DAR, she gained a commission from the surgeon general of the army, George M. Sternberg, to screen thousands of applications from aspiring nurses. McGee later became acting assistant surgeon general in

charge of the Nurse Corps Division. The army began hiring nurses under contract in March 1898, offering compensation of $30 per month and one daily ration. The surgeon general's initial restriction on women serving either in camps or overseas proved unsustainable in the face of disease, particularly the waves of typhoid and yellow fever that swept through army camps. Thus female contract nurses ended up playing a much more prominent role in the Spanish-American War than anyone had expected. Over 1,700 women, compared with only about a dozen men, served as contract nurses by the war's end.

Among the many who reported on the war were several women journalists, the best known being Anna Northend Benjamin and Teresa Howard Dean for *Leslie's* and Canadian Kathleen Blake Coleman for the *Toronto Mail and Express*. Coleman is believed to be the first accredited female war correspondent in the world. The *New York Journal, Chicago Record, New Orleans Picayune,* and *McClure's* also offered women's stories on the war with some regularity. Acclaimed photographer Frances Benjamin Johnston took pictures of war heroes such as the Rough Riders and Admiral George Dewey. The conflict and its imperialist aftermath became a potent theme for women writers, including Spanish authors Eva Canel and Emilia Pardo Bazán and American poets Frances E. W. Harper and Katherine Lee Bates. The most enduring U.S. image of the war, the public monument at Arlington National Cemetery called *The Hiker,* is the work of a woman: sculptor Theo Alice Ruggles Kitson, who created numerous other war memorials.

Lastly, women participated in public discussions. Although most women categorically supported the war as a humanitarian cause or a defense of national honor, others disagreed. Spanish women had staged a large antiwar demonstration in Zaragoza in the summer of 1896, demanding an end to poor men's conscription to put down the Cuban revolt. Women also led a firestorm of riots across Spain in May 1898 when the war drove up bread and flour prices. As vocal members of the peace movement and afterward of the Anti-imperialist League, U.S. women criticized the militaristic values and imperialist aggression that they believed the war enshrined. This too became a legacy of the Spanish-American War and laid the groundwork for more widespread dissent during World War I.

—*Laura R. Prieto*

See also Barton, Clara; Nurses, U.S. Army Nurse Corps in World War I

References and Further Reading

Freeman, Barbara M. 1989. *Kit's Kingdom: The Journalism of Kathleen Blake Coleman.* Ottawa: Carleton University.

Graf, Mercedes. 2001. Women Nurses in the Spanish-American War. *Minerva: Quarterly Report on Women and the Military* 19, no. 1 (Spring):3–38.

Hoganson, Kristin. 1998. *Fighting for American Manhood: How Gender Politics Provoked the Spanish-American and Philippine-American Wars.* New Haven, CT: Yale University.

Sarnecky, Mary. 1999. *A History of the United States Army Nurse Corps.* Philadelphia: University of Pennsylvania.

SPARTAN WOMEN

Role of women in the Spartan military state. By the sixth century B.C. the Greek state of Sparta had developed a unique military organization. Men of the elite Spartiate class engaged in no profession but war, and their whole lives were devoted to training and battle. This system, attributed to the legendary lawgiver Lycurgus, had profound implications for Spartan women. They were the state's military support staff par excellence, running estates and homes in their husbands' absence, producing future warriors of the highest possible quality, and reinforcing an ethic that preferred death to cowardice.

Unlike women in other Greek states, Spartiate females were rigorously educated from a young age. Their training included study of the classics, poetry, and philosophy but also intensive physical exercise because the Spartans believed that a strong, healthy woman was more likely to produce strong sons. Spartan girls learned to race, wrestle, throw the discus and javelin, and, in short, perform all the feats of their male counterparts except arms training. They married later than other Greek women, in their late teens, so they were prepared to take control of their households immediately (Spartan men lived in barracks until age forty, only occasionally visiting their wives). Both men and women seem to have been taught from a young age that their bodies were at the service of the state. Thus, it was apparently not uncommon for a husband to invite a stronger man to impregnate his wife, thereby producing a stronger future warrior of Sparta.

The Spartiate matron raised her daughters until their marriage and her sons until they moved to the barracks at age seven; therefore, she provided essential early ethical training. Most prominent in the ancient Greek sources concerning Sparta are mothers' exhortations to sons, encouraging them never to show cowardice. A Spartan mother is credited with handing her son his shield before he set out to battle with the laconic statement "With it or on it." The shield was the first thing a man dropped when running from the battlefield, but, conversely, the Greek round *hoplon* could be used to carry the bodies of the slain after the battle. Mothers were expected to show pride in sons who died for the state. There are accounts of Spartan women killing sons who had disgraced themselves and their family by showing cowardice in battle.

Spartan women were not trained to bear arms themselves. This is obvious from the panic when Thebans invaded Spartan territory in 369 B.C. at a time when the Spartan army was away. In times of crisis women could, however, play an important role in resistance. When Pyrrhus attacked in the mid-third century B.C., Archidamia, the grandmother of one of the two kings who simultaneously ruled Sparta, rallied the women and prevented the men from sending them to Crete for safety. (Sparta always had two kings, who descended from two families—the Agiads and the Eurypontids.) Women helped the soldiers dig a long trench as protection against Pyrrhus's war-elephants, and the next day they cheered the army on to victory.

—*Phyllis G. Jestice*

See also Greek Women and War in Antiquity

References and Further Reading

Pomeroy, Sarah B. 2002. *Spartan Women*. New York: Oxford University.

STARK, DAME FREYA (1893–1993)

English Voluntary Aid Detachment (VAD) volunteer, propagandist, and author. Stark served as a VAD worker during World War I and worked extensively with British intelligence during World War II.

Although her parents were English, Stark was raised in Italy. She began training as a nurse at St. Ursula in Bologna when Italy entered World War I but left nursing in 1915. After a broken engagement and illness, Stark traveled to England in 1916. She briefly worked as a censor before training with the VAD. She served as a VAD volunteer at Villa Trento in 1917 until her hospital unit retreated to Padua. She also served at various other English hospitals in Italy until the war's close.

Stark's involvement in World War II began as a correspondent with the British Foreign Office in Aden, Yemen, providing information on the Middle Eastern situation. In 1940 she visited Yemen, smuggling, translating, and showing British propaganda films to the elite. In 1940 she relocated to Cairo, Egypt, where she worked closely on propaganda with General Wavell, the commander in chief of the British eastern forces. She established the Brotherhood of Freedom, a largely social group that perpetuated Muslim and Christian ideals while advocating British interests. In 1941 Stark moved to Baghdad, Iraq, despite an intergovernmental crisis and a siege of the British Embassy that lasted from April to June. She traveled widely throughout the Middle East—Persia, Jerusalem, even Cyprus—and to India as well for her propaganda work.

In 1943 and 1944 Stark toured the United States and Canada. She gave speeches and socialized with influential people in an attempt to counteract Zionism. She encountered difficulty, however, due to anti-British sentiment in the United States and the unpopularity of the Colonial Office because of British involvement in India.

Stark eventually returned to her home in Italy, where she continued her propaganda work amid the ruins of the waning war and the collapse of fascism.

—*Barbara Penny Kanner*

See also Great Britain, Women in Service during World War I

References and Further Reading

Kanner, Barbara Penny. 1997. *Women in Context: Two Hundred Years of British Women Autobiographers, a Reference Guide and Reader.* New York: G. K. Hall.

Stark, Freya. 1961. *Dust in the Lion's Paw.* London: John Murray.

STEIN, EDITH (1891–1942)

Catholic nun and convert from Judaism who was murdered in a gas chamber at Auschwitz. Edith Stein, the daughter of a timber merchant, was born on October 12, 1891, in Breslau, Germany (now Wroclaw, Poland). Stein's father died when she was two, and she and her seven surviving siblings were raised by a strong and devout Orthodox Jewish mother. Stein, however, renounced Judaism and proclaimed atheism in 1904. She was among the first generation of German women to attend a university. She began her studies at the University of Breslau and continued them at Göttigen.

There she studied philosophy under Edmund Husserl. When Husserl moved to Freiburg, Germany, Stein, whose intellectual acuity had impressed him, moved as well and worked as his assistant. At Freiburg she earned her doctorate with highest honors. Drawn to Catholicism through her philosophical studies, Stein decided to convert while reading the autobiography of St. Theresa of Avila. She was baptized on January 1, 1922. She then relinquished her assistantship with Husserl to teach at a Catholic girls' school in Speyer. In 1932 she began teaching at the German Institute for Scientific Pedagogy, but in 1933, after the Nazis came to power, she was dismissed because of her Jewish ethnicity. The dismissal led her to take a step she had long contemplated. In 1934 Stein entered the cloistered Carmelite order in Cologne as Sister Teresa Benedicta of the Cross. In 1938, with the intensification of Nazi anti-Jewish measures, the order sent her to a convent in Echt in the Netherlands. The transfer did not save Stein. Germany invaded the Netherlands in May 1940. In 1942 leaders of the Catholic and Reformed churches in the Netherlands protested to the Nazi Reichs Commissioner Arthur Seyss-Inquart against the deportation of Dutch Jews. He informed them that if they did not publicize their protest, he would continue to make an exception for Jewish converts to Christianity. Nevertheless, when the Bishop of Utrecht issued a pastoral letter condemning the Nazi's anti-Jewish policy, Seyss-Inquart ordered the arrest and deportation of all Jewish Catholics (Rhodes 1973, 344–345).

On July 26, 1942, Stein and her sister Rosa, who had also converted to Catholicism, were seized and transported to Auschwitz. On August 9, 1942, they were killed in a gas chamber there. Edith Stein was canonized by Pope John Paul II on October 11, 1998. That the Catholic Church proclaimed Stein a saint angered some Jews because of Stein's status as a Jewish convert to Christianity who died in the Holocaust.

—*Bernard Cook*

See also Holocaust and Jewish Women

References and Further Reading

Garcia, Laura. 1977. Edith Stein—Convert, Nun, Martyr. *Crisis* 15 (June):32–35.

Rhodes, Anthony. 1973. *The Vatican in the Age of Dictators, 1922–1945.* London: Hodder and Stoughton.

Stein, Edith. 1991. *Edith Stein: Selected Writings by Edith Stein.* Springfield, IL: Templegate Publishers.

———. 1993. *Collected Works of Edith Stein,* vol. 5, *Self-Portrait in Letters, 1916–1942.* Translated by Josephine Koeppel. Washington, DC: Institute of Carmelite Studies Publications.

STIMSON, JULIA CATHERINE (1881–1948)

Chief nurse of American Red Cross Nursing (1918–1919) and director of nursing for the American Expeditionary Forces during World War I. Julia Catherine Stimson was born in 1881 in Worcester, Massachusetts. She was educated in St. Louis, Missouri, and in New York City and graduated from Vassar College in 1901. She entered nursing school in 1904 at New York Hospital and after graduation in 1908 worked at the Harlem Hospital in New York. From there she went to the Washington

A group of Red Cross nurses headed by the late Colonel Julia Stimson, Army Nurse Corps, during a parade in Paris, France, ca. 1920. (Bettman/Corbis)

University Hospital in St. Louis. In 1917 she joined the Army Nurse Corps and was named chief nurse of Base Hospital No. 21. She also served in that capacity in the British Expeditionary Forces Hospital No. 12 in Rouen, France. In April 1918 Stimson was appointed chief nurse of the American Red Cross in France and director of nursing of the American Expeditionary Forces. She supervised more than 10,000 nurses. She became dean of the Army School of Nursing in Washington, D.C., and superintendent of the Army Nurse Corps in 1919. In 1920, when nurses in the army were given relative rank, Stimson became the first woman to hold the rank of major. She was awarded the Distinguished Service Medal by the U.S. government, the British Royal Red Cross 1st Class, the French Medaille de la Reconnaissance Française and the Medaille d'Honneur de l'Hygiene Publique, and the International Red Cross Florence Nightingale Medal.

Stimson retired from the army in 1937 but continued in her work for the profession of nursing as president of the American Nursing Association from 1938 to 1944. She returned to active duty to assist with the recruiting of nurses during World War II. When army nurses were granted full rank she was promoted to colonel (retired) just six weeks before she died in September 1948.

Katherine Burger Johnson

See also Delano, Jane Arminda; Nurses, U.S. Army Nurse Corps in World War I

References and Further Reading

Aynes, Edith A. 1973. *From Nightingale to Eagle.* Englewood Cliffs, NJ: Prentice-Hall.

Stimson, Julia C. 1918. *Finding Themselves: The Letters of an American Army Chief Nurse in a British Hospital in France.* New York: Macmillan.

U.S. Army Center of Military History. 1995. *Highlights in the History of the Army Nurse Corps.* Washington, DC: U.S. Army Center of Military History.

STOBART, MABEL (1862–1954)

Set up hospitals for Bulgaria during the Balkan wars and on the western and Balkan fronts during World War I. Mabel Stobart was a supporter of female suffrage. She believed that in order to gain the right to vote women needed to demonstrate their active patriotism. She founded the Women's Sick and Wounded Convoy Troops (WSWCT) to provide help to soldiers at the front. The WSWCT sent women to Bulgaria in 1912 to assist Bulgarian soldiers in the First Balkan War. Stobart had approached Sir Frederick Treves, chairman of the British Red Cross Society, to allow the WSWCT to send women to Bulgaria. He had responded that there "was no work fitted for women in the Balkans" (Stobart 1935, 87). Lord Noel Buxton, however, agreed to have her accompany him to Bulgaria. Despite newspaper advertisements placed by the British Red Cross society advising women not to engage in the Bulgarian project, Stobart recruited fifteen British women volunteers—three doctors, six trained nurses, and six assistants. She and her volunteers were able, after a seven-day wagon trek over the Rhadope Mountains, to establish a hospital across the Turkish frontier at Kirk-Kilisse close to the fighting to aid wounded soldiers. Their effort was welcomed by the Bulgarian queen, Eleonora, a trained nurse who had tended to wounded soldiers during the Russo-Japanese War. Following the end of the First Balkan War, Stobart decided to disband her unit's operation. The three doctors, however, stayed behind and continued to work with the ill and, with the resumption of hostilities, with the wounded.

Although Stobart had spoken publicly against the impending war in August 1914, once Britain entered it she and Lady Muir McKenzie established the Women's National Service League (WNSL). Stobart argued, "Women are capable of taking a share, a serviceable share, in warfare, without inexpediency to any concerned, and even with direct benefit to all concerned"

(Stobart 1913, 212). The WNSL recruited volunteers to provide all of the skills necessary for the establishment of a military hospital operated entirely by women. On August 18 she headed for Brussels with her husband to prepare for the arrival of a WNSL unit. The rapid advance of the Germans preempted the operation. When Stobart attempted to reach Venlo in the Netherlands, having been given a pass by the German commandant in Brussels, she, her husband, and the unit chaplain were arrested as spies and almost summarily executed before being sent to Aachen, Germany, for trial. There a sympathetic military judge believed their story and sent them on to the Netherlands. After returning to England, Stobart led a WNSL unit to Antwerp, where they set up a hospital for wounded soldiers. After just ten days of operation, the Germans overwhelmed the city's defenses, and the hospital had to be evacuated. Stobart, who was undaunted, set up another WNSL hospital near Cherbourg, France, in November. This unit consisted of forty-five women, including six doctors, fifteen nurses, and ten orderlies as well as ambulance drivers and support personnel.

In February 1915 Stobart, feeling that her organizational work had been done, was drawn by news from Serbia to offer her services to the Serbian Relief Fund. In April she sailed to Salonika, Greece, with seven female doctors and eighteen trained nurses (Stobart 1935, 183). They set up their hospital at Kragujevatz and seven satellite dispensaries. The women had been in Serbia only three months when an orderly and a nurse died of typhus. In September Stobart was asked by the Serbians to command the First Serbian-English Field Hospital; the staff consisted of women from her WNSL unit and Serbians. Toward the end of October Stobart and the unit she commanded were forced to withdraw with the Serbian army and tend to the wounded during a three-month fighting retreat through Serbia, Montenegro, and Albania to the coast. She and the convoy she commanded reached Scutari on December 10, and from there she and her British personnel made their way home. In London Stobart was censured by the Serbian Relief Fund for, in her words, "having exceeded my instructions, and having led my Unit to unnecessary risks in accompanying the Army to the front" (Stobart 1935, 340).

—Bernard Cook

See also Inglis, Elsie, and the Scottish Women's Hospitals

References and Further Reading

Stobart, Mabel Annie Boulton. 1913. *War and Women, from Experiences in the Balkans and Elsewhere, by Mrs. St. Claire Stobart, Founder of the Women's Convoy Corps*. London: G. Bell and Sons.

———. 1935. *Miracles and Adventures: An Autobiography*. London: Rider.

STOWE, HARRIET BEECHER (1811–1896)

Prolific writer primarily remembered for her novel *Uncle Tom's Cabin*, which dealt with issues of slavery and was published in 1850. Harriet Beecher Stowe's writings intensified the debate on the subject of slavery that raged prior to the American Civil War. According to folklore, when President Abraham Lincoln met Stowe in 1862, he reputedly said, "So you're the little woman who wrote the book that started this Great War!" (Harrietbeecherstowe.org 2004).

Harriet Beecher was born into a devoutly religious family in Litchfield, Connecticut, the youngest of seven children. Her mother died when she was five, and she and her siblings were reared by her minister father, who physically and verbally abused them. At age twelve she was sent to the Hartford Female Seminary and placed under the tutelage of her oldest sister, a strict disciplinarian who soon had young Harriet assisting in teaching duties at the seminary.

In 1832 Harriet's father moved the family to Cincinnati, where he assumed the post of president of Lane Theological Seminary. It was in Cincinnati that Harriet Beecher joined a social and literary club called the Semi-Colons, which boasted many key literary figures as members. In 1836 she married Calvin Stowe, a widowed professor and Semi-Colon member who was nine years her senior. Harriet assumed the duties of wife and mother and took care of the family home, reared the children, and wrote articles for a number of magazines, journals, and newspapers. By the early 1840s her articles on domestic life, religion, temperance, politics, and gender issues made Harriet Beecher Stowe one of the most successful authors of her era.

Stowe became increasingly interested in the growing controversy surrounding the issue of slavery. Although she was not a fervent abolitionist, her book about the horrors of slavery, *Uncle Tom's Cabin,* became a huge literary success, despite the fact that abolitionist literature was very unpopular with many people at the time. The book was based on her research of antislavery literature, and its characters were drawn from actual escaped slaves the author met in Boston. There were many condemnations of the book, for which she published a rebuttal in *A Key to Uncle Tom's Cabin* in 1853. In 1856 she published another novel about slavery, *Dred: A Tale of the Great Dismal Swamp.* The author attracted the attention of many notable people, including Britain's Queen Victoria and the author and sociologist Harriet Martineau.

Stowe took vacation trips to Europe during the 1850s, possibly to escape the barrage of criticism aimed at her controversial works on the issue of slavery. Throughout the remainder of her life, however, she continued to write. In 1864 she and her husband returned to Connecticut, and from the late 1860s until the early 1880s the couple spent their winters in Florida, where she wrote descriptive accounts of that state. Calvin Stowe died in 1886, and Harriet died in 1896.

—*Leonard A. Steverson*

See also Civil War, American, and Women

References and Further Reading

Adams, John R. 1989. *Harriet Beecher Stowe.* Updated ed. Boston: Twayne Publishers.

Gilbertson, Catherine. 1937. *Harriet Beecher Stowe.* New York: D. Appleton-Century.

Harrietbeecherstowe.org. "Harriet's Life and Times." Harriet Beecher Stowe Center. http://www.harrietbeecherstowe.org/life (accessed September 29, 2004).

Henrick, Joan D. 1994. *Harriet Beecher Stowe: A Life.* New York: Oxford University.

STREET, JESSIE (1889–1970)

Feminist, peace campaigner, and political activist. Dubbed Red Jessie, Jessie Street was a leading figure on the Australian home front during the cold war. Born in Ranchi, India, Street grew up in New South Wales and studied at the University of Sydney. Following her attendance at the 1911 International Council for Women in Rome, Street became progressively concerned with social justice and equality for women. She was deeply involved in the work of the Equal Pay Committee; her 1935 pamphlet entitled *The Justice of Equal Pay and Equal Opportunity* can be found in the Papers of Jessie Street, in the National Library of Australia, Canberra. After World War I she founded the Sydney branch of the Australian League of Nations Union (ALNU) and became increasingly involved in the campaign for equal pay for women. In 1929 she was elected the first president of the United Association of Women (UAW). During World War II she was a prominent campaigner for peace and friendship as chair of the Women's Forum for Social and Economic Reconstruction (1941) and the Russian Medical Aid and Comforts Committee in New

South Wales (1941). Street initiated a national conference that resulted in the Australian Women's Charter (1943), and she led a delegation of thirteen women that introduced the charter resolution to parliament in 1944. As an Australian delegation member to the 1945 U.N. charter meeting in San Francisco, she promoted improvements in the status of women. In 1946 Street served as president of the Australian-Russian Society (later the Australian-Soviet Society). Her admiration for the USSR became obvious from the time of her first travel to that country in 1938 and again in March 1953, when Jessie was invited to attend Stalin's funeral in Moscow. As an active member of the controversial World Peace Council, Street was nominated as a delegate to the second World Peace Conference in Warsaw in 1950; she played a key role within the Sydney section of the Australian Peace Council until 1959. A victim of censure after contesting the legitimacy of British nuclear tests in Central Australia from 1952 to 1957, in later years Street remained a tireless defender of the Aboriginal cause through a campaign to grant Aborigines the right to vote. She died in Sydney on July 2, 1970. In 1989 the Jessie Street National Women's Library was founded to promote the fight for peace and social justice.

—*Jérôme Dorvidal*

See also McDowell, Mary Stone; Mead, Lucia Ames; Moore, Eleanor May; Olmsted, Mildred Scott; Onions, Maude

References and Further Reading

Radi, Heather. 1990. *Jessie Street: Documents and Essays.* Broadway, Australia: Women's Redress.

Sekuless, Peter. 1978. *Jessie Street: A Rewarding but Unrewarded Life.* Brisbane, Australia: University of Queensland.

Street, Jessie. Papers of Jessie Street, folder 7. National Library of Australia, Canberra.

STREETER, RUTH CHENEY (1895–1990)

Director of the U.S. Women's Marine Corps Reserve from February 1943 until she resigned her commission in December 1945. Born on October 2, 1895, in Brookline, Massachusetts, Ruth Cheney Streeter graduated from Bryn Mawr College in 1918. Between World Wars I and II, she held a variety of public posts in health and welfare services such as on the New Jersey State Relief Council and the New Jersey Board of Children's Guardians. As the international situation grew increasingly tense by 1940, she shifted more toward defense-oriented activities. In 1941 she chaired the Citizen's Committee on the Army and Navy for Fort Dix, New Jersey. A licensed pilot, Streeter was also the only female member of the Committee on Aviation for the New Jersey State Defense Council. These activities gave Streeter invaluable experience as a leader and administrator that would benefit her future role in uniform. Meanwhile, she raised four children, three of whom served in the U.S. military during World War II.

When the Japanese attacked Pearl Harbor millions of American men and women flocked to support the war effort. Among them was Streeter. She enlisted in the U.S. Navy's auxiliary organization called the Women Accepted for Voluntary Emergency Service (WAVES). Thomas Holcomb, commandant of the U.S. Marine Corps, resisted the inclusion of women in the corps. He bowed to pressure not only from the government and public but also from the real manpower shortages suffered by the corps. In February 1943, at forty-seven years of age, Streeter transferred from the WAVES to the recently authorized Women's Marine Corps Reserve (WMCR) and assumed the rank of major as its director. The U.S. Marine Corps eventually expanded to a strength of 475,000 officers and enlisted marines by war's end, of which 820 officers and 17,640 enlisted women served in the WMCR (Stremlow 1994, 17).

Major Streeter worked tirelessly to train the women recruits and integrate them into the corps as a whole. She selected only women with high qualifications for the corps. The basic training for women at Fort Lejeune, North Carolina, included the intensive drills and physical education expected of all marines, as well as target practice with small arms and antiaircraft artillery. The female marines replaced men who were needed in combat units in the Pacific. These women competently performed tasks in many military occupational specialties, such as clerical, administrative, maintenance, supervisory, and technical duties. In general, these women possessed education and professional qualifications greater than the men of similar active duty ranks. Members of the WMCR never participated as combatants in World War II.

Streeter brought a vision to her position that looked beyond the limited years of service. Women undoubtedly made significant contributions to the U.S. war effort while serving in the corps. In addition, Streeter hoped that women would acquire new skills and develop self-confidence that they could take with them into their postwar lives. Thus Streeter saw military service as a means of empowerment for women. For her military service Streeter received the Legion of Merit, the American Campaign Medal, and the World War II Victory Medal. Following the end of World War II in August 1945, Ruth Cheney Streeter continued to lead the WMCR until December 1945, when she resigned her commission as a colonel and returned to private life.

—David J. Ulbrich

See also United States, Marine Corps Women's Reserve

References and Further Reading

Meid, Pat. 1968. *Marine Corps Women's Reserve in World War II*. Washington, DC: Historical Branch, G-3 Division, U.S. Marine Corps.

Soderbergh, Peter A. 1992. *Women Marines: The World War II Era*. Westport, CT, and London: Praeger.

Stremlow, Mary V. 1994. *Free a Marine to Fight: Women Marines in World War II*. Washington, DC: History and Museums Division, U.S. Marine Corps.

SUDAN, WOMEN AND THE CIVIL WAR IN

Suffering of women during Sudan's civil war and ethnic cleansing. Civil war in the Sudan began shortly before independence from Great Britain in 1956 and lasted until 1972. It was renewed in 1983 and continued until 2004. The main issue driving the Sudanese civil war is the attempt of the fundamentalist Islamic governments in the north to impose *Sharia* (Islamic law) and the Arabic language on the whole country. The southerners, ethnically African, are either animist or Christian. They have resisted the religious imperialism of several Islamic governments. The groups in the south, however, have also fought each other over grazing lands and perceived tribal injustices.

Women in the Sudan have suffered in a variety of ways. The loss of family members and homelands has been the common lot of women in all parts of Sudan. The suffering has been greatest in the south, where violent death, disease, and starvation have killed great numbers of women and children. The psychological trauma has been devastating for many. Of those who have survived many are physically disfigured as well as emotionally scarred.

Rape has been used as a weapon against women and girls as young as seven years old. Some rapes have been random acts; however, rape has often been used as a matter of policy to disgrace women, destroy families, and sever tribal ties. In Darfur in northwestern Sudan during the early twenty-first century, "rape camps" contributed to the goal of ethnic cleansing of the Black-Africans via racial dilution. This has been cited as one of the justifications for calling that conflict genocide.

Human rights organizations have verified that southern women and girls have been abducted, taken to the north, and sold into slavery. Some women have been forcibly converted to Islam and married off. Boys under the age of seven are taken to the north and put into Islamic schools. Older males are slain if captured. Southerners, however, have also impressed young males into their guerrilla forces. The abuses suffered by southern women have been caused by combatants on both sides of the war.

In the decades of the civil war, homes and fields have been destroyed, crops have been seized, and hundreds of thousands of southerners have been displaced. Because African women are small-plot gardeners and the sole providers of food for their families, in subsistence economies this has been a serious loss. Seed and cultivating implements have been taken or destroyed, so if the women and children manage to escape the devastation of an attack on their village, there is nothing left when they return and no way to reestablish their livelihood.

Previous attempts to end the conflict had failed. On May 26, 2004, however, key protocols were signed by the government of Sudan and the principal south Sudanese rebel group, the Sudanese People's Liberation Army. The agreement called for a ceasefire, a power-sharing administration over three contested areas, and autonomy for the south for six years, to be followed by a referendum on independence.

Since 2003 the Darfur region in the northwestern part of Sudan has been the scene of terrible suffering of Black-African Muslim women at the hands of the Janjaweed, government-backed Arab militias. Rape and rape camps have been part of the anti-Black-African ethnic cleansing. The Black African Muslim women who conceive as a result of the gang rapes give birth to children who are labeled Janjaweed babies. The stigma remains with the mother and child forever. Such a child is called Devil on Horseback (the literal translation for the word *Janjaweed*) before he or she can even crawl.

One unexpected consequence of the civil war has been that some women in the south have been freed from traditional male dominance. With males either dead or gone some women have had to fend for themselves. Others have organized groups such as the Sudanese Women's Voice for Peace (SWVP); the Widows, Orphans, and the Disabled Rehabilitation Association of New Sudan (WODRANS); the New Sudan Woman's Federation (NSWF); and the Mundri Relief and Development Association (MRDA).

Women of the southern area have also engaged in armed conflict. Some have risen in the ranks of units into which they enlisted or into which they were forced. Some have become officers and noncommissioned officers. In 1984 the Sudanese People's Liberation Army, which led the resistance in the second part of the civil war, formed a Girls' Battalion, which subsequently disbanded. Since 1991 the participation of women in combat has been reduced. Former women soldiers have risen in the governmental units formed in the south.

—*Andrew Jackson Waskey*

See also Rape in War; Rwanda: Women and the Genocide

References and Further Reading

Fitzgerald, Mary Anne. 2002. *Throwing the Stick Forward: The Impact of War on Southern Sudanese Women*. Nairobi, Kenya: U.N. Development Fund for Women (UNIFEM).

Johnson, Douglas. 2003. *The Root Causes of Sudan's Civil Wars*. London: International African Institute.

Turshen, Meredeth, and Clotilde Twargiramariva, eds. 1998. *What Women Do in Wartime: Gender and Conflict in Africa*. Vol. 1. New York: St. Martin's.

SUMMERSKILL, EDITH CLARA (1901–1980), AND WOMEN'S HOME DEFENCE CORPS

Labour member of parliament (MP) and founder of the Women's Home Defence Corps in Great Britain during World War II. Born on April 19, 1901, Edith Clara Summerskill trained as a medical doctor, gaining political experience on the Middlesex County Council before entering the House of Commons in 1938 as a Labour MP representing Fulham West and then Warrington. An advocate of women's rights during the war, in the postwar years she served as parliamentary secretary for the Ministry of Food (1945–1950), as minister of national insurance (1950–1951), and as chair of the Labour Party (1954–1955). In 1961 Summerskill was granted a life peerage and entered the House of Lords. She died on February 3, 1980.

Summerskill's involvement in the issue of home defense stemmed from the British response in May 1940 to the threat of invasion: the establishment by the government of the Local Defence Volunteers. Renamed the Home Guard by Winston Churchill, this was a part-time, armed, volunteer defense force of men not in military service. By November 1940 female MPs from across the political spectrum were asking why women were excluded from the Home Guard. The most consistent and determined advocate was Edith Summerskill, who first raised the issue in June 1940. Her demands, however, were ignored, trivialized, or met with arguments pertaining to matters of principle, organization, or the supply of the force.

Summerskill's response was double-pronged. She maintained pressure on the War Office and the government, repeatedly demanding the right for women to learn to defend themselves and their homes through membership in the Home Guard. In the absence of any satisfactory response, she founded the Women's Home Defence Corps (WHD). This was a force in which women were trained to handle weapons and learned field craft in order to permit them to play a role in the defense of Britain in the event of an invasion.

Although there is evidence of women's units in the summer of 1940, the first references appear in War Office files from December 1940. In January 1942 the *Times* reported that women were learning to shoot in 30 WHD units, and by December 1942 there were said to be 250 such units with 10,000 members in London alone (Summerfield and Peniston-Bird 2000, 244). The WHD was not only an unofficial organization but also technically illegal because it was a uniformed force that provided weapons training and hence constituted a private army outside the authority of the Crown. The War Office chose not to instigate legal proceedings, however, to avoid public controversy, which could only result in raising the WHD's profile.

When conscription was introduced for the Home Guard in December 1941 and single women aged twenty to thirty became liable for service in the women's auxiliary forces, the illogicality of the exclusion of women from the force in a time of labor shortages was underlined. There is evidence that some Home Guard units had from the outset incorporated women, either in auxiliary capacities or by training them alongside men. In November 1941 the War Office issued an order reiterating that training of women as unofficial Home Guard units had not been authorized and stating explicitly that women were not to be instructed with Home Guard weapons or ammunition. In the face of localized practice, continued political pressure, and the labor shortage, however, the War Office drew up a scheme during 1942 to admit women to the Home Guard under specific terms.

Implemented in April 1943, the scheme involved "nominated women" who were to be suggested by recognized organizations such as the Women's Voluntary Service. These women were to be between the ages of 18 and 65 (preferably older than 45); they were not to wear uniforms apart from a plastic badge; and they were not to receive weapons training. Their role was to undertake noncombatant duties, including clerical work, cooking, and driving. With the assimilation of women from the WHD into the Home Guard, the pressure to train women for combat roles had successfully been thwarted. In spite of a subsequent name change to Home Guard Auxiliaries, women were never permitted membership under the same terms as men. Their numbers were officially capped; nonetheless, there were 32,000 Women Home Guard Auxiliaries when the Home Guard stood down in December 1944 (Central Statistical Office 1995). Despite women's ultimate inclusion in the force, the gender boundaries surrounding combat had been firmly redrawn.

—*Corinna Peniston-Bird*

See also Great Britain, Women in Service during World War II

References and Further Reading

Central Statistical Office. 1995. *Fighting with Figures*. Foreword by Anthony Montague Brown; text by Peter Howlett. London: Her Majesty's Stationery Office.

Summerfield, Penny. 2000. "She wants a gun not a dishcloth!" Gender, Service and Citizenship in Britain in the Second World War. Pages 119–134 in *A Soldier and a Woman: Sexual Integration in the Military*. Edited by Gerard J. DeGroot and C. M. Peniston-Bird. London: Pearson Education.

Summerfield, Penny, and Corinna Peniston-Bird. 2000. Women in the Firing Line: The Home Guard and the Defence of Gender Boundaries in the Second World War. *Women's History Review* 9(2):231–255.

———. Forthcoming. *Contesting Home Defence: Men, Women and the Home Guard in the Second World War*. Manchester, UK: Manchester University.

Summerskill, Edith. 1967. *A Woman's World*. London, Heinemann.

SUTTNER, BARONESS BERTHA SOPHIE FELICITA VON (1843–1914)

Winner of the 1905 Nobel Peace Prize. Baroness Bertha von Suttner was born Bertha Kinsky in Prague in the Austrian Empire on June 9, 1843. Her father, Count Franz Josef Kinsky von Chinic und Tettau, died before she was born. Her mother wasted her father's legacy at spas and casinos. Bertha became fluent in a number of languages and was known to European society but was forced to take a job as a governess to the young daughters of the Suttner family in Vienna. She fell in love with Arthur, one of the Suttner sons. The family strenuously objected to a marriage because of Bertha's poverty. Nevertheless, she and Arthur married and withdrew for nine years to the Caucasus, where Bertha had friends. They supported themselves giving language and music lessons but spent much time studying contemporary European developments. When Arthur had success writing articles about the Russo-Turkish War of 1877, the two turned to writing. After authoring four novels, the couple moved to Vienna, where Sophie wrote four more novels dealing with social issues before turning to nonfiction. In 1883 she published *Inventarium einer Seele* (Inventory of a Soul), a call for peace and international cooperation. In 1886 the Suttners briefly lived in Paris.

Though her husband, who shared her ideas, lived until 1902, Suttner completely eclipsed him. In Paris she renewed an acquaintance with Alfred Nobel, whom she encouraged to establish a peace prize. She also became acquainted with the International Arbitration and Peace Association, which greatly influenced her. She wrote *Machinenzeitalter* (Machine Age), in which she attacked nationalism and militarism. Her novel *Die Waffen nieder* (Lay Down Your Arms), published in 1889, established Suttner as a leading voice of the peace movement. In 1891 she founded the Austrian Peace Society, and in 1892 she was a founding member of the Bern Peace

Bureau. In 1899 she resided at The Hague during the first Hague Peace Conference and hosted a salon where she promoted her agenda for peace.

In 1905 Suttner was awarded the Nobel Peace Prize. She utilized the occasion to decry the barbarism of war and to call for arbitration. In subsequent lectures she advocated the unification of Europe to forestall war. For her efforts she was excoriated by German and Austrian nationalists. She died on June 21, 1914, thus sparing her the spectacle of the tragedy of World War I.

—*Bernard Cook*

See also Balch, Emily Green; Peace People Movement; Williams, Jody

References and Further Reading

Hamann, Brigitte. 1996. *Bertha von Suttner: A Life for Peace.* Translated by Ann Dubsky. Syracuse, NY: Syracuse University.

Lengyel, Emil. 1975. *And All Her Paths Were Peace.* Nashville, TN: T. Nelson.

Playne, Caroline Elizabeth. 1936. *Bertha von Suttner and the Struggle to Avert the World War.* London: G. Allen and Unwin.

Suttner, Bertha von. 1899 (1972). *Die Waffen nieder* [Lay Down Your Arms: The Autobiography of Martha von Tilling]. Translated by T. Holmes. New York: Garland Publishing.

———. 1910 (1972). *Memoiren von Bertha von Suttner* [Memoirs of Bertha von Suttner: The Records of an Eventful Life]. New York: Garland Publishing.

fellow Hungarians. Svobod's weapon of choice was a .303 British Enfield rifle, which was nearly as long as she was tall. It was a weapon she effectively used for killing the enemy.

Svobod belonged to the Hungarian resistance fighter band that was led by her husband, Janos Halasi. She was, in Hungarian fashion, sometimes called Janos Halasi (her husband's name) in the way that a woman in English-speaking countries could be called Mrs. John Smith when she is married to Mr. John Smith.

Svobod's unit operated in the northern mountains of Hungary. Her husband had acquired a wide reputation for wearing disguises. There were special operations in which he found it necessary to masquerade as a Roman Catholic or Orthodox priest when in areas with Serbian or Romanian populations. In August 1944 her husband was killed in action.

After the death of her husband, Maria Svobod took command of his unit. She led it on a number of operations against the Nazis. She was killed in battle in late 1944. She died a respected soldier and successful leader.

—*Andrew Jackson Waskey*

See also Senesh, Hannah

References and Further Reading

Pinter, Istvan. 1986. *Hungarian Anti-fascism and Resistance, 1941–1945.* Budapest: Akademiai Kiado.

Truby, J. David. 1977. *Women at War: A Deadly Species.* Boulder, CO: Paladin.

SVOBOD, MARIA (D. 1944)

Hungarian resistance fighter during World War II. Maria Svobod, despite her diminutive size, became a larger-than-life legend among her

SZABO, VIOLETTE (1921–1945)

British secret agent during World War II. Violette Szabo, code-named Louise, was a member of the British Special Operations Executive

Violette Szabo. (Hulton Archive/Getty Images)

(SOE) during World War II. She was born Violette Reine Elizabeth Bushell in France on June 26, 1921, to a British father and a French mother. Her family moved to England, where Violette attended school in Stockwell, Brixton, South London. She married Etienne Szabo, an officer of the Free French Forces, in August 1940 and joined the Auxiliary Transport Service (ATS) when her husband's unit was shipped to North Africa. Szabo had just given birth to a daughter when her husband was killed while fighting in El Alamein on October 24, 1942. Violette was recruited to work with the SOE and trained as a member of the secret First Aid Nursing Yeomanry (FANY) unit. The training included learning observation techniques, reading maps, and building physical endurance. Advanced training included weapons handling and learning self-defense methods.

Her first field operation near Rouen, France, lasted six weeks. She worked with Philippe Liewer (code-named Clement), a correspondent with the Havas news agency. She was briefly detained by military police while determining the number of operatives still working in the area. After she completed her first mission she returned to England and went to stay in the family cottage that now houses a museum dedicated to her memory. She returned to France in June 1944.

Szabo was captured near Limoges. Accounts vary describing her capture. Szabo had been traveling with Jacques Dufour, a member of the French Resistance, when they were trapped by German soldiers. Dufour managed to escape by hiding while Szabo barricaded herself in a house. Some accounts state she kept the Germans at bay in a lengthy gun battle; others believe the story of her bravery to be true but doubt the extent of the gun battle. Szabo was taken prisoner, placed in solitary confinement, and tortured to discover information about British operations in France. Even under torture, Szabo did not divulge anything related to the resistance or the location of operatives.

Szabo was put to death in 1945 at Ravensbrück; she was twenty-three years old. The war was nearing an end when her Nazi captors executed her along with Lillian Rolfe and Denise Bloch, fellow SOE agents. Violette Szabo was posthumously awarded the French Croix de Guerre and the British George Cross. Her George Cross citation reads in part, "Violette Szabo was continuously and atrociously tortured, but never by word or deed gave away any of her acquaintances or told the enemy anything of any value" (www.spartacus.schoolnet.co.uk/SOEszabo.htm). In 1947, Violette and Etienne Szabo's four-year-old daughter, Tania, received both medals for her mother's bravery. The Violette Szabo Museum is located in Wormelow at

Cartref House. A nature walk from Hereford-shire to the museum was dedicated to her memory in 2000. She was made a Member of the British Empire for her bravery.

—*Pamela Lee Gray*

See also Atkins, Vera H.; Ravensbrück

References and Further Reading

Binney, Marcus. 2002. *Women Who Lived for Danger: The Women Agents of the SOE in the Second World War.* London: Hodder and Stoughton.

Minney, Rubeigh James. 1956. *Carve Her Name with Pride.* London: Newnes.

Ottaway, Susan. 2002. *Violette Szabo: The Life That I Have.* Annapolis, MD: Naval Institute Press.

T

Tackaberry (Blake), Betty Guild (1920–)

U.S. Women Airforce Service pilot. Betty Guild Tackaberry (Blake), nicknamed Tack, graduated from the first class of Women Airforce Service Pilots (WASPs), class number 43-W-1, and served as a ferrying pilot while stationed in Long Beach, California, until the unit's deactivation. As a young girl in Hawaii, Betty Guild had dreamed of flying and devoured books about Charles Lindbergh and women pilots. At fourteen she attended a lecture given by famous pilot Amelia Earhart, who approached Guild and invited her to watch her flight the next day. Earhart's harsh language with her hangar mechanics prompted Guild's father to take Betty home before the flight, but the experience increased her fervor for aviation.

While in high school, flying remained Guild's passion, and she received informal lessons at John Rogers airfield in 1937. She later enrolled at the University of Hawaii to receive ground school instruction in the Civilian Pilot Training (CPT) program and was the first member of her class (which, apart from Guild, was all male) to fly solo. She earned her limited commercial license, flying tourists around the islands until the Japanese bombing of Pearl Harbor on December 7, 1941. She had received her instruc-

tor's rating and regular commercial license the previous afternoon, but civilian flights were immediately banned in Hawaii.

During the ensuing months, Guild worked at the captain of the navy yard's office in Pearl Harbor, logging positions of U.S. naval ships in the Pacific theater. In early February 1942 she married Robert Tackaberry, a naval officer who received orders to report to Philadelphia. She followed him but in November 1942 reported for WASP training at the Army Air Corps base in Houston, Texas. A member of the first class to train for the WASP, she acquired instruction in B-19, B-22, AT-6, P-51, and a twin-engine Cessna aircraft.

After graduation on April 24, 1943, Tackaberry reported to the Ferrying Command in Long Beach. Four days prior, her best friend, Cornelia Fort, was killed during flying exercises, but the incident failed to affect Tackaberry's determination to continue flying. While stationed in Long Beach, she first supervised cross-country flights of newer WASPs and then requested solo ferrying assignments, transporting aircraft directly from factories to other bases.

After the WASP disbanded on December 20, 1944, Tackaberry received instruction at the air force officer's training school in Orlando, Florida, and returned to California as a link (simulated flight) instructor for air force trainees. During this period, Tackaberry divorced her husband, and in 1945 she terminated her career as a link instructor to transport shrimp from New Orleans to California. She later married George Blake, an officer in the Air Transport Command, stopped flying after her marriage, and moved to Arizona. She remained there after the war, had three sons, and started various successful businesses in the ensuing decades.

Amy S. Balderach

See also Hobby, Oveta Culp; United States, Women Airforce Service Pilots

References and Further Reading

Blake, Betty. Interviewed by Deanie Parrish, November 11, 2001. Wings across America Project, Waco, Texas, and the WASP WWII Museum, Sweetwater, Texas. http://www.wasp-wwii.org/wings/information.htm (accessed November 18, 2004).

TALBOT, MARY ANNE (1778–1808)

British woman who fought as a sailor and soldier in male attire. Known as the British Amazon, Mary Anne Talbot was the sixteenth illegitimate child of Lord William Talbot, Baron of Hensol, colonel of the Glamorgan Shire Militia. Perhaps her father spurred her interest in the military. At any rate, as reported in her biography, at the age of fourteen she was seduced by an army captain, Essex Bowen, of the 82nd Regiment of the infantry. Some accounts state that she had fallen in love with him and married him. Disguised as a page, Mary Anne, calling herself John Taylor, accompanied Bowen to Port-au-Prince, Haiti (then St. Domingo), in the West Indies. There, Bowen ordered her to return to England and apparently threatened to sell her into slavery if she refused to become a regimental drummer.

As a drummer, Talbot fought in the siege of Valenciennes, France, in 1793. She was wounded, but Bowen was killed. Free of Bowen, Talbot, hoping to return to England, deserted the army and became a cabin boy on a French ship. The ship, which she had not realized was a privateer, was captured by the *Brunswick*. On the British ship, commanded by Admiral Lord Howe, she was promptly made a powder-monkey, carrying gunpowder to the ship's guns. Talbot was seriously wounded at the Battle of the Glorious First of June in 1794, for which she received a small pension. As soon as her wounds healed, she was once again at sea. This time she was captured by the French and spent eighteen months in prison.

After being freed in a prisoner exchange Talbot signed on a British merchant ship, the *Ariel*, captained by John Field. She claimed that she kept the ship's books, paid the men, and supervised the loading of cargo. She sailed to New York and Rhode Island, where she spent time with Field's family.

Talbot's gender was discovered when she returned to London in 1796. After being seized by a press gang, she revealed her gender to avoid going into battle again. After a short stint as an actor on Drury Lane, where she performed as a man, she was employed by the London publisher Sir Robert S. Kirby as his household servant. Kirby included an account of her adventures in his extremely popular Wonderful and Scientific Museum (1804) and later in the book *Life and Surprising Adventures of Mary Anne Talbot in the Name of John Taylor, a Natural Daughter of the Late Earl of Talbot, Related by Herself* (1809). It is not known if Kirby interviewed her or if she wrote the account herself. Because of its popularity, the book stayed in print until 1820. Talbot's wounds and imprisonment, however, took their toll on her health. She died in 1808 at the age of thirty, the year before Kirby published her story.

There are discrepancies in Talbot's story. Captain Bowen's name has never been found on army lists, which seems to indicate that his name was false or that he did not exist. In addition, the 82nd Regiment did not exist at that time.

—*Leigh Whaley*

See also Great Britain, Women in Service in the Seventeenth, Eighteenth, and Early Nineteenth Centuries

References and Further Reading

Druett, Joan. 2000. *She Captains: Heroines and Hellions of the Sea.* New York: Simon and Schuster.

Talbot, Mary Anne. 1809. *Life and Surprising Adventures of Mary Anne Talbot in the Name of John Taylor, a Natural Daughter of the Late Earl Talbot, Related by Herself.* London: R. S. Kirby.

TAMAR (1160–1213)

Queen of the kingdom of Georgia between 1184 and 1213. The eldest daughter of King Giorgi III (1156–1184), Tamar was made a co-regent in 1178 and succeeded her father six years later. Her accession, however, was not without difficulty. Powerful lords took advantage of the passing of the king to reassert themselves. Despite internal dissent, Georgia turned into a powerful kingdom and enjoyed major successes in its foreign policy. Between 1193 and 1194 Tamar led the Georgian army into southwestern Transcaucasia, and in 1195 she defeated a large Muslim coalition in the battle at Shamkhor (in modern Azerbaijan), allowing her to expand her sphere of influence. In 1203 she achieved another triumphant victory when a massive coalition of Muslim states, led by the sultan of Rum, was crushed at Basiani. Georgians annexed Ani, Arran, and Duin between 1201 and 1203, and in 1209 the combined armies captured the emirate of Kars (now in Turkey) while the mighty Armen-Shahs, the emirs of Erzurum and Erzinjan (also now in Turkey), and the north Caucasian tribes became the vassals. Georgian influence also extended to the southern coastline of the Black Sea, where the empire of Trebizond (now in Turkey), a Georgian vassal state, was established in 1204. Tamar then carried war into Azerbaijan and advanced as far as Tabriz, Qazvin, and Khoy in northern Iran between 1208 and 1210. In 1212 she successfully campaigned against mountaineers in the Caucasus. These victories brought Georgia to the summit of its power and glory, establishing a pan-Caucasian Georgian empire stretching from the Black Sea to the Caspian and from the Caucasus Mountains to Lake Van.

Tamar's political and military successes were accompanied by an equally impressive religious and cultural expansion throughout Asia Minor and the Holy Land. The stability and strong central authority of Tamar's reign facilitated the growth of towns and the development of trade and crafts. Tbilisi, with a population of some 100,000, became one of the largest cities in the Middle East and a center of regional and international trade linking China, Central Asia, and Europe. Tamar's reign also stimulated a renaissance of Georgian sciences and art. Numerous classical Georgian scholarly and literary works such as *Amiran-Darejaniani, Abdulmesia,* and *Tamariani* were produced both within Georgia and abroad while the arts of illumination of manuscripts and miniature painting reached their zenith. Georgian monasteries, generously sponsored by the queen, flourished throughout the Holy Land and Asia Minor. Finally, Shota Rustaveli's epic poem, *The Knight in the Panther's Skin,* was dedicated to Tamar; it remains the greatest cultural achievement of Georgia in that age.

—*Alexander Mikaberidze*

See also Guljamal-Khan(um); Kurmanjan-Datkha

References and Further Reading

Metreveli, Roin. 1992. *Tamar.* Tbilisi, Georgia: Metsniereba.

Qadagidze, Marine. 2001. *Tamar mepis droindeli matiane: Tskhovreba Mepet mepeta Tamarisi.* Tbilisi, Georgia.

Tamils, Women and the Conflict in Sri Lanka

Impact on women of the insurgency of the Liberation Tigers of Tamil Eelam, popularly known simply as the Tamil Tigers, which began in 1983 against the Sri Lankan government. The insurgents have asserted that the Sinhalese majority, which has dominated the Sri Lankan government since independence in 1948, has continued to marginalize the Tamil minority. In 1956, Sinhala was made the official language of Sri Lanka, and legislation formalized the preference given to Sinhalese in both educational and employment opportunities. In 1977, however, well before the current Tamil insurgency began, the Sri Lankan government revoked almost all of the laws that placed Tamils at a disadvantage. Nonetheless, the Tamil insurgents have sought to force the creation of a completely independent Tamil state in northern and eastern Sri Lanka. Although the northern districts largely controlled by the Tigers have traditionally been 90 percent Tamil, the eastern districts were only 40 percent Tamil at the beginning of the conflict. In 2003, during negotiations to resolve the conflict, the Tigers did indicate a willingness to consider the creation of a largely autonomous Tamil state within Sri Lanka, but they then undermined the truce established through the negotiations by conducting an escalating series of terror attacks against Sinhalese targets.

The conflict between the Tamil Tigers and the Sri Lankan military has cost almost 70,000 lives, forced more than a million Sri Lankans from their homes, and caused serious disruptions in the national economy. Moreover, the violence has not been restricted primarily to the Tamil-dominated sections of the country: the Tigers have waged a war of terror that has, in effect, transformed the entire nation into a war zone. The Tigers have not only assassinated government officials and military officers but also set off bombs at sites throughout the country. As a result, Sri Lanka's tourist industry, a major element of the nation's economy, has been dramatically affected. In combination with the Tamil insurgency, the extensive destruction caused by the 2005 tsunami has turned much of the eastern coast of Sri Lanka from a tropical paradise into a dangerous wasteland.

The Tamils have long dominated the states in southern India opposite Sri Lanka. Indeed, the Tamil presence in northern and eastern Sri Lanka originated with a Tamil invasion from the Chola Kingdom of southern India in the eleventh century. Beyond the ethnic and cultural differences between the warring parties, there are religious differences: the Tamils are largely Hindus, whereas the majority of the Sinhalese are Buddhists. In 1983 the long-standing antagonism between the two groups erupted into armed conflict. Under the leadership of Vilupillai Prabhakaran, the Tamil Tigers began a guerrilla campaign that initially targeted Sri Lankan government sites and officials. In response, the size of the Sri Lankan army was increased from 16,000 men to almost 75,000 men. Defense expenditures rose from 2.5 percent to 12.5 percent of the federal budget.

Although the Indian government initially supported the Tigers, providing them with matériel (including weapons) and funds, the government of Rajiv Gandhi (prime minister from 1984 to 1989) reversed this policy. It cut off aid to the Tigers and, with the consent of the Sri Lankan government, sent a peacekeeping force of 70,000 to the Tamil areas in 1987. The Tigers' strategy shifted from selective operations against specific targets to opportunistic guerrilla warfare and terror attacks against Sinhalese communities. In the middle of the night, Tamil guerrillas would surround a Sinhalese village and then systematically slaughter the inhabitants, typically with machetes and knives. The dark lore that began to accumulate around these attacks included the shocking fact that some of the most bloodthirsty of these killers were women. By 1990 the Tigers had also killed more than 1,000 Indian soldiers, and the Indian force was withdrawn from Sri Lanka. Then, in May 1991, one of the Tigers' suicide bombers assassinated Rajiv Gandhi.

By the early 1990s the Tigers were able to field a trained force of some 3,500 fighters, and they shifted strategy from guerrilla fighting to formal operations against the Sri Lankan army. Although the army was victorious in most pitched battles and overwhelmed several Tamil strongholds, it was unable to eliminate the Tigers, who proved adept at dispersing and reconstituting their forces and in recruiting new adherents from the Tamil population. Prabhakaran has become a very talented propagandist, and he has created around his uncompromising public persona a fanatical cult of personality with all sorts of religious overtones. The Sri Lankan army has reported that more than 600 Tigers have committed suicide by biting into cyanide capsules in order to avoid capture.

The Tigers have achieved even more international notoriety for their willingness to use women and children as both combatants and terrorists. About 30 percent of the Tigers have been women, and Tamil women have carried out approximately one-third of the suicide bombings organized by the Tigers. Indeed, Rajiv Gandhi was assassinated by a young woman: while seemingly offering him a sandalwood garland as a gift, she detonated the plastic explosives that killed not only the two of them but also fifteen others nearby.

The Tamils, for their part, have compiled a long catalog of atrocities committed against their people by the Sinhalese army. They assert that Tamil women have been gang-raped by Sinhalese troops and murdered with impunity. They report abductions of young women, who have been raped, tortured, and then murdered (United Nations Division of the International Federation of Tamils 1997).

Although they speak Tamil, members of Sri Lanka's Muslim minority (Muslims constitute about 7 percent of the country's population) have had tense relations with both the Tamil Tigers and the Sri Lankan government. Yet the escalating use of terror by Islamic insurgencies throughout the world—particularly the reliance on suicide bombers, whose numbers increasingly include women—has led many people to associate the Tamil Tigers with the Sri Lankan Muslims, an association that is stridently rejected by both groups. One of the points of contention between the groups has certainly been the Tigers' greater willingness to accord women a status more equal to that of men.

—*Martin Kich*

See also Terrorists, Women

References and Further Reading

Bloom, Mia. 2005. "Terror's Stealth Weapon: Women." *Los Angeles Times*, November 29, 2005. http://www.latimes.com/news/opinion/commentary/la-oe-bloom29nov29,0,3416302.story?coll=la-news-comment-opinions (accessed February 6, 2006).

Desmond, Edward W. 1987. "If This Is Peace . . . : A Four-Year War Officially Ends, but the Battle Could Rage On." *Time*, August 10.

———. 1991. "Sri Lanka's Tamil Tigers." *Time*, September 16.

Serrill, Michael S. 1988. "Sri Lanka Blood on the Ballot Box: A Savage Ethnic Rivalry Propels the Country toward Anarchy." *Time*, October 24.

Tamil Canadian: Tamil's True Voice. "Eliminate the Sinhala State Terrorism." 2006. http://www.tamilcanadian.com/eelam/massacres/ (accessed February 6, 2006).

United Nations Division of the International Federation of Tamils. 1997. "An Appeal to Chairperson and Delegates to the 53rd Sessions of the United Nations Commission on Human Rights," March-April 1997. http://www.tamilcanadian.com/pageview.php?ID=497&SID=91 (accessed February 6, 2006).

Walsh, James. 1991. "India: Death's Return Visit." *Time*, June 3.

TEODOROIU, ECATERINA (1894–1917)

The Joan of Arc of Romania. Ecaterina Teodoroiu was born in the northern part of the Oltenia region of Romania into a poor peasant family.

There were eight children in the family, and Teodoroiu's childhood was one of poverty and hardship. Having an extraordinary will and a strong character, she struggled to escape poverty and become a schoolteacher. After completing elementary school in her native village, she attended secondary school in Târgu Jiu and was able to continue her studies in Bucharest.

In 1913 during the Second Balkan War, Teodoroiu volunteered for a scouting group that assisted the Romanian military units. In August 1916, during the general mobilization as Romania entered World War I on the side of the Allies, Teodoroiu could not stand idle as her brothers went to war. She volunteered to tend to the wounded soldiers at the Târgu Jiu hospital.

The folk legend of the Virgin from Jiu originated with the battle at the Jiu River. On January 14, 1916, two companies of Bavarian mountain troops pushed to the Jiu bridge and threatened the defenseless city of Târgu Jiu. At that crucial moment Ecaterina Teodoroiu was the first Romanian woman to seize a weapon to save her country. Her action inspired the local population. The bridge was defended and the city saved from the Germans. Teodoroiu's action became a great symbol of Romanian national resistance against foreign invaders. Thus Ecaterina Teodoroiu became the Joan of Arc of Romania.

Subsequently serving as a volunteer in the same military unit with her brother Nicolae, she fought and became a heroic example for the other soldiers. At the beginning of November 1916, seeking revenge following the death of her brother, she fought in the Romanian effort to defend the Gorj region. After three days the Germans captured her unit. During a desperate clash, she shot a sentry and managed to escape. Fighting near the town of Filiasi on November 6, 1916, she was severely wounded in both legs by a mortar shell. She was evacuated with other wounded by hospital train to Moldavia. On March 19, 1917, she was granted the Romanian Military Medal of Honor and was promoted to second lieutenant. After recovering, Teodoroiu returned to combat. On August 22, 1917, she died in battle while leading her platoon during the great assault on Marasesti.

During her life Ecaterina Teodoroiu became a living legend and a patriotic icon, as was reflected in the April 17, 1917, edition of the newspaper *Romania* of Iasi: "Now, you, Caterina, have entered forever into the fairies' ring—dance of the brave legends of our nation." Her myth grew after the 1919 unification of Romania. On June 9, 1921, on the occasion of her reburial in the national unification monument in Târgu Jiu, a great national funeral was organized in her honor.

—*Miodrag Milin*

See also Marie, Queen of Romania

References and Further Reading

Grozea, Elsa. 1967. *Sublocotenentul Ecaterina Teodoroiu* [Sublieutenant Ecaterina Teodoroiu]. Bucharest: Editura Militari.

Mocioi, Ion. 1981. *Ecaterina Teodoroiu eroina poporului Român* [Ecaterina Teodoroiu: Hero of the Romanian People]. Craiova, Romania: Editura Scrisul Românesc.

TERRORISTS, WOMEN

Women who serve as supporters of terrorism and as agents of terror. Although the idea of female terrorists is surprising and even shocking to many people, women have been supporters, active participants, and even leaders in terrorist acts throughout history. In the modern era, female terrorists have been known in all parts of the world, although their motivation may differ from that of their male counterparts.

Statistical evidence based on arrests and other reports indicates that female participation in modern terrorism, particularly in leftist terrorist groups, has been notably high. In European terrorist groups, women have typically made up about a third of the membership (Hudson 1999, 82). At least one German terrorist group, Red Zora, recruited only women for numerous terrorist acts in the late 1970s and 1980s; the Norwegian terrorist group Valkyria also excluded males from membership. Women were prominent participants in the activities of most late-twentieth-century German terrorist groups, such as the Baader-Meinhof Gang, the Red Army Faction, and the June Second Movement. Female terrorists have been equally common in the Irish Republican Army; the Basque separatist group, Euskadi ta Askatasuna (ETA); various Italian terrorist groups; and the Kurdistan Worker's Party (PKK) in Turkey. Latin American insurgent groups have similarly recruited large numbers of women; the Sendero Luminoso (the Shining Path) and Tupac Amaru terrorist groups have reported that half their members are female. Colombian terrorist groups claim a large percentage of female participants; in the 1985 M19 (19th of April Movement) terrorist attack on Colombia's Palace of Justice, more than half the terrorists were women.

The United States has also had its share of female terrorists; about 8 percent of all persons indicted for terrorist crimes in the United States have been women (Hewett 2003, 69). In the 1970s Americans were familiar with photographs of the kidnapped heiress Patricia Hearst, posing next to the flag of the Symbionese Liberation Army with her assault weapon as she apparently prepared to carry out terrorist acts in California with the group, which had a large female component.

Nor has women's participation in terrorism been confined to Western societies. The Japanese Red Army and the religious terrorist group Aum Shin Rikyo have had numerous female members. North Korea has long-standing training programs for female terrorists, as revealed by Hyun Hee Kim, an infamous North Korean female terrorist who killed more than 100 people by bombing a South Korean airliner and who later recounted her training in a gripping book.

Female terrorists have appeared in Nepal, Sri Lanka, India, and elsewhere in Asia. Finally, the participation of women in terrorist attacks throughout the Muslim world has been increasing dramatically in the past few decades. It can generally be said that anywhere terrorists operate, there will be women supporting them and actively participating in their attacks.

Women are often prized participants in terrorist attacks because security forces are less likely to suspect them, and it is easier for women to infiltrate close to an intended target. Stereotypes about the natural role of women as life-givers and "the gentler sex" contribute to the image that women are less likely to resort to terrorism than men. There is also evidence that female terrorists are more likely to gain sympathy for their acts and to be punished less severely.

Although some scholars have opined that women are less likely than men to be leaders in terrorist acts, this does not appear to be the case. Prominent female terrorist leaders of modern times include: Dora María Téllez Argüello, who acted as second-in-command when a Sandinista terrorist unit attacked Nicaragua's National Palace in 1979; Suzanne Albrecht of the Red Army Faction, who arranged to assassinate a wealthy German businessman and family friend; Ulrike Meinhof of the Baader-Meinhof Gang, who committed suicide in prison in 1976 as an example to her followers; Soledád Iparraguirre of the ETA, who has plotted numerous terrorist attacks in Spain; and Fusako Shigenobu, who founded the Japanese Red Army, trained fellow terrorists all over the world, and evaded Japanese authorities for three decades.

The news media have prominently covered stories about female terrorists, raising awareness of their existence among the public and perhaps even encouraging other women to follow their example. In the 1970s, for example, Palestinian terrorist and hijacker Leila Khaled became internationally famous and a heroine in the Arab world when her photos appeared in major news media. The photos, in which a smiling Khaled posed with her assault rifle, purportedly convinced other Palestinian women to train as terrorists and may even have inspired writer John Le Carré to pen the best-selling novel *The Little Drummer Girl,* about an actress who pretends to be a female terrorist in order to infiltrate a terrorist network. Le Carré's book was made into a popular film, following a cinematic tradition of celebrating the acts of female terrorists, a tradition perhaps begun by the film *Battle of Algiers.* This 1966 film by Italian director Gillo Pontecorvo depicts a female Algerian terrorist slipping easily with her bombs through French security checkpoints after dressing provocatively and flirting with the male guards.

Although women have often been recruited for terrorist acts because security forces are less likely to suspect them, they have frequently been even more ruthless in action than male terrorists. Female terrorists have also been described as more focused and practical than male terrorists and able to use their social skills to keep groups focused on their goals. Christian Lochte, a German terrorism expert, has argued that female terrorists are generally more single-minded and dangerous than male terrorists and that, for safety reasons, "it is a good idea to shoot the women terrorists first" if security forces encounter both male and female terrorists at the same time (Hudson 1999, 89).

Female terrorists are often motivated by the same anger and desire for revenge that motivate male terrorists, but studies have found some significant gender differences. Female terrorists, for example, are often more committed to their cause, more idealistic, and more prone to turn to terrorism to please others or as a way to achieve others' unfulfilled needs. Feminist ideology has also motivated female terrorists and may explain in part their observed ruthlessness.

A special category of female terrorists is composed of female suicide bombers. The first female suicide bomber to successfully carry out a major bombing attack was Dhanu, a member of the Sri Lankan terrorist group Liberation Tigers of Tamil Eelam (LTTE, also known as the Tamil Tigers). She assassinated former Indian Prime Minister Rajiv Gandhi in 1991 by approaching him to offer flowers and then blowing herself up. She killed many bystanders as well. The Tamil Tigers have trained brigades of young girls in these techniques, and their female terrorists have carried out dozens of attacks.

Islamic terrorists have also made use of female suicide bombers. The first female Islamic suicide bomber appeared in Lebanon in the mid-1980s, when Syrian intelligence officers encouraged young Lebanese women to carry out suicide attacks against Israeli military units. The first known female Palestinian to engage in such attacks was Wafa Idris, who blew herself up in a store in Jerusalem in 2002, killing an elderly Israeli man and wounding more than 100 bystanders. She had been encouraged to commit her act by a speech made by Palestinian leader Yasser Arafat, who termed her a soldier in his "army of roses." Many other Palestinian women followed her example, and their exploits have been celebrated in Palestinian popular culture. In an interesting study of Palestinian women who have engaged in such attacks, author Barbara Victor has noted that these women have often been cajoled to carry out suicide attacks by male relatives or boyfriends who have convinced the women that, by carrying out a suicide bombing, they could atone for stains on their family honor or their inability to meet male social expectations (Victor 2003, 4, 19, 20, and 25).

In contrast, Chechen Black Widow suicide bombers have sought revenge against Russians who have killed their husbands or brothers in the wars in Chechnya, a breakaway province of Russia. These female terrorists, who sometimes dress in head-to-toe black attire with explosive belts around their waists, first came to prominence in 2002, when they seized a crowded Moscow theater in the middle of a performance and threatened to blow it up. The siege ended when Russian forces stormed the theater, killing most of the terrorists. Other Black Widows have been involved in numerous smaller terrorist attacks throughout Russia, but their specialty is causing mass casualties. According to Russian authorities, Chechen female terrorists destroyed two Russian airliners by planting bombs on them in 2004. Also in 2004, female Chechen terrorists participated prominently in the hostage crisis and massacre of more than 300 schoolchildren and teachers in Beslan, Russia. There have been some allegations, however, that some of these women were drugged or otherwise coerced into participating in their terrorist acts.

—*Margaret D. Stock*

See also Algeria, Women in the War of National Liberation; Baader-Meinhof Gang; Chechnya, Impact on Women of Wars in; Colombia, Women and Political Violence in; Islamic Resistance Movements, Women and; Latin America, Women in Guerrilla Movements in; Peru: Shining Path; Red Army Faction, West Germany, Women of the; Red Brigades, Italy, Women of the

References and Further Reading

Hewett, Christopher. 2003. *Understanding Terrorism in America from the Klan to Al Qaeda.* New York: Routledge.

Hudson, Rex A., et al. 1999. "Who Becomes a Terrorist and Why? Report on Profiling Terrorists." A report prepared by an interagency agreement by the Federal Research Division, Library of Congress, Marilyn Majeske, editor, and Andrea M. Savada and Helen C. Metz, project managers. http://www.loc.gov/rr/frd/pdf-files/Soc_Psych_of_Terrorism.pdf (accessed October 28, 2004).

Kim, Hyun Hee. 1993. *The Tears of My Soul.* New York: William Morrow.

Victor, Barbara. 2003. *An Army of Roses: Inside the World of Palestinian Women Suicide Bombers.* New York: Rodale.

Zedalis, Debra D. 2004. "Female Suicide Bombers." Strategic Studies Institute. http://www.carlisle.army.mil/ssi/pdffiles/PUB408.pdf (accessed October 28, 2004).

TERWIEL, MARIA (1910–1943)

Member of the German anti-Nazi resistance. Maria Terwiel was born in Boppard in the Rhineland on June 7, 1910. Her father was a Catholic and a senior civil servant, but because he was a Social Democrat, he was dismissed from his government post in 1933 after the Nazis came to power. The family then moved to Berlin. Because of her mother's Jewish ancestry, Maria was forced to give up studying law after the Nazis initiated their anti-Semitic program. She then took a job as a secretary in a textile factory. A dedicated Catholic, Maria joined the resistance group of Harro Schulze-Boysen. She distributed material critical of the regime and provided Jews with false passports. Arrested in the aftermath of the Nazi discovery of the Schulze-Boysen Red Orchestra group, she and her fiancé, Helmut Himple, were sentenced to death in January 1943 and were executed in August. In her last letter to her brother, who would die in an air raid, she wrote, "I have absolutely no fear of death. . . . Stay true to your principles and always stick together" (Leber 1994, 126).

—*Bernard Cook*

See also Harnack-Fish, Mildred; Schulze-Boysen, Libertas

References and Further Reading

Leber, Annedore. 1994. *Conscience in Revolt: Sixty-four Stories of Resistance in Germany, 1933–45.* Boulder, CO: Westview.

THADDEN, ELIZABETH VON (1890–1944)

Executed for her spiritual resistance to the Nazi state. Elizabeth von Thadden was born in East Prussia on July 29, 1890. Her family moved to an estate in Pomerania in 1905, and five years later, after the death of her mother, Elizabeth assumed the task of caring for her younger siblings and managing the household. She trained to be a teacher and after two teaching posts founded a Protestant boarding school near Heidelberg. In 1941 she was forced by the Nazis to hand over the direction of her school. She then worked for the Red Cross at soldiers' recreation centers.

Her convictions were conservative and Christian. She had a deep discomfort with the Nazis and sympathized with the Confessional Church, the evangelical opposition to the idolatry of the state. She invited a young man, recommended by friends, to a social at her home. He turned out to be a Gestapo agent who denounced von Thadden and her guests as defeatist opponents of the regime. She was arrested and sentenced to death. The charges were that her comments at the social gathering were detrimental to the morale of the troops and amounted to treason. She was executed on September 8, 1944.

—*Bernard Cook*

See also Ballestrem-Solf, Countess Lagi

References and Further Reading

Leber, Annedore. 1994. *Conscience in Revolt: Sixty-four Stories of Resistance in Germany, 1933–1945.* Boulder, CO: Westview.

THIRTY YEARS' WAR
(1618–1648)

A series of devastating conflicts within the Holy Roman Empire. The conflicts caused a virtual breakdown of the economy, as well as famines and pandemics. Poorly paid mercenary armies attempted to extract supplies from the population and thus often subjected it to considerable hardships. As the empire lost about one-third of its inhabitants, the Thirty Years' War must be regarded as one of the worst crises in German history.

Many civilians accompanied the mercenary troops. The baggage train of noncombatants could amount to more than half of the army's total strength. These noncombatants consisted in large part of women. Even though many of these women were at least part-time prostitutes, their role was much more complex. Women working as cooks, nurses, tailors, washerwomen, victualers, and dispensers of drink were an integral and indispensable part of the war economy. The camp followers received stolen goods or personally engaged in plunder. Many soldiers took their women and children with them. Part of the baggage train must be considered an accumulation of itinerant households. The women in the train were subject to military justice, and they were required to help fortify camps. Soldiers and officers who attempted to spare their female dependents this type of work caused considerable unrest. As a rule, the women and the whole train of noncombatants were under the surveillance of an officer who was misleadingly called *Hurenwaibel* (overseer of whores).

Military authorities tried to prevent sexual assaults on women in the countryside where the armies operated. Military justice imposed the death penalty for rape. Nevertheless, as it became more and more difficult for princes to pay their mercenary armies, discipline deteriorated. Rape by marauding soldiers seems to have been a common occurrence.

War propaganda used the imagery of gender. German Protestantism was depicted as a woman who turned to Gustavus Adolphus of Sweden for paternal protection. The pamphlets that described the conquest of the town of Magdeburg (maiden borough) used sexual references. They presented the city as a flirtatious girl who made fun of her would-be lovers until she was raped or forced to marry the general of the victorious army.

In his novel *Landstörtzerin Courasche* (1670) Grimmelshausen presented a camp follower as the negative heroine, an embodiment of worldliness. Usurping a male role, Courasche

(Courage) serves in the war as a female soldier. To her the war is an adventure and the opportunity to earn money. Courasche wins and loses a fortune in the war working in turn as a prostitute, a thief, a merchant, and a soothsayer . In his play *Mutter Courage und ihre Kinder* (Mother Courage and Her Children, 1941), Berthold Brecht turned Courasche into a tragic character. Even though Courage loses all of her children in the war, she is unable to overcome her own cynicism and regards the war simply as a business opportunity.

—*Johannes Dillinger*

See also France, Wars of Religion; Peasants' War

References and Further Reading

Meumann, Markus. 1996. Soldatenfamilien und uneheliche Kinder: Ein soziales Problem im Gefolge der stehenden Heere [Soldiers' Families and Illegitimate Children: A Social Problem in the Train of Standing Armies]. Pages 219–236 in *Krieg und Frieden [War and Peace]*. Edited by Bernhard Kroener and Ralf Proeve. Paderborn, Germany: Ferdinand Schoeningh.

Theibault, John. 1995. *German Villages in Crisis: Rural Life in Hesse-Kassel and the Thirty Years' War, 1580–1720*. Atlantic Highlands, NJ: Humanities.

When she was repatriated in October 1914, Thurstan lent her services to the Russian Red Cross and worked on the Polish front until 1915, when she was both wounded and taken ill with pleurisy.

After a brief respite in England, she was sent to Belgium as matron of a military hospital. In 1917 she transferred to a British dressing station at Coxyde where, despite being wounded again, her extraordinary work earned her the British Military Medal. She then went on to head a field ambulance unit in Macedonia before joining the Royal Air Force in 1918.

During World War II she served as an officer in the Women's Royal Naval Service. Following the war she commanded a refugee hospital in Carinthia, Austria, with the Prisoner of War and Refugee Department of the Allied Commission.

—*Barbara Penny Kanner*

See also Great Britain, Women in Service during World War I; Kea, Salaria; Spanish Civil War, Women and the

References and Further Reading

Thurstan, Violetta. 1915. *Field Hospital and Flying Column: Being the Journal of an English Nursing Sister in Belgium and Russia*. London: G. P. Putnam's Sons.

THURSTAN, VIOLETTA
(1879–1978)

A university-educated artist with an extensive military and nursing record. Violetta Thurstan served as a nurse in World War I, the Spanish Civil War, and World War II. Thurstan enlisted in the No. 46 Westminster Voluntary Aid Detachment (VAD) in 1913. In August 1914 the British Red Cross (BRC) sent Thurstan to Brussels, Belgium, as the head of a unit. She arrived just ahead of the German army and was subsequently taken prisoner and forced to work in German hospitals in Brussels and Charleroi.

TILLION, GERMAINE
(B. 1907)

French ethnologist and member of the Resistance during World War II. Germaine Tillion was the daughter of Lucien Tillion, a magistrate, and Émilie (Cussac) Tillion, also a member of the Resistance. Émilie Tillion was killed in the gas chamber at Ravensbrück concentration camp in 1945.

Born on May 30, 1907, in Allègre (Haute-Loire), Tillion studied ethnology at the Institut d'Éthnologie at the Sorbonne, and it was through her academic studies that she met future members of her Resistance network. Tillion went to Algeria in 1937 to do fieldwork among the Berbers of Chaouïas. She was there when France was defeated by the Germans. She returned to France as Marshal Philippe Pétain was signing the armistice.

Tillion opposed the Vichy regime from the start. She was therefore determined to put her career on hold and devote herself full time to the Resistance movement. In August 1940 a small network of Resistance fighters was formed in Paris, which Tillion named *Musée de l'homme* (Museum of Man) because its founding members were from the museum of that name and the network met clandestinely behind the museum's film room screen. This group was primarily composed of young left-wing intellectuals. Tillion and naturalist and escaped prisoner of war (POW) Boris Vildé were founders of the group, and art historian Agnès Humbert was in charge of recruitment. Other members of the group included Anatole Lewitsky, a Russian anthropologist, and Yvonne Oddon, a friend and colleague of Tillion. Tillion helped people get into unoccupied France by indicating places where the border could be crossed without German passes. In addition, she found people who would hide and feed evaders; she also supplied those fleeing with false papers. She enlisted teams of men and women to assist POWs in escaping from German camps in France. These prisoners included French, Asian, and African troops, as well as Jews.

Tillion was arrested on August 13, 1942. She was held at the Santé prison and then transferred to Fresnes. On October 21, 1943, she was deported to the Ravensbrück work camp, where her mother was also imprisoned. Tillion survived and was freed in April 1945, because Heinrich Himmler had made an agreement with the United States to exchange French prisoners for German prisoners who were interned in liberated France.

During her time in prison, Tillion managed to take copious notes about her life at Ravensbrück. These notes and further research resulted in her book *Ravensbrück* (1946). Tillion attended the Hamburg trials of those who ran Ravensbrück. She was distressed because she felt the facts were not accurately reported. According to Tillion, "The representation—re-presentation—of crimes followed its course, and I measured the deepening of the abyss being dug between what really happened and the uncertain re-presentation we call history" (Tillion 1975, 180).

—*Leigh Whaley*

See also France, Resistance during World War II, Women and; Ravensbrück

References and Further Reading

Lacouture, Jacques. 2000. *Le témoignage est un combat. Une biographie de Germaine Tillion* [Witness Is a Battle: A Biography of Germaine Tillion]. Paris: Seuil.

Reid, Donald. 2003. Germaine Tillion and Resistance to the Vichy Syndrome. *History and Memory* 15, no. 2 (Fall):36–63.

Tillion, Germaine. 1975. *Ravensbrück*. Translated by Gerald Satterwhite. Garden City, NY: Anchor.

"TOKYO ROSE" (IVA IKUKO TOGURI D'AQUINO) (1916–)

The nickname U.S. GIs fighting in the Pacific theater gave to an English-speaking Japanese radio announcer. Her sultry-voiced propaganda broadcasts were designed to weaken morale. In reality, there were many Tokyo Rose broadcasters engaged in different types of propaganda. Tokyo Rose was part myth and part reality. Nonetheless, a Japanese American woman, Iva Toguri, was labeled as Tokyo Rose and was convicted of treason but later pardoned.

Iva Toguri's first name in Japanese was Ikuko. She was born on July 4, 1916, in Los Angeles, California, to Japanese immigrant parents. Her father, Jun Toguri, reared her to be as "American" as possible. Iva Toguri attended the University of California at Los Angles (UCLA), earning a bachelor's degree in biology in 1940.

Toguri's parents had sent her to Japan in 1941 to help a sick aunt. In the haste to reach her aunt, she applied for a passport but was issued a Certificate of Identification instead because of the length of time needed to secure a passport. When Toguri arrived in Japan she found it difficult to adjust and wanted to return to California immediately. She could have become a citizen of Japan, but because of her loyalty to the United States, she refused official suggestions that she claim Japanese citizenship. By late 1942 Toguri was in a precarious position. Needing to support herself, she found a job as an English-language typist for Radio Tokyo. In November 1943 she was transferred from the typing pool to station NHK. There she worked with a broadcasting group led by Major Charles Cousens, an Australian prisoner of war with pro-American sympathies. Cousens chose Toguri for the job because she had very strong U.S. ties and because she had a voice unsuitable for pleasant broadcast listening.

After the occupation of Japan, reporters tried to find Tokyo Rose. A reporter for *Cosmopolitan* magazine located Toguri and offered her $2,000 to say that she was Tokyo Rose. In dire economic straits, she agreed to the sham, but *Cosmopolitan*'s editors refused to pay anything. U.S. authorities, however, acted, and Toguri was arrested and imprisoned at Sugamo Prison on a charge of treason. She was released when no solid evidence could be found to support the charge.

Toguri had been an announcer for the Tokyo-based program "Zero Hour," which broadcast music, the reading of letters by Allied prisoners, and some news. The female disk jockey called herself Orphan Ann. There was nothing in her broadcasts that was significant enough to qualify as propaganda.

Nevertheless, Iva Toguri was tried for treason in Federal District Court in San Francisco in July 1949. She had been arrested again on August 16, 1948, charged with "a treasonable act

Correspondents interview "Tokyo Rose," Iva Toguri, 1945. (National Archives)

. . . with an intent to betray the United States" while in Japan. Her arrest occurred despite the fact that she had been cleared by an investigation conducted by General Douglas MacArthur's staff after the war. Media agitation reflecting anti-Japanese sentiment had instigated the prosecution.

The pretrial investigations and Toguri's court case were tainted by prosecutorial misconduct. Witnesses were threatened, evidence was withheld, false testimony was given, and procedural rights were denied. Toguri's husband, Felipe d'Aquino, a Portuguese citizen of Japanese and Portuguese ancestry, tried to help her but was so intimidated by the harassment of federal officials that he returned to Japan and was never allowed to reenter the United States.

Toguri was acquitted of all charges except that "she spoke into a microphone about several ships that were sunk" (Duus 1990, 178). She was sentenced to ten years in prison and a fine. She served eight years. Following her release the federal government tried to strip her of her U.S. citizenship and to deport her. In 1977 President Gerald Ford granted her a pardon and restored her civil rights. She is the only American ever granted a pardon for a conviction of treason. Toguri lived in Chicago after her release from federal prison in 1958.

—*Andrew Jackson Waskey*

See also "Axis Sally"; "Lady Haw Haw"

References and Further Reading

Duus, Masayo. 1990. *Tokyo Rose, Orphan of the Pacific.* New York: Harper & Row.
Gunn, Rex B. 1977. *They Called Her Tokyo Rose.* Santa Monica, CA.
Howe, Russell Warren. 1990. *The Hunt for "Tokyo Rose."* Lanham, MD: Madison Books.

TOMARA, SONIA
(1897–1982)

First female war correspondent of World War II. Sonia Tomara was a Russian expatriate who fled St. Petersburg during the Russian Revolution. In France she found work as a secretary to the foreign editor of the French newspaper *Le Matin* and, because of his frequent absences, often took charge of the desk herself. She was soon plunged into international political reporting as well as financial affairs, which in 1928 led to writing a weekly financial review for the *New York Herald Tribune* and to an assignment with its Paris bureau.

During the 1930s Tomara covered the rise of Adolf Hitler and spent time in Nazi Germany, where she developed the reputation of being a shrewd political commentator. In 1937 she joined the *Herald Tribune* staff in New York; however, in 1939 she returned to Europe and became a roving correspondent. In September 1939 Tomara witnessed the German blitzkrieg in Poland and reported on the fall of Warsaw. She then moved to Paris and covered the German invasion of France. In June 1940 she was forced to flee the city on foot because of the imminent approach of the German armies. After the June 22, 1944, armistice and the establishment of the German-controlled French government at Vichy, Tomara escaped to Portugal and then to New York, where, after the important stories she had covered in Europe, her first major assignment was to write about a cat show. She later said it was humiliating, but it taught her something about reporting in the United States.

In 1942 Tomara received formal accreditation as a U.S. war correspondent. She was assigned to the Far East, where she covered the political and military situation in the China-Burma-India theater. She traveled extensively in the region and in December 1942 was in Calcutta when the Japanese bombed the city. In May 1943 she moved to China, where for three months she covered Nationalist Chinese military actions against Japan on the Yangtze River. In late 1943 Tomara left China, traveling first to Cairo and then on to Tehran, where she reported on meetings of the major powers. She was then reassigned to Algiers, where she spent six months covering the Allied Forces Headquarters in North Africa. In the summer of 1944 Tomara returned briefly to Paris, only to resign from the *Herald Tribune* in 1945 when she married U.S. federal judge William Clark, whom she met in Algiers.

—*Brett F. Woods*

See also Chapelle, Dickey; Emerson, Gloria; Fallaci, Oriana; Higgins, Marguerite; Hull, Peggy, pseud.; Journalists, American Women, during World War I; Luce, Clare Boothe; Schuyler, Philippa; Trotta, Liz; Watts, Jean

References and Further Reading

Collins, Jean E. 1980. *She Was There: Stories of Pioneering Women Journalists*. New York: Julian Messner.

Wagner, Lilya. 1989. *Women War Correspondents of World War II*. New York: Greenwood.

TOWER, ELLEN MAY
(1868–1899)

The first American woman to die on foreign soil in service to the United States. Ellen May Tower was the first nurse to die during the Spanish-American War and the first woman from Michigan to be honored with a military funeral—the third such in the United States.

Tower was born May 8, 1868, in Byron, Michigan, the daughter of Judge Samuel Spruce Tower, an American Civil War veteran, and Sarah S. Bigelow. She attended the Chaffee School and the Byron Village School, from which she graduated. The family moved to Onaway after her mother's death in 1880. Tower taught school in the Bancroft area and then worked for a female physician, Dr. Whealock. This revived her childhood dream of a nursing vocation.

Attending a nurses' training program at Detroit's Grace Hospital, the twenty-six-year-old Tower graduated on January 17, 1894, and began working at the Michigan School for the Blind in Lansing. After four years at the school, Tower returned to Grace Hospital for special training as a war nurse. She was made superintendent of nursing and became the first nurse to volunteer for duty with the U.S. Army during the Spanish-American War. After sending several letters to the surgeon general's adviser, Dr. Anita Newcomb McGee, Tower was accepted into the Daughters of the American Revolution (DAR) Hospital Corps, which acted as an examining board to help in hiring the most competent nurses to serve during the war.

After taking her oath on September 1, 1898, Tower, along with seventeen other nurses, was sent to Camp Wikoff at Montauk Point, New York, where she received thirty dollars a month and daily rations. There she earned the nickname the Camp Wikoff Angel for her devoted care of soldiers and her efforts to inform and console their families, whose concerns went unaddressed by the military. Tower was reassigned to San Juan, Puerto Rico, with four other nurses from Camp Wikoff. A few months after her arrival, Tower was the first nurse to contract typhoid fever. She died from acute pericarditis, ironically, the day before the Treaty of Paris was signed.

Dr. Sterling, who awarded Tower her nursing diploma, delivered Tower's eulogy at the Cass Avenue Methodist Episcopal Church. After her body lay in state at the Light Guard Armory in Detroit, 5,000 people, including many dignitaries, traveled to Bryon, where she was buried on January 17, 1899.

A ten-foot monument made by her cousin was placed at her grave in 1903 after friends, with help from the Women's Relief Corps, raised funds for its cost. A post office bearing her name was established near the village of Onaway, where her father resided. Tower was honored later that year when a new town, laid out west of Onaway, was named Tower in remembrance of her.

—*Rebecca Tolley-Stokes*

See also McGee, Anita Newcomb; Spanish-American War, Women and the

References and Further Reading

Graf, Mercedes H. Women Nurses in the Spanish-American War. *Minerva: Quarterly Report on Women and the Military* 19, no. 1 (Spring):3–27.

Michmarkers.com. "Ellen May Tower." Michigan Historical Markers. http://www.michmarkers.com/startup.asp?startpage=L1619.htm (accessed September 9, 2004).

Seward, Kathryn E., and Jennifer D. Freese Walkling. 1980. *The Village of Byron and Its Heroine, Ellen May Tower*. Privately printed.

Trauma and Brutalization Unleashed by World War I

Psychological and social impact of World War I. World War I resulted in unprecedented levels of psychological brutality and human devastation for both men and women. One of the symbols of modern warfare's incredible violence was the diagnosis of widespread mental injuries, called shell shock, war hysteria, or war neurosis by European doctors. These terms for what is today known as posttraumatic stress disorder were used following 1914 to describe myriad physical and psychological symptoms found in both men and women, ranging from tics, tremors, and paralysis to nightmares, heightened anxiety, uncontrollable aggression, and various emotional disorders. Medical debates over the causes of shell shock resulted in revisions of long-held assumptions about the connections between mental illness, gender, and social class. Shell shock was also a uniquely politicized wound. The problem of traumatic neurosis intensified existing social and political divisions over responsibility for the war, welfare for war victims, changes in gender norms and traditional values, and class tensions.

British and German doctors were the first to define shell shock in the early phases of the war, and their diagnoses reflected prewar assumptions about gender, social class, and the origins of mental illness. Before 1914 doctors widely assumed that mental illness was physiological in origin, and they constructed hysteria as an essentially female ailment, sometimes found in "unmanly" men across social classes, especially those allegedly weakened by urbanization and the erosion of traditional gender roles, or in working-class men who lacked self-control. Doctors also theorized that war would rejuvenate a society made increasingly decadent and that men and women behind the war would strengthen their nerves as they devoted themselves to national sacrifice and traditional authority and values. Warfare experienced at the Marne, the Somme, Verdun, and other sites of mass slaughter, however, resulted in an outbreak of widespread symptoms of neurotic disorders that crossed class lines, pushing psychiatrists to reevaluate their views on hysteria as primarily feminine or working-class in origin. The British army ultimately saw approximately 200,000 men with symptoms of traumatic neurosis, with the German and French armies suffering similar levels of such wounds.

Doctors first tried to restore masculinity through feminine tasks, including craftmaking and domestic chores, giving shell-shocked men a sense of confidence before they returned to a militarized, masculine environment that demanded discipline and obedience—namely, the front lines. Such treatment assumed that men first had to rebuild themselves through feminine paths of behavior before they could be restored to their essential, and superior, male gender identities. More severe cases were treated with electroshock therapy; when this failed, doctors experimented with forms of psychotherapy. This technique was most famously practiced by British doctor W. H. R. Rivers when he treated officers Siegfried Sassoon and Wilfred Owen, who expressed their war experiences in some of the most famous antiwar poetry of the century. In this context, Rivers acknowledged the essentially psychological nature of the wounds and the fact that even manly, healthy soldiers could be traumatized by the brutality and stress of modern combat.

Medical debates over the origins of shell shock evolved into politicized debates over responsibility for the consequences of the war and the significance of psychological trauma. Conservative interwar groups placed responsibility for shell shock on the men who suffered from it, targeting them as malingerers bent on escaping the trenches and acquiring a pension. Conservative politicians resisted paying welfare for traumatized men, and they called on women to practice traditional roles as nurturers—with assistance from the paternal authority of doctors—to restore a sense of discipline that would help men recover and become economically productive. More progressive political organizations, for example, the German Social Democratic Party (SPD), emphasized combat stress as primarily responsible for inflicting mental wounds and called for the expansion of state welfare institutions in providing health care, job retraining, and assistance for men reintegrating into work and family. Despite some conservative protests, British shell shock victims received substantial compensation for mental wounds in the wake of the *War Office Report on Shell Shock* (1922). Germany's 1920 National Pension Law also provided some of the most progressive approaches to war neurosis, defining it as a legitimate injury found in both men and women stressed by total war, entitling victims to state compensation.

As a result of defeat, Germany's political battles over war neurosis were particularly divisive and bitter. The SPD spearheaded the movement for more state spending for both men and women traumatized by war. Women SPD activists such as Alma Hissfeld and Martha Harnoss argued that working-class women were the most deeply traumatized by the war's effects, forcing them to struggle as single breadwinners in an economy that provided less pay to women while they tended to the emotional well-being of children and, eventually, mentally devastated men returning home. The SPD ultimately failed to bridge divisions between men and women, exacerbated by deepening pension cuts spearheaded by conservative parties in the midst of economic crisis. Men cut from the pension rolls by doctors and finance ministers resented women who continued to receive welfare for so-called hysterical disorders caused by the Great Inflation, the economic catastrophe of 1923 during which German currency lost almost all of its value and caused immense social misery.

Organizations further to the political left, for example, the German Communist Party, claimed that working-class men were actually the most resilient in the trenches, hardened by years of exploitation in prewar factories. Communist leaders asserted that the real hysterics were military officers and doctors who sadistically sent men to war, tortured them with electroshock treatment, and then labeled them unmanly

when they broke down under inhuman levels of stress. Communists argued that conservatives invented the concept of war hysteria and neurosis to deflect from their own responsibility in starting the war and to avoid paying its costs. When the Nazis came to power in 1933, they completely cut war neurotics from the pension rolls and blamed neurosis on welfare, democracy, pacifism, and the "new woman," all of which allegedly sapped men of their essential warrior instincts and masculine character.

Many doctors, state representatives, and lay critics feared that war neurosis was only the tip of deeper social and cultural disorders brought on by brutalization in total war. Psychiatrists in Germany testified in the Reichstag just after the armistice that war neurotics were responsible for an epidemic of moral deviance and disrespect for traditional gender roles and class hierarchies. The popular press published stories about sadistic men returning to the front as criminals, sex fiends, and murderous predators, fueling public fears that veterans could never be reintegrated into work and family. In *Sexual Life in the War* (1920), German journalist Hans Georg Baumgarth argued that soldiers brought their "primitive instincts" from the trenches and inflicted "bestial sexual acts" on their wives. Sexual passion and violence also rose in women, Baumgarth argued, leading to promiscuity, divorce, and domestic conflict.

German sexologist Magnus Hirschfeld claimed that the war stimulated latent violent instincts that threatened families and the social order. In *The Moral History of the World War* (1930), Hirschfeld pointed to the war as responsible for a rise in domestic violence and murders. The economic and sexual deprivations caused by the war, combined with fear and stress, led women to mimic the violence at the front in order to escape. Hirschfeld claimed that women who killed their abusive, emotionally unresponsive husbands who had just returned from the front were themselves secondary victims of the war. Though their experiences were different, Hirschfeld argued, both men and women suffered the same violent urges and psychological trauma stemming from the brutality of total war.

—Jason Crouthamel

See also France, World War I, Psychological Impact on French Women; Rape in War

References and Further Reading

Hagemann, Karen, and Stefanie Schüler-Springorum, eds. 2002. *Home/Front—The Military, War, and Gender in Twentieth Century Germany.* New York: Berg.

Leese, Peter. 2002. *Shell Shock: Traumatic Neurosis and the British Soldiers of the First World War.* New York: Palgrave Macmillan.

Micale, Mark S., and Paul Lerner, eds. 2001. *Traumatic Pasts: History, Psychiatry, and Trauma in the Modern Age, 1870–1930.* London: Cambridge University Press.

Showalter, Elaine. 1987. Rivers and Sassoon: The Inscription of Male Gender Anxieties. Pages 61–69 in *Behind the Lines—Gender and the Two World Wars.* Edited by Margaret Randolph Higonnet, Jane Jenson, Sonya Michel, and Margaret Collins Weitz. New Haven, CT: Yale University.

Whalen, Robert. 1984. *Bitter Wounds: German Victims of the Great War, 1914–1939.* Ithaca, NY: Cornell University.

TRAVERS, SUSAN
(1909–2003)

The only woman to serve in the French Foreign Legion. Daughter of a retired Royal Navy admiral, Travers led the rather inconsequential life of a socialite. After attending finishing school in Florence, she resolved to leave, in her words, "the humdrum reality of . . . life" and begin to pursue men as her "ticket to . . . wealth, and happiness," determined to "use my charms to my greatest advantage." Between 1929 and 1939 she indulged in "a heady decade of socializing" across Europe, "embarking," she wrote "on several affairs with wholly unsuitable men"

(Travers 2001). When war came in 1939, Travers joined the French Red Cross and became an ambulance driver. In 1940 she accompanied the French expeditionary force sent to help the Finns in the Winter War against the Russians. Later that year, shocked by France's collapse to Nazi Germany, she was determined "to do something of value on the front lines" (Travers 2001). After hearing a powerful broadcast by General Charles de Gaulle, calling for all French soldiers and others to join with his Free French, she went to his headquarters in London and joined the Free French forces. Attached to the 13th Demi-brigade of the Foreign Legion, she sailed for West Africa, where she witnessed the abortive attack on Dakar. She was then posted to Eritrea and took on the hazardous job of driving for senior officers, including Free French General Pierre Koenig. The desert roads were often mined and subject to enemy attack; she survived a number of crashes and was wounded by shellfire. As the only woman in her company, she was given the name La Miss. In the spring of 1942 her unit was sent to hold the bleak fort of Bir Hakeim, at the southern tip of the Allied defensive line in the western desert of North Africa. Fighting against overwhelming odds, the legionnaires—Travers among them—held out for fifteen days, turning Bir Hakeim into a French symbol of hope and defiance. With all ammunition and water exhausted, Koenig led a breakout at night through the minefields and three concentric cordons of German panzers that encircled the fort. Travers drove him to safety under intense fire. She was awarded the Croix de Guerre and the Ordre du Corps d'Arme for her actions in this feat. She remained with the Legion in Italy and France until the end of the war. In May 1945 she applied to officially join the Legion, taking care to omit her gender from the form. She was appointed an officer in the logistics division, becoming the only woman ever to serve with the Legion. In 1956 she was awarded the Medaille Militaire and in 1996 the Legion d'Honneur, in recognition of her bravery at Bir Hakeim.

—Alexander Mikaberidze

See also Nirouet, Collette

References and Further Reading

Porch, Douglas. 1991. *The French Foreign Legion: Complete History of the Legendary Fighting Force.* New York: HarperCollins.

Travers, Susan. 2001. *Tomorrow to Be Brave: A Memoir of the Only Woman Ever to Serve in the French Foreign Legion.* New York: Free Press.

TROTTA, LIZ

Reporter during the Vietnam and Yom Kippur Wars. Liz Trotta, winner of three Emmy Awards for television broadcasting and two Overseas Press Club Awards, worked in the early twenty-first century in syndicated news broadcasting. When she began her journalism career in 1965, she was relegated to articles classified as "topics of women's interest." These assignments included reporting on the wedding dress of Lynda Bird Johnson, President Lyndon Johnson's daughter, in 1967. Trotta fought the typecasting of female reporters and ended up, through sheer tenacity, covering the fighting front during the Vietnam War in 1968. She was the first U.S. female journalist to be assigned to report on tough news stories and battlefront war coverage. She returned to Vietnam on the tenth anniversary of the end of the war. Despite her excellence in reporting, Trotta lost her network news job due to age discrimination, something her male counterparts at the network did not face.

Liz Trotta graduated from Columbia University with an advanced degree in journalism. She began her career as a print journalist for the *Chicago Tribune* and *Newsday.* Her entry into broadcast news came in 1965 when she went to work for WNBC, the NBC affiliate in New York City. Trotta made her name in broadcast journalism by covering some of the most important stories of her lifetime, and in many ways she made possible the aspirations of today's female reporters.

Among the important stories Trotta covered was Senator Edward Kennedy's car accident at Chappaquiddick, where a campaign staff member was drowned in a car Kennedy was driving in June 1969. She reported on the George McGovern presidential campaign against Richard M. Nixon in 1972. Trotta again used her war correspondent skills in reporting on the Yom Kippur War in October 1973, exposing herself to mortar attack. When Iranian militants invaded the U.S. Embassy in Tehran on November 4, 1979, Trotta covered the hostage crisis, which at one point involved fleeing from a hostile crowd. In the early 1980s she wrote articles chronicling the media circus of the Von Bulow trial, in which husband Claus was accused of killing his heiress wife, Sunny, by drug injection. In 1983, with the U.S. invasion of Grenada, Trotta again covered the front lines of war on the island nation.

Trotta is known for her conservative views. After her dismissal from NBC in 1984, she held jobs at Hillman Periodicals, the Inter-Catholic Press Agency, *Long Island Press, Chicago Tribune, Newsday,* and the CBS Morning News. She lives in New York City, where she is a news analyst for the FOX News Channel and also serves as the New York bureau chief for the *Washington Times.* She occasionally teaches journalism, notably at Stern College of Yeshiva University. Trotta's conservative commentary continues to create heated debate.

—*Pamela Lee Gray*

See also Chapelle, Dickey; Emerson, Gloria; Fallaci, Oriana; Higgins, Marguerite; Hull, Peggy, pseud.; Journalists, American Women, during World War I; Luce, Clare Boothe; Schuyler, Philippa; Tomara, Sonia; Watts, Jean

References and Further Reading

Trotta, Liz. 1991. *Fighting for Air: In the Trenches with Television News.* New York: Simon and Schuster.

———. 1998. *Jude: A Pilgrimage to the Saint of Last Resort.* San Francisco: Harper.

TRÜMMERFRAUEN (RUBBLE WOMEN)

Tens of thousands of women, typically 16 to 45 years old, who removed debris from Germany's bombed-out cities after World War II. Demographic changes—over 3 million German men died in the war, and in 1945 over 11 million were prisoners in Allied camps—necessitated that women help clear the ruins. The work of the Trümmerfrauen (rubble women or women of the rubble) entailed removing rubble by hand, sorting building materials that could be reprocessed, disposing of materials that could not be recycled, cleaning mortar and cement from the salvaged material, and stacking stones and bricks for reuse.

Originally, occupation authorities forced families of National Socialist party members to clear rubble as part of the denazification process. The intense destruction of German cities, however, required authorities to compel larger sections of the populace to work removing debris. Almost all women ages 15 to 50 and men ages 14 to 65 were legally required to register with the unemployment office, although mothers of young children, students, and the disabled and sick were exempt from employment. The type of employment determined the level of ration card they received. Those involved in more strenuous labor, such as Trümmerfrauen, received a card that allowed them more calories per day. Immediately after World War II, each German received on average 1,100

Trümmerfrauen, or rubble women, in the British section of Berlin as they leave work for the day, 1948.
(Bettmann/Corbis)

calories per day, although the minimum daily requirement as set by the League of Nations was approximately 2,400 calories per day. During this time Germans also faced a lack of housing, crime, harsh winters without sufficient coal, political instability, and the threat of war between the Soviet Union and the United States.

Occupation and German authorities always viewed women as a temporary solution to Germany's postwar labor difficulties. Thus, they were prevented from seeking apprenticeships or higher positions within the construction industry, and health and safety officials and employers cared little for occupational injuries and other job-related health problems. Trümmerfrauen also earned less than male construction workers although Allied occupiers stated that contractors could pay women as much as men if they so desired. In reality, rubble cleanup was strenuous for women, and many did not hesitate to leave the construction industry after their mandatory service was finished or when they could find other means of supporting themselves and their families.

In the 1950s the Trümmerfrau gave way to the *Hausfrau* (housewife) as more women returned to domestic labor. This relieved many conservatives who thought that the hard work would spoil the gentle, feminine character of women and worried that women would forget their female duties, such as raising children and housework. Trümmerfrauen, however, became symbols for the creation of a new Germany after its destruction during the war and for the hard work and sacrifice that led to the *Wirtschaftswunder* (economic miracle). The pictures of devastated German cities and of women toiling among the ruins became symbols of Germany's suffering and victimization—not only for women but for men as well. In later generations, the Trümmerfrau became a symbol for the catastrophic consequences of war and the immediate postwar generation's lack of interest in confronting Germany's National Socialist past. Nevertheless, this criticism should not tarnish the amazing achievements of Germany's women during the country's reconstruction from 1945 to 1950.

—*Chad Wallo*

See also Germany, Women and the Home Front, World War II

References and Further Reading

Heineman, Elisabeth. 1996. The Hour of the Woman: Memories of Germany's "Crisis Years" and the West German National Identity. *American Historical Review* 101, no. 2 (April):354–395.

Höhn, Maria. 1997. Stunde Null der Frauen? Renegotiating Women's Place in Postwar Germany. Pages 75–87 in *Stunde Null: The End and the Beginning Fifty Years Ago.* Edited by Geoffrey J. Giles. Washington, DC: German Historical Institute.

Kuhn, Anette, ed. 1984. *Frauen in der deutschen Nachkriegszeit. Frauenarbeit 1945–1949* [*Women in the Postwar Period of Germany— Women's Work 1945–1949*]. Vol. 2. Düsseldorf: Schwann.

Polm, Rita. 1990. *"Neben dem Mann die andere Hälfte eines Ganzen zu sein!?" Frauen in der Nachkriegszeit—Zur Situation und Rolle der jüngeren Frauen in der Städten der Bundesrepublik (1945–1949)* ["Man's Other Half": Women in the Postwar Period—On the Situation and Role of Young Women in the Cities of the Federal Republic (1945–1949)]. Munster, Germany: Unrast.

T'SERCLAES, BARONESS ELIZABETH DE (NÉE SHAPTER) (1884–1978)

Ambulance driver and first-aid nurse during World War I in Belgium. Along with Mairi Chisholm, she established a frontline dressing station in Pervyse in November 1914, for which both women became renowned. Set up initially in a cellar and then in a series of abandoned houses, the post was not evacuated until the women were severely gassed in March 1918. Both were awarded the Chevaliers de L'Ordre de Léopold II in 1915 and given the British Military Medal in 1917.

Elizabeth (Elsie) Knocker (the future Baroness T'Serclaes) went to Belgium as a member of Dr. Hector Munro's Flying Ambulance Column in September 1914. The volunteer unit was made up of six men and four women, of whom she was the only trained professional nurse. The self-financing group aimed to help the Belgian medical service, which was in disarray after the German invasion. Knocker translated her skills as an avid motorcyclist to become an ambulance driver for the unit, which collected, treated, and transported wounded Belgian soldiers. After two months she became frustrated with the group's disorganization, and she and Chisholm resolved to set up an advanced dressing station a few hundred yards from the frontline trenches, where their skills would be put to better use.

Knocker recognized that it was vital for wounded soldiers to have immediate treatment for clinical shock to prevent deaths from minor injuries. She and Chisholm gave wounded Belgian soldiers prompt treatment and rest before the long, arduous ambulance journey to a field hospital. Just as the services of the Ambulance Corps had been rejected by the British War Office and the British, American, and French Red Cross, Knocker and Chisholm initially had difficulties obtaining permission and supplies for their advanced dressing station. As news of their efforts on the front lines spread, the Heroines of Pervyse were able to muster donations for the station through their newfound fame as well as their personal connections and the proceeds from lectures they gave in Britain on visits home.

Baroness T'Serclaes was born Elizabeth Blackall Shapter on July 29, 1884, in Exeter, Devon. In 1906 she married Leslie Duke Knocker. The couple's son, Kenneth Duke Knocker, was born in 1907, and the couple subsequently divorced. Privately educated, Knocker then undertook nurse's training at the Children's Hip Hospital, Sevenoaks, Kent, and trained as a midwife at Queen Charlotte's Hospital, London. In April 1916 she married Belgian pilot Baron Harold T'Serclaes, who died in 1919. After her evacuation from Pervyse in March 1918, she was an officer in the newly formed Women's Royal Air Force (WRAF) until it was disbanded at the end of the war. During World War II, the baroness was an assistant section officer in the WRAF, but she resigned when her son, a Royal Air Force pilot, was killed in action in 1942. She continued to be active in the Royal Air Force Benevolent Fund from 1949 to 1959, caring for the widows of airmen.

Her writings demonstrate her personal bravery and desire to be needed and esteemed, which she found in her wartime roles: "Only in time of war have I found any real sense of purpose and happiness," she wrote in her autobiography (T'Serclaes 1964, 213). Her experiences also reveal the initial official opposition to women's participation during World War I, as well as the greater freedom and opportunities available to women who could afford to volunteer their services in the war effort.

—Amy Bell

See also Chisholm, Mairi Lambert

References and Further Reading

Department of Documents, Imperial War Museum, London. Box P404 (Baroness T'Serclaes's war diaries, brief memoirs, press cuttings, and album containing drawings and signatures of distinguished visitors to the dressing station).

Mitton, Geraldine Edith, ed. 1917. *The Cellar-House of Pervyse: A Tale of Uncommon Things from the Journals and Letters of the Baroness T'Serclaes and Mairi Chisholm.* London: A & C Black.

T'Serclaes, Baroness. 1964. *Flanders and Other Fields: Memoirs of the Baroness T'Serclaes.* London: George Harrap.

TUBMAN, HARRIET
(CA. 1820-1913)

A child of U.S. slavery who would become the leading advocate of emancipation in her era. Though lacking any formal education, Harriet Tubman was a successful strategist, reformer, military spy, and suffragist. She is best known for her role as the leading "conductor" of the Underground Railroad.

Tubman was born in Maryland around 1820, although the exact date of her birth and her birthplace are unknown. Named Araminta Ross at birth, as a youngster she was both a domestic worker and a field hand. Around 1844 she married a freeman named John Tubman, though little is now known about their relationship. She desired to escape to the North, but her husband, who was already free, did not want to go and thus stayed behind.

She escaped to Philadelphia with the help of several people who hid her at various points on her arduous journey. She changed her name from Araminta Ross to Harriet Tubman. Philadelphia was home to the Philadelphia Society for the Promotion of the Abolition of Slavery, an organization that had set up a "railroad" system of transporting southern slaves, called "cargo," though various hiding places, called "depots," into the free areas of the North. This system, normally referred to as the Underground Railroad, appealed to Tubman, who began to take a major role in smuggling slaves into Philadelphia. In her role as a conductor of this system, traveling with the fugitives at night in order to avoid notice and capture, she came to be called Moses for her part in setting her people free.

In 1858 Tubman met one of the most fervent abolitionists of the era, John Brown. She developed a close relationship with and fully supported him, including assisting in the planning of the raid at Harper's Ferry, Virginia. Tubman had planned to be at the ill-fated raid, but due to changes of which she was not informed, she was not present.

Tubman, believing that the American Civil War would signal the end of slavery, enthusiastically supported the Union. She was asked by the governor of Massachusetts to help direct the transport of slave fugitives. She not only took on this task but also attended the wounded. In addition, she performed wartime espionage. She was attacked and injured in New Jersey by a train conductor who did not believe that she was a spy for the Union army.

Tubman returned home to Auburn, New York, and married a much younger former Union soldier. She continued to work on behalf of the rights of African Americans, especially the poor and aged. She also became very involved in the women's suffrage movement, despite her advanced age. She died in 1913 in abject poverty. Although she was never given a Civil War pension, she was provided military honors at her funeral. Because of the racial climate in the United States, it would be years before she received appropriate acknowledgment.

—*Leonard A. Steverson*

See also Civil War, American, and Women

References and Further Reading

Clinton, Catherine. 2004. *Harriet Tubman: The Road to Freedom.* New York: Little, Brown.

Humey, Jean M. 2003. *Harriet Tubman: The Life and the Stories.* Madison: University of Wisconsin.

Larson, Kate. 2004. *Clifford Bound for the Promised Land: Harriet Tubman, Portrait of an America Hero.* New York: Ballentine.

U

ULSTER, WOMEN DURING THE TROUBLES IN

The experience of women in Ulster, or Northern Ireland, during the three decades of "the Troubles" from 1968 to 1998. Women took on direct roles in the conflict as protesters, peace activists, militants, prisoners, and politicians. They also played indirect but equally important roles: as housewives who kept families together amid tragedy and upheaval; as churchwomen who strengthened their communities and supported the bereaved; and as quiet, sometimes secretive supporters of men on both sides involved in the fighting.

The Troubles began in 1968 with the first civil rights marches protesting discrimination against Catholics in housing, political representation, employment, and public services by the Protestant government. Following the Irish independence movement and the resulting partition of the Irish Republic in 1922, the six northern counties of Ulster remained part of the United Kingdom. Society in Ulster was segregated along sectarian lines: the indigenous Irish were traditionally Catholic, Republican, and Nationalist in religion and politics, many desiring either home rule or merger with the Irish Republic; those descended from the British colonialists who had settled in Ireland, however, were traditionally Protestant, Unionist, and Loyalist in their wish to remain a part of the United Kingdom and maintain a majority Protestant government. Women in large part fulfilled their traditional roles in families and churches, but these responsibilities did not prevent a large number of women from rising as leaders, organizers, and active participants in the conflict.

A militant Catholic leader whose career spanned the breadth of the Troubles was Bernadette Devlin McAliskey, who emerged as a leader in the student movement of the late 1960s. She was elected as a member of parliament at the age of twenty-one and became known for her electrifying speeches and her activism in marches and protests. She was jailed twice for inciting violence and gained notoriety when she struck Home Secretary Reginald Maudling in Parliament after he claimed that the Bloody Sunday incident of 1972, in which British paratroopers shot dead thirteen unarmed Catholic protesters, was provoked by the protesters. McAliskey and her husband survived serious gunshot wounds in an attempted assassination in 1981, but she persisted in her outspoken public persona, encouraging direct action and violent struggle against the injustices of the majority Protestant government of Ulster.

In contrast, other women organized a peaceful response to the violence and tragedy of the

Troubles. Monica Patterson, a Catholic, and Ruth Agnew, a Protestant, formed Women Together in 1970, drawing women from both communities to break up mobs, hold vigils and rallies, and support the families of those killed in the conflict. Another prominent peace movement was organized by Mairead Corrigan and Betty Williams in 1976 after a widely publicized incident in which Corrigan's three young nephews were hit and killed by a car after a British soldier shot its driver. The Peace People Movement was the result, and the organization initiated peace marches and rallies across the country and abroad. Corrigan and Williams were awarded the Nobel Peace Prize of 1976 for their work with Peace People.

The conflict of the Troubles was a feature of daily life in cities such as Belfast and Derry, where Catholic and Protestant paramilitaries were particularly active and the mostly Protestant police and military responded with force to Catholic agitation. Housewives assisted paramilitaries such as the Irish Republican Army (IRA) by providing safe houses, passing messages, and even alerting the neighborhood of police or military raids by banging metal trash can lids, a practice known as bin bashing. Other women participated as fighters within these paramilitaries, taking part in bombings, assassination plots, and street violence. Republican women were imprisoned at Armagh, where they participated in prison protests and rioting concurrently with their male counterparts imprisoned elsewhere. The activities of these women were often viewed in the context of women's traditional roles: a sympathetic view saw active women as exemplars of sacrifice, whereas the opposing view saw such activity as an example of the depths of depravity to which a group would go, using "even women" for violent ends.

As the Troubles raged on, the Northern Ireland Women's Rights Movement worked to challenge traditional gender stereotypes and to address problems unique to women, such as domestic violence, sex discrimination, and birth control. Founded in 1975, the movement operated as an umbrella organization for groups on both sides of the sectarian divide, bringing women together in common cause to improve their lives. Growing out of the movement was the Northern Ireland Women's Coalition, which sent two delegates, Monica McWilliams and Pearl Sagar, to the multiparty talks that resulted in the Belfast Agreement, or Good Friday Accord, in 1998, effectively bringing the Troubles to a close.

—Kristen L. Rouse

See also Devlin, Bernadette; Mowlam, Marjorie; Peace People Movement

References and Further Reading

Coogan, Tim Pat. 1996. *The Troubles: Ireland's Ordeal 1966–1996 and the Search for Peace.* Boulder, CO: Roberts Rinehart Publishers.

Galligan, Yvonne, Eilís Ward, and Rick Wilford, eds. 1999. *Contesting Politics: Women in Ireland, North and South.* Boulder, CO: Westview.

Morgan, Valerie. 1996. *Peacemakers? Peacekeepers? Women in Northern Ireland 1969–1995.* Londonderry, Northern Ireland: INCORE.

UNITED STATES, HOME FRONT DURING WORLD WAR I

The roles of women in the United States during World War I. During its years of neutrality, the United States was not immune to the arguments for and against its participation in the European conflict, and women played key roles on both sides of the debate. Fervent pacifists such as Jane Addams led the call for women to resist the lure of armed conflict and appealed to their uniquely female sensibilities—especially those linked to their maternal role—arguing that they had an obligation to object to the human sacrifice engendered by war. Hundreds of women joined the Mass Meeting for Peace on April 2, 1917, the day the United States declared war on Germany, and though large numbers of women continued their campaign of denouncing participation in the war, many feminists made the difficult decision to back the government once it pledged support to the Allies. Although she had been one of the founders of the Women's Peace Party in 1914 alongside Addams, Carrie Chapman Catt of the National Women's Suffrage Association was among those who favored U.S. intervention even before April 1917. Catt and her fellow suffragists hoped that women's participation in war work and patriotic activism would secure the vote and their equality.

The undercurrent of radical opinion and protest was strong enough to cause government leaders concern, and they lost no time in establishing a department to convince Americans to support the war effort. The Committee on Public Information, led by George Creel, was set up on April 13, 1917, and served as the government's propaganda bureau. Through films, posters, advertisements, and public speeches by celebrities and civic leaders, the committee encouraged women not to succumb to the temptation of keeping their sons and husbands at home. The pleas to women's patriotic selflessness went hand-in-hand with campaigns to encourage war economy in the home and war sacrifice in public. In June 1917 the National Food Administration, under Herbert Hoover, called on women to sign a pledge to conserve food through such schemes as Meatless Tuesdays and Wheatless Wednesdays. Within a month, 2 million housewives had signed the pledge cards. Public libraries were instrumental in this campaign through the Food Facts Library led by Edith Guerrier (Weigand 1989, 73).

The Committee on Public Information also enlisted the help of the movie industry, and although film historians have noted that features released between 1917 and 1918 were not overwhelmingly focused on war, films with war themes did strike a chord. The persona of patriotic American womanhood was perhaps best exemplified in Mary Pickford's *Little American* (1917) and *Johanna Enlists* (1918). Pickford, "America's Sweetheart," was also vigorously involved in campaigns to raise money for army ambulances and to encourage the purchase of Liberty Bonds. The Four-Minute Men, so called because these orators spoke for four minutes, were also a feature of the cinemas' contribution to the war effort. Before a movie was shown, one might hear the orators address topics such as "Food Conservation," "Why We Are Fighting," "The Second Liberty Loan," or "Maintaining Morals and Morale."

Posters featuring such seductive female images as the Christie girls recruited both men and women to the Allied cause. While men were encouraged to enlist in the army or the navy, women were confronted with diverse outlets for their patriotism, from joining knitting bees that made socks for soldiers to volunteering for work with the Red Cross as nurses, clerical workers, and canteen staff. Magazines such as *The Ladies' Home Journal*, which had a circulation of over 1 million, propounded the role of the patriotic middle-class homemaker in wartime through editorials, advertisements, and feature articles that provided advice on thrifty household management, from food preservation to dress economy. Approximately 6,000 young women joined the U.S. Expeditionary Force as telephone operators (the "Hello Girls"), stenographers, or typists; others chose from a variety of voluntary organizations to demonstrate their patriotism (Zieger 2000, 142). The Committee on Women's Defense Work of the Council of National Defense, set up in April 1917, was led by Dr. Anna Howard Shaw of the National American Women's Suffrage Association. It sought to coordinate the various voluntary contributions women could make to the war effort—from conserving food to sewing, gardening, selling war bonds, and generally boosting morale. The Women's Section of the Navy League recruited more than 11,000 women (269 in the marines) for clerical and communications positions left vacant by men. The army, albeit reluctantly, eventually employed over 30,000 women as nurses, clerks, translators, and welfare workers (Zieger 2000, 141–142).

World War I has been credited with causing unprecedented numbers of women to enter the labor market. However, though it is true that

1 million women took up war work in the expanding munitions industries, aircraft factories, and shipyards, only 5 percent were new hires (Abrahamson 1983, 95; Kennedy 1980, 285). The real change occurred in the type of employment. The 500,000 women who had previously been domestic servants, laundresses, or seamstresses or who had menial or unskilled factory experience were now assembling equipment, running lathes and drill presses, working in tool rooms and machine shops, and operating heavy equipment (Zieger 2000, 144). Although the war opened up opportunities for employment, the armistice shut the door on most of the gains. Many women lost their jobs in 1919, and despite the call by many activists for equal pay for equal work, trade unions were reluctant to admit women or to give them the same benefits as their male members. The Women in Industry Service, led by Mary Van Kleek, had hoped to secure rights for women workers but instead found itself increasingly up against blatant discrimination and flouting of employment laws.

Of all women on the home front, African American women had the least opportunity for war service or advanced employment. Voluntary organizations were made up exclusively of white, middle-class women, and government organizations hired few black women as clerical workers. Over 1,000 African American nurses who were registered with the Red Cross were rejected for service with the army, although some eventually were allowed to nurse wounded soldiers from the segregated black regiments when they returned stateside. Hundreds may have left the drudgery of domestic and agricultural work (particularly during the Great Migration north) for better opportunities in the factories, but African American women did the menial and more physically demanding work rejected by their white sisters in the manufacturing industries (Zieger 2000, 142).

The gendered and class-bound war effort of the U.S. home front was inimical to continued political dissent. To oppose the country's involvement in the war was not an easy path to follow. Those who dared question the official line were summarily threatened with prosecution and imprisonment. The societal pressure to conform, even to the level of buying Liberty Bonds, was enormous. The Selective Service Act, which established the first compulsory military draft since the American Civil War, went into force on May 18, 1917. The act not only provided for conscription but also made it an offense to dissuade anyone from registering for the draft. The Espionage Act followed soon after, on June 15, 1917, and targeted anyone who held antiwar sentiments or advocated radical social change. Thousands were indicted under this act, which had nothing to do with spying and everything to do with crushing dissent. The American Socialist Party and the Industrial Workers of the World (known as Wobblies) were especially targeted, as were so-called enemy aliens, particularly German immigrants and citizens of German descent. The anarchist Emma Goldman was arrested, tried, convicted, imprisoned, and eventually deported for her denunciation of the draft. Frances Witherspoon, executive secretary of the Bureau of Legal Advice from 1917 to 1920, worked tirelessly on behalf of conscientious objectors and others whose civil liberties were threatened by both acts.

The united and upbeat image of the U.S. home front in World War I as projected by wartime fiction, movies, and the now-iconic recruitment posters was only one facet of what was in reality a complex and contradictory society at war.

—*Jane Potter*

See also Addams, Jane; Catt, Carrie Chapman; Hello Girls; Posters, U.S., Images of Women in World War II

References and Further Reading

Abrahamson, James L. 1983. *The American Home Front: Revolutionary War, Civil War, World War I, World War II.* Washington, DC: National Defense University.
DeBauche, Leslie Midkiff. 1997. *Reel Patriotism: The Movies and World War I.* Madison: University of Wisconsin.

Karetzky, Joanne L. 1997. *The Mustering of Support for WWI by* The Ladies' Home Journal. Lewiston, NY: Edwin Mellen Press.

Kennedy, David M. 1980. *Over Here: The First World War in American Society.* New York: Oxford University.

Kennedy, Kathleen. 1999. *Disloyal Mothers and Scurrilous Citizens: Women and Subversion during World War I.* Bloomington: Indiana University.

Wiegand. Wayne A. 1989. *An Active Instrument for Propaganda: The American Public Library during WWI.* Westport, CT: Greenwood.

Zieger, Robert H. 2000. *America's Great War: WWI and the American Experience.* Lanham, MD: Rowman & Littlefield Publishers.

United States, Home Front during World War II

The mobilization of women in the United States during World War II. When the United States entered World War II, the need for increased production brought unprecedented numbers of women into the wage labor force. During the war, approximately 20 million women worked in defense production and civilian jobs; for 6.5 million of them, it was their first employment experience. For the first time in United States history, more married women than single women worked. In addition, the war brought a significant redistribution of women workers into jobs previously open only to men.

The War Manpower Division and the Office of War Information coordinated campaigns to encourage employers to hire women, to persuade the public that women should work, and to encourage women to work. Propaganda emphasized a woman's patriotic duty to work and linked her war work to the safety and victory of American troops. Publicity materials also assured women that they would be able to maintain their femininity and even compared the jobs they would be doing to cutting out patterns in sewing or following a recipe in cooking. Although many women did work for the patriotic reasons encouraged by the government, many also worked because their families needed their wages.

The U.S. Congress also debated possible solutions to the labor shortage. In 1942, House Resolution 6806 proposed to require women 18 to 65 to register under the Selective Training and Service Act. Other bills were proposed in the Senate between 1942 and 1943, including Senate Bill 666, known as the Austin-Wadsworth Bill or National War Service Act, which would have required women between the ages of 18 and 50 to serve in whatever industrial or agricultural job they were assigned. Pregnant women, those with children under 18, and those with incapacitated dependents were to be exempt. In the ensuing debates about the proposals, there was little congressional discussion specifically about drafting women and more debate about questions of drafting any civilian for wartime work, the proper means to execute such a draft, whether the proposal was an attack on unions, and whether such a draft was needed. Although polls of society found a majority in favor of an industrial draft, no legislation came to a vote.

The more than 3 million women who worked in defense production came to be known as Rosie the Riveters. The number of African American women in industrial work quadrupled during the war, but these women were often hired for the dirtiest or most dangerous jobs. Many women with specialized training in fields such as mechanics, engineering, or mathematics were not hired in their fields but were employed in less skilled and lower-paying jobs (Hartmann 1982, 60, 80–82).

Women in industrial jobs typically worked a forty-eight-hour workweek, six days a week. Many worked overtime hours; vacations and most holidays were canceled for the war's duration. All women workers felt intense pressure to perform well, both to ensure that faulty equipment did not result in a war death and to prove they were capable of doing the work traditionally done by men.

Women work in a tool production plant, Chicago. (Library of Congress)

Few areas of defense production were untouched by women. Approximately 85,000 women, organized into the Women Ordnance Workers division, worked directly for the Ordnance Department, where they loaded and fired weapons to test equipment and ammunition. Other women worked in dangerous munitions factories, often located in rural areas, where they produced bombs and ammunition. Shipbuilding was a deep-rooted industry long accustomed to an all-male workforce and was slow to take on women, but the numbers of vessels needed for the war meant that women also went to work in shipyards. The relatively new aircraft industry quickly employed women to work on stamp presses and to rivet. Women also performed heavy work in the steel and mining in-

dustries. Most women who worked in the railroad industries held clerical positions. In addition, female industrial workers performed such jobs as operating cranes to move tanks and artillery, guarding plants, operating hydraulic presses, driving tractors along assembly lines, and fighting fires in industrial accidents.

The need for childcare was a problem faced by many women and one that was never adequately addressed by industry or the government. At the beginning of the war, Works Progress Administration nurseries operated in some areas, and they continued to be run throughout the war by the Federal Works Agency. These childcare centers cost nearly $50 million and enrolled 130,000 children in more than 3,000 locations but were unable to meet the increasing demand. In 1942 Congress passed the Lanham Act to provide funds for childcare centers in communities most affected by war production. These centers provided daycare and after-school care for children between 2 and 14 years of age and spent $51.9 million on 3,102 centers for 600,000 children. Nonetheless, the facilities were not sufficient for the estimated 4.5 million children under the age of 14 in need of daycare in 1944. In many instances working mothers were blamed for the problem of childcare and were encouraged to fix it themselves by establishing babysitting networks and volunteering in childcare centers.

Throughout the war, no laws required equal pay for women workers. In 1944 the average salary for men was 50 percent higher than that for women. Part of the discrepancy derived from the low numbers of women in skilled and higher-paying positions, but even in unskilled positions women earned 20 percent less than did men in the same positions. Although polls showed a majority of the population supported equal pay for equal work and although the National War Labor Board ordered equal pay and frequently ruled in favor of equality in wage disputes, few employers paid equally. In some instances, employers segregated workers by gender so that they could say the workers performed different jobs. Although many of the women held union memberships, unions offered little wage protection.

For many women, though, the wages they earned were higher than what they had earned before the war or what they could earn in service jobs or office and sales work. Many women in civilian work, such as waitresses, teachers, and saleswomen, left their jobs for better-paying industrial jobs and consequently left their previous sectors short staffed. In addition, industrial jobs often provided benefits and social security, advantages that were especially valuable to African American women who left domestic service work for industry.

In addition to jobs in manufacturing or defense production, many women found wartime jobs in other sectors. In fact, approximately five times as many women worked in civilian employment than in the war industry, but much press coverage focused on women in war industry jobs. Many civilian positions previously closed to women were opened to them because of the labor shortage, including jobs as buyers and clerks in food stores, ushers in movie theaters, cashiers, drug clerks, elevator operators, meter readers, mail carriers, and cab drivers. At least 2 million women worked in clerical jobs, many in the federal government. Even women in the music industry found opportunities in all-girl bands.

Within the Office of Civilian Defense women directed salvage projects and blood drives, publicized victory gardens, ran the Civil Air Patrol, sold war bonds, and worked as ambulance drivers. In February 1945 there were 249 women in the Office of War Information's Overseas Operations Branch. They were stationed in New York, San Francisco, and Hawaii, producing radio propaganda, newsreels, films, and various publications for use in enemy or neutral countries. In the Office of Strategic Services more than 4,000 women did clerical work, deciphered radio traffic, translated documents, and debriefed agents who had been behind enemy lines.

More than 3 million women over 18 years old worked in the Women's Land Army either during their vacation time, for an entire summer, or for a few hours each day. By the summer of 1942 the proportion of women farmworkers had risen from 1 percent to 14 percent. These women were paid between $14 and $18 per week, much less than industrial women workers earned, especially considering that the average worker paid $10 per week for lodging and meals to the family with whom she lived or to the camp where she stayed. The Victory Farm Volunteers recruited close to 2.5 million high school girls for similar agricultural work from 1943 to 1945.

As the end of the war neared, the question arose as to what women working in industry and civilian jobs should do when the men returned. Beginning in 1943 the media ran articles encouraging women to leave their jobs at the end of the war and return to housework. Nevertheless, approximately 75 percent of respondents to a 1944–1945 survey said they expected to continue working after the war, including more than 50 percent of those who had been housewives before the war and more than 57 percent of married women who said they needed to keep working to support their families. Almost 95 percent of African American women expected to continue working after war (Hartmann 1982, 90).

By 1947 women had vacated 1 million factory jobs, 400,000 jobs in the federal government, 500,000 clerical positions, 300,000 jobs in commercial service, and 100,000 jobs in sales. Many women who remained in the wage labor force often did so by moving from blue-collar work to clerical jobs or jobs in the service sector. Even with the losses, however, nearly 17 million women remained in the labor force, a higher number than had been employed in 1940 (Hartmann 1982, 90–91).

In addition to work in the wage labor force, approximately 3.5 million volunteers worked in the Red Cross, shipping food parcels, collecting blood donations, aiding war refugees, acting as a communications link between families and relatives in the military, assisting servicemen and their families in filing for pensions and other benefits, and assisting wives and families of military personnel as they moved to different posts. The Production Department assembled and shipped kit bags containing soap, shoe cleaners, cigarettes, paper, and other goods to soldiers and prisoners of war and produced and shipped knitted garments to hospitals and civilian relief centers. Gray Ladies and nurse's aides worked in understaffed military hospitals to help relieve the nursing shortage. Volunteers in the First Aid Department of the Red Cross offered courses to help the civilian population deal with medical emergencies.

By 1944 approximately 1.5 million women volunteers in the United Service Organizations (USO) had established more than 3,000 clubs in the United States and overseas to meet the recreational and social service needs of troops and their families. USO camp shows also presented performances of well-known entertainers to military personnel. In the USO, unlike many other organizations, African Americans were included as volunteers and staff and as participants in shows and audiences. The USO also opened more than 300 clubs for African American troops and stationed workers in segregated bus and train stations and embarkation ports.

The American Women's Voluntary Services trained more than 350,000 women to drive ambulances, give first aid, and set up mobile kitchens and field hospitals in the event that the United States was bombed. In addition, women were trained in cryptography, mechanics, and translation, and they did relief work at military bases, worked with other organizations to sell war bonds, and provided services to military personnel and families.

Women who did not work outside the home also found their lives changed because of the war. Rationing changed homemaking as women devised substitutes to replace scarce goods such as sugar and red meat. Gas rationing limited how far women could drive to find groceries, supplies, and daycare and to run errands. In addition, women planted victory gardens and salvaged aluminum, tin, and rubber to be used in making war supplies.

Women also volunteered in a host of other organizations and aided the home front in numerous ways. The All-American Girls Professional Baseball League began in 1943 and provided sports entertainment as male baseball players served overseas. Female entertainers raised money by selling war bonds and promoted support of the war effort.

Other women opposed the war effort for reasons as diverse as not wanting to send their husbands or sons to war and opposition to President Franklin Delano Roosevelt or to Judaism. Many women pacifists worked in the Civilian Public Service program alongside male conscientious objectors.

—*Kara D. Vuic*

See also Conscientious Objectors in the United States during World War II

References and Further Reading

Bentley, Amy. 1998. *Eating for Victory: Food Rationing and the Politics of Domesticity.* Urbana: University of Illinois.

Carpenter, Stephanie A. 2003. *On the Farm Front: The Women's Land Army in World War II.* DeKalb: Northern Illinois University.

Gendergap.com. "Women in War Work." http://www.gendergap.com/military/usmil9.htm#war-work (accessed August 23, 2004).

Gluck, Sherna Berger. 1987. *Rosie the Riveter Revisited: Women, the War, and Social Change.* Boston: Twayne.

Hartmann, Susan M. 1982. *The Home Front and Beyond: American Women in the 1940s, American Women in the Twentieth Century.* Boston: Twayne.

Honey, Maureen, ed. 1999. *Bitter Fruit: African American Women in World War II.* Columbia: University of Missouri.

Milkman, Ruth. 1987. *Gender at Work: The Dynamics of Job Segregation by Sex during World War II—The Working Class in American History.* Urbana: University of Illinois.

Weatherford, Doris. 1990. *American Women and World War II: History of Women in America.* New York: Facts on File.

Yellin, Emily. 2004. *Our Mothers' War: American Women at Home and at the Front during World War II.* New York: Free Press.

UNITED STATES, MARINE CORPS WOMEN'S RESERVE (MCWR)

The service of women in the U.S. Marines. Although 305 women marine reservists served during World War I, the Marine Corps remained an all-male service until World War II. Resistant to the inclusion of women, the Marine Corps traditionally contended that it had a lower ca-

pacity than other services to absorb women because of its relatively high ratio of combat troops to support troops and that it considered women's presence as a threat to order and discipline among male soldiers.

On July 30, 1942, the navy bill, Public Law 689, authorized the establishment of both the Navy Women's Reserve and the Marine Corps Women's Reserve (MCWR). By February 13, 1943, Major Ruth Cheney Streeter—the wife of a prominent businessman, a pilot, a mother of four (including three sons in the service), and a leader for 20 years in New Jersey health and welfare work—had led the corps to attain its recruitment goal of over 18,000 women. Female reservists filled 87 percent of the enlisted jobs at Marine Corps headquarters during World War II and comprised one-half to two-thirds of the troops posted to many marine stations (Stremlow 1986, 101). They are credited with freeing the equivalent of one male marine division to fight.

World War II demobilization plans mandated dissolution of the MCWR by September 1946. The marines resisted momentum developing in other services to create permanent peacetime cadres of women in the military, claiming that women could fill too few positions in the postwar Marine Corps to justify the administrative costs. In a policy reversal, however, the Marine Corps commandant authorized the retention of a core group of women marines at headquarters assigned to clerical and administrative duty and created a postwar corps of reserves who could be called to active duty in the event of war or national emergency. These women remained the heart of the peacetime MCWR program until passage of the Women's Armed Services Integration Act of 1948, which established a permanent place for women in the U.S. armed forces.

At that time, faced with increased personnel needs and problems with the recruitment and retention of women, the Marine Corps gradually worked to improve women's status, utilization, acceptance, and integration. Three milestones provided impetus for women's increased presence: the war in Korea, the Women Marine Program Study Group of 1964, and the Ad-Hoc Committee on Increased Effectiveness of the Utilization of Women in the Marine Corps in 1973. By 1964, for example, women officers served in only 8 occupational fields, with about 70 percent in administrative billets. Only a handful were allowed to serve overseas, and most of those received assignment to Hawaii.

As a result of policy changes, 36 women marines served in South Vietnam during the Vietnam War, and by 1971, 9.3 percent, or 209 women, served overseas (Holm 1992, 217; Stremlow 1986, 87–88). In 1967 the marines further developed an expansion plan to bring the strength of the MCWR to 1 percent of the U.S. Marine Corps overall strength (2,750 women), with increased job and assignment opportunities and policy changes to improve enlistments and retention. In 1977 the corps dissolved gender-segregated, abbreviated 12-week basic training for women, and 22 female second lieutenants entered the 21-week basic course as members of Charlie Company (Stremlow 1986, 90). Separate command structures for women, historically administered by the director of women marines, transferred to other departments, leading to the abolishment of the directorship in 1977. In 1978 Margaret Brewer, the seventh and last director of women marines, became the first woman brigadier general in the Marine Corps, which was the last service to name a woman to an equivalent rank (Holm 1992, 278).

—Lee Ann Ghajar

See also Brewer, Lucy; Streeter, Ruth Cheney

References and Further Reading

Holm, Jeanne M. 1992. *Women in the Military: An Unfinished Revolution.* Rev. ed. Novato, CA: Presidio Press.
Stremlow, Mary V. 1986. *U.S. Marine Corps Women's Reserve: A History of the Women Marines, 1946–1977.* Washington, DC: U.S. Marine Corps, History and Museums Division Headquarters.

UNITED STATES, MILITARY SERVICE OF WOMEN IN WORLD WAR II

The direct contribution of women to the U.S. military during World War II. More than 350,000 women joined the U.S. armed services as auxiliaries and made significant contributions by functioning in more than 400 separate specialties during World War II, including not only work in the clerical fields but also service in logistical and technical fields (Meyer 1996, 76; Holm 1982). Women serving in the U.S. military during World War II replaced men who were then able to enter combat units.

Women have served in various capacities in every conflict in U.S. history. Most often, female nurses aided medics and doctors in military hospitals. This caregiving role represented a suitable and acceptable role for women to perform. Women in the United States struggled merely to gain basic civil rights, let alone the ability to serve in the military. Although they received the right to vote shortly after World War I, they were not truly emancipated, nor were they treated equally under the law. They had not gained parity with men in those jobs traditionally regarded as male. Men dominated the public, political, and economic spheres. Society expected males to be fathers, husbands, and protectors, with one specific male role being military service. Conversely, women occupied private, moral, and domestic spheres. Society expected them to be mothers, wives, and nurturers.

The U.S. military did allow several thousand women to join its ranks in World War I. Those women in uniform, however, were treated as auxiliaries and relegated to clerical work. They received neither equal rank nor equal pay. They served until the end of the conflict, after which they returned to civilian life. The U.S. military made no permanent place for women in its ranks. Women as regular soldiers, sailors, or marines went well beyond any socially acceptable gender roles.

As international tensions increased in the late 1930s, the U.S. military began laying plans for mobilization of men and material. Every resource could be and would be used in the coming conflict. By 1941 U.S. involvement in World War II seemed imminent. In April of that year, Representative Edith Nourse Rogers of Massachusetts introduced legislation to establish the Women's Army Auxiliary Corps (WAAC). Her bill was not passed until after the attack on Pearl Harbor. It was finally enacted in May 1942 with the caveats that the WAAC would only be 25,000 strong and that women serving in the WAAC would be separate from the regular military in terms of units, pay, status, and rank. Later in 1942 the U.S. Congress passed legislation making women part of reserves in both the U.S. Navy and Marine Corps. All branches of the military, as well as the U.S. Coast Guard, eventually added women to their rolls. Once called to active duty, they received parity with their male counterparts in pay, status, and rank.

The problematic juxtaposition of "soldier" and "women" emerged as the key issue in the first of year of World War II and would remain important throughout the conflict. How could women be allowed to serve in the masculine environment of the U.S. military yet still be able to maintain their acceptable feminine roles in society? Put more simply, how could women be soldiers? Many citizens, men and women alike, feared that making women into full-fledged soldiers would deprive them of their femininity. They might acquire masculine traits such as aggressiveness and assertiveness; these might even affect their sexual relations with men. Worse still, women in the military would be working in close proximity with one another and might even succumb to deviant sexual urges.

The massive personnel requirements of fighting a total war were a boon for women. Millions left the domestic sphere and entered the workforce. Personnel shortages also spurred the U.S. military to expand the number of women in uniform to more than 350,000 during the next 4 years. Women flocked to military recruiting stations for many reasons. The publicity and recruitment efforts appealed to their senses of patriotism, adventure, and sacrifice. A famous advertising quote, "Free a Man to Fight," attracted thousands of women to the military; many more women were turned away than accepted. They agreed to serve during the conflict and for 6 months after its end. Those who did join typically possessed much greater levels of experience and education than their male counterparts of similar rank. Many came from business, educational, and government backgrounds.

The commanders of each service's female component stand as examples of highly qualified individuals. All walked away from lucrative and rewarding careers to put on uniforms in 1942. Oveta Culp Hobby resigned as vice president of the *Houston Post* to become director of the WAAC, later renamed the Women's Army Corps (WAC). Mildred Helen McAfee left the presidency of Wellesley College in Massachusetts to lead the Women Accepted for Voluntary Emergency Service (WAVES), the navy's female contingent. Ruth Cheney Streeter held several positions in health and welfare services during the 1920s and 1930s before becoming director of Marine Corps Women's Reserve (MCWR). Dorothy C. Stratton served as dean of women and professor of psychology at Purdue University before entering the naval reserve and eventually leading the women reserves in the U.S. Coast Guard, known as SPARs (an acronym derived from the this service's motto, *Semper Paratus*—Always Ready). All these women rose to the rank of captain or colonel by the close of World War II.

The U.S. Army, with the personal support of Chief of Staff General George C. Marshall, formed the first units of females as part of the WAAC. Originally an auxiliary of 25,000 women, WAAC members did not receive recognized military rank, status, or privilege. They shouldered only clerical tasks at first. As the war lasted longer, however, the WAAC was renamed the Women's Army Corps in September 1943 and was given commensurate military recognition. New recruits went to training centers all over the nation, including Florida, Massachusetts, and Louisiana. Following boot camp, they found themselves stationed throughout the continental United States working in hundreds of military occupational specialties (MOS). Many of these were traditionally male jobs. The WAC eventually grew to 150,000 women by the conflict's end, of which some 16,000 served overseas in North Africa, Europe, and the Pacific (Holm 1992, 94, 98).

The U.S. Navy and the U.S. Marine Corps followed the army's lead in establishing their own women's components. The naval reserve was the conduit through which female recruits for these units passed. They went to Hunter College in New York City or Mount Holyoke College and Smith College in Massachusetts for their training. The women then either remained in the navy with the WAVES or transferred to the Marine Corps with the MCWR. The WAVES eventually expanded to 86,000 women by war's end. The Marine Corps included some 18,000 women marines (Holm 1992, 98).

The U.S. Coast Guard added its own female element in the SPARs. Most of the 12,000 SPARs stayed on the home front, where they performed clerical or support jobs. Others, however, moved into specialties that allowed them to do traditionally male work, and some did spend time overseas (Holm 1992, 98).

Women also flew military aircraft and worked on flight lines with the U.S. Army's Women in the Air Force (WAF), commanded by Elizabeth Bandel, or with the civilian Women Airforce Service Pilots (WASPs), headed by Jacqueline Cochran. Some 40,000 women in the WAF and another 1,000 WASPs ferried military aircraft across the continental United States (Holm 1992, 64). Beyond the glamorous life of a pilot, women in the WAF acquired skills in aircraft maintenance, air traffic control, and meteorology.

Women in every service faced varying levels of suspicion, discrimination, harassment, and abuse. They found themselves attempting to prove their worth as soldiers, while still maintaining their respectability as women. More often than not, male superiors and peers gradually discovered how competent and skilled the women soldiers, sailors, marines, and pilots were and eventually came to appreciate their contributions. The women not only performed clerical tasks such as stenography or office management but also worked in skilled and technical areas such as parachute rigging, engine maintenance, gunnery instruction, or radio operation. In all, women in the military performed more than 400 specialties. None of these was combat-related, though a few military women did come under enemy fire or were killed by enemy attacks.

Caucasian women faced many obstacles in the military because of their gender. African American women, however, faced still more because of race. Blacks were not accorded equal treatment in civilian society, and the situation in the military was no different. Approximately 4,000 highly qualified and patriotic "colored" or "Negro" women—as they were termed during World War II—found themselves in segregated WAAC units performing menial tasks such as housekeeping (Holm 1992, 78). Only late in the conflict did the other services allow African American women into their ranks.

Harassment emerged as one of the most difficult challenges for women in uniform. They could become objects of sexual advances and harassment from their counterparts or superiors. Smear campaigns against women erupted during World War II; these portrayed some servicewomen as lesbians and others as whores. Many in the United States worried that unfeminine qualities would be developed among these women and that this would cause a breakdown in the gender divisions within society as a whole. Exact numbers of lesbians in the military during World War II are not available. The suspicions and fears, however, proved to be unwarranted. Contrary to the allegations of the smear campaigns, the overwhelming majority of women in the army, navy, marines, and coast guard maintained high moral standards in their dress and conduct. They constructed their identities as women first and as soldiers second; this represented a means of separating the two antithetical gender roles. Any accusations of lesbianism or deviant behavior were handled quickly and quietly within the given service. The overwhelming majority of women in uniform, regardless of their sexual orientation, acquitted themselves with honor while on duty.

Harassment could also become physical in the form of rape: 971 convictions for sexual assault were handed down during World War II. Most of these occurred after the conflict ended when U.S. servicemen were in occupation units (Meyer 1996, 142). Unless the charge was made against an African American man, obtaining justice in a rape case proved almost impossible because sexual assault could be depicted as the victim's fault or otherwise trivialized as normal sexual intercourse. The rules and the culture protected the accused, rather than the accuser.

Despite the challenges, women in the U.S. military played a significant role in the nation's victorious war effort. According to Captain Winifred Quick Collins, a high-ranking officer in the WAVES during World War II, "Women could no longer be look upon as merely 'replacements.' The war years proved that the work they had done contributed much to the overall efficiency of the service. . . . Women demonstrated their usefulness, patience, and thoroughness by performing many duties equal to or better than the men had done" (Collins 1997, 90). Approximately 400,000 women, including nurses, served in the U.S. military. Among those, 470 deaths occurred, including 50 killed in action or by enemy gunfire. More than 1,600 military women received medals for meritorious service (Womensmemorial.org 2004).

When World War II ended, most servicewomen, like their male counterparts in the military, returned to their civilian lives. Nevertheless, their experiences and accomplishments in the war left lasting impressions on them. Some went back to work in business or government; others resumed their domestic roles as mothers and wives. A small number of women remained

on duty in the U.S. military; they received official recognition with passage of the Women's Service Integration Act in 1948. Since being recognized in this official way, women have worked for more equity and equality within the armed services.

—David J. Ulbrich

See also Cochran, Jacqueline; Eskimo Scouts; Hobby, Oveta Culp; Nurses, U.S. Army Nurse Corps in World War II; Streeter, Ruth Cheney; United States, Marine Corps Women's Reserve; United States, Navy Women's Reserve; United States, Women Airforce Service Pilots; United States, Women Reserves in the Coast Guard; United States, Women's Army Auxiliary Corps; United States, Women's Auxiliary Ferrying Squadron

References and Further Reading

Campbell, D'Ann. 1993. Women in Combat: The World War II Experience in the United States, Great Britain, Germany, and the Soviet Union. *Journal of Military History* 57 (April):301–323.

Collins, Winifred Quick, with Herbert M. Levine. 1997. *More Than a Uniform: A Navy Woman in a Navy Man's World.* Denton: University of North Texas.

Holm, Jeanne. 1992. *Women in the Military: An Unfinished Revolution.* Novato, CA: Presidio Press.

Litoff, Judy Barrett, and David C. Smith. 1994. *We're in This War, Too: World War II Letters from American Women in Uniform.* New York: Oxford University.

Meid, Pat. 1968. *Marine Corps Women's Reserve in World War II.* Washington, DC: U.S. Marine Corps, Historical Branch, G-3 Division.

Meyer, Leisa D. 1996. *Creating G.I. Jane: Sexuality and Power in the Women's Army Corps in World War II.* New York: Columbia University.

Treadwell. Mattie E. 1954. *U.S. Army in World War II: Special Studies—The Women's Army Corps.* Washington, DC: Department of the Army, Office of the Chief of Military History.

Womensmemorial.org. "Women in the United States Military." http://www.womensmemorial .org/historyandcollections/about.html (accessed Oct 31, 2004).

UNITED STATES, NAVY WOMEN'S RESERVE (WAVES)

Service of U.S. women in the navy reserve. On July 30, 1942, Public Law 689 authorized the Women's Reserve of the Navy for the duration of World War II and six months thereafter. The law took effect after seven months of disagreement between the navy, the executive branch, and the Congress over whether women should serve in the navy or with the service as auxiliaries. Called WAVES (Women Accepted for Volunteer Emergency Service), women in this unit received equal pay for equal rank as full members of the naval reserve. The law limited, however, the number of positions open to them in given ranks and gave women officers authority only over other women reservists. Mildred McAfee, president of Wellesley College and a liberal proponent of the rights and responsibilities of women, became the first WAVES director.

The navy originally intended that WAVES would fill administrative and clerical jobs in order to free men for duty at sea. As the war escalated and warfare became increasingly sophisticated, the navy continued to readjust perceptions about the capabilities of women, opening increasingly specialized positions to them in order to meet personnel needs. WAVES trained and worked in meteorology, aeronautical engineering, astronomy, radar operations and maintenance, ship design, navigation, intelligence, and other developing fields. By war's end, WAVES not only held jobs previously occupied by navy men but also performed hundreds of jobs that had not existed when the war began.

Navy officials realized that "lack of sufficient women service personnel [was] preventing the transfer of able-bodied males from billets which could be filled by women to duties in the combat areas" (Ebbert and Hall 1999, 97). Chafing at restrictions confining WAVES to duty in the contiguous United States, the navy petitioned Congress to remove geographic limitations. In response, Congress passed Public Law 441 in 1944, allowing WAVES to volunteer for assignment to Hawaii, Alaska, the Caribbean, and Panama.

By 1945, 86,000 women served as WAVES, and by war's end, women constituted roughly 2 percent of the navy. In the navy headquarters, however, 55 percent of the uniformed personnel were WAVES, and at Radio Washington—the nerve center of the navy's entire communications system—WAVES filled 75 percent of the positions. In 1945 the navy designated 80 women officers as naval air navigators and ordered 2 women officers to serve at the all-male U.S. Naval Academy. Between December 31, 1941, and August 31, 1945, 7 women officers and 62 enlisted women died while on active duty (Holm 1998, 73–74).

Although WAVES were authorized for demobilization six months after the end of World War II, the navy recognized a continuing need for women's services and joined with the U.S. Army in the struggle to secure a permanent place in peacetime for its women. In 1948 Public Law 625, the Women's Armed Services Integration Act, created permanent status for women in regular and reserve components of the armed forces and delineated the limitations and terms of their service. Although the act officially abolished the WAVES, the acronym continued in popular and official usage by both men and women until the early 1970s, when the navy eliminated a separate women's representative system and the office of assistant chief of personnel for women (Ebbert and Hall 1999, 125).

—*Lee Ann Ghajar*

See also United States, Military Service of Women in World War II

References and Further Reading

Ebbert, Jean, and Marie-Beth Hall. 1999. *Crossed Currents: Navy Women in a Century of Change.* Dulles, VA: Brassey's.

Holm, Jeanne M., and Judith Bellafaire, eds. 1998. *In Defense of a Nation: Servicewomen in World War II.* Arlington, VA: Vandamere Press.

United States, Opposition to U.S. Entry into World War II by Right-Wing American Women

U.S. isolationists at the time of World War II. With the outbreak of World War II in September 1939, tens of thousands of U.S. women of varying political stripes rushed to join the antiwar organizations that were sprouting throughout the country. Some female leaders on the political right took advantage of the antiwar sentiment to recruit women into their organizations, which were often referred to as mother's groups. Leaders such as Elizabeth Dilling, Catherine Curtis, Lyrl Clark Van Hyning, and Frances Sherrill drew women into their organizations by appealing to their patriotism and to their fears of losing loved ones in a foreign war. The Sherrill-led National Legion of Mothers of America, for example, established a "Mother's Creed" soon after the legion's founding in Los Angeles in October 1939. Prospective members pledged to aid the organization in its opposition to the sending of U.S. troops to fight in foreign lands, to support an active national defense program, and to oppose "subversive groups, whose object [was] the destruction of the American form of government" (Benowitz 2002, 139).

The legion's pledge was in keeping with the isolationist impulse of the U.S. people during the interwar years. Women signing the pledge felt both patriotic and confident that they were doing their best to save the lives of U.S. men. Time would reveal that Sherrill and others among the group's hierarchy broadly defined subversive groups to include almost anyone who did not agree with them. Initially, the legion attracted and accepted women of varied religious and ethnic backgrounds, and leaders claimed that 1 million members had signed the pledge during the organization's first month. Although the numbers were greatly exaggerated, with the help of William Randolph Hearst's publishing firm, thousands of women throughout the nation enthusiastically joined local chapters.

Legion membership began to decline by the summer of 1940. A power struggle had erupted within the organization in the spring, and by June 1940 some of the leaders who did not agree with Sherrill's prejudices against Jews and immigrants and her antipathy toward the Franklin Roosevelt administration were being pushed out of the group. Soon other leaders and some members-at-large began resigning due to their suspicions that the remaining legion officers were fascist sympathizers. When the turmoil subsided, the legion was a predominantly right-wing extremist organization.

On the East Coast Catherine Curtis, who was for a time associated with the legion, founded the Women's National Committee to Keep US Out of War in the fall of 1939. Curtis sometimes networked with other right-wing leaders, including Elizabeth Dilling, who headed the Chicago-based Patriotic Research Bureau, and Lyrl Clark Van Hyning, leader of We, the Mothers Mobilize for America, also based in Chicago. These women shared a hatred for the Roosevelt administration, Jews, Communists, and, to a lesser extent, the British. They accused these groups of conspiring to push the United States into war and urged their followers to help them fight this "conspiracy."

Although personal arguments would occasionally lead to rifts in the leaders' relationships, their antiwar groups would sometimes rally together around a cause. The congressional debate over the Lend-Lease bill in February 1941, which proposed that the United States lease supplies to money-strapped Britain, led to the Mothers' Crusade, a march on Washington by right-wing women's groups. Believing that Lend-Lease was but another step toward U.S. entry into the war, approximately 200 women paraded and protested on Capitol Hill. The bill's passage sent the women home angry in their defeat.

With the bombing of Pearl Harbor on December 7, 1941, the National Legion of Mothers of America disbanded, but other groups, including the Patriotic Research Bureau and We, the Mothers Mobilize for America, continued to protest the war. Only those women aligned with the extreme right remained in these organizations. Most right-wing U.S. women joined their fellow citizens in support of their country's efforts to defeat the Axis powers in World War II.

—*June Melby Benowitz*

See also Dilling, Elizabeth; National Legion of Mothers of America

References and Further Reading:

Benowitz, June Melby. 2002. *Days of Discontent: American Women and Right-Wing Politics, 1933–1945.* DeKalb: Northern Illinois University.

Jeansonne, Glen. 1996. *Women of the Far Right: The Mothers' Movement and World War II.* Chicago: University of Chicago.

UNITED STATES, WOMEN AIRFORCE SERVICE PILOTS (WASP)

Women pilots who flew military aircraft for the U.S. government during World War II. The Women Airforce Service Pilots (WASP) program was created on July 5, 1943. It later merged the Women's Auxiliary Ferrying Squadron (WAFS) and the Women's Flying Training Detachment (WFTD).

Jacqueline Cochran, director of women pilots, had specific standards for WASP applicants: they had to undergo a personal interview and a thorough military physical, meet height and age requirements, and have at least 35 hours of flight time. WASP training at Avenger Field near

Women's Airforce Service pilots, assigned to the Ferrying Division. (Bettmann/Corbis)

"WOMEN CAN FLY AS WELL AS MEN"

"Frankly, I didn't know in 1941 whether a slip of a young girl could fight the controls of a B-17 in the heavy weather they would naturally encounter in operational flying. Those of us who had been flying for twenty or thirty years knew that flying an airplane was something you do not learn overnight. But, Miss [Jacqueline] Cochran said that carefully selected young women could be trained to fly our combat-type planes. . . . Well, now in 1944, more than two years since WASP first started flying with the Air Forces, we can come to only one conclusion—the entire operation has been a success. [I]t is on the record that women can fly as well as men. . . . Certainly we haven't been able to build an airplane you can't handle. From AT-6's to B-29's, you have flown them around like veterans."

—General Henry H. "Hap" Arnold,
commander of the Army Air Forces and founder of the WASP program,
at the graduation ceremony of the last WASP class on December 7, 1944.
"Hap Arnold," Wasp on the Web.
http://www.wasp-wwii.org/news/press/arnold_press1.htm
(accessed February 10, 2006).

Sweetwater, Texas, lasted 5 months for each class of approximately 100 women. New classes began every 4 to 6 weeks. The flying portion of the training consisted of three phases: primary, basic (during which the women learned instrument flying), and advanced. WASP trainees also attended an extensive ground school, with classes in Morse code, navigation, simulated flight, aeronautics, math, physics, engine maintenance, and meteorology. Aviation Enterprises, Inc., a civilian company with a government contract, provided flight and ground school instructors as well as other staff needed to run the base. Chief Establishment Officer Leoti Deaton, along with 6 associate officers, carried out Cochran's orders. Military staff at Avenger Field comprised a commander, an adjutant, 9 officers in charge of giving army flight checks, 2 flight surgeons, and a physical director.

On the flight line, WASP trainees wore khaki zip-up GI jumpsuits nicknamed zoot suits. The women purchased their own dress uniforms, consisting of khaki pants, a white blouse, and an overseas cap. In April 1944 the WASP received official uniforms (in "Santiago blue," designed by Bergdorf-Goodman).

More than 25,000 women applied to join the WASPs. Of the 1,830 who were accepted, 1,074 got their wings. Following graduation, WASPs were sent to air bases around the country to ferry planes from factories to bases; to tow targets for ground-to-air and air-to-air gunnery training; to fly radar, strafing, and smoke-screen missions; to fly remote-control drone airplanes; and to test new aircraft and equipment. WASPs successfully flew aircraft that some male pilots refused to fly, such as the B-26 and B-29.

Many citizens were puzzled about the WASP program. Although detailed reports proved that many of the negative rumors and stereotypes about the women pilots were false, legislation designed to commission the WASP into the regular Army Air Force failed to pass Congress. On June 26, 1944, General Henry "Hap" Arnold announced that the WASP training program would be discontinued.

The last class of WASPs graduated on December 7, 1944; the program was officially disbanded on December 20, with 916 WASPs still on active duty. Thirty-eight WASPs died during the course of the program, 11 during training. In all, the WASPs flew over 60 million miles in almost every type of plane the military used. WASPs were not eligible for the GI Bill or other military benefits because they were considered civilian employees. Congress finally granted the WASPs military status in 1977.

—*Rebekah Crowe*

See also Cochran, Jacqueline

References and Further Reading

Douglas, Deborah G. 1990. *United States Women in Aviation: 1940–1985*. Smithsonian Studies in Air and Space no. 7. Washington, DC: Smithsonian Institution.

Merryman, Molly. 1998. *Clipped Wings: The Rise and Fall of the Women Airforce Service Pilots (WASPs) of World War II*. New York: New York University.

UNITED STATES, WOMEN RESERVES IN THE COAST GUARD (KNOWN AS SPARs)

Service of American women in the U.S. Coast Guard reserve force. On November 23, 1942, Public Law 773 established the Women's Reserve of the U.S. Coast Guard and authorized these women to serve ashore at stateside bases for the duration of World War II in order to free men for sea duty. The unit was nicknamed SPARs, an acronym drawn from the coast guard motto, *Semper Paratus*—Always Ready. The first 15 officers and 153 enlisted women withdrew from service in the U.S. Navy and entered the SPARs to form the nucleus of the new unit. Between 1942 and 1946 over 11,000 women volunteered for service (Holm 1998, 98).

In 1942 the duty and rank of women reservists was limited: lieutenant commander was the highest authorized rank, reserved for the director of the program, and no more than 18 women could serve as lieutenants. Dorothy Stratton, dean of women and professor of psy-

chology at Purdue University and the first commanding officer of the SPARs, recalled in 1992, " I had no command authority. All I had was the power of persuasion" (Thomson 1992, 1). In 1943 Congress elevated the SPAR director to the rank of captain.

Early SPAR volunteers trained at navy schools. By 1943, as the numbers of recruits grew, the coast guard leased the Palm Beach Biltmore Hotel in Florida for the duration of the war, transforming the luxury hotel into a boot camp, processing more than 7,000 enlisted women. SPAR officers became the first women to attend a military academy; beginning in 1943, the coast guard provided officer training for more than 700 women at the Coast Guard Academy in New London, Connecticut.

The first SPARs filled shore billets in every coast guard district of the continental United States. In late 1944 Congress expanded SPAR duty stations to include service in Alaska and Hawaii. Thirty-seven percent of SPAR officers held general-duty assignments, including administrative and supervisory work, and the majority of enlisted SPARs were assigned to clerical duties. Many, however, worked in specialized fields—for example, as chaplain's assistants, boatswain's mates, coxswains, radiomen, ship's cooks, vehicle drivers, and pharmacist's mates. The coast guard opened limited slots in aviation to women during World War II: 18 women became parachute riggers; 22 operated Link trainers (ground aviation trainers developed by Edward Link); and 12 were air-traffic control tower operators.

A small group of SPARs worked on one of the most highly classified and little publicized activities of the war effort: Long Range Aid to Navigation (LORAN), a newly developed system that enabled air- and surface-craft navigators to fix positions under all weather conditions. One officer and 11 enlisted SPARs selected for this classified duty trained at the Naval Training School at the Massachusetts Institute of Technology. Their work required standing twenty-four-hour watches, taking and recording radio signal measurements at two-minute intervals. The signals emanated from shore-based stations and were picked up by receiver–indicators installed on ships and planes. In 1943 the LORAN station at Chatham, Massachusetts, became the only all-woman station of its kind in the world (Holm 1998, 108).

By July 1947 SPARs were demobilized. However, during the Korean War 40 SPAR officers and enlisted women were recalled to active duty, and approximately 24 remained on extended active duty until retirement. Additionally, approximately 200 women volunteered to return to the service on extended active duty in the 1950s, and most stayed until retirement (Thomson 1992, 20).

—Lee Ann Ghajar

See also United States, Military Service of Women in World War II

References and Further Reading

Holm, Jeanne M., and Judith Bellafaire, eds. 1998. *In Defense of a Nation: Servicewomen in World War II.* Arlington, VA: Vandamere.

Thomson, Robin J. 1992. *The Coast Guard and the Women's Reserve in World War II.* Washington, DC: Coast Guard Historian's Office.

UNITED STATES, WOMEN'S ARMY AUXILIARY CORPS (WAAC)

Noncombat women's arm of the U.S. Army during World War II. The Women's Army Auxiliary Corps (WAAC) was established by the U.S. Congress on May 14, 1942, authorizing the army to enroll officers and enlisted women for noncombatant service. On May 16, 1942, Oveta Culp Hobby took the oath of office as director of the WAAC, with the relative rank of colonel. The legislation limited the corps as an auxiliary to the army rather than an integral part of it. The lack of full military status proved confusing, especially when the women began to serve overseas in December 1942 in North Africa but were ineligible to receive veterans' benefits. Auxiliary status was dropped when President Franklin D. Roosevelt signed legislation on July 1, 1943, to establish the Women's Army Corps (WAC) as an integral part of the wartime army.

Congresswoman Edith Nourse Rogers, a Republican from Massachusetts, initially introduced a bill in May 1941 to establish an all-volunteer women's corps to serve with the U.S. Army. General George C. Marshall, army chief of staff, encouraged and vigorously supported efforts to authorize women's participation in the army, and he selected Oveta Culp Hobby as the first director of the women's corps. Colonel Don C. Faith commanded the first WAAC training center, established at Fort Des Moines, Iowa, and on July 20, 1942, 440 women reported there to attend the 6-week WAAC Officer Candidate School. Ninety percent of the women in the first officer class had college training, and some had earned advanced degrees; many had been teachers. The average age of the officer candidates was 30; 99 percent had been employed. "You have a debt and a date," Director Hobby said in her address to the first officer candidate class several days later, "a debt to democracy, a date with destiny. . . . On your shoulders will rest the military reputation and the civilian recognition of this Corps" (Treadwell 1954; 58–59, 66).

Meanwhile, enlisted women attended the 4-week basic training course. The average age of the enlisted women was 24; over 60 percent had graduated from high school, and many had some college training. The WAAC basic and officer courses corresponded with courses for men except for the omission of combat subjects. The trainees drilled without weapons. The women studied military customs and decorum, army organization, first aid, supply, map reading, and defense against chemical and air attacks. They drilled and participated in parades and stood guard duty. Officer candidates also received training in WAAC company administration, leadership, voice and command, court-martial procedures, and mess management (Morden 1990, 7–8).

WAAC recruiting surpassed its initial goals, and by June 1943 WAAC strength reached 60,000 (including 5,000 officers) (Treadwell 1954, 765). Additional WAAC training centers were opened at Daytona Beach, Florida; Fort Oglethorpe, Georgia; Fort Devens, Massachusetts; and the combined Camps Polk and Ruston in Louisiana.

—*Sharon Ritenour Stevens*

See also Hobby, Oveta Culp

References and Further Reading

Morden, Bettie J. 1990. *The Women's Army Corps, 1945–1978.* Washington, DC: U.S. Government Printing Office.

Treadwell, Mattie E. 1954. *The Women's Army Corps.* United States Army in World War II Series. Washington, DC: U.S. Government Printing Office.

UNITED STATES, WOMEN'S AUXILIARY FERRYING SQUADRON (WAFS)

First group of women pilots to fly military aircraft for the U.S. government. In early 1940 Nancy Harkness Love, an experienced pilot, offered to recruit qualified female pilots for the recently created Ferrying Command Division of the Army Air Forces and was asked to compile a list of all U.S. women with commercial flight ratings. Love was not allowed to begin recruiting the pilots she had identified because of competition from Jacqueline Cochran, an award-winning aviatrix who also wanted to head a program of women pilots. Love and Cochran continued to have a strained relationship. In June 1942 Love again submitted her proposal for female pilots to serve as a part of the Air Transport Command's Ferrying Division. After a series of compromises, the revived Women's Auxiliary Ferrying Squadron (WAFS) proposal was forwarded to General Henry H. (Hap) Arnold on September 3, 1942. A week later Secretary of War Henry Stimson announced the creation of the WAFS, with Love as its director.

The original 27 WAFS pilots were hand-picked by Love, who insisted on higher standards for her group than the Army Air Forces used for men being recruited at the same time: the women had to be high school graduates between 21 and 35 years of age with 500 hours of flight time (50 of those within the preceding 12 months); have a Civil Aeronautics Administration 200-horsepower aircraft rating; and provide two letters of recommendation. Love had no intention of her pilots becoming part of the military. Her subordinates would work as civilian employees and only ferry small trainer and liaison-type airplanes. The women, as civilian employees, were paid $250 a month. The WAFS, after a brief orientation consisting of flight training and ground school, began ferrying planes on October 20, 1942. Love's pilots had to pay for their own uniforms, which consisted of an open-collared light gray shirt, slacks, and a gray-green belted jacket. Originally stationed at New Castle Army Air Force Base in Wilmington, Delaware, by February 1943 the WAFS were dispersed to Love Field in Dallas, Texas; to Romulus Field in Michigan; and to Long Beach, California. Still more bases were added later.

In August 1943 the WAFS were put under the control of Cochran, recently appointed director of women pilots, as part of a combined program called the Women Airforce Service Pilots (WASP). Love remained the head of the WAFS section of the WASP. By June 1944 all WASPs assigned to the WAFS section transferred back to the training command except for 123 women qualified to fly pursuit aircraft. Because all original 27 WAFS had commercial ratings and did not undergo the same military-style training as most of the WASPs, many of them never considered themselves WASPs.

—*Rebekah Crowe*

See also Cochran, Jacqueline; United States, Women Airforce Service Pilots; United States, Women's Auxiliary Ferrying Squadron

References and Further Reading

Douglas, Deborah G. 1990. *United States Women in Aviation: 1940–1985.* Smithsonian Studies in Air and Space no. 7. Washington, DC: Smithsonian Institution Press.

Keil, Sally Van Wagenen. 1979. *Those Wonderful Women in Their Flying Machines.* New York: Rawson, Wade.

UNITED STATES, WOMEN'S FLYING TRAINING DETACHMENT (WFTD)

First U.S. program to train women to fly military aircraft. On July 30, 1941, aviatrix Jacqueline Cochran submitted a proposal to General Henry (Hap) Arnold to organize a division of women pilots to assist the Army Air Forces by ferrying airplanes, but Arnold refused her idea. In early September 1942 Cochran learned that Nancy Harkness Love, another prominent pilot, was recruiting female pilots to ferry airplanes for the U.S. government. Cochran immediately contacted General Arnold, and on September 15, 1942, Cochran received permission to direct a training program for female pilots. This program would prepare the pilots to serve in the Women's Auxiliary Ferrying Squadron (WAFS) under Love.

Cochran enlisted the help of General Barton Kyle Yount, head of the Flying Training Command in Fort Worth, Texas, to help her find a location for the Women's Flying Training Detachment (WFTD). On November 3, 1942, Yount and Cochran picked Aviation Enterprises at Howard Hughes Field in Houston, Texas, as home to the WFTD, then part of the 319th Army Air Forces Flying Training Detachment (AAFFTD). Leoti Deaton, a Fort Worth Red Cross administrator and swimming instructor, became the WFTD staff executive.

The first class of 50 WFTD trainees arrived in Houston in October 1942. For the first month the women in this top-secret program lived in private homes and were transported to and from the base in white buses decorated with red-and-white striped awnings and edelweiss. The WFTD spent each day in flight training, ground school, and an hour or so of physical training, including learning to march. Training eventually lasted 30 weeks, with 210 hours of aerial instruction and 560 hours of ground school.

The Aviation Enterprises hangar had neither bathrooms nor a dining hall, so the WFTD had to march half a mile to the Houston Municipal Airport Terminal for their meals. As no uniforms were provided to the women during the first month of training, the only dress requirement on the flight line was a hairnet. By mid-December, however, khaki coveralls in men's sizes 40 to 46 were provided; the women called them zoot-suits. In late March 1943 Cochran announced that WFTD training would move to Avenger Field near Sweetwater, Texas. Four classes of WFTD consisting of 230 women received at least part of their training in Houston.

On April 5, 1943, Class 43-W-4 flew 26 WFTD trainer aircraft to Sweetwater as part of their flight instruction and continued their training there. The first class of 23 Woofteds, as the WFTD women referred to themselves, graduated in April 1943 and became part of the Women Auxiliary Ferrying Squadron. At graduation the women received bombardiers' "sweetheart" wings modified to include a shield and stylized ribbon engraved with the squadron and class numbers. Over 300 additional WFTD pilots became WAFS by the end of 1943. In July 1943 the WFTD merged with the WAFS to form the Women Airforce Service Pilots (WASP).

—*Rebekah Crowe*

See also Cochran, Jacqueline; United States, Women Airforce Service Pilots

References and Further Reading

Douglas, Deborah G. 1990. *United States Women in Aviation: 1940–1985*. Smithsonian Studies in Air and Space no. 7. Washington, DC: Smithsonian Institution Press.

Keil, Sally Van Wagenen. 1979. *Those Wonderful Women in Their Flying Machines*. New York: Rawson, Wade.

V

Van Devanter (Buckley), Lynda (1947–2002)

Vietnam combat nurse, founder and director of the Vietnam Veterans of America's Women's Project, and author of first autobiography by a female Vietnam veteran. Lynda Van Devanter was born into a politically conservative, Catholic family in 1947. She grew up in Arlington, Virginia, before she went on to nursing school in Baltimore. Shortly after her enlistment in the Army Nurse Corps in October 1968, she volunteered for deployment to Vietnam. From June 8, 1969, to June 7, 1970, she served consecutively with the 71st Evacuation Hospital and the 67th Evacuation Hospital as a nurse in the operating room. Her initial patriotism and Kennedy-inspired idealism quickly faded in the light of her experiences in Vietnam. As her tour of duty progressed, she became increasingly disillusioned, bitter, and alienated from her former values.

After her return to the United States and her honorable discharge from the army, she initially continued to work as a nurse in civilian hospitals. She was, however, increasingly affected by posttraumatic stress disorder, a psychological illness resulting from her war experiences, and she was finally forced to give up nursing. After a time of drug abuse, unemployment, intense psychological problems, and unsuccessful counsel-

ing, she got in touch with the Vietnam Veterans of America (VVA). Armed with a bachelor's degree in psychology from Antioch University, Van Devanter became the founding executive director of the VVA's Women's Project, which she headed from 1979 to 1984, and in the 1980s she married Tom Buckley. During her own therapy she began to write about her Vietnam experiences and finally published her autobiography, *Home before Morning: The True Story of an Army Nurse in Vietnam*, in 1983. It was the first autobiographical account of a female Vietnam veteran. The book reached a wide audience and encouraged many female veterans to start dealing with their own wartime memories. The book, however, was not undisputed among women veterans. Some former nurses accused Van Devanter of distorting her experiences for her own political goals; others defended her descriptions. Nevertheless, the publication of *Home before Morning* marked an important step toward the public recognition of female Vietnam veterans.

Even after her resignation as director of VVA's Women's Project, Van Devanter continued to lecture and write for numerous magazines and newspapers. During the Gulf War she also coedited a collection of writings by women veterans called *Visions of War, Dreams of Peace* (1991). For years Van Devanter suffered from several illnesses that were attributed to chemical exposure during the war. Nevertheless, she continued her work as long as possible. Lynda Van Devanter died at the age of fifty-five on November 15, 2002, from systemic collagen vascular disease, an illness most probably resulting from her exposure to poisonous chemical substances during the Vietnam War.

—Petra Feld

See also Vietnam, U.S. Women Soldiers in

References and Further Reading

Bates, Milton J. 1996. *Wars We Took to Vietnam: Cultural Conflict and Storytelling.* Berkeley: University of California.

Van Devanter, Lynda. 2001. *Home before Morning: The Story of an Army Nurse in Vietnam.* Amherst: University of Massachusetts.

VAN KLEECK, MARY
(1883–1972)

Industrial expert and social reformer who served as director of the U.S. Department of Labor's Women in Industry Service from 1917 through 1919. A graduate of Smith College, Mary van Kleeck became industrial studies director of the philanthropic Russell Sage Foundation in 1911. In addition, she joined the burgeoning social justice feminist movement, which used women's labor legislation as an opening wedge for the inclusion of all workers under the state's protection. Van Kleeck's pioneering studies on women bookbinders and artificial flowermakers in the United States established her national reputation as an industrial investigator. She became director of the Women in Industry Service after the United States entered World War I in April 1917.

Established by President Woodrow Wilson to both motivate women's participation in wartime industrial work and to establish labor standards for working women, the Women in Industry Service first concentrated on mobilizing women to replace the 4 million men entering military service. By early 1918 van Kleeck began promoting gender equality within the U.S. industrial workforce, a result of her concern that women workers' weekly salaries remained at most three-fourths the compensation paid to their male counterparts.

The Women in Industry Service's efforts, however, encountered indifference and even opposition from federal government officials. The National War Labor Board, which oversaw capital-labor relations, theoretically endorsed equal pay for men and women but in reality ignored van Kleeck's recommendations. In addition, during a special conference on working women held in October 1918, U.S. Secretary of Labor William Wilson refused to make equal pay a top priority. Thus gender wage inequality continued throughout the war.

Even so, by the time she left Washington, D.C., in the summer of 1919, van Kleeck had accomplished two important goals during her directorship of the Women in Industry Service. First, she successfully lobbied Congress to establish a permanent Women's Bureau in the U.S. Department of Labor and briefly served as its first director. Second, van Kleeck developed the idea of "industrial citizenship," which emphasized the continued improvement of both productivity and working conditions in the industrialized United States. Although postwar labor chaos and resurgent conservatism ended hopes of continuing the progress made during World War I, from 1927 through 1933 van Kleeck helped promote a successful hours-and-wages agenda for working women in New York. These advances established important precedents for the New Deal.

—John Thomas McGuire

See also United States, Home Front during World War I; United States, Home Front during World War II

References and Further Reading

Conner, Valerie Jean. 1983. *National War Labor Board: Stability, Social Justice, and the Voluntary State in World War I.* Chapel Hill: University of North Carolina.

McGuire, John Thomas. 2004. From the Courthouses to the State Legislatures: Social Justice Feminism, Labor Legislation, and the 1920s. *Labor History* 45, no. 2 (May):225–246.

VAN LEW, ELIZABETH LOUISE (1818–1900)

Union spy during the American Civil War. Elizabeth Van Lew was a crucial source of information for the Union army during the War between the States. Born October 15, 1818, Van Lew was the daughter of a prosperous hardware merchant, originally from Long Island, and his Philadelphian wife. Sent to a girls' school in Philadelphia, Van Lew absorbed abolitionist principles that guided her life, even after she returned to Richmond, Virginia, and acted as a popular society hostess in the family's mansion. In protest against the secession of Virginia, Van Lew donned mourning clothes, manumitted the family's slaves, and used her personal fortune to free many of their relatives. When prisoners began arriving from the Battle of Bull Run, she demanded access to them and provided many with crucial medical care, money, and food.

As Richmond citizens increasingly harassed Van Lew, she disguised her activities by becoming increasingly eccentric, wearing stained, ragged clothing and babbling nonsense as she walked throughout the city. Dismissed as "Crazy Betty," she was free to carry on with her Unionist plans, which by 1862 included acting as the head of an intelligence network, code-named Mr. Babcock, that relayed information from federal prisoners who made careful observations of Confederate strength and river traffic, as well as members of the German and Irish communities in Richmond. Van Lew even positioned a former servant as a waitress in the Confederate White House, from where the woman relayed sensitive material discussed at dinners and observed unguarded documents.

On February 9, 1864, 110 prisoners led by Colonel Thomas Rose tunneled out of Libby Prison in Richmond and sought help from Van Lew agents to return to Union lines. Van Lew concealed some of the men in a secret room in her house for 9 days while her agents smuggled out others. Fifty-nine successfully escaped to the north. Because of her intelligence information, especially from the Pennsylvania-born superintendent of the local railroad, Generals Ulysses S. Grant, George Meade, and Benjamin Butler had extensive knowledge of troop movements and Richmond's defenses. Van Lew's continued protests regarding the condition of federal prisoners resulted in the Kilpatrick-Dahlgren raid of February 6, 1864, which failed to rescue prisoners and ended in disaster. Feeling personally responsible, she retrieved Dahlgren's body and returned it to his family in the North.

By March 1865 her network of agents was so effective that Grant's headquarters at City Point, Virginia, received fresh produce daily from Van Lew's farm, along with intelligence. During the fall of Richmond, she worked tirelessly to save archives of Confederate documents and shielded slaves and her agents from an angry Richmond mob. Van Lew continued to live in Richmond but was a social outcast and suffered financial hardship because of her spending during the war. Grant, grateful for her assistance, made her his first presidential appointee in 1869, as postmistress of Richmond, but the job ended in 1877 when President Rutherford B. Hayes refused to continue the appointment. Resigning a humiliating clerkship in the Washington, D.C., post office, Van Lew lived the rest of her life on a generous annuity raised by relatives of men she aided during the Libby prison break, particularly the Revere and Reynolds families of Massachusetts. For the last twenty years of her life, she refused to pay taxes because, as a woman, she had no representation. Van Lew died at home in Richmond on September 28, 1900.

—*Margaret Sankey*

See also Civil War, American, and Women

References and Further Reading

Ryan, David P., ed. 1996. *A Yankee Spy in Richmond.* Mechanicsburg, PA: Stackpole.
Varon, Elizabeth. 2003. *Southern Lady, Yankee Spy.* New York: Oxford University Press.

VIANNAY, HÉLÈNE (1917–)

A founder of the clandestine newspaper *Défense de la France* during the World War II era. Hélène Mordkovitch Viannay was born in Paris, France, in 1917 to Russian parents. Her mother, originally from Siberia, arrived in France in 1908 after having been exiled from Russia by the czarist regime. Her father, a journalist, returned to Russia shortly after her birth. Viannay has credited her mother, who worked as a doctor, with her strong French patriotism because she passed on to her daughter her revolutionary ideas, especially those regarding an individual's right to self-expression.

After her mother's death in 1937, Viannay began to dedicate herself to antiwar efforts and opposition to the Nazi regime in Germany. Following the fall of France in 1940, Viannay, at the time a student of physical geography at the Sorbonne, joined the resistance effort at the urging of one of her professors, who then nominated her as the interim assistant for the department laboratory, a position that would prove valuable to Viannay's resistance efforts.

While part of the resistance movement, she, along with other students at the Sorbonne, joined in the production of the clandestine newspaper *Défense de la France,* which was edited by Philippe Viannay, whom she would marry in 1942. Hélène was placed in charge of the printing machine for the newspaper as well as its distribution, all of which she handled under the guise of doing research in the physical geography laboratory. Approximately 5,000 copies of the first issue of *Défense de la France* appeared in August 1941, and a total of 47 issues of the paper were published from 1941 to 1944; with its circulation peaking at over 450,000, it was the most widely circulated of the French clandestine newspapers during the resistance.

Following World War II, Hélène and Philippe Viannay ran Les Glénans, a sailing school in South Brittany. Following her husband's death in 1986, Viannay became chairwoman of the Défense de la France Association. In March 2002, Viannay was presented with the De Gaulle–Adenauer Prize for her efforts in furthering cooperation between France and Germany in the postwar era.

—Stephanie Longo

See also Borrel, Andrée; Fourcade, Marie-Madeleine; France, Resistance during World War II, Women and; Moreau-Evrard, Emilienne; Soulié, Geneviève; Tillon, Germaine

References and Further Reading

Feletin, Clarisse. 2004. *Hélène Viannay: L'instinct de résistance de l'occupation à l'école des Glénans* [Hélène Viannay: The Spirit of Resistance to the Occupation at the School of Glénans]. Paris: Editions Pascal.
Jackson, Julian. 2003. *France: The Dark Years, 1940–1944.* Oxford: Oxford University.
Thébaud, Veillon, and Françoise Thébaud. 1995. Hélène Viannay. CLIO: *Revue francophone d'histoire des femmes (Résistances and libérations en France, 1940–1945)* 1:1–32.

VIETNAM, U.S. WOMEN SOLDIERS IN

Women who served with the United States armed forces in Vietnam. About 10,000 U.S. female soldiers served during the Vietnam War (1965–1973). The majority, about 80 percent,

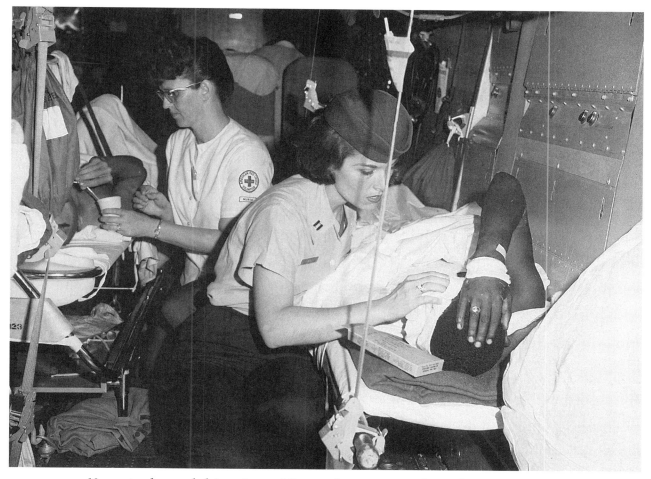

Nurses tend wounded American soldiers as they prepare to depart from a Vietnamese air base for the United States, 1967. (Bettmann/Corbis)

worked as medical personnel in the army or air force. But women were also deployed in non-medical positions, as secretaries for the Military Assistance Command, Vietnam, which was located in Saigon, and on U.S. bases throughout the country. They also served as air traffic controllers, photographers, cartographers, with the Army Signal Corps, in intelligence, and in other jobs requiring security clearance. All women held officers' ranks. With an average age of 23, the medical personnel in Vietnam were the youngest in the history of U.S. wars. Women were not subject to the draft; they joined the military voluntarily, and with a few exceptions, all female personnel deployed to Vietnam had volunteered for service in the war zone. Like their male peers, they served an individual 1-

year tour of duty in Vietnam, with the exception of the 36 female marines, who, like their male peers, had to stay 1 extra month. Women were not allowed to serve in combat units; they were officially classified as noncombatants by the military and not allowed to carry weapons. Nevertheless, female veterans experienced and described their situation as being at the receiving end of combat. Hospitals, for example, were not exempt from attacks by North Vietnamese forces.

Most women who joined the military and volunteered for service in Vietnam did so out of altruistic, patriotic, or idealistic notions; out of a sense of adventure; or following romantic, Hollywood-induced images of nursing in a war zone. Most were ignorant about the country and the actual military and political situation in Vietnam. The grim realities of the war zone hit them as soon as they landed. Many were shocked by the constant threat to all U.S. military personnel from guerrilla fighters, mines, or satchel charges. They were appalled by the hot climate, the smells, and the poverty. The peculiar nature of the Vietnam War, a war that had no front lines and consequently no safe rear area, made the U.S. bases and hospitals constant targets of guerrilla attacks. One of the eight female soldiers killed in Vietnam, First Lieutenant Sharon Lane, died during an enemy attack on the Evacuation Hospital at Chu Lai.

A few days after arriving in Vietnam, women were sent to their duty stations around the country. Nurses joined one of the nineteen medical facilities scattered throughout South Vietnam. On most of the bases, especially in the early war years, there were few provisions for female soldiers and no separate showers or latrines, and the post exchanges (PXs) did not cater to the specific needs of female soldiers.

Duty in the war zone proved to be vastly different from all scenarios nurses had been trained for in the States. The workload and the conditions they had to face in Vietnam exceeded all expectations. The medical facilities in Vietnam were typically connected with a specific unit or firebase. Usually, the hospital staff was notified of major operations and of the estimated number of casualties in advance. Under normal conditions, nurses worked twelve-hour shifts six days a week, but during "pushes," when battles were going on and a constant stream of wounded arrived at hospitals, the nurses stayed for days and nights on end. When the wounded arrived from the battlefield, the primary goal was to stabilize them, to operate on them, and to evacuate them to better-equipped large military hospitals at bases in Danang or Japan as soon as possible. Triage was often performed right on the helicopter pad. Nurses and doctors decided which patients were wounded so badly that they needed treatment at once, which ones could wait, and which were "expectants"—too severely wounded to survive. Due to the constant lack of doctors and the overload of patients, nurses quickly learned to carry out many tasks usually performed by doctors, including minor operations.

Nurses had to deal with mutilated, wounded, and dying GIs. Many nurses felt that they had to repress their emotions in order to function properly. Strategies such as not talking to the wounded soldiers about their private lives or even refusing to learn their names enabled the nurses to keep emotionally uninvolved and to regard their patients merely as bodies and not as individuals. In hindsight, many nurses judge their tour of duty as the most demanding and at the same time as the most satisfying year of their professional careers. For many, Vietnam represented the peak of professionalism, and any stateside employment with the strict hierarchical delineation of duties paled in comparison.

In their spare time, many women tried to help the civilian population by working in orphanages or U.S. aid programs. Initially, many women were interested in Vietnamese culture and tried to establish relations with Vietnamese civilians. Soon, however, they were confronted with the hostility of many South Vietnamese and their lack of enthusiasm for the United States and the anticommunist cause. The impossibility of distinguishing a South Vietnamese friend from a Viet Cong sympathizer or even from a North Vietnamese foe was a major problem for all U.S. forces, and many women developed a general feeling of mistrust toward the Vietnamese. Additionally, they often displayed racist attitudes similar to those of many male U.S. soldiers. In contrast to the altruistic stereotype of the nurse and the general image of the nonviolent, forgiving woman, female soldiers often shared their male counterparts' anger and hate for the Vietnamese, seeing them as responsible for the wounded U.S. soldiers who were their patients. In some cases, nurses even tried to avenge the deaths of soldiers on Vietnamese prisoners of war in their care.

Like many male soldiers, women grew more and more disillusioned as their tour of duty progressed. Many saw the official explanations for the involvement in Vietnam as not sufficiently convincing to justify the amount of suffering they witnessed. The war seemed insane and out of control, and government officials appeared either ignorant or consciously lying. Values such as patriotism or anticommunism, which many women had adhered to before they went to war, lost their validity.

To suppress the recurring memories and to endure the contradictions inherent in the war, many nurses used drugs, chain-smoked, and drank heavily in their leisure time, either alone or with their comrades. Many also became romantically involved with male soldiers or doctors. Those relationships were abruptly broken off when the tour of duty of either partner ended. Other nurses saw the men they had been dating brought into the hospital as casualties. Thus, most nurses preferred short-term, occasional affairs and avoided engaging in long-term relationships. Similar to their male peers in fighting units, many women described the intense comradeship as one of the most impressive and meaningful experiences of their entire tour of duty.

Women could not escape the negative and threatening aspect of living in the predominately male military system: many were sexually harassed by U.S. servicemen and reported problems from pranks to being threatened with disciplinary measures for refusing to engage in a sexual relationship with a superior officer. Female soldiers sometimes tried to avoid officers' clubs and invitations by fellow soldiers or officers and usually kept to themselves during their off-duty hours.

After their return to the states, women encountered the same problems as many male veterans: they were frequently confronted with indifference and even hostility by their families, friends, and U.S. society as a whole. The every-day problems of civilian society seemed trivial for women who were accustomed to life-and-death situations. Further, due to their war-related psychological problems, many woman veterans found it difficult to readjust to civilian life. Many suffered from posttraumatic stress disorder and used drugs or alcohol to numb their feelings and to repress the recurring nightmares and flashbacks of their time in Vietnam. All in all, about 25 percent of female veterans were affected by service-connected disabilities. In contrast to male veterans, many women, military as well as civilian, additionally felt that they were not entitled to call themselves veterans and had no right to their troubled emotions because they had not experienced what society, the military, and many male veterans saw as "the real war"—combat. Consequently, many women withdrew from their friends and family. They did not admit to being Vietnam veterans and therefore did not seek help for their problems.

In the years following the end of the war, the service of female soldiers in Vietnam was largely ignored in public discussions evolving about the war and warriors. Not even the veterans' organizations took note of the contribution of female soldiers or catered to the needs of female veterans.

In 1979 Lynda Van Devanter, a former Vietnam combat nurse, founded the Vietnam Veterans of America's Women's Project, which was explicitly designed to aid women veterans in coming to terms with their war experiences and to offer psychological help to overcome the problems they had faced since their return. In the 1980s female veterans began to lobby for their rights more intensely, and they gradually became part of the public memory of the war. Twenty years after the end of the Vietnam War, in 1993, the service of women in Vietnam was publicly recognized and honored by the dedication of the Vietnam Women's Memorial on the National Mall in Washington, D.C.

—*Petra Feld*

See also Van Devanter, Lynda

References and Further Reading

Bates, Milton J. 1996. *The Wars We Took to Vietnam: Cultural Conflict and Storytelling.* Berkeley: University of California.

Bigler, Philip. 1996. *Hostile Fire: The Life and Death of First Lieutenant Sharon Lane.* Arlington, VA: Vandamere.

Keen-Payne, Rhonda. 1998. United States: Nurses. Pages 741–752 in *Encyclopedia of the Vietnam War: A Political, Social, and Military History.* Vol. I. Edited by Spencer C. Tucker. Santa Barbara, CA: ABC-CLIO.

Smith, Winnie. 1992. *American Daughter Gone to War: On the Front Lines with an Army Nurse in Vietnam.* New York: Pocket Books.

Steinman, Ron, ed. 2000. *Women in Vietnam: The Oral History.* New York: TV Books.

Van Devanter, Lynda. 2001. *Home before Morning: The Story of an Army Nurse in Vietnam.* Amherst: University of Massachusetts.

VIETNAM, WOMEN IN THE BUDDHIST PEACE MOVEMENT

Efforts of Vietnamese women to restore peace to their country during the Vietnam War era. The impact of hostilities on their country and people led numerous Vietnamese women to take active roles in the peace movement despite the fact that many felt great ambivalence about entering the political arena. Driven by a desire to practice compassion by halting the conflict raging in their country, South Vietnamese Buddhists carried out a series of concerted challenges to the government of South Vietnam during the 1960s and 1970s. Vietnamese women also played an important part in these efforts to end the Vietnam War.

The antiwar commitment of these women grew out of traditional Buddhist beliefs regarding compassion and nonviolence, a desire to save their nation from a ruinous war, and the increased sense of empowerment they felt in the twentieth century. The women constituted the critical core of Buddhist efforts to end the war. Buddhist women participated in demonstrations, placed family altars in the streets, led students out of class to protest the war, made efforts to ameliorate the human impact of the conflict, and volunteered to immolate themselves to call attention to the plight of their people. Women who joined the peace movement also risked prison, defied social norms, endured enormous pain, placed themselves in jeopardy, and made shocking sacrifices to save their country.

Buddhist nuns ignored deeply held prohibitions against leaving their convents to agitate for peace, which aptly demonstrates the desperation that many nuns felt about ending the killing in Vietnam. Yet their entry into the public realm represented a significant departure from their normal roles. Most Vietnamese assumed that nuns would shun political activity, and a variety of Vietnamese, including monks and nuns, argued that Buddhist clerics should never express political opinions. In fact, nuns are seldom mentioned in histories of Vietnam Buddhism, which makes their emergence in the peace movement even more dramatic.

In the end, as many as twenty women immolated themselves to halt the conflict in South Vietnam. Unable to respond violently to provocations, they sacrificed themselves in the most dreadful fashion to honor the Buddha's injunction to practice compassion. Ultimately, by immolating themselves, many Buddhist women also declared their complete liberation from patriarchy and the world, becoming bodhisattvas in the process. Their willingness to die for peace serves as a poignant testament to the depth of feeling they had concerning the impact of the fighting on their people.

—*Robert J. Topmiller*

See also Baez, Joan Chandos; Balch, Emily Green; Fonda, Jane; Hobhouse, Emily; Peace People Movement

References and Further Reading

Topmiller, Robert J. 2002. *Lotus Unleashed: The Buddhist Peace Movement in South Vietnam, 1964–1966.* Lexington: University Press of Kentucky.

VIETNAM, WOMEN IN WAR AND RESISTANCE BEFORE 1954

Vietnamese legend, preserved in song, stories, and art, celebrates a long tradition of women warriors. Trung Trac and her sister Trung Nhi are remembered as leaders of a rebellion following the execution of Trung Trac's husband by the Chinese in A.D. 39. They raised an army of 80,000 and trained 36 women to serve as generals. One of their generals, Phung Thi Chihn, was reputedly pregnant when she led her troops into combat. She gave birth during battle, had her infant bound to her back, and, wielding a sword in each hand, continued to lead her troops. The success of the warrior Trung sisters led to the temporary collapse of Chinese authority in Vietnam. The Chinese governor, To Dihn, fled, and Trung Trac was hailed as Trung Vuong, the She-King. When the Chinese reasserted their control through a victorious campaign in A.D. 43, the sisters killed themselves rather than be captured.

The Vietnamese rose again against the Chinese in 248. According to Vietnamese tradition, their leader was Trieu Thi Trinh, a woman of tremendous energy and determination, who declared, "I wish to ride the tempest, tame the waves, kill the sharks. I want to drive the enemy away to save our people" (Bergman 1974, 54). This 20-year-old led an army composed of men and women. She was briefly successful, but when the Chinese were ultimately victorious, she too killed herself.

In the 1700s another woman, Bui Thi Xuan, led Tay Son rebels against the Nguyen dynasty.

They were temporarily victorious and established a reformist regime. When she was defeated and captured, the Vietnamese emperor Gia Long ordered her trampled to death by elephants, the degrading fate of women adulterers, and fed her heart, arms, liver, and lungs to his men in the hope that her courage would be ingested as well.

In the mid-nineteenth century the French established themselves in Vietnam. Vietnamese women played a prominent role in the anti-French resistance as they had in the anti-Chinese efforts. In 1907 Nguyen Thi Ba, a female innkeeper, poisoned 200 French soldiers. In 1931 in Nghe Ahn and Ha Tihn provinces, a guerrilla band of 120 fighters, 40 of whom were women, temporarily drove out local functionaries and established a short-lived soviet. When Nguyen Thi Ngia, a 23-year-old Nghe Tinh guerrilla fighter was captured, she cut off her tongue to avoid breaking under torture. Ming Khai, on the verge of death after being tortured by the French, wrote in her blood on the wall of her cell: "The sword is my child, the gun is my husband" (Jones 1997, 33). The French summarily executed the young guerrilla Vo Thi Sau before her fifteenth birthday. Vietnamese women continued this martial tradition, fighting both for and against the Viet Cong during the U.S. phase of the Vietnamese war. A Vietnamese saying states, "When the enemy comes, even the women should fight" (Bergman 1974, 32).

—*Bernard Cook*

See also China to 1911, Women Warriors in; India to 1857, Women Warriors in; Japan, Women Warriors in Ancient and Medieval Japan

References and Further Reading

Bergman, Arlene. 1974. *Women of Vietnam.* San Francisco: Peoples Press.

Buttinger, Joseph. 1958. *The Smaller Dragon: A Political History of Vietnam.* New York: Praeger.

Duiker, William J. 1982. Vietnam: War of Insurgency. Pages 107–122 in *Female Soldiers, Combatants or Noncombatants? Historical and Contemporary Perspectives.* Edited by Nancy Loring Goldman. Westport, CT: Greenwood.

Jones, David E. 1997. *Women Warriors: A History.* Washington, DC: Brassey's.

VIVANDIÈRES (ALSO KNOWN AS CANTINIÈRES) IN THE FRENCH ARMY

From 1792 until 1906 official auxiliaries of French army combat units. Throughout the medieval and early modern eras, there was a strong need for logistical support for military units above and beyond what armies could provide. This meant that most armies had a large number of camp followers who traveled with them and provided cooking, laundry, and sewing services. Often these camp followers were soldiers' wives and children, but others were prostitutes and assorted swindlers. The key problem for the high command was to get rid of the undesirable camp followers while retaining the desirable ones. By the 1780s many European armies had outlawed female camp followers. The French monarchy, however, made tentative attempts to regulate camp followers and make their status official, but these reforms were hardly under way when the French Revolution broke out in 1789. Starting in 1792 the new revolutionary government in France found itself at war with most of the rest of Europe. The size of the army increased dramatically, as did the number of camp followers. So many women and children began following the French armies that they hindered military operations. In April 1792 the French government passed a decree banning all women from the armies, except for two *vivandières* (dispensers of food) or *cantinières* (dispensers of drink) per regiment, who would act as official auxiliaries, selling food and drink and providing sewing and laundry services to the troops. The law deemed these vivandières to be essential to the operations of the armies.

The French army high command regarded vivandières as essential to the functioning of the army. They provided services that the army could not, and they helped prevent desertion by bringing alcohol, tobacco, home-cooked meals, and female company into the camp. All of these were things a soldier might otherwise leave camp to find. Each vivandière was required to be married to a soldier in the regiment in which she served. This helped prevent prostitution and the spread of venereal disease. The couple's children would be born in the field and grow up on campaign. They usually became soldiers or vivandières themselves on reaching adulthood. Starting in 1800 sons of vivandières were allowed to become *enfants de troupe* (children of the regiment). These boys received a uniform, half pay, and half rations from age two to sixteen, when they enlisted as private soldiers. This system remained in place until 1885 and provided an important source of pretrained manpower.

Vivandières performed many domestic tasks, but their chief role was to sell food and alcohol to the troops. Because they often ran a canteen, they were known interchangeably as cantinières. During combat many vivandières would walk through the front lines distributing brandy to the soldiers under fire. This helped soldiers keep their courage in the face of murderous fire. Some vivandières gave away liquor on battle days as a type of service to the nation. Many went further and personally fought the enemy, and others acted as battlefield nurses, tending the wounded and comforting the dying. Thousands of these women were killed or wounded themselves.

Once Napoleon Bonaparte seized power in France in 1799 the army expanded again, and the numbers of vivandières went up. Napoleon's ambitions brought him into conflict with the rest of Europe, and the resulting Napoleonic Wars lasted until 1815. Millions of men and women fought all across Europe. The chief development for vivandières during this time was the French army's long-term foreign service and the consequent cutting of almost all ties with French civilian society. Because French units were often abroad for years at a time, many French soldiers married foreign women, and they too became vivandières. By 1812 there were vivandières from almost every country in Europe serving in the French army. By 1815 the French army was defeated and largely disbanded. Most vivandières were thrown into poverty and unemployment, and there was fierce competition for the few remaining posts. Those who received positions had to prove their loyalty to the newly restored French monarchy; even so, gaining a vivandière post sometimes required patronage from the royal court.

The French invasion of Algeria in 1830 returned vivandières to new prominence. Many women served in the bitter guerrilla warfare there for the next forty years. In 1832 the government reorganized vivandière regulations, and from 1830 to 1840 it reorganized education for enfants de troupe, making it much more formal and uniform. During the same period vivandières began to wear French army uniforms that were distinctly feminine but patterned on the uniforms of their regiments. These included trousers, which were illegal for French women to wear at the time. Though the law was enforced on civilian women, vivandières broke it with impunity. The mid-nineteenth century saw vivandières held up as examples of fashion and feminine virtue; ironically these examples also smoked, drank, used firearms, and wore trousers. Although some French feminist movements such as the Vésuviennes adopted vivandières' dress, feminism was unknown within the vivandière corps, and the women's rights movement entirely passed them by. This likely occurred because all of the feminists' demands that mattered to military

A vivandière, *wearing Zouave regiment dress, during the Crimean War, 1855. (Library of Congress)*

women were already granted to them. There was no need, in their eyes, for any agitation. Unlike civilian women, vivandières could already own property, travel, exercise a profession, wear pants, and effectively divorce their husbands.

By the 1870s official opinion began to turn against vivandières. They served bravely in the 1870–1871 Franco-Prussian War, and many were killed, wounded, or captured. The high command, however, engaged in scapegoating for the French defeat, and vivandières came under unwarranted suspicion as potential spies. Members of the government complained that vivandières' wagons slowed columns and blocked roads. By 1875 the Ministry of War cut the number of active service vivandières in half. In 1879 the ministry cut vivandières by a further 33 percent and at the same time authorized units to hire male *cantiniers* in place of women. This resulted in the steady decline in the number of vivandières.

The following decade saw repeated discussions concerning completely suppressing vivandières, but traditionalists within the army high command blocked a final elimination. The so-called Three Year Law of 1889, which mandated three years of military service for all young men, created a moral and political environment that hastened the end of vivandières. Sons of the middle and upper classes now served as recruits, and alcoholism and venereal disease among them raised new public outcries against bad moral influences. By 1900 Minister of War Gaston A. A. Marquis de Gallifet ordered a ban on the sales of hard alcohol in all army canteens, cutting into the vivandières' profits. The same year, his replacement, Louis André, ordered noncommissioned officers to eat in official mess circles instead of in the vivandières' canteens, further eroding their ability to survive.

The final blow to vivandières came from the Dreyfus Affair, a scandal in which the French army proved largely hostile to the very existence of the French Republic. In response, the government passed the Two Year Law in 1905, which was designed to change the army from a largely professional, long-service entity into a short-term, citizen army composed of draftees serving two-year terms. The new idea was that the army would become a school for teaching citizenship, good morals, and love of country to every young man passing through. Vivandières, with their hereditary, long-service military families, epitomized the old professional army that the Republic wished to eliminate. As sellers of alcohol and as women in a men's world, vivandières represented a bad moral influence to many reformers at precisely the moment when moral purity seemed a life-and-death issue for the Republic. The Two Year Law mandated that all supply posts had to be reserved for male veterans who would serve as cantiniers, effectively eliminating vivandières.

To speed up the process, Minister of War Eugene Etienne ordered all commanders to report all vivandières "whose service has not been exempt from reproach and who for this reason or any other, they wish to replace" (Cardoza 2002, 21). The meaning of Etienne's message was clear: any vivandière could be replaced for any reason, and the minister of war was asking commanders to do it. A few vivandières managed to avoid termination until World War I, but by early 1906 they had been effectively eliminated as a group.

—*Thomas Cardoza*

See also American Revolution, Role of Women in the; Borginis, Sarah; Civil War, American, and Women; Etheridge, Anna; Great Britain, Women in Service in the Seventeenth, Eighteenth, and Early Nineteenth Centuries; Thirty Years' War

References and Further Reading

Cardoza, Thomas J. 2001. Stepchildren of the State: Educating Enfants de Troupe in the French Army, 1800–1845. *Paedagogica Historica* 37(3):551–568.

———. 2002. Exceeding the Needs of the Service: The French Army and the Suppression of Female Auxiliaries, 1871–1906. *War and Society* 20(1):1–22.

Rothenberg, Gunther E. 1978. *The Art of Warfare in the Age of Napoleon.* Bloomington: Indiana University Press.

VON RIEDESEL, FREDERIKE CHARLOTTE LUISE VON MASSOW

See Riedesel, Frederike Charlotte Luise von Massow von

von Suttner, Baroness
Bertha Sophie Felicita

See Suttner, Baroness Bertha Sophie Felicita von

von Thadden, Elizabeth
(1890–1944)

See Thadden, Elizabeth von

W

WAKE, NANCY (1912–)

Member of the French resistance and the British Special Operations Executive (SOE) during World War II. Nancy Wake was born in Roseneath, Wellington, New Zealand, in 1912, but her family moved to Sydney, Australia, when she was a baby. Her father was an Englishman who worked as a journalist, and her mother was a Maori. Nancy Wake worked as a nurse and then as a freelance journalist. She traveled widely and settled in Paris, where she met and married Henri Fiocca, a wealthy Frenchman from Marseilles. After the Nazi defeat of France in 1940, she served as a courier for the French resistance movement in Vichy-administered southern France. Wake helped fliers and prisoners escape over the Pyrenees Mountains into Spain. The Germans knew the elusive Wake as the White Mouse in recognition of her numerous disguises. After the Nazis offered a reward for her capture, she decided to leave for Britain. After she tried unsuccessfully to reach Spain, the Vichy government captured Wake. She escaped her captors, however, through an elaborate plan engineered by Patrick O'Leary, nicknamed the Scarlet Pimpernel of World War II.

The French section of the SOE recruited Wake after she arrived in England. Thirty-nine women working with the SOE, including Wake, were officially enrolled in the First Aid Nursing Yeomanry (FANY) to hide their advanced military training and espionage work. After her British training, Wake reentered France to organize the Maquis in preparation for the D-Day invasion. Her work was instrumental in the expansion of resistance volunteers and the mounting of guerrilla attacks on factories and military installations. She fought with troops in pitched battles in the Auvergne region of France and personally led raids on Gestapo headquarters.

She was one of the few SOE female operatives to survive after operating on such a large scale and for so long behind enemy lines. Her husband did not live through the war. He was captured in France, tortured, and executed in 1943 as punishment for working with the underground.

After the war Wake returned to Australia with her second husband, John Forward, a former operative. For her bravery, Nancy Wake was awarded the George Medal from the British government; the Resistance Medal, the Legion d'Honneur, and the Croix de Guerre from France; and the Medal of Freedom from the United States. She lived and worked in Australia until 2001, when she moved to London.

—Pamela Lee Gray

See also Atkins, Vera H.

References and Further Reading

Fitzsimons, Peter. 2001. *Nancy Wake: A Biography of Our Greatest War Heroine.* New York: HarperCollins.

WALKER, MARY EDWARDS (1832–1919)

Awarded the Congressional Medal of Honor for her service as a doctor during the American Civil War. Mary Edwards Walker was born on November 26, 1832, in Oswego, New York, the daughter of Alvah and Vesta Walker. Her father, a doctor, was an enthusiastic supporter of reform movements, including women's rights, especially for his five daughters. Mary graduated from the Syracuse Medical School in 1855. In 1856 she married another doctor, Albert Miller. They established a medical practice in Rome, New York. Their practice did not succeed, however, and they divorced after thirteen years. When the American Civil War erupted, Mary went to Washington to join the Union army as a doctor. When her attempt was refused, she volunteered to serve as an assistant surgeon. She served at Fredericksburg and Chattanooga. In September 1863 she was appointed assistant surgeon. In addition to her medical work, she served as a spy, crossing the battle lines into Confederate territory. In 1864 she was taken

---

MARY WALKER, MEDAL OF HONOR RECIPIENT

The Medal of Honor was presented to physician Mary Walker in 1865. The U.S. government revoked the award in 1917, but President Jimmy Carter restored it sixty years later. The proclamation accompanying the presentation of the award follows:

"Whereas it appears from official reports that Dr. Mary E. Walker, a graduate of medicine, 'has rendered valuable service to the government, and her efforts have been earnest and untiring in a variety of ways,' and that she was assigned to duty and served as an assistant surgeon in charge of female prisoners at Louisville, KY, under the recommendation of Major-Generals Sherman and Thomas, and faithfully served as contract surgeon in the service of the United states, and has devoted herself with much patriotic zeal to the sick and wounded soldiers, both in the field and hospitals, to the detriment of her own health, and has endured hardships as a prisoner of war four months in a southern prison while acting as contract surgeon; and

"Whereas by reason of her not being a commissioned officer in the military service a brevet or honorary rank can not, under existing laws, be conferred upon her; and

"Whereas in the opinion of the President an honorable recognition of her services and suffers should be made;

"It is Ordered. That a testimonial thereof shall be hereby made and given to the said Dr. Mary E. Walker, and that the usual medal of honor for meritorious services be given her."

Given under my hand in the city of Washington, D.C.,
this 11th day of November, A.D. 1865.
Andrew Johnson, President
"By the President:
Edwin M. Stanton, Secretary of War"
—www.astr.ua.edu/4000WS/WALKER.html.

Dr. Mary Edwards Walker. (National Archives)

prisoner by Confederate troops. She was imprisoned in Richmond for four months until she was exchanged with other doctors for a group of Confederate doctors. She was proud to be exchanged "man for man." She served during the Atlanta campaign and then as a doctor at a female prison and orphans' asylum in Tennessee. After the war she received a miserly pension, which was less than a widow's pension. On November 11, 1865, President Andrew Johnson awarded her the Congressional Medal of Honor, the highest military award of the United States.

In 1917 the U.S. Congress revoked her medal and those of 910 others, stating that the medals should be awarded only for actual combat. Walker refused to return her medal and proudly wore it until her death. It was posthumously restored in 1977. After the Civil War she wrote and engaged in speaking tours in support of women's rights, dress reform, and temperance.

—*Bernard Cook*

See also Civil War, American, Women in the Medical Services in the

References and Further Reading

Graf, Mercedes. 2001. *A Woman of Honor: Dr. Mary E. Walker and the Civil War.* Gettysburg, PA: Thomas Publications.
Snyder, Charles M. 1974. *Dr. Mary Walker: The Little Lady in Pants.* New York: Arno Press.
Walker, Dale L. 2005. *Mary Edwards Walker: Above and Beyond.* New York: Tom Doherty Associates.
Walker, Mary Edwards. 2003. *Hit: Essays on Women's Rights.* Amherst, NY: Humanity Books.

WARD, NANCY (CA. 1738–CA. 1824)

Native American warrior. Nancy Ward was the married name of a Cherokee woman whose birth name, *Nanye-hi* (One Who Goes About), was taken from *Nunne-hi* (Spirit People), the mythological name of the Cherokee. As a young person she was believed to possess spiritual powers. The identity of Nancy's father is uncertain. One story says that he was part Delaware or Lenni Lenap. Another version says that she was the daughter of an Irishman, Francis Ward. Nancy's second husband was also a Ward— Bryan (Briant) Ward, an English trader. They had a daughter, Elizabeth.

Nancy was born around the year 1738 in the Cherokee town of Chota, a site now covered by water behind the Telico Dam on the Tennessee River. Her mother, Tame Doe, was from the Wolf Clan and was a sister of Chief Attakullakulla.

Nancy married in her teens and had two children, Five Killer (*Hiskitihi*) and Catherine (*Kati*), with her husband Kingfisher, of the Deer Clan. She was with him when he was killed at the Battle of Taliwa (1755). His death so outraged her that she took up his musket and joined the battle. Her war song and action so inspired the remaining Cherokee warriors that they soon defeated the Creeks (Muskogees). After the battle Nancy was named *Ghighau,* which can be translated as Beloved Woman or in the form *Agigaue* as War Woman.

As a War Woman she was responsible for preparing the Black Drink used in the purification ritual for warriors preparing for war. She also had the power to prevent the execution of captives. On one occasion she saved the life of Lydia Bean, who was about to be burned at the stake by Cherokee warriors.

In keeping with the matrilineal tradition of the Cherokee, women played an important role in Cherokee town councils. Nancy was head of the women's council and a power in the council of chiefs. She had been educated by Moravian missionaries and was one of the Cherokee who favored good relations with whites. During the American Revolution she sent warning several times to frontier settlers that Cherokee war bands, instigated by British agents, were preparing to raid.

The 1819 Hiwassee Purchase by the United States forced Nancy to leave Chota. She moved to Womankiller Ford on the Ocoee River, where she operated an inn on the Federal Road. In 1923 the Nancy Ward Chapter (Chattanooga) of the Daughters of the American Revolution put a marker on her grave. The gravesite is in a park north of Benton, Tennessee, on the Ocoee River.

—*Andrew Jackson Waskey*

See also Nonhelema; Winema; Winnemucca, Sarah

References and Further Reading

Adams, Robert G. 1979. *Nancy Ward, Beautiful Woman of Two Worlds.* Chattanooga, TN: Hampton House Studios.
Sawyer, Susan. 2000. *More than Petticoats: Remarkable Tennessee Women.* Helena, MT: TwoDot.

WARTENBURG, COUNTESS MARION YORCK VON

See Yorck von Wartenburg, Countess Marion.

WASHINGTON, MARGUERITE PAT BEAUCHAMP WADDELL (B. 1900)

Member of the First Aid Nursing Yeomanry (FANY). Marguerite Washington served as a driver in World War I until an accident resulted in the amputation of her left leg. Through the use of a prosthetic limb, she was able to continue her FANY service during the interwar period and World War II. She received the French Croix de Guerre with Silver Star and the Belgian Civic Cross.

Washington joined FANY in 1913 and first began her war work in January 1915 at the Lamarck Hospital in Calais, working both as a Voluntary Aid Detachment (VAD) worker and bringing wounded from the trenches. In her spare time she joined other members of her unit as part of a group called the Fantastiks, which gave concert parties to nearby troops.

In 1916 she transferred to a special convoy unit of FANY ambulance drivers for the British Red Cross. Her main responsibility was the transport of supplies for the convoy. While on duty in May 1917, she lost her leg when her truck, which she had named Little Willie after Kaiser Wilhelm to reflect its temperamental nature, went out of control and smashed into an oncoming train. After a two-year convalescence she rejoined the FANY as adjutant in 1919.

Despite her disability, at the beginning of World War II Washington was asked to head a mobile volunteer FANY canteen convoy for the Polish army. She served in both France and Scotland.

—*Barbara Penny Kanner*

See also Black, Catherine; Great Britain, Women in Service during World War I; Haverfield, Evelina; Stobart, Mabel

References and Further Reading

Beauchamp, Pat. 1940. *Fanny Went to War.* London: G. Routledge & Sons.

———. 1942. *Eagles in Exile.* London: Maxwell, Love.

Popham, Hugh. 2003. *The F.A.N.Y. in Peace and War: The Story of the First Aid Nursing Yeomanry, 1907–2003.* Barnsley, South Yorkshire, UK: Leo Cooper; Pen and Sword Books.

WASHINGTON, MARTHA DANDRIDGE CUSTIS (1731–1802)

First lady of the United States as the wife of its first president, George Washington, for whom she was an invaluable ally during the Revolutionary War. Martha Dandridge was born June 2, 1731, at her father's plantation, Chestnut Grove, in Virginia. After a 1746 debut in Williamsburg, she married wealthy Daniel Parke Custis in May 1750 and bore him four children, two of whom survived his sudden death in July 1757. As a wealthy and socially influential widow, Martha chose to marry George Washington on January 6, 1759, having carefully studied him as a suitable stepfather and partner. Dandridge and Custis money allowed Washington to ascend Virginia's social ladder, spend lavishly on his estate at Mount Vernon, and purchase products from Great Britain. Martha Washington did not participate in the embargo against British goods and remained on polite terms with Royal Governor Lord Dunmore (John Murray) even during the tense years leading to the Revolution.

Martha, stunned by the death of her daughter Patsy from epilepsy in 1773, was not happy about Washington's acceptance of military command in the Revolution, but she hurried to join him when it became apparent that his enemies could interpret her absence as a weakness. Each year of the Revolution, Martha spent the winter with Washington in camp, bringing desperately needed medical supplies, clothing, and food, as well as organizing a social life that smoothed over differences between Washington, his subordinates, and their often-fractious wives. As the manager of a large plantation household, Martha was an expert on feeding, clothing, and managing large groups of people, and she served as a diplomatic emissary between the military camp and the sometimes hostile local community, organizing clothing drives and the collection of supplies. Much liked by the soldiers, Martha volunteered to have a smallpox inoculation to prove its safety to the troops, and she was affectionately addressed as Lady Washington.

After the war Martha was forced to deal with numerous visitors and the curious at Mount Vernon. The family's properties had been neglected during the war, and she struggled to right them while entertaining and dealing with Washington's political future. When he became president in 1789, she lived as first lady in New York and Philadelphia and set a respectable but elegant tone at her home, carefully balanced between a royal court and a casual social gathering. In the face of Washington's increasing alienation from his former soldiers, Martha was always available to veterans, distributing money and goodwill. At all times a warm maternal figure, Martha raised a large assortment of grandchildren, nieces, and nephews at Mount Vernon and the presidential residences.

Martha Washington survived her husband's death in 1799 by three years. She had been stunned by the defection of two of her slaves while she was living in Pennsylvania. She became convinced that the Mount Vernon slaves planned to murder her in order to gain the manumission promised at her death in Washington's will, and as a result, she freed them in 1800. Before her death she carefully burned all of her personal correspondence, diaries, and important documents, leaving few records about her life and relationships. She died at Mount Vernon on May 22, 1802, and was buried alongside her husband.

—*Margaret Sankey*

See also American Revolution, Role of Women in the

References and Further Reading

Bryan, Helen. 2002. *Martha Washington: First Lady of Liberty.* New York: John Wiley and Sons.

Clark, Ellen McCallister. 2002. *Martha Washington: A Brief Biography.* Mount Vernon: University of Virginia.

Conkling, Margaret. 1850. *Memoirs of the Mother and Wife of Washington.* Auburn, NY: Derby Miller.

WATTS, JEAN (1909–1968)

Canadian journalist and Communist Party activist who was the only woman to join the Mackenzie-Papineau Battalion, the Canadian contingent of the International Brigades, which fought on the Republican side in the Spanish Civil War.

Jean Watts was born into a wealthy Toronto family, but in the early 1930s she deserted her class to become a cultural activist and journalist with the Communist Party of Canada. She was working with the Communist Party at age twenty-three when she was arrested for distributing communist literature. In 1936 she used inherited wealth to help found the left-wing cultural magazine *New Frontier* and also joined the Theatre of Action, a left-wing theatrical troupe in Toronto. After the Spanish Civil War began in July 1936, Watts became determined to join the Republican forces, but the Communist Party's male leadership frowned on the idea of a woman joining the fray. The party agreed, however, to send her as a correspondent for its newspaper, the *Daily Clarion,* and to help Canadian Dr. Norman Bethune, who had established a blood transfusion institute in Madrid.

In January 1937 she reported to the International Brigades marshaling center in New York, where, she recalled, U.S. recruiters reacted with dismay, exclaiming, "My god, are they sending women?" (Interview 1627:1 in the Dorothy Livesay Collection, British Columbia Archives). After six months in Spain she grew disenchanted with her limited role as a correspondent. She never got to the front lines and instead seemed to be relegated to what Canadian newspapers at the time described as the "women's beat," covering culture, women and children, religion, and other human interest subjects. Frustrated, she demanded to join the Mackenzie-Papineau Battalion. Once accepted, she became its first and only female member and one of no more than a handful of Canadian women in the entire International Brigades. (Other Canadian women served with non-Canadian units.) She volunteered to be a truck and ambulance driver for the British Medical Unit and served at Hueta in Cuenca Province, working as a chauffeur and "grease monkey" and doing minor repairs. An attractive woman, Watts enjoyed the easy camaraderie of the male truck drivers and mechanics in the British Medical Unit. (The Royal Canadian Mounted Police showed some interest in her sexual orientation; one surveillance report described one of her "peculiarities" as "looks and dresses like a man" [Jean Watts file, National Archives of Canada, Canadian Security Intelligence Service Access to Information request 117–95]).

Watts returned to Canada in January 1938 and went to work with the Committee to Aid Spanish Refugees. She was forced to abandon this work in 1939 when the Communist Party became effectively illegal after Canada declared war on Germany, with which the Soviet Union had signed a nonaggression pact on August 23, 1939. In 1941 Watts joined the Canadian Women's Army Corps, an auxiliary women's unit of the Canadian military. She served within Canada and attained the rank of lieutenant before being discharged in 1946. After World War II she became a mother, and her involvement with the Communist Party declined, although she remained active with left-wing women's groups such as the Voice of Women. She committed suicide in 1968.

—Larry Hannant

See also Kea, Salaria; Street, Jessie

References and Further Reading

Parker, Douglas Scott. 1994. "Women in Communist Culture in Canada: 1932–1937." Unpublished master's thesis, McGill University, Montreal.

Sangster, Joan. 1989. *Dreams of Equality: Women on the Canadian Left, 1920–1950.* Toronto, Canada: McClelland and Stewart.

WERNER, RUTH (SONJA)

See Kuczynski, Ursula

WERTHEIMER, MARTHA (1890–1942)

Rescuer of Jewish children. Martha Wertheimer worked as a journalist for the *Offenbacher*

Zeitung in Frankfurt until she was fired because of Nazi anti-Jewish legislation. She became director of the office of children's affairs of the Frankfurt Jewish Community. She played a central role in the organization of the *Kindertransport* (children's transports) in 1938 and 1939. Approximately 10,000 Jewish children were transported out of Germany to refuge abroad. Though many were placed with families in the Netherlands and fell into the hands of the Nazis after the German conquest in May 1940, approximately 7,500 Jewish children from Germany were relocated to England, where they survived. The children were forced to travel without their parents and, in many cases, without their siblings, most of whom disappeared in the Holocaust. These refugee children were, of necessity, generally placed with non-Jewish families. Wertheimer accompanied a number of transports to England but always returned to Germany.

In Frankfurt, once the transports came to a halt because of the war, Wertheimer turned her attention to the Jews stranded in the Third Reich. She ran a soup kitchen and 8 homes for elderly Jews. On June 10 and 11, 1942, 1,042 Jews from Frankfurt and 450 from the surrounding area were rounded up for transport to the death camps in the east. Because of her work with the Jewish Community, the Gestapo ordered Wertheimer to take charge of organizing the group. She and the other Jews in this transport disappeared into the Nazi killing machine.

—Bernard Cook

See also Holocaust and Jewish Women

References and Further Reading

Interlog.com. "Dr. Martha Wertheimer—Rescuer of Children." Charlotte Opfermann, Women and the Holocaust. http://www.interlog.com/ ~mighty/special/Martha.htm (accessed October 25, 2003).

WEXFORD RISING, WOMEN OF

Role of women in the 1798 rebellion against English rule in Ireland. The Society of United Irishmen, a nationalist organization, was founded in 1791. Its goal was the liberation of Ireland from British rule, and a general rising of the Irish against the British was planned for 1798.

Bloody clashes occurred in villages to the west of Dublin. There were spontaneous and uncoordinated risings in Wexford, Antrim, and Down, but they had been crushed by the time a French force landed at Killala in County Mayo in August. Although the French were joined by many peasants, they were defeated in September. Women in the north were among the fighters and survivors. Betsy Grey of Granshaw, County Down, died in battle on June 13 at Ballinahinch with her brother and her lover, Willie Boal. The participation of women in these rebellions was particularly evident in the Wexford rising, which began on May 28. Led by Father John Murphy of Boolavogue, the rebels quickly gained control of County Wexford. The rebels were later defeated at Arklow and New Ross, and their forces were finally overrun at Vinegar Hill, near Enniscorthy, on June 21.

Women of Wexford played various roles. They supported their kin, smuggled ammunition, and sustained the rebels in battle by providing ammunition, drink, and succor. They fought, they were brutalized by the British, and they died. Confronting the growing sentiment of resistance, the British outlawed wearing of the color green in 1798. Wexford women who defied this order were reviled by British soldiers and had their offending ribbons, caps, and even petticoats ripped off. When Ann Ford of Garrysackle was confronted by a Hessian offended by her wearing of the green, she dispatched him

---

WEXFORD RISING

When the tyrant's hand was laid
Upon the true and brave,
In the tender pride of womenhood
They rose to help and save.
                    —John Keegan Casey

Then a figure rose above us,
'twas a girl's fragile frame,
And among the fallen soldiers there
She walked with eyes aflame,
And her voice rang o'er the clamour
Like a trumpet o'er the sea:
"Who so dares to die for Ireland,
Let him come and follow me."
                    —William Rooney,
              "Heroine of Ross (Mary Doyle)."
                    1789 Homepage,
    http://homepages.iol.ie/~fagann/1798/songs7.htm.

with a blow from the hammer she was carrying. At one point during an engagement with the British, Mary Doyle of Castleboro reputedly shamed the rebel men who were about to abandon an artillery piece by sitting on it and refusing to move unless they took the piece with them. At the Battle of New Ross, Mary Doyle, in the midst of the fighting, cut the cartridge belts off dead soldiers and passed them to the rebels and urged on faltering insurgents. She probably died as New Ross was overrun and burned.

Many women were involved in the climatic fighting when approximately 10,000 rebels—men, women, and children—gathered on Vinegar Hill. Women fought fiercely alongside their male relatives and died with them. Following the battle many surviving women were raped by the victorious British troops. After their defeat Michael Dwyer, Joseph Hall, and other surviving rebels took to the Wicklow Mountains. Peg Kavanagh was among the women who brought them food and information. Another courier was Susan Toole, the daughter of a blacksmith, who in addition to food and information brought the insurgents ammunition hidden in her dress.

—*Bernard Cook*

See also Ireland, Easter Rising of 1916; Ireland, War of Independence

References and Further Reading

Gahan, Daniel. 1995. *The People's Rising: Wexford, 1798.* Dublin: Gill & MacMillan.
————. 1997. *Rebellion! Ireland in 1798.* Dublin and Enniscorthy, Ireland: O'Brien Press/Comóradh '98.
Kavanagh, Patrick F. 1898. *A Popular History of the Insurrection of 1798: Derived from Every Available Record and Reliable Tradition.* Cork, Ireland: Guy.
Keogh, Dáire, and Nicholas Furlong, eds. 1998. *The Women of 1798.* Dublin. Four Courts Press.

WHITTLE, REBA ZITELLA (1919–1981)

A flight nurse for the U.S. Army who was captured by the enemy in 1944 when her plane crashed in German territory. Reba Zitella Whittle was the only U.S. female prisoner of war (POW) captured by the Germans during World War II. She was a POW for almost four months.

Born on August 19, 1919, Whittle requested a position as an army reserve nurse in June 1941. In January 1943 she applied for training with the Army Air Force School of Air Evacuation and was taught how to handle in-flight medical emergencies. On January 22, 1944, she began her European service with the U.S. military.

On September 27, 1944, Whittle, a second lieutenant, and her comrades from the 813th Aeromedical Evacuation Transportation Squadron in England were flying to pick up casualties from France. Whittle had already flown in forty missions, and she expected the current one to be routine. While flying over Aachen, their C-47 plane was shot down. Although she survived the crash, German soldiers captured her and marched her to a detention site.

Whittle was wounded in the crash, receiving a concussion and a deep forehead gash. When she was examined in a German hospital, the doctor admitted to being puzzled, saying, "Too bad having a woman as you are the first one and no one knows exactly what to do" (Kelly Patrick 2004). Her fiancé, Lieutenant Colonel Stanley Tobiason, received permission to do a voluntary search and rescue mission for Whittle but failed in his attempt. On October 6 she was transferred to the POW camp, Stalag 9C, at Meiningen, and while in captivity she nursed others. She was not officially acknowledged as a POW by the U.S. government, which found the situation highly embarrassing and a potential public relations nightmare. On January 25, 1945, she was sent to Switzerland, accompanied by members of the German Red Cross, and was then allowed to fly home.

The injuries sustained in the crash prevented Whittle from flying again, and the U.S. government requested that she not talk about her experiences, a typical practice to protect those still in captivity. She obeyed the orders. She seemed to display no bitterness about her experiences; her diary recorded many instances of German kindnesses. Whittle was promoted to first lieutenant but was then released from active duty in 1946.

She married Tobiason on August 3, 1945, and they raised two sons. They struggled to have POW status granted to Whittle, something that would not occur in her lifetime. She was, however, awarded the Purple Heart and the Air Medal in 1945. The second award, established in 1942, is given for meritorious achievement while participating in aerial missions.

Whittle spent several years during the 1950s seeking physical and psychological disability compensation and finally received a partial retirement settlement. She died of cancer on January 26, 1981, and was buried in the National Cemetery in San Francisco, California. In 1983 she was posthumously recognized as a POW, a designation that her husband said would have delighted her.

—*Kelly Boyer Sagert*

See also Bullwinkel, Vivian; Cornum, Rhonda

References and Further Reading

Military.com. "2nd Lt. Reba Whittle: Army Flight Nurse Was Only U.S. Woman POW in WWII Europe." Bethanne Kelly Patrick. http://www.military.com/Content/MoreContent?file=ML_whittle_bkp (accessed July 31, 2004).

WILHELMINA, QUEEN OF THE NETHERLANDS (1880–1962)

Queen of the Netherlands during World War II. In 1940 when Germany invaded the Nether-

Wilhelmina, Queen of the Netherlands. (Ridpath, John Clark, Ridpath's History of the World, 1901)

lands, Wilhelmina escaped to Great Britain and led the Dutch government-in-exile in London.

Wilhelmina Helena Pauline of Orange-Nassau was born on August 31, 1880, the daughter of King William III and his second wife, Queen Emma, who had been the German princess of Waldeck-Piermont. When Wilhelmina's father died in 1890, a special law was required to permit female succession. With its passage, Wilhelmina became queen. Her mother served as regent until Wilhelmina's eighteenth birthday.

Wilhelmina was a constitutional monarch but, unlike the kings and queens of England, had considerable governmental powers. During her first year as queen, she offered a palace at The Hague to the world as the site for the first Hague Conference, which met in 1899 in an effort to promote peace. The palace eventually became home to the International Court of Justice, which attempted to avoid conflict through international arbitration. When Wilhelmina was twenty, she gained international attention for intervening in the Boer War. Despite a British blockade of Boer Transvaal, the queen sent a Dutch warship to rescue the Boer president, Paul Kruger. In 1901 she married Hendrik, Duke of Mechlenburg-Schwerin. The marriage was an unhappy one, but it produced a daughter, Juliana, on April 30, 1909. Wilhelmina personally devoted herself to the upbringing of her daughter and at the same time became very wealthy through her investments, including those in Royal Dutch Shell.

When the Germans launched their Schlieffen Plan in August 1914, they decided not to violate Dutch territory. The Netherlands, though surrounded by German forces, was able to remain neutral, and following the collapse of the German war effort, Wilhelmina accorded Kaiser Wilhelm of Germany asylum in her country.

Germany did invade her kingdom on May 10, 1940. On May 13, following the advice of the Dutch government, Wilhelmina sent her daughter and others in her family to England on a British destroyer. The next day the Dutch military admitted its inability to stop the Germans. Wilhelmina had attempted to join her troops while they were still fighting near the coast in Zeeland, but the British ship she boarded at the Hook was ordered by the British navy to Harwich on the English coast. Wilhelmina was outraged, but after speaking with King George of Britain, she reluctantly agreed to join him in London. She stayed in England and led the Dutch government-in-exile. During the long German occupation of her country, Wilhelmina's weekly radio addresses encouraged the Dutch people to hope for liberation. The queen narrowly escaped injury when a German bomb hit her country residence in England. On her return to the Netherlands at the end of the war, she was welcomed by the people as the symbol of Dutch resistance to Nazism and of Dutch national identity. The queen toured the country on a bicycle, assessing the needs of her people and the reconstruction effort. Until the infrastructure was repaired and electricity was provided to the country, Wilhelmina did not allow heat or electricity to be turned on in her palace. Following her golden jubilee in 1948, the queen passed the crown to her daughter, Juliana. Wilhelmina died on November 28, 1962.

—*Bernard Cook*

See also Schaft, Jeannetje Joanna

References and Further Reading

Wilhelmina, H.R.H. Princess of the Netherlands. 1960. *Lonely but Not Alone.* Translated by John Peereboom. London: Hutchinson.

WILLIAMS, JODY (1950–)

Winner of the Nobel Peace Prize in 1997 for her effort to gain an international banning of land mines. Jody Williams, who was born on October 9, 1950, in Brattleboro, Vermont, was the founding coordinator of the International Campaign to Ban Land Mines (ICBL). Before earning a master's degree in International Relations at the Johns Hopkins School of Advanced International Studies, she had campaigned to educate the public about the policy of the U.S. government in Latin America. From 1986 to 1992 she was director of the nongovernmental organization (NGO) Medical Aid for El Salvador. In October 1992 the ICBL was set up with the assistance of six NGOs. As ICBL coordinator, she spoke about the problem of land mines before the United Nations, the European Parliament, and the Organization for African Unity. She coauthored a study based on field research in countries afflicted with the problem of land mines. In September 1997 her efforts bore fruit in an international treaty banning antipersonnel mines. The United States refused to support the treaty.

Land mines are an ongoing problem in areas that experienced civil war and ethnic conflict in the late twentieth and early twenty-first centuries. Especially plagued are Cambodia, Angola, Mozambique, Bosnia, Kosovo, Afghanistan, and Chechnya. Land mines kill and maim thousands of noncombatants annually.

—*Bernard Cook*

See also Balch, Emily Green; Peace People Movement; Von Suttner, Baroness Bertha Sophie Felicita

References and Further Reading

Roberts, Shawn, and Jody Williams. 1995. *After the Guns Fall Silent: The Enduring Legacy of Landmines.* Washington, DC: Vietnam Veterans of America Foundation.

WINEMA (TOBEY RIDDLE) (CA. 1848–1920)

Native American warrior and intermediary with the United States. Born about 1848 along the Link River in what is today Oregon, Winema's childhood exploits established her as a woman-chief among the Modoc Indians. As a young girl, Winema was paddling a canoe with several other children when the small boat was pulled into treacherous white water. Winema steered the canoe for several miles, keeping the others calm and giving them directions. Her bravery and stoicism in the face of danger, along with her exhibition of leadership, gave her status among the male warriors in her village. She was encouraged to learn from the men, acquiring proficiency with firearms, fist fighting, and hunting, as well as traditional female skills. She was perceived in adolescence to be a strong and powerful woman.

In 1862, at about the age of fourteen, Winema married a miner named Frank Riddle. Assuming the anglicized name Tobey Riddle, she adopted Euro-American dress and customs and was considered an excellent housekeeper by

white standards. In 1863 the couple had a son, Jefferson C. Davis Riddle, who would later write *The Indian History of the Modoc War.* The Riddles lived as trappers and farmers, becoming a significant part of the multicultural conflicts arising from Native American diaspora and white settlement. As interpreters and diplomats, the Riddles worked with the U.S. government and the Modoc Indians to establish peaceful relations.

The Klamath Reservation was a site of ethnic fighting, starvation, and disease. Diverse groups of indigenous people were placed together, and traditional rivalries prevented peaceful coexistence. By 1865 the Modocs, reduced to fewer than 300 individuals, were driven from the reservation by their long-standing enemies and more powerful neighbors, the Klamaths. During this period Tobey Riddle led an armed raid against the Klamaths to retrieve stolen livestock. Her bravery under fire brought her further prestige among the Modocs.

Led by Tobey Riddle's cousin Captain Jack, the Modocs lived off the reservation for four years. The Riddles helped negotiate their return, but by 1870 the Modocs once again left the Klamath Reservation. Frank and Tobey Riddle worked for the U.S. government, offering not only linguistic skills but also cultural interpretation and diplomatic advice. Relations between whites and the Modocs deteriorated. Raids led to the Modoc War in 1872.

On Good Friday, April 11, 1873, a peace commission met with Captain Jack in an effort to end the bloody fights in the Lava Beds. Tobey Riddle had warned the commissioners, including General E. R. S. Canby and A. B. Meacham, that their lives were in danger, but the army officers refused to heed her advice. Meacham was a friend of the Riddles. They had previously worked with him and appreciated his advocacy of Indian rights, as well as his enforcement of legal marriages between white men and Native American women. The Modocs attacked the U.S. delegation, killing Canby and several others. Tobey Riddle interceded and rescued Meacham.

Tobey Riddle survived the Modoc War and lived the remainder of her life near the Klamath Reservation. She died in 1920.

—*Dawn Ottevaere*

See also Nonhelema; Ward, Nancy; Winnemucca, Sarah

References and Further Reading

Dillon, Richard. 1973. *Burnt-Out Fires.* Englewood Cliffs, NJ: Prentice-Hall.

Meacham, Alfred Benjamin.1876. *Wi-ne-ma (the Woman-Chief) and Her People.* Hartford, CT: American Publishing.

Murray, Keith A. 1959. *The Modocs and Their War.* Norman: University of Oklahoma.

Quinn, Arthur. 1997. *Hell with the Fire Out: A History of the Modoc War.* Boston: Faber and Faber.

Riddle, Jefferson C. Davis. 1914. *The Indian History of the Modoc War.* Repr., Mechanicsburg, PA: Stackpole Books, 2004.

WINNEMUCCA, SARAH (CA. 1844–1891)

Native American army scout. Born about 1844 near the Humboldt Sink in what is today western Nevada, Sarah Winnemucca began life as *Thocmetony* (Shell Flower), daughter of Northern Paiute chief Old Winnemucca. Her early years were characterized by brief encounters and conflicting attitudes toward Euro-Americans. As settlers traveled through Northern Paiute subsistence areas, Sarah's maternal grandfather, Chief Truckee, worked with white landowners and the military as a powerful advocate for multiethnic cooperation. Old Winnemucca, however, initially resisted Truckee's acceptance of settlement, and Sarah's personal experience inspired an early fear of white populations.

When Sarah was six, Truckee took her, along with her mother and siblings, to live on a California ranch. Sarah's older sister Mary experienced many difficulties with the white men there, developing a strong dislike of Euro-Americans. Discrimination against indigenous populations, negative attitudes toward interracial marriage, and a frontier exchange economy utilizing Native American slaves and concubines created a tenuous existence for the Paiute women. At the same time, Sarah's older brothers Natchez and Tom gained both economically and socially from the livestock they acquired working on the ranch. For several years the family passed back and forth between white and Paiute society. When she was thirteen Sarah and her sister Elma were adopted by whites and worked in the town of Genoa for Major William Ormsby, becoming acquainted with the Indian agent system. Sarah grew to adulthood in this gender frontier and cultural borderland, establishing her ability to move between ethnic groups and traditional expectations.

The combination of gold, religion, land settlement, and cultural diversity made the late-nineteenth-century California-Nevada border a center of conflict. Miners, Mormons, ranchers, entrepreneurs, and Native Americans existed in a difficult cultural crucible. White settlers constantly encroached on Indian lands, creating bloody battles, retaliations, and diplomatic missions. The Northern Paiutes suffered from starvation and disease on and off the reservation as they struggled to adapt. Sarah Winnemucca found herself both an active participant and a cultural mediator in these ongoing clashes.

In the 1860 Pyramid Lake War, Sarah's patron, Major Ormsby, was killed, and her family became subject to more rigorous military oversight. Influenced by these experiences, Sarah began her life's work as an interpreter, scout, lecturer, and Native American rights advocate, providing a middle ground between government agents, the military, and Northern Paiutes. She was fluent in many languages, including Spanish, and had taught herself to read and write English. With these skills, she was able to travel between white settlements, reservations, and government centers, including Washington, D.C.

Sarah Winnemucca. (Library of Congress)

In 1868, as a scout and interpreter at Camp McDermit, Sarah Winnemucca worked with the U.S. Army, peacefully bringing in her father and his followers. She distributed rations to the displaced Paiute refugees and arranged transportation for the women and children. During the Bannock War in 1878 Sarah again worked as an army scout and an advocate for the Northern Paiutes. Her family, along with a number of others, found themselves trapped with Bannock insurgents. Sarah and her brother attempted to free them and help them to safety before the

army arrived. At the center of conflict her entire life, Sarah died on October 17, 1891.

—*Dawn Ottevaere*

See also Nonhelema; Ward, Nancy; Winema

References and Further Reading

Brooks, James. 2002. *Captives and Cousins: Slavery, Kinship, and Community in the Southwest Borderlands.* Chapel Hill: University of North Carolina.

Canfield, Gae Whitney. 1983. *Sarah Winnemucca of the Northern Paiutes.* Norman: University of Oklahoma.

Senier, Siobhan. 2001. *Voices of American Indian Assimilation and Resistance: Helen Hunt Jackson, Sarah Winnemucca, and Victoria Howard.* Norman: University of Oklahoma.

Zanjani, Sally. 2001. *Sarah Winnemucca.* Lincoln: University of Nebraska.

WITHERINGTON, PEARL
(B. 1914)

British special agent and a leader of the French Maquis during World War II. Pearl Witherington was born in Paris on June 24, 1914. When the war broke out she was working in Paris for the British air attaché and was engaged to a Frenchman, Henri Cornioley, who had been conscripted at the beginning of the war. Witherington, her widowed mother, and three younger sisters went south to Marseilles and were able to make their way to England by July 1941. In Britain Witherington joined the Women's Auxiliary Air Force and became a flight officer. She joined the Special Operations Executive, where her fluency in French was a valued asset. She was trained in the use of explosives and under the code name Marie was parachuted into occupied France on September 22, 1943. Witherington was assigned to serve as a courier for the Stationer network headed by Maurice Southgate. To her surprise, she discovered that Cornioley, who escaped from a German prisoner-of-war camp, was part of the network.

When Southgate was arrested by the Gestapo in May 1944, Witherington and Amédée Maingard stepped in. They divided the network into two sections. Witherington took over as leader of the new Wrestler network and had nearly 2,000 armed Maquis under her command. They carried out sabotage and even engaged German units. In support of the D-Day landing, her units disrupted the movement of German forces by attacking railways between Paris and Bordeaux. Witherington's Wrestler network and Maingard's Shipwright group interrupted the rail lines in the Indre department 800 times in June 1944 and completely severed German telephone lines around Orleans (Foot 1984, 389, 440). The Germans, who posted placards with Witherington's photograph, offered a million francs for her capture (Foot 1984, 381). On June 10 Witherington and approximately 150 of her Maquis were surrounded by Germans but survived a 14-hour firefight. Witherington herself did not fire; she saw her role as that of organizer and leader. She subsequently said, "I don't think it's a woman's role to kill" (Rossiter 1986, 180). Her reticence did not impair the performance of her network. At Issoudun on September 11, 1944, a large German force surrendered to Maquis units, including those led by Witherington.

Following the German withdrawal to the north and east, Witherington returned to Britain and subsequently married Cornioley. Although she was recommended for the Military Cross, it was not given to women. She was bestowed the civil Member of the British Empire (MBE) but returned it, stating that "she had done nothing civil" (Foot 1984, 48). She was then given an MBE–Military by the Air Ministry, and she accepted that award. She was also awarded the Legion of Honor, the Croix de Guerre, and the Medal of Resistance by the French government.

—*Bernard Cook*

See also Atkins, Vera H.

References and Further Reading

64-baker-street.org. "The WAAF Agents—Pearl Witherington," The Women of the Special Operations Executive. http://www.64-baker-street.org/agents/agent_waaf_pearl_witherington.html (accessed September 28, 2004).

Foot, Michael Richard Daniell. 1984 (1966). *SOE in France: An Account of the Work of the British Special Operations Executive, 1940–1944.* Frederick, MD: University Publications of America.

Rossiter, Margaret L. 1986. *Women in the Resistance.* New York: Praeger.

Spartacus Web. "Pearl Witherington." http://www.spartacus.schoolnet.co.uk/SOEwitherington.htm (accessed September 28, 2004).

WOHLAUF, VERA

A willing eyewitness to the Holocaust. Vera Wohlauf married Captain Julius Wohlauf on June 29, 1942, in Hamburg. Julius was second in command of the First Company of Police Battalion 101, consisting of policemen from Hamburg and assigned to Poland. He had taken special leave to celebrate his wedding with Vera, who was already pregnant. The couple had a belated honeymoon in the town of Józefów in eastern Poland, where Captain Wohlauf would direct an operation intended to exterminate the town's Jews. In addition to Vera, Lucia Brandt, wife of Lieutenant Paul Brandt of the same police battalion, was there. After some days the unit, accompanied by the four-months-pregnant Vera, moved toward Radzyn. Early on the morning of August 25, 1942, the battalion marched toward the town of Miedzyrzec to conduct a clearing operation and to organize the deportation of Jews to the Treblinka death camp. The Wohlaufs rode in the front of a truck beside the driver. At Miedzyrzec Captain Wohlauf ordered the killing of the sick and elderly, as they could not be sent to the railway station. Many were ordered to stand still in the town square and were killed at the slightest movement. Vera, who had been indoctrinated in the Hitler Youth, witnessed the battalion kill 960 people and deport Jewish men and women in a jam-packed train. In the evening she and Lucia Brandt joined others for a party with their spouses.

The operation continued until July 1943, with more killings and the shipment of 13,000 to Treblinka. Miedzyrzec came to be known as *Menschengeschenk* (human gift) by the Nazis. Although Vera did not take part in any killings, she was seen moving with a riding whip in the town's public square. The presence of the women was tolerated by the Nazi officers, but because Vera was pregnant, her presence was resented by Major Wilhelm Trapp, the battalion commandant. Afterward women were prohibited from being spectators at operations. But as they were living with their husband in married quarters, the wives were privy to all happenings by evening time. After the war Julius was imprisoned for 8 years. By the time of his release Vera had died.

—*Patit Paban Mishra*

See also Holocaust and Jewish Women

References and Further Reading

Browning, Christopher. 1993. *Ordinary Men: Reserve Police Battalion 101 and the Final Solution in Poland.* New York: HarperCollins.

Cosner, Sharon. 1998. *Women under the Third Reich: A Biographical Dictionary.* Westport, CT: Greenwood.

Goldhagen, Daniel Jonah. 1997. *Hitler's Willing Executioners: Ordinary Germans and the Holocaust.* New York: Random House.

WRNS

See Great Britain, Women's Royal Naval Service

Yorck von Wartenburg, Countess Marion (1904–)

Member of the anti-Nazi resistance Kreisau Circle. Marion Winter, after earning a law degree, married Count Peter Yorck von Wartenburg. Their apartment became the meeting place for the Kreisau Circle, which plotted the July 20, 1944, assassination attempt against Hitler. Peter Yorck von Wartenburg was arrested the day of the failed attempt. Following repeated interrogations he was tried on August 8, sentenced to death, and executed that same day. The countess had participated in all the major conferences of the Kreisau Circle and had attended its meetings at her residence. Her appeals to see her husband were denied, and she was arrested on August 10. She was incarcerated and interrogated at the Gestapo headquarters at Prinz-Albrecht Strasse. She was then transferred to the Moabit prison before her release in November.

After the war she served as a judge in Berlin and ultimately became a presiding judge of Berlin's Superior Court.

—*Bernard Cook*

See also Ballestrem-Solf, Countess Lagi; Thadden, Elizabeth von

References and Further Reading

Wickert, Christl, ed. 1994. *Frauen gegen die Diktatur: Widerstand und Verfolgung im nationalsozialistischen Deutschland* [Women against Dictatorship: Resistance and Persecution in National Socialist Germany]. Berlin: Hentrich.

Yorck von Wartenburg, Marion. 1982. Es ist eine gute Erfahrung für einen Strafrichter, das Gefängnis von innen zu kennen [It Is a Good Experience for a Criminal Judge to Know the Inside of a Prison]. Pages 131–141 in *Juristinnen: Berichte, Fakten, Interviews* [Female Jurists: Reports, Facts, Interviews]. Edited by Margarete Fabricius-Brand, Sabine Berghahn, and Kristine Sudhölter. Berlin: Elefanten Press.

———. 1985. Die Stärke der Stille: Erinnerungen an ein Leben im deutschen Widerstand [The Strength of Silence: Memories of a Life in the German Resistance]. Cologne, Germany: Diederichs.

YOUNG MEN'S CHRISTIAN ASSOCIATION (YMCA), WORLD WAR I

A service organization that assisted soldiers during World War I. The Young Men's Christian Association (YMCA) was founded in England in 1844 and was first organized in the United States in 1851. From the time of the American Civil War, the YMCA helped soldiers and civilians through social programs and entertainment. When the United States entered World War I in April 1917, the YMCA was the first of the civil or social welfare organizations to offer its services to the government. In August 1917 U.S. Commander in Chief John Pershing issued a general order supporting YMCA work among his troops.

The YMCA refocused from civilian to military operations and concentrated on serving soldiers in any way possible. It established permanent posts and staff in all 16 National Guard camps, setting up shop in huts that were to substitute for home, school, theater, and church. Soldiers thronged to these huts day after day, looking for the feel and comforts of home. Eventually the YMCA operated 4,000 huts and tents for recreation and religious services, and YMCA volunteers served snacks to those aboard 8,000 troop trains. YMCA volunteers worked as surgeons, nurses, chaplains, chaplains' assistants, and distributors of emergency medical supplies, food, and clothing. YMCA volunteers served on battlefields with horse-drawn canteens, built and staffed special kitchens in hospitals, brought books and prefabricated chapels to soldiers, taught enlisted men to read and write, maintained a hotel in England for soldiers on furlough, and provided free meals.

The YMCA had a paid staff of 26,000 men and women and 35,000 volunteers to attend to the spiritual and social needs of soldiers at home and abroad. Initially, the army needed every soldier in the ranks, so the YMCA willingly assumed the burden of running canteens. The YMCA operated 1,500 canteens and post exchanges under policies and restrictions that the army established until it took them over later in the war.

The YMCA operated 26 rest and relaxation leave centers in France, which accommodated 1,944,300 U.S. officers and enlisted men. In London the YMCA opened the Eagle Hut on September 3, 1917, and staffed it with about 800 volunteers. The Eagle Hut offered overnight accommodations and food for U.S. servicemen, and by February 1919 about 134,566 meals had been served. The YMCA had initiated overseas entertainment for the troops during the Spanish-American War, and it expanded this program during World War I. It mobilized 1,470 entertainers and sent them overseas to perform for the troops. It also organized educational programs for soldiers in Europe and after the war continued this effort by awarding 80,000 educational scholarships to veterans of World War I, an action that prefigured the GI Bill.

—*Kathleen Warnes*

See also Furse, Lady Katherine Symonds

References and Further Reading

Firstworldwar.com. The Eagle Hut. http://www .firstworldwar.com/atoz/eaglehut.htm (accessed March 15, 2004).

Hopkins, Charles Howard. 1951. *History of the YMCA in North America.* New York: Association Press.

Hungerford, Edward. 1920. *With the Doughboy in France: A Few Chapters of an American Effort.* New York: Macmillan.

Taft, William Howard, and Frederick Harris, eds. 1922. *Service with Fighting Men: An Account of the Work of the American Young Men's Christian Association in the World War.* New York: Association Press.

WorldwarI.com. "The History of the YMCA in World War I." Doughboy Center. Presented by the Great War Society, Captain Ralph Blanchard, USN, Ret. http://www.worldwarI .com/dbc/ymca.htm (accessed March 15, 2004).

Yugoslavia, Mother and Bride Images of Militant Serbian Nationalism

Mythic images inspiring militant Serbian nationalism. The theme of defeat at the hands of the Turks in Kosovo stands at the very heart of Serbian heroic poetry, and the mythical character of the mother of the Jugovic brothers represents the tragic motif of sacrifice for the lost freedom of the national state.

The mother is in fact the motherland of the nine brothers, who, in turn, are allegorical figures of martyred King Lazar's knights. They serenely led their 12,000 soldiers despite the prospect of their own imminent death on the Field of the Blackbirds in Kosovo in 1389.

Two black ravens, representing death and misfortune, bring the mother the torn hand of her youngest son, Damjan, still bearing his wedding ring, a symbol of new life and hope. The allegorical character of the mourning motherland, crushed by the loss of her sons, then fell down and disintegrated. She had sent her sons to death for their country and its freedom, all that was precious. Once these were lost on the Kosovo Plain, nothing remained to be valued and loved. Thus she dematerialized.

The other image of the motherland is the Kosovo Girl. She is the perpetual fiancée of the fallen hero, whose never-to-be-healed wounds she dresses in vain. Even when she seeks comfort under a green fir tree, it withers. The Kosovo Girl is the archetype of the unfortunate destiny of the Serbian Christian motherland during its armed confrontation with the aggressive Islam of the Middle Ages.

—*Miodrag Milin*

See also Yugoslavia, Women in the Military during World War II; Yugoslavia, Women and the Wars That Accompanied the Disintegration of Yugoslavia

References and Further Reading

Gjuric, Milos. 1918. *Smrt majke Jugovica. Knjicevno—filozofijska studija* [The Death of the Mother of the Jugovitch—A Philosophical Study]. Zagreb: Izdanja Grica.

Nogo, Rajko Petrov, ed. 1987. *Srpske junacke pjesme* [Serbian Heroic Poems]. 3rd ed. Belgrad: Beogradski Izdavacki Graficki Zavod.

Yugoslavia, Women in the Military during World War II

Significant role played by Yugoslav women in the Yugoslav Partisan resistance following the German conquest of Yugoslavia in April 1941. South Slav women had performed military service before; in 1858, for example, a battalion of women fought with the Montenegrin army against the Turks. It was the desperate situation during World War II, however, that led to the inclusion of so many women in the Communist Partisan forces. The initial Partisans came from the ranks of the Communist Party and the Communist Youth Organization. Many young, educated women were drawn to what they regarded as the liberating vision of the Communist Party. Most women Partisans, however, came from the peasantry, and 80 percent of Yugoslav women at the time were illiterate (Jancar-Webster 1990, 49, 65). Young women, motivated by camaraderie and a sense of purpose, enthusiastically volunteered for military action in the National Liberation Movement. Seventy percent of the women were under the age of 20, and the majority were Serbian (Jancar-Webster 1990, 48–49). Personal loss propelled many into the Partisan movement. Life was so perilous in occupied Yugoslavia that joining the Partisans seemed for many preferable to the insecurity of powerlessness. For many, joining the Partisans opened the prospect of new experiences and opportunities. Women learned to read and gained skills, which served them after the war if they survived. Many, however, did not. The casualty rate for female Partisans exceeded that for males.

One hundred thousand women served as soldiers in the National Liberation Army (NLA). Initially, 1 out of 10 NLA soldiers was a woman, but the proportion rose to 1 out of 8. In addition 2 million women were mobilized in the Anti-Fascist Front of Women (Anti-Fashisticki Front na Zenite, AFZ). These women ran local governments, provided support to the frontline fighters, and engaged in sabotage. According to Barbara Jancar, "From 1941 to 1945 8.5 percent of the total female population of Yugoslavia was killed or died" (Jancar 1982, 91). Twenty-five percent of the women who joined the NLA died, versus 11 percent for males, but there was an even higher casualty rate among the AFZ (Jancar 1982, 93). Though AFZ members were not formally soldiers, the war was a guerrilla one, and the front was elusive. When the Nazis and their allies overran villages, AFZ women fought and were killed or captured. Often capture led to rape, torture, and murder. Some have asserted that the higher casualty rate for women fighters resulted from their inexperience. Other observers, however, have asserted that the women, in general, fought more bravely than the men (Djilas 1977, 210).

Although 2,000 women did become officers in the NLA, women officers were few and predominantly limited to lower ranks. Of the 92 women fighters proclaimed national heroes by the postwar Yugoslav government, only 13 were officers, and 10 of these were political officers. Of these, only 3 served as unit commanders, and only 1 of these commanded a unit as large as a *ceta* (a detachment of approximately 300 fighters) (Jancar-Webster 1990, 92). Though there were more female fighters than female medics, women in the NLA disproportionately served in medical roles. In this guerrilla war, however, medics fought and died as regularly as other categories of combatants. After the victory of the Partisans, women were demobilized. Their participation in war, as far as the Yugoslav People's Army leadership was concerned, had been an emergency measure. When the Warsaw Pact forces invaded Czechoslovakia in August 1968, expedience again required the militarization of women. To deter Soviet intervention in Yugoslavia, the state organized the Territorial Defense Forces. Women as well as men were given military training in school, and two females became Territorial Defense Force generals. Women were also allowed to volunteer for service in what had previously been an all-male national army.

—*Bernard Cook*

See also Kufrin, Milka; Milosavljevi, Danica

References and Further Reading

Djilas, Milovan. 1977. *Wartime.* New York: Harcourt Brace Jovanovitch.

Jancar, Barbara. 1982. Yugoslavia: War of Resistance. In *Female Soldiers—Combatants or Noncombatants? Historical and Contemporary Perspectives.* Edited by Nancy Loring Goldman. Westport, CT: Greenwood.

Jancar-Webster, Barbara. 1990. *Women and Revolution in Yugoslavia, 1941–1945.* Denver, CO: Arden.

YUGOSLAVIA, WOMEN AND THE WARS THAT ACCOMPANIED THE DISINTEGRATION OF YUGOSLAVIA

Fate of women during the wars in the former Yugoslavia (1991–1999). The wars that arose from the breakup of Yugoslavia in the 1990s precipitated a humanitarian crisis of epic proportions. A vibrant multicultural and ethnically diverse society suddenly imploded, reflecting religious and ethnic feelings that were fueled by corrupt and ambitious politicians seeking to exploit these conflicts for their own ends. Women at all levels of society were caught in

Bosnian Muslim women cry as their relative is buried in Potocari, July 11, 2005. Relatives wept over more than 600 coffins of victims of the Srebrenica massacre, dug out of death pits at a ceremony to mark the tenth anniversary of Europe's worst atrocity in 50 years. The coffins contained the latest identified remains found in mass graves dug by Bosnian Serb forces to hide their slaughter of 8,000 Muslim men between July 11 and July 18, 1995. (Damir Sagolj/Reuters/Corbis)

savage fighting in which they were both the targets of and the justification for ethnic cleansing. How women suffered and how they responded reflects cultural, economic, social, and political issues that went to the heart of their position in Muslim, Serbian, and Croat communities and were central to the international response to the conflicts in Bosnia, Croatia, and Kosovo.

The Communist era marked a period of social, economic, and political stability that benefited women. Under Marshal Tito, Yugoslavia was an ordered society with clear rules and norms. In a socialist society with no capitalistic economic fluctuations, low divorce and child

mortality rates, and relatively low unemployment, ethnic and religious conflict was minimal. Serbs, Croats, and Muslims lived together, often in the same villages and neighborhoods, as they had for generations. Tito had established a delicate balance among Yugoslavia's ethnic groups, preaching an ideology of "peace and brotherhood." A complicated constitution had created six republics and two autonomous regions (within Serbia), tied together through their common loyalty to the president and reinforced by a repressive police state. Despite the high degree of political control from the top, Yugoslav women enjoyed comparative freedom and social equality. Higher education and the professions were open to them along with social services. Although they rarely reached the top of the ruling hierarchy, women were active in politics at the village, district, and provincial levels.

The stability of the Tito era evaporated following the president's death in 1980. Economic decay and drift led to rising unemployment that heightened both ethnic and gender tensions. Tito's successors tried rotating the presidency among the five ethnic republics, but this revolving-door system triggered conflicts among Yugoslavia's senior political figures and did not work. Ambitious politicians—most notably Slobodan Milosevic—revived ethnic nationalism for their own purposes. By the late 1980s Milosevic was using the Serb media to stir up Serbian nationalism along with anti-Croat and, particularly, anti-Muslim feelings. The Croats, led by Franjo Tudjman, a former general of the Yugoslav national army, responded with their own brand of nationalism. Tudjman was openly anti-Serb and anti-Muslim.

The brand of nationalism that Milosevic, Tudjman, and their adherents preached had heavily gendered overtones involving the subordination of women. The prevailing concern of these new ethnic-national ideologies with the establishment of cultural and religious values associated with an idealized past meant that women were to be assigned traditional roles. Foremost among these were responsibilities for the reproduction of the group and for the nurturing of cultural values and group identity. This new nationalism marked a revival and celebration of traditional gender codes and male power. Any notions of women's emancipation developed during the state socialist regime (better access to education, equal employment, equal pay, liberal abortion rights, and so forth) were demonized as unnatural and destructive to the group.

The effects of the wars surrounding Yugoslavia's dissolution were magnified by their sudden outbreak and, particularly in Bosnia, by the violent onslaught of the federal army and the Serb militias. Fighting had already occurred in June and July 1991 after Slovenia and Croatia declared independence from Yugoslavia. Hostilities erupted in the Bosnian capital, Sarajevo, in April 1992 after Bosnia and Herzegovina, with a plurality of Muslims and a majority of Muslims and Croats, also declared independence from Yugoslavia. Fearing the consequences of Bosnian independence and infused with nationalist propaganda and material support from Milosevic, the large Serb minority in Bosnia resorted to force.

The war's socioeconomic impact on women in Bosnia was immediate and devastating. The violence they faced was economic, social, and psychological as well as physical. Women in all of the affected areas had to deal with food shortages; loss of their homes due to shelling and bombing; dislocation; loneliness as their men were mobilized into the ethnic militias, killed in the fighting, executed, or sent into exile; and the possibility of being raped or murdered. They lived in constant fear for their own lives and futures as well as those of their families. If their men survived, women had to confront the reality of living with the psychological damage caused by their experiences.

Physical violence, most often in the form of the systematic rape of Muslim women in Bosnia by Serb forces, was central to the strategy of ethnic cleansing. Instances of women being specifically targeted in war zones is not new. In the case of the new ethnically-based nation building in the former Yugoslavia, however, this practice has a specific meaning. It was part of a massive gendered population transfer, if not outright genocide, that operated as a crucial symbolic and material element in the forging of new boundaries between ethnic collectives. This massive forced transfer resulted in women and children being exposed to various forms of violence. The worst attacks on women happened in the areas of the bloodiest fighting—those regions of Bosnia-Herzegovina and Croatia where Serbs, Croats, and Muslims had lived in close proximity to one another before Yugoslavia's collapse. The concept of women as symbols and reproducers or nurturers of the nation and its cultural identity made them important in the destruction of the opposing ethnic-national group. War reinforced the influence of religious traditionalism that demanded the withdrawal of women from policymaking positions where they might moderate the extreme nationalistic tendencies that surfaced in all of the camps. Thus Croatian nationalism gave the Catholic Church in Croatia greater influence, reinforcing its traditional view of the role of women. In Bosnia Islamic extremists demanded that women receiving aid cover their heads, a step toward keeping them "in their place" (Hunt 2004, 139). Women's subordinate status left them unprotected and made them targets. Reinforcing the practice of directing violence specifically toward women was the stigma that rape carried in highly patriarchal family structures. Men in all of the warring ethnic groups viewed their specific patriarchal family structures as the ideal they were fighting for. The effectiveness of this strategy—as well as its appalling human consequences—is reflected in the fact that nearly 70 percent of the refugees from the fighting in Bosnia-Herzegovina were women and children (Korac 1998, 163).

The suffering of these refugees and their portrayal in the Western news media generated pressures on the international community to intervene. The initial international reaction to the wars in the former Yugoslavia and reports of mass rape and ethnic cleansing was tentative and ineffective. The United States and the European Community both recognized Bosnia's independence. The United Nations sent small peacekeeping forces (mostly from the Netherlands, France, and Canada) to protect refugee sanctuaries and provide food and medical supplies to war victims. These measures did not deter Serb atrocities or protect refugees from marauding Serb forces. The United Nations recognized Bosnian independence and admitted Bosnia to the United Nations while barring Milosevic's rump Yugoslav state. The United Nations also ordered trade sanctions against Ser-

bia. The U.N. Security Council, however, refused to order the use of force. Similarly, the United States and the North Atlantic Treaty Organization (NATO) were reluctant to get involved militarily. An arms embargo against both sides hindered Muslim efforts to get weapons even as the Bosnian Serbs received arms from Serbia and Russia. This ineffective reaction on the part of the United Nations and the Western powers further undermined U.N. and NATO credibility among all of the warring ethnic factions, thus jeopardizing peace efforts. U.N. weakness was shown at its worst on July 11, 1995, when Serb forces entered a supposed U.N. safe zone in Srebrenica, pushed aside a small U.N. force, and rounded up 25,000 unarmed Muslim men, women, and children. They tortured and killed the men and boys, and the women and girls were forced to flee. The international outcry over the Srebrenica atrocity finally triggered military action by the United States and NATO that forced the Serbs into negotiations at Dayton, Ohio.

Exposed to the ravages of war and unable to rely on international efforts or protection from their own men, politically active women in Bosnia-Herzegovina and Croatia began to take matters into their own hands. Ironically, the wars and genocide that Serb and Croatian ethnic nationalists unleashed shattered the credibility of their notions of traditional women's roles and led to a heightened group consciousness among women on all sides. Their suffering led many into increased political and social activism.

Despite the gender-restrictive nationalist ideologies that pervaded all sides, the wars afforded women opportunities for service outside their traditional roles. Women with medical training as doctors and nurses were in demand to staff military hospitals. In these positions, they often helped negotiate local cease-fires to evacuate wounded soldiers and civilians. The absence of the male family head often left women in charge of harvesting crops and running family businesses.

The greatest opportunities for women, however, grew out of their suffering. Refugee camps in particular provided organizing opportunities for female activists. Women in the camps found that their efforts to find the basic elements of survival—food, clothing, housing, and money—depended on their sticking together and organizing. Local self-help groups such as the Association of Displaced Persons and Refugees of Bosnia and Herzegovina (formed during the siege of Sarajevo) not only facilitated communication among women in the camps but also served as avenues for refugee women to mobilize international human rights groups (such as Amnesty International) and women's organizations (such as Women Waging Peace) to help alleviate their plight and facilitate the peace process. Women's groups both on the scene and in the United States were active in contradicting the Balkan nationalists' contention that ethnic hatreds were deep-seated and inevitable, in agitating for stronger intervention in the wars of the former Yugoslavia, and in facilitating a peace process. Swanee Hunt, who served as U.S. ambassador to Austria from 1993 to 1997, was responding in part to reports from women in the refugee camps when she hosted negotiations and several international symposia to facilitate peace efforts in Bosnia-Herzegovina.

Despite intensifying female activism both in the war zone and internationally, women were excluded from the peace negotiations that commenced in Dayton, Ohio, in the fall of 1995. Many women activists believe that the warmakers intentionally shut them out of the Dayton talks because they feared women would give peace priority over nationalist aims. In any case, the Dayton negotiations allowed Serbian and Croatian nationalists to carve Bosnia up along unworkable ethnic lines. Most women activists were unhappy with the Dayton Accords because their implementation depended on the very elements responsible for the war to begin with. Although women comprised over half of the adult population of Bosnia, the elements charged with implementing the Dayton Accords did not seek or welcome their opinions. This omission undermined international peace efforts before, during, and after the Serb-Bosnian war. The Dayton negotiators ducked the war crimes issue by not requiring the parties to turn over Milosevic, Ratko Mladic (the senior commander of the Bosnian Serb army), and other accused war criminals to the Hague Tribunal for trial. In the view of many observers, the omissions of the Dayton Accords sent a signal to the Serb leadership that the international community would not take decisive action in the face of ethnic cleansing in other parts of the former Yugoslavia. Thus the same issues appeared in the brutal Serb attempt to stop the predominately Albanian–Muslim province of Kosovo from breaking away from Serbia in 1999—leading to a massive U.S.-NATO bombing campaign against Serbia.

The flaws of the Dayton Accords, as well as the hope they symbolized, galvanized women to organize to gain a greater voice in postwar Balkan politics and to create a stronger political and economic base to protect themselves. In June 1996, 500 women convened a meeting in Sarajevo to organize Women Transforming Themselves and Society. Funded by Women Waging Peace, it was the first effort following the Dayton agreement to bring citizens together across ethnic lines. The fall of Milosevic in the face of international economic sanctions and the Serbian withdrawal from Kosovo and his extradition to The Hague for war crimes trials (along with several other major accused war criminals) served as partial vindication for the victims of the Balkan wars of the 1990s. The success of the victims in highlighting their suffering is reflected in rulings from the World Court and the International Criminal Tribunal for the Former Yugoslavia that mass rape is a war crime. Their courage and resourcefulness in the face of horrific conditions and their development of a common sense of identity present a moving story. Their political significance for women in similar circumstances is even greater.

—*Walter Bell*

See also Markovic, Mirjana; Plavsic, Biljana; Rape in War

References and Further Reading

Cohen, Roger. 1998. *Hearts Grown Brutal: Sagas of Sarajevo.* New York: Random House.

Hunt, Swanee. 2004. *This Was Not Our War: Bosnian Women Reclaiming the Peace.* Durham, NC: Duke University.

Korac, Maja. 1998. Ethnic-Nationalism, Wars and the Patterns of Social, Political, and Sexual Violence against Women: The Case of the Post-Yugoslav Countries. *Identities* 5(2):153–171.

Kunovich, Robert M., and Katherine Deitelbaum. 2004. Ethnic Conflict, Group Polarization, and Gender Attitudes in Croatia. *Journal of Marriage and the Family* 66:1089–1107.

Ogata, Sadako. 2005. *The Turbulent Decade: Confronting the Refugee Crisis of the 1990s.* New York: W. W. Norton.

Power, Samantha. 2002. *A Problem from Hell: America and the Age of Genocide.* New York: Basic Books.

Z

ZANE, ELIZABETH (BETTY) (1766–1831)

Heroine of the Virginia frontier during what has been called the last battle of the American Revolution. Schooled in Philadelphia, sixteen-year-old Elizabeth Zane had recently returned to the town of Wheeling in Western Virginia. The town had been founded by her five brothers in 1769. When Zane returned from Philadelphia, she lived with her brother Ebenezer, whose cabin was located near Fort Henry. This garrison had already been used to defend against British and Indian attack in 1777.

One day in September 1782 a group of about 300 Indians and 50 British Rangers were spotted approaching the area. Betty and the rest of the townspeople were quickly herded into the fort as the attack began. Zane tended to the wounded and served food and drink. On the third day morale dwindled among the townsfolk as their supply of gunpowder petered out. Colonel Zane had a keg of gunpowder hidden in his cabin but did not know how to safely retrieve it. Betty Zane volunteered, saying she could run fast enough to make it to the cabin. She told her friends and neighbors that men were needed in the fort and that other women could help care for the wounded if anything happened to her. In the end it was agreed that she could make the attempt, and Zane removed her skirts so she could run faster. After she was let out of the fort she dashed the approximately 50-yard (45-meter) distance to the cabin, surprising enemy forces. On arrival at the cabin, she found the powder keg under the floorboards but realized it was too heavy to carry. She then packed the powder in a carpet that lay nearby. As she ran back to the fort with the powder wrapped in the carpet, she was fired on but arrived at Fort Henry unscathed except for a hole in her clothes where a bullet had grazed her. The townspeople used the new powder to hold off the attackers that night, and by the fourth day the Indians and British gave up and retreated.

Not much else is known about the remainder of her life. It is thought that she died in Ohio. Zane's story was first recorded in 1831, with the publication of Alexander S. Withers's *Chronicles of Border Warfare*. Her story was disputed by the last survivor of the siege at Fort Henry, who claimed Zane did not perform any heroics that day. Zane's legend later grew thanks to the great-grandson of Colonel Zane, the popular writer Zane Gray, who in 1903 wrote a fictional account of her life and heroics based on the actual events. The novel, called *Betty Zane*, helped cement a place for Zane in history.

—*Richard Panchyk*

See also American Revolution, Role of Women in the

References and Further Reading

Anticaglia, Elizabeth. 1975. *Heroines of '76*. New York: Walker.

Hintzen, William. 1995. Betty Zane, Lydia Boggs, and Molly Scott: The Gunpowder Exploits at Fort Henry. *West Virginia History* 55:95–109.

ZENOBIA, QUEEN OF PALMYRA (D. AFTER 274)

Warrior queen who fought against the Romans. In the third century Palmyra was a Roman client kingdom, a prosperous city on the Roman-Persian frontier that controlled several important caravan routes. The story of Palmyra's rebellion against Rome, led by Queen Zenobia (also Septima Zenobia and, in Aramaic, Znwbya Bat Zabbai), provides one of the very few examples of women actively engaging in battle in the ancient world.

Zenobia's husband, King Odenathus of Palmyra, was assassinated around A.D. 266. Zenobia, his second wife, then took power, officially as regent for her son Wahballat. She presented herself from the first as a warrior queen, claiming descent from Queen Cleopatra VII of Egypt.

Rome was in a chaotic state during this period. Emperor Valerian had been defeated and captured by the Persians in 260; worse, the empire had descended into a cycle of civil wars as rival generals fought for the imperial title. Zenobia soon began to take advantage of this Roman weakness, successfully claiming a number of neighboring Roman territories. By 269 Zenobia's general, Zabdas, had gained control of most of Egypt, and Zenobia herself annexed most of Syria. Her armies were victorious as far north as the Black Sea. Zenobia declared herself independent of Rome and claimed for herself the title of empress.

A lull in Rome's civil wars came with the reign of Emperor Aurelian (270–275). In 271 and 272 he turned his attention to the grievous losses in the eastern empire. A good general, he quickly reconquered Egypt and moved on to other lands Zenobia had taken. The Romans met the Palmyrene army of about 70,000 men and 1 woman near Antioch. Zenobia personally commanded the forces, riding her horse in the thick of battle—the only woman known to have done so in the Greco-Roman world. She maintained a minimum of propriety by transmitting her orders through her generals. Defeated by the more highly trained Roman troops at Antioch and again at Emesa, Zenobia took refuge in the city of Palmyra. She was soon captured while attempting to escape the city with her son.

Aurelian took the captive Zenobia back to Rome, where, following tradition, she was paraded in chains at his triumph in 274. Aurelian was apparently impressed by the queen and after the triumph allowed her to retire to a villa near Tivoli. She soon married a Roman senator and became noted for her frequent and elaborate entertainments in Rome. The queen spent the rest of her life quietly, and the year of her death is not known. Roman writers were fascinated by Zenobia. They compared her to Cleopatra VII and told of her beauty, chastity, learning, and enormous wealth.

—*Phyllis G. Jestice*

See also Roman Women and War

References and Further Reading

Stoneman, Richard. 1992. *Palmyra and Its Empire: Zenobia's Revolt against Rome*. Ann Arbor: University of Michigan.

ACRONYMS

AAFFTD	Army Air Forces Flying Training Detachment (U.S.)
AANS	Australian Army Nursing Service
ADF	Air Defense Forces (USSR)
AFF	American Friends of France (Comité Americain de Secours Civil)
AFL	Actresses' Franchise League
AFZ	Anti-Fascist Front of Women (Yugoslavia)
AIDS	Acquired Immunodeficiency Syndrome
ALNU	Australian League of Nations Union
AMES	Asociación de Mujeres Salvadreñas (Association of Salvadoran Women)
AMNLAE	Asociación de Mujeres Nicaraguenses "Luisa Amanda Espinoza" (Association of Nicaraguan Women "Luisa Amanda Espinoza")
AMPRONAC	Asociación de Mujeres ante la Problematica Nacional (Association of Nicaraguan Women Confronting the National Problem)
AMS	Auxiliary Military Service (UK)
ANAPO	National Popular Alliance (Colombia)
ANC	African National Congress (South Africa)
ANC	Army Nurse Corps (U.S.)
ANFASEP	Asociación Nacional de Familiares de Secuestrados (Relatives of the Disappeared) (Peru)
ANL	Army of National Liberation (Algeria)
AP	Associated Press
APA	Australian Peace Alliance
APO	Ausserparlamentarische Opposition (Extraparliamentary Opposition) (Germany)
ARC	American Red Cross
ATA	Air Transport Auxiliary (UK)
ATG	Alaska Territorial Guard (U.S.)
ATS	Auxiliary Territorial Service (UK); also Auxiliary Transport Service
AWAS	Australian Women's Army Service
BDF	Federation of German Women's Associations (Germany)

BFT	Bomber Flight Test Branch (U.S.)
BR	Brigate Rosse (Red Brigades) (Italy)
BRC	British Red Cross
CA	Church Army (UK)
CBCs	Comunidades Eclesiaticas de Base (Christian Base Communities) (El Salvador)
CBE	Commander of the British Empire
CBPP	contagious bovine pleuropneumonia
CCP	Chinese Communist Party
CND	Campaign for Nuclear Disarmament (UK)
CP	Communist Party
CPA	Communist Party of Australia
CPS	Civilian Public Service (U.S.)
CPT	Civilian Pilot Training program (U.S.)
CUC	Comité Unidad Campesina (Peasant Unity Committee) (Guatemala)
DACOWITS	Defense Advisory Committee on Women in the Services (U.S.)
DAG	Democratic Army of Greece
DAR	Daughters of the American Revolution
DBE	Dame Commander of the British Empire
DCPC	Direct Combat Probability Coding System (Risk Rule) (U.S.)
DDP	German Democratic Party (Germany)
DRC	Democratic Republic of the Congo (formerly Zaire)
EA	Ethniki Allilegyi (National Solidarity) (Greece)
EAM	Ethniko Apeleftherotiko Metopo (National Liberation Front) (Greece)
EDSNN	Ejército Defensor de la Soberanía Nacional de Nicaragua (Army in Defense of the National Sovereignty of Nicaragua)
EGP	Ejército Guerrillero de los Pobres (Guerrilla Army of the Poor) (Guatemala)
ELAS	Ellinikos Laikos Apeleftherotikos Stratos (Greek People's Liberation Army)
ELF	East London Federation of Suffragettes (UK)
ELN	Ejército de Liberación Nacional (National Liberation Army) (Colombia)
ENSA	Entertainment National Service Association
EPON	Eniaias Panelladikis Organosis Neon (United Panhellenic Organization of Youth) (Greece)
ETA	Euskadi ta Askatasuna (Basque Country and Freedom) (Spain)
EZLN	Ejército Zapatista de Liberación Nacional (Zapatista Army of National Liberation) (Mexico)
FANY	First Aid Nursing Yeomanry (UK)
FAR	Fuerzas Armadas Rebeldes (Revolutionary Armed Forces) (Guatemala)
FARC	Fuerzas Armadas Revolucionarias de Colombia (Revolutionary Armed Forces of Colombia)

FDLR	Forces Démocratiques de Liberation du Rwanda (Democratic Forces for the Liberation of Rwanda)
FEC	Far East Command Headquarters (U.S. and UK)
FFT	Fighter Flight Test (U.S.)
FMLN	Frente Farabundo Martí para la Liberación Nacional (Farabundo Martí National Liberation Front) (El Salvador)
FPO	Fareynigte Partizaner Organizatsie (United Partisan Organization) (Jewish)
FSA	Farm Security Administration (U.S.)
FSLN	Frente Sandinista de Liberación Nacional (the Sandinista National Liberation Front) (Nicaragua)
GAM	Grupo de Ayuda Mutua (Mutual Support Society) (Guatemala)
GPO	General Post Office
GUIW	General Federation of Iraqi Women
HIV	human immunodeficiency virus
HRF	Hero of the Russian Federation
HSU	Hero of the Soviet Union
IACHR	Inter-American Commission on Human Rights
ICA	Irish Citizen Army
ICBL	International Campaign to Ban Land Mines
ICW	International Congress of Women
ICWPP	International Committee of Women for Permanent Peace
IDF	Israeli Defense Force
INC	Indian National Congress
IRA	Irish Republican Army
JWOPY	Jewish Warring Organization of Pioneer Youth
KAU	Kenya African Union
KMT	Kuomingtang (Guomindang) Nationalist Party (China)
KPD	Kommunistische Partei Deutschlands (German Communist Party)
LORAN	Long Range Aid to Navigation (U.S.)
LTTE	Liberation Tigers of Tamil Eelam (Tamil Tigers)
LWV	Women's League of Voters (U.S.)
M19	19th of April Movement (Colombia)
MASH	Mobile Army Surgical Hospital Unit (U.S.)
MBE	Member of the British Empire
MCWR	Marine Corps Women's Reserve (U.S.)
MI5	Military Intelligence 5, Counterespionage (UK)
MIFTAH	Palestinian Initiative for the Promotion of Global Dialogue and Democracy
MOS	Military Occupational Specialties (U.S.)
MP	member of Parliament (UK)

MRDA	Mundri Relief and Development Association (Sudan)
MSTS	Military Sea Transport Service (U.S.)
MUFC	Mandela United Football Club (South Africa)
NAACP	National Association for the Advancement of Colored People (U.S.)
NACA	National Advisory Committee for Aeronautics (U.S.)
NATO	North Atlantic Treaty Organization
NAWSA	National American Women's Suffrage Association
NCO	noncommissioned officer
NEA	Newspaper Enterprise Association (U.S.)
NGO	nongovernmental organization
NLA	National Liberation Army (Yugoslavia)
NLMA	National Legion of Mothers of America (U.S.)
NSBRO	National Service Board for Religious Objectors (U.S.)
NSF/DFW	National Socialist Frauenschaft/Deutsches Frauenwerk (Women's Organization/Women's Work) (Germany)
NSK	Nasjonal Samlings Kvinneorganisasjon (National Gathering Women's Movement) (Norway)
NSWF	New Sudan Woman's Federation
NUWSS	National Union of Women's Suffrage Societies (UK)
OBE	Order of the British Empire (UK)
ORPA	La Organización del Pueblo en Armas (Organization of People in Arms) (Guatemala)
OSS	Office of Strategic Services (U.S. intelligence organization during World War II)
PDF	Panamanian Defense Forces
PFM	Popular Feminine Movement of Ayacucho (Peru)
PGT	Partido Guatemalteco del Trabajo (Guatemalan Labor Party)
PKK	Partiya Karkeren Kurdistan (Kurdistan Worker's Party) (Turkey/Iraq)
PLO	Palestine Liberation Organization
PLSK	Pomocnicza Lotnicza Sluzba Kobiet (Polish Auxiliary Air Force)
POW	prisoner of war
PX	post exchange
QAIMNS	Queen Alexandra's Imperial Military Nursing Service (UK)
RAANC	Royal Australian Army Nursing Corps
RAF	Rote Armee Faktion (Red Army Faction) (Germany)
RAF	Royal Air Force (UK)
RB	Red Brigades (Italy) (see BR)
ROC	Reserve Officer Candidate program (U.S.)
ROKWAC	Republic of Korea Women's Army Corps
RPF	Rwandan Patriotic Front

RSFSR	Russian Soviet Federated Socialist Republic
RTLM	Radio Tèlèvision Libre de Mille Collines (Rwanda)
RVV	Haarlemse Raad van Verzet (Haarlem Resistance Council) (Netherlands)
SACP	South Africa Communist Party
SAS	Special Air Services (UK)
SAWN	Spanish-American War Nurses (U.S.)
SD	Sicherheit Deinst (Nazi Security Service)
SIP	Sisterhood of International Peace
SL	Sendero Luminoso (the Shining Path) (Peru)
SOE	Special Operations Executive (British secret operatives during World War II)
SPARs	Women Reserves in the U.S. Coast Guard (from *Semper Paratus*—Always Ready)
SPD	Sozialdemokratische Partei Deutschlands (Social Democratic Party of Germany)
SS	Schutzstaffel (Defense Echelon) (Nazi Germany)
SSAFA	Soldiers', Sailors' and Airmen's Families Association
SWH	Scottish Women's Hospitals
SWSF	Scottish Women's Suffrage Federation
SWVP	Sudanese Women's Voice for Peace
TRC	Truth and Reconciliation Commission (Peru and South Africa)
UAW	United Association of Women (Australia)
UCLA	University of California at Los Angeles
UFR	Unión Feminista Revolucionario (Revolutionary Women's Union) (Cuba)
UNICEF	United Nations International Children's Emergency Fund
URNG	Unidad Revolucionaria Nacional de Guatemala (Guatemalan National Revolutionary Unity)
USAREUP	U.S. Army Headquarters, Europe
USMAG/ROK	U.S. Military Advisory Group/Republic of Korea
USO	United Service Organizations (U.S.)
USPD	Unabhängige Sozialdemocratische Partei Deutschlands (Independent Socialist Party) (Germany)
VAD	Voluntary Aid Detachment (Australia, UK)
VVA	Vietnam Veterans of America
WAAC	Women's Army Auxiliary Corps (UK, U.S.)
WAAF	Women's Auxiliary Air Force (UK)
WAC	Women's Army Corps (U.S.)
WAC(I)	Women's Auxiliary Corps (India) (UK)
WAF	Women in the Air Force (U.S.)
WAFS	Women's Auxiliary Ferrying Squadron (U.S.)
WASP	Women Airforce Service Pilots (U.S.)

WAVES	Women Accepted for Voluntary Emergency Service (U.S. Navy Women's Reserve)
WCCA	Wartime Civil Control Authority (U.S.)
WDM	World Disarmament Movement
WEC	Women's Emergency Corps (with fellow members of the Actresses' Franchise League [AFL])
WFTD	Women's Flying Training Detachment ("Woofteds") (U.S.)
WHC	Women's Hospital Corps
WHD	Women's Home Defense Corps (UK)
WILPF	Women's International League for Peace and Freedom
WLV	Women's League of Voters (U.S.)
WMCR	Women's Marine Corps Reserve (U.S.)
WNSL	Women's National Service League (UK)
WNWRA	Women's National War Relief Association (U.S.)
WODRANS	Widows, Orphans, and the Disabled Rehabilitation Association of New Sudan
WPA	Women's Peace Army (Australia)
WPA	Works Progress Administration (U.S.)
WRA	War Relocation Authority (U.S.)
WRAF	Women's Royal Air Force (UK)
WRL	War Resisters League (U.S.)
WRNS	Women's Royal Naval Service (referred to as the Wrens) (UK)
WSPU	Women's Social and Political Union (UK)
WSWCT	Women's Sick and Wounded Convoy Troops (UK)
WVS	Women's Volunteer Service (UK)
WWC	Women's Work Committee
WWM	Women's Workers' Movement
YMCA	Young Men's Christian Association

SELECT BIBLIOGRAPHY

Adie, Kate. 2003. *Corsets to Camouflage: Women and War.* London: Hodder and Stoughton (published in association with the Imperial War Museum, London). Written by a British war correspondent, this book deals primarily with the role of British women in war and the impact that war has had on the women of Britain in general. Many photographs are included.

Binney, Marcus. 2003. *The Women Who Lived for Danger: The Agents of the Special Operations Executive.* New York: HarperCollins. A study of the women who served in the British Special Operations Executive during World War II.

Blanton, DeAnna, and Lauren M. Cook. 2002. *They Fought Like Demons: Women Soldiers in the American Civil War.* Baton Rouge: Louisiana State University Press. The story of women who fought during the American Civil War. An additional source for this subject is Elizabeth D. Leonard, *All the Daring of the Soldier: Women of the Civil War Armies* (New York: W. W. Norton, 1999).

Bochkareva, Maria L., with Don Levine. 1919. *Yashka: My Life as a Peasant Officer and Exile.* New York: Frederick A. Stokes. This book purports to be an account of Bochkareva's life as recounted to Levine while she was in the United States. Because Bochkareva was illiterate, it can be assumed that Levine exercised a degree of creativity in the account.

Boyd, Belle. 1968 (1865). *Belle Boyd in Camp and Prison, Written by Herself.* Edited by Curtis Carroll Davis. New York: Thomas Yoseloff. The personal account of a famous Southern spy.

Brittain, Vera. 1978 (1933). *Testament of Youth.* London: Virago. The famous lament of a survivor from World War I.

Brysac, Shareen Blair. 2000. *Resisting Hitler: Mildred Harnack and the Red Orchestra— The Life and Death of an American Woman in Nazi Germany.* New York: Oxford University Press. The history of Harnack and the Red Orchestra resistance group in Nazi Germany.

Chang, Iris. 1997. *The Rape of Nanking: The Forgotten Holocaust of World War II.* New York: Basic Books. A notable book on this Japanese atrocity during World War II.

Cottam, Kazimiera J. 1980. "Soviet Women in Combat in World War II: The Ground Forces and the Navy." *International Journal of Women's Studies* 3, no. 4 (July-August 1980): 345–357. Other works by Cottam, a leading authority on the combat roles of Soviet women during World War II, include *Women in War and Resistance* (Nepean, Ontario, Canada: New Military Publishing, 1998) and *Soviet Airwomen in Combat in World War II* (Manhattan, KS: MA/AH Publishing, 1983).

De Pauw, Linda Grant. 1998. *Battle Cries and Lullabies: Women in War from Pre-history to the Present*. Norman: University of Oklahoma. A comprehensive study that should be read in conjunction with other works on the roles women have played in wartime.

DeGroot, Gerard J., and Corinna Peniston-Bird, eds. 2000. *A Soldier and a Woman: Sexual Integration in the Military*. Harlow, UK: Pearson Education. A study of women in the contemporary military.

Dombrowski, Nicole Ann, ed. 1999. *Women and War in the Twentieth Century*. New York: Garland. A compelling and useful series of papers from a conference at New York University. Of particular interest are articles on the Chinese Communist Army before 1949; on the rape of German women at the end of World War II; on women in the Soviet army; and on the internment of Japanese American women.

Farmborough, Florence. 1975. *With the Armies of the Tsar: A Nurse at the Russian Front, 1914–1918*. New York: Stein and Day. A fascinating account of the experiences of an English nurse in the service of the Russian army during World War I.

Fraser, Antonia. 1989. *The Warrior Queens*. New York: Knopf. Beginning with Boadicea, Fraser writes artfully of women military leaders, including Isabella of Spain, Elizabeth I, Catherine the Great, the Rani of Jhansi, Golda Meir, Indira Gandhi, and Margaret Thatcher.

Goldman, Nancy Loring. 1982. *Female Soldiers—Combatants or Noncombatants: Historical and Contemporary Perspectives*. Westport, CT: Greenwood. This book contains a number of excellent studies, including chapters on the former Yugoslavia, Algeria, Israel, and Vietnam.

Gundersen, Joan R. 1996. *To Be Useful to the World: Women in Revolutionary America, 1740–1790*. New York: Twayne. A helpful survey of the history of women during the Revolutionary era. According to Gundersen, the American Revolution "appears as a series of trade-offs. Women both gained and lost, but not equally, and one woman's gain might be intimately tied to another's loss."

Isakson, Eva, ed. 1988. *Women and the Military System*. New York: Harvester Wheatsheaf. An interesting compilation, including Marie-Aimee Helie-Lucas's "The Role of Women during the Algerian Liberation Struggle and After."

Jancar, Barbara. 1982. "Yugoslavia: War of Resistance." In *Female Soldiers—Combatants or Noncombatants? Historical and Contemporary Perspectives*. Edited by Nancy Loring Goldman. Westport, CT: Greenwood. This informative survey of the role of women in the Yugoslav Partisan movement has been expanded in Barbara Jancar-Webster, *Women and Revolution in Yugoslavia, 1941–1945* (Denver, CO: Arden, 1990). Jancar points out that despite their crucial performance in World War II, women were not given adequate recognition during that struggle and after the war were excluded from the Yugoslav military.

Jones, David E. 1997. *Women Warriors: A History*. Washington, DC: Brassey's. Despite this work's deficiencies as a historical study, Jones removes any doubts as to the fighting ability of women.

Kinchen, Oscar A. 1972. *Women Who Spied for the Blue and the Gray*. Philadelphia: Dorrance. A history of women spies in the service of the Union and the Confederacy during the American Civil War.

Laffin, John. 1967. *Women in Battle*. London: Abelard-Schuman. An interesting work but one that should be read with caution because legend and history are at times intermingled.

Leneman, Leah. 1994. *In the Service of Life: The Story of Elsie Inglis and the Scottish Women's Hospitals.* Edinburgh: Mercat. A biography of the important leader of the Scottish Women's Hospitals (SWHs). See also Eva Shaw McLaren, ed., *History of the Scottish Women's Hospitals* (London: Hodder and Stoughton, 1919), for personal memories of women who served in the SWHs.

Marlow, Joyce, ed. 1999. *The Virago Book of Women and the Great War, 1914–1918.* London: Virago Press. A useful compilation of contemporary newspaper articles, journal articles, and extracts from memoirs, arranged chronologically by year.

Matthews, Jenny. 2003. *Women and War.* Ann Arbor: University of Michigan Press. In photographs and text, Matthews depicts the roles that war has imposed on women around the world, including places such as Nicaragua, Sierra Leone, Afghanistan, Burma, Chechnya, Haiti, the United Kingdom, Guatemala, and Sudan.

Pennington, Reina. 2001. *Wings, Women and War.* Lawrence: University Press of Kansas. An authoritative and fascinating account of Russian women aviators during World War II.

Sandes, Flora. 1927. *The Autobiography of a Woman Soldier: A Brief Record of Adventure with the Serbian Army, 1916–1919.* London: H, F and G Witherby. The autobiography of a redoubtable medical volunteer who joined the Serbian army in World War I.

Saywell, Shelley. 1985. *Women in War.* Markham, Ontario: Penguin Books Canada. Compelling stories of women engaged in war in the twentieth century.

Stark, Suzanne J. 1996. *Female Tars: Women aboard Ship in the Age of Sail.* Annapolis, MD: Naval Institute Press. A lively account of women sailors on military vessels.

Stephenson, Jill. 2001. *Women in Nazi Germany.* Harlow, UK: Pearson Education. A comprehensive study of the experience of women in Nazi Germany, their role in World War II, and that conflict's impact on them.

Stobart, Mabel Annie Boulton. 1935. *Miracles and Adventures: An Autobiography.* London: Rider. The biography of a woman who spearheaded volunteer medical services both in the Balkan Wars and in World War I. Her *War and Women, from Experiences in the Balkans and Elsewhere, by Mrs. St. Claire Stobart, Founder of the Women's Convoy Corps,* with a preface by Viscount Escher, GCB (London: G. Bell and Sons, 1913), provides a Western glimpse into the Balkan Wars and recounts the accomplishments and trials of English women serving as volunteer medical workers with the Bulgarian army.

CONTRIBUTORS

Rafis Abazov
Harriman Institute, Columbia University
New York, NY

Carol Acton
St. Jerome University
Waterloo, Ontario
Canada

Susan R. Allan
Independent Scholar
Sydney
Australia

Nancy Fix Anderson
Loyola University, New Orleans
New Orleans, LA

Rolando Avila
University of Texas, Pan American
Edinburg, TX

Tracey J. Axelrod
Temple University
Philadelphia, PA

Anni P. Baker
Wheaton College
Norton, MA

Laura Balbuena-González
New School for Social Research
New York, NY

Amy S. Balderach
Baylor University
Waco, TX

Bethany A. Barratt
Roosevelt University
Chicago, IL

Roger B. Beck
Eastern Illinois University
Charleston, IL

Amy Helen Bell
Huron University College
University of Western Ontario
London, Ontario
Canada

Walter Bell
Lamar University
Beaumont, TX

Judith Bellafaire
Women in Military Service for America
    Memorial Foundation
Arlington, VA

June Melby Benowitz
University of South Florida, Sarasota-Manatee
Sarasota, FL

Christiana Biggs
Baylor University
Waco, TX

Avital H. Bloch
Center for Social Research, University of
  Colima
Colima
Mexico

Olivier Buirette
Université de Paris III, Sorbonne-Nouvelle
Paris
France

David Cahill
University of New South Wales
Sydney
Australia

Laura M. Calkins
Vietnam Archive, Texas Tech University
Lubbock, TX

Susanna Calkins
Searle Center for Teaching Excellence
Northwestern University
Evanston, IL

Aurélie Campana
Institut d'Etudes Politiques
Université Robert Schuman
Strasbourg
France

Thomas Cardoza
Truckee Meadows Community College
Reno, NV

Elaine Carey
St. John's University
Queens, NY

David M. Carletta
Michigan State University
East Lansing, MI

Dennis A. Castillo
Christ the King Seminary
East Aurora, NY

Jolynda Brock Chenicek
Florida State University
Tallahassee, FL

Rachael I. Cherry
Florida State University
Tallahassee, FL

Donna Coates
University of Calgary
Calgary, Alberta
Canada

Sara E. Cooper
California State University, Chico
Chico, CA

Kazimiera J. Cottam
Independent Scholar
Ottawa, Ontario
Canada

Brian E. Crim
Joint Personnel Recovery Agency
Ft. Belvoir, VA

J. Keri Cronin
Queen's University
Kingston, Ontario
Canada

Jason Crouthamel
Grand Valley State University
Allendale, MI

Rebekah Ann Crowe
Baylor University
Waco, TX

Page Dougherty Delano
Borough of Manhattan Community College
City University of New York
New York, NY

Johannes Dillinger
Universität Trier
Trier
Germany

Paul W. Doerr
Acadia University
Wolfville, Nova Scotia
Canada

Jérôme Dorvidal
Université Montpelier III
Montpelier
France

Megan Elias
Queensborough Community College
Bayside, NY

Nancy Driscol Engle
Eastern Washington University
Spokane, WA

Thomas M. Ethridge
Eastern Illinois University
Charleston, IL

Petra Feld
Johann-Wolfgang Universität
Frankfurt
Germany

Gilbert G. Fernandez
Tennessee Technological University
Cookeville, TN

Laura Finger
Houston Metropolitan Research Center
Houston, TX

Rachel Finley-Bowman
Delaware Valley College
Doylestown, PA

Andrew K. Frank
Florida Atlantic University
Boca Raton, FL

Lisa Tendrich Frank
Florida Atlantic University
Boca Raton, FL

Gregory Fremont-Barnes
Independent Scholar
Salisbury
United Kingdom

Lee Ann Ghajar
Women in Military Service for America
    Memorial Foundation
Arlington, VA

Amanda Gibbens
Lakeview Centennial High School
Dallas, TX

Pamela Lee Gray
Indiana University, Purdue University
Fort Wayne, IN

Christopher Griffin
Florida State University
Tallahassee, FL

Catherine D. Griffis
Loyola University Chicago
Chicago, IL

Richard Grossman
Northeastern Illinois University
Chicago, IL

Joan R. Gundersen
Independent Scholar
Aspinwall, PA

Larry Hannant
Camosun College and the University of
    Victoria
Victoria, British Columbia
Canada

Oliver Benjamin Hemmerle
Rumms Universität
Mannheim
Germany

Neil M. Heyman
San Diego State University
San Diego, CA

Marcie L. Hinton
Middle Tennessee State University
Murfreesboro, TN

Paula K. Hinton
Tennessee Technological University
Cookeville, TN

Charles F. Howlett
Molloy College
Rockville Centre, NY

Glen Jeansonne
University of Wisconsin, Milwaukee
Milwaukee, WI

Tricia Jenkins
Michigan State University
East Lansing, MI

Phyllis G. Jestice
University of Southern Mississippi
Hattiesburg, MS

Katherine Burger Johnson
University of Louisville
Louisville, KY

Barbara Penny Kanner
Center for the Study of Women, University of
    California, Los Angeles
Los Angeles, CA

Martin Kich
Wright State University, Lake Campus
Celina, OH

David Kieran
George Washington University
Washington, DC

Tonya M. Lambert
University of Alberta
Edmonton, Alberta
Canada

Eve-Marie Lampron
Université de Montréal
Montréal, Quebec
Canada

Caressa Lattimore
Baylor University
Waco, TX

Keith A. Leitich
North Seattle Community College
Seattle, WA

Claudia Lenz
Independent Scholar
Hamburg
Germany

Sarah Hilgendorff List
Independent Scholar
Reading, MA

Stephanie Longo
University of Scranton
Scranton, PA

David Luhrssen
University of Wisconsin, Milwaukee
Milwaukee, WI

John Thomas McGuire
College at Oneonta, State University of New
    York
Oneonta, NY

Howard N. Meyer
Independent Scholar
New York, NY

Alexander Mikaberidze
Independent Scholar
Santa Barbara, CA

Miodrag Milin
Tibiscus University
Timisoara
Romania

Dimitre Minchev
Bulgarian Association of Military History
Sofia
Bulgaria

Patit Paban Mishra
Sambalpur University
Burla, Orissa
India

Danelle Moon
San Jose State University
San Jose, CA

Irina Mukhina
Boston College
Boston, MA

Deanne Stephens Nuwer
University of Southern Mississippi
Hattiesburg, MS

Heather E. Ostman
Empire State College
State University of New York
New York, NY

Kazuo Ota
Tokyo Jogakkan College
Machida-shi, Tokyo
Japan

Dawn Ottevaere
Michigan State University
East Lansing, MI

Richard Panchyk
Independent Scholar
Westbury, NY

Edy M. Parsons
Iowa State University
Ames, IA

Corinna Peniston-Bird
Lancaster University
Lancaster
United Kingdom

Rubina Peroomian
University of California, Los Angeles
Los Angeles, CA

Lisa Porter
Cheekwood Museum of Art
Nashville, TN

Jane Potter
Wolfson College
Oxford
United Kingdom

Margaret Power
Illinois Institute of Technology
Chicago, IL

Cora Ann Presley
Georgia State University
Atlanta, GA

Laura R. Prieto
Simmons College
Boston, MA

J. Lyndsey Rago
University of Delaware
Newark, DE

Annette Richardson
University of Alberta
Edmonton, Alberta
Canada

Giselle Roberts
La Trobe University
Melbourne, Victoria
Australia

Joann M. Ross
University of Nebraska, Lincoln
Lincoln, NE

Jim Ross-Nazzal
Montgomery College
Houston, TX

Kristen L. Rouse
Tallahassee Community College
Tallahassee, FL

Markku Ruotsila
University of Tampere
Tampere
Finland

Kelly Boyer Sagert
Independent Scholar
Lorain, OH

Brian Sandberg
Medici Archive Project
Firenze
Italy

Margaret Sankey
Minnesota State University
Moorhead, MN

Estela Schindel
Freie Universität Berlin
Berlin
Germany

Marc L. Schwarz
University of New Hampshire
Durham, NH

Brenda L. Sendejo
University of Texas at Austin
Austin, TX

Mona L. Siegel
California State University, Sacramento
Sacramento, CA

Shawn Smallman
Portland State University
Portland, OR

Adam C. Stanley
Purdue University
West Lafayette, IN

Stephen K. Stein
University of Memphis
Memphis, TN

Sharon Ritenour Stevens
George C. Marshall Foundation
Lexington, VA

Leonard A. Steverson
Valdosta State University
Valdosta, GA

Pamela J. Stewart
Arizona State University
Tempe, AZ

Margaret D. Stock
U.S. Military Academy
West Point, NY

Gregory M. Thomas
Independent Scholar
New York, NY

Barbara L. Tischler
Horace Mann School
Bronx, NY

Rebecca Tolley-Stokes
East Tennessee State University
Johnson City, TN

Robert J. Topmiller
Eastern Kentucky University
Richmond, KY

Georgia Tres
Oakland University
Rochester Hills, MI

Pamela Tyler
North Carolina State University
Raleigh, NC

David J. Ulbrich
Temple University
Philadelphia, PA

Anastasia (Tasoula) Vervenioti
ASPAITE
Athens
Greece

Kara D. Vuic
Indiana University
Bloomington, IN

Michael C. Wallo
The Pennsylvania State University
University Park, PA

Margaret Ward
Democratic Dialogue
Belfast
Northern Ireland

Kathleen Warnes
University of Toledo
Toledo, OH

Andrew Jackson Waskey
Dalton State College
Dalton, GA

Leigh Whaley
Acadia University
Wolfville, Nova Scotia
Canada

Jacqueline Woodfork
Loyola University New Orleans
New Orleans, LA

Brett F. Woods
Independent Scholar
Santa Fe, NM

John R. Young
University of Strathclyde
Glasgow
Scotland

ABOUT THE EDITOR

Bernard Cook is Provost Distinguished Professor of History at Loyola University New Orleans. After studying at the Gregorian University in Rome and at the University of Marburg on a Fulbright Fellowship, he received his PhD in modern European history from Saint Louis University. He is the author of *Belgium: A History* and editor of *Europe since 1945: An Encyclopedia.*